THE
COMPLETE DICTIONARY
OF ABBREVIATIONS

THE COMPLETE DICTIONARY
OF ABBREVIATIONS

Robert J. Schwartz

THOMAS Y. CROWELL COMPANY
NEW YORK

MANUFACTURED IN THE UNITED STATES OF AMERICA

A Note to the Reader

Numbers in abbreviations are alphabetized as though spelled out, depending on whether cardinal ("one," etc.) or ordinal ("first," etc.). However, subscript numbers (as in chemical formulas) are disregarded.

The following are disregarded in alphabetizing: /, &, - (hyphen), "of," and "to." Abbreviations embodying them are placed immediately following other abbreviations consisting of the same letters. For example, "ac" is followed directly by "a/c" and "a of c."

Following the modern practice, no periods are used after abbreviations unless an abbreviation spells a word and is not written in solid capitals.

THE
COMPLETE DICTIONARY
OF ABBREVIATIONS

A

a abandon; abbreviation; about; absent; absolute; abutment; academician; academy; accommodate; account; accusative; acoustics; acre; acreage; acting; active; adagio; additional; address; adjective; adjutant; administration; administrator; administratrix; adult; advise; advice; aerial; afloat; after; afternoon; afterwards; age; air; airline; airplane; alternating; alto; amateur; America; among; ampere; and; Angstrom (unit); anhydrous; in the year of (*anno*—Latin); anode; anonymous; answer; before (*ante*—Latin); apartment; applicant; application; appointed; approved; aqueous; architect; are (metric); area; silver (*argentum*—Latin); army; aromatic; arrange; arrest; arrival; arteria; artificial; artillery; asbestos; assembly; assessed; assist; assistance; associate; association; assorted; assured; astigmatism; astronomy; at; atmosphere; atomic; attaché; attached; attendant; attention; attest; attorney; audit; auditor; author (*auteur*—French); (*autor*—Spanish); authority; automatic; to advance (*advancer*—French); avenue; aviation; aviator; axiom; axis; azimuth; azure

A absolute (temperature); alto (music); answer; Army—to be used in combination only; argon

aa antiaircraft; author's alteration

AA Aicoholics Anonymous

AAA Agricultural Adjustment Act (or Administration); American Automobile Association; antiaircraft artillery (US Army)

AAAS American Association for the Advancement of Science

AAC in the year before Christ (*anno ante Christum*—Latin)

AAM air to air missile (US Army)

AB able-bodied seaman; Bachelor of Arts (*Artium Baccalaureus*—Latin)

A/B joint stock company (*Aktiebolaget*—Swedish)

ABA American Bar Association; American Booksellers Association

AB&AR Atlanta, Birmingham, and Atlantic Railway

abbr, abbrev abbreviated; abbreviation

ABC Alcoholic Beverage Control; American Broadcasting Company; Argentina, Brazil, and Chile

Abl (*Abril*—Spanish)

A-bomb atomic bomb

ac acre; alternating current

a/c account

Ac actinium

AC Air Commodore; Aviation Cadet (US Army); Before Christ (*Aventi Cristo*—Italian)

a capp a capella (music)

acc acceleration; accept; acceptance (banking); accepted; accompanied; *accompagnamento* (music); according; account; accountant; accusative

accel accelerando (music)

accres accrescendo (music)

acct account; accountant

acct & aud accountant and auditor

ACCX Ansul Chemical Company (private car rr mark)

ack acknowledge; acknowledgment

ACL Acme Aluminum Alloys (NYSE)

ACLU American Civil Liberties Union

a c o anodal closing odor (medical)

a co against (*a cargo*—Spanish)

ACO Acme Steel Company (NYSE); Advisor on Combined Operations; Alpha Chi Omega (sorority); Automotive Club, Overseas

AC/OC Air Co-operation Command (RAF)

ACOFS, G-1 Assistant Chief of Staff, Personnel Division (US Army)

ACOFS, G-2 Assistant Chief of Staff, Military Intelligence Division (US Army)

ACOFS, G-3 Assistant Chief of Staff, Operations and Training Division, (US Army)

ACOFS, G-4 Assistant Chief of Staff, Supply Division (US Army)

ACOFS, WPD Assistant Chief of Staff, War Plans Division (US Army)

A Coll H Associate of the College of Handicraft

A Com Associate in Commerce

ACOM Aviation Chief Ordnanceman (US Navy)

A-Com-In-C Air-Commodore-in-Chief

A Comm Air Commodore

ACOS American College of Osteopathic Surgeons

acoust acoustics

ACP American College of Physicians; Anti-Comintern Pact; Associate of the College of Preceptors; Associated Church Press; Association of Correctors of the Press

a&cp anchors and chains proved (shipping)

ACPA American College Personnel Association; American Concrete Pipe Association; Asbestos Cement Products Association; Associate of the Institution of Certified Public Accountants

ACPM American Congress of Physical Medicine

ACPRA American College Public Relations Association

acpt acceptance (banking)

ACPT accept (US Army)

acq acquired

ACR Admiral Commanding Reserves (Great Britain); Alpha Chi Rho (Fraternity); American Cable & Radio (NYSE); American College of Radiology; American Criminal Reports (legal)

ACRA Associate of the Corporation of Registered Accountants

ACRD Airfield and Carrier Requirements Department

1

acre-ft acre-foot
ACRL Association of College and Reference Libraries
ACRM Aviation Chief Radioman (US Navy)
ACRMA Air Conditioning and Refrigerating Machinery Association
ACR Off Office of Admiral Commanding Reserves (Great Britain)
ACRR American Council on Race Relations
ACRTLF Association of Colored Railway Trainmen and Locomotive Firemen
acs anodal closing sound (medical)
ACS Acting Commissary of Subsistence; Additional Curates Society; Allied Chiefs of Staff; Alpha Chi Sigma (fraternity); American Cancer Society; American Ceramic Society; American Chemical Society; American College of Surgeons; American Colonization Society; Association of Cutlers and Scalers
A/CS Aircraft Security Vessel
AC of S Assistant Chief of Staff
ACSA American Coal Sales Administration; American Cotton Shippers Association; Association of Collegiate Schools of Architecture
ACSC Association of Casualty and Surety Companies
ACSCE Association of Civic Service Clubs Executives
ACSD American Council of Style and Design; Assistant Comptroller of Stores Department
ACSI American Cancer Society, Inc
ACSM American Congress on Surveying and Mapping
ACSMA American Cloak and Suit Manufacturers Association
ACSMH Association of Clerks and Stewards of Mental Hospitals
ACSN Association of Collegiate Schools of Nursing
a/cs pay accounts payable
AC Sqn Army Cooperation Squadron (RAF)
ACSR aluminum cable steel reinforced; American Council for Soviet Relations
a/cs rec accounts receivable
ACSSN Association of Colleges and Secondary Schools for Negroes
act. acting; active voice (grammatical); actinium; active; actuary
ACT Air Cargo Transport; Air Council for Training; Arnold Constable Corporation (NYSE); Association of Cine-Technicians; Australian Capital Territory; Australian College of Theology
a cta on account (a cuenta— Spanish)

ACTC Art Class Teachers' Certificate; Annual Conference of Trades Councils
actg acting
actg chf acting chief
actg sec acting secretary
ACTH adrenocorticotropic hormone
ACTMNY Association of Cotton Textile Merchants of New York
ACTU Association of Catholic Trade Unionists; Australian Council of Trade Unions
act. wt actual weight
a-cu alto-cumulus
ACU American Congregational Union; Association of College Unions; Auto-Cycle Union
ACUSA Assistant Chief of United States Air [Staff]
acv actual cash value
ACVAFS American Council of Voluntary Agencies for Foreign Service
ACVC American Council of Venture Clubs
ACVX American Cider and Vinegar Company (private car rr mark)
a c w alternating continuous waves (radio)
ACW Aircraftwoman; American Chain of Warehouses; Apostolate of Christ the Worker
ACWA Amalgamated Clothing Workers of America; Associate of the Institute of Costs and Works Accountants
ACWE American Cotton Waste Exchange
ACWW Associated Country Women of the World
ACY Akron, Canton & Youngstown Railway Company, The (rr mark); American Cyanamid Company (NYSE)
AC&Y Akron, Canton, & Youngstown Railway Company
ACYD Association of Cotton Yarn Distributors
a d active duty (US Army); adagio; leisurely (music); adapted; adaptor; adde, add (photography); adverb; advertisement; air dried (lumber); airdrome; ambulance driver; average deviation; right angle (angle droit— French)
ad aerodrome; after date
Ad Adam; Aldebaranium
AD Aden Airways Limited; Administrative Department; Administrative Division; Aerodynamics Department; Air Defense; Air Director; Air Division; Alpha Delta (society); American Decisions (legal); Appellate Division (legal); Archduke; Armament Depot; Army Dental Corps; Assembly District;

in the year of our Lord (Anno Domini—Latin); let here be added (addatum— Latin); on the (an der— German)
ADA Adams (J. D.) Manufacturing Company (NYSE); Admiralty Draughtsmen's Association; American Dairy Association; American Dehydrators Association; American Dental Association; American Diabetes Association; American Dietetic Association; Americans for Democratic Action; Assistant Director of Artillery; Assistant District Attorney; Atomic Development Authority
ADAC Art and Design Advisory Council
Ad An at the year (ad annum— Latin)
adap adapted
ADAP Assistant Director of Administrative Planning (military); Assistant Director of Army Psychiatry
ADATS Assistant Director of Auxiliary Territorial Service
ADAVAL advise of availability (US Army)
ADAWS Assistant Director of Army Welfare Services
ADC Advance delivery of correspondence; Airdrome Defense Corps; Aide-de-Camp; Alaska Defense Command; Amateur Dramatic Club; American Distilling Company (NYSE); Army Dental Corps; Assistant Director of Contracts (military)
ADC Gen Aide-de-Camp General
ADCI American Die Casting Institute
add. adding; addition; additional; address
ad deliq to fainting (ad deliquium— Latin)
addend to be added (addendum— Latin)
Add. ER Addams' Ecclesiastical Reports (legal)
addit addenda; addition (additiones—Latin)
addnl additional
ADDNR Assistant and Deputy Director of Naval Recruiting
addns, alts, & reprs additions, alterations, and repairs
addsd addressed
ADE Andes Copper Mining Company (NYSE)
ADEA Assistant Director of Expense Accounts (naval)
ADEE addressee (US Army)
ad eund to the same degree (ad eundem gradum—Latin)
ad ex to extreme (ad extremum—

Latin)
Adf Adolf
ADF African Defense Federation;
after deducting freight; Alexandra
Day Fund
ADFI American Dog Feed Institute
ad fin at, or to, the end (*ad finem*—
Latin)
ADG Assistant Director General
ADGB Air Defense of Great Britain
adgo adagio (music)
adhibend to be used (*adhibendus*—
Latin) (pharmacy)
ad h l to this place, on this passage
(*ad hunc locum*—Latin)
ADHP Assistant Director of Hygiene
and Pathology (military)
ADI Air Distribution Institute; American Documentation Institute; Animal Defenders, Incorporated; International Diplomatic Academy
(*Académie Diplomatique International*—French)
ad Inf without limit (*ad infinitum*—
Latin)
ad Init at the beginning (*ad initium*
—Latin)
ad Int in the meantime (*ad interim*
—Latin)
adj adjacent; adjective; adjoining
[landowners](legal); adjourned; ad-
judged; adjunct; adjustment
Adj Adjutant
ADJA Adjunct in Arts
adj sp adjustable speed
djt Genl Adjutant General
Ad Jus Adam's Justiciary Reports
(legal)
ADL Admiral Corporation (NYSE)
ad Lat out of Latin (*aus dem
Lateinischen*—German)
Adlb Adelbert
ad lib as much as you like (*ad
libitum*—Latin)
ad lit to the letter (*ad litteram*—
Latin)
ad loc at the place (*ad locum*—
Latin)
ADLS Air Delivery Letter Service
adm admission; administration; ad-
ministrative; administrator
Adm Admiral, Admiralty
ADM Annual Delegate Meeting;
Archer-Daniels-Midland Company
(NYSE)
ADMA American Drug Manufacturers
Association; Aviation Distributors
and Manufacturers Association
Adm Ct Admiralty Court
Adm & Ecc Admiralty and Ecclesi-
astical (legal)
ADM Affiliated Dress Manufactur-
ers, Inc; American Dry Milk Insti-
tute
ADMIN administration (US Army)
admastr administrator

adminstrn administration
ADMM Association of Dandyroll and
Mould Makers
admon administration (*adminis-
tracion*—Spanish)
Adm Rev Very Reverend (*admodum
reverendus*—Latin)
ADMS Assistant Director of Medical
Services
ADMSG advise by electrically
transmitted message (US Army)
adm(tr)x administratrix (legal)
ADN Aden (IDP)
ADNA Assistant Director of Naval
Accounts
ADNC Assistant Director of Naval
Construction
ADNI Assistant Director of Naval
Intelligence
ADO Air Defense Officer
ADOF Assistant Director of
Ordnance Factories
Adolph & E Adolphus & Ellis'
English King's Bench Reports
(legal)
adop adoption (legal)
ADOS Assistant Director of
Ordnance Services; Assistant Di-
rector of Ordnance Stores
ADP Air Defense Position (RAF);
Alpha Delta Phi (fraternity); Alpha
Delta Pi (sorority); Assistant Di-
rector of Pathology (military)
A Dpo Aircraft Depot
ADPTS Assistant Director of Phys-
ical Training and Sports
adr address (*adresse*—German,
Norwegian)
Adr Adrian
ADR American Depositary Re-
ceipts; Assistant Director of Re-
mounts
ADRA Animal Diseases Research
Association
ADRDE Air Defense Research and
Development Establishment
adrm airdrome
ads at the suit (*ad sectam*—Latin);
autograph document signed
AdS Academy of Science (*Académie
des Sciences* —French)
ADS Advanced Dressing Station;
Allied Mills, Inc. (NYSE); Alpha
Delta Sigma; Anglo-Danish Society;
Animal Defense Society
ADSA American Dairy Science As-
sociation
ADSHPDAT advise shipping date
(US Army)
ADS&T Assistant Director of
Supplies and Transport
ADSTKOH advise stock on hand of
(US Army)
ADT American District Telegraph;
the same day (*an demselben tage*—
German); any desired thing; As-

sistant Director of Transport
(technical)
ADTA American Dental Trade Association
AD Tr Assistant Director of Transportation
ADUI Architects' & Draftsmen's
Union, International
ad us. according to custom (*ad
usum*—Latin)
adv advance; advanced; advent;
adverb; adverbially; against
(*adversus*—Latin); advertisement;
advisory; advocate
ADV Advance Aluminum Castings
(NYSE)
ad val according to value (*ad
valorem*—Latin)
adv chgs advance charges
adven adventurer
adv frt advanced freight (shipping)
Adv Gen Advocate General
advl adverbial
advnced cse advanced course
adv poss adverse possession (legal)
ADVS Assistant Director of Veterinary Services
advt advertisement
advtg advantage; advertising
ADW Assistant Director of Works
(British Territorial Army)
ADWS Assistant Director of War-
like Stores
ADX Adams Express Company
(NYSE)
ae adult education; after end
(shipbuilding); agricultural engineer; army education
AE All England; American Embassy;
Angström unit (*Angströmeinheit*—
German); George Russell (pen name)
AE third class ships in Lloyd's Reg-
ister
A&E Adolphus and Ellis (law re-
ports); Aircraft and Engine (avia-
tion license)
AEA Actors Equity Association;
Agricultural Education Association;
Air Efficiency Award; Air-Way
Electric Appliance Corporation
(ASE); Amateur Entomologists As-
sociation; American Economic As-
sociation; Automotive Electric As-
sociation
AEAA Association of Export Ad-
vertising Agencies
AEAF Allied Expeditionary Air
Force
AEAI Auctioneers and Estate
Agents Institute
AEB Art Exhibitions Bureau
AEC Army Educational Corps; As-
sociation of Education in Citizen-
ship; Association of Education
Committees; Associated Equipment
Company; Atlantic and East Caro-

lina Railway Company (rr mark); Atomic Energy Commission (United States); Society of Writers Who Served in the War (*Association des Écrivains Combattants*—French)

A & E Corp Ca American and English Corporation Cases (legal)

AECS Association of Established Civil Servants

AECSF Admiralty Established Civil Servants' Federation

AECX American Extract Company (private car rr mark)

A Ed Associate in Education

AED Air Equipment Department; Alpha Epsilon Delta (society); Associated Equipment Distributors

Ae E Aeronautical Engineer

AEF Allied Expeditionary Force; American Economic Foundation; American Education Fellowship; American Expeditionary Forces; French Equatorial Africa (*Afrique Equatoriale Française*)

AEF Sib Vets AEF Siberian Veterans

aeg sick (*aeger*—Latin)

AEG United Electricity Company (*Allgemeine Elektrizitäts-Gesellschaft*—German)

AEGM Anglican Evangelical Group Movement

AEI Alpha Epsilon Iota (society)

AEIC Association of Edison Illuminating Companies

AEIOU It is given to Austria to rule whole world (*Austriae est imperare orbi universo*—Latin)

AELI American Export Lines, Inc

AEM American Meter Company (NYSE)

A-E-M plan architect-engineer-manager plan

AENF Allied Employers' National Federation

Aen Nas "Brazen Nose"—Brasenose College, Oxon (*Aenei Nasi*—Latin)

A & E NS Adolphus & Ellis' English Queen's Bench Reports, New Series (legal)

A Ent O Area Entertainments Officer (military)

AEO Area Education Officer (military)

AEOS Ancient Egyptian Order of Sciots

AEP Alpha Epsilon Phi (sorority); Alpha Epsilon Phi (fraternity)

AE and P Ambassador Extraordinary and Plenipotentiary (Diplomatic)

AEPEM Association of Electronic Parts and Equipment Manufacturers

AEPX Appalachian Electric Power Company (private car rr mark)

aeq equal (*aequalis, aequales*—Latin)

aer aeronautics

AER Aero Supply Manufacturing Company (NYSE); Association for Education by Radio

AERA American Educational Research Association; Associate Engraver of the Royal Academy; Automotive Engine Rebuilders Association

AERAF Societe Africaine de Transportes Tropicaux (Air Africaine)

AERI Agricultural Economics Research Institute

AERM1c Aerographer's Mate First Class (US Navy)

AERM2c Aerographer's Mate Second Class (US Navy)

AERM3c Aerographer's Mate Third Class (US Navy)

aero aeronautics

AERO Aero O/Y (Finnish Airlines); Association of Electronic Reserve Officers

Aero E Aeronautical Engineer

AEROF Aerological Officer (US Navy)

aeron aeronautics

AERONAVES Aeronaves de Mexico

aer[o]p aeroplane

aero sq aero squadron

AEROTEC Aerotechnique

A & ERRC American and English Railroad Cases (legal)

AES American Electrochemical Society; American Electroplaters Society; American Eugenics Society; Artillery Equipment School

AESC American Engineering Standards Committee

AESD Association of Engineering and Shipbuilding Draughtsman

AESLA Associate of Experimental Station Laboratory Association

AESSO Assistant Embarkation, Supply and Stores Officer

A-E Sud Anglo-Egyptain Sudan

AESX North American Car Corporation (private car rr mark) Staley Manufacturing Company (private car rr mark)

aet or **aetat** aged; of age (*anno aetatis suae*—Latin)

AET Alien Enemy Tribunals; American Encaustic Tiling Company (NYSE)

AETA American Educational Theatre Association

A et M Arts and crafts (*Arts et Métiers*—French)

AEU Amalgamated Engineering Union; Artists Equity Association

aevia alleluia (music)

AEW Appalachian Electric Power Company (ASE)

AEX American Export Lines, Inc (NYSE)

a f advanced freights; anticipated freights; audio frequency (radio); commercial correspondence in favor (*a favor*—Spanish)

Af Africa; African

AF Admiral of the Fleet; Agricultural Farm; Air Force; Air France; Alcoholic Foundation; Allen Foundation; Altman Foundation; American Car & Foundry (NYSE); Anderson Foundation; Anglo-French; French Academy (*Académie Française*—French); French Army (*Armée Française*—French); Army form; Auerbach Foundation

A and F August and February

AFA Academy of Fine Arts; Actors Fund of America; Advertising Federation of America; Air Force Association; Air Force Auxiliary; Amateur Fencing Association; Amateur Football Association; American Federation of Arts; American Forestry Association; American Foundrymen's Association; Associate in Fine Arts; Associate of the Faculty of Actuaries; Associate of the Faculty of Arts; Association of Federal Architects; Auditor Freight Accounts

AF & AM Ancient Free and Accepted Masons

AFAS Air Force Aid Society; Associate of the Faculty of Architects and Surveyors

AFB Air force base (US Army); American Foundation for the Blind

AFBF American Farm Bureau Federation

AFBMA Anti-Friction Bearing Manufacturers Association

AFBS American and Foreign Bible Society

a f c auditor freight claims; automatic frequency control (radio)

AFC Air Force Cross; American Finance Conference; Army Finance Center (US Army); Association Football Club; Association of Flooring Contractors; Association of Floor Constructors; automatic frequency control (radio)

AFCA Armed Forces Chemical Association; Armed Forces Communication Association; Assistant Freight Claim Agent

AFCI Associates of the Food and Container Institute

AFCTM Associated Fur Coat and Trimming Manufacturers

AFCU American and Foreign Christian Union

AFD Association of Food Distributors; Doctor of Fine Arts
AFDCS Association of First Division Civil Servants
AFDOUS Association of Food and Drug Officials of the United States
AFDU Air Force Development Unit
AFE Airfleets Inc (NYSE)
AFEA American Farm Economic Association
aff affairs; affectionately; affirmatively; affirming; postage (*affranchisement*—French)
AFF Army Field Forces
AFFA Air Freight Forwarders Association
affd affirmed
aff etr foreign affairs (*affaires étrangères*—French)
affett tenderly (*affetuoso*—music)
affl affiliated to; affluent (geography)
affme most tenderly (*affezionatissimo*-music)
affrett affrettando (music)
afft affidavit
Afg Afghanistan
AFGE American Federation of Government Employees
Afgh Afghanistan
AFGM American Federation of Grain Millers
AFGWUNA American Flint Glass Workers Union of North America
AFH American Foundation for Homeopathy
AFHTWTA Amalgamated Felt Hat Trimmers' and Wool Trimmers' Association
AFHW American Federation of Hosiery Workers
AFI Agence Française Indépendante, Ltd (French); Air Filter Institute; Associate of the Faculty of Insurance; Atlantic Refining Company (NYSE)
AFIA American Foreign Insurance Association
AFIED Armed Forces Information and Education Division
AFII American Federation of International Institutes
AFL Air Force List; American Federation of Labor
AFLA Amateur Fencers League of America; American Foreign Law Association; Association of Fire Loss Adjustors
AFLCA American Fur Liners Contractors Association
AFLD air field (US Army)
AFM Air Force Medal; American Federation of Musicians
AFMA American Feed Manufacturer's Association; American Fur Merchants Association

AFMBT Artificial Flower Manufacturers Board of Trade
AFMC Allied Foreign Ministers' Conference
afme airframe
AFMH American Foundation for Mental Hygiene
afmo yours truly (*afectisimo*—Spanish)
AFN French North America (*Afrique Française du Nord*—French)
AFO Anti-Fascist Organization (Burma); Army Forwarding Officer
AFOC Auditor Freight Overcharge Claims
AFPE American Foundation for Pharmaceutical Education
AFPH American Federation of the Physically Handicapped
AFPI American Forest Products Industries
AFPS Armed Forces Press Service (US Army)
AFPTU Association Football Players and Trainers' Union
A f r Auditor of freight receipts
Afr Africa; African
AFr Anglo-French
AFR Armed Forces Radio
AFRA American Federation of Radio Artists
AFRAeS Associate Fellow of the Royal Aeronautical Society
AFRKB American Federation of Retail Kosher Butchers
AFRS Armed Forces Radio Service (US Army)
afs sender (*afsender*—Danish)
AFS Alles & Fisher, Inc. (NYSE); Amalgamated Film Studios; American Field Service; Anglo-Finnish Fisheries Society; Animal Feeding Stuffs; Associate of the Faculty of Secretaries; Atlantic Ferry Service; Auxiliary Fire Service; Department of Administrative and Financial Services (UN Secretariat)
AFSA American Flight Strips Association
AFSC American Federation of Soroptimist Clubs; American Friends' Service Committee
afsd aforesaid (legal)
AFSF Airborne Forces Security Fund
AFSG American Foundation Studies in Government
AFSWP Armed Forces Special Weapons Project (US Army)
aft after; afternoon
AFT American Federation of Teachers; American Manufacturing Company (NYSE); Auditor freight traffic

AFTC American Fair Trade Council
AFTM American Foundation for Tropical Medicine; Assistant Freight Traffic Manager; Associated Fishing Tackle Manufacturers
aftwd afterward
AFU Advanced Flying Unit
AFUS Air Force of the United States (US Army)
AFV armored fighting vehicle
AFW Army Field Workshop
AFWA Air Force with Army (US Army)
AFWAL American Federation of Women's Auxiliaries of Labor
AFWESPAC American Forces, Western Pacific
Ag agricultural; agriculture; atomic weight (*Atom gewicht*—German); August; joint stock company (*Aktiengesellschaft*—German); silver (*argentum*--Latin)
A g to the left (*à gauche*—French)
AG Accountant General; Adjutant General; Agent General; Air Gunner; Allegheny Ludlum Steel (NYSE); Assemblies of God; Attorney General; Auditor General; Authors' Guild
a-g anti-gas
AGA Abrasive Grain Association; Air Routes and Ground Aids; American Gas Association; American Genetic Association; American Glassware Association; to a pleasant sourness (*ad gratum aciditaem*—Latin)
A g b any good brand
AGB Adjutant General's Branch
AGBF Artists' General Benevolent Fund
AGBI Artists' General Benevolent Institution
AGBPS Association of Governing Bodies of Public Schools
AGBU Armenian General Benevolent Union
a g c automatic gain control
AGC American Gas & Electric (NYSE)
AGCA Associated General Contractor of America
AGCX Vendome Tank Car Company (private car rr mark)
Agcy agency
agd agreed
AGD Accountant General's Department; Adjutant General's Department; Alpha Gamma Delta (sorority)
AGDC Assistant Grand Director of Ceremonies (Freemasons)
AGDec Attorney General's Decisions (legal)
AGDL Attorney General of the

Duchy of Lancaster
AGE Affiliated Gas Equipment (NYSE)
AGF Adjutant General to the Forces; American Golf Foundation; Army Ground Forces
Agfa *Aktiengesellschaft für Anilin-fabrikation* (German) photographic company
AGFA Assistant General Freight Agent
aggr aggregate
AGI American Geological Institute
agito agitatedly (*agitato*—music)
AGL Aero Geral Ltda
AGM Amalgamated Sugar Company (NYSE); Annual General Meeting
AGMA American Guild of Musical Artists; Athletic Goods Manufacturers Association
agn again
AGN Agnew-Surpass Shoe Stores Ltd. (common stock, ASE)
AGO Adjutant General's Office; American Guild of Organists; Anglo-Lautaro Nitrate (NYSE)
AGO A Anglo-Lautaro Nitrate Corporation (ASE)
AG Op Attorney General's Opinions (legal)
AGOS air-ground operations system (US Army)
AGP Anglo-Iranian Oil Company Ltd. (ASE)
AG & QMG Adjutant General and Quartermaster General
agr agriculture, agricultural; agriculturalist
AGR Alpha Gamma Rho (fraternity)
AGRM Adjutant General of the Royal Marines
AGR MAT Agricultural Mortgage Bank (ASE)
agrost agrostology
AGRS American Graves Registration Service (US Army)
agrt agreement (legal)
AGRY Alliance for Guidance of Rural Youth
AGS aero gun sights; air ground section (US Army); Alabama Great Southern Railroad Company; American Gem Society; American Geographic Society; American Goat Society; American Gynecological Society; Assistant Grand Sojourner (freemasons); Spalding (A.G.) & Bros., Inc (NYSE)
AGSA Aerovias Guest
AGSM Associate of the Guildhall School of Music
AGSMI American Gold Star Mothers, Inc
AGSS American Geographical and Statistical Society, American Gold Star Sisters

agst against
AGSX Alabama-Georgia Syrup Company (private car rr mark)
agt agent
AGT Alabama Gt. South. Railroad Ord. (NYSE)
Agt-Gen Agent General
AGU American Geophysical Union
Agua Aguascalientes
a g v anilin gentian violet
AGVA American Guild of Variety Artists
AGVL Agent General for Victoria in London
a g w actual gross weight (railroad)
AGW Atlantic, Gulf & West Indies Steamship (NYSE)
AGWI Atlantic, Gulf, West Indies (shipping)
a h after hatch; agricultural homestead; ampere-hour (electricity); hypermetropic astigmatism (medicine); hour angle (*angle horaire*—French)
AH. Allis-Chalmers Manufacturing Company (NYSE); in the Hebrew year (*anno Hebraico*—Latin); in the year of hegira (*anno hegira*—Latin)
a&h accident and health (insurance)
AHA American Heart Association; American Historical Association; American Hospital Association; American Hotel Association
AHAA American Hearing Aid Association
AHAUS Amateur Hockey Association of the United States
AHC Army Hospital Corps
AHCC American Hungarian Chamber of Commerce
AHCP Arab Higher Committee of Palestine
AHD American Agricultural Chemical (NYSE)
AHDGA American Hot Dip Galvanizers Association
AHEA American Home Economics Association
AHEI American Hardwood Exporters, Inc (Webb Association)
AHF American Heritage Foundation; American Hobby Federation
AHFI Associated Health Foundation, Inc
AHHS American Hackney Horse Society
AHI American Honey Institute; Animal Health Institute
a h l at this place (*ad hunc locum*—Latin)
AHL American Hockey League; Anglo-Hellenic League
AHLI American Home Lighting Institute
AHM Association of Headmasters
AHMA American Hardware Manu-

facturers Association
AHMI Appalachian Hardwood Manufacturers, Inc
AHMIT Association of His Majesty's Inspectors of Taxes
AHMOA Amalgamated Horse and Motor Owners' Association
AHMS American Home Missionary Society
ahp air horsepower
AHP Alpha Portland Cement Company (NYSE)
AHQ Air Headquarters; Allied Headquarters; Army Headquarters
AHR American Hard Rubber Company (NYSE)
AHRGB Association of Hotels and Restaurants of Great Britain
AHS American-Hawaiian Steamship (NYSE); American Hearing Society; American Helicopter Society; American Horticultural Society; American Humane Society; Anglo-Hungarian Society; in the year of human salvation (*anno humanae salutis*—Latin)
AHSA American Highway Sign Association; American Horse Shows Association
AHT Adam Hat Stores Inc (common stock, ASE)
a h v at this word (*ad hanc vocem*—Latin)
AHWC Associate of Heriot-Watt College (Edinburgh)
ai aircraft interception (radar); all iron
AI Aaland Islands; Admiralty Islands; Agricultural Institution; Air-India Limited; Imperial Highness (*Altesse Impériale*—French); American Institute; Anthracite Institute; Anthropological Institute; Athletic Institute; Auctioneers' and Estate Agents' Institute; in the year of the discovery (*anno inventionis*—Latin)
A & I accident and indemnity
AIA Aircraft Industries Association of America; American Institute of Accountants; American Institute of Actuaries; American Institute of Architects; Anglo-Indian Association; Archaeological Institute of America; Associate of Institute of Actuaries; Associate of Institute of Architects; Authors' Insurance Association
AIAA Aircraft Industries Association of America; American Industrial Arts Association; Architect Member of the Incorporated Association of Architects and Surveyors; Association of International Advertising Agencies
AIAE Associate Institution of Auto-

mobile Engineers

AIAESD American International Association for Economic and Social Development

AI Arb Associate of the Institute of Arbitrators

AIAS Associate Surveyor Member of the Incorporated Association of Architects and Surveyors

AIAS Quan Associate Quantity Surveyor Member of the Incorporated Association of Architects and Surveyors

AIB Accidents Investigation Branch (RAF); American Institute of Baking; American Institute of Banking

AIBA American Industrial Bankers Association

AIBD Associate of the Institute of British Decorators

AIBNRM American Institute of Bolt, Nut, and Rivet Manufacturers

AIBS American Institute of Biological Sciences

AIC Acting Inspector of Constabulary; Allied International Investing Corporation (ASE); American Institute of Chemists; American Institute of Cooperation; Associate of the Institute of Chemistry

AICB Association of Insurance Company Buyers

AICCP Association of Interstate Commerce Commission Practitioners

AICE American Institute of Chemical Engineers; American Institute of Consulting Engineers; Associate of Incorporated Institution of Commercial Engineers; Associate of the Institution of Civil Engineers

AICNY American Institute of City of New York

AICO Association of Insurance Committee Officers

AICS Associate of the Institute of Chartered Shipbrokers

AID Aeronautical Inspection Directorate; Aircraft Inspection Department; Aircraft Intelligence Department; American Institute of Decorators; Army Intelligence Department; Artificial Insemination Donor

AIDC American Industrial Development Council

AIEE American Institute of Electrical Engineers; Associate of Institution of Electrical Engineers

AIF Allied Invasion Forces; Australian Imperial Forces

AIFD American Institute of Food Distribution

AI Fire E Associate Institute of Fire Engineers

AIFM Medical Women's International Association

AIFR American Institute of Family Relations

AIG Accident Investigation; Adjutant Inspector General; Assistant Inspector General

AIGA American Institute of Graphic Arts

AIGBI Archaeological Institute of Great Britain and Ireland

AIGCM Associate of Incorporated Guild of Church Musicians

AIGT Association for the Improvement of Geometrical Teaching

AIH International Association of Hostelries (*Association Internationale de l'Hotellerie*—French)

AIHA American Industrial Hygiene Association; Associate of the Institute of Hospital Almoners

AIHS International Academy of the History of Science

AII Anglo-India International; Altrusa International, Inc.; American Interprofessional Institute; Austrian Institute, Inc.

AIIA Associate of the Institute of Industrial Administration

AIIC American Institute for Intermediate Coinage

Aik Aikens' Vermont Reports (legal)

AIL Air Intelligence Liaison; Airways (India) Ltd; American Institute of Laundering; Associate of the Institute of Linguists

AILO Air Intelligence Liaison Officer

AI Loco E Associate of the Institution of Locomotive Engineers

AIM American Institute of Management; Africa Inland Mission

AIMA as interest may appear (insurance)

AI Mar E Associate of the Institute of Marine Engineers

AIME American Institute of Mining and Metallurgical Engineers; Associate of the Institution of Marine (Mechanical, Mining) Engineers

AIML All-India Moslem League

AIMM Associate of the Institution of Mining and Metallurgy

AIMTA Associate of the Institute of Municipal Treasurers and Accountants

AIMU American Institute of Marine Underwriters

AIN Addressograph-Multigraph (NYSE); American Institute of Nutrition

AINA Associate of the Institution of Naval Architects

A Inst CE Associate of the Institution of Civil Engineers

A Inst P Associate of the Institute

of Patentees; Associate of the Institute of Physics

A Inv in the year of invention (*anno inventionis*—Latin)

AIOB Associate of the Institute of Builders

AIOC Anglo-Iranian Oil Company

AIODOT Association of Intelligence Officers in the Department of Overseas Trade

AIOW Association of Independent Optical Wholesalers

AIP American Institute of Physics; American Institute of Planners

AIPA Associate of the Institute of Incorporated Practitioners in Advertising

AIPC International Association for Bridge and Structural Engineering

AIPE American Institute of Park Executives; Associate of the Institution of Production Engineers

AIPO American Institute of Public Opinion

AIPR American Institute of Public Relations; Association of International Publishers Representatives

AIPT Assistant Inspector of Physical Training (military)

AIR Ainsworth Manufacturing Corporation (ASE); airworthiness; American Institute of Refrigeration; Thai Airways Company, Ltd.

AIRA Air Attaché (US Army)

AIRARMUNIT Aircraft Armament Unit (US Navy)

AIRCREY Air Ceylon Limited

AIREA American Institute of Real Estate Appraisers

air hp air horsepower

AIR INTEL air intelligence (US Army)

AIRLO Air Liaison Officer (US Army)

AIROH Aircraft Industries Research Organization on Housing

AIRORIEN Orient Airways Ltd.

AIRXRS American Industrial Radium and X-Ray Society

AIS Allied Information Service; American Ice Company (NYSE); Anglo-Italian Society

AISA Associate of Incorporated Secretaries Association

AISBDS Associated Iron, Steel, and Brass Dressers of Scotland

AISC American Institute of Steel Construction; Associate of the Incorporated Staff Sight-Singing College

AISE Association of Iron and Steel Engineers

AISF All-Indian Student Federation

AISI American Iron and Steel Institute; America-Italy Society, Inc; Associate of Iron and Steel Institute

Al San E Associate of the Institution of Sanitary Engineers

Al Struct E Associate of the Institute of Structural Engineers

AIT International Touring Alliance

AITA All-Indian Temperance Association

AITCC Assistant Inspector of Training Corps and Cadets

AITM American Institute of Tack Manufacturers

AIU Aero Insurance Underwriters

AIUPCW Amalgamated Industrial Union of Packing Case Workers

AIWC All-India Women's Conference

AIWM American Institute of Weights and Measures

AIWPHSA American Institute of Wholesale Plumbing and Heating Supply Associations

aj Ajax

AJ Alaska Juneau Gold (NYSE); Associate Justice

Aja Ajaccio, Corsica

AJC American Jewish Committee; American Jewish Conference; American Jewish Congress

AJDC American Joint Distribution Committee

AJHS American Jewish Historical Society

AJI Associate Jewelers, Inc

AJIL American Journal of International Law

AJLA Association of Junior Leagues of America

AJOJ April, July, October, January (quarter months)

AJPM Jesus through Mary (*Ad Jesum per Mariam*—Latin)

AJR Artemus-Jellico Railroad Company (private car rr mark)

AJRC American Junior Red Cross

AJS American Journal of Science; American Judicature Society

AJSM Association of Jute Spinners and Manufacturers (Scottish)

AJWMA American Jeweled Watch Manufacturers Association

AK Army Corps (*Armee Korps*—German); old fighters (*Alte Kämpfer*—German)

a k a also known as

Akad Akademie

AKB Akron Brass Manufacturing Company (NYSE)

AKC American Kennel Club; Associate of King's College (London)

Akc B-ve joint stock company (*Akcines bendrove*—Lithuanian)

Akc Dvo joint stock company (*Akciova drustvo*—Yugoslavian)

Akc Spol joint stock company (*Akciova spolecnost*—Czechoslovakian); joint stock company (*Spolka Akeyjna*—Polish)

AKD Alpha Kappa Delta (society)

AKFM Association of Knitted Fabrics Manufactures

AKFMI Association of Knitted Fabric Manufacturers, Inc

AKGMM Association of Knitted Glove and Mitten Manufacturers

AKK Alpha Kappa Kappa (fraternity)

AKL Alpha Kappa Lambda (fraternity)

AKO Atlas Tack Corporation (NYSE)

AKP Alpha Kappa Psi (fraternity)

A kr Austrian kronen (monetary unit)

AKS Arkansas Natural Gas (NYSE)

Aktb joint stock company (*Aktiebolaget*—Swedish)

Akt-Ges joint stock company (*Aktiengesellschaft*—German)

al alley

a l after delivery (*après livraison*—French); air letter; all lengths (lumber); autograph letter; other persons (*alie*—Latin); other things (*alia*—Latin)

aL on the river Lahn (*an der Lahn*—German)

Al aluminum

AL Air Lines; American League (baseball); American Legion; Anglo-Latin; annual lease; Architectural League; Army List; light-year (*année lumière*—French); United Air Lines, Inc. (NYSE); in the year of light (*anno lucis*—Latin)

Ala Alabama

ALA Agriculture Labor Administration; All American Airways, Inc. (ASE); Allied Lines Association; Amalgamated Lithographers of America; American Legion Auxiliary; American Library Association; Assistant Legal Advisor; Associate of the Library Association; Authors League of America; Automobile Legal Association

ALAA Associate of London Association of Certified and Corporate Accountants

ALACAI Affiliated Ladies Apparel Carriers Association, Inc

ALAFC Associated Latin-American Freight Conferences

ALA Jrs American Legion Auxiliary Juniors

ALAM Association of Licensed Automobile Manufacturers

Alas Alaska

Ala Sel Cas Alabama Select Cases (legal)

Alaska Co Alaska Codes (legal)

Alb Albania; Albanian; Albany; Albemarle; Albert; Alberta; Albion; white (*albus*—Latin)

Al B aluminium bronze

ALB Automobile Labor Board; Boston & Albany Railroad Company (NYSE)

ALBA American Leather Belting Association

Alban of St. Albans

ALBE Air League of the British Empire

Alb Law J Albany Law Journal

Albr Albrecht

alc alcohol

ALC American Life Insurance Convention; American Lutheran*Church; The Atlantic Coast Line Company (ASE)

ALCA American Leather Chemists Association

ALCD Associate of the London College of Divinity

alchem alchemy

ALCM Associate of the London College of Music

Alc & Nap Alcock and Napier's Irish King's Bench Reports (legal)

ALCOA Aluminum Company of America

alcoh alcohol; alcoholic; ethyl alcohol

ALCX Aluminum Company of Canada Limited (private car rr mark)

ald alderman

Ald Alden's Condensed Reports (legal); Aldine (printing)

ALD Agricultural Lime Department; Allied Laboratories, Incorporated (NYSE); Alpha Lambda Delta (society)

ALDA Air Line Dispatchers Association (AFL)

ALE Allied Products Corporation (NYSE)

al ed in another edition (*alia editione*—Latin)

Alex Alexander

Alf Aifonso; Alfred; Alfredian

ALF American Leprosy Foundation

Alg Algerian; Algernon; Algiers

ALG Advanced Landing Ground (RAF); Aluminum Goods Manufacturing Company (ASE)

ALGCU Association of Land Grant Colleges and Universities

ALGERIE Societe Algerienne de Constructions Aeronautiques (AIR ALGERIE)

ALGFO Association of Local Government Financial Officers

ALGNI Agent in London for Government of Northern Ireland

Alh Alhambra

AL of H American Legion of Honor

ali elsewhere (*alibi*—Latin)

ALI Agricultural Limestone Institute; Aluminum Ltd (NYSE); American Ladder Institute; American Law

Institute; American Library Institute; Argyll Light Infantry; Automotive Lift Institute

ALIC Association of Life Insurance Counsel

ALIMDA Association of Life Insurance Medical Directors of America

alk alkaline

ALK Alaska Airlines, Inc (NYSE)

alky alkalinity

Al L Alsace-Lorraine

ALL Adams-Millis Corporation (NYSE)

Alleg Allegheny; allegorical; allegory

Allem German (Allemand—French)

Allg general; universal (allgemein—German)

Allgtto Allegretto (music)

Allln Allinson, Pennsylvania, Superior and District Court (legal)

All N B Allen's New Brunswick Reports (legal)

allo rather lively (allegro—music)

all' ott an octave higher than written (all' ottava—Italian)

All. Ser Allahabad Series, Indian Law Reports (legal)

All. Tel Cas Alien's Telegraph Cases (legal)

ALM Alabama & Vicksburg Railway Company (NYSE); American Legion of Merit; Arkansas & Louisiana Missouri Railway Company (rr mark); Master of the Liberal Arts (Artium Liberalium Magister—Latin)

ALMA American Lace Manufacturers Association; Association of Licensed Automobile Engineers (Canada)

almc almanac

ALMT allotment (US Army); Association of London Master Tailors

ALNY Architectural League of New York

ALO Admiralty Liaison Officer; Air Liaison Officer

ALOA Amalgamated Lithographers of America

ALOI Associated Luncheonette Owners, Inc

ALOT allotted (US Army)

ALOX The Alberta Linseed Oil Company, Limited (private car rr mark)

ALP Alabama Power Company (NYSE); ambulance loading post (US Army); American Labor Party; Alpes Provence (France)

ALPBC American League of Professional Baseball Clubs

Alph Alphonse

alr otherwise (aliter—Latin)

ALR Amalgamated Leather Companies (NYSE); American Law Reports

ALS American Lumber Standards; Associate of the Linnaean Society; autograph letter signed

AL&S Alton and Southern Railroad (rr mark)

al seg to the sign (al segno—music)

ALSW Associated Law Societies of Wales

alt alteration; alternate; alternating; alternative; Highness (Altesse—French); altitude; alto

alt ... alt the one ... the other (altera ... altera—pharmacy)

ALT Aer Lingus Teoranta

Alta Alberta (Canada)

alt dieb alternate days (altemis diebus—Latin)

alt eg my other self (alter ego—Latin)

altern hor every two hours (alternis horis—pharmacy)

alt id another exactly the same (alter diem—Latin)

alt of inst alteration of instruments (legal)

Altun Alton Railroad Company

ALTPEM Association of Lift Truck and Portable Elevator Manufacturers

Alt&S Alton and Southern Railroad

Al Tel Ca Allen's Telegraph Cases (legal)

alum aluminum; alumnus

Alum Yalen Alumni of Yale College (Alumni Yalensia—Latin)

ALUSLO Naval Liaison Officer (US Navy)

ALUSNA Naval Attaché at ... (US Navy)

ALUSNOB Naval Observer at ... (US Navy)

a l w arch loop whorl (medicine).

ALWS allowance (US Army)

alz alzamento (music)

am. ammeter (electricity); amperemeter; amplitude; meter angle; minesweepers (US Navy)

Am. America; American; ametropia (medicine); ammonium; ammunition; Amos (Biblical); amyl; before noon (ante meridium—Latin)

Am americium

AM Albert Medal; Air Marshal; air ministry; air medal (US Army); admiral (amiral—French); African Missions (Lyons Society of); amplitude modulation; Armour & Company (Illinois) (NYSE); Army Manual; Associate Member; on the Maine (am Main—German); Hail Mary (Ave Maria—Latin); Master of Arts (Artium Magister—Latin); Mutual Assurance (assurance mutuelle—French); the wonderful year (1666)

(mirabilis—Latin); in the year of the world (annus mirabilis—Latin)

a-m ampere-minute

A/M on the Mainz River (Am Mainz—German)

(A/M) Specialist in Aviation Medicine (naval)

A & M ancient and modern (hymns)

A and M agricultural and mechanical

AMA Academy of Model Aeronautics; Acoustical Materials Association; Agricultural Marketing Administration; American Management Association; American Medical Association; American Missionary Association; American Monument Association; American Motorcycle Association; American Municipal Association (PACH); American Mutual Alliance; Assistant Masters Association; Assistant Mistresses Association; Automobile Manufacturers Association

AMAA Adhesives Manufacturers Association of America; Armenian Missionary Association of America; Army Mutual Aid Association

AMAB Air Ministry's Accident Branch

Amad Amadeus

AMAI Aircraft Manufacturers Association, Inc; Arena Managers Association, Inc

amal amalgam; amalgamated

Am Assn Sci American Association for the Advancement of Science

Amb Ambassador; Ambrose; ambulance

Amb(l) Ambler's (Law Reports)

AMB American Bantam Car (NYSE); Bachelor of Mechanic Arts

Am Benk R American Bankruptcy Reports (legal)

AMBBA Associated Master Barbers and Beauticians of America

Amb & C Ambassadors and Consuls

Amb Co Ambulance Company

AM Brit IRE Associate Member of the British Institution of Radio Engineers

AMC Agricultural Mortgage Corporation; American International Corporation (NYSE); American Maritime Cases; American Mining Congress; American Music Conference; Armed Merchant Cruiser; Army Medical Center; Art Masters Certificate; Association of Municipal Corporations; Coastal Mine Sweepers (US Navy)

AMCBWNA Amalgamated Meat Cutters and Butcher Workmen of North America

AMCCW Association of Manufacturers of Chilled Car Wheels

Am Cont American Continent
Am Corp Cas American Corporation Cases (legal)
AMCP Associated Medical Care Plans
Am Cr Rep American Criminal Reports (legal)
Am Cr Tr American Criminal Trials (legal)
AMCS Aberdeen Medico-Chirurgical Society
AMCSUS Association of Military Colleges and Schools of the United States
am. cur. a friend of the court (legal) (*amicus curiae*—Latin)
Am Cyc American Cyclopedia
AMD Administrative and Miscellaneous Duties (RAF); Air Matériel Department; Amalgamated Master Dairymen, Inc; Army Medical Department
AMDB Agricultural Machinery Development Board
AMDC Assistant Marshal of the Diplomatic Corps
Am Dec American Decisions (legal)
AMDG to the greater glory of God (*ad majorem Dei gloriam*—Latin)
Am Dig American Digest (legal)
AMDP Department of the Air Member for Developments Production
amdt amendment
AME African Methodist Episcopal; American Machine & Metals, Inc (NYSE); Association of Municipal Employers
AMEC African Methodist Episcopal Church
AMECZ antimechanized (US Army)
AMEE Associated Municipal Electrical Engineers
AMEI American Macaroni Export Institute
AMEIC Associate Member of the Engineering Institute of Canada
AMEIGGS Amalgamated Machine, Engine and Iron Grinders and Graziers Society
AMEM African Methodist Episcopal Mission
amend. amendment
Am & Eng Corp Cas American and English Corporation Cases (legal)
Amer America; American
Amer AA American Automobile Touring Alliance
Amer GS American Geographical Society
Amer Jur American Jurist (legal)
Amer Law Reg (N S) American Law Register, New Series (legal)
Amer Law Rev American Law Review (legal)
AMES Air Ministry Experimental Station

Am Ex American Express
AMEZC African Methodist Episcopal Zion Church
AMF air mail field; American Factors, Ltd (NYSE); American Machine & Foundry (NYSE); Australian Military Forces
AMFIE Association of Mutual Fire Insurance Engineers
AM1c Aviation Metalsmith First Class (US Navy)
umg among
AMG Allied Military Government; American Music Guild; Artists Managers Guild
AM-G Assistant Major-General
AMGO Assistant Master General of Ordnance
AMGOT Allied Military Government of Occupied Territory
AMHA American Motor Hotel Association
Amh Coll Amherst College
AMHIS American Marine Hull Insurance Syndicate
Am Hist Rev American Historical Review
AMI American Meat Institute; American Military Institute; Ancient Monuments Inspectorate; International Masonic Association; Associate Member Institution of Automobile Engineers
AMI Ae E Associate Member of Institution of Aeronautical Engineers
AMIAMA Associate Member of the Incorporated Advertising Managers Association
AMICE Associate Member of Institution of Civil Engineers
AMI Chem E Associate Member of the Institution of Chemical Engineers
AMIEE Associate Member of the Institution of Electrical Engineers
AMIEI Associate Member of the Institution of Engineering Inspection
AMI Fire E Associate Member of the Institute of Fire Engineers
AMI Gas E Associate Member of the Institution of Gas Engineers
AMI Loco E Associate Member of the Institution of Locomotive Engineers
Am Ind American Indian
Am Ins Rep American Insolvency Reports (legal)
AM Inst BE Associate Member of the Institution of British Engineers
AM Inst CE Associate Member of the Institution of Civil Engineers
AM Inst Chem E Associate Member of the Institution of Chemical Engineers
AM Inst EE Associate Member of the Institution of Electrical Engi-

neers
AM Inst Gas E Associate Member of the Institution of Gas Engineers
AM Inst M & Cy E Associated Member of the Institution of Municipal and County Engineers
AM Inst T Associate Member of the Institute of Transport
AM Inst TE Associate Member of the Institution of Transport Engineers
Am ISCL American Iraqi Shipping Company Limited
AMI Tec E Associate Member of the Institute of Technical Engineers
AMI Mar E Associate Member of the Institute of Marine Engineers
AMIME Associate Member of the Institution of Mining Engineers
AMI Mech E Associate Member of the Institution of Mechanical Engineers
AMI Min E Associate Member of the Institution of Mining Engineers
AMINA Associate Member of the Institution of Naval Architects
AMIPE Associate Member of the Institution of Production Engineers
AMIS American Marine Insurance Syndicate
AMISE Associate Member of the Institution of Sanitary Engineers
AMI Struct E Associate Member of the Institution of Structural Engineers
AMIT Associate Member of the Institute of Transport
AMIWE Associate Member of the Institution of Water Engineers
Am Jour Pol American Journal of Politics (legal)
Am Jour Soc American Journal of Sociology (legal)
AMK American Seal-Kap Corporation (NYSE)
AMKITU Amalgamated Moulders and Kindred Industries Trade Union
AML American Mission to Lepers
Am Law J (NS) American Law Journal, New Series (legal)
Am Law Mag American Law Magazine (legal)
Am Law Rec American Law Record (legal)
Am Law Reg American Law Register (legal)
AMLBO Association of Master Lightermen and Barge Owners
Am L Cas American Leading Cases (legal)
Am L of H American Legion of Honor
Am L Rev American Law Review (legal)
Am LTR American Law Times Reports (legal)

AMM American Metal Company (NYSE); Master of Mechanic Arts
AMM1c Aviation Machinist's Mate First Class (US Navy)
AMMI American Merchant Marine Institute; Associated Millinery Men, Inc
AMMLA American Merchant Marine Library Association
AMMO ammunition (US Army)
ammon ammonia
AMMR American Medical Mission to Russia
AMM2c Aviation Machinist's Mate Second Class (US Navy)
AMM3c Aviation Machinist's Mate Third Class (US Navy)
AMNH American Museum of Natural History
AMN Inst E Associate Member of the National Institute of Engineering
AMNS Air Ministry News Service
Am Num Arch. Soc American Numismatic and Archaeological Society
AMO Administrative Medical Officer; Air Ministry Order
amo friend (*amigo*—Spanish)
AMOAI Automatic Music Operators Association, Inc
AMORC Ancient Mystical Order Rosae Crucis (Rosicrucian Order)
amorph amorphous
AMOX Alamo Tank Car Company (private car rr mark)
amp amperage; ampere
AMP Air Member for Personnel; American Military Police; American Writing Paper Corporation (NYSE)
AMPA American Machine and Parts Association; American Manganese Producers Association; Associated Motion Picture Advertisers
AMPAS Academy of Motion Picture Arts and Sciences
AMPC Auxiliary Military Pioneer Corps
AMPH amphibian; amphibious (US Army)
AMPP Association of Motion Picture Producers
Am Prob Rep American Probate Reports (legal)
AMPS Army Mine Planters Service; Army Motion Picture Service; Auxiliary Military Pioneer Corps
AMPX Ark-Mo Plant Food Company, Inc (private car rr mark)
AMQ American Maracaibo Company (NYSE)
AMR American Airlines, Inc (NYSE)
AMRD Aircraft Maintenance and Repair Department
AMRE Air Ministry Reconnaisance Department
Am Rep American Reports

Am RR Cas American Railway Cases (legal)
AMRS Air Ministry Radio Station
AMRX American Refrigerator Transit Company (private car rr mark)
AMS American Mathematical Society; American Meteorological Society; American Sumatra Tobacco (NYSE); Ancient Monuments Society; Army Map Service; Army Medical Service; Army Medical Staff; Assistant Military Secretary; Assurance Medical Society
AMSA Artificer and Mechanical Staff Association; Associated Manufacturers of Saddlery Accessories
AM 2C Aviation Metalsmith Second Class (US Navy)
AMSEF Anti Minesweeping Explosive Float
AMSH Association for Moral and Social Hygiene
AMSO Air Member for Supply and Organization
Am Soc CE American Society of Civil Engineering
Am Soc ME American Society of Mechanical Engineers
AMSS Assistant Masters in Secondary Schools Inc
Amst Amsterdam
Am St Paps American State Papers
Am St Rept American State Reports
AMSUS Association of Military Surgeons of the United States
amt amount
AMT Air Mail Transmission; Air Member for Training; American Investment (Illinois) (NYSE)
AMTC Academic Member of Trinity College of Music, London; Art Masters' Teaching Certificate
AMTDA American Machine Tool Distributors Association
AMTEA American Machine Tool Export Associates
AM Tech I Associate Member of the Technological Institute of Great Britain
AM 3c Aviation Metalsmith Third Class (US Navy)
AMTNA American Music Teachers' National Association
Amtorg Amtorg Trading Corporation (Russia)
AMTPI Associate Member of the Town Planning Institute
AMTRAC amphibious tractor (US Army)
AMU American European Securities (NYSE)
A Mus (TCL) Associate of Music (Trinity College, London)
AMUUS Association of Marine Underwriters of the United States

AMV Aluminum Industries, Inc (NYSE)
Am Vet Coll American Veterinary College
AMVETS American Veterans of World War II
AMW Actual Measurement Weight (railway)
AMWA American Medical Women's Association
AMWR Air Ministry War Room
AMWSA Associated Manufacturers of Washable Service Apparel
AMWWM Association of Manufacturers of Wood-Working Machinery
AMY American Laundry Machinery (NYSE)
AMZ American Seating Company (NYSE)
an. above-named; anonymous; before (*ante*—Latin); the year (*anno*—Latin)
a n acid number; arrival notice
An. actinon (chemistry)
AN air natural cooled; Air Reduction Company (NYSE); American Navy; Apalachicola Northern Railroad Company (rr mark)
A-N Anglo-Norman
Ana Anacosta
ANA Air Navigation Act; American Nature Association; American Naturopathic Association; American Numismatic Association; American Nurses Association; Anacon Lead Mines Limited (ASE); Associate of National Academy; Associate of the National Academy of Design; Association of National Advertisers; Australian National Airways; Australian Natives Association
anac anachronism
ANACA Army, Navy and Air Force Comforts Association
Anacr Anacreon; Anacreontic
ANADP Association of North American Directory Publishers
anaes anaesthesia; anaesthetic
anal analogous; analogy; analysis; analytic; analyze
analyt analytical
Anast Anastasius
anat anatomical; anatomy
ANAX Anaconda Copper Mining Company (private car rr mark)
ANB Anglo-California National Bank (NYSE)
anc ancient
ANC Airlines Negotiating Committee; American News Company (NYSE); Army Nurse Corps; before the birth of Christ (*ante Nativitatem Christi*—Latin)
ANCA Armenian National Council of America

ANCAM Association of Newspaper Classified Advertising Managers
AMCBWNA Amalgamated Meat Cutters and Butcher Workmen of North America
an cc anodal closure contraction (medicine)
ANCE American National Cooperative Exchange
AN C-in-C Allied Naval Commander-in-Chief
anct ancient; anciently
and. slow and graceful (*andante*—music)
And. Andorra; Andrè; Andrew
AND Air Navigation Directions; Andes; Andromeda (constellation)
&c and so forth (*et cetera*—Latin)
ANDES Aerovias Nacionales del Sur
ando rather quicker than "andante" (*andantino*—music)
And Theol Sem Andover Theological Seminary
ANFBA American National Fur Breeders Association
ANFM August, November, February, May (quarter months)
Anfr question (*Anfrage*—German)
ang angular; angle; concerning (*angôende*—Danish, Norwegian)
ANG Anglesey (Wales, England); Anglice; Angola; Air National Guard; American Natural Gas Company (NYSE); American Newspaper Guild
Ang & Dur Angell & Durfee's Reports (legal)
angew used as (*angewandt*—German)
Ang-Fr Anglo-French
Ang-I Anglo-Italian
angl in English (*anglice*—Latin)
Angl Anglia; Anglican; Anglicized
Angl Ch Anglican Church
Ang-Sax Anglo-Saxon
ANGUS Air National Guard of the United States
ANGX Arkansas Fuel Oil Company (private car rr mark)
ANHSO Ashmolean Natural History Society of Oxfordshire
anhyd anhydrous
a n i international normal atmosphere (*atmosphère normale internationale*—French)
anim animated (*animato*—Italian) (music)
ANL Allen Industries, Inc (NYSE)
ANLSA American National Live Stock Association
Anm note (*Anmerkung*—German)
anm remark, observation (*anmaerkning*—Danish)
ANMB Army and Navy Munitions Board
ann annales; annals (*annalen*—

German); annual; annuity; annum; in the year (*anno*—Latin); year (*annus*—Latin)
Ann Cas American and English Annotated Cases (legal)
anniv anniversary
annot annotated; annotation; annotator
ann rep annual report
Ann. St Annotated Statutes (legal)
Annunc Annunciation [of the Virgin Mary]
anny annuity (legal)
ANO Air Navigation Orders; Austin, Nichols & Company, Inc (NYSE)
anon anonymous; anonymously
Anorg inorganic (*Anorganisch*—German)
ANP Anderson-Prichard Oil Corporation (NYSE)
ANPA American Newspaper Publishers' Association
ANPP Association of Negro Press Photographers
ANPX Anchor Petroleum Company (private car rr mark)
anr another (legal)
ANR American Negligence Reports (legal); Angerman Company Inc (common stock, ASE)
ANRC American National Red Cross
ANRJA American National Retail Jewelers Association
ANRPB American National Resources Planning Board
a n s autograph note signed
ans answer; answered
Ans Anselm
ANS Admiralty Naval Staff; Air Navigation School; American Numismatic Society; Anglo-Netherlands Society; Army Nursing Service
ANSA Agenzia Nazionale Stampa Associata (Italian press agency)
ANSETT Ansett Airways Pty., Ltd
ANSIA Army-Navy Shipping Information Agency
ANSS Associate of Normal School of Science
Anstr Anstruther's Reports
ant. antiphon; antiquarian; antique; antiquities; antonym; antrim
Ant. Antarctica; Anthony; Antigua; Antlia; Antoine; Anton; Antonia
ANTA American National Theatre and Academy
Ant. & Cl Antony and Cleopatra
ANTFA Allied Non-Theatrical Film Association
Ant. Fed. Anti-Federalist
ant. frt anticipated freight (shipping)
anthol anthology
Anth Anthony
Anth NP Anthon's Nisi Prius (legal)
anthrop anthropological; anthropology
antilog antilogarithm

Anto Anthony (*Antonio*—Spanish)
ant. pit. anterior pituitary (medicine)
ANU Army and Navy Union
ANUDE United Nations Economic Development Administration (UNEDA)
ANUUS Army and Navy Union of the United States
Anw employment (*Anwendung*—German)
ANWC American Newspaper Women's Club
ANZAC, Anzac Australian and New Zealand Army Corps
a o and others; army officer; army order; obtuse angle (*angle obtus*—French)
AO Accounting Officer; Administration Officer; Alpha Omega (fraternity); Asphalt Institute; Aviacion y Comercio, South America; in the year of the order (*Anno Ordinis*—Latin)
a/o account of
A & O April and October
AOA Administration of Operations Activities (American); Air Officer in Charge of Administration; American Optometric Association; American Ordnance Association; American Orthopaedic Association; American Orthopsychiatric Association; American Osteopathic Association
AOAC Association of Official Agricultural Chemists
AOB Antediluvian Order of Buffaloes
AOC Aircraft Operating Company (Ltd); Airport Operators Council; American Optical Company (NYSE); Army Ordnance Corps; attached to other correspondence; Auditor of Overcharge Claims; in the year of the Creation (*anno Orbis Conditi*—Latin)
AOCBAF Air Officer Commanding Base Air Forces
AOC-In-C Air Officer Commanding-in-Chief
AOCS American Oil Chemists Society
AOCX Aluminum Ore Company (private car rr mark)
AOD Advanced Ordnance Department; Army Ordnance Department; Ancient Order of Druids
AOE Associated Elec Indus ADR (NYSE)
AOER Army Officers' Emergency Reserve
AOF Ancient Order of Foresters; French West Africa (*Afrique Occidentale Française*—French)
AOFB Ancient Order of Frothblowers
AOGB American Outpost in Great Britain
AOH Alliance of Honour; Ancient

Order of Hibernians

AOHA American Osteopathic Hospital Association; Ancient Order of Hibernians in America

a o l v automatically operated inlet valve

AOM Academy of Medicine; Association of Operative Millers; Master of Obstetric Art

AOM1C Aviation Ordnanceman First Class

AOML Association of Officers of the Ministry of Labour

AOM2C Aviation Ordnanceman Second Class

AOM3C Aviation Ordnanceman Third Class

A1 first class

AOP Alpha Omicron Pi (sorority)

AOPA Aircraft Owners and Pilots Association

AOPA American Potash & Chemical Corp. (ASE)

aor aorist (grammar)

a/or, &/or, and/or either "and" or "or"

AOR Anchor Post Products, Inc (NYSE)

AOS Agricultural Organization Society; Air Observer School; Ancient Order of Shepherds; Army Ordnance Stores; American Oriental Society

AOSA Admiralty Overseeing Staff Association; Association of Official Seed Analysts

AOSE American Order of Stationary Engineers

AOSC Association of Officers of the Supreme Court

AOSEA American Office Supply Exporters Association

AOSS Fellow of the American Oriental Society (*Americanae Orientalis Societatis Socius*—Latin)

AOT Association of Officers of Taxes

AOTA American Occupational Therapy Association

AOTC Accountant Officers' Technical Course

AOU American Ornithologists' Union; Aquila Airways Limited

AOUW Ancient Order of United Workmen

AOW Articles of War

AOX Associated Oil Company (private car rr mark)

AOY American Colortype Company (NYSE)

ap above proof (spirits); accounts payable; additional premium; advanced post; aft perpendicular (naval engineering); apothecary; apostle; apostleship of prayer; arithmetical progression; armor-piercing shell; army pensions;

aside (*aparte*—Spanish); atmospheric pressure; atomic power; before noon (*aamupäivällä*—Finnish); druggist (*Apotheker*—German); separately (*aparte*—Spanish)

AP Aero Portuguesa; Alpha Phi (sorority); Alpha Psi (fraternity); American Power & Light (NYSE); Associated Presbyterian; Associated Press

a/p authority to pay; authority to purchase

A&P Atlantic and Pacific

a p a axial pressure angle (gears)

AFA Agricultural Publishers' Association; All Peoples' Association; American Pharmaceutical Association; American Philological Association; American Physiotherapy Association; American Poultry Association; American Press Association; American Prison Association; American Protective Association; American Psychiatric Association; American Pulpwood Association; Auxiliary Police Association

APART Alliance of Pan American Round Tables

APB anti-personnel bomb

APBA American Power Boat Association

APBPA Association of Professional Ball Players of America

APC alien property custodian; American Parents Committee; American Publishers Conference; Army Pay Corps; Asiatic Petroleum Company; assistant principal chaplain; Association of Private Camps; Atlas Powder Company (NYSE)

APCA American Planning and Civic Association

APCC American-Portuguese Chamber of Commerce

APCI Association of Pulp Consumers, Inc

APCK Association for Promoting Christian Knowledge (Church of Ireland)

APCL Air Pullmans Croydon, Limited

APCM Association of Portland Cement Manufacturers

APCN in the year after Christ's birth (*Anno Post Christum Natum*—Latin)

APCO Associated Police Communication Officers

APCX Atlas Powder Company (private car rr mark)

APD Admiralty Press Division; Air Personnel Department; American Metal Products (NYSE); Alpha Phi

Delta (fraternity); Army Pay Department

APE Apex Electrical Manufacturing Company (common stock, ASE)

APEA American Photo-Engravers Association

APEC American Provisions Export Co. (Webb Association)

APEM American Protestant Episcopal Mission

APERS antipersonnel (US Army)

APEX Apex Oil Company (private car rr mark)

APF Anglican Pacifist Fellowship; Association of Pacific Fisheries; Association of Puddlers and Forgemen of Great Britain

APFC American Plant Food Council

AP1C Aviation Pilot First Class (US Navy)

AP2C Aviation Pilot Second Class (US Navy)

APG American Platform Guild; Army Proving Grounds; Gresham Professor of Astronomy

aph aphorism

APH anterior pituitary hormone

APHA American Protestant Hospital Association; American Public Health Association

aphet aphetic

APHX Apache Powder Company (private car rr mark)

API Alabama Polytechnic Institute; American Petroleum Institute; American Potash Institute; armor-piercing incendiary (US Army)

APIC American Petroleum Industries Committee

APIDEP International Protestant Loan Association

APIM International Professional Association of Medical Practitioners

APIS Agricultural Price Insurance Scheme

APJA Appliance Parts Jobbers Association

ap JC in the year after Christ (*après Jésus-Christ*—French)

APK Ayrshire Collieries Corporation (common stock, ASE)

APKC Associated Pot and Kettle Clubs

Apl April

APL American President Lines

APLA American Patent Law Association

APLE Association of Public Lighting Engineers

apm apomict

APM American Presbyterian Board of Foreign Missions; Assistant Paymaster; Assistant Provost-Marshal

APMA American Pharmaceutical Manufacturers Association; Associated Pants Manufacturers

Association; Automatic Phonograph Manufacturers Association

APMC Allied Political and Military Commission

apo empowered attorney (*apoderado* —Spanish); apogee (astronomy)

APO Acting Pilot Officer; African People's Organization; air post office; Alpha Phi Omega (society); Army Post Office

APOB Aerograph Observation (US Navy)

apoc apocalypse; apocrypha

apog apogee

apos apostrophe

apost apostle

apoth apothecary

app apparatus; apparent; apparently; appellate; appendix; applied; appointed; apprentice[d]; approved; approximation

APPA American Paper and Pulp Association; American Pork Producers Association; American Public Power Association

App Cas Beng Sevestre and Marshall's Bengal Reports (legal)

appd approved

App DC Appeals, District of Columbia (legal)

App Div Appellate Division

app&e appeal and error (legal)

appatis having been approved (*approbatis*—Latin)

appl appeal (legal); applicable [to]; application (US Army); applied (to)

applicand to be applied (*applicandus* —Latin) (pharmacy)

applicat let it be applied (*applicatur*—Latin) (pharmacy)

appln application

APPM Association of Publication Production Managers

APPMSA American Pulp and Paper Mill Superintendents Association

App NZ Appeal Reports, New Zealand (legal)

appr appreciation; apprentice

appro approbation; approval

approx approximate; approximately; approximation

appt appoint (legal); appointment

apptd appointed

appurts appurtenances (legal)

appx appendix

apr after (*après*—French)

ápr April (*április*—Hungarian)

APR air priority (US Army); Atlantic and Pacific Railroad

APRA Alianza Popular Revolucionaria Americana (Peru); American Public Relations Association; Automotive Parts Rebuilders Association

APRC in the year after the building

of Rome (*anno post Roman conditam* —Latin)

a pri beforehand (*a priori*—Latin)

APRISTA member of APRA

APROP appropriate (US Army)

approx approximate(ly)

APRW Association of Puerto Rican Workshops

Aps Apus (constellation)

a p s autograph poem signed

APS Aberdeen Philosophical Society; Aborigines Protection Society; Academy of Political Science; American Peace Society; American Philosophical Society; American Physical Society; American Protestant Society; Anglo-Portuguese Society; Army Postal Service; Assistant Private Secretary; Associate of the Pharmaceutical Society; Preparatory Schools Association

APSA American Political Science Association

Ap Sed Apostolic See (*Apostolica Sedes*—Latin)

Ap Sed Leg legate of the Apostolic See (*Apostolicae Sedis Legatus*— Latin)

APSFSL Assistant Private Secretary to the First Sea Lord

APSGB Associate of the Philosophical Society of Great Britain

APSI American Philatelic Society, Inc

APSL Acting Paymaster Sub Lieutenant

APSO Association of Postal Supervising Officers

APSS Academy of Political and Social Science; Army Printing and Stationery Services

APT appoint(ed) or (ment) (US Army)

apt apartment (pl. apts.)

APTA American Physical Therapy Association

APTC Allied Printing Trades Council; Army Physical Training Corps

APTI Association of Principals of Technical Institutions

APU Army Postal Unit (US Army)

APUB American Public Utilities Bureau

APUC Association for Promoting the Unity of Christendom

APW A.P.W. Products Company (NYSE)

APWA All Pakistan Women's Association; American Public Welfare Association; American Public Works Association

APWPL Association of Public Wharfingers of the Port of London

APX Albro Packing Company, The (private car rr mark)

aq aqueous; water (*aqua*—pharmacy)

Aq Aquila (constellation)

a q achievement quotient; any quantity

aq bull boiling water (*aqua bulliens* —Latin)

AQC Associate of Queen's College (London)

aq cal hot water (*aqua calida*— Latin)

aq com tap water (*aqua communis*— Latin)

aq dest distilled water (*aqua destillata*—Latin)

aq ferv boiling water (*aqua fervens* —Latin)

aq gel cold water (*aqua gelida*— Latin)

aqic may his soul rest in Christ (*anima quiescat in Christo*—Latin)

AQM Assistant Quartermaster

AQMG Assistant Quartermaster General

Aqr Aquarius

aq tep lukewarm water (*aqua tepida* —Latin)

a r administrative ruling; aerial reconnoiterer; analytical reagent; analyzed reagent; annual return; autonomous republic

ar arrive; arrives

AR Appointments Register; Augustinian Recollect Fathers; Arabia; argon (chemistry); aryl; Aerolineas Argentinas; American Reports; American Smelting & Refining (NYSE); Army Regulations; Atlantic Reporter (legal); Queen Anne (*Anna Regina*); Regional Association (of WMO); Royal Highness (*Altesse Royale*—French); in the year of the reign (*Anno Regni* —Latin); silver (*argentum*—Latin)

a/r all rail; all risks

A/R at the rate of (US Army)

ARA Abbreviated Registered Address (postal); Agricultural Research Administration (America); Air Reserve Association; Amateur Rowing Association; American Railway Association; American Relief Association; American Remount Association; Artists Representatives Association; Associate of the Royal Academy, London

Arab. Arabia; Arabian; Arabic

ARAC Associate of the Royal Agricultural College

arach arachnology

ARAD Associate of the Royal Academy of Dancing

ARAE American Retail Association Executives

ARAeS[1] Associate of the Royal Aeronautical Society (and Institution)

ar agt army agent
ARAL Associate of the Royal Academy of Literature
Aram Aramaic
ARAM Associate of the Royal Academy of Music
ARAS Associate of the Royal Aeronautical Society
Arb works (*Arbeiten*—German)
ARB Army Retiring Board (US Army)
ARBA American Road Builders Association; Associate of the Royal Society of British Artists; Associated Retail Bakers of America
arb arbitrary
Arb & aw arbitration and award (legal)
ARBBA American Railway Bridge and Building Association
ARBC Associate, Royal British Colonial Society of Artists
arbor. arboriculture
ARBS Associate of the Royal Society of British Sculptors
arbtrn arbitration
arbtror arbitrator
Arc. Arctic; with the bow (*arcato*—music)
ARC Aero Research Committee; Agricultural Research Council; Alpha Rho Chi (fraternity); Amerada Petroleum (NYSE); American Railway Cases (legal); American Red Cross; American Rehabilitation Committee; Asthma Research Council; Automobile Racing Club
ARCA Aeronca (aircraft); American Rice Growers Cooperative Association; Associate of the Royal Cambrian Academy; Associate of the Royal Canadian Academy; Association of Railway Claim Agents; Associate of the Royal College of Art
ARCB Association of Reserve City Bankers
ARCBA American Rabbit and Cavy Breeders Association
ARCC American-Russian Chamber of Commerce
ARCCC American Red Cross Camp Club
Arc. Circ Arctic Circle
ARCE Academical Rank of Civil Engineers
ARCEC All Russian Central Executive Committee
arch. archaic; archaism; archery; Archibald; archipelago; architect; architectural; architecture; Court of Arches, England (legal)
archaeol archaeological; archaeology
Archb N P Archbold's Nisi Prius Law (legal)
Archb Pr Archbold's Practice (legal)
Archb Pr K B Archbold's Practice

King's Bench (legal)
Archbp Archbishop
Arch. E Architectural Engineer
Archld Archdeacon (*Archidiaconus*—Latin)
Archlprb Archpriest (*Archipresbyter*—Latin)
archlt architect; architectural; architecture
arch. nav naval architecture (*architecture navale*—French)
Arch. Surg Archives of Surgery
archtl architectural
ARCI American Railway Car Institute; Associate of the Royal Colonial Institute; (Great Britain)
ARCM Associate of the Royal College of Music
ArCO aromatic acyl radical
ARCO Associate of the Royal College of Organists
ARCOC American Red Cross Officers' Club
ARCOS Anglo-Russian Co-operative Society
ARCS Associate of the Royal College of Science; Associate of the Royal College of Surgeons
ARCUS Associated Retail Confectioners of the United States
ard ardito (music)
ARDA American Rabbit Dealers Association
ARDC American Racing Drivers Club
ARDTOA Admiralty and Royal Dockyards Technical Officers' Association
ARE Associate of the Royal Society of Painter-Etchers and Engravers
AREA American Railway Engineering Association; American Recreational Equipment Association
ARF Advertising Research Foundation; Aid to Russia Fund; American Radio Forum; American Relief for France; Armenian Revolutionary Federation; Armour Research Foundation
arg argent (heraldry)
Arg Argentina; Argentine; Argyll; Argyllshire
ARG Argo Oil Corporation (NYSE)
Arg Rep Argentine Republic
ARH ammunition railhead; Anchor Hocking Glass Corporation (NYSE)
ARHA Associate of the Royal Hibernian Academy
Ari Aries (constellation)
ARI Affiliated Restaurateurs, Inc; Aluminum Research Institute; Aluminum Roofing Institute; American Refractories Institute
ARIB Asphalt Roofing Industry

Bureau
ARIBA Associate of the Royal Institute of British Architects
ARIC Associate of the Royal Institute of Chemistry
ARICS Professional Associate Royal Institution of Chartered Surveyors
Arist Aristotle
arith arithmetic; arithmetical
Ariz Arizona
Ark. Arkansas
ARL Arundel Corporation (NYSE); Association of Research Libraries
ARLX Armour Refrigerator Line (private car rr mark)
Arm. Armagh; Armenian; armoric; armature
Ar M Master of Architecture (*Architecturae Magister*—Latin)
ARM armament (US Navy); Armstrong Rubber Company (NYSE); Assistant Resident Magistrate; Aviation Radioman
ARMA army attaché (US Army)
ARM A Armstrong Rubber Company ("A") (ASE)
ARMD armored (US Army)
Armen Armenian
ARM1c Aviation Radioman First Class (US Navy)
ARMLO army liaison officer (US Army)
Armr Sergt Armorer Sergeant
ARMS Associate of the Royal Society of Miniature Painters
Arms. Br P Cas Armstrong's Breach of Privilege Cases, New York (legal)
ARM2c Aviation Radioman Second Class (US Navy)
arm' armament
ARM3c Aviation Radioman Third Class (US Navy)
ARMX Armco Steel Corporation (private car rr mark)
Arn Arnold; Arnold's English Common Pleas Reports (legal)
Arn & Hod B C Arnold & Hodges' English Bail Court Reports (legal)
ARNO Association of Retired Naval Officers
Arnot Cr C Arnot's Criminal Cases, Scotland (legal)
ARO army routine order; Associated Road Operators (Ltd); Aro Equipment Corp. (ASE); Asian Relations Organization
AROTC Air Reserve Officers' Training Corps (US Army)
AROX Air Reduction Company, Inc (private car rr mark)
ARP Air Raid Precautions (superseded by C.D. Civil Defence) (British); Air Raid Protection; Associated Reformed Presbyterian

arp° arpeggio (music)
ARPO Air Raid Precautions Officer
ARPS Associate of the Royal Photographic Society
ARR Artloom Carpet Company (NYSE); in the year of the Sovereign's reign (*Anno Regni Regis*—Latin)
ARRC Associate of the Royal Red Cross
arrgt arrangement
ARRL American Radio Relay League
arr n arrival notice
ars arsenal
ARS Admiralty Recruiting Service; Aeroplane Repair Section; Argus Cameras, Inc (NYSE); American Radium Society; American Recreation Society; Army Recreational Service (US Army); American Rocket Society; American Rose Society; in the year of our redemption (*anno reparatae salutis*—Latin)
ARSA Allied Railway Supply Association; Associate of the Royal Scottish Academy; Associate of the Royal Society of Antiquaries; Associate of the Royal Society of Arts
AR San I Associate Royal Sanitary Institute
ARSCM Association of Roller and Silent Chain Manufacturers
ARSL Associate of the Royal Society of Literature
ARSM Associate of the Royal School of Mines
ARSS Fellow of the Royal Society of Antiquaries (*Antiquariorum Regiae Socius*—Latin)
ARSW Associate of the Royal Scottish Society of Painters in Water-colours
art. article (*artículo*—Spanish); (*Artikel*—German); artificer; artificial; artillery; artist
Art. Artemisia; Artemus
ART American Refrigerator Transit Company (private car rr mark)
ARTA Assistant Regional Technical Adviser
ARTC Associate of the Royal Technical College, Glasgow
Art. E Artificer Engineer
Arth Arthur; Arthurian
Artic Clerl articles of the clergy (legal)
Articuli sup Chart articles upon the charters (legal)
artill artillery
arts. articles
Arts D Doctor of Arts
ARTUC Anglo-Russian Trade Union Committee
arty r artillery reconnaissance
ARU American Railway Union;

American Republics Corporation (NYSE)
arv esteemed (*arvoisa*—Finnish)
ARV American (Standard) Revised Version (of the Bible); Arvin Industries, Inc (NYSE)
ARVA Associate Incorporated Association Rating and Valuation Officers
ARW Air Raid Warden
ARWA Associate of the Royal West of England Academy
ARWAF Army personnel assigned and or attached as individuals or units for duty w/Air Force
ARWS Associate, Royal Society of Painters in Water Colours
ARZ American Safety Razor Corporation (NYSE)
a s air speed; automatic sprinkler; assistant secretary; assistant surgeon; at sight
as. astigmatism (medicine); asymmetric; astronomy
As arsenic
As. Asia; Asian; Asiatic
AS. Academy of Science; African Star (decoration); Agricultural Society; Air Service; Air Staff; American-Spanish; anonymous firm (*Anonim Suket*—Turkish); Anthropological Society; apprentice seaman; Aristotelian Society; Arkansas State (college); Armco Steel Corporation (NYSE); Associate in Science; Avicultural Society; in the year of salvation (*anno salutis*—Latin)
a/s after sight; alongside (shipping); care of (*aux soins de*—French)
A/S joint stock company (*Aktieselskabet*—Danish); joint stock company (*Aktsia selts*—Estonian); joint stock company (*Akziun Sabeedriba*—Finnish); joint stock company (*Aktieselskapet*—Norwegian)
A&S Abilene & Southern Railway Company (rr mark)
A-S Anglo-Saxon; anti-submarine
ASA Acoustical Society of America; Actuarial Society of America; Alaska Airlines; Alpha Sigma Alpha (sorority); Amateur Swimming Association; American Schools Association; American Society of Agronomy; American Standards Association; American Statistical Association; American Stockyards Association; American Surgical Association; Armenian Students' Association; Army Security Agency; Auditors of Sheriffs' Accounts
A & SA Atlanta & Saint Andrews Bay Railway Company (rr mark)

ASAA Amateur Softball Association of America; Area Section of the Automobile Association; Associate of the Society of Incorporated Accountants and Auditors
ASACU Anti-Socialist and Anti-Communist Union
ASAE American Society of Agricultural Engineers
ASAHC American Society of Architectural Hardware Consultants
ASAI American Sightseeing Association, Inc
ASAM Associate of the National Society of Art Masters
ASAMPE Allied States Association of Motion Picture Exhibitors
ASAP American Society of Animal Production; as soon as possible (US Army)
Asaph of St. Asaph
ASAPS Anti-Slavery and Aborigines Protection Society
ASAS American Society of Agricultural Sciences
A Sax Anglo-Saxon
asb asbestos
ASB Amalgamated Society of Brassworkers; Asbestos Manufacturing Co. (NYSE)
ASBA American Soy Bean Association; Association of Ship Brokers and Agents
asb c asbestos covered
ASBC American Society of Biological Chemists; American Society of Brewing Chemists
ASBE American Society of Bakery Engineers; American Society of Body Engineers
ASBO Association of School Business Officials
ASBPA American Shore and Beach Preservation Association
ASBSMR Amalgamated Society of Boot and Shoe Makers and Repairers
A Sc Associate in Science
A S C automatic selectivity control
ASC Agnes Scott College; Aircraft Supply Council; Albany State College; Allied Staff Chiefs; Allied Supreme Council; Amalgamated Society of Coopers; American Silk Council; American Society of Cinematographers; American Stores Company (NYSE); Anglo-Soviet Committee; Army Service Corps; Assessors for Shipping Casualties; Associated Ship Chandlers
ASCA American Schools and Colleges Association; American Speech Correction Association
ASCAP American Society of Composers, Authors, and Publishers
ASCB Army Sports Control Board

ASCC American Society for Control of Cancer; American Swiss Chamber of Commerce

asc dr right ascension (*ascension droite*—French)

ASCE American Society of Civil Engineers

ASCEA American Society of Civil Engineers and Architects

ASCL American Sugar Cane League

ASCLU American Society of Chartered Life Underwriters

ASCM Association of Sprocket Chain Manufacturers

ASCS American Society of Corporate Secretaries

A/S Cse anti-submarine course

ASCX Amalgamated Sugar Company, (private car rr mark)

AScW Association of Scientific Workers

ASCWC Associated Societies for the Care of Women and Children

ASD Armament Supply Department (US Navy); Association of Steel Distributors

a/s de care of (*aux soins de*—French)

ASDIC Allied Submarine Detection Investigation Committee; Anti-Submarine Device International Committee

ASDJ American Society of Disk Jockeys

ase air standard efficiency

ASE Amalgamated Society of Engineers; Anti-submarine Establishment (US Navy); Army School of Education; Associate of the Society of Engineers; American Stock Exchange

ASEE American Society for Engineering Education

ASEF Association of Stock Exchange Firms

ASEX Armour Stock Express (private car rr mark)

asf amperes per square foot

ASF American Scandinavian Foundation; Army Service Forces; Association of State Foresters; Automotive Safety Foundation

ASFB Amalgamated Society of Farriers and Blacksmiths

ASFLH American Society of the French Legion of Honor

ASFTB Atlantic Seaboard Freight Tariff Bureau

ASFX American Steel Foundries (private car rr mark)

ASG assign(ed) or (ment) (US Army); Assistant Solicitor General; Assistant Surgeon General

ASGB Aeronautical Society of Great Britain; Anthroposophical Society of Great Britain

ASGBI Anatomical Society of Great Britain and Ireland

asgd assigned

asgmt assignment

As. H hyperopic astigmatism (medicine)

ASH Ashland Oil & Refining Company (NYSE)

A&SH Argyll and Sutherland Highlanders

ASHA American School Health Association; American Social Hygiene Association; American Student Health Association

ashp airship

ASHPS American Scenic and Historic Preservation Society

ASHS American Society for Horticultural Science

ASH & VE American Society of Heating and Ventilating Engineers

ASI Air Services of India; airspeed indicator; Alaska Salmon Industry; American Specification Institute

ASIA American Stone Importers Association; Associate of Society of Incorporated Accountants

ASIL American Society of International Law

ASJSA American Society of Journalism School Administrators

ASK Aspinook Corp. (The) (common stock, ASE)

ASL Acting Sub-Lieutenant; American Society in London; Anti-Strike Law (United States); Architectural Society of Liverpool

ASLA American Society of Landscape Architects

ASLE American Society of Lubricating Engineers

ASLE and F Associated Society of Locomotive Engineers and Firemen

ASLI American Savings & Loan Institute

ASLIB Association of Special Libraries and Information Bureaux

ASLP Amalgamated Society of Lithographic Printers

ASLRA American Short Line Railroad Association

ASLV life insurance (*assurance sur la vie*—French)

ASLW Amalgamated Society of Leather Workers; Auxiliary Society of Lace Workers

asm assembly

ASM Aerovias Sud Americana, Inc; air to surface missile (US Army); American Society for Metals

ASMA American Ski Manufacturers Association

asmblr assembler

A/S MD Anti-Submarine Material Department

ASME American Society of Mechanical Engineers

ASMEA American Spring Manufacturers Export Association (Webb Association)

ASMMA American Supply and Machinery Manufacturers Association

ASMP American Society of Magazine Photographers; American Society of Magazine Publishers; Association of Screen Magazine Publishers

asmt assortment

ASN American Society of Naturalists; army service number; Asiatic Steam Navigation Co.; Assistant Secretary of the Navy

ASNA Advertising Specialty National Association

ASNE American Society of Naval Engineers; American Society of Newspaper Editors

ASNLH Association for the Study of Negro Life and History

ASNOS Anti-fascist Council of National Liberation of Serbia (*Antifasisticka Skupstina Narodnog Oslobodjenja Srbije*)

ASO Air Associates, Inc. (N. J.) (common stock, ASE); Assistant Section Officer (WAAF)

ASOFA Assistant Secretary of the Army (US Army)

ASP accepted under protest— of bills (*accepté sous protêt*—French); Air Stores Park; Alpha Sigma Phi (fraternity); American Society of Photogrammetry; ammunition supply point (US Army); Automatic Steel Products (NYSE)

ASPA American Society for Public Administration (PACH)

ASPB Armed Services Petroleum Board (US Army)

ASPC Anglo-Saxon Petroleum Company

ASPCA American Society for Prevention of Cruelty to Animals

ASPDA Association of State Planning and Development Agencies

ASPEA American Soda Pulp Export Association (Webb Association)

ASPF Association of Superannuation and Pensions Fund

asph asphalt

asph mac asphalt macadam

ASPI Associated Serum Producers, Inc.

Asp. MC Aspinall's Maritime Cases (legal)

ASPO American Society of Planning Officials

A spol and company (A *spolecnost* —Czechoslovakian)

ASPPA Armed Services Petroleum Purchasing Agency

asppc accepted under protest for account—of bills (*accepté sous protêt pour compte*—French)

ASPPR Association of Sugar Producers of Puerto Rico

ASPRS American Society of Plastic and Reconstructive Surgery

ASPT Army School of Physical Training

ASR Air-Sea Rescue Service; American Sugar Refining (NYSE)

ASRE American Society of Refrigerating Engineers

ASRS Amalgamated Society of Railway Servants

ASRX American Sugar Refining Company, The (private car rr mark)

ass. assay; assembly; assistant; association; assortment

Ass. Assyria(n); book of Assizes (legal)

ASS Acts of the Saints (*Acta Sanctorum*—Latin); American Sociological Society; Anglo-Spanish Society; Anglo-Swedish Society; Anti-Slavery Society; Army Signal School; Assistant Secretary of State

Ass. Jerus Assizes of Jerusalem (legal)

ASSA Association of Supervisors of Sorting Assistants (G.P.O.)

ASSAB Atlantic States Shippers Advisory Board

ASSBT American Society of Sugar Beet Technologists

ASSC Air Service Signal Corps

assce assurance

Ass. Com Gen Assistant Commissary General.

assd assessed; assigned; assured

ASSE American Society of Safety Engineers; American Society of Sanitary Engineering

ASSEA Assistant Secretary of State for Economic Affairs

ASSET Association of Supervisory Staffs and Engineering Technicians

ASSI Association for the Study of Snow and Ice

assigt assignment

assim assimilated

assist. assistant

assmt assessment

assn(s) assign(s); assignee(s); association(s)

assnce assurance

assnd assigned

assoc associate; association

Assoc I Min E Associate of the Institute of Mining Engineers

Assoc INA Associate of the Institution of Naval Architects

Assoc Inst T Associate of the Institute of Transport

Assoc ISI Associate of the Iron and Steel Institute

Assoc MICE. Associate Member of the Institution of Civil Engineers

Assoc (M) Inst Gas E Associate (Member) of the Institute of Gas Engineers

Assoc S Associate in Science

Assoc St J Associate of the Order of St John of Jerusalem

assoc w associated with

ASSR Autonomous Soviet Socialist Republic

asst assessment; assistant

ASST assist (US Army)

asst bus. mgr assistant business manager

Asst Cash. Assistant Cashier

Asst Chf Assistant Chief

Asst Com Gen Assistant Commissary General

Asst Commr Assistant Commissioner

asstd assented; assorted

Asst Lib. Assistant Librarian

Asst Sec War Assistant Secretary of War

Asst Surg Assistant Surgeon

ASSU American Sunday School Union

ass'y assembly

Assyr Assyria[n]

Assyriol Assyriology

ast astrology; astronomy

Ast Assistant (US Navy)

A s t Atlantic standard time

AST Alpha Sigma Tau (sorority)

A-St Alto-Stratus (clouds)

ASTA American Seed Trade Association; American Society of Technical Appraisers; American Society of Travel Agents; American Spice Trade Association; American Surgical Trade Association

ASTE American Society of Tool Engineers

ASTHO Association of State and Territorial Health Officers

ASTM American Society for Testing Materials; American Society for Testing Metals; American Society of Trade Movement; American Society of Tropical Medicine

ASTMA American Steel Tire Manufacturers Association

ASTP Army Specialized Training Program

astrol astrologer; astrological; astrology

astron astronomer; astronomical; astronomy

astrophys astrophysical; astrophysics

ASTRP Army Specialized Training Reserve Program

ASTT American Society of Traffic and Transportation

ASTUC Anglo-Soviet Trades Union Committee

ASTWKT Amalgamated Society of Textile Workers and Kindred Trades

ASU Amalgamated Stevedores' Union; American Snowshoe Union; American Students' Union; Area Service Unit (US Army)

ASUUS Amateur Skating Union of the United States

ASV an aeronautical radar

ASW Association of Scientific Workers.

AS&W American Steel and Wire Company Gauge

ASWA American Steel Warehouse Association

ASWAF arms and services on duty with Air Force (US Army)

A/S WD Anti-submarine War Division

ASWH advise soldier write home (US Army)

ASWW Amalgamated Society of Wood Workers

ASX American Smelting & Refining Company (private car rr mark); Associated Laundries of America (NYSE)

ASXRT American Society of X-Ray Technicians

asy asylum

ASYFA Anglo-Soviet Youth Friendship Alliance

asym asymmetric; asymmetrical

ASZ American Society of Zoologists

at. airtight; atmosphere; atomic; attorney

At astatine

a t revert to the original time (*a tempo*—music); air temperature; air transport

A t Atlantic time

AT Admiralty Trawler; Alien Tribunals; Old Testament (*Altes Testament*—German); American Tobacco Company (NYSE); Old Testament (*Ancien Testament*—French); Appellate Tribunals; Archtreasurer; American Translation (Bible)

a/t anti-tank

A/T American Terms (grain trade);

at-% atomic per cent

ATA Aetna Ball & Roller Bearing (NYSE); Air Force Training Auxiliary; Air Transport Auxiliary; Amateur Trapshooting Association; Army Temperance Association; American Taxicab Association; American Teachers Association; American Title Association; American Transit Association; American Tree Association; American Trucking Association; American

Tunaboat Association; Army Transportation Association; Associate in Technical Affairs

ATAA Advertising Typographers Association of America; Air Transport Association of America

ATAAI Advertising Typographers Association of America, Inc

ATABW American Trade Association for British Woollens

ATAE American Trade Association Executives

ATAM Automotive Trade Association Managers

ATAS Air Transport Auxiliary Service

ATAU Air Transport and Allied Undertakings

ATB aeration test burner (heating); anti-tank battery

ATBA American Toll Bridge Association

ATBI Allied Trades of the Baking Industry

a t c aerial tuning condenser

ATC Air Traffic Control; Air Training Corps; Air Transport Command; Air Transport (Canadian) Convention; Area Traffic Commissioner; Art Teachers' Certificate; Automatic Telephone Company

ATCA Air Traffic Conference of America (division of the Air Transport Association); Air Training Corps of America; Associated Traffic Clubs of America

ATCC Air Training Corps Cadet

ATCH attach (US Army)

atchd attached

ATCL Associate of Trinity College (of Music), London

ATCX Ace Tank Car Company (private car rr mark)

ATDS Association of Teachers of Domestic Science

atdt attendant

ATE Atlantic City Electric (NYSE)

a tem a tempo

ATEMA American Tanning Extract Manufacturers Association

ATEX Teas Extract Company (private car rr mark)

ATFAC American Turpentine Farmers Association, Cooperative

ATFP Alliance of Television Film Producers

a t g anti-tank gun

ATG Assoc. Tel. & Tel. (NYSE)

ATG A Associated Tel. & Tel. Co. ("A") (ASE)

At-Gen Attorney-General

At Gew atomic weight (*Atomgewicht* —German)

ath athletic

Ath Athabasca; Athenaeum; Athenian; Athens; Athol

athw athwartship

a t i aerial tuning inductance

ATI American Toy Institute; Asbestos Textile Institute; Asphalt Tile Institute; Associate of the Textile Institute; Association of Technical Institutions

ATK attack (US Army)

Atk Atkyn's English Chancery Reports (legal)

Atl Atlanta; Atlantic; Atlantic Reporter (legal)

ATL American Tariff League; Atlantic Coast Fisheries Co. (The) (ASE)

ATLA Air Transport Licensing Authority

ATLNC Association of Teachers of Language in Negro Colleges

Atl O Atlantic Ocean

ATLX Armour Tank Line (private car rr mark)

atm atmosphere; atmospheric

ATM Army Training Memorandum; Assistant Traffic Manager; Associated Tobacco Manufacturers

ATMC Alloy Tank Manufacturers Council

ATMEA American Tire Manufacturers Export Association

atm pr atmospheric pressure

ATMX United States Atomic Energy Commission, New York, N. Y. (private car rr mark)

at. no. atomic number

ato courteous (*atento*—Spanish)

ATO Alpha Tau Omega (fraternity); Altorfer Brothers Co. (common stock, ASE)

ATOA American Tung Oil Association; Associated Tavern Owners of America

Atomgew atomic weight (*Atomgewicht*—German)

aton atonement

ATP army training program (US Army)

ATPI American Textbook Publishers Institute

a tps army troops

a t r aircraft trouble report; anti-tank regiment

a t r i m a as their respective interests may appear

a t s air training scheme; animal tub sized (paper); anti-tetanic serum; at the suit of (legal)

ATS Aeronautical Training Society; Air Technical Service; Alpha Tau Sigma (fraternity); American Television Society; American Tract Society; Army Transport Service; Associate of Theological Study; Associate of the Theological Senate (Congregational); Associates Investment Company (NYSE); Aux-

iliary Territorial Service

ATSA Aero Transportes

ATSC Associate of the Tonic Sol-Fa College

ATSEFI Auxiliary Territorial Service Expeditionary Force Institutes

ATSF Atchison, Topeka & Santa Fe Railway, The (rr mark)

AT&SF Atchison, Topeka and Santa Fe Railway Company

att attach; attaché; attached; attention; attorney

AT&T American Telephone & Telegraph Company

ATTA American Tin Trade Association

atten attention

attestn attestation

attg attending

Att-Gen Attorney-General

ATTI Association of Teachers in Technical Institutions

ATTN attention (US Army)

attrib attribute; attributed [to]; attributive

ATTS Amalgamated Typefounders' Trade Society

ATTX American Turpentine & Tar Company Ltd. (private car rr mark)

atty attorney

Atty & C attorney and client (legal)

Atty Gen Op Attorney Generals' Opinions, United States (legal)

ATU Alcohol Tax Unit; Automatic Washer Company (NYSE)

at. vol atomic volume

ATW Amalgamated Textile Warehousemen; American Theatre Wing; Athey Products Corporation (NYSE)

at. wt atomic weight

at. y ss very truly yours (*atento y seguro servidor*—Spanish)

a u angstrom unit; astronomical unit

au author

Au gold

AU Acadia University (Canada); Actors' Union; Alfred University; Allen University; American University; in the year of the city [of Rome] (*Anno Urbis*—Latin); Atlantic Union

A/U attached unassigned (US Army)

AUA Allied Underwear Association; American Unitarian Association; Associated Unions of America

AUAW Amalgamated Union of Asphalt Workers

AU of B American University of Beirut

AUBBER Associated University Bureau of Business and Economic Research

AUBLS American Uniform Boiler Law Society

Aub Theol Sem Auburn Theological Seminary

AUC year from the building of Rome (*anno urbis conditae*—Latin)

AU of C American University of Cairo

Auch Auchinleck's Manuscript Cases (legal)

aucte by the authority (*auctoritate*—Latin)

AUCTU All Union Council of Trade Unions

aud audit; auditor

AUD Aldens, Incorporated (NYSE)

aud disb auditor disbursements

Aud-Gen Auditor-General

Aud Treas Dept Auditor of the Treasury Department

Aufdr imprint (*Aufdrucke*—German)

Aufl edition (*Auflage*—German)

Aug augment (ative); augere (increase—pharmacy); August (*Augusztus*—Hungarian); (*Augusti*—Swedish); Augustus

auj today (*aujourd'hui*—French)

AUM air to underwater missile (US Army); Automatic Canteen Company of America (NYSE)

a u n free from marking (commercial) (*abseque utta nota*—Latin)

AUPM American United Presbyterian Missions

AUPX Austin Powder Company (private car rr mark)

Aur Aurelius

AUR Automatic Voting Machine (NYSE)

aurin an ear cone (pharmacy) (*aurinarium*—Latin)

auristill ear drops (pharmacy) (*auristillae*—Latin)

a u s done as above (*actum ut supra*—Latin) (legal)

AUS Ambassador of the United States; Army of the United States

Aus Austin; Austria; Austrian

Ausl export (*Ausländisch*—German)

AUSS Assistant Under Secretary of State

Aust Austin's English County Court Cases (legal)

Aust-Hung Austria-Hungary; Austro-Hungarian

Austl Australia; Australasia

Aust LT Australian Law Times (legal)

Ausw quantity (*Auswage*—German)

aut author (*auteur*—French, autore—Italian); autograph; automobile; automatic

AUT Association of University Teachers

auth authentic; authoress; authorized; authority

AUTHGR authority granted (US Army)

Auth Ver Authorized Version (of the Bible)

AUTMV automotive (US Army)

auto. automatic; automotive

autog autograph[ed]

au tr aural training

autref formerly (*autrefois*—French)

AUU Association of Urban Universities

aux auxiliary; auxiliary craft

auxfs auxiliary fire station

av April (*avril*—French); attorney (*avocat*—French); avenue; average; avoirduprois (weight); credit (*avoir*—French)

Av Aveyron (French department)

a v acid value; atomic volume; he,she, lived so many years (*annos vixit*—Latin); to the value of (*ad valorem*—Latin)

a/v average

AV Artillery Volunteers; Authorized Version

A v/a at sight (*a la vista*—Spanish)

AVA Administration of Veterans' Affairs; American Vocational Association

AVAL available (US Army)

a v c automatic volume control (radio)

AVC American Veterans Committee; Army Veterinary Corps; Artillery Volunteer Corps; Association of Vitamin Chemists

AVCM Associate of Victoria College of Music

avd deceased (*avdøde*—Norwegian)

AVD A B C Vending Corporation (NYSE); Army Veterinary Department; Army Victualling Department

AVDA American Venereal Disease Association

a v e automatic volume expansion

ave avenue

AVE Aerovias Venezuela Europe

AVENSA Aerovia Venezolanas

avert. notification (*avertissement*—French)

AVFR available for reassignment (US Army)

avg average

AVG American Volunteer Group

AVGAS aviation gasoline (US Army)

AVI Association of Veterinary Inspectors

AVIANCA Aerovias Nacionales de Colombia

avdp avoirdupois

av l average length (lumber)

A-VL Anti-Vivisection League

AVL Aroostook Valley Railroad Company (rr mark)

AVM Air Vice Marshal

AVMA American Veterinary Medical Association

avn aviation

AVN Air Vietnam

AVNOJ Anti-Fascist Council of National Liberation of Yugoslavia (*Antifašističko Veče Narodnog Oslobodjenja Jugoslavije*—Yugoslavian)

AVO Administrative Veterinary Officer

AVOIL aviation oil (US Army)

AVPA American Vencer Package Association

AVRE Armoured Vehicles Royal Engineers

AVS Anti-Vivisection Society; Army Veterinary Service

av sec aviation section

av w average width (lumber)

AVWWII American Veterans of World War II

a w all water (transportation); all widths (lumber); atomic weight

a/w actual weight

AW Ahnapee & Western Railway Company (rr mark); Article of War (US Army); automatic weapons (US Army); outside diameter (*äussere weite*—German)

AWA American Warehousemen's Association; Aluminum Wares Association; American Wine Association; American Women's Association; Aviation Writers Association

AWAA American Watch Assemblers Association

AWAFBF Associated Women of the American Farm Bureau Federation

AWAIUU Automobile Workers of America, Internation Union, United

AWAMD American Warehousemen's Association, Merchandise Division

AWAVI Adviser on War Administration to the Viceroy of India

AWB Association of Women Broadcasters

AWC Acting Wing Commander; Agricultural Wages Committee; Air War College; American Women's Club; American Wool Council; Anaconda Wire & Cable (NYSE); Army War College (U.S.A.); Army Welfare Committee

AWCA American War Correspondents Association

AWCT Association of Wireless and Cable Telegraphists

AWE Acme Wire Company (ASE)

AWF American Wildlife Foundation

AWG American wire gauge; Art Workers' Guild

AWHA Australian Women's Home Army

AWHRC American Women's Hospital Reserve Corps

AWIMA American Washer and Ironer Manufacturers Association

AWK American Water Works Company

(NYSE)
a w l artesian well lease
A&WI America and West Indies Station (US Navy)
AWM American War Mothers
AWMA Aluminum Window Manufacturers Association; American Walnut Manufacturers Association; American Weldment Manufacturers Association
AWO Army Welfare Officer; Atlas Plywood Corporation (common stock, ASE)
AWMOAI Affiliated Washing Machine Operators Association, Inc
AWOI American Waterways Operators, Inc.
AWOL absent (absence) without leave (US Army)
AWP Angostura-Wuppermann Corporation
A&WP Atlanta and West Point Railroad Company
AWPA American Wood Preservers Association
AWS Aircraft Warning Service; Air Weather Service (US Army); American Welding Society; Army Welfare Services

AWSVC Air Warning Service (US Army)
AWSX Alan Wood Steel Company (private car rr mark)
AWTAO Association of Water Transportation Accounting Officers
AWTD Air and Water Transport Division; Air Warfare Training Division (US Navy)
AWU Australian Workers' Union
AWVS American Women's Voluntary Services
AWWA American Water Works Association
AWWPA American Wire Weavers Protective Association
awy airway
ax. axiom; axis
AX Atlantic Coast Line Railroad Company (NYSE)
AXD Alpha Xi Delta (sorority)
AXS Smith (Alexander), Inc (NYSE)
AXSIGCOMM axis or axes of signal communication (US Army)
AY Allegheny & Western Railway (NYSE)
AYA Austrian Youth Association

AYC Alexandra Yacht Club; Austrian Youth Congress
AYD American Youth for Democracy
AYH American Youth Hostels
AYHA American Youth Hostel Association
AYL Anderson, Clayton & Company (NYSE); As You Like It
AYM Ancient York Mason
ayn MII the same author (ayni MDellif—Turkish)
Ayr Ayrshire
az azimuth; azure (heraldry); nitrogen (azote—French)
aZ on credit, on account (auf Zeit —German)
AZ Aerolinee Italiane Internazionali (ALITALIA); Alpha Zeta (society); Atlas Corporation (NYSE)
AZC American Zionist Council
AZI American Zinc Institute
Az Is Azores Islands
Azo Azores
AZO Alpha Zeta Omega (fraternity)
AZR Aigle Azur
AZX American Zinc Company of Illinois (private car rr mark)

B

b at the, with the (beim—German); at, with (bei—German); bachelor; bacillus; balboa; ball; base; bass; battle; bay; beam; bill, good for (billet, bon—French); blessed (beato—Spanish); boils; boils at; boliviano; bolivai; bonida
b/ bag, bale
B Baldwin-Lima-Hamilton (NYSE); Bancus (the common bench—legal); Baumé; Belgium; Bey (Turkish); Bible; bishop (chess); British; boron
b a sand bath (balneum arenae—Latin)
ba bachelor
b/a billed at
Ba barium
BA atomic bomb (Bombe Atomique —French); French department (Basses-Alpes); Bachelor of Arts (Baccalaureus Artium—Latin); Belt Association; Board of Agriculture; Board of Air; Boeing Airplane (NYSE); British Academy; British America; British Army; British Association (for the advancement of Science); British Association screw-thread; Buenos Aires; Buffalo Ankerite Gold Mines (NYSE); Bureau of Advertising; Burma; Buisson Ardent—The

Burning Bush (Freemason); Boys Apparel and Accessories Manufacturers Association
Baa Baal, Baalam
BAA Basketball Association of America; Billiard Association of America; British Acetylene Association; British Archaeological Association; British Astronomical Association; Bachelor of the Art of Architecture
BAAS British Association for the Advancement of Science
Bab Babington (botany); Babylonian
BAB Babbitt (B.T.), Inc (NYSE)
BABA Bachelor of Arts in Business Administration; Boys Apparel Buyers Association
Ba & Be Ball & Beatty's Irish Chancery Reports (legal)
BABI Broadcast Advertising Bureau, Inc
Bac Baccalaureus (bachelor)
BAC Bellanca Aircraft Corporation (NYSE); Board of the Air Council; Board of the Army Council; Boeing Aircraft Company; Business Advisory Council; British Aircraft Constructors; British Association of Chemists; British Automatic Company
BACAL Butter and Cheese Association Ltd
BAcc Bachelor of Accounting
BACC[BSF] Billiards Association Control Council [and Billiards for the Services Fund]
BACH Bachelor of Arts in Chemistry
back. backwardation (securities)
BACS Blue Albion Cattle Society
bact bacteriological; bacteriology; bacterium (medicine)
bacter bacteriologist
BAD Base Air Depot
B Adm Eng Bachelor of Administrative Engineering
B A E Belfast Association of Engineers; Bureau of Agricultural Economics (U.S.A.)
BAEA British Actors' Equity Association
BA Educa Bachelor of Arts in Education
BAEF Belgian American Educational Foundation
B Aero E Bachelor of Aeronautical Engineering
BAF Banff Oil Ltd (NYSE); British Air Force
BAFT Bankers Association for Foreign Trade
BAG baggage (US Army) Beaux Arts Gallery

B Agr Bachelor of Agriculture (*Baccalaureus Agriculturae*)

BAGS Buenos Aires and Great Southern (railroad)

B Ag Sc Bachelor of Agricultural Science

BAGX Bloch & Guggenheimer, Inc (private car rr mark)

BAHU Bureau of Accident and Health Underwriters

BAI Bachelor of Engineering (*Baccalaureus Artis Ingeniariae*)

Bail. Bailey's Law Reports (legal)

Bail. Eq Bailey's Equity Reports (legal)

Bals Bahama Islands

BAIU British Association for International Understanding

BA J Bachelor of Arts in Journalism

BAK Baker-Raulang Company (NYSE)

BAKX Belle Alkali Company (private car rr mark)

bal balance; ballet

Bal Baluchistan

BAL Baldwin Securities (NYSE); Bonanza Air Lines, Inc

Bald. Baldwin

Balf Balfour's Practice (legal)

ball. ballast

Ball. Coll Oxon Balliol College, Oxford

BALL British Association for Labour Legislation

B Alp Basses-Alpes (French Department)

BALPA British Air Line Pilots' Association

bals balsam (*balsamum*—Latin) (pharmacy)

BALS Bachelor of Arts in Library Science

Balt Balthasar; Baltimore

BAMCL British Aircraft Manufacturing Company Limited

BA Mus Ed Bachelor of Arts in Music Education

Banc Sup King's Bench (*Bancus Superior*) (legal)

bank. banking

BANK International Bank for Reconstruction and Development

bank clgs bank clearings

bankcy bankruptcy (legal)

bank debs. bank debits

Bank. and Ins R Bankruptcy and Insolvency Reports (legal)

Banks. Banks' Reports (legal)

Bann Bannister's Reports (legal)

Bann & A Pat Ca Banning & Arden's Patent Cases (legal)

BA Nurs Bachelor of Arts in Nursing

BAO Bachelor of Obstetrics; Base Account Officer; British American Oil (NYSE)

BAOR British Army of the Rhine

BAOX British American Oil Company Ltd, The (private car rr mark)

b à p bills payable (*billets à payer* —French)

bap baptism; baptized

BAP Beta Alpha Psi (fraternity)

Bapt Baptist

bar. baritone; barometer; barometric; barque; barrel; barrister; bills receivable (*billets à recevoir*—French)

Bar. Barbados; Barbara; Baruch

B Ar Bachelor of Architecture

BAR Book Auction Records; British Association of Refrigerators; Browning automatic rifle

B&Ar Bangor and Aroostook Railroad Company

Bar. & Ad Barnewall & Adolphus' King's Bench Reports (legal)

Barb. Barbour's Supreme Court Reports (legal)

Barb. Abs Barbour's Abstracts (legal)

Barb. Ark. Barber's Reports, Arkansas (legal)

Barb. Ch Barbour's Chancery (legal)

BARBLN barrage balloon (US Army)

Barb. SC Barbour's Supreme Court Reports (legal)

B Arch. Bachelor of Architecture

BARM British Admiralty Repair Mission

Bar. N Barnes' Notes (legal)

Barn. Barnard

Barn. & Ald Barnewall & Alderson's King's Bench Reports (legal)

Barn. Ch Barnardiston's English Chancery Reports (legal)

b&arp bare and acid resisting paint

barr barrister

B & ARR Boston and Albany Railroad

bars. barrels

Bart Baronet; Bartholomew

Bart El Cas Bartlett's Congressional Election Cases (legal)

Bart's St. Bartholomew's Hospital, London

bas basso (music)

Bas Basilius; Basutoland

BAS Basic Refractories, Inc (NYSE); Berkshire Archaeological Society; Bessemer Acid Steel; Brewers' Association of Scotland

BA Sc Bachelor of Agricultural Science; Bachelor of Applied Science

BASI Brown Animal Sanatory Institution

BA Sp Bachelor of Arts in Speech

bat. battalion; battery; battle; battleship (US Navy)

Bat. Batavia

BAT Bank of Algeria and Tunis; Butler Air Transport Pty. Ltd; Technical Assistance Board (TAB)

BATC Building Apprenticeship and Training Council

bat. chg battery charging

BAT[Co.] British-American Tobacco [Company]

Bat. Dig. Battle's Digest (legal)

BATM British Admiralty Technical Mission

BATRECON battle reconnaissance (US Army)

batt battery (*batterie*—French)

BAU British Association unit

Bav Bavaria; Bavarian

BAW Babcock & Wilcox Company (NYSE); British Acetylene and Welding Association

BAYX Bay Chemical Company (division of Morton Salt Co) (private car rr mark)

b b bail bond; ball bearings; balloon barrage; bank book; bank note (*billet de banque*—French); baseball; base on balls; basketball; bearer bonds; black-bordered (stationery); branch bill; break bulk

b and b bed and breakfast

BB Bitter and Burton (beer); Blue Book; B'nai B'rith; Boys' Brigade; Bureau of the Budget; Burning Bush (freemasonry); b and better (lumber)

BBA Bachelor of Business Administration; Barristers' Benevolent Association; Big Brothers of America; British Bankers' Association; British Beekeepers' Association

BBAI Bermuda Benevolent Association, Inc

b b b bed, breakfast, and bath

BBB bankers' blanket bond; Beta Beta Beta (society); extra very black (of pencils)

BBBC British Boxing Board of Control

b b c baseball club; bromobenzyl cyanide (gas)

BBC Big Ben Council; Block and Bridle Club; British Broadcasting Corporation; Burry Biscuit Corporation (NYSE)

BBCUA Barbers & Beauty Culturists Union of America

BEE Bachelor of Electrical Engineering

BBFC British Board of Film Censors

BBH battalion beachhead (US Army)

BBIA Billiard and Bowling Institute of America

BBII Brass and Bronze Ingot Institute

B Bisc Bay of Biscay
bbl barrel
BBL Big Brothers League
bbls/day barrels per day
BBMA British Brush Manufacturers' Association; British Button Manufacturers' Association
BBMG Bristol Board Manufacturers Group
BBO Barber Oil Corporation (NYSE)
b b s box bark strips (lumber)
BBS Bachelor of Business Science
BBSI Beauty and Barber Supply Institute
BBTB Brush and Broom Trade Board
B Bus Ad Bachelor of Business Administration
b c bad character; balloon command; bank clearing; basso continuo (music); battery commander; bayonet cap; bolt circle broadcast band; building congress
BC Bachelor of Chemistry; Bachelor of the Classics; Bachelor of Commerce; Bachelor of Surgery; Bankruptcy Court; Beaver College; Before Christ; Belgian Congo (Africa); Bennington College; Board of Control; Boston College; Bowdoin College; Bristol Channel (shipping); British Cinemas; British Columbia; British Commonwealth; British Corporation (naval engineering); British Council; Burnham Committee (education); Butte Copper & Zinc Company (NYSE)
b/c bill for collection; board of customs
B & C Barnewall and Cresswell (Law Reports); building and contents (insurance)
B of C Board of Customs; Bureau of Customs
BCA Banco de los Andes (ASE); Bank Charter Act; Birth Control Association; Boys' Clubs of America; British Caravan Association; British Charities Association; British Continental Airways; Buddhist Churches of America; Bureau of Current Affairs
BCASS British Chartered Accountants Students' Society
BCB Bakers' Conciliation Board
BCC Bail Court Reports (legal); Belfast City Commission; British Council of Churches; British-Czechoslovak Centre; Brunswick-Balke-Collender Company (NYSE)
BCCCUS British Commonwealth Chamber of Commerce in the United States
BCCS British Council of Christian Settlements

BCCUS Belgian Chamber of Commerce in the United States
BCD bad conduct discharge (US Army); Belfast and County Down (railway); Bituminous Coal Division (United States)
BCDA Biscuit and Cracker Distributors Association
BCE Bachelor of Chemical Engineering; Bachelor of Civil Engineering; Board of Customs and Excise; British Commonwealth and Empire
BCECC British—Central-European Chamber of Commerce
BCEIUA Building and Civil Engineering Industries Uniformity Agreement
BCFT Beechcraft (aircraft)
BCG Calmette-Guérin bacillus (medicine)
BCGA British Commercial Gas Association; British Cotton-Growing Association
bch bunch
Bch Burchard
B Ch Bachelor of Surgery (Baccalaureus Chirurgiae—Latin); Barbour's Chancery Reports (legal)
BCH Beech Creek Railroad Company (NYSE)
B Ch D Bachelor of Dental Surgery (Baccalaureus Chirurgiae Dentalis)
B Chem E Bachelor of Chemical Engineering
Bches-du-R Bouches-du-Rhône (French department)
B Chir Bachelor of Surgery
B Chrom Bachelor of Chromatics
BCI Bituminous Coal Institute; Bureau of Contract Information (insurance); Butchers' Charitable Institution
BCIRA British Cast Iron Research Association
bc l broadcast listener
BCL Bachelor of Canon Law; Bachelor of Civil Law
BCLA Broadmoor Criminal Lunatic Asylum
BCM Blackheath Conservatoire of Music; British Commercial Monomark; British Consular Mail
BC & M Belgian Congo and Mandate
BCMA Brattice Cloth Manufacturers Association; British Corset Manufacturers' Association
BCMAA Biscuit and Cracker Manufacturers Association of America
BCMC Bureau Central Militaire de Circulation
BCMS Bible Churchmen's Missionary Society
BCN British Celanese (NYSE); British Commonwealth of Nations

BCO Bank Clerks' Orphanage; Bolsa Chica Oil Corporation (NYSE)
B & Co D (R) Belfast and County Down (railway)
b coeff block coefficient (naval engineering)
BCOG British College of Obstetricians and Gynaecologists
B Com Bachelor of Commerce
B Com Sc Bachelor of Commercial Science
B Comm Bachelor of Commerce
b cont basso continuo (music)
BCP Bachelor in City Planning; Blue Cross Plan (Hospital Insurance, United States); Book of Common Prayer; British Col. Power (NYSE)
BCPA British Commonwealth Pacific Airlines
BCP B Brit. Columbia Pw. Corp. Ltd ("B" Stock) (ASE)
BCP E British College of Physical Education
BCPM Baruch Commission on Physical Medicine
BCPW British Committee for Polish Welfare
BCRI Bituminous Coal Research, Inc
BCS Bachelor of Chemical Science; Bachelor of Commercial Science; Battle Cruiser Squadron; Bengal Civil Service; British Ceramic Society; British Colonial Secretary
BCSO British Central Scientific Office (Washington)
BCT Baker Charity Trust
BCTC Building and Construction Trades Council
BCURA British Coal Utilization Research Association
BCW Bedford College for Women (London); Bureau of Child Welfare
BCWA British Cotton Waste Association
BCWIUA Bakery & Confectionery Workers' International Union of America
BCX Beech Aircraft Corporation (NYSE); Brown Company (private car rr mark)
BCYCAS British Columbia and Yukon Church Aid Society
b d back dividends; bank debits; bank dividends; bank draft; base diameter; battle dress; bills discounted (banking); boom defense; brass disc (plumbing); twice a day (bis in die—pharmacy)
bd beaded (plumbing); board; boulevard; bound; bundle; volume (band—German)
b/d barrels per day; brought down (accounting)

BD base depot or bomb disposal (US Army); United States (*Birlesik Devletler*—Turkish)

BDA British Dental Association

BDAE Barrow and District Association of Engineers

BDBJ Board of Deputies of British Jews

b d c bottom dead center (engineering)

BDC Burma Defence Council

BD & C British Dominions and Colonies

BDCT Board of Directors of City Trusts

BDD Boom Defence Department

BDDRE Brigadier and Deputy Director of Royal Engineers

Bde brigade; volumes (*Bände*—German)

Bde-Maj Brigade-Major

B Des Bachelor of Design

BDE Bomber Development Establishment

BDES British Dominions Emigration Society

bd ft board foot

bdg binding (book trade)

BDGH Base Depot and General Hospital

B DI Bachelor of Didactics

b d l bearing deviation indicator; both days inclusive

BDI Bandini Petroleum Company (NYSE)

BDK Black & Decker Mfg Company (NYSE)

bdl bundle(s)

bdl bk s bundled bark strips (lumber)

BDL British Drama League

BDM Births, Deaths, and Marriages; League of German Girls (*Bund Deutscher Mädel*—German)

BDO Boom Defense Officer (naval)

B D & O Blackham, Dundas & Osborne's Nisi Prius Reports (legal)

Bdr Bombardier; Brigadier

B Dr Art Bachelor of Dramatic Art

Bdr-Gnr Bombardier-Gunner

bd rts bond rights (securities)

BDRY boundary (US Army)

bds boards (bookbinding); bonds; bundles

BDS Bachelor of Dental Surgery; Bomb Disposal Squad

B D Sc Bachelor of Dental Science

BDST British Double Summer Time

BDU Bomb Disposal Unit

BDW Baldwin Rubber Co. (common stock, ASE)

Bdx Bordeaux (France)

b e bacillary emulsion (medicine)

Bé Baumé (hydrometer)

Be beryllium (chemistry)

B/E bill of entry

BE Bachelor of Education; Bachelor of the Elements; Bachelor of Elocution; Bachelor of Engineering; Bank of England; Benguet Consol. Mining (NYSE); Bill of Exchange; Board of Education; Boston Elevated Railway (NYSE); British Embassy; British Empire; Buddhist Era; Bureau of Explosives; Bachelor of Expression

b & e beginning and ending

B of E Bank of England; Board of Education (obsolete); Board of Estimate

BEA Barn Equipment Association; Brassfounders' Employers Association; British East Africa; British Engineers' Association; British Esperanto Association; British European Airways, Corporation

BEAC British European Airways Corporation

BEAIRA British Electrical and Allied Industries Research Association

BEAMA British Electrical and Allied Manufacturers' Association

Beau Beaufort; Beauregard

Beav Beavan's (Law Reports)

Beav & Wal Ry Cas Beavan & Walford's Railway and Canal Cases (legal)

bec because

BEC Beckman Instruments, Inc (NYSE)

BECC British Empire Cancer Campaign

Bech Bechuanaland

BECX Buffalo Electro-Chemical Company, Inc (private car rr mark)

B Ed Bachelor of Education

BED. Bachelor of Elementary Didactics

BEDA British Electrical Development Association

B Ed In Phys Ed Bachelor of Education in Physical Education

Beds. Bedfordshire (English County)

BEDT Brooklyn Eastern District Terminal

B Educ Bachelor of Education

Bee. Bee's United States District Court Reports (legal)

BEE Bachelor of Electrical Engineering; British Empire Exhibition; British Employers' Executive

Bee. Adm Bee's Admiralty (legal)

BEF Basic Energy Foods (United States); Best Foods, Inc (NYSE); Bonus Expeditioncry Force; British Empire Forces; British Employers' Federation; British Expeditionary Force

befe before (legal)

beg. begin; beginning

BEG Berghoff Brewing Corporation (NYSE)

BEGTS Book Edge Gilders' Trade Society

BEI Board of Education Inspectorate

BEIA Board of Education Inspectors' Association

beif, beiflgd [sent] herewith (*beifolgend*—German)

belgeb bound (in with something else) (*beigelbunden*—German)

Beibl supplements (Beiblätter—German)

BEK Beck (A. S.) Shoe Corporation (common stock, ASE)

bel below

Bel Belgian; Belgium; Belinda; Belgrade; Belgravia

BEL Bachelor of English Literature; Belden Manufacturing Company (NYSE); British Empire League

B El Eng Bachelor of Electrical Engineering

Belg Coug Belgian Congo

Belg pat. Belgian patent

Beling & Van Beling & Vanderstraaten's Ceylon Reports (legal)

Bell Ap Ca Bell's Scotch Appeals (legal)

Bell CHC Bell's Reports, Calcutta High Court (legal)

Bell H C Bell's Reports, High Court (legal)

Bell Sc Dig Bell's Scottish Digest (legal)

BELRA British Empire Leprosy Relief Association

BEM Beaunit Mills, Inc (NYSE); British Empire Medal

BEMA Bakery Equipment Manufacturers Association

BEMCSLF Board of Education of the Methodist Church, Student Loan Fund

ben blessing (*benedictio*—Latin)

Ben. Benjamin

BEN Benrus Watch Company Inc (NYSE)

BENA British Empire Naturalists' Association

Ben. Assoc Beneficial Associations (legal)

BENCOM Bentley's Complete Phrase Telegraphic Code

B en Dr Bachelor of Laws (*Bachelier en Droit*—French)

Bened Benedict

Benedic (liturgical), canticle from Psalm ciii

BENELUX Belgium-The Netherlands-Luxemburg

benevol benevolence (*benevolentia*—Latin)

Beng Bengali

B Eng Bachelor of Engineering

B Eng A Bachelor of Agricultural Engineering

B Eng Physics Bachelor of Engineering Physics

Beng LR Bengal Law Reports (legal)

Benj Benjamin

Benl & Dal Benloe & Dalison's Common Pleas Reports (legal)

Ben Mon Ben Monroe's Reports, Kentucky (legal)

Benn & H Cr Cas Bennett & Heurd's Leading Criminal Cases (legal)

Ben. NI Bengal Native Infantry

BENSEC Bentley's Second Phrase Telegraphic Code

Bent. Bentley's Reports (legal)

BEO Board of Economic Operations (United States)

BEPO British Empire Producers' Organization

BEPX Belcher Oil Company (private car rr mark)

beqd bequeathed (legal)

beqt bequest (legal)

Ber Beranger; Berlin; Bermuda

ber computed (berechnet—German)

berat Ing consulting engineer (beratender ingenieur—German)

Ber Is Bermuda Islands

Berk Berkeley

Berks Berkshire (English county)

Bern Bernard; Bernard's Church Cases (legal)

Bert. Bertram

BERSEAPAT Bering Sea Patrol

Berw Berwick (Scotland)

bes especially (besonders—German); in charge of (besorgt—German)

BES Bachelor of Engineering Science; Bradford Engineering Society; British Ecological Society

BESA British Engineering Standards Association

B ès A Bachelor of Arts (Bachelier ès Arts—French)

beschn condensed (Beschnitten—German)

B ès L Bachelor of Letters (Bachelier ès Lettres—French)

BESL British Empire Service League (Canadian Legion)

BESL Aux British Empire Service League Auxiliary

Bess. Bessemer

BESS Bank of England Statistical Summary

B ès S Bachelor of Science (Bachelier ès Sciences—French)

best. order (bestellung—German)

bet. between

BETAA British Export Trade Advertising Association

Beth. Bethel; Bethlehem

betr concerning (betreffs, betreffend—German)

BETRO British Export Trade Research Organization

betw between

BEU Beau Brummell Ties, Inc (NYSE); British Empire Union

bev bevel

Bev & M Bevin & Mill's Reports (legal)

BEW Board of Economic Warfare

Bey Beyrout

bez respecting, with reference to (bezüglich—German)

Bez district (Bezirk—German)

bezw respectively (bezichungsweise —German)

b f bankruptcy fee; bass frequency (basse fréquence—French); beat frequency; beer firkin; bloody fool (colloquial); bold face (type); blank flange (plumbing); blind flange (plumbing); firkin of butter; in good faith (bona fide—Latin)

bf brief (legal)

BF Bachelor of Finance; Bachelor of Forestry; Bache Foundation; Banque de France; Brez Foundation; British Forces; Buchanan Foundation; Budd Company (NYSE); Buhl Foundation; Burus Federation; Byram Foundation

BFA Bachelor of Fine Arts; Brass Forging Association; British Fellmongers' Association; British First Army; British Footpaths Association

BFA In Dr Art Bachelor of Fine Arts in Dramatic Art

BFAC Burlington Fine Arts Club

BFAD British First Airborne Division

BFA Ed Bachelor of Fine Arts in Education

BFA Sp Bachelor of Fine Arts in Speech

BFA Mus Bachelor of Fine Arts in Music

BFA PS Bachelor of Fine Arts in Painting and Sculpturing

BFB British Flight Battalion; "Bundles for Britain"

BFBPW British Federation of Business and Professional Women

BFBS British and Foreign Bible Society

BFC Bellefonte Central Railroad Company; British Free Corps; Buffalo Forge Company (NYSE)

BFCAA Birmingham and Five Counties Architectural Association

BFCS British Friesian Cattle Society

BFCX Berger Foods Company (private car rr mark)

BFD Brown-Forman Distillers Corporation (NYSE)

BFDC Bureau of Foreign and Domestic Commerce

BFG Brad Foote Gear Works (NYSE)

BFHMF British Felt Hat Manufacturers' Federation

BFI British Film Industries; British Film Institute; Business Forms Institute

B1c Boilermaker First Class (US Navy)

BFIX Borden's Farm Products Division of the Borden Company (private car rr mark)

BFMP British Federation of Master Printers

b f o beat frequency oscillator

BFPO British Field Post Office

BFS Bankruptcy Fee Stamps; British Flight Student; Booth Fisheries Corporation (NYSE)

BFSLA Bankers Federal Savings and Loan Association

BFSS British and Foreign Sailors' Society; British and Foreign School Society

BFT Baptist Foundation of Texas

BFTA British Fur Trade Alliance

BFUP Board of Fire Underwriters of the Pacific

BFUW British Federation of University Women

BFWPS Billingsgate Fish Workers' Protection Society

BFX Best Foods Inc (private car rr mark)

b g bank guard; basso generale (music); bay gelding (turf)

bg bag; bearing; being

BG Birmingham Gauge (wire); Bren gun; Brigadier General; Briggs Mfg. Company (NYSE); British Grenadiers; British Guiana; Bulgaria

b/g bonded goods

BGA Barre Granite Association; British Gliding Association

Bg Adj Brigade Adjutant

BGAL British Guiana Airways Ltd

BGB [Associated] Booksellers of Great Britain

Bg C Brigade Commander

BGC Bailiff Grand Cross (freemasonry)

B Gen Brigadier-General

B G Ed Bachelor of General Education

BGG Briggs & Stratton Corporation (NYSE)

BGGS Brigadier General General Staff

BGH Burroughs Adding Machine (NYSE)

bght bought

BGM Bethnal Green Museum; British Gallantry Medal

Bgmstr 1c Buglemaster First Class

Bgmstr 2c Buglemaster Second Class

BGRA British Greyhound Racing Association

bgs bags

BGS Beta Gamma Sigma (fraternity); Bigelow-Sanford Carpet (NYSE);

Bombing and Gunnery School; Brigadier General Staff; British Goat Society

Bg Sf P O Brigade Staff Petty Officer

BGSU Bowling Green State University

BGT Bridgeport Gas Light Co. (The) (ASE)

B Gu British Guiana

b h bay horse; brown horse (racing); candle-hour (*bougie-heure*—French)

BH beachhead (US Army); bulkhead; Bachelor of Humanics; Barnardo's Homes; Base Hospital; Bridewell Hospital; British Honduras; Burlington House

B/H bill of health (shipping); Bordeaux to Hamburg inclusive (shipping)

"BH" horse or horse and carriage express (rr car)

B of H Band of Hope; Board of Health

b h a base helix angle (gears)

BHA British Homeopathic Association; British Hospitals Association; British Humane Association

B'ham Birmingham

BHARAT Bharat Airways Ltd

BHB Bush Term. Bldgs. (NYSE)

BHC British High Commissioner

BHCIUAJ Barbers, Hairdressers & Cosmetologists International Union of America, the Journeymen

bhd bulkhead

B & H Dig. Bennett & Heard's Digest

B'head Birkenhead

BHI British Horological Institute

BHK Bohack (H. C.) Company Inc (common stock, ASE)

BHL Bachelor of Hebrew Literature; Bohn Alum. & Brass Corporation (NYSE)

BHN Brinell Hardness Number; Brotherhood of the Holy Name (of Jesus)

B/HNHPS Brighton and Hove Natural History and Philosophical Society

B Hond British Honduras

bhp brake horse power; bishop

bhpric bishopric

BHQ Brigade Headquarters

BHRI Brewers Hop Research Institute

BHRMA British Hemp Rope Manufacturers' Association

BHRS Bedfordshire Historical Record Society

BHS British Homeopathic Society; Business Historical Society

BHT Brotherhood of the Holy Trinity; Bureau of Highway Traffic; Burkart (F) Manufacturing (NYSE)

BHTA British Herring Trade Association

BHTD Bureau of Hygiene and Tropical Diseases

Bhu Bhutan

BHW Bell & Howell Company (NYSE)

BHWJAC Brighton-Hove-Worthing Joint Airport Committee

BHY Belding Heminway Company (NYSE)

B Hy Bachelor of Hygiene

BI Balearic Islands; Board of Investigation; British India

bi bicycle

b i bodily injury; buffer index (insurance); business interruption

Bi bismuth

BI British India; Brookings Institution; cooperative buying organization (*Begarnes Inkopacentral*—Swedish); National Biscuit Company (NYSE)

B & I Bankruptcy and Insolvency Cases (legal)

BIA Bicycle Institute of America; Board of Immigration Appeals; Braille Institute of America; Bristle Institute of America; Bureau of Insular Affairs; International Anti-Militarist Bureau against War and Reaction (IAMB)

BIAA Bee Industries Association of America

BIAE British Institute of Adult Education

bib. drink (*bibe*—Latin)

Bib. Bible; Biblical

B & IB Billing and Instruction Book

Bib. Clk Bible Clerk (Oxford)

bibliog bibliographer; bibliographical; bibliography

Bibl Mun Municipal library (*Bibliothèque Municipale*—French)

BIC Benchers of the Inns of Court; British Institute of Cinematographers; British Insulated Cables; International Containers Bureau

B I C live in Christ (*bibas in Christo*—Latin)

bicarb sodium bicarbonate

BICL British India Commonwealth League

b i d twice a day (*bis in die*—pharmacy)

BIDAC bids acceptance

ble battery (*batterie*—French)

BIE Bureau of Intercultural Education; International Bureau of Education (IBE)

bien biennial (botany)

BIF British Industries Fair

Big. Bignell's Reports (legal)

BIH International Time Bureau

BII Biosophical Institute, Inc

BIIA British Institute of Industrial Art

bij jewels (*bijoux*—French); successor (Latvian)

BIK Bickford's, Inc. (Md.) (common stock, ASE)

BIL Belgian Institute in London; billet (US Army); British-Italian League

bild background (*bildung*—German)

bill, billds billiards

Bills & N bills and notes (legal)

bi m bi-monthly

BIM Bolivia Inland Mission; British Institute of Management

Bin. Binney's Pennsylvania Reports (legal)

BIN Binks Manufacturing Company (NYSE)

BINA International Bureau of Automobile Standardization

biochem biochemistry

Biochem Jour Biochemical Journal

biog biographer; biographical; biographically

Biogeog biogeography

biol biologic; biological; biologist

BIOS British Intelligence Objectives Sub-Committee

BIOWAR biological warfare (US Army)

BIP British Institute in Paris; British Institute of Philosophy

BIPM International Bureau of Weights and Measures

BIPO British Institute of Public Opinion

BIR Bird & Son, Inc (NYSE); Board of Inland Revenue; British Institute of Radiology

Birds. St Birdseye's Statutes (legal)

BIRE British Institution of Radio Engineers

BIR T Board of Investigation and Research-Transportation (United States)

bis bissextile; twice (*bis*—French, Italian, Latin)

Bis Bismarck; bismuth; Bissell's United States Circuit Court Reports (legal)

BIS Bank for International Settlements; Bishop Oil Company (NYSE); Boiler Institute, Steel; British Information Service

Bis Arch Bismarck Archipelago

Bisc Biscayan

BISF British Iron and Steel Federation

BISNC British India Steam Navigation Company

BIT Bureau International de Travail (International Labor Office)

BITAC International Bus and Lorry Transport Office (now: International Road Transport Union)

bitm bitumen

bitum bituminous

BIV bivouac (US Army)

BIW Bath Iron Works Corporation

(NYSE)
BIWF British Israel World Federation
b j ball joint; brass jacket; bump joint (plumbing)
BJ Bachelor of Journalism
BJA Burlap & Jute Association
BJAEMA Beater, Jordan and Allied Equipment Manufactures Association
BJC Byron Jackson Company (NYSE)
BJIC Bacon Joint Industrial Committee
B Jon Ben Jonson (author)
bk backwardation; bank; bark; block; book
b k bilge keel; blue key
Bk Black's United States Supreme Court Reports (legal); berkelium
BK Blaw-Knox Company (NYSE); signal used to interrupt a transmission in progress (QS)
BKA Bee Keepers' Association
bkbndr bookbinder
bkcy bankruptcy (legal)
bk comr bank commissioner
bk ex book exchange
bkg banking; bookkeeping
bk lr black letter
BKP Buckeye Pipe Line Company (ASE)
bkpt bankrupt
BKR Barker Bros Corporation (NYSE)
BKR1c Baker First Class (US Navy)
bks banks; barracks; books
BKS British Kinematograph Society
bkt bracket
bkt[s] basket[s]
BKX Blaw-Knox Company (private car rr mark)
b l base line; bill lodged (banking); black letter; breech-loading gun
bl bale; wind instruments, musical (*Bläsinstrumente*—German); blessed; block; blue
Bl company (*Bölük*—Turkish); newspaper (*Blat*—German)
BL Bachelor of Law; Bachelor of Letters; Basutoland; Black Leghorn (poultry); Bodleian Library (Oxon); bomb line (US Army); Brazilian Tract. Lt & Pw Company Ltd (ASE); British Legion;
B/L bill of lading
b & l ball and lever (plumbing)
BLA Bachelor of Landscape Architecture; Bachelor of Liberal Arts; Bilateral Agreements; Blauner's (NYSE); British Liberation Army
bl a among other things, or others (*bland amst, bland andra*—Swedish); among others (*blant annet*—Norwegian)
BLACC British and Latin American Chamber of Commerce

Bla Ch Bland's Maryland Chancery Reports (legal)
Blackst Blackstone's Commentaries (legal)
Blackf Blackford's Indiana Reports (legal)
Blackw Cond Blackwell's Condensed Reports (legal)
B & L Assn Building & Loan Association
Blatch Pr Cas Blatchford's Prize Cases
B/L att bill of lading attached
BLB Boys' Life Brigade
BLBSB Better Light, Better Sight Bureau
BLCA Bellanca (aircraft)
Bl C C Blatchford's United States Circuit Court Reports (legal)
Bl Com Blackstone's Commentaries (legal)
BLCX Bernuth, Lembcke Company, Inc (private car rr mark)
BLD Bullard Company (NYSE)
bldg building
Bldg E Building Engineer
BLE Brotherhood of Locomotive Engineers
B&LE Bessemer and Lake Erie Railroad Company
BLEA British Labour Esperanto Association
BL Ex SMA British Limbless Ex-Servicemen's Association
BLG Burke's Landed Gentry (England)
Blg enclosure (*Beilage*—German)
BLH British Legion Headquarters
BLI Bachelor of Literary Interpretation; Bliss & Laughlin, Inc (NYSE)
BLJ Bachelor of Letters in Journalism
blk black; block; bulk
BLK Blockson Chemical Company (NYSE)
BLL Bachelor of Laws (*Baccalaureus Legum*—Latin); Bell Aircraft Corp (NYSE)
blle bottle (*bouteille*—French)
BLItt Bachelor of Letters (*Baccalaureus Litterarum*—Latin)
b l m kiss the hand (*besa la mano*—Spanish)
BLMA Brake Lining Manufacturers Association
BLMAS Bible Lands Missions Aid Society
BLMRA British Leather Merchants Research Association
BLN balloon (US Army)
BLO Brillo Manufacturing Company, Inc. (NYSE); Bulolo Gold Dredging, Ltd (NYSE)
BLO A Brillo Mfg. Co., Inc. ("A") (ASE)

BLOF British Lace Operatives' Federation
b l p kiss the feet (*besa los pies*—Spanish)
b l r breech-loading rifle
BLR Blair Holdings Corporation (NYSE)
bls bales; barrels
BLS Bachelor of Library Science; Bureau of Labor Statistics (United States); greeting to the well-wishing reader (*Benevolenti lectori salutem*—Latin)
BL & SP Butter, Lard, and Salt Provisions (railway)
blt built
BLT battalion landing team (US Army)
BLTDA Burley Leaf Tobacco Dealers Association
BLTJC British Lace Trade Joint Committee
BLV British Legion Village
blvd boulevard
b m bearing magnetic; bench mark; bending moment; board measure (lumber); brass mounted (plumbing); breech mechanism; brown mare (racing); to the well-deserving (*bene merenti*—Latin); bowel movement (medicine)
BM Bachelor of Medicine; Beach Master (RAF); Bishop and Martyr; Blessed Mary (*Beata Maria*—Latin); of blessed memory (*Beatae Memoriae*—Latin); of happy memory (*Bonae Memoriae*—Latin); Bon Ami (NYSE); Brigade Major; British Monomark; British Museum; Bronze Medallist; Brotherhood Movement; Brown-McLaren Mfg Company (NYSE); Burgomaster; miik (rr car); monitors (US Navy designation for foreign ships)
B&M Boston and Maine Railroad
b of m bill of material
BMA Bobbin Makers' Association; British Marine Aircraft; British Medical Association
B Maj Brigade Major
BMB Broadcast Measurement Bureau
BMC British Match Corporation; Bureau of Motor Carriers
BMCat British Museum Catalogue
BMCI British Mosquito Control Institute
BMCRC British Motor Cycle Racing Club
BMCX Brown-Miller Company (private car rr mark)
BMDM British Museum Department of Manuscripts
BME Bachelor of Mechanical Engineering; Bachelor of Mining Engineering; Bachelor of Music Education; Birmingham Electric Company

(NYSE)

B Mech E Bachelor of Mechanical Engineering

B Med Bachelor of Medicine

b m e p brake mean effective pressure (engineering)

B Met Bachelor of Metallurgy

B Met E Bachelor of Metallurgical Engineering

BMF Brandeis Memorial Foundation

BMI Barley and Malt Institute; Battelle Memorial Institute; Birmingham and Midlands Institute; Book Manufacturers Institute; Broadcast Music Incorporated; Burma Mines, Ltd (ASE)

B Min E Bachelor of Mining Engineering

BMJ British Medical Journal

BML Burma Mines, Ltd., (NYSE)

B mld Breadth moulded (naval engineering)

BMMA Beverage Machinery Manufacturers Association

BMN British Merchant Navy

b m p brake mean power (engineering)

BMPIUA Bricklayers, Masons & Plasterers Union of America

BM PSM Bachelor of Music in Public School Music

BM SM Bachelor of Music in School Music

BMPX The Borden Company Manufactured Products Division (private car rr mark)

b m r basal metabolism rate (medicine)

BMR Boston & Maine (NYSE)

BMRR Boston and Maine Railroad

BMS Baptist Missionary Society; British Medical Society; British Missionary Society; British Mycological Society

BMSE Baltic Mercantile and Shipping Exchange

BMSMWS Birmingham and Midland Sheet Metal Workers' Society

BMSS Birmingham and Midlands Scientific Society

BMT Beit Memorial Trust; Brooklyn-Manhattan Transit

B Mt to the well deserving (Bene Merenti—Latin)

BMTB Button Manufacturing Trade Board

BMTC Business Men's Training Corporation

BMTD Bureau of the Mint, Treasury Division (United States)

BMU Book and Magazine Union

B Mus Bachelor of Music; British Museum

B Mus E Bachelor of Music Education

BMV Blessed Mary the Virgin (Beata Maria Virgo—Latin)

BMWA Building and Monumental Workers' Association

BMWE Brotherhood of Maintenance of War Employees (United States)

BMY Bristol-Myers Company (NYSE)

bn baron; battalion; been

b n bank note

BN all between . . . and . . . (used after a question mark to request a repetition) (QS); Bachelor of Nursing; Borden Company (NYSE); British Navy

BNA Basle Nomina Anatomica; Belgian News Agency; Brazil Nut Association; British North America; Burma National Army

BNB British North Borneo

BNC Bingham's New Cases (legal); Brasenose College, Oxford

BNCA British National Cadet Association

BNCICC British National Committee of the International Chamber of Commerce

bnd bound

BND Bond Stores, Inc (NYSE)

bndg binding

Bnf Braniff (airline)

BNF Brand Names Foundation; Braniff International Airways, Inc

BNHAS Burton-on-Trent Natural History and Archaeological Society

BNHPS Birmingham Natural History and Philosophical Society

Bn HQ Battalion Headquarters

BNHS Buteshire Natural History Society

BNI Bengal Native Infantry

BNK Bangor & Aroostook Railroad (NYSE)

BNL Beneficial Loan Corporation (NYSE)

BNOC British National Opera Company

Bn RO Battalion Routine Orders

BNS Bachelor of Naval Science; Benson & Hedges (NYSE); Bristol Naturalists' Society

Bnss Baroness

BNSS Bournemouth Naturalists' and Scientific Society

BNU Beech-Nut Packing Company (NYSE)

BNX Benolite Corporation (private car rr mark); Westinghouse Electric Corporation, Benolite Department (private car rr mark)

b o back order; bad order; body odor (colloquial); branch office; broker's order; buyer's option

b/o brought over (accounting)

BO Bachelor of Oratory; Baltimore & Ohio Railroad Company (NYSE); Board of Ordnance; Burma Office

B&O Baltimore and Ohio Railroad Company

BOA British Olympic Association; British Optical Association; British Osteopathic Association; British Overseas Airways

BOAC British Overseas Airways Corporation

BOAFG British Order of Ancient Free Gardeners

BOB Bureau of Budget

BOBF Bank Officers' Benevolent Fund

b o c back outlet central (plumbing)

Boc Boccaccio

BOC Board of Customs; British Ornithologists' Club; British Oxygen Company

BOCA Building Officials Conference of America

BoCS Bombay Civil Service

B&OCT Baltimore and Ohio Chicago Terminal Railroad Company

b o d biochemical oxygen demand

BOD Base Ordnance Depot

Bodl Lib Bodleian Library (Oxon.)

b o e back outlet eccentric (plumbing)

BOE Board of Education

BOF Bell of Freedom (Lithuania)

Bog. Bogota

BOG Bank Officers' Guild; Brigade of Guards; Borg (George W.) Corporation (NYSE)

Boh Bohemia; Bohemian

BOH Band of Hope

BOI basis of issue (US Army); boiler (US Navy)

BOIG Boeing (aircraft)

boil. boiling

BOJ Bourjois, Inc (common stock, ASE)

bol bolivar (Venezuelan money); boliviano (Bolivian money); pill (bolus—Latin)

Bol Bolivia; Bolivian

BOK Book-of-the-Month Club, Inc (NYSE)

BOL Bachelor of Oriental Languages

Bom Bombardier

BOM bombing (US Navy); Bureau of Mines

Bomb. L R Bombay Law Reporter (legal)

Bomb. Sel Cas Bombay Select Cases (legal)

Bom CS Bombay Civil Service; Bombay Staff Corps

b l s beaded one side (lumber)

Bon Bonaparte

Bo'ness Borrowstounness

Boni Boniface

bon mem of happy memory (bonae memoriae—Latin)

BONS Berlin Overseas News Service

BOP Boys' Own Paper

BOQ bachelor officers' quarters (US

29

Army)
bor boron; borough
BOR Battalion Orderly Room; Borg-Warner Corporation (NYSE)
BORD Bordeaux (France)
B&O RR Baltimore & Ohio Railroad
Bos Bosphorus
BOS American Bosch Corporation (NYSE)
Bo SC Bombay Staff Corps
bos'n boatswain
Bost Boston; Bostonian
bot botanical; botanist; botany; bottom; bought
BOT Board of Trade; Brotherhood of Teamsters
Bot Gaz Botanical Gazette
BOU British Ornithologists' Union
boul boulevard
BOWO Brigade Ordnance Warrant Officer
BOWX Bowman Dairy Co. (private rr mark)
b p base pitch (gears); bed plate; base plate; below proof (spirits); bill of parcels; bill(s) payable; boiling point; foot candle (bougie-pied—French); boiler pressure; borough president; brick protected (insurance); brass plug (plumbing); by-pass (plumbing); the public good (bonum publicum—Latin)
bp birthplace; bishop; much (beaucoup—French)
BP Bachelor of Pharmacy (Baccalaureus Pharmaciae—Latin); Bachelor of Philosophy (Baccalaureus Philosophiae—Latin); Bachelor of Painting; Baden-Powell [Lord]; base point (US Army); Blind Post (GPO); Blue Peter (flag); Bombing Post; Boston & Providence Railroad Corporation (NYSE); British Patent; British Pharmacopoeia; British Public; Most Holy Father (Beatissime Pater—Latin); Union Bag & Paper Corporation (NYSE)
b/p blueprint
b&p bare and painted (shipbuilding)
BPA Biological Photographic Association; Birds Protection Act; Blind Persons Act; Bonneville Power Administration (United States); British Philatelic Association; railway post office (Bahn Post Amt—German)
BPAA Bowling Proprietors Association of America
b p b bank post bill[s]; blanket position bond (insurance)
BPBDIA Bill Posters, Billers & Distributors, International Alliance of
BPBI Book Publishers Bureau, Inc
BPBMF British Paper Box Manu-

facturers' Federation
BPC British Pharmaceutical Codex; British Purchasing Commission
bpd barrels per day
B Pd Bachelor of Pedagogy (Baccalaureus Pedagogiae—Latin)
BPD British Society of Poster Designers
BPE Bachelor of Physical Education
B Pe Bachelor of Pedagogy (Baccalaureus Pedagogiae—Latin)
b p f good for ... francs (bon pour ... francs—French)
BPF British Pacific Fleet; British Plastics Federation
B Ph British Pharmacopeia
B Pharm Bachelor of Pharmacy
B Phil Bachelor of Philosophy (Baccalaureus Philosophiae—Latin)
BPI Bureau of Public Inquiries; Booksellers' Provident Institution; Building Products Institute
BPICA Permanent International Bureau of Motor Manufacturers (PIBMM)
BPIR Booksellers' Provident Institution and Retreat
BPIX Budlong Pickle Company (private car rr mark)
bpl birthplace
BPMA Blotting Paper Manufacturers Association; Book Paper Manufacturers Association
BPMC Batch Pasteurizer Manufacturers Council
BPMF British Pottery Manufacturers' Federation
BPNMA British Plain Net Manufacturers' Association
B & PNR Bosanquet & Puller's New Reports (legal)
BPOE Benevolent and Protective Order of Elks
BPOWBGF British Prisoners of War Books and Games Fund
BPR Brown's Parliamentary Reports (legal)
BPS British Phrenological Society; British Press Service; British Psychological Society
BPSM Bachelor of Public School Music
BPSMS British Psychological Society Medical Section
BPSO Base Personnel Staff Officer (RAF)
Bp Suff Bishop Suffragan
BPT battle practice target (naval); Beta Pi Theta (society); Boston Personal Property Trust (NYSE)
BPW Quebec Power Company
BPWC Blind Persons' Welfare Committee; Business and Professional Women's Club
BPWMA Buff and Polishing Wheel Manufacturers Association

BPX Bond Pickle Company (private car rr mark)
B Py Bachelor of Pedagogy
bq barque
BQ British Amer. Tob., (NYSE)
BQB Brit-Amer. Tob. Co. Ltd (ASE)
BQMS Battery Quartermaster Sergeant
BQ Pr B Brit-Amer. Tob. Co. Ltd. (Pref. Bearer) (ASE)
BQR Brit-Amer. Tob. Co. Ltd. (ADR's)
bque barque
b r bank rate; bill of rights; boiler room; boiling range; border regiment; builder's risk; bill rendered
br branch; brand; brass; bridge; brief; brig; broché (sewn— of books); bronze; brother; brown; bugler; latitude (breite—German)
B/R bill[s] receivable; Bordeaux-Rouen (grain trade); Builders' Risks
Br bratschen (music); Brazil; Brazilian; Britain; brother (Bruder—German); brothers (Breca—Yugoslavian; Brocia—Polish; Brahli—Latvian; Broderva—Swedish; Brodrene—Danish; Brohali—Lithuanian); viola (Bratsche—German) (music); bromine
BR Bankruptcy Reports (legal); Book of Reference; King's Bench (Bancus Regis—Latin); Queen's Bench (Banco Reginae—Latin); British Railways
BRA Boy Rangers of America; Building Renovating Association
brach to the arm (brachio—pharmacy)
Brad. Bradford's Surrogate Reports (legal)
Bradw Bradwell's Appellate Reports (legal)
Br Am British America(n)
BRAMA British Rubber and Allied Manufacturers' Association
Brayt Brayton's Vermont Reports (legal)
Braz Brazil; Brazilian
BRBA Bristol Royal Blind Asylum
BRC British Research Council; Business Reply Card
BRofC Belt Railway Company of Chicago
BRCA Brotherhood of Railway Carmen of America
Br Col British Columbia
Br Cr Ca British Crown Cases (legal)
BRCS British Red Cross Society
brd board
BRD Broadway-Hale Stores (NYSE)
BRE Bachelor of Religious Education; Bureau of Railway Economics
breach of p breach of the peace (legal)
b rec bills receivable

Brec Brecknockshire (Wales)
b rend bill rendered
Bret Breton
brev brevet; brevier (type)
Brev Brevard's Reports (legal)
breveté sgdg patented without Government guarantee (*sans garantie du gouvernement*—French)
Brev Ju Brevia Judicialia (Judicial Writs) (legal)
brew. brewer; brewing
Brewst Brewster's Reports (legal)
brf brief (legal)
BRF British Road Federation; Burke Relief Foundation
Br Fed. Dig. Brightly's Federal Digest (legal)
Br & For. St Paps British and Foreign State Papers
brg bearing
BRG bridge (US Army)
br g brown gelding
BRGHD bridgehead (US Army)
Br Gu British Guiana
brh brush holder
B Rh Bas-Rhin (French Department)
Br Hond British Honduras
Br I British India
B-RI Burlington-Rock Island Railroad Company
Brick. Dig. Brickell's Digest
Brig. brigade; Brigadier
Brig. Gen Brigadier General
Brig. Maj Brigade-Major
brill. brilliantly (*brillante*—music)
Brit Cr Cas British Crown Cases (legal)
Brit Mus British Museum
Brit Pat. British Patent
Brit Pharm British Pharmacopœia
Britt *Britanniarum*—of all the Britains (on coins)
BRK Brach (E. J.) & Sons(NYSE)
brklyr bricklayer
brkmn brakeman
BRKT Bracker (naval construction)
BRL bomb release line (US Army)
BRLSI Bath Royal Literary and Scientific Institution
BRM ACF-Brill Motors Company (NYSE)
BRMA Board of Registration of Medical Auxiliaries
BRMAVOFI Bureau of Raw Materials for American Vegetable Oils and Fats Industries
BRO Brigade Routine Order
Bro Adm Brown's United States Admiralty Reports (legal)
Bro CC Brown's Chancery Cases (Law Reports)
Brock Cas Brockenbrough's Cases (legal)
brok brokers (legal)
Bro (Pa.) Browne's Pennsylvania Reports (legal)

Bro PC Brown's Cases in Parliament (Law Reports)
bros brothers
brot brought
BR & PR Buffalo, Rochester and Pittsburg Railroad
BR & R Brown & Rader's Missouri Reports (legal)
BRS Borne Scrymser Company (NYSE); Bristol Record Society; Building Research Station; Business Reply Service
BRSA Brotherhood of Railroad Shopcrafts of America; Brotherhood of Railroad Signalmen of America
BSIU British Society for International Understanding
BRSL British Record Society Limited
Br Som British Somaliland
BRSU British Railway Stockholders' Union
BRT Brotherhood of Railroad Trainmen; gross registered tonnage (*Brutto-Register-Tonnen*—German); Burton-Dixie Corporation (NYSE)
Brt fwd brought forward (accounting)
Brth Berthold
BRTTS British Roll Turners' Trade Society
Bru Brunei; Bruno
bryol bryology
BRZ Breeze Corporations, Inc (Common stock, ASE)
b s balance sheet; battleship; battle squadron; boiler survey (shipbuilding); bottom settlings; broadcasting station; buffer survey
BS Bachelor of Science; Bachelor of Surgery; Bethlehem Steel Corporation (NYSE); Biochemical Society; The Biometric Society; Birmingham Southern Railroad Company; Bishop Suffragan; black squad (stokers); Blessed Sacrament; Blind School; Blue Shade (paper); Boy Scouts; British Standard; Brontë Society; Building Society
b/s bags; bales; bill of sale; bill of store (commerce)
b&s beams and stringers (lumber); bell and spigot (plumbing); brandy and soda
B2c Boilermaker Second Class (US Navy)
b7d buyer 7 days to take up (stocks)
B & S Best and Smith (law reports); Brown and Sharpe (wire gauge)
BSA Bachelor of Agricultural Science (*Baccalaureus Scientiae Agriculturalis*—Latin); Bibliographical Society of America; Big Sister Association (United States); Birmingham Small Arms; Botanical Society of America; Boy Scouts of America; Boy Scouts' Association; British

South Africa; British School at Athens; British Spiritualists' Association
BSAA Bachelor of Science in Applied Arts; British School of Archæology (Athens)
BSAC British South Africa Corps; Brotherhood of Shoe and Allied Craftsmen
BSAE Bachelor of Science in Aeronautical Engineering; Bachelor of Science in Administrative Engineering; Bachelor of Science in Agricultural Engineering; British School of Archaeology (Egypt)
BS Aero Adm Bachelor of Science in Aeronautical Administration
BS Aero E Bachelor of Science in Aeronautical Education; Bachelor of Science in Aeronautical Engineering
BS Agr Bachelor of Science in Agriculture
BS Agr Ed Bachelor of Science in Agricultural Education
BS Agr Eng Bachelor of Science in Agricultural Engineering
BSAI British School of Archælogy (Iraq)
BSAJ British School of Archæology (Jerusalem)
BSAP British South Africa Police
BS App Arts Bachelor of Science in Applied Arts
BSAR British School of Archæology (Rome)
BS Arch. Bachelor of Science in Architecture
BS Arch. Engr Bachelor of Science in Architectural Engineering
BS Art Ed Bachelor of Science in Art Education
BSAS British Ship Adoption Society
BSB British Standard Beam
BS BA Bachelor of Science in Business Administration
BS Biol Bachelor of Science in Biology
BSBS British Sugar Beet Society
BS Bus. Bachelor of Science in Business
BS Bus. Adm Bachelor of Science in Business Administration
BS Bus. Ed. Bachelor of Science in Business Education
BS Bus. and Public Adm Bachelor of Science in Business and Public Administration
BSc Bachelor of Science (*Baccalaureus Scientiae*—Latin)
BSC Bachelor of Christian Science; Bachelor of Science in Commerce; Bengal Staff Corps; Bethlehem Steel Company (ASE); British Standard Channel; British Sugar

Corporation; British Supply Council

BSCA British Society of Chartered Accountants

BSCC British Service Charities Committee

BS CE Bachelor of Science in Civil Engineering

BS C and E Bachelor of Science in Commerce and Economics

BS ChE Bachelor of Science in Chemical Engineering

BS Chem Bachelor of Science in Chemistry

BS Chem Eng Bachelor of Science in Chemical Engineering

BS Com Ed Bachelor of Science in Commercial Education

BS Com Eng Bachelor of Science in Commercial Engineering

BS Comm Bachelor of Science in Commerce

BS Comm Eng Bachelor of Science in Commercial Engineering

BSCNA British Supply Council in North America

BSCP Brotherhood of Sleeping Car Porters

BSCPL Bribery and Secret Commissions Prevention League

bsd particularly (*besonders*—German)

BSD Bachelor of Science in Dentistry; Bachelor of Didactic Science (*Baccalaureus Scientiae Didacticae* —Latin); British School of Dowsers

BSE Boston Stock Exchange; Botanical Society of Edinburgh; Botany School of Edinburgh; Boston Edison Company (ASE)

BSEA British School of Egyptian Archæology

BSECBI Botanical Society and Exchange Club of British Isles

BS Ec and Bus. Adm Bachelor of Science in Economics and Business Administration

BS Econ Bachelor of Science in Economics

BS Ed Bachelor of Science in Education

BS Ed Music Super Bachelor of Science in Education, Music Supervision

BS Ed—Phys Ed Bachelor of Science in Education—Physical Education

BS E Engr Bachelor of Science in Electrical Engineering

BSEIU Building Service Employees International Union

BS Elem Ed Bachelor of Science in Elementary Education

BSEM Bachelor of Science in Engineering of Mines

BS Engr Bachelor of Science in Engineering

BS Engr Phys Bachelor of Science in Engineering Physics

BSF Birdsboro Steel Fdry. & Mach. (NYSE); British Standard Fine (screw threads)

b s fc brake specific fuel consumption

BS For. Bachelor of Science in Forestry

BSFS Bachelor of Science in Foreign Service; British Society of Franciscan Studies

BSG Black, Starr & Gorham (NYSE); British Standard Gauge

BSGA British Sports and Games Association

b s g d g patent without government guarantee (*breveté sans garantie du gouvernement*—French)

BS Gen Bus. Bachelor of Science in General Business

BS Gen Ed Bachelor of Science in General Education

BS Gen Eng Bachelor of Science in General Engineering

BS General Home Econ Bachelor of Science in General Home Economics

BS Geol Bachelor of Science in Geology

BS Group Work Admin Bachelor of Science in Group Work Administration

BS Group Work Ed Bachelor of Science in Group Work Education

bsh bushel

BSH Bush Terminal Company (NYSE)

BSHC Board of State Harbor Commissioners; British Social Hygiene Council

BS Health Ed Bachelor of Science in Health Education

BS Health and Phy Ed Bachelor of Science in Health and Physical Education

BS Home Econ Bachelor of Science in Home Economics

BS Home Econ Ed Bachelor of Science in Home Economics Education

BS Hyg Bachelor of Science in Hygiene

BSI British Standards Institution

BSIE Bachelor of Science in Industrial Engineering

BS Ind Ed Bachelor of Science in Industrial Education

BS Ind Engr Bachelor of Science in Industrial Engineering

BS Jrnl Bachelor of Science in Journalism

bskt basket

BSL Bachelor of Sacred Literature; Bachelor of Science in Law; bomb safety line (US Army); Botanical Society of London

Bs./L bills of lading

BSLA Bachelor of Science in Landscape Architecture

BS Lab Tech Bachelor of Science in Laboratory Technology

BSLA and Med Bachelor of Science in Liberal Arts and Medicine

BSLA and Nurs Bachelor of Science in Liberal Arts and Nursing

BSL Arch. Bachelor of Science in Landscape Architecture

BS Lib Arts Bachelor of Science in Liberal Arts

BS Lib Service Bachelor of Science in Library Service

BSLS Bachelor of Science in Library Science

BSL&W Beaumont, Sour Lake & Western Railway Company

BS Light Bldg Industry Bachelor of Science in Light Building Industry

BSM Bachelor of Sacred Music; Bachelor of School Music; Battery Sergeant-Major; Boy Scout Movement; Bronze Star Medal (US Army); Bruck Mills, Ltd (ASE)

BSMA Blue Star Mothers of America

BSME Bachelor of Science in Mechanical Engineering; Bachelor of Science in Mining Engineering

BS Mech Arts Bachelor of Science in Mechanical Arts

BS Mech E Bachelor of Science in Mechanical Engineering

BS Mech Ind Bachelor of Science in Mechanical Industries

BS Med Bachelor of Science in Medicine

BS Med Sc Bachelor of Science in Medical Science

BS Med Tech Bachelor of Science in Medical Technology

BS Met. Eng Bachelor of Science in Metallurgical Engineering

BS MS Bachelor of Science in Military Science

BS Mus Bachelor of Science in Music

BSNA Bureau of Salesmen's National Associations

BS N Ed Bachelor of Science in Nursing Education

BS Nurs Bachelor of Science in Nursing

BSO Bailey Selburn Oil & Gas Ltd. (ASE); Beta Sigma Omicron (sorority); Boston Symphony Orchestra

BSP Pan American Sanitary Bureau (PASB); British Socialist Party; British Standard Pipe (screw threads)

BSPA Bachelor of Science in Public Administration; Bachelor of

Science in Practical Arts
BSPAL Bachelor of Science in Practical Arts and Letters
BSPE Bachelor of Science in Petroleum Engineering; Bachelor of Science in Physical Education
BS P Educ Bachelor of Science in Physical Education
BS Phar Bachelor of Science in Pharmacy
BSPHN Bachelor of Science in Public Health Nursing
BS Phys Bachelor of Science in Physics
BSPSM Bachelor of Science in Public School Music
BS Public Adm Bachelor of Science in Public Administration
BSR Beta Sigma Rho (fraternity); British School at Rome
BSRA British Shipbuilding Research Association; British Silk Research Association
BS Rad Tech Bachelor of Science in Radiological Technology
BSRE Bachelor of Science in Religious Education
BS Ret Bachelor of Science in Retailing
BSRTB Boot and Shoe Repairing Trade Board
BS Ry ME Bachelor of Science in Railway and Mechanical Engineering
BSS Barium Steel Corp. (NYSE); British Sailors' Society; British Standard Specification
BS Sc Bachelor of Science in Science
BS School LS Bachelor of Science in School Library Science
BS School Mus Bachelor of Science in School Music
BS School Supv Bachelor of Science in School Supervision
BSSE Bachelor of Science in Sanitary Engineering
BS Sec St Bachelor of Science in Secretarial Studies
BSSH Blinded Soldiers' and Sailors' Hostel
BSSO British Society for the Study of Orthodentics
BS Soc Bachelor of Science in Sociology
BS Sp Bachelor of Science in Speech
BSSP Benevolent Society of St. Patrick
b'st ballast
B/St bill of sight (commerce)
BSTC Bay State Teachers College
BS Tech Bachelor of Technical Science
BSSW Bachelor of Science in Social Work
BST Best & Co., Inc (NYSE); British summer time

BS Textile Eng Bachelor of Science in Textile Engineering
BS Voc Ed Bachelor of Science in Vocational Education
BSVMA Bank and Security Vault Manufacturers Association
BSW British Standard Whitworth (screw threads)
bs & w basic sediment and water
BSWCC British Short Wave Correspondence Club
BSWU Boot and Shoe Workers Union
b t bankers' turnover; baronet; berth terms (shipping); board of trade; boat; bomber transport; bought; brevet trust
bt brevet; gross (tonnage) (brut—French)
Bt Benedict's United States District Court Reports (legal)
BT Baltimore Transit Company (NYSE); British Togoland (Africa)
BTA Binder Twine Association; Board of Tax Appeals (United States)
BTC Bachelor of Textile Chemistry; Battery Training Corps; Bell Telephone Company of Canada (The) (ASE); Bicycle Touring Club
BTAF British Tactical Air Force
BTAMS British Trans-Atlantic Air Mail Service
BTC of C Board of Transport Commissioners of Canada
bté patent (breveté—French)
BTE Bachelor of Textile Engineering
BTEF Book Trade Employers' Federation
BTE&S Bureau of Transport Economics & Statistics
BTF British Trawlers' Federation
BTG Bespoke Tailors' Guild
BTGCA Burley Tobacco Growers Cooperative Association
BTH British Thomson-Houston
BThU British Thermal Unit
BTI Broaching Tool Institute
BTJ Board of Trade Journal
BTJC Building Trade Joint Council
btk buttock
btl bottle
BTL British Temperance League; Butler Brothers (NYSE)
BTL.X W. H. Barber Company (private car rr mark)
BTM British Trades Mission
BTMA British Toy Manufacturers' Association; British Typewriter Manufacturers' Association
btn battalion
BTN Bastian-Blessing Company (NYSE)
BTNPF Board of Trustees of the National Police Fund
BTO Big Time Operator (slang);

bombing through overcast; Brigade Transport Officer; Building Trades Operatives
BTP Beta Theta Pi (fraternity)
BTPO Board of Trade Patents Office
BTPTS Building and Town-Planning Technical Staff
BTRY battery (US Army)
BTS Bible Translation Society; Blood Transfusion Society; Board of Theological Studies
b 2 s beaded two sides (lumber)
BTSES Board of Trade Survey and Emigration Staff
BTSOOA Board of Trade Survey Outdoor Officers' Association
bttns battens
BTU Balloon Training Unit; Board of Trade Unit; British Thermal Unit
btwn between
bty battery (military)
bu bureau; bushel (s); bread unit; brick unprotected (insurance)
Bu butyl (normal butyl)
BU Baptist Union; Baylor University; Boston University; Brooklyn Union Gas Company (NYSE); Brown University (Rhode Island); Bucknell University
BUA British Undertakers' Association
BUAER Chief of the Bureau of Aeronautics
BUAV British Union for the Abolition of Vivisection
buck. buckram
Bucks. Buckinghamshire (English County)
BUCL Baptist Union Corporation Limited
Budd Buddhism; Buddhist
BUDOCKS Chief of the Bureau of Yards and Docks
BUF British Union of Fascists
buginar nasal bougie (pharmacy) (buginarium—Latin)
build. building
BUK Bunker Hill & Sullivan Mng. & Conc. Co. (Common stock, ASE)
bul bulletin
Bulg Bulgar; Bulgaria; Bulgarian
bull. bulletin
BUMED Bureau of Medicine and Surgery (US Navy)
BUORD Bureau of Ordnance (US Navy)
BUP British United Press
BUPERS Bureau of Naval Personnel (US Navy)
bur bureau; buried
Bur Burma; Burnett's Reports (legal)
BUR Burlington Mills Corp. (NYSE)
burg burgess; burgomaster
burl burlesque

Burr. Burrow's (Law Reports)

burs bursar

Bur Stds National Bureau of Standards

bus. busbar; bushel[s]; business; omnibus

BUSANDA Bureau of Supplies and Accounts (US Navy)

Busb Cr Dig. Busbee's Criminal Digest (legal)

Busb Eq Busbee's Equity Reports (legal)

BUSHIPS Bureau of Ships (US Navy)

Bus. Mgr Business Manager

BUSS Bristol University Spelœological Society

BUTD British Union Temperance Department

b v book value; boom vessel; for example (*by voorbeeld*—Dutch); vapor bath (*balneum vaporis*—Latin)

BV Bible Version (of the Psalms); Blessed Virgin (*Beata Virgo*—Latin); Bureau Veritas (international Register for Shipping and Aircraft); Your Holiness (*Beatudo Vestia*—Latin)

B & V Beling & Vanderstraaten's Reports, Ceylon (legal)

BVA Bachelor of Vocational Agriculture; Blinded Veterans Association; Bulova Watch Company (NYSE)

B-ve company (*Bendrove*—Lithuanian)

BVI Better Vision Institute

BVM Blessed Virgin Mary (*Beata Virgo Maria*—Latin)

bvt brevet

bvtd breveted

b w please turn page (*bitte werden*—German); biological warfare; brass washer (plumbing); butt weld (plumbing)

BW Baldwin-Wallace (college); Black Watch; Board of Works; Bonded Warehouse

BWA Barrack Wardens' Association; Bedstead Workers's Association; British Waterworks Association; Building Waterproofers Association

BWAA British Women's Ambulance Association

Bway Broadway

BWB Brown & Bigelow (NYSE)

BWC Board of War Communications; British War Cabinet; Bureau of Water Carriers

BWCF British War Comforts Fund

BWCX Berwind White Coal Mining Company (private car r r mark)

BWF British Wool Federation

BWG Birmingham Wire Gauge

BWGMSB Bright Wire Goods Manufacturers Service Bureau

BWHC British Women's Hospitality Committee

BWI British West Indies; British Women's Institute; British Workmen's Institute

BWIA British West Indies Airways

bwk brickwork; bulwark

BWMCMA British Wholesale Mantle and Costume Manufacturers' Association

BWMS British Wireless Marine Service

BWMUI Broom & Whisk Makers Union, International

BWN Brown Company (Common stock, ASE)

BWN III Pr Brown Company ($3 Second Pref.) (ASE)

BWN V Pr Brown Company ($5 Conv. First Pref.) (ASE)

BWR Brown Rubber Company Inc. (Common stock ASE)

BWRA British War Relief Association

BWRL Bureau of War Risk Litigation

BWRS British War Relief Society

BWS British Watercolour Society; Brown Shoe Company, Inc (NYSE)

BWSCS Bath and West and Southern Counties Society

BWTA British Women's Temperance Association

BWTAU British Women's Total Abstinence Union

BWTX Big West Oil Company of Montana (private car rr mark)

BWVAI British War Veterans of America, Inc

BWVF British War Victims Fund

bx box (pl bxs); flexible armored cable

Bx Brix

BX express (rr car); Bendix Aviation Corp. (NYSE)

BY Bucyrus-Erie Company (NYSE)

BYAX Byerlyte Corporation (private car rr mark)

by c battery commander

BYC Brewers Yeast Council

Byelo SSR Byelorussian Soviet Socialist Republic

BYK Bayuk Cigars Inc (NYSE)

BYPU Baptist Young People's Union

BYU Brigham Young University

Byz[ant] Byzantine; Byzantium

Bz benzene; benzoyl C_6H_5CO—; BzH, benzaldehyde; BzOH, benzoic acid

BZ order blank (*Bestellzeitel*—German)

bzgl in regard to (*bezüglich*—German)

bzw and/or (*bezichungsweise*—German); respectively (*bezichungsweise*—German)

C

c about (*circa*—Latin); calorie (small); candle; carton; cavalry; cathode; caught; cent; centime; centimeter; century; chapter; chemistry; child; city; cloudy (nautical); code; cold (water); commander; company (*compagnia*—Italian); conductor; constable; contralto (music); corps; count;created; creative; crowned; cubic; current; cylinder; hundredweight; velocity

C Captain; Carl; Carlo; Catechism; Catholic; Celsius; Celtic; center (of stage); Centigrade (thermometer); centum; Chancellor; Chancery; Charles; Charlotte; chemical constant; chief; Chrysler Corporation (NYSE); church circuit; coefficient; collected only at outstations (railway); Command (paper); Common Meter (hymns); Common Time (music); compound (*compositus*—Latin) (pharmacy); confessor; Conservative; coulomb (electricity); Cuba; Curie's constant; specialist in Chemical Defense (naval); Cyrus; carbon

C/ account (*cuenta*—Spanish)

C/- case; coupon; currency

Ɔ (inverted C), 500

ca about (*circa*)

c a alternating current (*courant alternatif*—French); capital account; chronological age; claim agent; consular agent; credit account; current account; with the bow (*coll'arco*—music)

Ca calcium; company (*Compagnia*—Italian); cancer (medicine)

CA Army Corps (*Corps d'Armée*—French); bromobenzyl cyanide (gas—United States); cascade amplifier (radio); Catering Adviser; Catholic Association; Cemeteries Association; Central America; Ceylon Association; Chartered Accountant; Chief Accountant; China Association; Church Army; Church Assembly; Church Association; Classical Association; Clerk of Arraigns (legal); College of Arms (Heralds' College); Combined Baggage and Passenger (rr car); Command Accountant (military); Commercial Agent; Commercial Aviation; Companies Act; Comptroller of Accounts; Confederate Army; Consultant-Adviser; Consolidated Cigar Corporation (NYSE); Counterpoise Aerial; County Alderman; Coupons Attached; Court of Appeal; Croquet Association; Current Account; Cyprus Association; heavy cruisers (US Navy)

C/a open account (*cuenta abierta*—Spanish)
C/A close annealed
C & A Chicago and Alton Railroad Company (rr mark)
C of A Certificate of Accounts
CAA Central African Airways Corporation; Council of African Affairs
CAAA Canadian Association of Advertising Agencies; College Art Association of America
CAAI Caribbean-Atlantic Airlines Incorporated
CAAM Civil Aeronautics Authority Manual
CAAN Continental Advertising Agency Network
CAASF Canadian Army Active Service Force
cab. cabalistic; cabinet
CAB Canadian Armoured Brigade; Canadian Association of Broadcasters; Citizens' Advice Bureau; Civil Aeronautics Board; Conciliation and Arbitration Board; Consumers Advisory Board; Yellow Cab Company (NYSE)
cabwk cabinetwork
CABX Cabot Carbon Co. (private car rr mark)
CAC Administrative Committee on Co-ordination (ACC); Calaveras Cement Company (NYSE); Carnegie Alumni Clan; Carter (J. W.) Company (Common stock, ASE); Central Advisory Committee; Civilian Affairs Committee; Coast Artillery Corps; Congressional Agricultural Committee; Constable Art Club; County Agricultural Committee; Criminal Appeal Court; Crown Agents for the Colonies
CACA Central and Associated Chambers of Agriculture
CACC Colombian-American Chamber of Commerce
CACS Commission of Assembly of the Church of Scotland
CACU Coastal Artillery Co-operation Unit

CACUBO Central Association of College and University Business Officers
cad. cadence (*cadenza*—music) cadet
c-à-d that is to say; namely (*c'est-à-dire*—French)
CAD Capital Administration (NYSE); cash against documents; Colonial Audit Department; Crown Agents' Department; Combined Baggage and Buffet (rr car)
cadav cadaver
CADETRON Cadet Practice Squadron (US Coast Guard)
Cadwal Cadwallader
CADX Cadillac Tank Car Company (private car rr mark)
Cae Caelum (constellation)
C Ae Commission for Aerology
CAEA California Alkali Export Association
CAEF Chemical and Allied Employers' Federation
C Ae M Commission for Aeronautical Meteorology
CAERM Chief Aerographer's Mate (US Navy)
Caern Caernarvonshire
Caes Cæsar
cæt par other things being equal (*caeteris paribus*—Latin)
CAF Coastal Air Force; Cost-Assurance-Freight; Curates' Augmentation Fund
CAG Civil Air Guard; Comptroller and Auditor General
CAGA Catholic Actors' Guild of America
CAGE California Almond Growers Exchange
CAGI Compressed Air and Gas Institute
C Ag M Commission for Agricultural Meteorology
CAGWU County Agricultural and General Workers' Union
cah book (*cahier*—French)
CAH Cambridge Ancient History
CAI Canadian Industries, Ltd (ASE); Colonial Airlines, Inc; Committee of Americans, Inc
Cai Caines' Term Reports (legal)
CAIA Council Against Intolerance in America
Cai Cas Caines' New York Cases in Error (legal)
Cai Coll Caius College, Cambridge
Caines Cas Caines' Cases (legal)
C Air C Caribbean Air Command
Caith Caithness (County in Scotland)
Cai T R Caines' Term Reports (legal)
cal rate and tone diminished (*calando*—music); caliber; calorie

Cal calcium; Calends (*Calendae*—Latin); California; calomel (pharmacy); kilogramme-calories (unit of heat, 1,000 gram-calories)
CAL caliber (US Army); Canadian Airways, Ltd; Continental Air Lines, Inc (NYSE)
calc calculate
calcd calculated
calcn calculation
Cald Caldwell's Reports (legal)
Caled Caledonia[n]
calef warm it (*calefiat*—pharmacy)
Calif California
CALLIGB Central Association of the Lime and Limestone Industry of Great Britain
calm. calmato (music)
Cal St Pap Calendar of State Papers
Calv Calvin
Calva Calvados (French department)
CALX Calco Chemical Division, American Cyanamid Company (private car rr mark)
Cam Cambridge; Camelopardus (constellation); Cameroons; camouflage; camphor
CAM Cannon Mills Company (NYSE)
C Am Central America
camb cambric
Camb Ant. S Cambridge Antiquarian Society
Camb Obs Cambridge Observatory
Camb R Cambridgeshire Regiment
Cambs Cambridgeshire (county in England)
Camd S[oc] Camden Society
CAMDG Civil Assistant to Medical Director General (naval)
Camn Highrs Cameron Highlanders
Camp. Campeche
can. cancellation; canto; cantoris
Can. Canada; Canadian; Canon
CAN. Canada Bread Company, Ltd (ASE)
Canc Chancellor (*Cancellarius*—Latin)
canclg canceling
Can. Exch Canada Exchequer Reports (legal)
Can. F Canadian French
Can. FA Canadian Freight Association
Can. Is. Canary Islands
Canpac Canadian Pacific Railway
Can. pat. Canadian patent
Can. Res Canon Residentiary
cant. singable, in songlike manner (*cantabile*—music); canto
Cant. Canterbury, Canticles; Cantonese
Cantab of Cambridge (*Cantabrigiensis*—Latin)
Cantuar (Archbishop of) Canterbury (*Cantuariensis*—Latin)

CANX Canfield Tank Line Company (private car rr mark)
CAO Chief Accountant Officer
cap. capacity; capital; capitalize; capitol; captain; chapter (*capitulo* —Spanish; *capitulum*—Latin); foolscap (paper); head (*caput*—Latin)
CAP California Electric Power Company (NYSE); Capital Airlines, Incorporated; cash against policy (insurance); chloroacetophenone (tear gas); Chief Aviation Pilot (US Navy); Civil Air Patrol
capel chapel (*capella*—Latin)
capiend to be taken (*capiendus*—pharmacy)
Capⁿ Captain (*capitán*—Spanish)
caps. capital letters; capsule (pharmacy)
CAPS Civil Assistant Personal Services (naval)
caps. amylac a cachet (*capsula amylacea*—pharmacy)
caps. gelat a gelatine capsule (*capsula gelatina*—pharmacy)
CAPT captain (US Army)
CAPWJP Community Action for Post-War Jobs and Profits
CAPX Capital City Products Company (private car rr mark)
capy capacity
car. carat; carpentry; carrier
Car. Carlow; Carina (constellation); Carolina; Carolus (legal)
CAR. Capital Airlines (NYSE)
Car Acct Car Accountant
carb carbon
Card. Cardiganshire; Cardinal
card. cardamom
CARE Cooperative for American Remittances to Europe
ca resp a form of writ (*capias ad respondendum*—legal)
Carib Caribbean
CARIBSEAFRON Caribbean Sea Frontier (US Navy)
Carliol (Bishop of) Carlisle
Carm, Carmarths Carmarthenshire
Carn Carnarvonshire
Caro Caroline
carp. carpenter; carpentry
CARR carrier (US Army)
C & ARR Chicago and Alton Railroad (now Alton Railway Corporation)
carrd fwd carried forward (accounting)
Car Ser Agt Car Service Agent
cart. cartage
Carth Carthage
cas castle; casualty
Cas Casimir; Casey's Reports (legal); Cassiopeia (constellation)
CAS Cambridge Antiquarian Society; Casualty Actuarial Society; Castle

(AM) & Company (NYSE); Cathcart Art Society; Chief of the Air Staff; Children's Aid Society; collected alongside ship (railway); Colonial Administrative Service; Congress of Archæological Society; Fellow of the Connecticut Academy (*Connecticutensis Academiæ Socius*—Latin)
ca sa a writ of execution (*capias ad satisfaciendum*—legal)
CASBO Conference of American Small Business Organizations
Cas C L Cases in Crown Law (legal)
cash. cashier
CASO Canada Southern Railway (rr mark)
Cass Dig. Cassel's Digest (legal)
Cast. Castile
Cas w Op Cases, with Opinions (legal)
cat. catafalque; catalogue[d]; cataplasm; catechism; cattle; caught
Cat. Catalan
CAT. Canadian Atlantic Oil Company Ltd (ASE); category (US Army); Civil Air Transport; Technical Assistance Committee (TAC)
Catal Catalan; Catalonian
cath cathedral; cathode
Cath Catherine; Catholic
Cathol Eastern ecclesiastical dignitary (*Catholikos*)
CATK counterattack (US Army)
CAU Congress of American Unions
caus causation; causative
CAUSA Compania Aeronautica Uruguaya
c a v the court desires to consider (*curia advisare vult*—Latin) (legal)
cav cavalier (*cavaliere*—Italian); cavalry
CAV Calvan Consolidated Oil & Gas Company Ltd (ASE)
cav[t] a form of writ (*caveat*—Latin) (legal)
cavu ceiling and visibility unlimited
CAWA Civil Aviation Wireless Association
CAWB Central Agricultural Wages Board
CAY Carey (Philip) Manufacturing Company (NYSE)
Cb columbium (chemistry)
c b cash book; cast brass; col basso (music); common battery; contrabass
CB Belgian Congo; Cape Breton; Cash Book Customs Bureau; Cavalry Brigade; Centliore Brewing Corporation (NYSE); Central Battery (telephone); Center of Buoyancy; Chantrey Bequest; Chief Baron; Common Bench (law re-

ports); Companion of the Order of the Bath; Confidential Book; confined to barracks; Construction Battalion (US Army); Cotton Board; counter-battery; county bill (banking); county borough; currency bond; large cruisers (US Navy)
c & b caught and bowled (cricket)
C by B collected or delivered by barge (railway)
C of B confirmation of balance (banking)
CBA Caribbean Atlantic Airlines, Inc; Consumer Bankers Association; Council for British Archæology
CBAA Corset & Brassiere Association of America
CBAT Central Bureau for Astronomical Telegrams
CBBA Covered Button and Buckle Association
c b c complete blood count
CBC Canadian Broadcasting Corporation; Carbon County Railway Company (rr mark); Carr-Consolidated Biscuit Company (ASE); Christian Brothers' College; Columbia Broadcasting Corporation; Cotton Board Commission; County Borough Council
c b d cash before delivery
CBE Commander of the Order of the British Empire; Cooper-Bessemer Corporation (NYSE)
CBEI Carbon Black Export, Inc (Webb Association)
CBEL Cambridge Bibliography of English Literature
CBF Colonial Bishoprics' Fund
CBFAA Customs Brokers and Forwarders Association of America
CBFC Central Bank for Crops
CBFCE Central Board of Finance of the Church of England
C Bgmstr Chief Buglemaster
C B&H Continent between Bordeaux and Hamburg (shipping)
CBI Cape Breton Island; Children's Branch Inspector; China, Burma, India; Committee of the Brick Industry; Consumer Banking Institute
CBII Carbonated Beverages Institute, Inc
c bk check book
CBK Carey, Baxter & Kennedy, Inc (ASE)
c bl unlimited authority (*carte blanche*—French)
CBL Cable Electric Products, Inc (ASE); Conemaugh & Black Lick Railroad Company (rr mark)
CBM Chesebrough Manufacturing Company (Common stock, ASE); Chief Boatswain's Mate
c b m constant boiling mixture

how Cooperative for American Relief Every where

cbm cubic meter

CBN carbine (US Army); Columbian Carbon Company (NYSE)

CBNA Business Newspapers Assn. of Canada

CB(NS) Common Bench, New Series (Law Reports)

CBO Counter-Battery Officer

CBP Chantrey Bequest Purchase; Chi Beta Phi (society); Commission for Bibliography and Publications

CB & P Cork, Blackrock and Passage (railway)

CB & Q Chicago, Burlington and Quincy (railroad)

CB & QRR Chicago, Burlington & Quincy R.R. Company

cbr counterbore

CBR Cuba Railroad Company (NYSE)

CBRA Copper and Brass Research Association

CBRTD Cotton Board's Recruitment and Training Department

CBS central battery signal (telephone); Church Building Society; Columbia Broadcasting System; Confraternity of the Blessed Sacrament

CBSA Clay Bird Shooting Association

CB & SEC Cork, Bandon, and South-East Coast (railway)

CBSRA Council of British Societies for Relief Abroad

CBT Chicago Board of Trade

cbtmkr cabinetmaker

CBTRY counterbattery (US Army)

CB 2 s center bead two sides (lumber)

CBU City & Suburban Homes Company (ASE)

CBX Canadian Breweries Ltd. (private car rr mark)

c by t collected or delivered by truck

cc account current (*compte courant* —French); carbon copy; cash credit; cast copper; center to center; civil commotions (insurance); compass course; continuation clause (insurance); continuous current; contra credit; cubic centimeter(s); cupping glass (*cucurbita cruenta*—medical); direct current (*courant continu*—French)

CC cadet captain; Caius College (Cambridge); Camel Corps; Camp Commandant; Canal Commission; Cape Colony; Caterpillar Club; Catholic clergyman; Catholic curate; Chamber of Commerce; Chancery Cases (Law Reports); change of course (navigation); Charity Commission; Chess Club; Chief Clerk; Chief Constructors (naval);

Chief Controller (ATS); Christian community; Circuit Court; Citizens' Conference; City Council[or]; Civil Commotions; Civil Court; Claims Commission (military); Clerk of the (Privy) Council; Climbing Club; Coaching Club; Coal Commission; Coastal Command (RAF); Cobden Club; combat command (US Army); Commercial Credit (NYSE); Cricket Club; Crown Clerk; Cruising Credits; customs charges; Cycling Club; confined to camp (RAF); Connecticut College; Consular Clerk; Continuation Clause (insurance); Contraband Control; Controllers Congress (part of National Retail Dry Goods Association); Convocation of Canterbury; Cordwainers' Company; County Clerk; County Commissioner; County Council[or]; cyanogen chloride

C.C. Celestial Canopy (freemasonry)

c/c current account (*cuenta corriente*—Spanish)

C/C running account (*conte corrente* —commerce)

c&c coal and coke

C of C Chamber of Commerce; Controller of Communications (RAF); course of construction (insurance)

c to c center to center

CCA Calcium Chloride Association; Canadian Colonial Airways; Canal Carriers Association; Catalin Corp. of America (ASE); Central Chamber of Agriculture; Chief Clerk to the Admiralty; Circuit Court of Appeals; Citrus Corporation of America; City Caterers' Association; Coal Charges Account; Colliery Craftsmen's Association; Commission for Convenient Armaments; Congregational Church Aid; Consumers' Co-operative Association; Controller of Civil Aviation; County Councils Association; County Court of Appeals; Court of Criminal Appeal; United States Circuit Court of Appeals Reports (legal)

C&CA Canton & Carthage Railroad Company (rr mark)

CCAA Chefs de Cuisine Association of America

CCAI Carpenter Contractors Association, Inc; Controlled Circulation Audit, Incorporated

CCAQ Consultative Committee on Administrative Questions

C Cass Supreme Court of Appeal (*Cour De Cassation*—French)

CCAU Common Council for American Unity

CCB Canadian Custom Bonded; Con-

nexional Candidates' Board; Cotton Control Board; County Courts Branch

CCBP Combined Communication Board Publications (US Army)

CCBS Clear Channel Broadcasting Service

CCBX Carbide and Carbon Chemicals Company (private car rr mark)

c c c cathodal closing contraction (medicine)

CCC Central Control Commission; Central Criminal Court; Christ's College, Cambridge; Civilian Conservation Corps (United States); Clerk Controller Company (NYSE); Clerk to the County Council; Club Cricket Conference; Commodity Credit Corporation; Congregational Christian Churches; Corpus Christi College (Oxford); Cosmopolitan Correspondence Club; County Cricket Club

CCCA Corps Commander Coast Artillery

CC Chr Chancery Cases Chronicle (legal)

CCCI Community Chests and Councils, Inc

CCCJ Committee of County Court Judges

CCCNY Chinese Chamber of Commerce of New York

CCCR Co-ordinator of Commercial and Cultural Relations

CCCS Colonial and Continental Church Society

CCCSF Chinese Chamber of Commerce of San Francisco

CCC & StLR Cleveland, Cincinnati, Chicago and St. Louis Railroad

CCCUS Cuban Chamber of Commerce in the United States

CCCX Continental Carbon Company (private car rr mark)

CCDNL Central Council for District Nursing in London

CCDU Coastal Command Defence Unit (RAF)

CCE Caines' Cases in Error (legal)

CCEE Committee of European Economic Co-operation (CEEC)

CCEL Central Council of Economic Leagues

CCEX Chipman Chemical Company, Inc (private car rr mark)

CCF Canadian Car and Foundry Company; Coal Charges Fund; Congregation of the Brothers of Charity; Co-operative Commonwealth Federation (Canada)

CCFMS Canadian Congregational Foreign Missionary Society

CCFSA Certified Cold Fur Storage Association

CCI Carman & Company, Inc (NYSE);

Collegiate and Commercial Institute; Commandant and Chief Instructor, Equitation School (military); Co-operative Club International; International Chamber of Commerce (*Chambre de Commerce Internationale*—French)

CCIA Commission of the Churches on International Affairs

CCICMS Council for the Co-ordination of International Congresses of Medical Sciences

CCIEU Citizens Conference on International Economic Union

CCIF International Telephone Consultative Committee

CCIR Catholic Council for International Relations; International Radio Consultative Committee (*Comité Consultatif International des Radio-communications*—French)

CCIT International Telegraph Consultative Committee (*Comité Consultatif International Télégraphique*—French)

CCIX Consolidated Chemical Industries Inc (private car rr mark)

CCJ Circuit Court Judge; Congregation of Sacred Heart of Jesus (*Congregatio Cordis Jesu*—Latin)

CCJO Consultative Council of Jewish Organizations

CCK Campbell's Creek Railroad Company (rr mark); Crown Cork & Seal Company, Inc (NYSE)

cckw counterclockwise

C Cl Commission for Climatology; coinsurance clause

CCL Carolina, Clinchfield & Ohio Railway (NYSE)

C Cls Court of Claims

C Cls R Court of Claims Reports

CCLX Crystal Car Line (private car rr mark)

ccm centimeters

c cm cubic centimeter

CCM Chief Carpenter's Mate (US Navy); Continental Commercial Corporation (common stock, ASE)

CCMA Card Clothing Manufacturers Association; Cedar Chest Manufacturers of America; Commander of Corps of Medium Artillery; Cotton Card Makers' Association

CCMLC Chief, Chemical Corps (US Army)

CCMX Crossett Chemical Company (private car rr mark)

CCNA Controlled Circulation Newspapers of America

CCNRA Central Council of National Retail Associations

CCNS Chief of the Canadian Naval Staff

CCNX Catalin Corporation of America (private car rr mark)

CCNY Carnegie Corporation of New York; College of the City of New York

CCO Charity Commissioners' Office; Chief of Combined Operations; County Comforts Organization

CC&O Carolina, Clinchfield and Ohio Railway (rr mark)

CCOX Chickasha Cotton Oil Company (private car rr mark)

CCP Chancellor of the Chamber of Princas; Chief Commissioner of Police; Code of Civil Procedure; Consolidated Coppermines (NYSE); Court of Common Pleas

CCP A California Canning Peach Association; Coal Consumers Protective Association; Court of Customs and Patent Appeals (Reports)

CCPI Consultative Committee on Public Information

CCPX Crown Central Petroleum Corporation (private car rr mark)

CCR Common Code of Regulation; Continental Car-Na-Var Corporation (common stock, ASE); Crown Cases Reserved

CCRC County Court Rule Committee

CCRP Central Council for Rivers Protection

C Cr P Code of Criminal Procedure

CCS Casualty Clearing Station; Ceylon Civil Service; Cleveland, Cin. Chi. & St. L. Railway (NYSE); Combined Chiefs of Staff; Corps of Chartered Secretaries

CCSFI Canned Chop Suey Foods Industry

CCSM Consultative Committee on Statistical Matters

CCSTD Chief Commissary Steward (US Navy)

CC Supp City Court Reports, Supplement New York (legal)

CCT Canada Cement Company, Ltd (common stock, ASE); Central California Traction Company (rr mark); Chicago Community Trust; Clarkson College of Technology

c/cta whose account (*cuya cuenta*—Spanish)

c/cte account current (*cuenta corriente*—Spanish)

CCTI Central Council of International Touring

CCTO Chief Clinical Tuberculosis Officer

CCT Pr Canada Cement Co., Ltd. (6½% Redeemable Pref.) (ASE)

CCU Consolidated Railroad of Cuba (NYSE)

CCUS Chamber of Commerce of the United States

cc vv illustrious men (*clarissimi viri*—Latin)

CCX Columbian Carbon Company (private car rr mark); Continental Copper & Steel Ind (NYSE)

cd canned; cash discount; catalogued; certificate of deposit (securities); command; commissioned; cord; coned; dividend (*cum dividendo*—Latin)

Cd cadmium

CD Canada Dry Ginger Ale (NYSE); Chancery Division; Chief of Division; Civil Defense; Coast Defense; Colonial Dames; Compass Department (naval); contagious diseases; Council for Democracy; Diplomatic Corps (*Corps Diplomatique*—French); current density (electricity)

C/D Commercial Dock; Consular Declaration

c/d care of (*cargo de*—Spanish); carried down

c & d collected and delivered; collection and delivery

C of D Certificate of Deposit

CDA Catholic Daughters of America; Civil Defense Act; Cia. Dominicana de Aviacion; Clergy Discipline Act; Coast Defence Artillery; College Diploma in Agriculture; Colonial Dames of America; Compass Department of the Admiralty; Contagious Diseases Act

CDAAA Committee for the Defense of America by Aiding the Allies

CD Acts. Contagious Diseases Acts

CDAS Civil Defense Ambulance Service

CDC Canadian Dental Corps; Chairman of the Development Commission; Civil Defense Committee; Course and Distance Calculator

CD&C Cumberland Railway & Coal Company (private car rr mark)

CDCDSCA Children's Dress, Cotton Dress, and Sportswear Contractors Association

CDD certificate of disability for discharge (US Army); Council for the Disposition of the Dead; Cunningham Drug Stores (NYSE)

CDE Civil Director of Economics (military); Belgian decoration (*Croix des Évadés*); Colon Development Company, Ltd (ASE)

c de g center of gravity (*centre de gravité*—French)

C de G *Croix de Guerre* (French decoration)

CDF Civilian Defense Forces; Combined distribution frame (telephone)

CDFEA California Dried Fruit Export Association

CDFS Civil Defense Fire Service

cd ft cord foot (feet)

CD(G)S Civil Defense (General) Services

CDH College Diploma in Horticulture; Commonwealth Department of Health (Australia); Continental-Diamond Fibre (NYSE)

CDI Childs Company (NYSE); Cutting Die Institute; International Law Commission (ILC)

CDIRU Canadian Division Infantry Reinforcement Unit

c div cum dividend (NYSE)

CDJC County Donegal Joint Committee (railway)

CDKX Cliffs Dow Chemical Company (private car rr mark)

Cdl Cardinal

CDL Canine Defense League; Council of the Duchy of Lancaster; Corby (H.) Distillery Ltd., (NYSE)

CDLX California Dispatch Line (private car rr mark)

CDNA Canadian Daily Newspaper Association

CDO Colonial and Dominions Offices

CDP Chi Delta Phi (society)

CDR Cornell-Dubilier Electric (NYSE)

CDRC Civil Defense Regional Commissioner

CDRD Chemical Defense Research Department

Cdre Commodore

CDRM Chatham Division Royal Marines

Cd RMG Commissioned Royal Marine Gunner

CDRS Civil Defense Reserve Service

cds cards

CDS cash on delivery service; Civil Defense Services

Cd SB Commissioned Signals Boatswain

CDSI China Defense Supplies Incorporated

CDSO Companion of the Distinguished Service Order

Cd SO Commissioned Supply Officer

Cdt Commandant

CDT Carnegie Dunfermline Trust

CDU Churchmen's Defense Union

c d v visiting card (carte de visite—French)

CDV Civil Defense Volunteers

CDVO Civilian Defense Volunteer Offices

CDWS Civil Defense Wardens' Service

CDX Cudahy Packing Co. (private car rr mark)

Ce cerium

c e buyer's risk (caveat emptor—Latin); chronometer error; commutator end; compass error

CE Canada East; Canon Emeritus; Cessna Aircraft Company (NYSE); Chancellor of the Exchequer; Chemical Engineer; Chi Epsilon (society); Chief Engineer; Christian Endeavor; Church of England; Civil Engineer; Commercial Engineer; Common Era; compression engine; Consumption Entry (commerce); Corps of Engineers (US Army); counter-espionage; Customs and Excise

C&E (Erie) Chicago and Erie Railroad Company

c&e clothing and equipage

C of E Church of England; Company of Engineers (Irish)

CEA Atomic Energy Commission (AEC); Canadian Electrical Association; Church Extension Association; Cinematograph Exhibitors' Association; Civil Engineer Adviser (military); Commodity Exchange Administration; Council for Educational Advance; Council of Economic Advisers; County Education Authority; European Confederation of Agriculture

CEAA Chorus Equity Association of America

CEAC Chemical Engineering and Applied Chemistry; Colonial Economic Advisory Committee

CEACES Church of England Advisory Council of Empire Settlement

CEAEO Economic Commission for Asia and the Far East (ECAFE)

CEAUS Coal Exporters Association of the United States

CEB Central Electricity Board; Chief Engineer's Branch; Child Evacuation Bureau; Church Evangelical Board

CEC Canadian electrical code; Church Education Corporation; Church Estates Commissioners; Civil Engineering Contractors; Civil Engineering Corps; Consolidated Engineering Corporation (NYSE); Contributors' Executive Committee

CECCB Civil Engineering Construction Conciliation Board

cechy corporation (Polish)

CED Committee for Economic Development

CEDC Citizen's Emergency Defense Conference

CEE Calamba Sugar Estate Inc (NYSE); Customs and Excise Establishment; Economic Commission for Europe (ECE)

CEEC Committee of European Economic Co-operation

CEF Canadian Expeditionary Force; Child Education Foundation; Chinese Expeditionary Force

CEG Central Aguirre Sugar Company (NYSE)

CEH Currency Exchange Headquarters; Cutler-Hammer, Inc (NYSE)

CEI Cycle Engineers' Institute; International Electro-technical Commission (Commission Électrotechnique internationale—French)

C & EI Chicago and Eastern Illinois Railroad (rr mark)

CEIP Carnegie Endowment for International Peace

cel celebrated; celibate

Cel Celebes; Celsius (thermometric scale—same as Centigrade)

Celt. Celtic

cem cement; cemetery

CEM Chief Electrician's Mate (US Navy); College of Estate Management; Compo Shoe Machinery (NYSE)

CEMA Council for the Encouragement of Music and the Arts; Conveyor Equipment Manufacturers Association; European Council for Economic Mutual Aid (Molotov Plan)

cemb harpsichord (cembalo—Italian)

CEMF counter-electro-motive force (electricity)

CEMS Church of England Men's Society

CEN Centaurus (constellation); Central Airlines, Inc

cen centennial; center; central; century

Cen Am Central America

cen eccl ecclesiastical censure (censura ecclesiastica—Latin)

C Eng-in-CD Civil-Engineer-in-Chief's Department (naval)

cent. cental or quintal; centiare; centime; central; centrifugal; century; a hundred (centum—Latin)

Cent. Centigrade

Cent. Cub. cubic centimeter (centimètre cube—French)

Cent. Dig. Century Digest

centf centrifugal

cent. htg central heating

centg centigrade

centr hydr-él hydro-electric exchanges (centrales hydro-électriques—French)

CENX Central Chemical, Division of Wilson Company, Inc (private car rr mark)

CEO Claude Neon, Inc (common stock, ASE); Command Education Officer; Command Entertainments Officer; Corps Education Officer
Cep Cepheus (constellation)
CEP Chemical Engineering Progress (a publication)
CEPA Ceramic Equipment Producers Association
CEPAL Economic Commission for Latin America (ECLA)
CER Central Illinois Light (NYSE); Chinese Eastern Railway; European Broadcasting Conference
CERA Chief Engine-room Artificer (naval)
ceram ceramics
Cer E Ceramic Engineer
cereol a urethral bougie (cereolus—pharmacy)
cert certain; certificate; certified; certify; certiorari
Cert AIB Certificated Associate of the Institute of Bankers
cert inv certified invoice
c e s central excitatory state
CES Central Employment Service; Christian Endeavour Society; Christian Evidence Society; Committee on Economic Security (United States); County Experimental Station; Central Ohio Steel Products Company (ASE)
CESA Canadian Engineering Standards Association; Customs and Excise Surveyors' Association
CESSI Church of England Sunday School Institution
CESS Inst Church of England Sunday School Institute
Cestr of Chester (Cestrensis—Latin)
CET Casualty Evacuation Train; Central-Ill. Securities Corporation (NYSE)
Cet Cetus (constellation)
cet par other things being equal (ceteris paribus—Latin)
CETS Church of England Temperance Society
CEU Christian Endeavour Union; Constructional Engineering Union; Co-operative Employees' Union
CEW Central Power & Light (Texas) (NYSE)
CEWA Customs and Excise Watchers' Association
CEWC Council for Education in World Citizenship
CEWMS Church of England Working Men's Society
CEX Corn Exchange Bank Tr (New York) (NYSE)
Cey[l] Ceylon[ese]
CEY Century Electric Company (NYSE)
CEZMS Church of England Zenana

Missionary Society
cf calf (bookbinding); compare (confer, conferatur—Latin)
c f center field (baseball); center of flotation; cost and freight; illustrated (cum figurus—Latin); cattle feeding (railway)
Cf californium
CF Campbell Foundation; Colorado Fuel & Iron Corporation (NYSE); Columbia Foundation; Commonwealth Fund; Corresponding Fellow; Comédie Française (France); Cowles Foundation; Cranbook Foundation; most illustrious woman (clarissima femina—Latin); Chaplain of the Fleet; Chemical Foundation; Cleveland Foundation
c&f cost and freight
C of F Chaplain of the Fleet (naval); Companions of the Forest
CFA Alexian Brothers (Latin); Canadian Freight Association; Central Freight Association; cost-freight-assurance; Counter Freezer Association; French African Colonies (Colonies Françaises d'Afrique—French)
C of F of A Companions of the Forest of America
CFAT Carnegie Foundation for the Advancement of Teaching
CFB Combined Food Board (United States); Corporation of Foreign Bondholders
CFC Chief Consolidated Mining Company (ASE); Chief Fire Controlman; Christian Frontier Council; Congregation of Fathers of Charity; Consolidated Freight Classification
CFCO Cinematograph Film Control Order
CFDA Cooperative Food Distributors of America
CFE California Fruit Exchange
CFF California Packing (NYSE)
CFG Corn Products Refining Company (NYSE)
CFGE California Fruit Growers Exchange
CFGI Camp Fire Girls, Inc
CFGSA Cutlery Forgers and General Stampers' Association
CFI Chief Flying Instructor (RAF)
c f i cost, freight, and insurance
CFIX Colorado Fuel & Iron Corporation, The (private car rr mark)
CF(J) Chaplain to the Forces (Jewish)
CFL Canadian Federation of Labour; Clinchfield Coal Corporation (NYSE); Committee for Liberation
c f m cubic foot (feet) per minute
CFM Children's Fund of Michigan; confirm (US Army)
CFMD Coastal Forces Material

Department
CFMUA Cotton Fire & Marine Underwriters Association
CfO channel for orders (shipping); coast for orders (shipping)
CFP Brothers of the Poor of St. Francis
CFPC Canadian Field Park Company
CFPX Chartrand's Traffic Service (private car rr mark)
CFR Code of Federal Regulations; Cooperative Fuel Research; Council on Foreign Relations
CFRDD Colonial Forest Resources Development Department
CFRX Chicago Freight Car & Parts Company (private car rr mark)
CFS Central Flying School; Clergy Friendly Society
c ft cubic foot (feet)
CFT Croft Company (NYSE)
CF(TA) Chaplain to the Forces (Territorial Army)
CFTB Central Freight Tariff Bureau
CFTC Confederation of Christian Workers (Confédération Française des Travailleurs Chrétiens—French)
CFTMA Caster and Floor Truck Manufacturers Association
CFU Camden Fire Insurance Association (ASE); Croatian Fraternal Union
CFX Xavierian Brothers (Congregatio Fratrum Xaverianorum—Latin)
CG Captain General; Captain of the Guard; Central Georgia Railway (rr mark); Coldstream Guards; Columbia Gas System (NYSE); Commanding General (US Army); Commissary General; Conference of Governors (United States); Consul General; Croix de Guerre (French medal); left side (côté gauche—French); phosgene (carbonyl chloride); wholesale trade (commerce de gros—French)
c g center of gravity; centigram
C & G Columbus & Greenville Railway Company (rr mark)
c g a cargo's proportion of general average (insurance)
CGA Compressed Gas Association; Cornish Guild of America; Country Gentlemen's Association
C of Ga Railway Central of Georgia Railway
CGAX Cumberland Gasoline Corporation (rr mark)
CGB Consolidated Gas Electric Light & Power (NYSE)
CGC Calavo Growers of California; City and Guilds College; Coast Guard Cutter
CGCD Citizens' Guild for Civil Defense

CGCX Consolidated Food Processors, Inc (private car rr mark)
C G'ds Coldstream Guards
cge carriage; charge
CGE Chicago & Eastern Illinois Railroad (NYSE); Controller General of Economy (military)
C Gen Chaplain-General
CGG Chicago Pneumatic Tool (NYSE)
CGH Cape of Good Hope; Clevite Corporation (NYSE)
CGIT Canadian Girls in Training
CGL Coast Guard League
CGM Chief Gunner's Mate (US Navy); Conspicuous Gallantry Medal; Cornucopia Gold Mines (NYSE)
CGMA Compressed Gas Manufacturers Association
cgo cargo; contango
CGO Chicago & Southern Air Lines (NYSE)
CGPA Council of Guidance and Personnel Associations
CGPC Coast Guard Patrol Cutter
CGPDTM Comptroller General of Patents, Designs and Trade Marks
CGQ Cariboo Gold Quartz (NYSE)
CGR Coast Guard Reserve; Consolidated Grocers Corporation (NYSE)
CGS centimetre-gramme-second; Chief of the General Staff; Chief of General Staff in the Field; Commissary General of Subsistence; Department of Conference and General Services (UN Secretariat)
CGSC Command and General Staff College (US Army)
cgse centimetre gram second-electromagnetic (system)
C&GS Sch Command and General Staff School
CGT Compagnie Générale Transatlantique (The French Line); Consolidated Gas Utilities Corporation (NYSE); General Confederation of Labor (*Confederation Generale du Travail*—French)
CGTU General Federation of United Labor (*Confederation General du Travail Unitaire*—French)
CGTX Canadian General Transit Company, Ltd (private car rr mark)
CGW Chicago Great Western Railway Company (rr mark)
CGX Calor Gas Company (private car rr mark)
ch candle hours; chain; chairman; chancery; chapter; chaldron; champion (dogs); check; chemical; chemistry; chest; chestnut; chief; child; children; chirurgeon; choice; choir; church; clearinghouse; courthouse; customhouse; horsepower (*cheval-vapeur*—French); room (*chambre*—

French); surgery (*chirurgie*—French)
Ch Chaldee; China; Chinese
CH Captain of the Horse; chaplain (US Army); Companion of Honor; concentration of hydrogen ions (in moles per liter); Continental Can Company (NYSE); Member of the Order of the Companions of Honour (England)
I CH First Chronicles (Bible)
II CH Second Chronicles (Bible)
CHA Catholic Hospital Association; Chamaeleon (constellation); Charon; Co-operative Holidays' Association
Cha Ca Cases in Chancery (legal)
Ch Acct Chief Accountant
Ch Acct Off. Chief Accounting Officer
chal heat (*chaleur*—French)
CHAL Cambridge History of American Literature
cham chamomile (medicine)
chamb chamberlain; chambers
Cham Comm Chamber of Commerce
champ. champion; championship
Chanc Chancellor; Chancery
chap. chaplain; chapter (pl chaps.)
Chap. Gen Chaplain-General
Ch App Cas Chancery Appeal Cases (legal)
Chap. St J Chaplain of the Order of St John of Jerusalem (England)
char. character; charity; charter; charterer
Char. Mar. Charente-Maritime (French Department)
chart. a powder (*charta*—pharmacy)
Chat. Chattanooga
Chauc Chaucer
chauf chauffeur
CHAX Chartrand's Traffic Service (private car rr mark)
CHB Chain Belt Company (NYSE)
Ch B Bachelor of Surgery (*Chirurgiae Baccalaureus*—Latin)
chbrs chambers
CHC Chaplain Corps; Clerk to the House of Commons
chc chokecoil
ch clk chief clerk
Ch C Chancery Court; Christ Church
Ch ca Cases in Chancery (law)
Ch Coll Christ's College (Cambridge)
Ch D Chancery Division (law); Doctor of Chemistry
ch d'aff chargé d'affaires
Ch E Chemical Engineer
CHEL Cambridge History of English Literature
chem chemical[ly]; chemistry
chem e chemical engineer[ing]
Ches[h] Cheshire (county, England)
Chev Chevalier; Cheves' Law Reports (legal); chevron

Chey Cheyenne (Wyoming)
chf chief
Ch of F Chaplain of the Fleet
CHFA Cooperative Health Federation of America
CHFC Carnegie Hero Fund Commission
Chf Con Chief of Construction
chfd chamfered
Chf E Chief Engineer
chftn chieftain
ch fwd charges forward
ch g chestnut gelding
chg change; charge
chg acct charge account
chgd changed; charged
chges ppd charges prepaid
CHGFA cost chargeable to fund authorization (US Army)
CHGPAA costs chargeable to purchase authorization advice (US Army)
Ch Gun Chief Gunner
CH&H Continent between Havre and Hamburg (shipping)
ch hist church history
Chi Chicago
CHI Chicago and Southern Air Lines; Chicago Corporation (NYSE)
Chia Chiapas
Chih Chihuahua
Ch-in-C Chaplain-in-Chief
Chino-Jap Chino-Japanese
Chip. D D. Chipman's Vermont Reports (legal)
Chir Doct Doctor of Surgery (*Chirurgiae Doctor*—Latin)
chirurg chirurgical
Ch J Chief Justice
Chl Chile
CHL Cambridge Higher Local (Examination); Chile Copper Company (NYSE)
chlo chloride; chloroform
Ch M Master of Surgery (*Chirurgiae Magister*—Latin)
Ch Mar. Charente Maritime (French Department)
Cho Chosen (Korea)
CHO Checker Cab Manufacturing Corporation (NYSE)
c/h/o cannot hear of
choc chocolate
chor choral; chorister; chorus
chp championship
CHP Charis Corporation (NYSE)
ch ppd charges prepaid
chq cheque
CHQ Corps Headquarters
chr chrestomathy; chromobacterium (medicine)
Chr Christ; Christian; Christine; Christopher
Chr Coll Cam Christ's College, Cambridge
Chr Rep Chamber Reports (legal)

chron   chronicle; chronological; chronologically; chronology
Chron   Chronicles (Biblical)
I Chron   I Chronicles (Bible)
II Chron   II Chronicles (Bible)
chrs   chambers (legal)
Chrtrs   Charterers
CHS   Cushman's Sons (NYSE)
ch sent.   chancery sentinel (legal)
CHSGBI   Clydesdale Horse Society of Great Britain and Ireland
CHSSC   Central Hospital Supply Service Committee
Ch St JJ   Chaplain of the Order of St. John of Jerusalem
cht   chest
CHT   Chicago Towel Company (NYSE)
ch tr   choir training
chtrd frt   chartered freight (shipping)
chtrr   charterer
CHU   centigrade heat unit
ch v Français   continental horse-power (cheval-vapeur français—French)
CHW   Chamberlin Company of America (NYSE)
c h w   constant hot water
chwdn   churchwarden
CHX   Cutler-Hammer, Inc (private car rr mark)
CHY   Cherry-Burrell Corporation (NYSE)
chy   charity
cl   cirrus
c I   cast iron; corrugated iron
CI   California Ink Company Inc (NYSE); Captain-Instructor (naval); Cereal Institute; Chain Institute; Channel Islands; Chief Inspector; Chief Instructor; Chlorine Institute; Civitan International; Colour Index (British book); Commander-Instructor (naval); Continental Baking Company (NYSE); Copper Institute; Cordage Institute; Cosmopolitan International; cost insurance; counter intelligence (US Army); Crown of India; Czechoslovakia Institute; Minneapolis Gas Company (NYSE)
c/I   certificate of insurance
c & I   cost and insurance
cia   company (companhia—Portuguese, compañía—Spanish)
CIA   Caribbean International Airways Ltd; Central Intelligence Agency (US Army); Central Institute of Art; Chief Inspector of Accidents (Air Ministry); Chief Inspector of Armaments; China Institute of America; Cigar Institute of America; Construction Industries Association; Controllers Institute of America; Cork Institute of America; Cotton Importers Association; Cotton In-

dustries Association (Canada); Cotton Insurance Association; International Confederation of Agriculture (ICA)
CIAA   Colored Intercollegiate Athletic Association
CIAC   Council for Inter-American Cooperation
CIAD   Central Institute of Art and Design
CIAI   Cigar Institute of America, Inc
CIAM   Chief Inspector of Ancient Monuments; International Congress of Modern Architecture (Congrès International de l'Architecture Moderne—French)
CIAMAC   International Conference of Associations of Disabled Soldiers and Ex-service Men
CIANA   Latin American Commission for Air Navigation
CIB   Corporation of Insurance Brokers; Credit Interchange Bureau
CIBAD   Combat Infantryman Badge (US Army)
Cic   Cicero
CIC   Canadian Infantry Corps; Capital Issues Committee; Cedar Rapids & Iowa City Railway Company (rr mark); Chinese Industrial Cooperatives; Combat Information Center (on United States ships); Commander in Chief; Counter Intelligence Corps (US Army); International Hunting Council; International Agricultural Co-ordination Commission
Cicestr   of Chichester (Cicestrensis—Latin)
CICM   Congregation of the Immaculate Heart of Mary
CICR   International Committee of the Red Cross (ICRC)
CID   Committee of Imperial Defence; Council of Industrial Design; Criminal Investigation Department
CIDALC   International Committee for the Diffusion of Artistic and Literary Works by the Cinematograph
CIDDA   Chief Inspector under Dangerous Drugs Act
CIDEC   Ibero-American Confederation of Catholic Students
CIE   Captain's imperfect entry (Customs); Companion of the Order of the Indian Empire; company (compagnie—French)
CIEA   Conference of Independent Exhibitors Associations
CIEC   International Council of Commerce Employers
CIEE   Civil Institute of Electrical Engineers
CIER   Commission for International Educational Reconstruction
c I f   cost, insurance, and freight

CIF   Chief Inspector of Factories; International Council of Women
c I f & c   cost, insurance, freight, and commission
c I f c & I   cost, insurance, freight, commission, and interest
c I f & e   cost, insurance, freight, and exchange
c I f & i   cost, insurance, freight, and interest
c I f i & e   cost, insurance, freight, interest, and exchange
c I f L t   cost, insurance, and freight, London terms
CIGR   International Commission on Agricultural Engineering (ICAE)
CIGRE   International Conference on Large Electric Systems
CIGS   Chief of the Imperial General Staff
CIHU   Canadian Infantry Holding Unit
CII   Carpet Institute, Inc; Chartered Insurance Institute; Chlorine Institute, Inc
CIIA   Canadian Institute of International Affairs
CIK   Chickasha Cotton Oil Company (NYSE)
CIL   certificate in lieu of (US Army); Chicago, Indianapolis & Louisville Railway Company (rr mark)
CIM   Chicago & Illinois Midland Railway Company (rr mark); China Inland Mission; Congo Inland Mission; International Convention concerning the Transport of Goods by Rail; International Music Council (IMC)
CI Mech E   Companion of the Institute of Mechanical Engineers
CIMO   Commission for Instruments and Methods of Observation
C Imp Ex   Société Française Continentale d'importation et d'exportation
CIN   Cincinnati Gas & Electric (NYSE); Cincinnati Stock Exchange
CINA   International Commission for Air Navigation (ICAN)
CINC   Commander in Chief (US Army); Commander in Chief (US Navy)
CINCAF   Commander in Chief, Asiatic Fleet (US Navy)
C-in-CHF   Commander-in-Chief, Home Forces
CINCLANT   Commander in Chief, Atlantic Fleet (US Navy)
CINCPAC   Commander in Chief, Pacific Fleet (US Navy)
CINCPOA   Commander in Chief, Pacific Operations Area (US Navy)
Cinn   Cincinnati
CINO   Chief Inspector of Naval Ordnance

CIO Committee for Industrial Organization; Congress of Industrial Organizations

CIOIC Interim Commission for the International Trade Organization (ICITO)

CIOS International Committee of Scientific Management (ICSM)

CIP Catholic Institute of the Press; Central Illinois Public Service Company (NYSE); International Poplar Commission

CIPA Chartered Institute of Patent Agents; Permanent International Commission of Agricultural Associations (PICA); Permanent Inter-American Anti-Locust Committee

CIPAP Authority is granted to make such changes in above itinerary and to proceed to such additional places as may be necessary for accomplishment of this mission (US Army)

CIPM International Committee of Weights and Measures

CIPO International Committee for Bird Preservation (ICBP)

CIPRA Cast Iron Pipe Research Association

CIPRI Cast Iron Pressure Pipe Institute

CIPSH International Council for Philosophy and Humanistic Studies (ICPHS)

cir circuit; circular; circulation; circumference

Cir Circinus (constellation); circus

CIR circular (US Army); Intergovernmental Committee on Refugees (IGCR)

CIRAF International High-Frequency Broadcasting Conference

cir bkr circuit breaker

Circ Ct Circuit Court

circe circumstance

Circ J Circuit Judge

circm circumference

CIRF Cork Industries Research Foundation

CIRM International Radio Maritime Committee

cir mils circular mils (wire measure)

CIS Chartered Institute of Secretaries; Commercial Insurance Scheme; Continental Insurance Company (NYSE)

c i s central inhibitory state

CISA Cairy Industries Supply Association

CISAE International Congress of Anthropological and Ethnological Sciences

CISC International Federation of Christian Trade Unions (IFCTU)

CISL International Confederation of Free Trade Unions (ICFTU)

CISPR Special International Committee of Radioelectric Interference

c I t cleaning in transit; compression in transit

cit citation; cited; citizen; citrate

CIT California Institute of Technology; Carnegie Institute of Technology (NYSE); CIT Financial Corporation (NYSE); International Rail Transport Committee; Inter-American Confederation of Workers

CITA International Confederation of Agricultural Engineers and Technicians

CITI International Confederation of Intellectual Workers (ICIW)

City Ct R City Court Reports (legal)

City Ct R Supp City Court Reports, Supplement (legal)

City H Rec City Hall Recorder (legal)

CIUNA Coopers International Union of North America

CIUSS Catholic International Union for Social Service

civ civil; civilian; civilization; civilized

CIV Century Investors, Inc (NYSE); City Imperial Volunteers; Colonial Imperial Volunteers; International Convention concerning the Transport of Passengers and Baggage by Rail

Civ Code Civil Code (legal)

Civ Eng Civil Engineer

Civ Engin Civil Engineering

CIV Pr Century Investors, Inc. (Conv. Pref.) (ASE)

Civ Proc Rep Civil Procedure Reports, New York (legal)

Civ Serv Civil Service

CIW Carnegie Institution of Washington; Chicago & Illinois Western Railroad (rr mark)

CIXL Canadian Industries Ltd (private car rr mark)

c | converse joint (plumbing)

cj conjectural

CJ body of law (*corpus juris*—Latin); Chief Judge; Chief Justice; Congregation of Josephites; United States Pipe & Foundry (NYSE)

CJ Can. body of the canon law (*Corpus Juris Canonici*—Latin)

CJ Civ body of the civil law (*Corpus Juris Civilis*—Latin)

CJFWF Council of Jewish Federations and Welfare Funds

CJM Code of Military Justice (*Code de Justice Militaire*—French); Congregation of Jesus and Mary (Eudist Fathers); World Jewish Congress (WJC)

CK Collins & Aikman Corporation (NYSE)

CKB Cacquot Kite Balloon

CKI Crown Cork International (NYSE)

CKL Clark Equipment Company (NYSE)

CKP Cockshutt Farm Equipment (NYSE)

cks casks; checks

ckt circuit

ckw clockwise

c l carload lots; center line; civil law; cut lengths (plumbing); carload

cl centiliter (*centilitro*—Spanish); clarinet; class (of a stock); classical; clause; cloth; clove (wool, 7 lbs.); legal procedure (*curso legal*—Spanish)

Cl Claude; chlorine

CL Canadian Legion; carload (US Army); Carnegie Libraries; Cheshire Lines (railway); Civil Lord (Admiralty); Colgate-Palmolive-Peet Company (NYSE); Commander of the Order of Leopold (Belgium); Conditional Lease; Conversion Loan; *Crédit Lyonnais*; light cruisers (US Navy); I am closing my station (QS)

c/l cash letter; craft loss (shipping)

c&l canal and lake

cla clause (*clausula*—Latin)

Cla Clackmannan (county in Scotland); Clare College, Cambridge

CLA Central Landowners' Association; Civil Lord of the Admiralty

clar clarinet (*clarinetto*—Italian) (music)

Clar Clarence; Clarencieux (King of Arms); Clarendon (type)

Clarke Ch Clarke's Chancery (legal)

claro clarinet (*clarino*—Italian)

clartto clarinet (*clarinetto*—Italian)

Clas Catholic Ladies' Aid Society; classify(ication) (US Army)

class. classic; classical; classification

class. myth. classical mythology

class. rev classical revue

CLAUSA Christian Labor Association of the United States of America

Clb Caleb

CLB Church Lads' Brigade; Club Aluminum Products (NYSE)

CLBGA California Lima Bean Growers Association

CLC Canadian Atlantic Oil (NYSE); Canners League of California

C & lc Capitals and lower case (typography)

Cl Coll Clare College (Cambridge)

CLCX Cornwell Chemical Corporation (private car rr mark)

cld called (bonds); cleared; colored; cost laid down

CLD Council of Labour and Defence

CLE Council of Legal Education

Clem Clemens; Clemen's Reports (legal); Clement

Cleop Cleopatra

cler clerical; clergy

clerg clergyman

cl ex cloth extra

CLF Cleveland-Cliffs Iron Company (NYSE)

Cl & F[in] Clarke and Finnelly (Law Reports)

CLH Claussner Hosiery Company (NYSE); Cross of the Legion of Honor (croix de la légion d'honneur —French)

cl ht ceiling height

CLI City of Lima (Republic of Peru) (ASE)

Clif Clifford's United States Circuit Court Reports (legal)

CLII Central Location Index, Inc

climatol climatological; climatology

clin clinic; clinical

Clin Sci Clinical Science

clk clerk; clock

Clk O Clerk in Orders

CLK Clark (D.L.) Company (NYSE)

cl L classical Latin

CLL Continental Oil (NYSE)

CLLA Commercial Law League of America

CLM Coleman Company, Inc (NYSE); Commander of the Legion of Merit

CLN colon (US Army)

CLNY Consumers League of New York

CLO Celotex Corporation (NYSE); clothing (US Army); Coach Lace Institute

CLOX Canada Linseed Oil Mills, Limited (private car rr mark)

CLP car loading point; Columbia River Packers Association (NYSE); Commonwealth Land Party

CLPA Common Law Procedure Act

Cl Qu Classical Quarterly

clr color

cl&r canal, lake, and rail

CLR Clarostat Manufacturing Company (NYSE); Central London Railway; City of London Rifles; clearing (US Army); Committee of Land Registry; Common Law Reports

CLRX Chas. L. Read & Company, Inc (private car rr mark)

Cls Claudius

CLSC Chautauqua Literary and Scientific Circle

cl sg class singing

CLSS Chautauqua Literary and Scientific Society (United States)

clt collateral trust (bonds)

CLT code language telegram; Consolidated Mining & Smelting (NYSE)

CLTX Coltexo Corporation (private car rr mark)

CLU Chartered Life Underwriter; Civic Liberties Union (United States); Cluett, Peabody & Company, Inc (NYSE)

Clun The Monks of Cluny (Cluniacenses)

CLUSA Cooperative League of the United States of America

CLWS Canadian Legion War Service

CLX Crossett Lumber Company (private car rr mark)

c m center matched (lumber); church missionary; circular mil (wire measure); corresponding member; court-martial; metric caret (caret metrique—French); common stock; middle classes (classes moyennes —French); tomorrow morning (cras mane—pharmacy)

Cm curium

CM Certificated Master or Mistress; Master of Surgery (Chirurgiae Magister—Latin); Church Missionary; common meter (music); Congregation of the Missica; court-martial (US Army); Crosley Motors, Inc (NYSE); Cruiser Minelayer (naval)

c/m call of more (NYSE)

C/M co-operative movement

cm² square centimeter

cm³ cubic centimeter

C&M Cork and Macroom (Railway)

Cma Camilla

C Ma Canis Major (constellation)

CMA Cable Makers' Association; Candle Manufacturers' Association; Cia Mexicana de Aviacion; Cinema Managers' Association; Clothespin Manufacturers of America; Construction Men's Association; Convector Manufacturers Association; Creameries of America, Inc (NYSE); Crucible Manufacturers Association; comma (US Army)

CMAA Casket Manufacturers Association of America; Cigar Manufacturers Association of America; Clock Manufacturers Association of America; Club Managers Association of America; Cocoa Merchants Association of America; Crown Manufacturers Association of America

CM A6 Commission for Aeronautical Meteorology (French)

CMAS Clergy Mutual Assurance Society

c m b very respectfully (literally, whose hands I kiss) (cuyas manos beso—Spanish)

CMB Central Midwives' Board; Coal Mines Board; Coastal Motor Boat; Combined Munitions Board; Controlled Mining Base

CMC Chairman of Maritime Commission (United States); Coastal Minelayers (US Navy); County Magistrates' Court

CMCE Central Michigan College of Education

CM Coll Church Missionary College

CMCW Calvinistic Methodist Church of Wales

cmd Command paper (with number following); common meter double (music)

CMD Coal Mines Department; Colonial Medical Department; Mastery in Surgery, Dublin (Chirurgiae Magister —Latin)

cmdg commanding

CME Columbia Machinery & Engineering (NYSE)

CMEC Colored Methodist Episcopal Churches

CMEE Chief Mechanical and Electrical Engineer (RAF)

CMF Cement Makers' Federation; Central Mediterranean Force; Colonial Military Forces; Commonwealth Military Forces; Missionary Sons of the Immaculate Heart of Mary (Cordis Mariae Filius—Latin)

CM1c Carpenter's Mate First Class (US Navy)

CMFO Control of Motor Fuel Order

CMG Companion of the Order of St. Michael and St. George; Congressional Medal for Gallantry (United States)

CMGATC Calvinistic Methodist General Assembly Temperance Committee

CMH Combined Military Hospital; Congressional Medal of Honor; Corporal Major of Horse (Household Cavalry)

CMHQ Canadian Military Headquarters

CMI Can Manufacturers Institute; Canis Minor (constellation)

CMIA Coal Mining Institute of America; Cultivated Mushroom Institute of America

CMIC Central Mining and Investment Corporation

CMII Can Manufacturers Institute, Inc; Coin Machine Industries, Inc

CMIUA Cigar Makers International Union of America

CMJ Church Mission to Jews

CMK Carnation Company (NYSE)

cml commercial

CML chemical (US Army); Commercial

CMM Chief Machinist's Mate (US Navy); Commission for Maritime Meteorology; Community Public Service (NYSE)

CMMA Clay Machinery Manufacturers Association

CM Mh Missionaries of Marianhill

CMML Christian Missions in Many Lands

CMO Chicago, St. Paul, Minneapolis and Omaha Railway Company (rr mark); Chief Maintenance Officer (RAF)

CMOMM Chief Motor Machinist's Mate (US Navy)

CMOS Cigarette Machine Operators' Society

cmp compromise

CMP Canadian Magazine Post; Champion Paper & Fibre Company (NYSE); Commissioner of Metropolitan Police; Controlled Materials Plan; Corps of Military Police

CMPA Certified Milk Producers of America; Magazine Publishers Association of Canada

cm pf cumulative preferred (stocks)

cmps centimetres per second

C&M Pty Care and Maintenance Party (RAF)

CMPX Chemical Products Corporation (private car rr mark)

CMQ Coal Mining and Quarrying

c m r continuous maximum rating

CMR Cape Mounted Rifles; Continental Motors Corporation (NYSE); continuous maximum rating

CMRA Chemical Market Research Association

CMRB Citizens Medical Reference Bureau

c m s to be taken tomorrow morning (cras mane sumendus—pharmacy)

CMS Church Missionary Society; Commission for Synoptic Meteorology (CSM) (of WMO); Consumers Power Company (NYSE)

CMSA Canning Machinery and Supplies Association

cm/sec centimetres per second

CMStP&P Chicago, Milwaukee, St. Paul and Pacific Railroad Company

CMSX Consolidated Mining and Smelting Company of Canada, Limited, The (private car rr mark)

CMTC Citizens Military Training Camp

CM2c Carpenter's Mate Second Class (US Navy)

CM3c Carpenter's Mate Third Class (US Navy)

cmttee committee

CMU MAT. Cons. Municipalities of Baden (ASE)

CMW Canadian Marconi Company (NYSE)

CMWX Commodities Car Company Inc (private car rr mark)

CMX Chromium Mining & Smelting Corporation (private car rr mark)

CMZ Cincinnati Milling Machine (NYSE)

CMZS Corresponding Member of the Zoological Society

c n circular note; consignment note; cosine of the amplitude; credit note; new account (compte nouveau —French); tomorrow night (cras nocte—Latin)

cn canon

CN Canadian National Railways; Central News; chloracetophenone (tear gas); Code Napoleón; New York Central Railroad (NYSE)

CNA Chief Naval Adviser; Colonial Airlines, Inc (NYSE)

CNAC China National Aviation Corporation

CNAS Chief of Naval Air Services

CNB Canadian Breweries (NYSE)

Cnc Cancer (constellation)

CNC Catalan National Council; Czech National Committee

CNCA Cia Nacional Cubana de Aviacion; Czechoslovak National Council of America

CND Canadian Dredge & Dock Co. Ltd (Common stock, ASE)

cne captain (capitaine—French)

CNG Canadian Naval Gunboat; Consolidated Natural Gas Company (NYSE)

CNGB Chief, National Guard Bureau (US Army)

CNH Central Hudson Gas & Electric (NYSE); Committee for the Nation's Health

CNI Chief of Naval Information (Admiralty); Clinton Foods, Inc (NYSE); Commissioner for Northern Ireland

CNJ Central Railroad Company of New Jersey (rr mark)

CNK A MAT. Central Bank of German State & Prov. Bks. (ASE)

CNK B MAT. Central Bank of German State & Prov. Bks. (ASE)

CNL Committee of National Liberation; Consolidated Retail Stores, Inc (NYSE)

CNLA Council of National Library Associations

CNLAI National Committee of Liberation for North Italy (Comitato Nazionale di Liberatione per l'Alta Italia)

CNO Canada Southern Oils (NYSE); Chief Nursing Officer; Chief of Naval Operations

CNO&TP Cincinati, New Orleans and Texas Pacific Railway Company

CNO V Canada Southern Oils Ltd. (Registered Form) (ASE)

CNOX Canadian Oil Companies,

Ltd. (private car rr mark)

CNP Chief of Naval Personnel (Second Sea Lord—British Admiralty); Crown Central Petroleum (NYSE)

CNR Canadian National Railways; Chief Naval Representative; Civil Nursing Reserve; Conseil National de la Resistance (France); Container Corporation of America (NYSE)

CNRRA Chinese National Relief and Rehabilitation Administration

CNRX Conroe Creosoting Company (private car rr mark)

CN Ry Canadian Northern Ry

CNS Canada Southern Railway; (NYSE); Chief of the Naval Staff (First Sea Lord—British Admiralty)

CNV City Investing Company (NYSE)

CNW Chicago and North Western Railway Company (rr mark)

CNWMS Chester and North Wales Medical Society

CNWT Commander of the North-West Territories

c o coupon off; open account (compte ouvert—French)

co coinsurance; colon; company; county

Co cobalt

CO Cabinet Office; Camouflage Officer; Capacity Office; Cemented only (of envelopes); Chesapeake & Ohio Railway (NYSE); Chi Omega (sorority); Colonial Office; Commanding Officer (US Army); Command Orders; Commissioner for Oaths; Commissioner's Office; Open account (compte ouvert— French); conscientious objector; Criminal Office; Crown Office; General call to all stations (QS); Combined Baggage, Mail and Passenger (rr car)

c/o care of; carried over; cash order

C&O Chesapeake and Ohio Railway Company

C of O Chief of Ordnance

Coa Coahuila

COA California Olive Association; Coal Owners' Association; Certificated Officers' Association (Port of London Authority); College of Arms; Commonwealth of Australia

coad coadjutor

Coad Bp coadjutor bishop

coam coaming

cobq may he rest with all good souls (cum omnibus bonis quiescat— Latin)

COC Chamber of Commerce; Clergy Orphan Corporation; Columbus & Southern Ohio Electric (NYSE); Combined Operations Command;

Corps of Commissionaires; Crown Office in Chancery

coch amp(l) tablespoonful (*cochleare amplum*—Latin) (pharmacy)

cochl a spoonful (*cochleare*—Latin) (pharmacy)

coch mag a large spoonful (*cochleare magnum*—Latin) (pharmacy)

coch med a dessertspoonful (*cochleare medium*—Latin) (pharmacy)

coch parv a teaspoonful (*cochleare parvum*—Latin) (pharmacy)

Cochr Cochran's Nova Scotia Reports (legal)

co claim counterclaim (legal)

COCX California Cotton Oil Corporation (private car rr mark)

cod. code; codex; codification

COD cash on delivery; Central Ordnance Depot; Chamber of Deputies; collect on delivery; Concise Oxford Dictionary

CODAN coded weather analysis (US Navy)

Cod. Arg Codex Argenteus

Cod. Civ Code Civil

codd codices

Code N Code Napoléon

Code Rep Code Reporter (legal)

Cod. Jur Civ Justinian's Code (*Codex Juris Civilis*—Latin) (legal)

codl codicil (legal)

Cod. Theodos Codex Theodorianus (legal)

COE Cone Mills Corporation (NYSE)

COEAC Cabinet Office Economic Advisory Council

co-ed co-educational

coeff coefficient

Co Ent Coke's Entries (legal)

COF Catholic Order of Foresters; French Olympic Committee (*Comité Olympique Français*—French)

COFCH Chief of Chaplains (US Army)

Cof Dig. Cofer's Digest (legal)

COFENGRS Chief of Engineers (US Army)

coff cofferdam

COFF Chief of Finance (US Army)

COFI Chief of Information (US Army)

COFORD Chief of Ordnance (US Army)

COFRON Coastal Frontier (US Navy)

COFS Chief of Staff (US Army)

COFSPS Chief of Special Services (US Army)

COFT Chief of Transportation (US Army)

cog(n) cognate (with); cognizant

COG. Congoleum-Nairn, Inc (NYSE)

COH Commodore Hotel, Inc (NYSE)

COHC Clerks and Officers of the House of Commons

COHQ Combined Operations Headquarters (naval *and* RAF)

COI Central Office of Information; certificate of origin and interest; Co-ordinator of Information

coins. cl coinsurance clause

COK Cook Paint & Varnish Company (NYSE)

col colatitude (navigation); collected; collector; college; collegiate; colonel; colonial; col(on)y; color; colored; column; counsel; strain (*cola*—Latin)

Col Colorado; Colossians; Columbia

COL Colonel (US Army); Colorado Springs Stock Exchange

col c with (accompanying) the voice (*col canto*—Italian) (music)

Col-Comdt Colonel-Commandant

Col Corp Color Corporal

Coldm Gds Coldstream Guards

Colem Cas Coleman's Cases (legal)

Col Gd Color Guard

Colim Colima

coll collateral; colleague; collect; collection; collector; college; collegian; collegiate; colloquial(ly)

collab collaborating; collaboration; collaborator

coll barg collective bargaining (banking)

coll cl collision clause (insurance)

coll conc collection of the councils (*collectio conciliorum*—Latin)

collect. collective

Coll Goth. Collegiate Gothic

Coll/L collection letter

coll'otta with an octave higher (*coll'ottava*—Italian) (music)

collr collector

Col L Rev Columbia Law Review

coll tr collateral trust

collun a nose wash (*collunarium*—Latin) (pharmacy)

collut a mouth wash (*collutorium*—Latin) (pharmacy)

coll vol collective volume

collyr an eye lotion (*collyrium*—Latin) (pharmacy)

coln column

Colo Colorado

colog cologarithm (mathematics)

col p with the principal part (*colla parte*—Italian) (music)

Col Sergt Color Sergeant

col v(o) with the principal voice (*colla voce*—Italian) (music)

COLX Collins Construction Company (private car rr mark)

com comedy; comic; comfrey (botany); comma; commander; commentary; commerce; commercial; commissary; commission; committee;

commodore; common; commoner; commonly; commune; communicate[d]; communication[s]; community; commutator

Com Commonwealth; Communist; commission merchant (*comisionista*—Spanish); partner (silent) (*Comanditario*—Spanish)

COM Crowley, Milner & Company (NYSE)

COMAC Comité d'Action Militaire (France)

COMAIRLANT Commander Air Force, Atlantic (US Navy)

Com Arr Committee of Arrangements

comb. combination; combine[d]; combining; combustible

comb. liqu liquid fuel (*combustibles liquides*—French)

com carr common carrier

COMCRULANT Commander Cruisers, Atlantic (US Navy)

COMD Combined Operations Material Department

COMDGOF Commanding Officer (US Navy)

Com E Commercial Engineer

Com Ed Committee on Education

Com Err The Comedy of Errors

com & exp commission and expenses

Com Fin. Committee on Finance

Com H Committee of the House

coml commercial

Com Law Common Law

Com Merch Commission Merchant

Com Mil Aff Committee on Military Affairs

COMINCH Commander in Chief of United States Fleet

Comintern Communist International

comis commissary (*comisario*—Spanish)

COMISCO International Co-operating Organization of the Socialist Parties

Comm Agt Commission Agent

commem commemorative

commod commodity

commt commencement

Com Off. commissioned officer

comp companion; comparative; compare; comparison; compensating; compilation; compiled; composer; composition; compositor; compound; compensation (insurance); comprehensive (insurance); comprising

COMP composite (US Army)

compa company (*compañía*—Spanish)

compar comparative; comparison

comp asph compressed asphalt

Comp Dec Comptroller of the Treasury's Decisions

---

* COD – Commonwealth organization of Democrats. Source – Boston Globe 5/28/62 in existence about a year.

compd strand compressed strand
compenson compensation (legal)
comp g compressed gas
Comp Gen Comptroller General
Comp Gen Dec Decisions of the Comptroller General of the United States
compl complement; complementary; complete; compliment
complt complainant
compp compounds
comp p compression pressure
comp r compression ratio
Comp Stat Compiled Statutes
compt rend. reports (*comptes rendus*—French)
com pts common points
Com Serg Commissary Sergeant
Com SP Committee on State Prison
Com Sub. Commissary of Subsistence
COMPT comptroller (US Army)
compt compartment; comptometer
comptr comptroller
Comst Comstock (legal)
Com Ver Common Version (Bible)
Comy Gen Commissary General
COMZ communications zone (US Army)
con concerning; concentrate; concentration; concerto; conclusion; concerts; conics; conformist; connection; console; consolidated; consolidation; consort (*conjux*—Latin) (legal); continued; continuously rated; conversation; in opposition to, against (*contra*—Latin)
Con Consul
Concertm Concertmaster
conch. conchological; conchology
con cr contra credit
COND condition (US Army)
cond condense(r); conditional; conduct; conducted; conductor; conductivity (electricity)
condens condensation
conf compare (*confer*—Latin); conference; confessor
confed confederation
Confed Confederate
Conf Pont Confessor and Bishop (*Confessor Pontifex*—Latin)
Cong Congregational; Congregationalist; Congress; Congressional; gallon (*congius*—Latin)
Cong Rec Congressional Record (legal)
Congr Orat Congregation of the Fathers of the Oratory of St. Philip Neri (Oratorian Fathers)
conj conjugation; conjunction; conjunctive
conjunct. conjunctivitis
conn. connected; connection; connotation

Conn. Connecticut
CONN Connellan Airways Ltd
connt bill of lading (*connaissement*—French)
conn. w connected with
CONPY contact party (US Army)
conq conquer; conqueror
Conr Conrad
cons consecrated; consecration; consecutive; consequence; consequent; conservation; conservatory; consigned; consignment; consolidated; consonant; constable; constabulary; constitution; construction; consulting
Cons Conservative; Consolidated (stocks); Constitution[al]
consec ds consecutive days
con sect. conic section
Cons-Gen Consul-General
consgt consignment
consciae of conscience (*conscientiae*—Latin)
Cons Mus Conservatory of Music
conso advice (*consejo*—Spanish)
consol consolidated
Consols Consolidated Annuities (British Government stock)
conson consideration (legal)
Cons Reg Consular Regulations
cons sp constant speed
CONST construction (US Army)
const constable; constant; constituency; constitution; constitutional
Const Constantine
CONSTAB constabulary (US Army)
constr constructed; construction
Const US Constitution of the United States (legal)
const w construed with
consultn consultation (legal)
Con Sur Connoly's Surrogate (legal)
cont containing; contano (music); contents; continue; continuo (music); continuous; contract; contrary; control; controller
Cont Continent; Continental
contag contagious
Cont (AH) Continent, Antwerp-Hamburg range (shipping)
contbd contraband; contributed
contbg contributing
Cont (BH) Continent, Bordeaux-Hamburg range (shipping)
contbns contributions
cont bon mor contrary to good manners (*contra bonos mores*—Latin) (legal)
contce continuance (legal)
contd contained; continued
contemp contemporary
contg containing
Cont (HH) Continent, Havre-Hamburg range (shipping)
cont hp continental horsepower

contin let it be continued (*continuetur*—Latin) (pharmacy)
contn continuation
contr contract; contracted; contraction; contractor; contradict; contradiction; contralto; contrary; controller
contrib contribution; contributor
contrib val contributory value (insurance)
contt contract
Cont US&C Continental United States and Canada
conv convenient; convent; convention; conversation; convert; convertible; convict; convocation
convalesc convalescent
convce conveyance (legal)
convd converted
CONVN convenient(ce) (US Army)
convte useful (*conveniente*—Spanish)
CONX Continental Oil Compnay (private car rr mark)
COO Chief Ordnance Officer
cook. cookery
co-op co-operation; co-operative
Co-op Dig. Co-operative Digest, United States Reports (legal)
Coop. Tenn Ch Cooper's Tennessee Chancery Reports (legal)
COORD coordinate (US Army)
cop. copper; copulative
Cop. Copernican; Coptic
COP Combined Operations Personnel; Co-operative Party
COPA Cia Panamena di Aviacion
copart counterpart (legal)
COP EC Conference on Christian Politics, Economics, and Citizenship
copr copyright
COPR Copper Range Railroad Company (rr mark)
Copt Coptic
COPX Consolidated Products Company (private car rr mark)
cor body (*corpus*—Latin); cornet; coroner; correction; corrective; correlative; correspondence; correspondent; corresponding; corrupt; corruption
c or d by t or b collected or delivered by truck or barge
Cor Corinthians; Cornelia; Cornelius; Coroner; Corsica
I Cor I Corinthians (Bible)
II Cor II Corinthians (Bible)
COR Crystal Oil Refining Corporation (NYSE)
Cord. Cordelia
CORDOVA Cordova Air Service, Inc
Coriol Coriolanus
Cor Mem Corresponding Member
Corn. Cornish; Cornwall

Corn. LQ Cornell Law Quarterly

Corn. Univ Cornell University

Co R (NY) Code Reporter, New York (legal)

coroll corollary

corp to the body (*corpori*—Latin) (pharmacy); corporal; corporation

Corp Ch Coll Corpus Christi College

Corp Jur body of law (*Corpus Juris*—Latin) (legal)

corr correct; corrected; correction; correlate; correlative; correspondence; correspond[ent]; corresponding; corrugated; corrupt[ed]; corruption; things needing correction (*corrigenda*—Latin)

CORR correspond(ence) (US Army)

Corr Fell Corresponding Fellow

Corr Mem Corresponding Member

corrte current (*corriente*—Spanish)

corrupt. corrupted; corruption

Cor Sec Corresponding Secretary

C&O Ry Chesapeake & Ohio Railway Company

cos companies; cosine (mathematics); counties; countries

COS cash on shipment; Chamber of Shipping; Charity Organization Society; Chief of Staff; civilian occupational specialty (US Army); College of the Sea (Seafarers' Educational Service); Controller of Ordnance Services; Controller of Overseas Supplies; Copperweld Steel Company (NYSE)

co sa as above (*come sopra*—music)

cosec cosecant (mathematics)

COSFPS Commons, Open Spaces and Footpaths Preservation Society

cosh hyperbolic cosine (mathematics)

cosmog cosmographical; cosmography

co so. as above (*come sopra*—music)

Coss Consuls, in the time of the Consuls (*Consules, Consulibus*—Latin)

COSX Mid-Continent Petroleum Corporation (private car rr mark)

cot. cotangent (mathematics)

COT Coty, Inc (NYSE)

coth hyperbolic cotangent

COTS Central Officers' Training School

COTT Central Organization for Technical Training

Cott MSS Cottonian Manuscripts (British Museum)

COU Courtaulds, Ltd (ASE)

coun counsel

coup. coupler

cour of the current month (*courant*—French)

Cout Dig. Coutlée's Digest (legal)

cov covenant

c o v cross-over value

Cov G Covent Garden

Cow. Cowen's New York Reports (legal)

Cow. Cr R Cowen's Criminal Reports (legal)

Cow. NY Cowen's New York Reports (legal)

Cowp Cowper's (Law Reports)

cox coxswain (maritime)

coy. company

COY Consolidated Royalty Oil Company (NYSE)

c p candle power; carriage paid; center of pressure; centipoise; chemically pure; circular pitch; close pattern (plumbing); colla parte (music); compare; constant potential; constant pressure; coupling; coupon; custom of the port

CP Canadian Pacific Railway (rr mark); Canadian Press; Cape Province (South Africa); Cardinal Point; Car Park; Car Post; Carter, Paterson and Co.; Central Press; Central Provinces (India); Centre Party; Certification of Purchase; Chamber of Princes (India); change point (survey); Charter Party; Chi Phi (fraternity); Chi Psi (fraternity); Chief of Police; Chief Patriarch (freemasonary); Chief Psychologist (US Army); Civil Procedure; Clarendon Press; Clerk of the Peace; Code of Procedure (legal); College of the Pacific; College of Preceptors; Command Post; Common Pleas (legal); Common Prayer; Communist Party; Congregation of the Passion (*Congregatio Passionis*); Contract and Purchase Department (naval); Convict Prison; Crystal Palace; General call to two or more specified stations (QS)

C/P Charter Party; custom of port (grain trade)

CPA Calico Printers' Association; Canadian Pacific Air Lines. Ltd; Canned Pea Association; Catholic Parents' Association; Catholic Press Association; Certified Public Accountant; Civilian Production Administration; Chartered Patent Agent; Church Pastoral-Aid Society; Civilian Production Agency; Clay Products Association; College Protestant Association; Council of Personnel Administration; Cumberland and Pennsylvania Railroad Company (rr mark)

CPAA Poster Advertising Association of Canada

CPAGA California Prune and Apricot Growers Association

CPAS Catholic Prisoners' Aid Society; Conference of Pharmaceutical Association Secretaries

cpb center of pressure back

CPB Contractors Pump Bureau

CPC Chief Postal Censor; City Police Commissioner; City Police Court; Clerk of the Privy Council; Communist Party Congress; Compassionate Posting Committee; Congo Protestant Council; Council of Peoples' Commissars; Cumberland Presbyterian Church; Curtis Publishing Company (NYSE)

CPCC Cerebral Palsy Coordinating Council; Clerk of the Peace and of the County Council

CPCECA Customs Port Clerks and Excise Clerks' Association

CPCF Committee of the Permanent Charity Fund

CPCIZ Permanent Committee of International Zoological Congresses

CPC&N certificate of public convenience and necessity

CPCU Certified Property and Casualty Underwriter

CPCX Cosden Petroleum Corporation (private car rr mark)

cp cycle constant pressure cycle

cpd compound

CPD Capital City Products Company (NYSE); charterers pay dues (shipping); Civilian Personnel Division (US Army); Common Pleas Division (Law Reports); Contract and Purchase Department (Admiralty)

CPDE Compagnie Parisienne de Distribution de l'Electricité

CPDX Capital Packing Company (private car rr mark)

CPE College of Physical Education

c pen penal code (*code penal*—French)

CPF Colt's Manufacturing Company (NYSE); Provisional Frequency Board (PFB)

c p f f cost plus fixed fee

CPFX Champion Paper and Fibre Company (private car rr mark)

CPG Cotton Piece Goods

CPGB Central Practitioners of Great Britain; Communist Party of Great Britain

CPH certificate of public health

CPHM Chief Pharmacist's Mate (US Navy)

CPHTA Central Public House Trust Association

CPI Cinchona Products Institute;

Crop Protection Institute

CPIA Contracting Plasterers International Association

CPIMCO Preparatory Committee of the Inter-Governmental Maritime Consultative Organization

CPIRA Carbon Paper and Inked Ribbon Association

CPJGB Council of Polish Jews in Great Britain

cpl carpel (botany)

Cpl Corporal

CPL Carolina Power & Light Company (ASE)

Cple Constantinople

cplg coupling

CPLX Currie Products Limited (private car rr mark)

cpm common particular meter (hymns); cycles per minute

CPM Chief Principal Matron; Common Photographer's Mate (US Navy); Cosden Petroleum Corporation (NYSE)

CPNLGC Conference of Presidents of Negro Land-Grant Colleges

CPO Chief Petty Officer (naval); Chief Provision Officer; Command-Post Officer

CPOIR Preparatory Commission for the International Refugee Organization

cp on coupon on (bonds)

CPP Commissioner of Police and Prisons

CPPA Coated Processed Paper Association; Periodical Press Association of Canada

CPPS Society of the Precious Blood (Congregatio Pretiosissimi Sanguinis—Latin)

CPQ Code of Civil Procedure, Quebec (legal)

cpr copper

C Pr Code of Procedure (legal)

CPR Canadian Pacific Railway; Chief Parachute Rigger (US Navy); civilian personnel regulations (US Army)

CPRB Combined Production and Resources Board

CPRC Central Price Regulation Committee

CPRE Council for the Preservation of Rural England

C Prep counter-preparation

C Prtr Chief Printer (US Navy)

CPRW Combined Photographic Reconnaissance Wing

CP Ry Canadian Pacific Railway Company

cps cycles per second; centipoises

CPS Cambridge Philosophical Society; Church Patronage Society; Clerk of Petty Sessions; Congregational Publishing Society; Columbia Pictures Corporation (NYSE)

CPSI Council of Profit Sharing Industries

CPSX California Cedar Products Company (private car rr mark)

cpt let him take (capiat—Latin) (pharmacy); counterpoint

Cpt Captain

CPT Committee for the Promotion of Temperance

CPTP Civil Pilot Training Program

CPU Church Peace Union

CPVX Cook Paint & Varnish Company (private car rr mark)

CPX Central Packing Company, Inc (private car rr mark); command post exercise (US Army); Copper Range Company (NYSE)

CPY Clopay Corporation (NYSE)

CQ charge of quarters (US Army)

CQA Chalk Quarrying Association

CQD come quick, danger

CQM Chief Quartermaster (US Navy)

CQMS Company Quartermaster-Sergeant

c r account rendered (compte rendu —French); center of resistance; class rate; company's risk; current rate; reports (comptes rendus—French)

cr created; creation; credit; crescendo; crochet; crown; cruiser

CR Caledonian Railway; Cambrian Railway; cathode-ray; Central Railway; Central Registry; Chemical Reviews (a publication); Chief Ranger (of the Ancient Order of Foresters); cold rolled (steel sheets); Congregation of the Resurrection; Commendation Ribbon (US Army); compression ratio; compulsory registration; Congressional Republicans (United States); Connaught Rangers; Consumers Research; Copper Range Railroad Company (rr mark); Costa Rica; Crane Company (NYSE); crossroad (US Army); currency regulation; current rate; Keeper of the Rolls (Cestos Rotulorum); King Charles (Cawllus Rex); Queen Caroline (Carolina Regina)

Cr Cranch's Reports (legal); chromium

c/r for account and risk of (cuenta y riesgo—Spanish)

c&r canal and rail; canal and river

C of R Comminuty of the Resurrection

CRA Commander, Royal Artillery; California Redwood Association; Corona Australis (constellation)

CRAFA Comrades of the Royal Air Force Association

CRALOG Council of Relief Agencies Licensed for Operations in Germany

cran craniological; craniology

craniom craniometry

Cr App Criminal Appeal (Law Reports)

CRASC Commander Royal Army Service Corps

CRAT Colonel, Royal Artillery Training

CRB Convention of Royal Burghs; Corona Borealis (constellation); County Road Board (Scotland)

CRBI Cab Research Bureau, Inc

c r c closed roller check

CRC Canadian Railway Commission; Central Resistance Council; Christian Reformed Church; Civil Rights Congress; Coordinating Research Council

Cr Ca Criminal Cases (Law Reports)

crca cold rolled close annealed (steel)

CRCC Canadian Red Cross Committee

Cr C C Cranch's United States Circuit Court Cases (legal)

Cr Code Criminal Code (legal)

CRCS Clerks Regular of the Congregation of Somaschi

CRDX Central West Refrigerator Dispatch (private car rr mark)

CRE Commander, Royal Engineers; Congress of Racial Equality

CRECON counterreconnaissance (US Army)

cres becoming louder (crescendo—music); crescent

cres sub. pond. virt virtue increases under a burden (crescit sub pondre virtus—Latin)

CRF Cancer Research Fund; Continental Foundry & Machine (NYSE)

CRFO Chief Regional Fire Officer

CRG Coro, Inc (NYSE)

CRGX Midland Cooperative Wholesale, Cushing Refining Division (private car rr mark)

CRH Casualty Receiving Hospital; Chelsea Royal Hospital

CRHO Chief Road Haulage Officer

CRI Chicago River & Indiana Railroad Company (rr mark); Committee for Reciprocal Information (United States); Italian Red Cross (Croce Rossa Italiana); International Red Cross (Croix-rouge Internationale—French)

Cri Crimean

CR&I Chicago River and Indiana Railroad Company

CRiC Canons Regular of the Immaculate Conception; Commercial Radio International Committee

crim criminal

Crim L Rep Criminal Law Reporter (legal)

criminol criminology

CRI&P Ry Chicago, Rock Island & Pacific Railway Company

crit criterion; critic; critical; criticized; criticism

c r l cotton rubber-lined (fire hose)

CRL Canon[s] Regular of the Lateran; Chemical Research Laboratory; Conservators of the River Lea

CRL X Cudahy Refrigerator Line, The (private car rr mark)

CRM Chief Radioman (US Navy)

c r m counter radar measures

CRMA Cloth Reel Manufacturers Association; Commercial Refrigerator Manufacturers Association

CRMB Combined Raw Materials Board

CRMD Clerks Regular of the Mother of God

CRMI Clerks Regular Ministering to the Infirm (Camillians)

CRMX Cristales Mexicanos (private car rr mark)

CRN Canadian Canners, Ltd. (common stock, ASE)

CR&N Carolina & Northwestern Railway Company (rr mark)

CRNS Code Reports, New Series (legal)

CRNX Coosa River Newsprint Company (private car rr mark)

CRO cathode-ray oscilloscope; Claims and Records Office; Command Routine Order[s]; Consumer Rationing Order; Corps Routine Order[s]; Criminal Record Office

Croat. Croatia; Croatian

Cro Car. Croke's (Law Reports)

Crom Cromwell

CROP Christian Rural Overseas Program

cross. crossing

Cr P Criminal Procedure (legal)

CRP Calendar of the Patent Rolls (*Calendarium Rotulorum Patentum*) (legal); Canons Regular Premonstratensian; Central Railroad of Pennsylvania (rr mark); Creole Petroleum Corporation (NYSE)

CRR Carrier Corporation (NYSE); Curia Regis Roll; Clinchfield Railroad Company (rr mark)

CRR of NJ Central Railroad Company of New Jersey

c r s cold-rolled steel

CRS Camp Reception Station (US Army); Carpenter Steel Company (NYSE); Catholic Record Society; Ceremonial and Reception Secretary; Cooperative Recreation Ser-

vice; Container Recovery Service

CRSI Concrete Reinforcing Steel Institute

Crsp Crispian; Crispin; Crispus

crt court; crate; crater

CRT Certain-teed Products Corporation (NYSE); Chief Radio Technician

crtkr caretaker

crtr courtier

CRTS Curtiss (aircraft)

CRTX Continental Turpentine & Rosin Corporation Inc (private car rr mark)

CRU Corroon & Reynolds Corporation (NYSE)

cru cruiser

CRUIT Recruiting Office

CRUZEIRO Air Service of the Southern Cross (*Servicos Aereos Cruzeiro do Sul*)

crv corvus

CRYPTO cryptography(ic) (US Army)

cryst crystal; crystalline; crystallized; crystallography

Cs cesium

C&S Chicago & Southern Air Lines Inc

C of S Chief of Staff; Church of Scotland; Commissioner of Ships; Comptroller of Stamps; Courts of Survey

c to s carting to shipside

C SS CC Congregation of the Sacred Hearts of Jesus and Mary

C&S Ry Co Colorado & Southern Railway Company

CSSR Congregation of the Most Holy Redeemer

CSSS *Congregatio Sanctissimi Salvatoris* (Brigittine Congregation)

C St PM&O Chicago, St. Paul, Minneapolis & Omaha (rr)

c t cable transfer; certified teacher; commercial traveler

ct carat; caught (cricket); cent; circle; circuit; county; court; a hundred (*centum*—Latin); the present month (*courant*—French); current

C/T cable transfer; California Terms (grain trade)

CT California terms; Candidate in Theology; center tap (of a winding); Central time; central territory (shipping); Chadwick Trust (Promotion of Sanitary Science); Chief Telegrapher (US Navy); code telegrams; collateral trust; combat team (US Army); Crabtree Trustees; conning tower (submarines); cypher telegram

cta with the will annexed (*cum testamento annexo*—Latin)

CTA Chicago Transit Authority (ASE); Colored Trainmen of America; Continuation Teachers' Association

CTAL Confederation of Latin American Workers

c tant with the same amount of (*cum tanto*—Latin) (pharmacy)

Ct App Court of Appeals

Ct App NZ Court of Appeals Reports, New Zealand (legal)

CTAU Catholic Total Abstinence Union

CTB Chain Trade Board; Chief of Tariff Bureau; College of Teachers of the Blind; Commercial Traffic Bulletin (US Army); Corset Trade Board

c t c corn trade clauses

CTC Canadian Transport Commission; Capital Transit Company (NYSE); Centralized Traffic Control; Chief Turret Captain; Citizens Training Corps; Civil Technical Corps; Confederation of Chilean Workers; Cyclists' Touring Club

CTCB Coal Trade Conciliation Board

CTCHI Committee of Ten Coal and Heating Industries

Ct Cl Court of Claims, United States (legal)

Ct Cls R Court of Claims Reports

Ct Com Pleas Court of Common Pleas

CTCX California Tank Car Line (private car rr mark)

CTD Central Training Depot (WRENS); Classified Telephone Directories; Cotton Trade Deputation

CTDAA Custom Tailors and Designers Association of America

cte account (*compte*—French)

ctee committee

Ctesse Countess (*Comtesse*—French)

ctf certificate; certified; certify

CTF Chaplain to the Territorial Forces

CTGA Committee on Temperance of the General Assembly (of the Church of Scotland)

ctge cartage

CTH Corporation of Trinity House

C Theod the Theodosian Code (*Codex Theodosianus*) (legal)

CTI Cotton Textile Institute

CTK Official Czech Press Agency (in London)

ctl cental (100 lb. weight)

c t l constructive total loss (shipping)

CTL Continental Steel Corporation (NYSE)

c t l o constructive total loss only (insurance)

CTM Chief Torpedoman's Mate (US Navy); World Engineering Conference

CTMA Collapsible Tube Manufacturers Association; Cutting Tool Manufacturers Association

ctmo centesimo; centimo

ctn carton; cotangent

CTN Canton Railroad Company (rr mark)

cto concerto (music); fourth (*cuarto* —Spanish)

CTO Central Telegraph Office; Compulsory Tillage Order; Cotton Trade Organization; Cuban Tobacco Company Inc (NYSE)

CTP Pr Central Maine Pw. Company (3.50% Pfd.) (ASE)

C Tps Corps Troops

ctr center

CTR Caterpillar Tractor Company (NYSE)

ctrs centers

ctrsgd countersigned

ctrsig countersignature

CTS Catholic Truth Society

CTSE Chicago, Terre Haute & Southeastern Railway Company (rr mark)

ct stp certificate stamped (securities)

CTT City Auto Stamping Company (NYSE)

cttee committee

CTUS Carnegie Trust for the Universities of Scotland

ctvo centavo

CTX Caterpillar Tractor Company (private car rr mark); Consolidated Textile Company (NYSE)

CTY Century Ribbon Mills, Inc (NYSE)

cu cubic; cube

Cu copper

CU Cambridge University; Camouflage Unit; Central Eureka Mining (NYSE); Church Union; Citizens Union; Clark University; Close-up (films); Colgate University; Congregational Union; Consumers Union; Cooper Union; Cornell University; Creighton University; Curaçao; Customs Union

CUA Catholic University of America; Confederated Unions of America

CUAC Cambridge University Athletic Club

CUAFC Cambridge University Association Football Club

cub. cubic

CUB Cuban Atlantic Sugar Company (NYSE)

CUBANA Cubana de Aviación

CUBC Cambridge University Boat Club

CUCC Cambridge University Cricket Club; Cambridge University Cruising Club

cu cm cubic centimeter(s)

CUD Cudahy Packing Company (NYSE)

CUDS Cambridge University Dramatic Society

CUEW Congregational Union of England and Wales

CUFC Cambridge University Football Club

cu ft cubic foot (feet)

CUG Curtis Manufacturing Company (NYSE)

CUGB Catholic Union of Great Britain

CUGC Cambridge University Golf Club

CUHC Cambridge University Hockey Club

cu in. cubic inch[es]

cuis cuisine

cuj of which (*cujus*—Latin)

CUJC Coal Utilization Joint Council

cujusl of any (*cujuslibet*—Latin)

CUKT Carnegie United Kingdom Trust

CUL Cambridge University Library; Curtis Lighting Corporation (NYSE)

CULC Cambridge University Lacrosse Club

cult. cultivated (botany)·

CULTC Cambridge University Lawn Tennis Club

cu m cubic meter

cum cumulative

CUM Cambridge University Mission

CU-M Colliery Under-Managers

Cumb Cumberland (county in England)

cum div with dividend (*cum dividend* —Latin) (NYSE)

cum int with interest

cu mm cubic millimeter

cum pref cumulative preference (NYSE)

cum rts with rights (NYSE)

cu mu cubic micron

CUMS Cambridge University Musical Society

CUMX Cuero Cotton Oil & Manufacturing Company (private car rr mark)

CUN Cuneo Press, Inc (NYSE)

CUNA Credit Union National Association

CUOTC Cambridge University Officers' Training Corps

CUP Cambridge University Press

cu pf cumulative preferred (stocks)

cur. currency; current

Cur. Curaçao

cur. adv vult the court wishes to be advised (*curia advisari vult*—Latin)

CURFC Cambridge University Rugby Football Club

Cur. Ov Ca Curwen's Overruled Cases (legal)

CURR current; currency (US Army)

Current. Ct Dec Current Court Decisions (legal)

Curt. CC Curtis' United States Circuit Court Decisions (legal)

Curt. Dig. Curtis' Digest (legal)

CURUFC Cambridge University Rugby Union Football Club

Curw RS Curwen's Revised Statutes (legal)

CUSAAF Chief of the United States Army Air Force

cusec cubic feet per second

Cush Cushing's Massachusetts Reports (legal)

CUST custody(ian) (US Army)

custod custodian

CUUS Consumers Union of United States

cu yd cubic yard

cv chief value; constant volume (cycle); convertible; horsepower (*cheval-vapeur*—French); tomorrow evening (*cras vespere*— pharmacy); with the voice (*colla voce*—music)

CV aircraft carriers (US Navy); Cape Verde Islands; Central Vermont Railway, Inc (rr mark); clearing volume; combat vehicle (US Army); Common Version (Bible); Commercial Solvents Corporation (NYSE)

CVA Central Vermont Airways; City Valuers' Association

CVB aircraft carriers, large (US Navy)

CVC Central Valuation Committee

cv cycle constant volume cycle

c v d cash against documents (commerce)

cv db convertible debentures (securities)

CVE aircraft carriers, escort (US Navy)

c v k center vertical keel

CVL aircraft carriers, light (US Navy)

C Vn Canes Venatici (constellation)

CVO Commander of the Royal Victorian Order

c voc colla voce (music)

c v l s center vee one side (lumber)

cv pf convertible preferred (securities)

CVR Chicago Rivet & Machine Company (NYSE)

CVS Central Violeta Sugar Company, (NYSE)

cvt convertible (securities)

CVt Central Vermont Railway, Inc

c v 2 s center vee two sides (lumber)

CVX Cleveland Electric Illum. Company (NYSE)

cw clockwise rotation; commercial weight; connected with

CW Canada West; carrier wave (broadcasting); Chemical Warfare; Child Welfare; churchwarden; commercial weight; Commissions and Warrants Department (Admiralty); Common Wealth; company's wagon; continuous waves (telephone); Curtis-Wright Corporation (NYSE)

C of W College of Wooster

CWA Civil Works Administration; Communications Workers of America; Congress of Women's Auxiliaries

CWAC Canadian Women's Army Corps; Christian Women's Association of Canada

CWB Central Welsh Board

CWBC Credit Women's Breakfast Club

CWC Circle Wire & Cable Corporation (NYSE)

C&WC Charleston & Western Carolina Railway Company

CWCCI Crayon, Water Color and Craft Institute

CWCUSA Country Women's Council, United States

CWD civilian war dead

CWDA Colonial Welfare and Development Act

CWDF Colonial Welfare and Development Fund

CW Dud C. W. Dudley's Law Equity Reports (legal)

CWE Commonwealth Edison Company (NYSE)

CWEA Copper Wire Engineering Association

CWEX Commonwealth Edison Company (private car rr mark)

: w f cross wind force (navigation)

CWG Communist Workers Group

CWGA California Walnut Growers Association

CWH Cream of Wheat Corporation (The) (NYSE)

CWI Chicago & Western Indiana Railroad Company (rr mark); Cooperative War Industry

C & WI RR Chicago & Western Indiana Railroad Company

CWL Cable and Wireless Limited; Catholic Women's League; Cornwall Railroad Company (rr mark)

CWLA Child Welfare League of America

CWM Common Wealth Movement

CWMA Chemical Ware Manufacturers' Association

CWNA Canadian Weekly Newspapers Association

c w o cash with order

CWO Chief Warrant Officer (US Army); Commissioned Officer from Warrant rank (naval); Commissioner of Works Office; Crown Drug Company (NYSE)

CWOSD Commissioner of Works Supplies Division

CWP Chicago, West Pullman & Southern Railroad (rr mark); Civilian Works Program (United States)

CWPA Canvas Water Proofers Association

CWPX Consolidated Water Power & Paper Company (private car rr mark)

CWR Cabinet War Room; California Western Railroad (rr mark); Central Western Region

CWRTB Cotton Waste Reclamation Trade Board

CWS Central Wireless Station (RAF); Chemical Warfare Service (United States); Churchwardens' Society; Co-operative Wholesale Society

CWSI Church World Service, Inc

CWSS Carbon Wrench Statistical Service

cwt hundredweight (100 pounds in United States, 112 pounds in Great Britain)

CWT Campbell, Wyant & Cannon (NYSE); Central war time

CWTC Chicago World Trade Conference

CWTI Civilian War Time Injuries

CWU Chemical Workers' Union

CWUI Chemical Workers Union, International

CWVI Catholic War Veterans, Inc

CWWW Council for Women War Workers (Australia)

CWX Crystal Springs Water Company, Inc (private car rr mark)

cx convex

CX Colorado & Southern Railway Company (NYSE)

CXC Clorox Chemical Company (NYSE)

CXM Climax Molybdenum Company (NYSE)

CXP Central Explorers Ltd (NYSE)

cy capacity; county; currency; cycle; cylinder

Cy cyanogen (chemistry)

CY City Products Corporation (NYSE)

cyath a glassful (cyathus — Latin) (pharmacy)

cyath amp a tumbler (cyathus amplus — Latin) (pharmacy)

cyath vinos a wineglassful (cyathus vinosus — Latin)

cyc cycles [per second]; cycling; cyclopaedia

Cyc Cyclopedia of Law and Procedure

CYC Canadian Youth Congress; Corinthian Yacht Club

CYCX Pennsylvania-Conley Tank Line (private car rr mark)

CYE Calgary & Edmonton Corporation (NYSE)

Cyg Cygnus (constellation)

CYI Coty International Corporation (NYSE)

cyl cylinder; cylindrical

Cym Cymric

Cymb Cymbeline

CYMS Catholic Young Men's Society of Great Britain

CZ Canal Zone; Caprivi Zipfel; Celanese Corporation of America (NYSE); combat zone (US Army); Czechoslovakia

Czerw June (Czerwiec — Polish)

D

d customs (douane — French); date, daughter; day; dead; debit; deceased; deciduous (botany); declination; decree (decretum); degree; delete (dele); departs;

departure; deserted; deserter; dextro; dextrorotary; diameter; died; dime; diopter; discharged; distance; doctor; dollars; dominant; dorsal; dose; drama; drizzling

(nautical); dyne; leader (dux — Latin); right (droit — French)

D steamship (Dampfschiff — German)

d a deposit account; depositor's account; direct action (electricity);

of the said year (*dicti anni*—Latin); this year (*dette ar*—Norwegian)

d ä senior (*den äldre*—Swedish); that is (*det är*)

d A Sr. (*der Ältere*—German); this year (*dette Âr*—Danish)

Da Danish

DA Deccan Airways, Ltd ; Decimal Association; Defense Act; Department of Agriculture; Department of the Army; Di-phenylchlor-arsine (tear gas); Diploma in Anaesthetics; Diploma of Edinburgh College of Art; Direct Action (RAF); District Attorney; Division Association; Doctor of Arts; Dominion Atlantic Railway Company (rr mark); Draughtsmen's Association; Dining (rr car)

D/A days after acceptance; deposit account; discharge afloat (shipping); documents against acceptance; documents attached

D of A Daughters of America; Director of Artillery

DAA Diploma of the Advertising Association; Domestic Allotment Act; Durene Association of America

DAAG Deputy Assistant Adjutant General

D[A]A & QMG Deputy [Assistant] Adjutant and Quartermaster General

DAB Dictionary of American Biography; German Pharmacopoeia (*Deutsches Aporthekerbuch*—German)

dac deductible average clause (insurance)

DAC Deputy Assistant Censor; District Advisory Committee; Durex Abrasives Corporation

DACG Deputy Assistant Chaplain General

DACX Darling & Co (private car rr mark)

DAD Deputy Assistant Director; Documents against discretion

DADG Deputy Assistant Director General

DADOS Deputy Assistant Director of Ordnance Services

DADQ Deputy Assistant Director of Quartering

DAE Doctor in Aesthetics; Director of Air Equipment (naval); Director of Army Education

DAF Desert Air Force

DAFS Director of Army Fire Services

D/AFS Department of Administrative and Financial Services

DAFW Directorate of Air Force Welfare

dag dekagramme

DAG Deputy Adjutant General;

Deputy Attorney General

D Agr Doctor of Agriculture

Dah Dahomey

D A H disordered action of the heart (medicine)

DAI Director of Aeronautical Inspection; Division of Applications and Information

Daily Trans Daily Transcript

DAIS Directorate of Aeronautical Inspection Services

DAJAG Deputy Assistant Judge Advocate General

Dak Dakota; Dakota Territory Reports (legal)

DAL Delta Air Lines, Inc

Dall Dallas' United States Supreme Court Reports; Dallas' Pennsylvania Reports (legal)

Dall SC Dallas' United States Supreme Court Reports (legal)

dal s dal segno (music)

DALX Dominion Alkali & Chemical Company, Ltd (private car rr mark)

dam. dekameter

DAM Director of Air Material (naval)

D Am E Dictionary of American English

DAMGO Deputy Assistant Master General of Ordnance

DAMP Department of the Air Member for Personnel

DAMR Director of Aircraft Maintenance and Repair (naval)

DAMS Deputy Assistant Military Secretary

DAMSO Department (or Deputy) of the Air Member for Supply and Organization

DAMT Department of the Air Member for Training

Dan. Daniel (Biblical); Danish Danube; Danzig

Dan. & Ll Danson & Lloyd's Mercantile Cases (legal)

DAN MAT Danzig Port & Waterways Board (ASE)

dand to be given (*dandus*—Latin) (pharmacy)

DAP Directorate of Accident Prevention (RAF); Director of Administrative Planning; Director of Aircraft Production; Director of Air Personnel (RAF); Director of Army Psychiatry; Draft Assembling Point; documents against payment

DAPM Deputy Assistant Provost Marshal

DAPS Director of Army Postal Services

DAQMG Deputy Assistant Quartermaster General

DAR Daughters of the American Revolution; Defense Air Reports

(United States); Directorate of Armament Requirements (RAF); Director of Army Requirements

D Arch. Doctor of Architecture

darst readiness (*darstellung*—German)

Dart Coll Dartmouth College

DAS Davison Chemical Corporation (NYSE); delivered alongside ship (railway); Department of Agriculture (Scotland); Director of Armament Supplies; Dramatic Authors' Society

DASD Department of the Army Shipping Document (US Army)

DA/SM Director Anti-Submarine Material

DASO District Armament Supply Officer

Dass Dig. Dassler's Kansas Digest (legal)

DA/SW Director of Anti-Submarine Warfare

dat dative

DATC Director of Air Training Corps

DATI Department of Agriculture and Technical Instruction for Ireland

DATO Disbursing and Transportation Office (US Navy)

DATS Director of Auxiliary Territorial Service

dau daughter

DAUD Director of Anti U-Boat Division

Dauph Dauphin County Reports

Dav David

DAV Davidson Brothers, Inc (NYSE); Disabled American Veterans

DAV Aux Disabled American Veterans Auxiliary

d a v c delayed automatic volume control

DAVRS Director of Army Veterinary and Remount Services

DAVSF Disabled American Veterans Service Foundation

DAWS Director of Army Welfare Services

DAWT Director of Naval Air Warfare and Flying Training

DAX Diamond Alkali Company (private car rr mark)

DAY Dayton Rubber Company (NYSE)

DAZ *Deutsche Allgemeine Zeitung* (German newspaper)

db day book; debenture; decibel (unit of sound)

d b double-breasted

DB Bachelor of Didactics; Bachelor of Divinity; Deals and Battens (timber trade); Dental Board; divebomber; Doernbecher Manufacturing (NYSE); Domesday Book; double

bottoms (naval); Buffet (rr car)
D/B date of birth
D&B Dun & Bradstreet
d b a doing business as
DBA Doctor of Business Administration
d-bass double-bass
DBB deals, battens, and boards (timber trade)
db clg double-beaded ceiling (lumber)
DBD Director of Bomb Disposal
DBE Dame Commander of the Order of the British Empire
d b h diameter breast-high
D Bib. Douay Bible
dbk drawback (commerce)
DBK Dobeckmun Company (NYSE)
dbl double
d bl in this paper (*dieses blattes*— German)
dblr doubler
dbm decibel meter
DBM Director of Bureau of Mines
DBMA Distillate Burner Manufacturers Association
d b n of the goods not (yet administered) (*de bonis non*—Latin)
db part. double-beaded partition (lumber)
db pull draw bar pull
DBR Dominion Bridge Company (NYSE)
Dbre December (*Décembre*—French, *Diciembre*—Spanish)
db rts debenture rights (securities)
DBST Double British Summer Time
DBW Dow Brewery Ltd (NYSE)
d c dead center; depth charge; deviation clause (insurance); direct current (electricity); double column (accounting); repeat (*da capo*—music)
DC After Christ (*dopo Cristo*— Italian); death certificate; De Candolle (botany); decontamination; Defense Credits; Departmental Committee; depth charge; Deputy Chief; Deputy Commandant; Deputy Consul; Development Commission; Diplomatic Corps; Direct Current; Disarmament Conference; Disciples of Christ; District Court; District of Columbia; Divisional Controller; Divisional Court; Ph₂AsCN (a toxic smoke gas); Cafe (rr car); Dartmouth College; Delta Chi (fraternity); Delway Connecting Railroad Company (rr mark)
d/c cash (*dinero contante*—Spanish)
D&C District and County Reports
D of C Daughters of the Confederacy
D and C Dean and Chapter
DCA anti-aircraft defence (*défense contre aéronefs*—French); Deputy

Chief Architect; Director of Civil Affairs (military); Director of Civil Aviation; Divisional Catering Officer
DCADA District of Columbia Alley Dwelling Authority
DC Ae Diploma of the College of Aeronautics
d cap. double foolscap (paper)
DCAS Deputy Chief of the Air Staff; Division of Central Administration Services
DCASR Department of the Controller of American Supplies and Repair
DCB Defense Communications Board; Diocesan Chaplains Board; Distant-Control Boat (naval)
d cc double concave
DCC Diocesan Consistory Court; Double cotton covered (electric conductors)
DCCUS Dominican Chamber of Commerce of the United States
DCCX Davison Chemical Company (private car rr mark)
DCD Daitch Crystal Dairies (NYSE); Director of Compass Department (Admiralty)
DCDMA Diamond Core Drill Manufacturers Association
DCE Deputy Cl ef Engineer; Deputy City Engineer; Doctor of Civil Engineering
DCF deal-cased frame (carpentry)
DCG Department of the Controller General; Deputy Chaplain-General
DCGS Department of Conference and General Services; Deputy Chief of the General Staff (military)
D Ch Doctor of Surgery (*Doctor Chirurgiae*—Latin)
DCH Diploma in Child Health
D Ch O Diploma in Ophthalmic Surgery
DCI Des Moines and Central Iowa Railway Company (rr mark)
DCIGS Deputy Chief of the Imperial General Staff (military)
DCIS Department of Commercial and Intelligence Statistics
DCJ District Court Judge
DCL Dean and Chapter Library; Director of Contract Labor; Doctor of Civil Law; Lunch Counter Lounge Car (rr car)
DCLI Duke of Cornwall's Light Infantry
DCM Department of Coins and Medals (British Museum); Distinguished Conduct Medal; District Court-Martial; Drumhead Court-Martial
DCMA Dry Color Manufacturers Association
DCMS Deputy Commissioner of

Medical Services
DCN Dana Corporation (NYSE)
DCNA Deputy Chief Naval Adviser
D Cn L Doctor of Canon Law
DCNO Deputy Chief Nursing Officer
DCNS Deputy Chief of Naval Staff
DCO Diploma of the College of Optics; District Capacity Office; Divco Corporation (NYSE); draft collection only; Duchy of Cornwall Office
DCOD Director Combined Operations Division
DCOFS Deputy Chief of Staff (US Army)
DCOFSADMIN Deputy Chief of Staff for Administration (US Army)
DCOFSPCO Deputy Chief of Staff for Plans and Combat Operations (US Army)
DCOMD Director Combined Operations Material Department
DCOP Director Combined Operations Personnel
D of Corn LI Duke of Cornwall's Light Infantry
DCOS Department of the Controller of Ordnance Services
DCP Diploma in Clinical Pathology; Director of Coal Production; Director of Convict Prisons
DCPX Dacar Chemical Products, Inc (private car rr mark)
DCR Diocesan Chancellor and Registrar; District Chief Ranger (Ancient Order of Foresters)
DCRD Department of the Controller of Research and Development
DCRE Deputy Commandant Royal Engineers
DCREOS Department of the Controller of Repair, Equipment and Overseas Supplies
DCRHO Deputy Chief Road Haulage Officer
DCRS Devon and Cornwall Record Society
DCS Deputy Chief of Staff; Deputy Clerk of Session; Director of Clothing and Stores (military); Distillers Corp-Sagrams (NYSE); Doctor of Christian Science; Doctor of Commercial Science; Dyers' and Colourists' Society
DC of S Deputy Chief of Staff
DCT Depth Charge Thrower; Doctor of Christian Theology
DCTD Directors of Commodity and Technical Divisions
DCVO Dame Commander of the Royal Victorian Order
DCW Deputy Chief Warden
DCWC Diocesan Child Welfare Committee
DCWX Detroit Chemical Works

(private car rr mark)

d cx double convex

DCX Diamond Alkali Company of California (private car rr mark)

d d days after date (bills of exchange); days' date; delayed delivery; demand draft; double deck; dry dock (shipbuilding); given by (*dono dedit*—Latin); today's date (*de dato*—Latin) (legal)

dd dedicated; delivered; delivered at docks

DD Daily Double; death duties; deep drawing (steel sheets); Department of Defense (US Army); Discharged dead (naval); dishonorable discharge; Doctor of Divinity (*Divinitatis Doctor*—Latin); Dockyard Department (naval); duPont (E.I.) de Nemours (NYSE); Diner Dormitory (rr car)

d/d dated; delivered at docks; demand draft; divorce division; domicile to domicile

D d he gave to God (*Deo dedit*—Latin)

d and d drunk and disorderly

D of D Director of Dockyards

DDA Dangerous Drugs Act; Dental Dealers of America

DDALV Days' delay en route authorized chargeable as leave (US Army)

DDALVP Days' delay en route authorized chargeable as leave provided it does not interfere with reporting on date specified and provided individual has sufficient accrued leave (US Army)

DDATS Deputy Director of Auxiliary Territorial Service

D=day a predetermined date; date of Allied invasion of France (World War II)

DDCA Deputy Director of Civil Affairs (military)

DDD Comprehensive Dishonesty, Disappearance and Destruction Policy (insurance); Delta Delta Delta (sorority); Director of Dockyards Department; gives, devotes, dedicates (*dat, dicat, dedicat*—Latin); he gave and consecrated as a gift (*dono dedit dedicavit*—Latin)

d d In d from day to day (*de die in diem*—Latin)

DDDS Deputy Director of Dental Services (military)

DDE Deputy Director of Equipment (RAF)

DDG Deputy Director General

DDGCA Department of Director General of Civil Aviation

DDGMP Department of the Director

General of Munitions Production

DDGTA Deputy Director General of the Territorial Army

DDHP Deputy Director of Hygiene and Pathology (military)

DDL *Det Danske Luftfartselskab* (Danish Aviation Company)

DDM Doctor of Dental Medicine

DDMI Deputy Director of Military Intelligence

DDMOI Deputy Director of Military Operations and Intelligence

DDMS Deputy Director of Medical Services

ddo dispatch discharging only

D Docks. Director of Docks Service

DDS Deaf and Dumb Society; Deputy Director of Science (military); Doctor of Dental Science; Doctor of Dental Surgery

DDSD Deputy Director of Staff Duties (military)

DD&Shpg dock dues and shipping

DDSP Deputy Director of Selection of Personnel (military)

DDS&T Deputy Director of Supplies and Transport

ddt deduct

DDT dichloro-diphenyl-trichloro-ethane (insecticide); duplex-drive tank

DD of T Director, Division of Traffic

DDTA Deputy Director, Territorial Army

DDTI Deputy Director of Tactical Investigation (military)

DDV Deputy Director of Vehicles

d e double entry (accounting); this is, (*det er*—Norwegian)

DE Used to separate the call sign of the station called from the call sign of the calling station (QS); Dail Eireann (Lower House of the Eire Parliament); deckled edges (paper); Deere & Company (NYSE); destroyer escort; Director of Engineering (naval); Director of Equipment; Doctor of Education; Doctor of Engineering; Doctor of Entomology; Duke Endowment; Dynamic Engineer; Diner without Kitchen (rr car)

D and E Davis and Elkins (college)

D of E Director of Education

DEA Davis Escape Apparatus; Dockyards Expenses Accounts; deacon; Deady's United States District Court Reports (legal)

DEAA Department of Egyptian and Assyrian Antiquities

deaur let it be gilded (*deauretur*—Latin) pharmacy

deb debenture; debut; debutante; debit

Deb Deborah

DEB Dental Examining Board (naval)

DEBK debark (US Army)

dec deceased; decimal; decision; declaration; declared; declension; declination; decorative; decrease; deduct (*decort*—German)

DEC Door Export Company

DECA Department of Economic Affairs

decd deceased (legal); declared

Dec Dig. American Digest, Decennial Edition (legal)

decid deciduous (botany)

decis decision

Decl of Ind Declaration of Independence

declon declaration

decn decontamination

Dec O Ohio Decisions (legal)

decoct. decoction (*decoctum*—Latin)

decomp decomposition

DECON decontaminate (US Army)

D Econ Sc Doctor of Economic Science

decor decoration

decupl decuplicate

DECX Duval Engineering & Contracting Company (private car rr mark)

ded dedicated

DED Director of Education Department (Admiralty)

D Ed Doctor of Education

deduct. deduction

DEE Director of Electrical Engineering

def defendant; deferred (shares); deficit; defined; definite[ly]; definition

Def deferred (of stocks or shares—NYSE)

defl deflation; deflection

defs definitions

deft. defendant (legal)

deg degree

deglut to be swallowed (*deglutiendus*—Latin) (pharmacy)

De GM & G De Gex, Macnaghton and Gordon (Law Reports)

DEI Dutch East Indies

DEIDP Department of Engraving, Illustration, Design and Painting

dekag dekagram

del delegate; delegation; delete; deliberation; he drew it (*delineavit*—Latin)

Del Delaware; Delphinus (constellation)

DELACCT delinquent account (US Army)

Del Ch Delaware Chancery Reports (legal)

deld delivered

dele   delete (*deleatur*—Latin)

delib   deliberation

delic   delicatamente (music)

deliquesc   deliquescent

delt   he drew it (*delineavit*—Latin)

dely   delivery

dem   demand; democracy; democratic; demurrage; demy (size of paper)

Dem   Democrat; Democratic

DEM   Director of Extramural Department

DEMA   Diesel Engine Manufacturers Association

DEML   detached enlisted men's list (US Army)

demob   demobilization

Demol   Demolombe's Code Napoléon (legal)

demon.   demonstrative

DEMS   Defensively equipped merchant ship; Director of Equipment for Merchant Ships

Dem Sur   Demarest's Surrogate (legal)

den   denotation; denotatively

Den.   Denbighshire (Wales); Denio's New York Reports (legal); Denmark

DEN   Director of Engineering (Royal Australian Navy)

Denb   Denbighshire (Wales)

D Eng   Doctor of Engineering

D Eng   Doctor of Engineering Science

denom   denomination

dent.   dental

Dent. Hyg   Dental Hygienist

DEO   Divisional Education Officer; Divisional Entertainments Officer

DEOWW   Disabled Emergency Officers of the World Wars

dep   depart; department; departure; deponent; deposed; deposit; depot; deputy; laid to rest (*depositus*—Latin); since (*depuis*—French)

dép   deputy (*député*—French); French department (*département*)

Dep-Adv-Gen   Deputy-Advocate-General

depart.   department

Dep Commr   Deputy Commissioner

dep ctf   deposit certificate (securities)

depend.   dependency

Dep Eng-in-Ch   Deputy Engineer-in-Chief

depilat   depilatory (*depilatorium*—Latin) (pharmacy)

deposn   deposition (legal)

Dep prov   member of the provincial parliament (*deputato provinciale*—Italian)

dept   department; deponent; depot; deputy; French territorial division (*département*—French)

deputn   deputation

der   last (*dernier*—French); deriva-tion; derivative; derived; of the last month (*dernier*—French)

Derb(s)   Derbyshire

Derby.   Derbyshire (county in England)

dermatol   dermatology

des   designate; designation

Des   Desaussure's South Carolina Equity Reports (legal)

DES   Delta Espilon Sigma (society); destroyer (US Navy); Detroit Steel Corporation (NYSE); Director of Educational Services (RAF); Director of Engineering Stores (military)

desc   descendant; describe; discount (*descuento*—Spanish)

descron   description

descto   discount (*descuento*—Spanish)

desid   desiderata; desideratum

desig   designate

desp   despatch

dess   dessiatine

dest   destra (music); destroyer (naval)

destn   destination

det   detach; detachment; detail; detective; determine; let it be given (*deturi*—Latin) (pharmacy)

d e t   double end trimmed (lumber)

DETA   Divisao de Exploraçao dos Transportes Aereos

detd   determined

determn   determination

detn   detention

Deut   Deuteronomy (Biblical)

dev   deviation; develop

Dev   Devonshire (England)

DEV   development (US Army); De Vilbiss Company (NYSE); Holly Development Company (NYSE)

Dev Ct Cl   Devereux's Reports, United States Court of Claims (legal)

dev lgth   developed length

Devon   Devonshire (county in England)

DEW   Delaware Power & Light Company (NYSE); distant early warning (radar)

DEWD   Director of Economic Warfare Division

D Ex-SMF   Deafened Ex-Servicemen's Fund

dext   right (*dexter*—Latin)

dez   dezembro (Portuguese)

D/F   direction finding (US Army)

d/f   days from date (*dias fecha*—Spanish)

d f   dead freight (shipping); direction finder; double front; federal district (*distrito federal*—Spanish)

DF   Dean of Faculty; Defender of the Faith (*Defensor Fidei*—Latin);

Destroyer Flotilla; Development Fund; diamond flap (of envelopes); Dickens Fellowship; direction-finder; Doctor of Forestry; Dodge Foundation; door in flat (theater); disposition form (US Army)

DFA   Dairy Farmers' Association; Division Freight Agent; Drop Forging Association

DFAC   Dried Fruit Association of California

DFC   Distinguished Flying Cross

DFEC   Douglas Fir Export Company

DFFX   Durkee Famous Foods, a division of the Glidden Company (private car rr mark)

DFM   Director of Freight Movement; Distinguished Flying Medal

DFMR   Dazian Foundation for Medical Research

DFMS   Domestic and Foreign Missionary Society

d forg   drop forging

DFPA   Douglas Fir Plywood Association

DF Stn   Direction-Finding Station

DFSWO   Department of the Financial Secretary of the War Office

dft   defendant; draft

DG   Associated Dry Goods Corporation (NYSE); declaration of war (*déclaration de guerre*—French); degaussing (naval); Delta Gamma (sorority); DiGiorgio Fruit Corporation (NYSE); Director General; Divisional General; double-gummed (of envelopes); Dragoon Guards; Dramatists Guild; by the grace of God (*Dei gratia*—Latin); thanks to God (*Deo gratias*—Italian); Grill Room (rr car)

DGC   Dangerous Goods Classification (railway); Duty Group Captain

DGDC   Deputy Grand Director of Ceremonies (freemasonry)

DGF&JB   De Gex, Fisher, & Jones' English Bankruptcy Reports (legal)

DGI   Director General of Information; Date Growers Institute

DGIAB   Durable Goods Industries Advisory Board

dgl   alike (*desgleichen*—German); ditto (*desgleichen*—German); such (*dergelike*—Dutch)

DGLS   Douglas (aircraft)

DGM   Detroit Gasket & Manufacturing Company (NYSE)

DGMS   Director General of Medical Services

DGMW   Director General of Military Works

Dgn   Dragoon

DGO   Diploma in Gynaecology and Obstetrics; Director General of

Organization (RAF)

DGP Director General of Production (Air Ministry); Directorate General of Postings (RAF)

DGR Denver & Rio Grande Western (NYSE); Director of Graves Registration

d g s double green silk covered (electric conductors)

DG St J Dame of Grace of the Order of St John of Jerusalem (England)

DGW Directorate General of Works (RAF)

DGWIP Director General of Weapons and Instruments Production

DGY Detroit Gray Iron Foundry (NYSE)

d h deadhead (freight); dead heat (racing)

DH Department of Hygiene; Director of Hygiene; double-hung (windows); Delaware & Hudson Company (NYSE)

d&h dressed and headed (lumber)

dha good luck (*dicha*—Spanish)

DHC Defense Homes Corporation

DHCA Director of Home Civil Aviation

D&HCo Delaware and Hudson Railroad Corporation

D Hgs Director of Hirings Service

DHI Dunhill International, Inc. (NYSE)

DHL Doctor of Hebrew Literature

DHM Detroit Hardware Manufacturing (NYSE)

DHMPGTS Department of His Majesty's Procurator General and Treasury Solicitor

dho said (*dicho*—Spanish)

DHOB Durham Hosiery Mills ("B" common stock) (ASE)

DHQ Division Headquarters (US Army)

D & H RR Delaware & Hudson Railroad Company

DHS Defense Homes Corporation (United States); Department of Health for Scotland; Detroit, Hillsdale & South Western Railway (NYSE)

DHWS Defense Health and Welfare Service (United States)

D Hy Director of Hygiene; Doctor of Hygiene

DHY Develet Hava Yollari Genel Mudurlugu (airline)

d i diplomatic immunity

DI daily inspection (aircraft); Deputy Inspector; Director of Infantry; District Inspector; Divisional Inspector

D/I Director of Intelligence (US Army)

D of I Director of Intelligence

dia diagram; diameter

DIA Date Industries Association; Design and Industries Association, Diamond Alkaki Company (NYSE)

dial. dialect[al]; dialectic[al]; dialogue

diam diameter

diap diapason (music)

DIB Department of Information and Broadcasting (India)

dic December (*dicembre*—Italian; *diciembre*—Spanish)

DIC Dairy Industry Committee; Diploma of Imperial College; Director of Infestation Control

DICEA Division for the Investigation of Cartels and External Assets

Dick. Dickens' English Chancery Reports (legal)

DICST Diploma of Imperial College of Science and Technology

dict dictated; dictation; dictator; dictionary

dicta dictaphone

DICX Dry Ice Refrigerator Line (private car rr mark); Merchants Despatch Transportation Corporation (private car rr mark); Pure Carbonic Company (private car rr mark)

did. didactic

DID Detail Issuing Depot

DIDA Director of Intelligence Division of the Admiralty

DIE Diploma of the Institute of Engineering

dieb alt every other day (*diebris alternis*—Latin) (pharmacy)

diet. dietetics

difce difference

difclt difficult

difclty difficulty

diff difference; different; differential

diff calc differential calculus (mathematics)

dig. digest

Dij Dijon (France)

dil dilute

dild diluted

dilet dilettante

diln dilution

dim. dimension; diminutive; dimissory; a half (*dimidium*—Latin) (pharmacy); getting softer (*diminuendo*—Italian) (music); Sunday (*dimanche*—French)

DIM Denver and Intermountain Railroad Company (rr mark); District Inspector of Musketry

DIN Deutsche Industrie Normal (photography); Diana Stores Corporation (NYSE)

D Ing. Doctor of Engineering (*Doctor [Artis] Ingeniariae*—

Latin)

DIO Directorate of Intelligence (Operations) (RAF)

dioc diocesan; diocese

dioc conf diocesan conference

Dioc Sem Diocesan Seminary

dioc syn diocesan synod

DIPAB Dress Industry Price Adjustment Bureau

Dip. diploma; diplomacy; diplomatic

dipl diplomat

DIL Distillers Company Ltd. (ASE)

diplom diploma[cy]; diplomatic

dir directed; direction; director

DIR Directorate of Intelligence (Research) (RAF)

D & IR Duluth and Iron Range Railroad Company (private car rr mark)

dir-conn direct-connected

diron direction (legal)

dis disciple; discipline; disconnect; discount; distance; distant; distribute; discontinued (bookselling)

DIS Directorate of Intelligence (Security)

DISB disburse (US Army)

disbs disbursements

disbs &/or ant. earns. disbursements and/or anticipated earnings (insurance)

disc. discount; discovered; discoverer; discovery

DISCH discharge (US Army)

dischge discharge (legal)

discreoni to the discretion (*discretioni*—Latin)

discron discretion (legal)

disct discount

DISI Dairy Industries Society, International

disp dispensary; dispensatory; dispense; disperse; number, part of (*dispensa*—Italian)

DISP dispose(ition) (US Army)

displ displacement

diss dissenter; dissertation

dist distance; distant; distinguish; district

Dist Atty District Attorney

Dist Chf District Chief

Dist Comdr District Commander

Dist Ct District Court

distd distilled

Dist Eng District Engineer

disting distinguish; distinguishing

Dist J District Judge

Dist Mgr District Manager

DISTR distribute(ion) (US Army)

Dist R District Railway

Dist Rep District Reports (legal)

disy disyllabic

DIT Detroit Institute of Technology; Drexel Institute of Technology

div diverse (*divers*—French);
divide[d]; dividend; divine;
divinity; divisi (music); divisibility;
division; divisor

DIV Diversey Corporation (NYSE)

Div Eng Division Engineer

divide dividend (*dividende*—French)

div in pt aeq divide into equal parts
(*divide in partes aequales*—Latin)
(pharmacy)

divs dividends

d j dust jacket (books); junior
(*der Jüngere*—German); of this
year (*dieses Jahres*—German)

DJ Dejay Stores, Inc. (NYSE);
District Judge; Divorce Judge;
Doctor of Law (*Doctor Juris*—
Latin)

D & J December and June

DJAG Deputy Judge Advocate
General

DJC Doehler-Jarvis Corporation
(NYSE)

DJS Doctor of Juridical Science

dk deck; dock

DK Dormitory, Kitchen Car (rr car)

DKA Decca Records, Inc. (NYSE)

DKE Delta Kappa Epsilon
(fraternity)

dkg dekagram; decking (lumber)

dkl dekaliter

dkm dekameter (metric); monuments
(*denkmäler*—German)

dkm² square dekameter (metric)

dkm³ cubic dekameter (metric)

DKP Kitchen Car (rr car)

dks dekastere

dkt docket

dkyd dockyard

d l demand loan

dl deciliter; part; volume (*deel*—
Dutch)

DL day letter; dead load; Delaware,
Lackawana and Western Railroad
(NYSE); Deputy Lieutenant
(England); Director of Labor;
Doctor of Law; dog license;
Double Ledger; driver's license;
Buffet Lounges (rr car)

D of L Duchy of Lancaster

D lat difference in latitude

DLB Deposit Liquidation Board

DLC Doctor of Celtic Literature;
Disaster Loan Corporation; Lunch
Counter Car (rr car)

dld delivered

DLGA Decorative Lighting Guild of
America

DLI Durham Light Infantry

DLIA Dental Laboratories Institute
of America

D Lit Doctor of Literature

D Litt Doctor of Literature (Oxon)
or Letters (Cambridge)

dIM of the current month (*des*

laufenden Monats—German)

DLM Daily List of Mails (G.P.O.);
Director of Liaison and Munitions

dlM of the current month (*des
laufenden Monats*—German)

dlo dispatch loading only

d lo difference of longitude
(navigation)

DLO Dead Letter Office; Diploma in
Laryngology and Otology;

d long. difference of longitude

DLOX Dominion Linseed Oil
Company Ltd. (private car rr mark)

DLP Dunlop Rubber Ltd. (NYSE)

dlr dealer; dollar

DLR Dominion Law Reports

DLS Doctor of Library Science

dls/shr dollars per share

DLT Daily Letter Telegram

DLVR deliver(y) (US Army)

dlvy delivery

DL&W Delaware, Lackawanna and
Western Railroad Company

DLX Dryson's Limited (private car
rr mark)

DLY Duraloy Company (NYSE)

dm decameter; decimeter; draft
molded

d M of the instant (*dieses Monato*
—German); this month (*denne
Maaned*—Danish)

DM² square decimeter

DM³ cubic decimeter

DM dedicated to the souls of the
departed (*Dis manibus* [*sacrum*]
—Latin); Defence Minister; Deputy Master; *destra mano* (with the
right hand—music); Diphenylar-
sinechlorarsine (adamsite, NH
$(C_6H_4)_2AsCl$—tear gas); Director of Mechanization; disconnect-
ing manhole (sanitary engineering);
Dispatch of Mails; Doctor of Mathematics; Doctor of Medicine; Doctor
of Music; Dome Mines, Ltd (NYSE);
Durham Miners (Union of); light
mine layers (US Navy)

D&M Detroit and Mackinac Railway
Company

d&m dressed and matched (timber)

D of M Director of Music

DMA Dental Manufacturers of America

DMAA Diamond Manufacturers Association of America; Direct Mail
Advertisers Association

DMAAI Direct Mail Advertising Association, Inc

DMB Defense Mediation Board
(United States); Director of Merchant Shipbuilding

DMBL demobilize (US Army)

DMD Doctor of Dental Medicine
(*Dentariae Medicinae Doctor*—

Latin); Doctor of Mathematics
and Didactics

DMDG Department of the Medical
Director-General (naval)

DME Director of Mechanical Engineering (military)

D Med Doctor of Medicine

D Met Doctor of Metallurgy

DMG Deputy Master General
(military)

DMHS Director of Medical and
Health Services

DMI Director of Military Intelligence; Day Mines, Inc (NYSE)

DMIAAI Diamond Manufacturers and
Importers Association of America,
Inc

DMIR Duluth, Missabe & Iron Range
Railway Company (rr mark)

DMJS December, March, June, September (quarter months)

DML demolition (US Army); Doctor
of Modern Languages

d mld depth moulded (naval engineering)

DMMC Department of Metallurgy and
Metallurgical Chemistry

DM & N Duluth, Missabe & Northern
Railway Company (rr mark)

dmnstr demonstrator

DMO Director of Maritime Operations (RAF); Director of Military
Operations

DMOI Director of Military Operations and Intelligence

DMP Director of Manpower Planning

DMQ Director of Movements and
Quartering

DMR Department of Medical Radiology; Director of Merchant Ship
Repairs; Division of Monetary Research

DMRE Diploma in Medical Radiology and Electrology

DMRF Debs Memorial Radio Fund

DMS consecrated to the souls of
the departed (*Dis manibus sacrum*
—Latin); Deputy Military Secretary; Director of Medical Services;
Director of Military Survey; Director of Mine-Sweeping Division; Directorate of Microgram Services
(RAF); Doctor of Medical Science;
Dominion Stores, Ltd (NYSE)

DMSS Director of Medical and Sanitary Services

DMST demonstrate(ion) (US Army)

DMT Director of Military Training

DMU Danish Cons. Municipal Loan
(ASE); Des Moines Union Railway
Company (rr mark)

D Mus Doctor of Music

DMWD Director of Miscellaneous
Weapons Development Department

DMY Dresser Industries, Inc (NYSE)

dn delta amplitude; down

DN Diamond Match Company (NYSE); to our Lord (*Domino Nostro—*Latin)

D/N debit note; delta amplititude

D of N Director of Navigation

DNA Director of Naval Accounts

DNAD Director of Naval Air Division

DNAO Director of Naval Air Organization

DNB *Deutsches Nachrichten Buro* (Official German News Agency); Dictionary of National Biography; dinitrobenzene

DNC Democratic National Committee; Director of Naval Construction

Dne customs (*douane—*French)

DNE Director of Naval Equipment

DNF Dominion Naval Forces

DNG Dutch New Guinea

DN and G[R] Dundalk, Newry and Gruenore (railway)

DNHAS Dorset Natural History and Archæological Society

DNHS Durham Natural History Society

DNI Director of Naval Intelligence

D of '98 Daughters of '98

DNMS Director of Naval Medical Services

DNMTB Drift Nets Mending Trade Board

DNO Director of Naval Operations

DNPP Our Lord the Pope (*Dominus noster Papa Pontifex—*Latin)

DNR Department of National Revenue; Director of Naval Recruiting

DNSPD Divisions of Naval Staff Plans Division

DNT dinitrotoluene

Dnus Lord (*Dominus—*Latin)

d o outside diameter

do. delivery order; the same (*ditto—*Italian); Dornier (German aeroplane); dissolved oxygen

DO day-old; Deemed Oath; Delta Omega (society); Delta Omicron (music society); Designs Office; Diploma in Osteopathy; Diploma of Ophthalmology; direct order; Director of Organization; Directorate of Operations (RAF); District Office; Divisional Officer; Divisional Orders; Doctor of Optometry; Doctor of Oratory; Doctor of Osteopathy; Dominions Office; Duty Officer; Cafe Observation (rr car)

d o a dead on arrival

DOA Deutsche-Ost-Afrika-Linie (German East Africa Steamship Line); Documents on Acceptance

DOAE Department of Oriental Antiquities and Ethnology (British Museum)

doc document; docket; doctor

DOC Bureau of Documents (UN Secretariat); Department of Ceramics; Department of Circulation; Director of Cleansing; Director of Contracts (military); Directorate of Camouflage; District Officer Commanding; Dr. Pepper Company (NYSE); Duchy of Cornwall

DOCA Director of Overseas Civil Aviation

Doc Eng Doctor of Engineering

doct document (legal); doctor

docum document

documᵗᵒ document (*documento—*Spanish)

DOD Dodge Manufacturing Corporation (NYSE)

DOD(F) Director of Operations Division (Foreign)

DOD(H) Director of Operations Division (Home)

D Oec Doctor of Economics (*Doctor Oeconomiae—*Latin)

DOES Director of the Office of Economic Stabilization (United States)

DOFS day of supply (US Army)

dogm dogmatic

dol dolce (music); dollar

DOL Doctor of Oriental Languages

dol urg when the pain is severe (*dolore urgente—*Latin) (pharmacy)

dolcis very softly (*dolcissimo—*Latin) (music)

dolent part to the afflicted part (*dolenti parti—*Latin) (pharmacy)

dom domestic; domicile; dominion

Dom [belonging] to the Lord (*Dominicus—*Latin); Dominic; Dominica; Dominion; Sunday (*Domingo—*Spanish)

DOM Department of Metalwork; Director of Music; Dominguez Oil Fields Company (NYSE); God the best and greatest (*Deo optimo maximo—*Latin); God the Master, or Lord, of all (*Dominus omnium Magistu—*Latin)

Dom Bk Domesday Book

DOMC Diploma in Ophthalmology, Medicine and Surgery

Dom Can Dominion of Canada

Dom Econ Domestic Economy

Dom Ex domestic exchange

Dom Proc In the House of Lords (*Domus Procerum—*Latin)

Dom Rep Dominican Republic

DOMS Diploma in Ophthalmic Medicine and Surgery; Doctor of Orthopædic Medicine and Surgery

DOMX Dothan Oil Mill Company (private car rr mark)

Don Donegal (Ireland)

DOO Directing Ordnance Officer (military); Director of Organization; Duty Operations Officer

d o p developing out paper; documents on payment

DOPBM Department of Oriental Printed Books and Manuscripts (British Museum)

dopp ped doppio pedale (music)

dor doric; dormitory

Dor Dorado (constellation); Dorothy

DORA Defense of the Realm Act

Dord Dordogne (French Department)

Dors Dorsetshire

dos dose (pharmacy)

DOS Director of Ordnance Services; Director of Stores (naval); Doctor of Optical Sciences; Domestic Finance Corporation (NYSE)

DOT Department of Overseas Trade; Department of Textiles; Director of Operational Training

D/OT Director of Organization and Training (US Army)

Doug Douglas (legal); Douglas' Michigan Reports (legal)

DOV double oil of vitriol

dow dowager

DOW died of wounds (US Army); Dow Chemical Company (NYSE)

DOWB Department of Works and Buildings; Director of Works and Buildings

Down. Downing College, Cambridge

DOWX Dow Chemical Company (private car rr mark)

DOX Derby Oil Company (private car rr mark)

doz dozen

d p diametral pitch (gears); direct port (shipping); distributing point; double pole (switch); drip proof

dp deep

DP Cerro de Pasco Corporation (NYSE); Delta Phi (fraternity); Delta Psi (fraternity); Democratic Party; by direction of the President (US Army); Director of Pathology; Director of Postings (RAF); displaced persons; distributing point (US Army); Doctor of Pharmacy; Doctor of Philosophy; double pole; duty paid; The House of Lords (*Domus Procerum*); Dining and Parlor (rr car)

D/P documents against [or for] payment (banking); double pole

D&P development and printing (photography)

D of P Degree of Pocahontas; Director of Planes (Admiralty)

D P A deferred payment account

DPA Delta Phi Alpha (society); Diploma in Public Administration; Directorate of Policy (Air Ministry); Discharged Prisoners' Aid; Disney Professorship of Archaeology; Doctor of Public Administration; Diner Lounge (rr car)

D/PA Director of Personnel and Administration (US Army)

d In p æ divide into equal parts (*divide in partes æquales*—Latin) (pharmacy)

DPAS Discharged Prisoners' Aid Society

DPB Defence Purchasing Board; Department of Printed Books (British Museum)

d p b deposit passbook (banking)

DPC Defense Plant Corporation; double paper covered

DPCX Dewey Portland Cement Company (private car rr mark)

DPD Delta Phi Delta (society); Department of Prints and Drawings (British Museum); Director of Plans Division

D of PD Director of Plans Division

d p d t double pole, double throw

DPE Delta Phi Epsilon (sorority)

DPET Director of Pre-Entry Training

DPF Deferred Pay Fund

d p h diamond pyramid hardness

D Ph Doctor of Philosophy

DPH Diploma in Public Health, Doctor in Public Health

D Pharm S Diploma of the Pharmaceutical Society

D Phil Doctor of Philosophy

DPHP Director, Post Hostilities Plans

DPHy Doctor of Public Hygiene

DPI Department of Production and Inspection; Director of Public Information; Director of Public Instruction

DPII Dairy Products Improvement Institute

DPIX Distillation Products Industries, a division of Eastman-Kodak (private car rr mark)

DPJS Department of Prisons and Judicial Statistics (Scotland)

DPK Delta Psi Kappa (society)

dpl diplomat; diplomat

DPL Dayton Power & Light (NYSE)

DPLO Director of Principal Librarian's Office

DPM Deputy Prime Minister; Deputy Provost Marshal; Diploma in Psychological Medicine; Director of Production Management

DPMO Deputy Principal Medical Officer

dpn diamond pyramid [hardness] number

dpo depot

d p o distributing post office

D/PO Director of Plans and Operations (US Army)

DPP Director of Public Prosecutions

DPR Director of Public Relations; District Probate Registry; Dominions Provincial Relations

d p r double lapping of pure rubber

D Pro GM Deputy Provincial Grand Master (freemasonry)

DPS Department of the Permanent Secretary; Department of Public Safety; Director of Personal Services; Director of Postal Services

d p s double pole snap switch

DPSK Department of the Private Secretary to the King

DPSS Director of Printing and Stationery Services

d p s t double-pole single throw

dpt depth; department; deponent

DPTS Director of Physical Training and Sports (naval)

DPTX D.P. Tafe (private car rr mark)

DPUSSA Department of the Permanent Under Secretary of State for Air

DPUSSW Department of the Permanent Under Secretary of State for War

DPW Department of Public Works; Director of Prisoners of War

DPX Reconstruction Finance Corporation (private car rr mark)

d q direct question

DQMG Deputy Quartermaster General

DQMS Deputy Quartermaster Sergeant

DQU Duquesne Light (NYSE)

dr debit; debtor; doctor; door; drachm (pharmacy); drain; drama; drawer; drawn; dresser; drive; driver; drum; drummer; law (*droit*—French)

Dr doctor (*Doktor*—German)

D R daily report (insurance); Daughters of the Revolution; dead reckoning; Defense Regulations; debenture rights; Diploma in Radiology; District Railway; District Registry; Division of Reports; dock receipt; Drill Regulations; rural dean (*decanus ruralis*—Latin); National Distillers Products (NYSE)

D/R date of rank (US Army); deposit receipt

dra doctor (feminine) (*doctora*—Spanish); doctress (*doutora*—Portuguese)

Dra Draco (constellation)

DRA Director of Royal Artillery; Dude Ranchers Association

DRAC Director of the Royal Armoured Corps

dram. dramatic; dramatist

dram. pers the characters or actors

in a play (*dramatis personae*—Latin)

dr ap apothecaries' dram

dr av avoirdupois dram (pharmacy)

DRB Druggists Research Bureau

Dr Bot Doctor of Botany

Dr Chem Doctor of Chemistry

DRCM Dutch Reformed Church Mission

DRCOG Diploma of Royal College of Obstetricians and Gynaecologists

DRD Deputy Regional Director; Director of Recruiting and Demobilization

DRDX Duredo Company (private car rr mark)

DRE Director of Radio Equipment; Divisional Road Engineer; Doctor of Religious Education

Dr Eng Doctor of Engineering

drftsmn draftsman

drg drawing

DRG Dragon Cement Company (NYSE)

DR-G Deputy Registrar-General

D & RG Denver & Rio Grande Western Railroad

drgl similar things, alike (*derg le ichen*—German)

DRGM *Deutsches-Reichsgebrauchsmuster* (German registered design)

D & RGWRR Co Denver & Rio Grande Western Railroad Company

DRH Driver-Harris Company (NYSE)

Dr Hy Doctor of Hygiene

DRI Davenport, Rock Island and North Western Railway Company (private car rr mark); drip-proof (electric engineering)

Dr J Doctor of Law (*Doctor Juris*—Latin)

Dr JU Doctor of Both Laws (*Doctor Juris utriusque*—Latin)

DRL Drilling & Exploration Company (NYSE); Drought Relief Loans

DRLS Despatch Rider Letter Service

Dr Med Doctor of Medicine (*Doctor Medicae*—Latin)

DRMO Deputy Regional Medical Officer

Drn drawn

Dr Nat Hist Doctor of Natural History

Dr Nat Phil Doctor of Natural Philosophy

Dr Nat Sc Doctor of Natural Science

Dro duty (*derecho*—Spanish)

DRO Daily Routine Order; Deep Rock Oil Corporation (NYSE); Departmental Regional Officer; Director of Recruiting and Organization; Divisional Recruiting Officer; Divisional Routine Order

DRP *Deutsches Reichspatent* (German patent); *Deutsche Reichspost* (German imperial post)

Dr PH Doctor of Public Health; Doctor of Public Hygiene

Dr Phil Doctor of Philosophy (*Doctor philosophiae*—Latin)

Dr Phys Sc Doctor of Physical Science

Dr Rer Nat Doctor of natural science (*Doctor Rerum Naturalium*—Latin)

Dr Rer Pol Doctor of Political Science (*Doctor Rerum Politicarum* —Latin)

drs drawers

DRS Devoe & Raynolds, CI A (Common stock, NYSE); Devon Record Society; Director of Repair Service

Dr Sci Doctor of Science

drsmkr dressmaker

DRT Detroit & Cleveland Navigation (NYSE)

Dr und Vrl printed and published by (*Druck und Verlag*—German)

Dr Univ Par Doctor of University of Paris

D of Ry Director of Railways

ds days; document signed; double screen (plumbing); double sweep (plumbing); drop siding (lumber); in (*dans*—French); repeat from the sign (*dal segno*—Italian) (music)

Ds dysprosium; God (*Deus*—Latin)

DS Defense Secretary; Delius Society; Demolition Squad; Dental Surgeon; Department of State; Deputy Secretary; detached service (US Army); direct steamer (railway); Directing Staff; Director of Signals; Director of Supplies; distance surveillance (US Army); Doctor of Science; Dugdale Society

D/S double-screened (coal trade)

d/s days after sight; delivery service (express)

d & s demand and supply

D of S Daughters of Scotia

DSA division service area (US Army); Deputy Scientific Adviser; Deputy-Secretary to the Admiralty; District Staffs' As-ociation; Duluth, South Shore and Atlantic Railroad Company (rr mark)

DSAI District Surveyors' Association Incorporated

DSANY Diamond Setters Association of New York

DS Doctor of Science

D Sc Doctor of Science

DSC Defense Supplies Corporation; Distinguished Service Cross; Doctor of Surgical Chiropody

d s c double-silk-covered

DSCA Department of Security Council Affairs

DSCAEF Deputy Supreme Commander Allied Expeditionary Force

DSD Delta Sigma Delta (fraternity); Doctor of Science and Didactics

DS Hyg Doctor of Science in Hygiene

DSDX Dairy Shippers Despatch Company (private car rr mark)

DSE Delta Sigma Epsilon (sorority); Detroit Stock Exchange

D & SE[R] Dublin and South-Eastern [Railway]

dsgl ditto (*desgleichen*—German)

DSI Distilled Spirits Institute; Drinking Straw Institute

DSIA Diaper Service Institute of America

DSIR Department of Scientific and Industrial Research

DSJ differential space justifier

DSL Dominion Steel & Coal (NYSE)

D&SL Denver and Salt Lake Railway Company

DSL X Canada & Dominion Sugar Company Ltd (private car rr mark)

DSM Distinguished Service Medal; Doctor of Sacred Music

D&SM dressed and standard matched (lumber)

dsmd dismissed

DSN Dennison Manufacturing Company, CI A (common stock, NYSE)

DSN D Dennison Manufacturing Company (ASE)

DSO Companion of the Distinguished Service Order; Distinguished Service Order; District Staff Officer; Donora Southern Railroad Company (rr mark)

D/SOA Department of Social Affairs

DSOC Deputy Signal Officer in Chief

dsp died without issue (*decessit sine prole*—Latin)

DSP Detroit Steel Products (NYSE); Delta Sigma Phi (fraternity); Delta Sigma Pi (fraternity)

d spec design specification

DSPLN discipline(ary) (US Army)

dsq discharged to sick quarters

DSR Delta Sigma Rho (society); Director of Scientific Research

ds s documents signed

DSS Diploma in Sanitary Science; Doctor of Holy Scripture (*Doctor Sacrae Scripturae*—Latin); Doctor of Social Science

DSS&A Duluth, South Shore and Atlantic Railway Company

DST Director of Supplies and Transport; Doctor of Sacred Theology; Double Summer Time; Daylight Saving Time

D StJ Dame of Justice (or of Grace) of the Order of St. John of Jerusalem

dstn destination

DS/VD Director of Salvage Department

DSVP Director of Small Vessels Pool

D Svy Director of Survey

DSWV Director of Special Weapons and Vehicles

dt debit (*doit*—French); draft

d t delirium tremens; double throw (switch); double time; duration tetany (medicine)

DT American Radiator & SS Corporation (NYSE); Daily Telegraph; deferred telegram; Detroit Terminal Railroad Company (rr mark); Director of Transport; Doctor of Theology

DTA District Traffic Agent; Divisao de Exploraçao dos Transportes Aereos

DTC Deputy Theatre Commander; Deputy Town Clerk; Dominion Tar & Chemical (NYSE)

DTCX Dominion Tar & Chemical Company Ltd. (private car rr mark)

d t d let such a dose be given (*detur talis dosis*—Latin) (pharmacy)

DTD *Dekoratie voor Trouwe Dienst* (South African decoration); Delta Tau Delta (fraternity); Delta Theta Phi (fraternity); Director of Technical Development; Director of Trade Division

DTDX Texas Division of Dow Chemical Company (private car rr mark)

DTE Detroit Edison Company (NYSE)

D Ter Dakota Territory

DTG date time group (US Army)

DTh Doctor of Theology (*Doctor Theologiae*—Latin)

DTH Diploma in Tropical Hygiene

D Theol Diploma in Theology; Doctor of Theology

DTI Dial Test Indicator (RAF); Director of Tactical Investigation

DT&I Detroit, Toledo and Ironton Railroad Company

d t m duration time modulation

DTM Diamond T Motor Car Company (NYSE); Diploma in Tropical Medicine; Director of Torpedoes and Mining Department; Doctor of Tropical Medicine

DTM and H Doctor of Tropical Medicine and Hygiene

dt mld draft moulded; molded draft

DTO District Transport Officer

D&TSL Detroit and Toledo Shore Line Railroad Company

D2S&CM Dressed two sides and center matched (lumber)

D2S&M Dressed two sides and

matched (lumber)
D2S&SM Dressed two sides and standard matched (lumber)
DTR Division of Tax Research
DTS Director of Tank Supplies
DTSD Director of Training and Staff Duties Division (naval)
DTT Director of Technical Training
DTV Detroit-Michigan Stove Company (NYSE)
DTX Dominion Textile (NYSE)
Dtzd dozen (*Dutzend*—German)
d u died unmarried
Du Duchy; Duke; Dutch
DU Dalhousie University (Canada); Delta Upsilon (fraternity); De Paul University; Drake University; Drew University; Duke University; Depauw University; Duquesne University
dub. doubting (*dubitans*—Latin); dubious (*dubius*—Latin)
Dub. Dublin (Ireland)
DUBD Director of Unexploded Bombs Department
DUBDD Director of Unexploded Bomb Disposal Department
Dud. (Ga) Dudley's Georgia Reports (legal)
DUDAT deadline or due date (US Army)
DUK Duke Power Company (NYSE)
DUM Dublin University Mission
Dumb. Dumbarton (Scotland)
Dumf Dumfries (Scotland)
dun. dunnage
Dunc Duncan
Dunelm (Bishop of) Durham
D Univ Doctor of the University (*Docteur de l'Université*—French)
duo. duodecimo (books)
dup duplicate
DUP Duplan Corporation (NYSE)
dup! duplicate
DUPX DuPont de Nemours & Company (private car rr mark)
Dur Durango; Durham
DUR Duro-Test Corporation (NYSE);
Durf Durfee's Reports (legal)
Durh LI Durham Light Infantry
DUSA Defence Union of South Africa

Dut Dutch
Dutz dozen (*Dutzend*—German)
DUVCW Daughters of Union Veterans of the Civil War
DUX Donner-Hanna Coke Corporation (private car rr mark)
DV Dixie Cup Company (NYSE); Douay Version (of Bible); God willing (*Deo volente*—Latin)
d v double vibration
d/v days sight (*dias vista*—Spanish) (commercial)
DVC MAT Dept. of Cauca Valley (ASE)
DVG Davega Stores Corporation (NYSE)
DVH Diploma in Veterinary Hygiene
DVL Duval Sulphur & Potash Company (NYSE)
dvm he died during his mother's lifetime (*decessit vita matris*—Latin)
DVM Doctor of Veterinary Medicine
DVMS Doctor of Veterinary Medicine and Surgery
DVO Devon Leduc Oils Ltd (NYSE)
dvp died in his father's lifetime (*decessit vita patris*—Latin)
dvr driver
d v s that is (*det vil si*—Norwegian); (*det vil sige*—Danish); (*det vill säga*—Swedish)
DVS Doctor of Veterinary Science; Doctor of Veterinary Surgery
DVSM Diploma in Veterinary State Medicine
DVY Davenport Hosiery Mills, Inc (NYSE)
d w dead weight; drive well (plumbing); dust wrapper (books)
DW Deck Watch (naval); Dock Warrant; Duke of Wellington's West Riding Regiment
D/W dock warrant
DWA Director of War Archives; double wire armored (electric cables)
DWAAF Director of Women's Auxiliary Air Force
d w c deadweight capacity
DWD Director of Wreck Dispersal Department (naval)

dwg drawing; dwelling
DWG D W G Cigar Corporation (NYSE)
dwg-ho dwelling-house (legal)
DWI Descriptive-Word Index; Director of Office of War Information; Dutch West Indies
dwn down
DWP Duluth, Winnipeg & Pacific Railway (rr mark)
DWPUA Diamond Workers Protective Union of America
DWR Duke of Wellington's Regiment
DWS Department of Water Supply
d w s double white silk (covered cable)
DWSA Deputy War Shipping Administrator (United States)
DWSG&E Department of Water Supply, Gas and Electricity
dwt pennyweight
d w t deadweight tonnage
d w t f [publications] daily and weekly till forbidden
DWTMC Domestic Water Tank Manufacturers Council
dx double cash ruled (stationery); distance; static (radio)
DXC Penn-Dixie Cement Corporation (NYSE)
DXW Dome Exploration (Western) (NYSE)
d y junior (*den yugre*—Swedish)
dy delivery; dockyard; penny (nails)
Dy dysprosium (chemical)
DY Dryden Paper Company (NYSE); duty (US Army)
Dy Eng-in-Chief Deputy Engineer-in-Chief
DYM Daystrom, Inc (NYSE)
dyn dynamics; dynamite; dynamo
DYO Derby Oil Company (Kansas) (NYSE)
DYRMS Duke of York's Royal Military School (Dover)
d z zenith distance (*distance zénithale*—French)
dz dozen; hundredweight (kilograms) (*doppelzentner*—German)
DZ Delta Zeta (sorority); Department of Zoology; Doctor of Zoology; drop zone (US Army)
dzne dozen (*douzaine*—French)

E

e eccentricity (of eclipse); educated; efficiency; elasticity; eldest; electromotive force (of cell); errors; excellence; excellent

(E) Equipment Branch Officer (RAF); Specialist in Ear, Nose and Throat Surgery
E Earl; Earth; East; Eastern; Elo-

histic; elocution; emmetropia (ophthalmic); emmetropic (ophthalmic); Engineer [ing]; English; Erie Railroad Company (NYSE);

Excellency; 2nd class (merchant) ship in Lloyd's Register; US Army and Navy symbol for excellence and efficiency

ea each; ends annealed (plumbing)

E.A.A. entered apprentice (free-masonry)

EA Economic Adviser; Educational Age; Egyptian Army; Electrical Artificer; Enamel Association; Enemy Aircraft; English Association; Esperanto Association

E & A Ecclesiastical and Admiralty (legal)

E/A enemy aircraft

EAA Export Advertising Association

EAAI Export Advertising Association, Inc

EAAL European and American Airways Limited

EAC Economic Advisory Council; Eire Air Corps; Engineering Advisory Committee; European Advisory Commission; Exhibitors Advisory Council

EACC Ecuadorean-American Chamber of Commerce

EAD Employment Association for the Defective; Exchequer and Audit Department; extended active duty (US Army)

EAFC Eastern Association of Fire Chiefs

EAK Kenya Colony and Protectorate (IDP)

EAL Eastern Air Lines (NYSE)

EAM Equipment Ammunition Magazines; Greek National Liberation Front (*Ethnikon Apeleutherotikon Metopon*)

EANA Esperanto Association of North America

e a o n except as otherwise noted

EAPAUS Employment Agencies Protective Association of the United States

EARC Eastern Association of Rowing Colleges

EAS Essex Archæological Society; Estimated Air Speed (RAF)

easemt easement

East Rep Eastern Reporter (legal)

EAT Eastern Air Transport; Tanganyika Territory (IDP)

EAU Uganda (IDP)

EAZ Zanzibar (IDP)

eb eastbound; boiling point (*point d'ébullition*—French)

Eb Ebenezer

EB Encyclopædia Biblica; Encyclopædia Britannica; Equipment Branch (RAF)

E & B Ellis and Blackburn (law)

EBA Educational Buyers Association

EBAX Ethyl Corporation (private car rr mark)

EBC European Brewery Convention; Exchange Buffet Corporation (NYSE)

EBCX The E. Berghausen Chemical Company (private car rr mark)

Eben Ebenezer

EBF Economic and Business Foundation

Ebh Eberhard

E b N east by north

e b 1 s edge bead one side (lumber)

EBS Edinburgh Bibliographical Society; Electric Bond & Share Company (NYSE); English Bookplate Society

E b S east by south

EBSRI Eye Bank for Sight Restoration, Inc

EB2S Edge bead two sides (lumber)

EBUSW Executive Board of United Steel Workers

e c enamel-covered; for example (*exempli causa*—Latin)

Ec Ecclesiastes (Bible); Ecuador

EC earth closet; East African Airways Corporation; East Central; East Coast; Eastern Command; Ecclesiastical Commissioner; Education Committee; Eighty Club; Electric Current; Electricity Commission; Embarkation Commandant; Emergency Chaplain (US Army); Engineer-Captain; Engineering Corps; English Cases; English Chancery (legal); Episcopal Church; Established Church; Exchange Control

e/c emergency charges; on account (*en cuenta*—Spanish); extended coverage

ECA Department of Economic Affairs (UN Secretariat); Economic Cooperation Administration

ECAC Eastern College Athletic Conference

ECAFE Economic Commission for Asia and the Far East

E&CB1S Edge and center bead one side (lumber)

E&CB2S Edge and center bead two sides (lumber)

ecc and so forth (*eccetera*—Italian)

ECC Ecclesiastical Courts Commission; electrical continuous cloth

ECCCA Education Committee of County Councils Association

eccles ecclesiastical; ecclesiological; ecclesiology

Eccles Ecclesiastes (Biblical)

Eccles Com Ecclesiastical Commissioners

Ecclus Ecclesiasticus (Biblical)

ECCP East Coast Coal Port

ECE Economic Commission for Europe

ece extended coverage endorsement (insurance)

ECFL Emergency Crop and Feed Loans

e c g electro-cardiogram (medicine)

ECGB East Coast of Great Britain (shipping)

ECGD Export Credits Guarantee Department

ech echelon (military)

ECI East Coast of Ireland (shipping)

ECIPFA Enameled Cast Iron Plumbing Fixtures Association

ECITO European Central Inland Transport Organization

écl lighting (*éclairage*—French)

ECLA United Nations Economic Commission for Latin America

eclec eclectic

ECLOF Ecumenical Church Loan Fund

e c m ends center matched (lumber)

ECM Electric Controller & Manufacturing Company (NYSE)

ECME Economic Commission for the Middle East

ECNR Executive Council for National Recovery

ECO Ecclesiastical Commissioners' Office; electron-coupled oscillator (radio); Elliott Company (NYSE); European Coal Organization

ecol ecological; ecology

e con on the contrary (e *contra*—Latin)

econ economical; economics; economist; economy

econ dom domestic economy (*économie domestique*—French)

econ pol political economy (*économie politique*—French)

econ r rural economy (*économie rurale*—French)

ECOSOC United Nations Economic and Social Council

ECOX Eagle Cotton Oil Company (private car rr mark)

ECPD Engineers Council for Professional Development

ECSX Scurlock Tank Car Company (private car rr mark)

ECTC East Carolina Teachers College

ECU English Church Union

Ecua Ecuador

ECUK East Coast of the United Kingdom (shipping)

E&CV1S Edge and center V one side (lumber)

E&CV2S Edge and center V two sides (lumber)

ECW Emergency Conservation Work

ed edition; editor; educated; extra

duty; former, foregoing (*edellinen*—Finnish)

• d executive document; existence doubtful; extra dividend

Ed [Edw, Edwd] Edward

ED Consolidated Edison of N. Y. (NYSE); Doctor of Engineering; Eastern Department; Education Department; Efficiency Decoration (England); Electrical Department (naval); Employment Department; Engineering Department; Engineering Division; Entertainments Duty; Establishment Department; Estate Duties; ex-dividend (NYSE)

EDANC Engineers, Draftsmen & Associates, National Council

Ed B Bachelor of Education

EDB Economics Defense Board

EDC European Defense Community; Express Dairy Company

EDCMR effective date of change(s) on morning reports (US Army)

edcn education

Ed Cr Edwards' New York Chancery (legal)

EDCX Ethyl-Dow Chemical Company (private car rr mark)

edd editions (*editiones*—Latin)

Ed D Doctor of Education

EDD English Dialect Dictionary

EDE Empire District Electric Company (NYSE)

Edenburgen of Edinburgh (*Edenburgensis*—Latin)

EDES Ellinikos Demokratikos Ethnikos Stratos (Greek Democratic National Army)

EDFTGA Eastern Dark-Fired Tobacco Growers Association

Edg Edgar

Edin Edinburgh

Ed in Ch Editor in Chief

Edm Sel Cas Edmonds' New York Select Cases (legal)

Ed M Master of Education

Edm Edmund

Edn Edwin

EDO Eastern District Office; Estate Duty Office

EDR Emsco Derrick & Equipment (NYSE)

EDRX El Dorado Refining Company (private car rr mark)

EDS E. D. Smith's New York Common Pleas (legal); English Dialect Society

EDST Eastern daylight saving time

EDT Eastern daylight time

educ educated; educational

Edw Ch Edwards' Chancery (legal)

• e eased edges (lumber)

EE Boston Edison Company (NYSE); Early English; Electrical Engineer; Employment Exchange; errors

excepted; Experimental Establishment (RAF); Your Reverence (*Euer Ehrwürden*—German)

E-E Envoy-Extraordinary

E to E End to end (plumbing)

EEA Engineering Employers' Association

EEAM Workers' National Liberation Front (Greece)

EEC Eastern Corporation (NYSE); East Erie Commercial Railroad (rr mark); Electrical Export Corporation

EEF Egyptian Expeditionary Force; Engineering Employers' Federation; Exchange Equalization Fund

EEG Electroencephalogram; Electrographic Corporation (NYSE)

EEI Edison Electric Institute; essential elements of information (US Army)

EE & MP Envoy Extraordinary and Minister Plenipotentiary

E Eng Early English

EENT eye, ear, nose, (and) throat

EEP Epsilon Eta Phi (society)

E Equat Afr Eastern Equatorial Africa

EER English Ecclesiastical Reports (legal)

EETS Early English Text Society

EE UU The United States (*Estados Unidos*—Spanish)

• f extra fancy; extra fine

EF Ehrmann Foundation; Emerson Foundation; Expeditionary Force

EFA Economic and Financial Adviser; Empire Forestry Association; English Forestry Association

eff efficiency; efficient

EFF effective (US Army)

effy efficiency

EFHTC Eno Foundation for Highway Traffic Control

EFIB Eastern Freight Inspection Bureau

• Fl ells Flemish (measurement)

EFLA Educational Film Library Association

EFMG Electric Fuse Manufacturers Guild

EFPA Educational Film-Producers Association

• Fr ells Frer (measurement)

E Fris East Frisian

EFTD Economic, Financial and Transit Department

eftf successor (*efterfolger*—Norwegian)

eftr successor (*efterträdare*—Swedish)

efts children (*enfants*—French)

EFU Eastern Gas & Fuel Association (NYSE)

EFU Pr Eastern Gas & Fuel Asso-

ciates (4½% Pfd) (ASE)

• g [all] edges gilt; eggs in hatching; the former (*eerstgenvemde*—Dutch); for example (*exempli gratia*—Latin); of a like kind (*ejusdem generis*—Latin)

Eg Egypt; Egyptian; Egyptology

EG edge grain (timber); Embroiderers' Guild; Employers' Group Associates (NYSE); expert gunner (US Army)

EGA Export Guarantees Act

Egb Egbert

• g e water, gas, electricity (*eau, gaz, électricité*—French)

egl church (*église*—French)

EGM Egypt General Mission; Empire Gallantry Medal

EGMRSA Edible Gelatin Manufacturers Research Society of America

EGP Eagle-Picher Company (NYSE)

Egt Egypt

EGUHM Extra Gentleman Usher to His Majesty

eh honored (*ehrenhalber*—German); English Hymnal

EHC Emergency Housing Corporation

EHF extremely high frequency

EHFA Electric Home and Farm Authority

EHMA Electric Hoist Manufacturers Association

ehp effective horsepower; electric horsepower

e h t extra-high tension

e h v extra-high voltage

E/I endorsement irregular (banking)

EI East India; East Indian; East Indies

EIA East Indian Association; Empire Industries Association; Engineering Institute of America

EIB Export-Import Bank

EIBAD Expert Infantryman Badge (US Army)

EIBW Export-Import Bank of Washington

EIC East India Company; Engineering Institute of Canada

EICS East India Civil Service; East India Company's Service

EID East India Docks

Eig property (*Eigenschaft*—German)

8bre octobre (French)

8/40 Soc The Society of 8 Horses and 40 Men (*La Société des 8 Chevaux et 40 Hommes*

8° octavo

8ve octave

E-in-C Engineer-in-Chief

E Ind East Indian

einschl including, inclusive (*einschliesslich*—German)

EIR Eire (Southern Ireland); East

Indian Railway
EIS East India Service; Educational Institute of Scotland
EITA Electric Industrial Truck Association
EJC Engineers Joint Council
EJ&E Elgin, Joliet and Eastern Railway Company
EJN Endicott Johnson Corporation (NYSE)
EJR East Jersey Railroad and Terminal Company (rr mark)
EJ & S East Jordan & Southern Railroad (rr mark)
ejusd of the same (*ejusdem*—Latin)
e K after Christ [AD] (*etter Kristi*—Norwegian)
EK Eastman Kodak Company (NYSE)
EKA Eureka Corporation Ltd (NYSE)
EKCX Eastman Kodak Company (private car rr mark)
ekg electro-cardiogram (medicine)
EKN Eta Kappa Nu (fraternity)
EKR East Kent Regiment
eks example (*eksempel*—Danish)
EKSX E Kahn's Sons Company, Cincinnati, Ohio (private car rr mark)
EKSTC East Kentucky State Teachers College
EKTX E. Kahn's Sons Company Tank Cars (private car rr mark)
EKU Eureka Pipe Line Company (The) (ASE)
el east longitude; elected; electric; element; elevated; elevated railway; elevation; or (*ellev*—Norwegian)
El Elias; Queen Elizabeth (legal)
EL East Lothian; Eastern League (baseball); Eastern Lines; Emergency Legislation; Engineer-Lieutenant (naval); equipment list (US Army); Eucharistic League
e lact with milk (e *lacte*—Latin) (pharmacy)
EL AL El Al, Israel Airlines, Ltd
E Lan R East Lancashire Regiment
ELAS Ellinikos Laikos Apeleutherotikos Stratos (Greek Popular Liberation Army)
ELASNA Evangelical Lutheran Augustana Synod of North America
ELCA Evangelical Lutheran Church of America
EL Cr Engineer Lieutenant Commander
ELCX Elkland Leather Company, Inc (private car rr mark)
eld eldest
elec electric; electrical; electricity; electuary
electrn electrician

electrochem electrochemistry
électron electronics (*électronique*—French)
electrophys electrophysical
Elekt electricity (*Elektrizität*—German)
elem element; elementary
elev elevation
EL G El Paso Natural Gas Company (NYSE)
Eli Elias; Elijah
ELI Elmira Water, Light & Railroad Company (ASE)
ELIM eliminate (US Army)
Elis Elizabeth
ell. or (*eller*—Swedish)
ellipt elliptical[ly]
Eliz Elizabeth
ELLIS Ellis Air Lines
el lt electric light
ELM element (US Army)
ELO Ecole (spéciale) des Langues Orientales (vivantes); (Special) School of Oriental Langauges
E long East longitude
elong elongation
ELR East Lancashire Regiment; East London Railway; Export Licensing Regulations
ELS Escanaba and Lake Superior Railroad Company (rr mark)
ELT European Letter Telegram
ELW El Dorado Oil Works (NYSE)
ELz Elzevir
em afternoon (*eftermiddag*—Danish) (*eftermiddag*—Norwegian) (*eftermiddagen*—Swedish); electromagnetic; expanded metal; radium emanation; emanation (chemistry); embargo; eminence; eminent
Em Emily; Emma; Emmanuel
EM Earl Marshal; Eastern Massachusetts St. (NYSE); Edward Medal; Engineer Manager; Engineer of Mines; enlisted men (US Army); Headquarters (*État-Major*—French); Master of the Horse (*Equitum Magister*—Latin)
EMA Embroidery Merchants Association; Evaporated Milk Association; Envelope Manufacturers Association
EMAI Embroidery Merchants Association, Inc
emb embankment; embargo; embassy; embroidered; embryology
EMB embark (US Army); Embroidery Manufacturers Bureau
EMC Emporium Capwell Company (NYSE); equalibrium moisture content
EMCNY Export Managers Club of New York
EMCX Eastern Corporation (private

car rr mark)
emdp electromotive difference of potential
EMEA Electrical Manufacturers Export Association
emer emergency
Emer Emeritus
E Met. Engineer of Metallurgy
emf electromotive force
EMF erythrocyte maturing factor
EM1C Electrician's Mate First Class (US Navy)
E-MG General Headquarters (*État-major général*—French)
EMI Elec. & Musical Indus (NYSE)
EMICO International Co-ordination Committee for European Migratory Movements
Emigr Chap. Emigration Chaplain
EMJ Engineering and Mining Journal
EMK electromotive force (*Elektromotorische Kraft*—German)
EML Eastern Malleable Iron Company (NYSE); equipment modification list (US Army)
Emm Emmanuel College (Cambridge)
emp a plaster (*emplastrum*—Latin) (pharmacy)
Emp Emperor; Empire; Empress
EMP Empire Millwork Corporation (NYSE)
emp agcy employment agency
empd employed
emph emphasis; emphatic
EMPL emplacement (US Army)
EMPX Emmart Packing Company (private car rr mark)
EMR Emerson Electric Manufacturing Company (NYSE)
EMS Emergency Medical Service
EM2C Electrician's Mate Second Class (US Navy)
EM3C Electrician's Mate Third Class (US Navy)
emu electromagnetic units
emul an emulsion (*emulsio*—Latin) (pharmacy)
en ethylenediamine
e n exceptions noted
enam enameled
ENA English Newspaper Association
enc enclosed;
Enc Brit Encyclopaedia Britannica
ENCMP Economists National Committee on Monetary Policy
encour encouragement
ency encyclopedia;
Ency Bibl Encyclopaedia Biblica
end. endorse; endorsed; endorsement
en dd with date of (*en date du*—French)
end. guar endorsement guaranteed (banking)
energ forcibly (*energicamente*—

Italian) (music)

en fav de in favor of (*en faveur de*—French)

eng engaged; engine; engineer; engineering; engraving

Eng England; English

Eng Ad English Admiralty (legal)

Eng-Capt Engineer-Captain

Eng Ch English Chancery (legal)

Eng-Cmdr Engineer-Commander

Eng D Doctor of Engineering

Eng Eccl English Ecclesiastical Reports (legal)

engg engineering

Eng law & us. English law and usage (insurance)

Eng-Lt-Comdr Engineer-Lieutenant-Commander (naval)

Eng ORC Engineer Officers Reserve Corps

engr engineer

Eng RC Engineer Reserve Corps

Eng Rear-Adm Engineer Rear-Admiral

Eng Ru Ca English Ruling Cases (legal)

enl enlarged; enlisted

ENL enlist (US Army)

Eno January (*Enero*—Spanish)

en rep a in reply to (*en réponse à*—French)

Ens Ensign

ENSA Entertainments National Service Association (Great Britain)

ent entertainment; entomology; entomological; past (*entinen*—Finnish)

ENT enter; entrance (US Army)

EN & T Ear, Nose and Throat

enth containing (*enthaltend*—German)

entom entomological; entomology

entomol entomological

entspr corresponding (*entsprechend*—German)

Ent Sta Hall Entered at Stationers' Hall

Entsteh origin (*Entstehung*—German)

env about (*environ*—French); envelope

Env Ext Envoy Extraordinary

ENW Elgin National Watch Company (NYSE)

ENX Eaton Manufacturing Company (NYSE)

enz and so forth (*en zoo voort*—Dutch)

e o by authority of his office (*ex officio*—Latin)

EO Easter offerings; Education Officer; Engineer-Officer (RAF *and* naval); Entertainments Officer; Equipment Officer; errors and omissions; Excise Office; Executive Officer

EOCI Electric Overhead Crane Institute

e o d every other day

EOD entry on duty (US Army)

E&oe errors and omissions excepted

e o h p except otherwise herein provided

e o m end of month; every other month

EOM Egyptian Order of Merit

e o o e error or omission excepted (*erreur ou omission exceptée*—French)

EORC Engineer Officers' Reserve Corps

EORX Cities Service Oil Company (private car rr mark)

EOS Edison Bros. Stores, Inc (NYSE)

e o t enemy-occupied territory

e p earned premium; electric primer; electrically polarized; electroplate; end point (distillation); epistle; in passing (*en passant*—French)

ep letter (*epistola*—Latin); estimated position (navigation); first edition (*editio princeps*—Latin); extended play; electric power

Ep Bishop (*Episcopus*—Latin)

EP Eddy Paper Corporation (NYSE); entrucking point (US Army); Examiner of Plays

E and P Extraordinary and Plenipotentiary

EPA Emergency Powers Act; Empire Parliamentary Association; Empire Press Agency; Entertainments Protection Association; Evangelical Preachers' Association

EPAA Educational Press Association of America; Employing Printers Association of America

EPB Fort Pitt Brewing Company (NYSE)

EPC Educational Policies Commission; Economic Policy Committee; electroplate on copper

EPD Excess Profits Duty; may he rest in peace (*en paz descanse*—Spanish)

EPDA Emergency Powers Defense Act; Exhibit Producers and Designers Association

EPEAA Employing Photo-Engravers Association of America

Eph Ephraim; Ephesians (biblical)

epil epilogue

Epiph Epiphany

Epis Episcopal; Episcopalian

epit epitaph; epitome

e p l extreme pressure lubricant

EPNS electro-plated nickel silver

EPNX El Paso Natural Gas Company (private car rr mark)

EPO Ekco Products Company (NYSE)

e pp before noon (*edellä puolenpäivän*—Finnish)

EPR Erie & Pittsburgh Railroad (NYSE)

EPT Excess Profits Tax

EPTS existed prior to service (US Army)

EPU Empire Press Union

Epus Bishop (*Episcopus*—Latin)

EPWM electroplate on white metal

EPX El Pino, South America (private car rr mark)

eq equal; equivalent; equalize; equation; equipment; equitable; equity (legal); equivalent

Eq Equator; Equerry; Knights (*Equites*—Latin)

EQ Equitable Office Building (NY) (NYSE)

Eq Af Equatorial Africa

Eq Ca Ab Equity Cases Abridged

Eq Cas Abr Equity Cases Abridged (legal)

eqpt equipment

Eqpt O Equipment Officer

eqt equation time (navigation)

EQT Equitable Gas Company (NYSE)

eq tr equipment trust (bonds)

EQU Equity Corporation (NYSE)

equin equinox

EQUIP equipment (US Army)

equiv equivalent

e quol veh in any vehicle (*e quolibet vehiculo*—Latin) (pharmacy)

e quov liq in any liquid (*e quovis liquido*—Latin) (pharmacy)

EQU Pr Equity Corp. (The) (Merged Corp.) ($2 Conv. Pfd.) (ASE)

Er erbium; Eric

ER East Riding (Yorkshire); East River; Easter Region; King Edward (*Edwardus Rex*); Emergency Reserve; engine room; expert rifleman (US Army); external resistance; Here (QS)

ERA Emergency Relief Administration; Engineer Rear-Admiral; Engine-Room Artificer (naval)

Erb request (*Erbitten*—German)

ERC Engineers Reserve Corps; English Red Cross; Enlisted Reserve Corps (US Army); Evangelical and Reformed Church

ERCX Elk Refining Company (private car rr mark)

EREP Greek Workers' Reformist Party

ER et I Edward King and Emperor (*Edwardus Rex et Imperator*—Latin)

ERGAS Greek Workers' Union

erh heated (*erhitzt*—German)

Erie Erie Railroad Company

Erit Eritrea

erm ermine

Ern Ernest

ERO A Ercole Marelli Electrical Manufacturing Company (ASE)

ERP Emerson Radio & Phonograph (NYSE); European Recovery Program

Err & App Error and Appeals (legal)

erron erroneous; erroneously

ERU English Rugby Union

ERV English Revised Version (Bible)

ERX Excelsior Refineries Ltd. (private car rr mark)

e s eldest son

es example (esempio—Italian)

ES Eastern Sugar Associates (NYSE); Electrical Radio Training School; Electrochemical Society; electrostatic (system); electrostatic; ells Scotch; engine-sized (of paper); Entomological Society; Eugenics Society; exclusive of sheeting (railway); extra series; Exchange Students

e s c by decree of the Senate (ex senatus consulto—Latin)

ESA Electrolysis Society of America

ESAI Euthanasia Society of America, Inc

ESAUS Export Screw Association of the United States

ESB Economic Stabilization Board; Electric Storage Battery (NYSE)

ESBA East side Boys Association

esc escadrille; discount (escompte —French)

ESC Esquire, Inc (NYSE)

eschat eschatological; eschatology

escrit writing (escritura—Spanish)

escte discount (escompter—French)

Esdr Esdras (biblical)

ESE East-Southeast

ESF Eastern Sea Frontier

ESG English Standard Gauge

esim for example, e.g. (esimerkiksi —Finnish)

Esk Eskimo

ESL Eastern Steamship Lines

ESLJ East St. Louis Junction Railroad (rr mark)

ESM Ends standard matched (lumber)

ESMA Engraved Stationery Manufacturers Association

ESN Elastic Stop Nut Corporation (NYSE)

esp especially

Esp Esperanto

ESP Eta Sigma Phi (society); Extra-Sensory perception (psychology)

ES Pr Eastern Sugar Associates ($5 Pfd. Shs. of Beneficial Interest) (ASE)

espress espressivo (music)

Esq or Esqr Esquire

e s r effective signal radiated

ESR East Surrey Regiment; Essex Scottish Regiment of Canada

ess essence

Ess Essex (county in England)

ESS Economic Situation Survey

essay. essayist

est established; estate; establishment; estimated; estuary

Est Esther; Estonia

EST Eastern Standard Time; Eastern States Corporation (NYSE); Eastern Summer Time; Empire Social Telegram

EST A Pr Eastern States Corp. ($7 Pfd. Ser. "A") (ASE)

EST B Pr Eastern States Corp. ($6 Pfd. Ser. "B") (ASE)

estda esteemed (letter) (estimada— Spanish)

este estate

estg estimating

estn estimation

est wt estimated weight

ESTX Eston Chemicals, Inc (private car rr mark)

esu electrostatic unit

ESU English Speaking Union

ESUUS English Speaking Union of the United States

Et ethyl

ET Easter Term; Eastern Telegraph Company; Eastern Time; Educational Training; Electric Auto-Lite Company (NYSE); Electric Telegraph; Egypt (IDP); English text; English translation; Entertainments Tax; Equipment Trust; Expander Tube (type of wheel brake); electric transcription

e t a estimated time of arrival

ETAB Employers Test Administration Bureau

Etabs Establishments (Establissements—French)

et al and elsewhere (et alibi— Latin); and others (et alii—Latin)

etc and so forth (et cetera—Latin)

ETC Eastern Telegraph Company

ETCX Tennessee Eastman Company of Eastman Kodak Company (private car rr mark)

e t d estimated time of departure

eth ethical; ethics

Eth Ethiopia; Ethiopic

ethnog ethnography

ethnol ethnology

ETI Electric Tool Institute

ETL Eastern Trunk Line; Essex Terminal Railway (rr mark)

ETLX Export Tank Lines (private car rr mark)

ETN equipment table nomenclature (US Army)

ETO European theater of operations (military); European Transport Organization; Express Transportation Order

EtOH ethyl alcohol

ETOUSA European Theater of Operations, US Army

ETS expiration term of service (US Army)

et seq and the following

ETSTC East Texas State Teachers College

ETSX Schoenwald, E. T. (private car rr mark)

Et2O ether

ETU Electrical Trades Union

et ux and wife (et uxor—Latin)

ETX Elmar Tank Line Company (private car rr mark)

etymol etymology

Eu Europe; European; europium; Eustace

EU Emory University; Ethical Union; Evangelical Union; the United States (los Estados Unidos —Spanish)

E-U United States (États-Unis— French)

EUA Eastern Underwriters Association; United States of America (Etats-Unis Amérique—French)

EUBC Evangelical United Brethren Church

Eucl Euclid

Eug Eugene

Eugo Eugenio

EUI United States of Indonesia (USI)

EUK Eureka Williams Corporation (NYSE)

EUMC Enameled Utensil Manufacturers Council

euphem euphemism

Eur Europe; European

EUS eastern United States

Eust Eustace

ev evangelical; possible (eventuell —German); enclosed and ventilated

e v electron volt; escort vessel

E v Rights reserved (Eingang vorbehalten—German)

E V English Version (Bible)

EVA Engineer Vice Admiral

evac evacuated; evacuation

EVAC evacuate (US Army)

evang evangelist; evangelical; gospel (evangelium—Latin)

evap evaporate

evapd evaporated

evapn evaporation

evce evidence (legal)

eve. evening

Evel Evelina

event. possibly (eventuell—German)

e viv disc departed from life (e vivis discessit—Latin)

evol evolution

EV1S Edge Vee one side (lumber)

EVR Eversharp, Inc (NYSE)
evtl perhaps (eventuell—German)
EV2S Edge Vee two sides (lumber)
EVW European Voluntary Worker
evy every
EVY Evans Products Company (NYSE)
EW enlisted woman or women (US Army)
EWA Ewa Plantation Company (NYSE); East and West Association; Education Writers Association; Wiggins Airways
EWB Bliss (E. W.) Company (NYSE)
EWD Economic Warfare Division (naval)
EWHA Eastern Women's Headwear Association
EWO Electrical and Wireless Operators (RAF); Essential Work Order
EWS Emergency Water Supply
EWT Eastern war time
ex examined; example; excellent; except; exception; exceptional; exchange; excluding; exclusive; excursion; executed; executive; exempt; exercise; export; extra; extract (extractum—Latin); out of; excluding
Ex Exchange; Exeter; Exodus (Biblical)
EX experiment; experimental (US Navy)
exag exaggerated; exaggeration
EXAM examine (US Army)
exam examine; examined; examination
examg examining
ex aq in water (ex aqua—Latin) (pharmacy)
Ex B/L exchange bill of lading
Exc Excellency; excellent; except; exception; exciter; excommunication; he engraved it (excudit—Latin)
Exch exchange; exchequer

ex champ. ex-champion
excl exclamation; excluded; excluding; exclusive[ly]
excldg excluding
excoe excommunication (excommunicatione—Latin)
Ex Coll Oxon Exeter College of Oxford
Ex Com Executive Committee
ex cp ex coupon
exd examined
ex div without dividend
ex doc executive document
exec executed; executive; execution; executor
exec bd executive board
exec clk executive clerk
exec off. executive officer
Exet Exeter College (Oxford)
ex fcy extra fancy
ex gr for example (exempli gratia—Latin)
exh exhaust; exhibit; exhibition
exhib let it be given (exhibiatur—Latin) (prescription)
ex hvy extra heavy (plumbing)
ex int not including interest
ex lib ex-library; from the books of (ex libris—Latin)
Exmo Excellency (Excellentissimo—Portuguese)
exmr examiner
ex n ex new (excluding the right to new shares—NYSE)
Ex O Executive Order
Exod. Exodus (Bible)
ex off. by authority of his office (ex officio—Latin)
Exon [signature of] Bishop of Exeter
exp expansion; expedition; expense; experiment; expiration; explanation; export; exportation; exported; express; expression
ex p on one side only (ex parte—Latin) (legal)

EXPED expedite(ion) or (ionary) (US Army)
expl explosion; explained; explanation; explanatory; example (exemple—French)
exploit. exploitation
exp o experimental order
expr express; expressive; expressing; expression
expt experiment
ex pte on one side only, ex parte (legal)
exptl experimental
exptr exporter
exr executor
ex rel by the relation of (legal) (ex relatione—Latin)
exrx executrix
exs expenses
ex Sd by decree of the Senate (ex Senatus decreto—Latin)
ext extend; extension; exterior; external; extinct; extra; extract; extreme
extd extracted
ex temp sp ex tempore speaking
extend. to be spread (extendendus—Latin) (pharmacy)
extern externally
ex tm in accord with the testament of (ex testamento—Latin)
extn extraction
extrad extradition
extraord extraordinary
extrem extremity
exx examples; executrix
Exx excellency (Exzellenz—German)
Ez Ezekiel; Ezra
EZ Easy Washing Machine, Cl B (NYSE)
EZAACMO Eastern Zone Army Air Corps Mail Operations
Ezech Ezechiel
Ezek Ezekiel (Bible)

F

f born (född—Norwegian) (född—Swedish); family; farad (electric unit); father; fathom; felon; female; filament (radio); halfpenny (fillér—Hungarian); fire alarm; firm (pencils); fleet; focal distance; force; folio; for (fór—Norwegian); frequency; following
F fluorine; Fahrenheit
FA Factory Act; Fatties Anonymous; Felt Association; Field Artillery; Financial Adviser; Fleet Auxiliary;

Football Association; Food Administrator; frame aerial; Freight Agent; Freight Association; fugacity (of gases)
f&a fore and aft
fA last year (forrige Aar—Danish)
F/A free astray (shipping)
F&A February and August
F of A Foresters of America
faa free of all average (shipping)
FAA Fatal Accidents Act; Fellow of the American Association for

the Advancement of Science; Fellow of the Central Association of Accountants; Fifth Avenue Association; Fleet Air Arm (England); Foreman's Association of America
FAAAS Fellow of the American Association for the Advancement of Science; Fellow of the American Academy of Arts and Sciences
FAAG First Advertising Agency Group
FAAR Fellow of the American

Academy in Rome

fab free on board (*franco á bord*—French); (*frei an bord*—German); manufacturing plant (*fabrique*—French)

fabr fabrication

Fab Soc Fabian Society

fac an exact copy (*factum similis*—Latin); facsimile; fast as can (shipping); façade (construction)

FAC facility(ies) (US Army); Farmers' Action Council; Federal Advisory Council; Federal Aviation Commission; Federated Admiralty Contractors; Foreign Affairs Committee (US Army)

FACA Federal Alcohol Control Commission

FACCA Fellow of the Association of Certified and Corporate Accountants

FACD Fellow of the American College of Dentists

facet. facetiaé; facetious

FACI Folk Arts Center, Inc

FACP Fellow of the American College of Physicians

FACS Fellow of the American College of Surgeons

fact. bill; invoice (*factura*—Spanish)

FAD free air delivered

Faer Faeroe Islands

FAF Fresh Air Fund; forage acre factor (grazing)

fag. fagotto (music)

FAGO Fellow of the American Guild of Organists

FAGS Fellow of the American Geographical Society

FAI Fellow of the Auctioneers' Institute; Fellow of the Chartered Auctioneers' and Estate Agents' Institute; Frontiers of America, Inc; International Abolitionist Federation; International Aeronautic Federation

FAIA Fellow of the American Institute of Architects

FAIC Fellow of the American Institute of Chemists

FAII Fellow Australian Insurance Institute

FAJ Fajardo Sugar Company (NYSE)

Fakt invoice (*Faktura*—German)

FAL Facilitation (ICAO); Falstaff Brewing Corporation (NYSE); Frontier Airlines, Inc

Falk Is. Falkland Islands

FALPA Fellow of the Incorporated Society of Auctioneers and Landed Property Agents

fal set falsetto (music)

fal sif falsification

fam familiar; family; famous; field ambulance

FAM Family Finance Corporation (NYSE); Federal Air Mail; Florida Agricultural and Mechanical (college); Foreign Air Mail; Free and Accepted Mason; Free Austrian Mission; free at mill

FANY First Aid Nursing Yeomanry

FANYS First Aid Nursing Yeomanry Service

FAO finish all over; Fleet Accountant Officer; Food and Agriculture Organization

FAP First Aid Post

FAPS Fellow of the American Physical Society

faq fair average quality; free alongside quay

faqs fair average quality of season

far. farad; farriery; farthing

FAR Fargo Oils Ltd. (NYSE)

FARA Foreign Agents' Registration Act

fas firsts and seconds (American lumber); free alongside ship

FAS Federation of American Scientists; Fellow of the Anthropological Society; Fellow of the Antiquarian Society; Fellow of the Society of Actuaries in Scotland; Fellow of the Society of Arts; Food Advice Service

FASA Fellow of the Acoustical Society of America; First Auditor of Sheriff's Accounts

FASB Fellow Asiatic Society of Bengal

fasc a bundle (*fasciculus*—Latin); number, part (*fasciolo*—Italian)

FASC Foreign Affairs Sub Committee

FASE Fellow of the Antiquarian Society of Edinburgh

FASL Fellow of the Anthropological Society of London

fath fathom

FAV Fairchild Camera & Instrument (NYSE); favorable (US Army)

FAVO Fleet Aviation Officer

FAWAI Fishermen & Allied Workers of America, International

fb flat bar; fog bell; fullback

FB Fenian Brotherhood; film bulletin (US Army); Fire Brigade; Fishery Board; Flying Boat; Free Baptists; freight bill

F&B fumigation and bath (US Army)

FBA Federal Bar Association; Federal Business Associations; Fellow of the British Academy; Fibre Box Association

FBAA Fellow of the British Association of Accountants and Auditors; Fur Brokers Association of America

FBAS Fellow of the British Association of Secretaries

fbc fallen building clause (insurance)

fbcw fallen building clause waiver (insurance)

FBCX Folev Butane Company, Inc (private car rr mark)

fbd freeboard (shipping)

FBDFCP Federation of Bleachers, Dyers, Finishers and Calico Printers

FBE Follansbee Steel Corporation (NYSE)

FBEA Fellow of the British Esperanto Association

FBH fire brigade hydrant; free on board, harbor

FBI Federal Bureau of Investigation; Federation of British Industries

f bk flat back (lumber)

fbm feet board measure (board feet)

FBOA Fellow of the British Optical Association

FBOU Fellow of the British Ornithologists' Union

FBP final boiling point

FBPC Foreign Bondholders Protective Council

FBRL final bomb release line (US Army)

FBRX Fiske Brothers Refining Company (rr mark)

FBS Fellow of the Botanical Society

FBSE Fellow of the Botanical Society of Edinburgh

FBSI Fellow of the Boot and Shoe Industry

FBSM Fellow of the Birmingham School of Music

FBU Fire Brigades Union

f c bequeathed in trust (*fidei commissum*—Latin) (legal); follow copy (printing); foot candle; for cash

FC fair cutting (building); Farmers' Club; Federal Cabinet; Federal Cases (legal); Feint and Cash (account book rulings); Ferry Command (RAF); Fifth Column; Films Council; fire cock; fire control; Fisheries Convention; Fishmongers' Company; Fleming Committee; Food Conference; Food Controller; Football Club; Foreign Commissioner; Forestry Commission; Free Church (Scottish); Free Collection; French Cameroons (Africa); Frequency Changer (films); frozen credits; Fuel Control; form (and) class

F∴ C∴ Fellow Craft (freemasonry)

FCA Farm Credit Administration Fellow of the (Institute of) Chartered Accountants; Film Council of America; Freight Claim Agent

FCAB Fire Companies' Adjustment Bureau

FCAC Federal Council of American

Churches

FC Adj Freight Claim Adjuster

FCAO Farm Credit Administration Operations

fcap foolscap

FC Aud Freight Claim Auditor

FCB Fabian Colonial Bureau; Freight Container Bureau

FCBA Federal Communications Bar Association

FCC Federal Commissions Cable/ Radio; Federal Communications Commission; Federal Council of Churches; Central Railway (*Ferro-Carril Central*); First Class Certificate; Food Control Committee; Four Corners Club; Free Church Council

FCCCA Federal Council of the Churches of Christ in America

FCCNY Foreign Commerce Club of New York

FCCS Fellow of Corporation of Certified Secretaries

FCCUS French Chamber of Commerce of the United States

FCDA Federal Civil Defense Administration

FCE Florida Citrus Exchange; Foreign Currency Exchange

FCEX Fruit Growers Express Company (private car rr mark)

FCGGMA Federation of Cash Grain Commission Merchants Associations

FCGI Fellow of the City and Guilds of London Institute

FCI Fellow of the Institute of Commerce; Finance Corporation for Industry; International Federation of Dog Breeders

FCIA Fellow of the Corporation of Insurance Agents

FCIB Fellow of the Corporation of Insurance Brokers; Foreign Credit Interchange Bureau

FCIC Federal Crop Insurance Corporation

FCII Fellow of the Chartered Insurance Institute

FCIS Fellow of the Chartered Institute of Secretaries

FCM Ferrocarril Mexicano (Mexican Railway) (rr mark)

FCNL French Committee of National Liberation

fco fair copy; frank (*francisco*— Spanish); post free (*franco*— Italian)

FCO Federation of Colliery Officials; Fellow of the College of Optics; Fellow of the College of Organists; Fire Control Officer; Fleet Constructor Officer

FCOG Fellow of the College of Obstetrics and Gynecology

FCP Fellow of the College of Preceptors

fcp foolscap (paper)

FCR Fire Control Room; full cold rolled (steel sheets)

FCRF Federated China Relief Fund

fcs francs; free of capture and seizure (shipping)

FCS Fellow of the Chemical Society; *Ferro-Carril Sud* (Southern Railway); Fire Control School

fcsad free of capture, seizure, arrest and detainment (shipping)

FCSC Food and Civil Supplies Commissioner

FCSI Fellow of the Chartered Surveyors' Institute

fcsrcc free of capture, seizure, riots and civil commotions (shipping)

FCT fraction thereof (US Army); Federal Capital Territory (of Australia); Federal Co-ordinator of Transportation

FCTA Federal Central Technical Authority

FCTB Fellow of the College of Teachers of the Blind

FCTCSC Flue Cured Tobacco Co-operative Stabilization Corporation

FCU Federal Credit Unions (United States)

FCUS Federal Credit Union System

FCWA Fellow of the Institute of Cost and Work Accountants

fcy pks fancy packs

FCX Fuelane Corporation (private car rr mark)

f d before this, previously (*för detta*—Swedish)

fd field; flight deck (aircraft carriers); focal distance; framed (building); fund

Fd Ferdinand

FD Central Foundry Company (NYSE); Defender of the Faith (*Fidei Defensor*—Latin); Factory Department; Faculty Department; Federal Debt; Finance Department (US Army); forced draught; free delivery; free discharge; free dispatch; free docks; frequency doubler (radio)

f & d faced and drilled (plumbing); freight and demurrage (shipping)

FDA Food and Drug Administration; Food Distribution Administration

FDAI Furniture Deliverers Association, Inc

Fd Amb Field Ambulance

FDB Fighter Dive Bomber

Fd Bde Field Brigade

Fd Bty Field Battery

f d c mint condition (*fleur de coin*) (numismatics)

FDC fire direction center (US Army);

Foreign Department Conversion

FD&C Food Drug and Cosmetic (Act)

FDCA Fish Distributors Cooperative Association

Fd Coy. Field Company

FDD free of charge (*franc de droits*—French)

FDEX Fruit Growers Express Company (private car rr mark)

FDFDA Fur Dressers and Fur Dyers Association

FDFU Federation of Documentary Film Units

fdg funding (NYSE)

FDGI Fur Dressers Guild, Inc

FDHO Factory Department, Home Office

Fd Hyg Sec Field Hygiene Section

FDI Fir Door Institute; International Dental Federation

FDIC Federal Deposit Insurance Corporation

FDIF Women's International Democratic Federation (WIDF)

FDL Foremost Defended Localities

fd ldg forced landing (RAF)

FDM Food Machinery & Chemical (NYSE)

FDMA Fibre Drum Manufacturers Association

fdn foundation

FDO Fleet Dental Officer

FDP Florida Power Corporation (NYSE)

Fd PO Field Post Office

FDR Franklin Delano Roosevelt

fdry foundry

FDS Federated Department Stores (NYSE)

fe first edition (books); flanged ends (plumbing)

f é current year (*folyó évi*—Hungarian)

F e Flemish ells (measurement)

Fe ferrum (iron)

FE Far East[ern]; Federal Estimates; Forest Engineer

FEA Flints Export Agency; Fashion Exhibitors of America; Federal Economic Administration; Firemen's Employment Association; Foreign Economic Administration; French Equatorial Africa

FEACCI Far East-America Council of Commerce and Industry

Feb February (*február*—Hungarian) (*Februar*—Norwegian); (*Februari*— Swedish); (*Februar*—Danish)

FEBANYC Foreign Exchange Brokers Association of New York City

Febb February (*Febbrais*—Italian)

feb dur while fever continues (*febre durante*—Latin) (medicine)

fec faith, hope, charity (*foi, espér-*

ance, charité—French)

FEC Far East Conference; First Edition Club; Florida East Coast Railway Company; Fuel Efficiency Committee

FECB Foreign Exchange Control Board

Fed. Federal; Federalist; federated; federation

FED Froedtert Corporation (NYSE)

Fed. Aud Federal Auditor

Fed. Bar. J Federal Bar Association Journal

Fed. Cas Federal Cases

fed. cas no federal case number (legal)

Fed. Mal St Federated Malay States

Fed. Reg Federal Register

Fed. Supp Federal Supplement

FEE Foundation for Economic Education

Feet bm feet board measure

FEF French Expeditionary Force

FEHC Federal Emergency Housing Corporation

FEI Farm Equipment Institute

FEIS Fellow of the Educational Institute of Scotland

Fel Felix

FEL Felt & Tarrant Manufacturing Company (NYSE); Full Employment League

fel mem of happy memory (felicis memoriae—Latin)

FELX Fels & Company (rr mark)

fem female; feminine

FEMA Fire Extinguisher Manufacturers Association; Foundry Equipment Manufacturers Association

FEMAUS Flavoring Extract Manufacturers Association of the United States

FEN Fairchild Engine & Airplane (NYSE)

F Eng Forest Engineer

FENSA Film Entertainments National Service Association

FEO Fleet Engineer Officer

FEP Federated Petroleums, Ltd. (NYSE)

FEPC Fair Employment Practices Committee

Fer Ferdinand; Fermanagh (county, Ireland)

FER Foreign Exchange Restrictions

FERA Federal Emergency Relief Administration

Ferd Ferdinand

Ferndo Fernando

ferr railroad (ferrovia—Italian)

Fernspr telephone (Fernsprecher—German)

fertz fertilizer

ferv boiling (fervens—Latin)

FES Fellow of the Entomological Society; Fellow of the Ethnological Society

FESO Federal Employment Stabilization Office

fest festival

FEST Federation of Engineering and Shipbuilding Trades [of the United Kingdom]

FEU Federated Engineering Union

feud. feudalism

fev February (fevereiro—Portuguese)

fév February (février—French)

FEWA Farm Equipment Wholesalers Association

f o y for ever yours

ff file finish; fixed focus; folded flat; folios; following pages; the following (folgende—Danish)

F f to be continued (Fortsetzung folgt—German)

FF Falk Foundation; Farm Foundation; Fianna Fail (Eire); Field Foundation; Filene Foundation Fleet Fighter (RAF); Ford Foundation; Franklin Foundation; Free French; Friendship Fund; Frontier Force; Fuller Fund; Most Fortunate Brothers (Felicissimi Fratres—Latin); thick fog (nautical)

f & f furniture and fixtures (insurance)

F of F Firth of Forth

F to F face to face (plumbing)

FFA Fellow of the Faculty of Actuaries; Foreign Freight Agent; Future Farmers of America

f f a free foreign agency (shipping); free from alongside

FFAS Fellow of the Faculty of Architects and Surveyors

FFAUSC Federation of French Alliances in the United States and Canada

FFC Fire Force Commander; Fly Fishers' Club; Foreign Funds Control; free from chlorine

fff as loud as possible (fortississimo—music)

FFF Friends of the Fighting Forces

FFFI Frozen Food Foundation, Inc

FFGT firefighter(ing) (US Army)

FFHMA Full-Fashioned Hosiery Manufacturers of America

FFI Fellow of the Faculty of Insurance; Freight Forwarders Institute; French Forces of the Interior; French Independence Front (Front Français de l'Indépendance—French); Frozen Food Institute

F1C Fireman First Class (US Navy)

FFL fast freight line; Free French Forces (Forces Françaises Libres —French)

FFLI Frozen Food Locker Institute

ffly faithfully

FFMC Federal Farm Mortgage Corporation

FFPS Fellow of the Faculty of Physicians and Surgeons

FFPSG Fellow of the Faculty of Physicians and Surgeons, Glasgow

F Fr Free French

FFR Fellow of the Faculty of Radiologists

FFS Food Fair Stores, Inc (NYSE)

FF Sc Fellow of the Faculty of Sciences

FFV First Families of Virginia

FFWVI Federation of French War Veterans, Inc

FFY Fanny Farmer Candy Shops (NYSE)

fg suburb (faubourg—French)

f g fully good

FG Federal Government; field gun; Fine Gael (Ireland); fine grain (leather); Fire Guards; flat grain (timber); Foot Guards;(military); frictionglazed (paper)

fga foreign general average (marine insurance); free of general average

FGA Foreign General Agent

FGCM Field General Court-Martial

FGCSSWA Federation of Glass, Ceramic & Silica Sand Workers of America

FGEX Fruit Growers Express Company (private car rr mark)

f g f fully good, fair

FGI Fashion Group, Inc; Fellow Institute of Certificated Grocers

FGJA Federal Grand Jury Association

fgn foreign

FGO Fellow of the Guild of Organists; Fleet Gunnery Officer

FGS Fellow of the Geological Society; Friends of the Golden State

FGSA Fellow of the Geological Society of America

fgt freight

FGTSA Fur Garment Traveling Salesmen's Association

f h fog horn; fore hatch (shipping); flat head (plumbing); make a draught (fiat haustus—Latin) (pharmacy)

FH Fellowship Homes; fire hydrant; free harbor

fha date (fecha—Spanish)

FHA Farmers' Home Administration; Federal Housing Administration; Fellowship Holidays Association; Future Homemakers of America

FHAA Field Hockey Association of America

FHAS Fellow of the Highland and Agricultural Society

fhb family hold back (colloquial)

fhdo dated (*fechado*—Spanish)

FHI Freedom House, Inc

FHIX Fruit Growers Express Company (private car rr mark)

FHK Shattuck (Frank G.) Company (NYSE)

FHLB Federal Home Loan Banks

FHLBA Federal Home Loan Bank Administration

FHLBB Federal Home Loan Bank Board

fhld freehold

f hosp field hospital

FHP friction horsepower

FHR Federal House of Representatives (Australia)

FHRPEA Florida Hard Rock Phosphate Export Association

FHS Fellow of the Historical Society; Foundling Hospitals Schools

fhv former (*forhenvaerende*—Danish)

f i for instance

FI Bureau of Finance (UN Secretariat); Falkland Islands; farm insurance; Farðe Islands; Fellow of the Institute of Chemistry; Freedom International (association)

fia full interest admitted

FIA Factory Insurance Association; Fellow of the Institute of Actuaries; Fellow of the Institute of Auctioneers; International Automobile Federation (IAF)

FIAA Fellow Architect Member of the Incorporated Association of Architects and Surveyors

FIAC Fellow of the Institute of Company Accountants; Inter-American Federation of Automobile Clubs

FIADEJ International Federation of Associations of Newspaper Managers and Publishers

FiAe S Fellow of the Institute of Aeronautical Sciences

FIAI Fellow of the Institute of Arbitrators (Inc)

FIAMA Fellow of the Incorporated Advertising Managers' Association

FI Arb Fellow of the Institute of Arbitrators

FIAS Fellow Surveyor Member of the Incorporated Association of Architects and Surveyors; Fellow of the Institute of Aeronautical Sciences

FIAT *Fabbrica Italiana Automobile Torino* (Italian automobile manufacturer); Field Information Agency, Technical

f i b free into barge; free into bunker (coal trade)

FIB Fellow of the Institute of Bankers; Food Investigation Board

FIBD Fellow of the Institute of British Decorators

f i c freight, insurance, carriage

FIC Federal Insurance Corporation; Federation of Insurance Council; Fellow of the Institute of Chemistry

FICA Factory Inspectorate and Canteen Advisers; Fellow of the Institute of Chartered Accountants; Food Industries Credit Association

FICB Federal Intermediate Credit Banks

FICE International Federation of Children's Communities

FICI Fellow of International Colonial Institute

FICM International Federation of Motor-Cycling Clubs

FICS Fellow of the Institute of Chartered Shipbrokers

fict fictional; pottery (*fictilis*—Latin)

fid fidelity; fiduciary

FID Fellow of the Institute of Directors; Fidelity & Deposit Company, Md (NYSE); Field Intelligence Department; International Federation for Documentation

FIDA International Federation of Women Lawyers

Fid Def Defender of the Faith (*Fidei Defensor*—Latin)

FIDIC International Federation of Consulting Engineers

FIDO Fog Investigation Dispersal Operation

FIEJ International Federation of Newspaper Publishers and Editors

FIF Fellow of the Institute of Fuels

fi fa have it executed—a writ (*fieri facias*—Latin) (legal)

fig. figurative; figuratively; figure (*figur*—Danish)

FIG International Federation of Surveyors (IFS)

FIGCM Fellow of the Incorporated Guild of Church Musicians

FIH Fellow of the Institute of Hygiene

f-II brothers (*fratii*—Rumanian)

FII Fellow of the Imperial Institute; Food Institute, Inc.

FIIA Fellow of the Institute of Industrial Administration

FIIG Federation of Private and Semi-Official International Organizations established (Geneva)

FI Inst Fellow of the Imperial Institute

FIJ Fellow of Institute of Journalists; International Federation of Journalists

FIJL International Federation of Free Journalists (IFFJ)

FIL Fellow of Institute of Linguists;

filter (US Army)

fil filament

filt filter

FIMS International Medico-Athletic Federation

FIMTA Fellow of the Institute of Municipal Treasurers and Accountants

fin. finance; financial; finished (*finis*—Latin)

Fin Finland; Finnish

Fin Adv Financial Adviser

F Inc ST Fellow of the Incorporated Society of Shorthand Teachers

FINEBEL France, Italy, Netherland, Belgium and Luxemburg (Economic Agreement)

Finn Finnish

Fin Sec Financial Secretary

F Inst P Fellow of the Institute of Physics

f i o free in and out (shipping)

FIO Fellow of Institute of Ophthalmic Opticians

FIOB Fellow Institute of Builders

FIOCES International Federation of Organizations for School Correspondence and Exchanges

FIP Fellow of the Institute of Physics; Fire Association of Philadelphia (NYSE)

FIPA International Federation of Agricultural Producers (IFAP)

FIPESCO International Federation of Secondary Teachers

FIPI Fellow of the Institute of Patentees (Inc)

FIPO Orient Press International Federation

FIPRESCI International Federation of the Cinematographic Press

FIPS Fellow of the Incorporated Phonographic Society; Fellow of the Institute of Private Secretaries; Fellow of the Photographic Society

fir. firkin

f l r floating-in rates (transportation)

FIR Firestone Tire & Rubber Company (NYSE)

1st Lt First Lieutenant

1st Sgt First Sergeant

FISA Fellow of the Incorporated Secretaries Association

FISAC Inter-American Federation of Societies of Authors and Composers

FISC Fur Industry Salvage Commission

FISE Fellow of the Institution of Structural Engineers; United Nations International Children's Emergency Fund (UNICEF)

fit. fabrication in transit; free in truck; free of income tax

FIT Fashion Institute of Technology

FITCA International Federation of

Commercial Motor Users

FITEC International Federation of Thermalism and Climatism

FIU forward interpretation unit (US Army)

FIUS French Institute in the United States

5tette quintett (music)

f l w free in wagon

FIWT Fellow of the Institute of Wireless Technology

FJ American Steel Foundries (NYSE)

FJI Fellow of the Institute of Journalists

FJQ Fedders-Quigan Corporation (NYSE)

f k flat keel (shipbuilding)

f K before Christ (før Kristus—Norwegian)

Fk Frank

FK Frankenmuth Brewing Company (NYSE)

FKC Fellow of King's College

FKCL Fellow of King's College, London

FKM Fairbanks, Morse & Company (NYSE)

FKQCPI Fellow of the King's and Queen's College of Physicians, Ireland

FKRX Flintkote Company of Canada, Ltd., The (private car rr mark)

FKS Franklin Simon & Company (NYSE)

FKS Pr Franklin Simon & Co. Inc. (4½% Conv. Pfd.) (ASE)

f l a false reading (falsa lectio—Latin)

fl flourished (floruit—Latin); flute; flute lead (gears); full load; flauto (music); floor; florin; flour; flourished (floriut—Latin); flower (flores—Latin);fluid (flurdus—Latin)

Fl Flamen; Flanders; Flemish; Florida; liquid (Flüssigkeit—German)

FL Flag Lieutenant (naval); Flight Lieutenant; Flotilla Leader; Friends of the Land; Fuller (George A.) Company (NYSE)

F L A do it by the rules of the art (fiat lege artis—Latin) (pharmacy); Federal Loan Agency; Federation of Local Authorities; Fellow of the Library Association; First Lord of the Admiralty; Fluorescent Lighting Association

Fla Florida

FLAA Fellow London Association of Certified Accountants

flag. flageolet (music)

flak anti-aircraft gunfire

(Flug[zeug]abwehrkanone—German)

FLAS Fellow of the Land Agents' Society

FLB Federal Land Banks

FLC Flag Lieutenant Commander

FLCM Fellow of London College of Music

FLD field (US Army)

fld flowered (botany)

fldg avg fielding average

fl dr fluid dram (apothecaries')

Fl e Flemish ell (measurement)

FLEA Foremen's League for Education and Association

Flem Flemish

FLETRABASE Fleet training base (US Navy)

flex flexible

flg flange; following

FLGA Fellow Local Government Association

flgd flanged

FLGS Fellow of the Local Government Association

fl hd flat head

Flints. Flintshire (county in Wales)

FLJ Jacobs (F. L.) Company (NYSE)

Fll liquids (Flüssigkeiten—German)

fl ld floor load

f l n following landing numbers (shipping)

Flo Florence

FLO Florsheim Shoe Co., Cl A (common stock, NYSE)

Fl O Flight Officer

FLOA Federal Licensed Officers Association

fl oz fluid ounce (apothecaries')

FLP fighting landplane (US Navy)

fl pl in full bloom (flore pleno—Latin)

fl prf flame-proof (electrical engineering)

fl pt flash point

flr florin

flrs flowers (botany)

FLRX Fabrica de Jabon "LaReinera" (private car rr mark)

FLS Fellow of the Linnean Society; Florence Stove Company (NYSE)

FLSA Fair Labor Standards Act

flt filter; flight; float

FLT fleet (US Navy)

Flt Comdr (RAF) Flight Commander

Flt Lt Flight Lieutenant

fltr floater (insurance)

Fltr-Serg-Nav Flight-Sergeant-Navigator (RAF)

Flt-Sgt Flight Sergeant (RAF)

FLUG Flugfeiag Islands, H. F. (Iceland Airways, Ltd.)

fluor fluorescent

flüss liquid (flüssig—German)

fly. flyweight (boxing)

FLY Flying Tiger Line, Inc. (NYSE)

FLZO Farband-Labor Zionist Order

fm farm; fathom; form; from; before noon (formiddag—Norwegian); (förmiddagen—Swedish); fine measurement; housewife (femmes de ménage —French); make a mixture (fiat mistura—Latin) (pharmacy); married women (femmes mariées—French)

FM Federated Malay States; field magnet; field manual (US Army); Field Marshal; Flight-Mechanic; Foreign Mission; Fraternity of Physicians (Fraternitas medicorum —Latin); Frequency Modulation (radio)

F&M Franklin and Marshall College

FMA Felt Manufacturers Association; File Manufacturers' Association; Flour Mills of America (NYSE); Forging Manufacturers Association; Frequency Modulation Association

FMAN February, May, August, November (quarter months)

FMANU World Federation of United Nations Associations (WFUNA)

FMB Federal Maritime Board

FMBSA Farmers and Manufacturers Beet Sugar Association

FMC Farm Mortgage Corporation; Ford Motor Company of Canada, Cl A (NYSE)

FMC A Ford Motor Co. of Can. Ltd. (Class "A" Non-Vt) (ASE)

FMC B Ford Motor Co. of Can. Ltd. (Class "B" Voting) (ASE)

FMCNA Foreign Missions Conference of North America

fmd foot-and-mouth disease

FMEA Flour Millers Export Association; Friction Materials Export Association

FMEF Flour Milling Employers' Federation

FMF Fleet Marine Force (US Navy); Food Manufacturers' Federation

FMFIC Federation of Mutual Fire Insurance Companies

FMGJ Federation of Master Goldsmiths and Jewelers

FMI International Monetary Funds (Fonds Monétaire International— French); Sons of Mary Immaculate (Filii Mariae Immaculatae—Latin)

fmm magnetomotive force (force magnétomotrice—French)

FMMA Floor Machinery Manufacturers Association

fmn formation

FMO Federal-Mogul Corporation (NYSE); Fleet Mail Office; Fleet Medical Officer

FMPE Federation of Master Process Engravers

FM Prot Fine-mesh-cover protected (electrical engineering)

fms fathoms

FMS Federal Mining & Smelting Company (NYSE); Federated Malay States; Fellow of the Medical Society; Marist Brothers

FMT Federal Fawick Corporation (NYSE)

FMTS World Federation of Scientific Workers (WFSW)

FMTX Freeport Mexican Fuel Oil Corporation (private car rr mark)

FMYX Yorke & Sons, Limited, F. M. (private car rr mark)

fn footnote

f n national holiday (*fête nationale*—French)

FN Front National (France); St. Louis-San Francisco Railway (NYSE)

FNA Friars National Association

FNAA Fellow of the National Association of Auctioneers, House Agents, Rating Surveyors and Valuers

FNBA Fellow of the North British Academy

fnd found

FND National Democratic Front (*Frontul National Democratic*—Rumania)

fndd founded

fndg founding

fndn foundation

fndr founder

FNFA Fellow of the National Federation of Accountants

FMFIC Federation of Mutual Fire Insurance Companies

FNFL Free French Naval Forces (*Forces Navales Françaises Libres*—French)

FNGDA Farmers National Grain Dealers Association

FNI Fellow of the National Institute of Sciences (India)

FNL Fansteel Metallurgical Corporation (NYSE)

FNMA Federal National Mortgage Association

fnp fusion point; melting point

FNU United Nations Forces (*Forces des Nations Unies*—French)

fo besides (*för övriglil*—Swedish); firm offer; for orders; free overside (shipping); fuel oil; full out terms (grain trade); folio; faced only

FO Federal Official; Field Officer, (naval); Flag Officer (RAF); Flintkote Company (NYSE); Flying Officer; Foreign Office; full organ (music); Federal Office

FOA Faculty of Advocates; Foreign Operations Administration

FO Adj Freight Overcharge Adjuster

f o b free on board

FOBX Fruit Growers Express Company(private car rr mark)

f o c free of charge; free on car

FOC Father of the Chapel; Federation Organization Committee; Ford of Canada; from own correspondent

fo'c'sle forecastle

f o d free of damage

FOE Ferro Corporation (NYSE); Fraternal Order of Eagles; Friends of Europe

FOF Ford Motor of France (NYSE)

F Offr Field Officer

FOGA Fashion Originators Guild of America

FOGAI Fashion Originators Guild of America, Inc.

fohc free of heart center or centers (lumber)

FOIC Flag Officer in charge (naval)

f o k free of knots (lumber)

FOKX British American Oil Company Ltd. (private car rr mark); Fidelity Oil Company (private car rr mark)

fol folio

FOL follow (US Army)

FOLA Latin American Odontological Federation

folg following (*folgend*—German)

FOLNOAVAL following items not available (US Army)

f u m fault of management (insurance); from and with (*fra og med*—Norwegian)

FOO Forward Observation Officer (RAF)

f o q free on quay (shipping)

f o r free on rail; free on road

For. Formosa

for. foreign; forester; forestry; fornax; forte (music)

for'd forward

FORF forfeit(ure) (US Army)

forf author (*forfatter*—Danish)

förf author (*författare*—Swedish); authoress (*författarinna*—Swedish)

forg forged; forgery

form. formation; former; formula

For. Min Foreign Minister

formn foreman; formation

formul formulary

For. Rel Foreign Relations of the United States

fort. fortification; fortified

f o r t full out rye terms (grain trade)

fortif fortification

fortis as loud as possible (*fortissimo*—music)

Forts. continuation (*Fortsetzung*—German)

FORTSK for task force (US Army)

forwn forewoman

forz forzando (music)

f o s free on station; free on steamer

FOS Fisheries Organization Society

f o t free on tax; free on truck

found. foundation; founded

40/8 Soc The Society of 40 Men and 8 Horses (La Société des 40 Hommes et 8 Chevaux—French)

4/ 4ths r d c four-fourths running-down clause (insurance)

4° quarto

4-H head, heart, hands, health

4-P four-pole (electricity)

4th Div Assn Fourth Division Association

4tette quartette (music)

FOUSA Finance Office, United States Army (US Army)

f o w first open water (shipping) free on wagon

FOX Fox (Peter) Brewing Company (NYSE)

f p face plate; fine paper; fixed price; flame-proof; foot pound; former pupil(s); forward perpendicular; fully paid; freezing point; flame protected

Fp melting point (*Fusionspunkt*—German)

FP American & Foreign Power (NYSE); faithful performance bond; Fascist Party; field punishment; floating policy; foreign policy; free port; fully paid (premium); frame protected (insurance)

fpa free of particular average (marine insurance)

FPA Federal Power Act; Family Planning Association; Food Production Administration; Foreign Policy Association; Foreign Press Association

FPA (AC) Free of Particular Average (American Conditions)

FPA(EC) Free of Particular Average (English Conditions)

FPB Fort Pitt Brewing Company (common stock) (ASE)

FPBAA Folding Paper Box Association of America

FPC Federal Personnel Council; Federal Power Commission

f p c for private circulation

FPDX Forest Products Chemical Company (private car rr mark)

FPF French Protestant Federation

FPHA Federal Public Housing Authority

F PhS Fellow of the Philosophical Society of England

F Phys S Fellow of the Physical Society

FPI Federal Prison Industries; Flexible Packaging Institute

f pil make a pill (*fiat pilula*—Latin) (pharmacy)

f p l l full premium if (vessel) lost (insurance)

f pl face plate

FPL final protective line (US Army); Florida Power & Light Company (NYSE); Forest Products Laboratory

fpm feet per minute

FPMO Free of Poundage Money Order

FPMPMA Fountain Pen and Mechanical Pencil Manufacturers Association

FPO fleet post office (US Navy)

FPRA Financial Public Relations Association

FPRL Forest Products Research Laboratory

fps feet per second; foot-pound-second (physics)

FPS Fellow of the Pathological Society; Fellow of the Philharmonic Society; Fellow of the Philological Society; Fellow of the Philosophical Society; Fellow of the Physical Society (London)

fpsps feet per second per second

FPTA Fruit and Produce Trade Association

FPVPC Federation of Paint and Varnish Production Clubs

FPX Fidelity-Phenix Fire Insurance Company (NYSE)

f r freight release; reducing flame (*flamme réductrice*—French); right-hand page (*folio recto*—Latin)

fr father; fragment; frame; franc; free; frequent; friar; from; fruit (botany); brother (*frater*—Latin)

Fr Father (church use); Frances; Francis; French; Friday; francium

FR Federal Register; Federal Reporter (legal); flash ranging (US Army); Forest Reserve; Fuel Research; fully registered; Furness Railroad; Roman Forum (*Forum Romanum*—Latin)

F/R Fighter Reconnaissance (RAF); freight release

f&r feed and return (plumbing)

FRA Fleet Reserve Association; Francisco Sugar Company (NYSE)

FRAeS Fellow of Royal Aeronautical Society

FRAG fragment (US Army)

frag fragile; fragmentary

fragm fragment[s]

FRAHS Fellow of the Royal Australian Historical Society

FRAI Fellow of the Royal Anthropological Institute

FRAM Fellow of the Royal Academy of Music

Frank. Frankish

FRAS Fellow of the Royal Asiatic Society; Fellow of the Royal Astronomical Society

FRASB Fellow of the Royal Asiatic Society of Bengal

FR Assn Fleet Reserve Association

FR Assn Aux Fleet Reserve Association Auxiliary

frat fraternity

FRAUD fraudulent (US Army)

FRB Federal Reserve Board

FR Bk Federal Reserve Bank

FRBS Fellow of Royal Botanic Society; Fellow of Royal Society of British Sculptors

FRC Facilities Review Committee; Famine Relief Committee; Federal Radio Commission; Federation of Rambling Clubs; Foreign Relations Committee

f r & c c free of riots and civil commotions (insurance)

FRCI Fellow of the Royal Colonial Institute

FRCM Fellow of the Royal College of Music

FRCO Fellow of the Royal College of Organists

FRCOG Fellow of the Royal College of Obstetricians and Gynaecologists

FRCP Fellow of the Royal College of Physicians, London

FRCPE Fellow of the Royal College of Physicians, Edinburgh

FRCPI Fellow of the Royal College of Physicians of Ireland

FRCS Fellow of the Royal College of Surgeons

FRCSc Fellow of the Royal College of Science

FRCSE Fellow of the Royal College of Surgeons, Edinburgh

FRCSI Fellow of the Royal College of Surgeons, Ireland

FRCSL Fellow of the Royal College of Surgeons, London

FRCVS Fellow of the Royal College of Veterinary Surgeons

FRD Federal Rules Decisions; Ford Motor Ltd. (England) (NYSE); Foreign Relations Department; free rural delivery

FR Dist Federal Reserve District

FRDX Ford Motor Company (private car rr mark)

fre invoice (*facture*—French)

FREB Federal Real Estate Board

FR Ec S Fellow Royal Economic Society

Fred. Frederic, Frederick

freebd freeboard

freehd freehand

Fr e French ell (measurement)

FR Ent S Fellow of the Royal Entomological Society

freq frequent; frequentative

FREQ frequent; frequency (US Army)

Fr Eq Afr French Equatorial Africa

freq m frequency meter

fres brothers (*frères*—French)

FRES Fellow of Royal Empire Society; Fellow of Royal Entomological Society

FRFPS Fellow of Royal Faculty of Physicians and Surgeons

FRFPS[G] Fellow of the Royal Faculty of Physicians and Surgeons of Glasgow

FRGS Fellow of the Royal Geographical Society

frgt freight

Fr Gu French Guiana

FRHS Fellow of the Royal Historical Society; Fellow of the Royal Horticultural Society

Fri Friday

FRI Fellow of the Royal Institution; Food Research Institute

FRIA Fellow of the Royal Irish Academy

FRIBA Fellow of the Royal Institute of British Architects

FRIC Fellow of the Royal Institute of Chemistry

FRICS Fellow Royal Institution of Chartered Surveyors

Fries. Friesic

FR Ind Ch French Indochina

Fris Frisia (Friesland), Frisian

Frisco San Francisco

FRITALUX France, Italy, Benelux (Nations)

frk Miss (*fröken*—Swedish)

Frk Miss (*Frøken*—Danish) (*Frøken*—Norwegian)

Frl Miss (*Fräulein*—German)

frl fractional

frld foreland

frm framing (lumber)

FRMCS Fellow of the Royal Medical and Chirurgical Society

FR Met S Fellow of Royal Meteorological Society

frmn formation

frmnta fermentation

FRMS Fellow of the Royal Microscopical Society

FRM ST Finland Residential Mtge. Bank (ASE)

FRNS Fellow of the Royal Numismatic Society

FRNSA Fellow of the Royal School of Naval Architecture

FRO Fleet Recreation Officer; Food Rationing Order

f r o f fire risk on freight

front. frontispiece

FRP Federation of Railway Progress

FRPS Fellow of the Royal Photographic Society

FRPSL Fellow of the Royal Philatelic Society, London

frs francs (French monetary units); fruits (botany)

FRS Federal Reserve System; Fellow of the Royal Society; Friends' Relief Service; Fuel Research Station

FRSA Fellow of the Royal Society of Arts

FRSAI Fellow of the Royal Society of Antiquaries in Ireland

FR San I Fellow Royal Sanitary Institute

FRSC Fellow of the Royal Society, Canada

FRSE Fellow of the Royal Society of Edinburgh

FRSGS Fellow of the Royal Scottish Geographical Society

FRSI Fellow of the Royal Sanitary Institute

FRSL Fellow of the Royal Society of Literature; Fellow of the Royal Society, London

FRSM Fellow of the Royal Society of Medicine

FRSNA Fellow of the Royal School of Naval Architecture

FRSNZ Fellow of Royal Society of New Zealand

Fr Som French Somaliland

FRSS Fellow of the Royal Statistical Society

FRSSA Fellow of Royal Scottish Society of Arts; Fellow of Royal Society of South Africa

FRSSI Fellow Royal Statistical Society of Ireland

FRSSS Fellow of the Royal Statistical Society of Scotland

fr st fracto-stratus clouds (meteorology)

frt freight; fruit

Frt Assn Freight Association

frt ppd freight prepaid

FRTX Rives Transportation Company (private car rr mark)

FRUI Fellow of the Royal University of Ireland

frum of the brothers (fratrum—Latin)

frust in small pieces (frustillatim—Latin)

FRVA Fellow of the Incorporated Association of Rating and Valuation Officers

FRVIA Fellow of the Royal Victorian Institute of Architects

Fr W Afr French West Africa

FRZS Scot Fellow of the Royal Zoological Society of Scotland

fs facsimile; film strip; forged steel

FS Fabian Society; Faraday Society; Fee Stamp; Field Security; Field Service; Finance Section; Financial Secretary; Fleet Surgeon; Flight Sergeant (RAF); Florida Southern (college); Forest Service; Forged Steel; French Somaliland (Africa); Fresno State (college); Friendly Society; Fruitarian Society; please forward (faire suivre—French); Financial Statement

f/s factor of safety; foot-second

Fs Francis

F/S financial statement

FSA Farm Security Administration; Federal Securities Act; Federal Security Agency; Fellow of the Society of Antiquaries; Fellow of the Society of Arts; Flax Spinners' Association; Friendly Societies Act

FSAA Family Service Association of America; Fellow of the Society of Incorporated Accountants and Auditors

FSAI Fellow of the Society of Antiquaries of Ireland

FSAL Fellow of the Society of Antiquaries of London

FS Arch Fellow of Society of Architects

FSAS Fellow of the Society of Antiquaries of Scotland

FSC Brothers of the Christian Schools (Christian Brothers); Foundation for the Study of Cycles; Franklin Stores Corporation (NYSE)

FSCC Federal Surplus Commodity Corporation

FSCJ Congregation of the Sons of the Sacred Heart of Jesus

FSCW Florida State College for Women

FSE Fellow of Society of Engineers

FSEC Federal Securities and Exchange Commission

F2c Fireman Second Class (US Navy)

FSEF Foreign Service Educational Foundation

FSEII Food Service Equipment Industry, Inc.

F Sgt Flight Sergeant (RAF)

FSGT Fellow of the Society of Glass Technology

FSH Fishmann (M. H.), Company, Inc. (NYSE); follicle-stimulating hormone

FSHC Federal Subsistence Homesteads Corporation

FSI Fellow of the Sanitary Institute; Fellow of the Surveyors' Institution; Free Sons of Israel

FSLA Federal Savings and Loan Association

FSLIC Federal Savings and Loan Insurance Corporation

FSM World Federation of Trade Unions (WFTU)

FSMA Foundry Supply Manufacturers Association; Fruit and Syrup Manufacturers Association

FSMBUS Federation of State Medical Boards of the United States

FSMC Fellow of the Spectacle Makers' Company

FSN fiscal station number (US Army)

FSO Field Security Officer (military); Fleet Signals Officer (naval)

F Sp flash spotting

FSR Field Service Regulations

FSRA Federal Sewage Research Association

FSRC Federal Surplus Relief Corporation

FSS Fellow of the Statistical Society

FSSc A Fellow of the Society of Science and Art of London

FS Sec Field Security Section

FSSI Fellow of the Statistical Society of Ireland

FSSU Federated Superannuation Scheme for Universities

f st forged steel

FST First National Stores (NYSE)

FSTI Formed Steel Tube Institute

F Supp Federal Supplement (legal)

FSWA Federation of Sewage Works Associations

FSWMA Fine and Specialty Wire Manufacturers Association

FSWO Financial Secretary to the War Office

FSWX Flamingo Water Company (private car rr mark)

FSX Fryer & Stillman, Inc., Denver, Colorado (private car rr mark)

f t full terms; fume tight

ft faint; feint (account book ruling); flat (paper); foot or feet; fort; fortified; foretop; let it be made (fiat—Latin) (pharmacy)

ft² square foot

ft³ cubic foot (feet)

FT feet, foot, or firing table (US Army); Freeport Sulphur Company (NYSE); French Togoland (Africa)

f & t fire and theft (insurance)

FTA Federation of Tax Administrators; Food Tray Association; Future Teachers of America

FTAAWUA Food, Tobacco, Agricultural & Allied Workers Union of America

FTB Fleet Torpedo Bomber; Freight Tariff Bureau

ft b m feet board measure (lumber)

ft-c foot-candle

FTC Federal Trade Commission; Federal Trade Zones Board; Freight Traffic Committee

ft & c feint and cash (account books)
FTCD Fellow of Trinity College, Dublin
FTCL Fellow of Trinity College of Music, London
F T C M Fellow Toronto College of Music
FTCX Frazier Brokerage Company (private car rr mark)
ftd fortified
FTD Florists' Telegraph Delivery; Freight Traffic Department
FTDA Florists Telegraph Delivery Association
FTF Fur Trade Foundation
ftg filting; footing
FTH Firth Carpet Company (NYSE)
F3c Fireman Third Class (US Navy)
fthm fathom
FTI Facing Tile Institute; Fellow of the Textile Institute
ft-l foot-lambert
FTL Flying Tiger Lines, Inc.; full truck loads (railway)
ft-lb foot-pound
FTLX Fagan Tank Line (private car rr mark)
FTM Freight Traffic Manager; frequency time modulation
ft/min feet per minute
ftn fortification
FTNS field trains (US Army)
FTO Fleet Torpedo Officer
ft pulv subtil make a fine powder (*fiat pulvis subtilis*—Latin) (pharmacy)
ftr fitter
FTR fighter (US Army); Fruehauf Trailer Company (NYSE)
FTS Forged Tool Society
ft-sec foot-second
ft/sec feet per second
ft s m feet surface measure (lumber)
ft-tn foot-ton
FTW free trade wharf

FTX Frontier Tank Car Company, Inc. (private car rr mark)
FTZ Federal Trade Zone
fu frame unprotected (insurance)
FU Federal Union; Fordham University; Furman University
FUA Farm Underwriters Association
FUM fumigate (US Army)
FUND International Monetary Fund
fu p fusion point
f up follow up
FUPOSAT follow-up on supply action taken (US Army)
fur furlong; furnished; further
FURN furnish, furniture (US Army)
furng furnishing
furr furrier; further
Fus Fusilier
FuSf to be continued and concluded (*Fortsetzung und Schluss folgen*— German)
fut future; futures (exchange)
FUW Federation of University Women
f v on the back of the page (*folio verso*—Latin)
fvda esteemed (*favorecida*—Spanish)
FVPA Flet Veneer Products Association
f w face width (gears); full or card weight pipe (plumbing)
FW Field Worship (military); Focke-Wulf (German airplane); Fresh Water; full weight
F&W feeding and watering (shipping)
FWA Factories and Workshops Act; Federal Works Administration; Free World Association
FWAA Football Writers Association of America
fwb four-wheel brake; free-wheel bicycle; front wheel brakes;
FWB Free-Will Baptists
FWC Foster Wheeler Corporation

(NYSE)
FWCC Friends' World Committee for Consultation
f&w chg feeding and watering charge (transportation)
fwd fresh water damage (shpg); four-wheel drive; forward
FWD Four Wheel Drive Auto Company (NYSE)
FW&D Fort Worth and Denver Railway Company (rr mark)
FWDA Federal Wholesale Druggists Association
FW&DC Fort Worth and Denver City Railway Company
fwdg forwarding
fwdr forwarder
FWDX Fort Worth—Denver (private car rr mark)
FWO Fleet Wireless Officer
FWSAB Federation of Women shareholders in American Business
FWT fair wear and tear (US Army)
fx foreign exchange
fxle forecastle (naval)
FY Fiscal year (US Army)
FYK First York Corporation (common stock) (ASE)
FYKPr First York Corporation ($2 Div. Pfd.) (ASE)
FYP Five-year Plan; Four-year Plan
Fys physics (*Fysik*—German)
fz accented (*forzando*—Italian) (music)
Fz Franz
FZ Fitz Simons & Connell D. & Dock (NYSE)
FZA Fellow of the Zoological Academy; Fitzsimmons Stores, Ltd., CI A (NYSE)
FZS Fellow of the Zoological Society
FZS Scot Fellow Zoological Society of Scotland

G

g acceleration of gravity; center of gravity; game; gage; gelding; general intelligence (psychology); gold; good; gram; gross; guide; guinea; gulf; gynoeicium; specific gravity conductance
G Gains; German; Germanic; Greyhound Corporation (NYSE); Guineas Gulf; Gunnery (naval)
(G) Air Gunner Officer; Genitourinary [Specialist]
g/ cheque (*giro*—Spanish)

G-1 personnel and administration (US Army)
G-2 intelligence (US Army)
G-3 operations and training (US Army)
G-4 logistics (supply) (US Army)
Ga gallium; Georgia
GA Gamma Alpha (society); Garrison Adjutant; General Aircraft Limited; General Assembly (Church of Scotland); Geographical Association; Geologists' Association; Georgia Railroad (rr mark); Glen

Alden Coal Company (NYSE); Golfing Association; Government Actuary; Graduate in Agriculture; grate area; Group Adviser; Gunmakers' Association; Gypsum Association
G/A general average (insurance)
GAAWD Gunnery and Anti-Aircraft Warfare Division
GAC Gamewell Company (NYSE); Gamma Alpha Chi (society)
GACL Guernsey Aero Club Limited

G/A con General Average contribution (insurance)
GAD Government Actuary's Department; Guards' Armoured Division
Ga Dec Georgia Decisions (legal)
G/A dep general average deposit (insurance)
GAE General Air Express
Gael. Gaelic
GAEX General American—Evans Company (private car rr mark)
g a h games at home
GAHS Galway Archaeological and Historical Society
GAI Gair (Robert) Company, Inc. (NYSE)
GAJ Guild of Agricultural Journalists
gal. gallon (pl. gals.); general (général—French)
Gal. Gallison's Reports (legal); Galway (Ireland); Galatians (Biblical); Galen
GAL Gdynia-America Line; General Aircraft Limited; Guinea Airways Ltd.
gal. cap. gallon capacity
Gall. Gallison's Reports (legal)
galv galvanic; galvanism; galvanized
galv I galvanized iron
Galw Galway
gam gamut
Gam Gamaliel; Gambia
GAM General American Investors Company (NYSE)
GAMP General Administration Ministry of Pensions
GAMX General American Transportation de Mexico (private car rr mark)
GAO General Accounting Office
goof gummed all over flap (of envelopes)
GAP Great Atlantic & Pac. Tea (NYSE)
GAPAN Guild of Air Pilots and Navigators of Great Britain
GAPCE General Assembly of the Presbyterian Church of England
GAP Pr Great Atlantic & Pacific Tea Co. of Amer. (Md.) (7% 1st Pfd.) (ASE)
gar garage
GAR garrison (US Army); Garrett Corporation (NYSE); Grand Army of the Republic; Group Advisory Representative
G Arch. Graduate in Architecture
Gard N.Y. Rept Gardenier's New York Reporter (legal)
garg gargle (gargarisma—Latin) (pharmacy)
GARIOA Government and Relief in Occupied Areas
GARX General American Refriger-

ator Express Company (private car rr mark)
GAS gasoline (US Army)
gas. ftr gas fitter
gas. & sc general average, salvage, and special charges (insurance)
Gast Gaston
GASX General American Stock Express (private car rr mark)
GAT Greenwich Apparent Time
GATT General Agreement on Tariffs and Trade
GATX General American Tank Line (private car rr mark)
G Aud General Auditor
GAUFCC General Assembly of Unitarian and Free Christian Churches
Gaul. Gaulish
GAWA German-American Writers' Association
GAWX General Aniline & Film Corporation, General Aniline Works Division (private car rr mark)
gaz gazette; gazetted; gazetteer
g b glider bomb; gold bonds; guide book
GB Gaumont-British; Granby Consolidated (NYSE); Great Britain; gunboat (naval); Gun-Bus (RAF)
GBA Governing Bodies Association
GBBA Glass Bottle Blowers Association
GBC General Board of Control; Greif Brothers Cooperage (NYSE)
GBCW Governing Body of the Church in Wales
GBD General Builders Supply (NYSE)
GBD Pr General Builders Supply Corp. (5% Conv. Pfd.) (ASE)
gbe gilt bevelled edges (bookbinding)
GBE Knight (or Dame) Grand Cross of the Order of the British Empire
GBFX Green Bay Food Company (private car rr mark)
GBG General Baking Company (NYSE); Guernsey (IDP)
GB&I Great Britain and Ireland
GBIB Gorsedd of Bards of the Isle of Britain
GBJ Jersey (IDP)
GB/L Government bill of lading (US Army)
GBL Goebel Brewing Company (NYSE)
GBM Isle of Man (IDP)
GBMA Golf Ball Manufacturers Association
g b o goods in bad order
gbr usual (gebräuchlich—German)
GBS George Bernard Shaw; Government Bureau of Standards
GBSNCA Greater Blouse, Skirt, and Neckwear Contractors Association

GBSX Great Bear Spring Company (private car rr mark)
GBT Gilbert (A.C.) Company (NYSE)
GBW Green Bay & Western Railroad Company (NYSE)
GBX General Box Company (NYSE)
GBY Malta (IDP)
GBZ Gibraltar (IDP)
GC General Candy Corporation (NYSE); Gentleman Cadet; George Cross; Goldsmiths' College; Gold Coast; Golf Club; Good Conduct; Goucher College; Government Chemist; Grand Chancellor; Grand Chaplain; Grand Chapter; Grand Conductor; Grand Cross; Greek Church; Greene Committee (mining); Grinnell College; Group Captain (RAF); gun carriage; gun control; gun cotton; [Knight] Grand Cross; [Knight] Grand Commander; great circle
GCA Garden Club of America; General Claim Agent; General Contractors' Association; Geneva Convention Act; ground control approach
g-cal gram-calorie
G Capt Group Captain (RAF)
GCB General Council of the Bar; Giro Central Bank (German Savings Bank); Knight Grand Cross of the Order of the Bath
GCBS General Council of British Shipping
GCC General Commission on Chaplains; General Council of Congress; Girton College, Cambridge; Gonville and Caius College (Cambridge)
GCCA Greater Clothing Contractors Association
GCCX Gaylord Container Corporation (private car rr mark)
g c d greatest common divisor (mathematics)
GCD Great Circle Distance
gcf greatest common factor (mathematics)
GCFLH Grand Cross of the French Legion of Honour
GCG Grand Captain General; Grand Captain Guard
GCH [Knight] Grand Cross of Hanover
G Ch The Gardeners' Chronicle
GCI Ground Control Interception (radar)
GCIAA Granite Cutters International Association of America
GCIB German Commercial Information Bureau
GCIE Knight Grand Commander of the Order of the Indian Empire
GCLH Knight Grand Cross of the

Legion of Honour; Grand Chancellor of the Legion of Honor (*Grand Chancelier de la Legion D'Honneur*—French)

GCLX Glaser, Crandell Company (private car rr mark)

gcm greatest common measure

GCM General Court-Martial

GCMG Knight Grand Cross of the Order of St. Michael and St. George

GCMI Glass Container Manufacturers Institute

GCN Greenwich Civil Noon (navigation)

GCNVF Gold Coast Naval Volunteer Force

GCO Grand Chapter of Officers; Gun Control Officer (naval)

G Com Grand Commander; Grand Commandery

G Cp Graduate in Chiropody

GCPA Gas Companies' Protection Association

GCR General Cigar Company (NYSE)

GCS Game Conservatory Society; Green Cross Society

GC&SF Gulf, Colorado and Sante Fe Railway Company

GC & TPA Garden Cities and Town Planning Association

GCSG Knight Grand Cross of St. Gregory the Great

GCSI Knight Grand Commander of the Order of the Star of India; Game Conservation Society, Inc

GCSS Knight Grand Cross of St. Sylvester

GC St J Bailiff (or Dame) Grand Cross of the Order of St. John of Jerusalem

GCT general classification test (US Army); Greenwich civil time

GCU Glass Cutters' Union

GCUS Governors' Conference of the United States

GCVO Knight Grand Cross of the Royal Victorian Order

GCW Garden City Western Railway Company (rr mark)

GCX General Chemical Division, Allied Chemical & Dye Corporation (private car rr mark)

gd good delivery; gravimetric density; granddaughter; good; ground; guard (railway)

Gd Gadolinum (chemistry)

GD gave delivery; General Department; general discharge (US Army); General Duties (Forces); Graduate in Divinity; Grand Deacon (freemasonry); Grand Duchess; Grand Duchy; Grand Duke; Guild of Designers

g-d gravimetric density

G&D Galvanized and dipped (plumbing)

Gd A gauged arch (building)

GDA gun defended area (US Army)

GDB General Duties Branch (RAF)

GDC Gardner-Denver Company (NYSE); Governmental Defense Council; Grand Director of Ceremonies (freemasonry)

g d e gilt deckled edge (stationery); large training division (*grande division d'ecole*—French)

gde vit great speed (*grande vitesse*—French)

GDHSE guardhouse (US Army)

Gdns gardens; guardians

GDPX Gas del Pacifico (private car rr mark)

gds goods

GDS Glenmore Distilleries, Cl B (NYSE)

GDS B Glenmore Distilleries Co. ("B" Com) (ASE)

Gdsm Guardsman

GDY General Dynamics Corporation (NYSE)

ge gilt-edged (finish); gilt edges; (bookbinding); gauge; weight unit (*gewichtseinheit*—German)

GE Garrison Engineer; General Election; General Electric Company (NYSE); Ground Engineer

Ge germanium (chemistry)

geb born (*geboren*—German); bound (*gebunden*—German) (bookbinding)

GEB General Education Board

Gebr Brothers (*Gebroeders*—Dutch)

GEC General Electric Company

ged gedämpft (music)

gef kindly (*gefälligst*—German)

GEG Gamma Eta Gamma (fraternity)

geg against (*gegen*—German)

gegr founded (*gegründet*—German)

Geh contents (*Gehatt*—German); Privy Councillor (*Geheimrat*—German)

gek characterized (*gekennzeichnet*—German)

GEL Gellman Manufacturing Company (NYSE)

gem geminate

Gem Gemini (constellation)

gen gender; general; generic; genealogy; genetics; genital; genitive (grammar); genus

Gen General; Genesis (Biblical); Geneva

GEN General Telephone Corporation (NYSE)

Gen Aud General Auditor

gen av general average (marine insurance)

geneal genealogical; genealogy

Gen Hosp General Hospital

Gen Led General Ledger

Gen Man General Manager

genn January (*gennaie*—Italian)

GENR generate (US Army)

Gen St General Statutes (legal)

Gen Supt General Superintendent

gent gentleman

geny generally

Geo George; Georgia

GEO Central of Georgia Railway (NYSE)

geod geodesy; geodetic

Geod E Geodetic Engineer

Geo Dec Georgia Decisions (legal)

Geof Geoffrey

geog geographical; geographic

Geogr Rev Geographical Review

geol geologist; geology

Geol E Geological Engineer

Geo LJ Georgetown Law Journal

geom geometer; geometric; geometry

geophys geophysical; geophysics

ger gerund; gerundive (grammar)

Ger Germany; Gertrude

GER Gerity-Michigan Corporation (NYSE); Great Eastern Railway

Geref Reformed Calvinist (*Gereformeerde*—Dutch)

Ger pat. German patent

ges entire (*gesamt*—German); registered trade-mark (*gesetzlich geschützt*—German)

Ges association (*Gesellschaft*—German)

GES General and Estimates Section; gilt-edged securities; Gloucestershire Engineering Society

Gesch history (*Geschichte*—German)

Ges Gesch patented (*gesetzlich geschützt*—German)

gest died (*gestorben*—German)

GESTAPO Nazi Secret Police (*Geheime Staatspolizei*—German)

Gew weight (*Gewicht*—German)

gewöhnl usually (*gewöhnlich*—German)

Geww weights (*Gewichte*—German)

GEX General Electric Company (private car rr mark)

GEZ State Publishing House (*Gosudarstvennoe Knigoizdatelstvo*—Russian)

GF boys and girls (*garçons et filles*—French); French Guides (*Guides de France*—French); General Foods Corporation (NYSE); Government Form (shipping); Grand Fleet; Grazing Farm; Grant Foundation; Guggenheim Foundation

G & F Georgia & Florida Railroad (rr mark)

g f a good fair average

GFA General Freight Agent; Grain Futures Administration
GFD General Freight Department
GFDNA Grain and Feed Dealers National Association
GFG Governor's Foot Guard
GFM Government furnished material (US Army)
GFN General Finance Corporation (NYSE)
GFN A Pr General Finance Corporation (5% Pfd. "A") (ASE)
GFO General Freight Office; Gulf, Mobile & Ohio Railroad (NYSE)
GFP German Secret Police (*Geheime Feldpolizei*—German)
GFR German Federal Republic
GFS Girls' Friendly Society
GFT Greenfield Tap & Die Corporation (NYSE)
GFTU General Federation of Trade Unions
GFWC General Federation of Women's Clubs
GG Gamma Globulin (polio treatment); Girls' Guildry; Grenadier Guards; Ground Gunner (RAF)
g g d great granddaughter
GGMA Glassine and Greaseproof Manufacturers Association
GGNI Governor General of Northern Ireland
g gr great gross
g g s great grandson
GGS German General Staff
G/h gilt head
gh grazing homestead
GH general hospital (use in combination only) (US Army); Gibraltar to Hamburg (shipping)
GHA Greenwich hour angle
GHC German High Command
GHG Governor's Horse Guard
GHH Helme (Geo. W.) Company (NYSE)
GH&H Galveston, Houston and Henderson Railroad Company (rr mark)
GHM Gotham Hosiery Company Inc (NYSE)
GHP Grand High Priest
GHQ General Headquarters
GHV Gleaner Harvester Corporation (NYSE)
gl gill (measure)
GI gastrointestinal; general inducted (U.S. military); general issue; Gideons International; Gimbel Brothers, Inc (NYSE); (Royal) Glasgow Institute of Fine Arts; Government issue; Gunner Instructor
GIA Garuda Indonesian Airways Ltd; Gemological Institute of America; Goodwill Industries of

America; Gummed Industries Association
Gib Gibraltar
GIB Gibson Refrigerator Company (NYSE)
GIBAIR Gibraltar Airways Ltd
Gibr Gibraltar
GI Fire E Graduate of the Institution of Fire Engineers
GIFS Gray Iron Founders Society
Gilb Gilbert
Gilb CP Gilbert's Common Pleas
Gilp Gilpin's United States District Court Reports (legal)
GI Mech E Graduate of the Institution of Mechanical Engineers
Gin and It. Gin and Italian [Vermouth]
G in N Graduate in Nursing
GIO Gas Identification Officer; Guild of Insurance Officials
GIP Great Indian Peninsular (Railway)
gir girder
Gir Gironde (French department)
GIS General Mills, Inc (NYSE); Greater India Society; Guides' International Service
g i t grooved for iron tongues
Giun junior (*Giuniore*—Italian)
GJC Grand Junction Canal
GJD Grand Junior Deacon (freemasonry)
Gk Greek
GK General Cable Corporation (NYSE); unlimited partnership (*Gomei Kaisha*—Japanese)
GKA Garter King of Arms
GKC Gilbert Keith Chesterton
gl gill; glass; glory (*gloria*—Latin); gloss; old (*gammel*—Danish)
g/l grams per liter
Gl glucinum
GL Government Laboratories; Graduate in Law; Grand Lodge (freemasonry); Great Lakes Dredge and Dock Company (NYSE); Ground level; Gun Layer; Gun Licence
GLA General Longshoremen's Association
Glamorg Glamorganshire (county in Wales)
Glas Glasgow
GLB Globe-Union, Inc (NYSE)
GLC Gaylord Container Corporation (NYSE)
GLCC Gas Light and Coke Company
gld guild
GLD Gladding, McBean & Company (NYSE)
GLE General Electric, Ltd. (NYSE)
GLER General Electric Co. Ltd. (ASE)
GLI General Time Corporation

(NYSE); glider (US Army)
GLK Great Lakes Oil & Chemical (NYSE)
GLMMM Grand Lodge of Mark Master Masons (freemasonry)
GLN Glidden Company (NYSE)
GLO ground liaison officer (US Army)
gloss glossary
Glos Gloucester; Gloucestershire (English county)
GLP General Fireproofing (NYSE)
GLS Gypsy Lore Society; Grand Lodge of Scotland (freemasonry)
GLSA General Live Stock Agent
GLSTM Graduate of the London School of Tropical Medicine
GLSX Great Lakes Steel Corporation (private car rr mark)
GLT Greetings Letter Telegram (Empire Social Telegram)
GLW Corning Glass Works (NYSE)
GLZ General Bronze Corporation (NYSE)
gm gram
g m general merchandise; general mortgage; grade marked (lumber)
GM General Manager; General Motors; Geological Museum; George Medal; Gold Medallist; Grand Master (freemasonry); gun metal; guided missile (US Army)
GMA Grocery Manufacturers of America
GMAA Gold Mining Association of America
GMAC General Motors Acceptance Corporation
G Man Government man
GMB Good merchantable brand; Grand Master Order of the Bath
GMBE Grand Master of the Order of the British Empire
GmbH Limited Liability Company (*Gesellschaft mit beschränkter Haftung*—Germany)
Gmc Germanic
GMC General Medical Council; Gray Manufacturing Company (NYSE)
GMD geometric mean distance
GMF Glass Manufacturers' Federation; Goodman Manufacturing (NYSE)
GM1C Gunner's Mate First Class (US Navy)
GMIE Grand Master of the Order of the Indian Empire
GMITPM Gorgas Memorial Institute of Tropical and Preventive Medicine
GMKP Grand Master of the Knights of St. Patrick
GML Gypsum Lime & Alabastine, Canada Ltd. (ASE)

GMMG Grand Master of the Order of St. Michael and St. George

GM&NRR Gulf, Mobile & Northern Railroad Company

GMO Gorham Manufacturing Company (NYSE)

GM&O Gulf, Mobile and Ohio Railroad Company (rr mark)

GMP Grand Master of the Order of St. Patrick

GMPR General Maximum Price Regulation

g m q good marketable quality

GMS Gospel Missionary Society

GM2C Gunner's Mate Second Class (US Navy)

GMSI General Milk Sales, Inc; Grand Master of the Order of the Star of India

GMT General American Trans (NYSE); Greenwich mean time; Greenwich meridian time

GM3C Gunner's Mate Third Class (US Navy)

GMU Gospel Missionary Union

g m v gram-molecular volume

GMW General Metal Workers

gn guinea

Gn General (Genel—Turkish)

GN Graduate Nurse; Great Northern Railway (NYSE)

GNB Gould-National Batteries (NYSE)

GNCEW General Nursing Council of England and Wales

gnd ground

GNF Gannett Newspaper Foundation

GNH Grand National Hunt (sport)

GNI Great Northern Iron Ore, (NYSE)

GN of I (R) Great Northern Railway of Ireland

GNIB German Newspaper Information Bureau

G-NP chemical agent, nonpersistent (US Army)

gnr gunner (military)

GNR Great Northern Railway

gns guineas

GNT Government land grant (bonds)

GNTC Girls' Naval Training Corps

GNY General Alloys Company (NYSE)

GNYE Greater New York Fund

GO General Officer; General Order; great organ (music); Group Officer; (WAAF); Grumman Aircraft Engineering (NYSE); Gulf Oil Corporation (NYSE); gummed only (of envelopes)

g o b good ordinary bonds; good ordinary brand

GOB Gobel (Adolf), Inc (NYSE)

gobo government (gobierno— Spanish)

gobr governor (gobernador— Spanish)

GOC General Officer Commanding; General Operating Committee; Greek Orthodox Church

GOC-in-C General Officer Commanding-in-Chief

GOL Goldblatt Brothers, Inc (NYSE)

GOM Grand Old Man (William Ewart Gladstone)

Gonz Gonzalez

GOP Girls' Own Paper; Grand Old Party (Republican)

GOPX Gas-Oil Products, Inc (private car rr mark)

Gord H Gordon Highlanders

g org grand-orgue (music)

G Org Grand Organist (freemasonry)

GOS Gossard (H.W.) Company (NYSE)

Goth. Gothic

GOU General Outdoor Advertising (NYSE)

gov government; governmental

Gov Governor

Gov-Gen Governor-General

Gov Pr Off. Government Printing Office

GOW Georgia Power Company (NYSE)

GOWVIPr Georgia Power Co. ($6 Pfd) (ASE)

GOX Godchaux Sugars, Inc (NYSE)

GOX A Godchaux Sugars, Inc. ("A" Stk) (ASE)

GOX B Godchaux Sugars, Inc ("B" Stk.) (ASE)

GOX Pr Godchaux Sugars, Inc. ($4.50 Pr. Pfd) (ASE)

g p galley proofs (printing); grateful patient; general practitioner; great primer

gp group

GP Gallup poll; general paralysis; general practitioner; general purpose; German patent; glory be to the Father (Gloria Patri—Latin); Graduate in Pharmacy; great primer (type)

G-P chemical agent, persistent (US Army)

GPA Alderney (IDP); General Passenger Agent; Glycerine Producers Association

GPB Gamma Phi Beta (sorority)

Gp C Group Captain (RAF)

GPC Gatineau Power Company (NYSE); General Purposes Committee

Gp Comdr Group Commander (RAF)

GPCT George Peabody College for Teachers

GPCX General Petroleum Corporation (private car rr mark)

gpd gallons per day; grams per denier

GPD General Passenger Department

Gp E Geophysical Engineer

GPEX General American–Pfaudler Corporation (rr mark)

gph gallons per hour

G Ph Graduate in Pharmacy

GPH General Acceptance Corporation (NYSE)

GPI general paralysis of the insane

GPKT Grand Priory of the Knights of the Temple

GPLD government property, lost or damaged (US Army)

gpm gallons per minute

GPM Grand Past Master (freemasonry)

GPMA Gas Pump Manufacturers Association; Groundwood Paper Manufacturers Association

GPMM Grain Processing Machinery Manufacturers

GPN General Paint Corporation (NYSE)

GPO General Post Office; Government Printing Office

GPOA Guild of Prescription Opticians of America

GPP Great Northern Paper Company (ASE)

GP Pr Graham–Paige Corp. (5% Conv. Pfd) (ASE)

GPR to the genius of the Roman people (Genio Populi Romani— Latin); Glider Pilot Regiment

gps gallons per second

GPT General Portland Cement (NYSE)

GPU Government Political Organization (Soviet Russian secret state police) (Gosudarstvennoe Politicheskoe Upravlenie— Russian)

G Pur Grand Pursuivant (freemasonry)

GPV General Public Service (NYSE)

GPVEH general purpose vehicle (US Army)

GPV VI Pr General Public Service Corp. ($6 Pfd) (ASE)

GPW Green Mountain Power Corporation (ASE)

GPX Georgia Pine Turpentine Co. Division of The Glidden Company (private car rr mark); Glidden Company, The Naval Stores Division (private car rr mark)

GPY General Plywood Corporation (NYSE)

GPY Pr General Plywood Corp. (5% Conv. Pfd.) (ASE)

GQG General Headquarters (Grand Quartier-Général—French)

GQs General Quarters (naval)

gr grain; grammar; grammarian;

grammatically; gramme; grand; gravity; great; grind; groschen; gross

Gr grade; Grand (title); Granenhorst (entomology); gray (botany); greater; Grecian; Greece; Greek; Gunner

GR General Reconnaissance; General Regulations; General Reserve; Gloucestershire Regiment; Gold Reserve; Grand Recorder; Grand Registrar; Green Room; King George (*Georgius Rex*—Latin); King William (*Gulielmus Rex*—Latin); Republican Guard (*Garde Républicaine*—French); General Reserve (US Army); Goodrich (B.F.) Company (NYSE); Grasse River Railroad Corporation (rr mark); Greece (IDP)

G/R grooved roofing (lumber)

GRA Governmental Research Association

grad graduate; graduated

Grad IAE Graduate Institution of Automobile Engineers

gram. grammar; grammatical

gram. sch grammar school

gran granary; granular; granulated

grat gratification; gratify

Grat Grattan's Virginia Reports (legal)

grav gravure

graz gracefully (*grazioso*—Italian) (music)

GRB Grayson-Robinson Stores, Inc. (NYSE)

Gr Brit Great Britain

Grc Greece

GRC Granite City Steel Company (NYSE); General Railway Classification; Greek Red Cross

Gr Ca Grant's Cases (legal)

Gr Capt Group Captain (RAF)

GRCM Graduate of the Royal College of Music

GRCX Gulf Oil Corporation (private car rr mark)

grd ground; guaranteed

Gr D Grand Duchess; Grand Duchy; Grand Duke

GRD Gray Drug Stores, Inc. (NYSE)

grdns guardians

GRE Greenland (US Navy)

G Reg Grand Registrar (freemasonry)

Greg Gregory

Gren Grenada

Gren Gds Grenadier Guards

GRF Golden Rule Foundation

gr gro great gross

GRH Greer Hydraulics, Inc. (NYSE)

g r i guaranteed retirement income (insurance)

GRI George, King and Emperor (*Georgius Rex Imperator*—Latin)

Grif L Reg Griffith's Law Register, (legal)

GRL General Instrument Corporation (NYSE)

grm grammar; gramme

GRMN Grumman (aircraft)

GRN Green (H.L.) Company, Inc. (NYSE)

Grnld Greenland

gro grocer; gross; group

GRO General Register Office; General Routine Orders; Grocery Store Products Company (NYSE)

GROBDM General Register Office for Births, Deaths and Marriages

gross t gross tonnage

Grot Grotius

Gr Prod grain products

GRR Gabriel Company (NYSE)

GRREG graves registration (US Army)

Gr Rev Greek Revival

grs grains; grandson

GRS General Railway Signal (NYSE); General Reconnaissance School

GRSM Graduate of the Royal Schools of Music (London)

grs t gross tons

GRSX National Car Company (private car rr mark)

gr r t gross register tonnage

gr t m gross ton mile

Grtn Gärtner (botany)

Gru Grus (constellation); General Recruiting Unit

GRUCOM Group Commander (US Navy)

Grudz December (*Grudzién*—Polish)

GRV Grand Rapids Varnish Corporation (NYSE)

gr wt gross weight

GRX General Refractories Company (NYSE)

GRYX Grace Co., John H. (private car rr mark)

gs gauss; grandson; guineas; German silver

g s ground speed (aviation)

GS Bureau of General Services (UN Secretariat); General Secretary; General Service; General Staff (US Army); general strike; Geographical Society; Geological Survey; Georgia State College; Gillette Company (NYSE); Gold Standard; Golfing Society; government stock; Grammar School; Grand Scribe (freemasonry); Grand Secretary (freemasonry); Grand Sentinel (freemasonry); Grand Sentry (freemasonry); Grand Steward (freemasonry); ground speed

G/S general support (US Army)

GSA Genetics Society of America; Geological Society of America; General Services Administration; Girl Scouts of America

GSB Grand Standard Bearer; Grand Sword Bearer (freemasonry)

GSBA Grand Street Boys Association

GSC General Staff Corps (US Army); Grain Stabilization Corporation; Gymnasium Seating Council

GSCX Gulf States Creosoting Company (private car rr mark)

GSD Gamma Sigma Delta (fraternity); Goodall-Sanford, Inc. (NYSE); Grand Senior Deacon (freemasonry)

GSE Gamma Sigma Epsilon (society); Geological Society of Edinburgh

G Sec Grand Secretary (freemasonry)

GSF Gun and Shell Factory (military)

GS&F Georgia Southern and Florida Railway Company

GSFC General Superintendent of Freight Claims

GSGB Geological Survey of Great Britain

GSH General Shoe Corporation (NYSE); glutathione

GSI Geological Survey of India

G&SI Gulf and Ship Island Railroad Company

GSIO General Staff Interpreter Officer (military)

GSK Gamble-Skogmo, Inc. (NYSE)

GSL Geological Society of London

gsm good sound marketable

GSM Garrison Sergeant Major; Geological Survey and Museum; Golden State Inc. (NYSE); Gold Star Mothers; Guildhall School of Music

GSN(C) General Steam Navigation (Company)

GSO General Staff Officer

GSP good service pension

GSR Great Southern Railway (Erie)

GSS general service schools (US Army)

GSSX Goar's Service & Supply (private car rr mark)

Gst Gustave; Gustavus

GST Georgia School of Technology; Gilchrist Company (NYSE); Greenwich Sidereal time (navigation)

GSU general signals use

GSUSA General Staff, United States Army

GSW General Steel Wares, Ltd. (NYSE); Great Western Sugar Company (NYSE); gunshot wound

G&SWR Glasgow and South-Western Railway

GS&WR Great Southern and Western

Railway (Ireland)
GSX Gold & Stock Telegraph Company (NYSE)
gt drop (gutta—pharmacy); gilt; great; gun turret (military); gutta
g t gas-tight; gilt top (bookbinding); gross ton (shipping)
GT Good Templar; Goodyear Tire & Rubber (NYSE); Grand Tiler (freemasonry); Grand Treasurer (freemasonry); Greetings Telegram; gross ton; part by weight (Gewichtsteil—German)
GTA graphic training aid (US Army)
Gt Br Great Britain
g t c good till canceled or countermanded (brokerage)
gtd guaranteed
GTD General Traffic Department
GTE General Precision Equipment (NYSE)
gt gr great gross
Gth Gunther
g t m good this month
GTM General Traffic Manager
GTMO Guantanamo (US Navy)
GTREC Goodyear Tire and Rubber Export Company
GT Ry Grand Trunk Railway System
GTS Guantanamo Sugar Company (NYSE)
gtt drops (guttae—pharmacy)
GTU Gulf States Utilities Company

(NYSE)
g t w good this week
GTW Grand Trunk Western Railroad Company (rr mark)
GTY Grant (W.T.) Company (NYSE)
GU Compania Guatemalteca de Aviacion; General Realty & Utilities (NYSE); genitourinary; Georgetown University; Gonzaga University
G&U Grafton & Upton Railroad Company (rr mark)
Guad Guadeloupe
Guan Guanajuato
guar guarantee; guarantor
Guat Guatemala
Guer Guerrero
Gui Guiana
gun. gunner; gunnery
GUT A Guantanamo & Western Railroad Company (ASE)
gutt drop or drops (gutta or guttae —Latin) (pharmacy)
g u v correct and complete (gerecht und vollkommen—German)
GUX Grand Union Company (NYSE)
GUY General Public Utilities (NYSE)
g v gravimetric volume
GV Goldfield Consol. Mines (NYSE)
GVZ Pr General Outdoor Advertising Co. Inc. (6% Pfd.)

GWB Griesedieck Western Brewery (NYSE)
GWBX Griesedieck Western Brewery Company (private car rr mark)
GWD Gar Wood Industries, Inc (NYSE)
GWEX Western Division, The Dow Chemical Company (private car rr mark)
GWF Galveston Wharves (private car rr mark)
GWI Grinding Wheel Institute
GWMC Galvanized Ware Manufacturers Council
GWP Government White Paper
GWR Great Western Railway
GWRy of Can Great Western Railway of Canada
GWSF Georgia Warm Springs Foundation
GWU George Washington University
GWVA Great War Veterans' Association (Canada)
GXP Georgia-Pacific Plywood Company (NYSE)
GY General Tire & Rubber Company (NYSE)
GYK Giant Yellowknife Gold Mines (NYSE)
gym gymnasium; gymnastic
GYN Gynecology
gynecol gynecological, gynecology

H

h hail; harbor; hard; hardness; has; have; headquarters; heat; h [beam]; height; high; hits (baseball); horse; hot; hour (heure—French); house; hull; hundred; husband; hydrant; hydraulics; intensity of magnetic field
H Henry; Hupp Corporation (NYSE); hydrogen
H¹ protium
H¹⁺ proton
H² heavy hydrogen
H³ tritium
H° hydrogen in concentration
h a heir apparent; helix angle (gears); this year (hoc anno— Latin); this year's (hujus anni— Latin)
HA Hautes-Alpes (French department); Headmasters Association; Headmistresses' Association; Heavy Artillery; High Angle (gunnery); Historical Association; Hockey Association; Holophane Company, Inc (NYSE); Horse Artil-

lery; hour angle (navigation)
HAA Heavy anti-aircraft
hab habitation; he lives (habitat— l.atin)
Hab Habakkuk (Biblical)
HAB high-altitude bombing
hab corp produce the body (habeas corpus—Latin)
hab fac poss that you give him possession (habere facias possessionem—Latin)
habit. habitat
habt let him have (habeat—Latin) (pharmacy)
HAC Honourable Artillery Company; House Appropriations Committee (Congress)
HACC Holland-American Chamber of Commerce
hack. hackney
hac noct tonight (hac nocte—Latin) (pharmacy)
HACX Canada Packers Ltd (private car rr mark)
HA or D Havre, Antwerp or Dun-

kerque (grain trade)
HAF Helms Athletic Foundation
Hag Haggai (Bible)
HAG hold for arrival of goods
Hai Haiti
hairdrsr hairdresser
Hal Halifax; halogen
HAL Halliburton Oil Well Cementing (NYSE); Hamburg-America Line; Haupt Abteilungs Leiter (Chief Section Leader—Nazi party, Germany); Hawaiian Airlines, Ltd.
Hal Law Halsted's New Jersey Law Reports (legal)
Hals Halsted's New Jersey Reports (legal)
Ham. Hamlet, Prince of Denmark
HAM Heart of Africa Mission; Hymns Ancient and Modern; heavy automotive maintenance (US Army)
Han Handy's Ohio Reports (legal); Hanover
HANA Helvetia Association of North America
Handelsbol trading company

(*Handelsbolaget*—Swedish)
Handelsges trading company
  (*Handelsgesellschaft*—German)
Handelsmij trading company
  (*Handelsmaatschappij*—Dutch)
Handelsver commercial association
  (*Handelsvereeiging*—Dutch)
Hants Hampshire (county in
  England)
ha'p'orth halfpennyworth
h app heir apparent
Har Harold
HAR harbor (US Army); New York
  & Harlem Railroad Company
  (NYSE)
Har & Gill Harris & Gill's Maryland
  Reports (legal)
harm. harmony
Harp Harper's Law Reports (legal)
harps. harpsichord
Hart Hartley's Reports (legal)
Harv Harvard University
Harv L Rev Harvard Law Review
Hask Haskell's United States
  Circuit Court Reports (legal)
HAT Hat Corporation of America
  (NYSE)
HAUC Health and Accident Under-
  writers Conference
hav haversine (mathematics)
HAV Harvard Brewing Company
  (NYSE); Himalayan Aviation Ltd.
Hav PEI Haviland's Reports,
  Prince Edward Island (legal)
Haw Hawaiian (US Navy)
Hawl Cr R Hawley's American
  Criminal Reports (legal)
HAWSEAFRON Hawaiian Sea
  Frontier (US Navy)
HAY Hayes Industries, Inc. (NYSE)
Hay & Haz Hayward & Hazelton
  Circuit Court (legal)
Hayw Haywood's Reports (legal)
haz hazard
Hb haemoglobin
HB half-breadth; hard and black;
  heavy bomber (RAF); hit by ball;
  hollow back (lumber); Humble Oil
  & Refining Company (NYSE)
H & B Humboldt and Bonpland (bot-
  any)
HBA Hoist Builders Association
HBAX Hirsch Bros. & Company
  (private car rr mark)
HBC Hudson's Bay Company
HBCC House Banking and Currency
  Committee (United States)
HBFTB Hair, Bass and Fibre
  Trade Board
H bk hollow back (lumber)
HBK Hathaway Bakeries, Inc
  (NYSE)
HB & K (botany), Humboldt, Bon-
  pland, and Kunth
HBLO Home Base Ledger Office

HBM His (or Her) Britannic Majesty
H-bomb hydrogen bomb
hbr harbor
HBS Halifax Building Society;
  harbor boat service (US Army);
  Henry Bradshaw Society; herring-
  bone strutting (building)
HBSS Hospital Bureau of Standards
  and Supplies
HBSX Haskins Brothers & Company
  (private car rr mark)
H & BT Huntingdon & Broad Top
  Mountain Railroad & Coal Company
  (private car rr mark)
HB&T Houston Belt & Terminal
  Railway Company
H&BV Houston & Brazos Valley
  Railway Company (rr mark)
HBX Hately Brothers Company
  (private car rr mark)
hc hand cut (of envelopes); held
  covered (marine insurance); for
  the sake of honor (*honoris causa*
  —Latin); hot and cold (water)
h & c hot and cold
HC Calumet & Hecla, Inc. (NYSE);
  habitual criminal; Hague Conven-
  tion; Halcyon Club; Hamilton Col-
  lege; Hannibal Connecting Railroad
  Company (rr mark); Harvard College;
  Headmaster Commander; Headmas-
  ters' Conference; Heralds' College;
  High Church; High Commissioner;
  High Court; Hockey Club; Holy
  Communion; Home Counties;
  House Committee; Household
  Cavalry; House of Commons;
  House of Correction; Housing
  Committee; Hunterian Club; out of
  competition (*hors concours*—
  French)
HCA High Conductivity Association;
  Hobby Clubs of America
HCAAS Homeless Children's Aid
  and Adoption Society
hcap handicap
HCC High Commissioner for
  Canada; Holy Cross College;
  Horticultural Co-ordination Com-
  mittee; hydraulic cement concrete
HCCX Hercules Cement Corpora-
  tion (private car rr mark)
HCE here lies buried (*hic conditus*
  —Latin); High Commissioner for
  Eire
HCF highest common factor (mathe-
  matics); Honorary Chaplain to the
  Forces
HCH Hecht Company (NYSE)
HCHI Hand Chain Hoist Institute
HCI Order of the Hashimite Chain
  of Iraq
HCIED High Commissioner for India
  Education Department
HCJ High Court of Justice

HCK Hancock Oil Company (NYSE)
CI A
h c l high cost of living
HCM His Catholic Majesty
HCMTB Hat, Cap and Millinery
  Trade Board
H Com High Commissioner
H Con Res House Concurrent Reso-
  lution (Congress)
hcp handicap
HCP High Commissioner for the
  Philippines
HCPNI Hardware Cloth and Poultry
  Netting Institute
HCPTR helicopter (US Army)
HCR High Chief Ranger (Ancient
  Order of Foresters); High Court
  Reports, India (legal)
HCRNWP High Court Reports,
  Northwest Provinces (legal)
HCS Hallé Concerts Society; Home
  Civil Service; Home Cure Service
HCUSA High Commissioner for the
  Union of South Africa
hd head; hogshead; hydrodome
h d on going to bed (*hora decubitus*
  —Latin) (pharmacy); hard-drawn
  (metallurgy); hearing distance; high
  density (cotton); high pressure
  (*hochdruck*—German); horse drawn;
  hourly difference (navigation)
HD Harbour Defence; Hawaiian De-
  partment; Home Defence; honorable
  discharge; Hudson Bay Mg & Sm
  (NYSE); Husband's Divorce
HDA Hydrographic Department, Admiralty
hdbk handbook
HDC Hawaiian Defense Command
HDI House Dress Institute
hdkf handkerchief
hdlg handling
HDM high-duty metal
HDMA Hardwood Dimension Manufacturers Association
hdn harden
HDN Heyden Chemical Corporation
  (NYSE)
H Doc House Document (Congress)
HDP Hinde & Dauch Paper Company
  (NYSE)
hdqrs headquarters
HDS Horder's, Inc (NYSE)
Hds M Her Majesty (*Hendes Ma-
  jestæt*—Danish)
hdwd hardwood (lumber)
hdwe hardware
HDX Hooker-Detrex Incorporated
  (private car rr mark)
h e hub end (plumbing); this, that is
  (*hic est*—Latin)
He helium
He. Heinkel (German airplane)
HE heat engine; Heinz Endowment;
  high explosive; His Eminence; His

Excellency; Hydraulics Engineer
Heb Hebrews (Bible)
hebdom a week (*hebdomada*—Latin)
(pharmacy)
Hebr Hebrews (Biblical); Hebrides
hect hectare (*hectarea*—Spanish);
hectoliter
Hect Hector
hectog hectogramme
hectol hectoliter
hectom hectometer
HED Headquarters (US Navy)
HEH His Exalted Highness
HEI Heat Exchange Institute
HEIC Honourable East India Company
HEICS Honourable East India Company's Service
heir app heir apparent
heir pres heir presumptive
Heisk Heiskell's Reports (legal)
Hel Helvetia (Switzerland)
HEL Hartford Electric Light Company (NYSE)
Hellen Hellenic; Hellenistic
Hen. Henry
Hen. V; —VIII King Henry V; —VIII
1 Hen. IV, etc. First Part of King Henry IV, etc.
Hen. & Mun Hening & Munford's Virginia Reports (legal)
HEO Higher Executive Officer
HEPC App Hydro-Electric Power Commission approved
HEPX Hydro-Electric Power Commission of Ontario (private car rr mark)
her. heir (*heres*—Latin); heraldry
Her. Heraldry; Hercules
HER Helena Rubenstein, Inc (NYSE)
HER A Helena Rubinstein, Inc (Class "A" Stock) (ASE)
herb. herbarium (botany)
herb. recent. of fresh herbs (*herbarum recentium*—Latin) (medicine)
Herb. Herbert
herds. heirs (*herdeiros*—Portuguese)
hereds heirs (*herederos*—Spanish)
Heref Herefordshire
herpet herpetology
herst manufacture (*herstellung*—German)
Herts Hertfordshire
HERX American Car Corporation (private car rr mark)
HES Hydro Electric Securities Corporation (common stock, ASE)
HEU hydroelectric units
HEW Hewitt-Robins, Inc (NYSE)
hex. hexachord; hexagon; hexagonal
hf half
Hf hafnium
HF Haig's Fund; Hayden Foundation; Haynes Foundation; Heckscher Foundation; high frequency;

Holiday Fellowship; Holy Family;
Holy Father; Home Fleet; Home
Forces; Home Front; Hyde Foundation
HFA Heavy Field Artillery
HFAC House Foreign Affairs Committee
HFARA Honorary Foreign Associate of the Royal Academy
hf-bd half-binding; half-bound; high-frequency band
h f c high-frequency current
HFC Household Finance Corporation (NYSE)
HFCAUS Hatters Fur Cutters Association of the United States
hf cf half-calf
hf cl half cloth binding (books)
HFD Hunt Foods, Inc (NYSE)
HFDF High Frequency Detecting and Finding
hfg heat [of vaporization]
hf h half hard (steel)
HFI Hard Fibres Association
HFIX Hunt Foods, Inc (private car rr mark)
hfm hold for money
hf mor half morocco
HFMRA Honorary Foreign Member of the Royal Academy
HFO Hygrade Food Products Corporation (NYSE)
HFRA Honorary Foreign Member of the Royal Academy
HFSC Home Furnishings Style Council
hfst chapter (*hoofdstuk*—Dutch)
hg hectogram; heliogram
Hg Hugo; mercury
HG *Haute-Garonne* (French department); His (Her) Grace; higher grade; High German; Holy Ghost; Home Guard; Horse Guards
H & G Harris & Gill's Maryland Reports (legal)
HGA Hereditary Grand Almoner (freemasonry); Hobby Guild of America; Hotel Greeters of America
HGCC Household Goods Carriers Conference
HGCX Home Gas Corporation (private car rr mark)
HGDH His (or Her) Grand Ducal Highness
HGFX Northern Refrigerator Line, Inc (private car rr mark)
HGMM Hereditary Grand Master Mason (freemasonry)
HGO II ST Hugo Stinnes Industries, Inc (Md.) (ASE)
hgt height
HGW Herbert George Wells (author)
hh leaves (*hojas*—Spanish); heavy hydrogen (deuterium)
HH gentlemen (*Herren*—German);

Haig Homes; half hard (metallurgy);
Hampshire Hunt (Foxhounds); His
(Her) Highness; His Holiness (*the Pope*); Houdaille-Hershey (NYSE)
H/H Havre to Hamburg (grain trade)
h to h heel to heel
HHA Hickory Handle Association
HHCX Champlin Refining Company (private car rr mark)
hhd hogshead
HHD Doctor of Humanities
hhf household furniture (insurance)
HHFA Housing and Home Finance Agency
hh g household goods
HHH very hard (of pencils)
H-hour a predetermined hour
hi hectoliter
HI American Hide & Leather (NYSE); Hawaiian Islands; here lies (*hic jacet*—Latin); horizontal interval; Hampton Institute; Hat Institute; Holton Inter-Urban Railway Company (rr mark); Hydraulic Institute
HIA Handkerchief Industry Association; Highway Industries Association; Hobby Institute of America; Horological Institute of America; Hospital Industries Association
HIAS Hebrew Sheltering and Immigrant Aid Society of New York
Hib Hibernian
HIB Hibbard, Spencer, Bartlett (NYSE)
HIC Herring Industry Council
Hid. Hidalgo
Hier Jerusalem (*Hierosolyma*—Latin)
HIF Housing Insurance Fund
HIG Higbie Manufacturing (NYSE)
highrs highlanders
HIGOG US High Commissioner for Germany
HIG Pr Higbie Manufacturing Company (5% Conv. Pfd.) (ASE)
HIH His (or Her) Imperial Highness
HIJMS His Imperial Japanese Majesty's Ship
hik hiking
Hikakuten Proprietorship (Japanese)
Hil Hilary
HIL Heileman (G.) Brewing Company (NYSE)
Hilt. Hilton's Common Pleas Reports (New York) (legal)
HIM. His (or Her) Imperial Majesty
Hind. Hindi; Hindu; Hindustan
HINLHBS Hunting Improvement and National Light Horse Breeding Society
H-ion hydrogen ion (chemical)
Hip. Hippolyte; Hippolytus
HIP Hawaiian Pineapple Company Ltd (NYSE); Health Insurance Plan

Hipp Hippocrates

HIPX Hawkeye Produce Company (private car rr mark)

HIR Walker(Hiram)-Gooderham & Worts g (NYSE)

HIS. Historical Division (US Army); here lies buried (*hic iacet sepultus* —Latin)

hist historic; history

Hist MSS Com Historical Manuscripts Commission

hiv winter (*hiver*—French)

HJ here lies (*hic jacet*—Latin); Hitler Youth (*Hitler Jugend*)

H & J Harris & Johnson's Maryland Reports (legal)

HJHX H.J. Heinz Company (private car rr mark)

HJMX Sterling Fuels (private car rr mark)

HJ Res House joint resolution

HK Chamber of Commerce (*Handels Kammer*—German); Hong Kong (IDP); House of Keys

HKA Hong Kong Airways, Ltd.

hkf handkerchief

HKH His Royal Highness (*Hans Kongelige Højhed*—Norwegian)

HKM Harbison-Walker Refrac. Company (NYSE)

HKR Hooker Electrochemical Company (NYSE)

HKSRA Hong Kong—Singapore Royal Artillery

hk tls Haikwan taels (weight measure)

h l in this place (*hoc loco*—Latin); of this place (*hujus loci*—Latin)

hl hectoliter; holy, Saint (*heilig*— German)

HL *Haute-Loire* (French Department); Headmaster-Lieutenant (naval); Hecla Mining Company (NYSE); Honours List; House of Lords; Howell Electric Motors Company (NYSE); hotel license (liquor)

H of L House of Lords

HLB Home Loan Bank; Homes for Little Boys

HLBB Home Loan Bank Board

HLC Headmaster Lieutenant-Commander (naval); House of Lords Cases (Law Reports)

HLF Hallicrafters Company (NYSE)

Hlg halogen

HLI Highland Light Infantry

HLL Hollander (A.) & Son, Inc (NYSE)

HLM headlamp mask

HLMX H.L. Mills (private car rr mark)

HLN Holland Furnace Company (NYSE)

HLO Holly Oil Company (NYSE)

HLOUK Headquarters and Liaison Officer in the United Kingdom

HLP Hall (C.M.) Lamp Company (NYSE)

HLPR Howard League for Penal Reform

HLPX Houston Lighting & Power Company (private car rr mark)

hl qc at the usual time and place (*hora locoque consuetis*—Latin)

HLR Heller (Walter E.) & Company (NYSE)

HL Rep. House of Lords Reports (legal)

HLR IV Pr Heller (Walter E.) & Company (4% Pfd.) (ASE)

HLR Pr Heller (Walter E.) & Company (5½% Pfd.) (ASE)

hls holes

HLT Hilton Hotels Corporation (NYSE)

Hlw half-bound cloth (*Halbleinwand* —German)

HLYX Holly Sugar Corporation (private car rr mark)

h m handmade; in this month (*hoc mense*—Latin)

Hm Herman; measurement standard (*Hohlmass*—German)

hm hand-made (paper); hectometer[s]

hm² square hectometer

hm³ cubic hectometer

HM Harbour Master; *Haute-Marne* (French department); Head Master; Head Mistress; His Majesty (*Hans Majestat*—Swedish) (*Hans Majestæt* —Danish) (*Hans Majestet*— Norwegian); Her Majesty; Home Mission; Homestake Mining Company (NYSE); Master of Humanities

H & M hit-and-miss (lumber)

HMA Hair Manufacturers' Association; Headmasters' Association; His Majesty's Airship

HMAA Horse and Mule Association of America

HMAC His Majesty's Aircraft Carrier; House Military Affairs Commission (United States)

HMAF His (or Her) Majesty's Armed Forces

H Maj:t His Majesty (*Hans Majestät* —Swedish)

HMAS His (or Her) Majesty's Australian Ship

HMBDV His Majesty's Boom Defence Vessel

HMC Headmasters' Conference; His (Her) Majesty's Customs; Historical Manuscripts Commission; Homes for Motherless Children

HMCIS His Majesty's Chief Inspector of Schools

HMCN His Majesty's Canadian Navy

HMCNA Home Missions Council of North America

HMCS His Majesty's Canadian Ship

HMCSC His Majesty's Civil Service Commissioners

hmd hydraulic mean depth

HMD Hammond Instrument Company (NYSE); His Majesty's Drifter

HMDBA Hollow Metal Door and Buck Association

HMF Haslemere Musical Festival; Hastings Manufacturing Company (NYSE); Hauliers' Mutual Federation; His Majesty's Forces

hmg greatest common divisor (*l'heure* [*moyenne*] *de Greenwich*— French)

HMG heavy machine gun (US Army)

HMH His Majesty's Household

HMHMH His Majesty's Household Master of the Horse

HMHS Hereditary Master of the Household of Scotland; His Majesty's Hospital Ship

HMHX Tank Car Corporation of America (private car rr mark)

HMI His Majesty's Inspector

HMIE His Majesty's Inspector of Explosives

HMIS His (or Her) Majesty's Inspector of Schools

HML Hammermill Paper Company (NYSE)

hmlt hamlet

HMMA Hydraulic Machinery Manufacturers Association

HMML His Majesty's Motor Launch

HMMMS His Majesty's Motor Mine Sweeper

HMO Hercules Motors Corporation (NYSE)

HMOW His (or Her) Majesty's Office of Works

HMP hand made paper; he erected this monument (*hoc monumentum posuit*—Latin)

HMRT His Majesty's Rescue Tug

HMS His (Her) Majesty's Service; His Majesty's Ship; Home Missions Society

HMSA Hardware Manufacturers Statistical Association

HMSAS His Majesty's South African Ship

HMSO His Majesty's Stationery Office

HMT His Majesty's Trawler

HMW Hamilton Watch Company (NYSE)

HMX Hyman-Michaels Company (private car rr mark)

HMY U. S. Hoffman Machinery (NYSE)

HN north hemisphere (*Hémisphère Nord*—French)

Hn nitrogen mustard gas

HNB Horn & Hardart Baking Company (N. J.) (ASE)

Hnos brothers (*Hermanos*—Spanish)

Hnos en Liq brothers in liquidation (*Hermanos en Liquidación*—Spanish)

HNU Honolulu Oil Corporation (NYSE)

HNW Hein-Werner Corporation (NYSE)

HNZ Heinz (H. J.) Company (NYSE)

ho house

Ho holmium

HO olive oil (*Huile d'Olives*—French); Head Office; Home Office; Hostilities Only; Houston Oil Company of Texas (NYSE)

HOC House of Charity; House of Commons

HOD Hebrew Order of David

HOE A Hoe (R.) & Company Inc (Class "A" Stock) (ASE)

Hoff Ch Hoffman's New York Chancery Reports (legal)

Ho For. Home Forces

HOKX Hooker Electrochemical Company (private car rr mark)

HOL Hollinger Cons. Gold Mines (NYSE); House of Lords

HOL C Home Owners Loan Corporation

Holl Holland

Holl p Dutch patent (*Holländisches patent*—German)

HOLUA Home Office Life Underwriters Association

HOM Hoskins Manufacturing Company (NYSE)

homœo homœopathic; homœopathy

Homer. Homeric

hon honorary; honorable; honorably

HON Honolulu; Honolulu Stock Exchange

Hond Honduras

Hon FRAM Honorary Fellow Royal Academy of Music

Hon Life M Inst Gas E Honorary Life Member of the Institute of Gas Engineers

Hon MIAE Honorary Member Institution Automobile Engineers

HONO Honolulu (US Navy)

Hon RAM. Honorary Member Royal Academy of Music

hons honors

Hon Sec Honorary Secretary

Hon Treas Honorary Treasurer

Hopk Ch Hopkins' New York Chancery Reports (legal)

hor horizon; horology

Hor Horace; Horologiun (constellation)

HOR Horn & Hardart Company (NYSE)

hor decub at bedtime (*hora decubitus*

—Latin) (pharmacy)

hor intermed at intermediate hours (*horis intermediis*—Latin) (pharmacy)

horlz horizontal

h or m hit-or-miss (lumber)

horol horological; horology

hort horticultural; horticulture

Hos Hosea (Biblical)

HOS Howard Stores Corporation (NYSE)

hosp hospital

Hosp Sergt Hospital Sergeant

Hosp Stew. Hospital Steward

HOU Houston Lighting & Power Company (NYSE)

Houst Houston's Delaware Reports (legal)

HOV Hoover Ball & Bearing Company (NYSE)

how. howitzer (military)

How. Howard's United States Supreme Court Reports (legal)

How. App Howard's Court of Appeals Cases (legal)

How. Pr Howard's New York Practice Reports (legal)

howr however

h p half-pay; heir presumptive; high power; high pressure; high priest; hire purchase; horse-power; horizontal parallax; hot-pressed (paper)

HPACCNA Heating, Piping and Air Conditioning Contractors National Association

HPAX Hunter Packing Company (private car rr mark)

HP BPMI Hair Pin and Bob Pin Manufacturers Institute

HPC Hercules Powder Company (NYSE)

HPCX Hercules Powder Company, Inc (private car rr mark)

h-p cyl high-pressure cylinder

HPG Hall (W. F.) Printing Company (NYSE)

hp-hr horsepower-hour

HPI Hardwood Plywood Institute

hp n horsepower nominal

h pres heir presumptive

h-press high pressure

HPT American Home Products (NYSE)

HPX Houston Packing Company (private car rr mark)

h q see this (*hoc quaere*—Latin)

HQ Headquarters

HQBA Headquarters Base Area (RAF)

HQFC Headquarters Fighter Command (RAF)

HQSRN Headquarters Staff of the Royal Navy

hr height (*hauteur*—French); hour

Hr Mr. (*Herr*—German, Herr—

Norwegian)

HR hard rolled; Highland Railway; Home Rule; Hot rolled (steel sheets); House of Representatives; International Harvester (NYSE)

h-r high resistance

H of R House of Representatives

Hra Mr. (*Herra*—Finnish)

HRA Honorary Royal Academician; Hotels and Restaurants Association

HRB Highway Research Board

HRC Harnischfeger Corporation (NYSE); Holy Rosary Confraternity; House Rules Committee (United States)

HRCA Honorary Member of the Royal Cambrian Academy

hrd hard

hrdty heredity

HRE Holy Roman Emperor; Holy Roman Empire

HREBIU Hotel and Restaurant Employees & Bartenders International Union

H rept House report

H res House resolution

HRF Hat Research Foundation

HRF Hussmann Refrigerator Company (NYSE)

HRH His (Her) Royal Highness; Home of Rest for Horses

HRHA Honorary Member of the Royal Hibernian Academy

HRI Holt Radium Institute; Honorary Member of the Royal Institute of Painters in Water Colours

HRIP here rests in peace (*hic requiescit in pace*—Latin)

HRL Hormel (Geo. A.) & Company (NYSE)

Hrm Herman

HRN Hearn Department Stores (NYSE)

hrnar hereinafter

HRP holding and reconsignment point (US Army)

hrs heirs; hours

Hrs Hussars

HRS hot-rolled steel; Hires (Charles E.) Company (NYSE)

HRSA Honorary Member of the Royal Scottish Academy

hrsg published (*herausgegeben*—German)

Hrt CC heart cubical content (lumber)

Hrt FA heart facial area (lumber)

Hrt G heart girth (lumber)

hrtwd heartwood (lumber)

HRWMC House of Representatives Ways and Means Committee

h s hemstitched; at bedtime (*hora somni*—Latin) (pharmacy); here is buried (*hic sepulus or situs*—Latin); homestead selection; in this sense (*hora somni*—Latin)

Hs Hans

HS Hakluyt Society; hand-starter; Harbour Service; Harleian Society; Harveian Society; *Haute-Saône* (French department); heating surface; high school; high speed; Home Secretary; Honorary Secretary; Hospital Saturday; hospital ship; Hospital Sunday; house surgeon; Hunterian Society; mustard gas (di-chloro-di-ethyl-sulphide); South Hemisphere (*hémisphère sud* —French)

H&S Harris & Simrall (legal); headquarters and service (US Army)

HSA Hispanic Society of America; Hospital Savings Association

HSC Higher School Certificate; Home Security Circular; Home Service Corps; Honourable Society of Cymmrodorion

hse here lies buried (*hic sepultus* (or *situs*) *est*—Latin)

HSF Harness and Saddling Factory; Hospital Saturday Fund

hsg housing

HSH His (or Her) Serene Highness

HSK Honourary Surgeon to the King

HSKPG housekeeping (US Army)

h s l very soluble hot (*heiss sehr löslich*—German)

HSL Hercules Steel Products (NYSE); Huguenot Society of London

HSM Hart Schaffner & Marx (NYSE); His (Her) Serene Majesty

HSMAA Hack Saw Manufacturers Association of America

HSPA Hawaiian Sugar Planters Association

HSS Fellow of the Historical Society (*Historiae Societatis Socius*— Latin); Stinnes (Hugo) Corporation (NYSE)

HST Holly Stores (NYSE)

HSTX Hinckley & Schmitt (private car rr mark)

HSU Hardin-Simmons University

HSY Hershey Chocolate Corporation (NYSE)

t full page plate (*hors texte*— French); heel to toe; high tension; high tongue; at this time (*hoc tempore*—Latin); under this title (*hoc titulo*—Latin)

ht a draught (*haustus*—Latin) (pharmacy); heat; height

Ht Harriet

HT half-time survey; Hawaiian Territory; high tide; high treason; hired transport; Holy Trinity; Horsed Transport; Hudson Motor Car (NYSE)

H&t hardened and tempered

hta until (*hasta*—Spanish)

HTA Horticultural Trades Association

h-t b high-tension battery

HTB Hollow-ware Trade Board

HTCX Harbor Tank Line Company (private car rr mark)

HTE Holyrood (Amenity) Trust, Edinburgh

Hte Gar Haute-Garonne (French department)

Hte L Haute-Loire (French department)

Hte M Haute-Marne (French department)

Htes Pyr Hautes-Pyrénées (French department)

Hte Saô Haute-Saône (French department)

Hte Sav Haute-Savoie (French department)

htofore heretofore

HTPX Thiessen Pickle Company (private car rr mark)

H Trin Holy Trinity

h t s half-time survey

hts heights

HTS high tensile steel; House Territories Subcommittee; Hutchinson Sugar Plantation Company (NYSE)

ht wkt hit wicket (cricket)

HTX Houston Tank Car Company (private car rr mark)

H Ty Hawaiian Territory

HTY Holt (Henry) & Company (NYSE) Inc

Hu Harvard University; Howard University; Hubert; Hughe's United States Circuit Court (legal); Hugh; Hugo; Humphrey

HUB Hubbell (Harvey), Inc (NYSE)

HUCR highest useful compression ratio

HUCX Huron Portland Cement Company (private car rr mark)

hum. humble; humorous

Hum. the Humanities (*Humaniori*— Latin); humanitarian; Humphrey

hun hundred

hund hundred

Hung. Hungarian; Hungary

hunth hundred thousand

HUNTS Huntingdonshire (county in England)

HUR Hurd Lock & Mfg. Company (NYSE)

Huss Hussars

HUT Huttig Sash & Door Company (NYSE)

HV hard valve (radio); Haute-Vienne (French department); Havana Lithographing Company (NYSE); heavy (US Army); high velocity (guns); High Voltage

h w hit wicket; head water; high water

HW Howe Sound Company (NYSE)

Hwb handy dictionary (*Handwörterbuch*—German)

HWCX Halliburton Oil Well Cementing Company (private car rr mark)

h w l not very soluble hot (*heiss wenig löslich*—German)

HWMC House Ways and Means Committee

HWMX Walker & Sons, The H. W. (private car rr mark)

HWNA Hosiery Wholesalers National Association

HWO Hotel Waldorf-Astoria (ASE)

H'wood Hollywood

HWOST high water ordinary spring tides

HWRX Hi-Way Refineries, Ltd (private car rr mark)

HWSX Walker & Sons, Limited, Hiram (private car rr mark)

HWX Wilcox Oil Company (private car rr mark)

HWY highway (US Army)

HXR Hudson & Manhattan R. R. (NYSE)

hy heavy; hydraulic; hygiene

HY Hitler Youth (*Hitler Jugend*)

Hya Hydra (constellation)

HY ART Heavy Artillery

hyb hybrid

HYB Hayes Mfg. Corporation (NYSE)

hyd hydraulic; hydrographic; hydrostatic

hydraul hydraulics

Hydrarg mercury (*Hydrargyrum*— Latin)

hydro hydropathic establishment

HYDRO Hydrographic (US Navy)

hydrodyn hydrodynamics

hydrog hydrographic

hydros hydrostatics

hyds hydraulics

hydt hydrant

hyg hygiene; hygienic

HYGX North American Car Corporation (private car rr mark)

HYI Hydrus (constellation)

HYMA Hebrew Young Men's Association

hymnol hymnology

hyp hypothesis; hypothetical

Hypo Hyposulphite of soda

hypoth hypothesis; hypothetical

HYTX Hygrade Food Products Corporation (private car rr mark)

HZ Hazeltine Corporation (NYSE)

Hz His Excellency, His Majesty (*Hazretleri*—Turkish)

HZT Hazel-Atlas Glass Company (NYSE)

HZX Hegeler Zinc Company (private car rr mark)

I

i in (*im*—German); indicated; infantry; intensity; intransitive; that (*id*—Latin)

I candle power; direct current; (electric) current (in amperes); Idaho; Emperor, Empress (*Imperator, Imperatrix*—Latin); imperial; incisor (dentistry); Independent (politics); inspector; institute; institution; Intelligence; interpole; Interpreter (RAF); iodine; Ireland; Irish; island; isle; Italian; Italy and Italian colonies; Jesus

Ia Iowa

IA first quality; Imperial Airways; Incorporated Accountant; Indian Army; Infected Area; Institute of Actuaries; International Angstrom (physics); Iraqi Airlines; Isle of Arran

iA by order of (*im Auftrage*—German)

I/A Isle of Anglesey

I of A Instructor of Artillery

IAA Incorporated Accountants and Auditors; Incorporated Association of Architects and Surveyors; Insurance Accountants Association; International Acetylene Association; International Apple Association

IAAA Institute of Air Age Activities; Irish Amateur Athletic Association

IAAAA Intercollegiate Association of Amateur Athletes of America

IAAB Inter-American Association of Broadcasters

IAAM Incorporated Association of Assistant Masters; International Association of Auditorium Managers

IAARC International Administrative Aeronautical Radio Conference

IAB Industrial Advisory Board

IABA Inter-American Bar Association

IABPAI International Association of Blue Print and Allied Industries

IABSOIW International Association of Bridge, Structural & Ornamental Iron Workers

IAC Intelligence Advisory Committee; Iranian Airways Co.

IACB International Association of Convention Bureaus

IACCP Inter-American Council of Commerce and Production

IACD International Association of Clothing Designers

IACDHW International Association of Cleaning & Dye House Workers

IACP International Association of Chiefs of Police

IACS International Academy of Christian Sociologists; International Annealed Copper Standard

IACSU International Association of Casualty and Surety Underwriters

IAD Inland Steel Company (NYSE)

IAE Institution of Automobile Engineers

IAEI International Association of Electrical Inspectors

IAEL International Association of Electrical Leagues

IAES International Association of Electrotypers and Stereotypers; International Association Exchange Students

IAF Indian Air Force; Indian Armoured Formation; International Automobile Federation; Italian Air Force

IAFC International Association of Fire Chiefs

IAFE International Association of Fairs and Expositions

IAFF International Association of Fire Fighters

IAG Institute of American Genealogy; International Association of Geodesy

IAGFCC International Association of Game, Fish, and Conservation Commissioners

IAGLO International Association of Governmental Labor Officials

IAGM International Association of Garment Manufacturers

IAH International Association of Hydrology

IAHA Inter-American Hotel Association

IAHDRUM Industrial Association of House Dress, Robe, and Uniform Manufacturers

IAI International Association for Identification

IAIABC International Association of Industrial Accident Boards and Commissions

IAIC International Association of Insurance Counsel

IAICM International Association of Ice Cream Manufacturers

IAL Imperial Airways Limited; Imperial Arts League; International Arbitration League; Irish Academy of Letters

IALA International Auxiliary Language Association

IAM International Association of

Machinists; International Association of Meteorology

IAMA Irish Association of Municipal Authorities

IAMB International Anti-Militarist Bureau Against War and Reaction; International Association of Microbiologists

IAMCA International Association of Milk Control Agencies

IAMFS International Association of Milk and Food Sanitarians

IAOC Indian Army Ordnance Corps

IAOS Irish Agricultural Organization Society

IAP Institute of Agricultural Parasitology; Iota Alpha Pi (sorority)

IAPES International Association of Public Employment Services

IAPGWB Incorporated Association for Promoting the General Welfare of the Blind

IAPI Institute of American Poultry Industries

IAPO International Association of Physical Oceanography

IAQR International Association on Quaternary Research

I Arb Institute of Arbitrators

IARO Indian Army Reserve of Officers

IARU International Amateur Radio Union

IARVO Incorporated Association of Rating and Valuation Officers

IAS Incorporated Association of Surveyors; Indicated Air Speed; Institute for Advanced Study (United States); Institute of the Aeronautical Sciences; International Association of Seismology; Irish Archaeological Society

IASAC International Affiliation of Sales and Advertising Clubs

IASAP Intercollege Association for Study of the Alcohol Problem

IASC Inter-American Safety Council

IASCI International Associated Sports Clubs, Inc.

IASI Inter-American Statistical Institute

IASM Independent Association of Stocking Manufacturers

IATA International Air Transport Association

IATC International Air Transport Convention (or Conference); International Association of Torch Clubs

IATME International Association of Terrestrial Magnetism and Electricity

IATS Inspector of Auxiliary Territorial Service

IATSE International Alliance of Theatrical Stage Employes and Moving Picture Machine Operators of the United States and Canada

IAU International Astronomical Union

IAUPL International Association of University Professors and Lecturers

IAV International Association of Vulcanology

IAWA International Association of Wood Anatomists

IAWEC International Alliance of Women for Equal Citizenship

IAZ inner artillery zone (US Army)

ib in the same place (*ibidem—Latin*)

IB Iberia, Cia Mercantil Anonima de Lineas Aereas; Illinois Brick Company (NYSE); Immigration Branch; in bond; Incendiary Bomb; inner bottom (shipbuilding); Intelligence Branch; Invoice Book; iron body (plumbing)

IBA Independent Bankers Association; Institute of British Architects; International Brigade Association; Irish Bleachers' Association

IBAA Investment Bankers Association of America

IBAPT Incorporated British Association of Physical Training

IBAU Institute of British-American Understanding

IBB International Brotherhood of Bookbinders

IBBDFH International Brotherhood of Blacksmiths, Drop Forgers & Helpers

IBBISBHA International Brotherhood of Boilermakers, Iron Ship Builders and Helpers of America

IBC Independent Business Council; International Broadcasting Corporation

IBCA International Baby Chick Association

IBD Institute of British Decorators

IBE Institute of British Engineers; International Bureau of Education

IBEN Incendiary Bomb with Explosive Nose

IBEW International Brotherhood of Electrical Workers

IBF Institute of British Foundrymen

IBFME International Brotherhood of Foundry and Metal Employes

IBFO International Brotherhood of Firemen and Oilers

IBG International Boxing Guild

IBH initial beachhead (US Army)

IBI Insulation Board Institute

IBIA Institute of British Industria Art

ibid in the same place (*ibidem—Latin*)

IBK Institute of Bookkeepers

IBL Institution of British Launderers; Intelligence Branch and Library

IBM International Brotherhood of Magicians; International Business Machines (NYSE)

i b o invoice book outward

i b p initial boiling point

IBP Institute of British Photographers

IBRC International Business Relations Council

IBRD International Bank for Reconstruction and Development

IBRL initial bomb release line (US Army)

IBRM Institute of Boiler and Radiator Manufacturers

IBS International Bible Students

IBSA Inanimate Bird Shooting Association; International Bible Students' Association

IBSS Imperial Bureau of Soil Science

IBST Institute of British Surgical Technicians

IBTT International Bureau for Technical Training

i bu imperial bushel

IBU International Broadcasting Union

i c ice-chest; index conection (navigation); in charge; internal combustion; internal connection; between meals (*inter cibos—Latin*) (pharmacy)

ic icon (plate engraving)

i/c in charge of

IC Brothers of Christian Instruction (La Mennais Brothers); Fathers of the Institute of Charity; Illinois Central Railroad Company (rr mark); Imperial Conference; inductive coupling; Industrial Court; information center (US Army); Inspiration Consolidated Copper (NYSE); Institute of Charity; Institute of Chemistry; internal combustion (engine); International Conference; International Corps; Interceptor Command

I-C Indo-China

ICA Ice Cream Alliance (Ltd); Imperial College of Agriculture (West Indies); Institute of Chartered Accountants; Institute of Company Accountants; International Chefs Association; International Chiro-

practors Association; International Civil Aircraft; International Claim Association; International Colonisation Association; International Co-operative Alliance; International Confederation of Agriculture; International Co-operative Alliance; International Culinarians Association; Interstate Commerce Act; Irish Cyclists' Association

ICAA Investment Counsel Association of America

ICAAAA Intercollegiate Association of Amateur Athletes of America

ICAE International Conference of Agricultural Economists; International Commission on Agricultural Engineering

ICAF Industrial College of the Armed Forces (US Army)

ICAN International Commission for Air Navigation

ICAO International Civil Aviation Organization

ICBP International Committee for Bird Preservation

ICC International Chamber of Commerce; International Correspondence College; Interstate Commerce Commission

ic&c invoice cost and charges

ICCA Infants and Children's Coat Association

ICCASP Independent Citizens Committee of the Arts, Sciences and Professions

ICCE International Council of Commerce Employers

ICCH International Commodity Clearing House

ICCICA Interim Co-ordinating Committee for International Commodity Arrangements

ICC Spec'n Interstate Commerce Commission Specification

ICCSSM Industrial Council of Cloak, Suit and Skirt Manufacturers

ICD With Jesus Christ as Leader (Jesu [*iesu*] Christo Duce—Latin)

ICE Institute of Christian Education; Institution of Chemical Engineers; Institution of Civil Engineers

Ice. Iceland[ic]

ICEF International Children's Emergency Fund

ICEI Internal Combustion Engine Institute

Icel Icelandic

ICES International Council for the Exploration of the Sea

ICESA Interstate Conference of Employment Security Agencies

ICF Irwin Charity Foundation; Italian Catholic Federation

ICFB International Catholic Film Bureau

IC4A Intercollegiate Association of Amateur Athletes of America

ICFTU International Confederation of Free Trade Unions

ICHAM Institute of Cooking and Heating Appliance Manufacturers

ichth ichthyological; ichthyology

ICI Imperial Chemical Industries; International Commission on Illumination

ICIA International Crop Improvement Association

ICIE International Council of Industrial Editors

ICITO Interim Commission for the International Trade Organization

ICIW International Confederation of Intellectual Workers

ICJ International Court of Justice

ICL Carriers & General Corporation (NYSE)

ICMA International Circulation Managers Association; International City Managers Association; International Congresses for Modern Architecture

ICMI Ice Cream Merchandising Institute

ICMICA International Catholic Movement for Intellectual and Cultural Affairs

ICN in Christ's name (in Christi nomine—Latin); International Council of Nurses

ICO International Chemistry Office

ICOM International Council of Museums

Icon. iconographical; iconography

ICPHS International Council for Philosophy and Humanistic Studies

ICR Illinois Central Railroad; Irish Chancery Reports (legal); Island Creek Cocl Company (NYSE)

ICRC International Committee of the Red Cross

ICRE International Council of Religious Education

ICRF Imperial Cancer Research Fund; International Cancer Research Foundation

ICRR Illinois Central Railroad System

ICS Imperial College of Science; Indian Civil Service; International College of Surgeons; Institute of Chartered Shipbrokers; International Correspondence Schools

ICSAB International Civil Service Advisory Board

ICSH interstitial cell-stimulating hormone

I C S M International Committee of Scientific Management

ICSU International Council of Scientific Unions

ICSW International Conference of Social Work

ICT inflammation of connective tissue (medicine); International Critical Tables; Jesus Christ, our protector (Jesu [Iesu] Christo Tutore—Latin)

ICTA Imperial College of Tropical Agriculture; International Cooperative Trading Agency

ICTUS Counselor at Law (iurisconsultus—Latin)

ICU International Code Use (signals)

ICW International Council of Women; interrupted continuous waves

ICWG International Co-operative Women's Guild

ICWSG Infants and Children's Wear Salesmen's Guild

ICWU International Chemical Workers Union

ICZ Isthmian Canal Zone

id identification; the same (idem—Latin)

Id Idaho; Ides (Idus—Latin)

i d induced draught (draft); inside diameter; internal diameter

ID Inniskilling Dragoons; Institute of Directors; Intelligence Department; Institute of Distribution; Intelligence Division (US Army); Interior Department

i D in the form of steam (im Dampf—German)

Ida. Idaho

IDA Idaho Power Company (NYSE); Import Duties Act; Independent Druggists' Alliance; with the guidance of Immortal God (Immortalis Dei auspicio—Latin)

IDAA Industrial Diamond Association of America; Industrial Soap Association

IDAC Import Duties Advisory Committee

IDB illicit diamond buyer

idc Completed a course at, or served for a year on the staff of the Imperial Defence College (naval)

IDC Imperial Defence College; International Danube Commission

IDCD Inter-Departmental Committee on Dentistry

IDDA Inspectors under Dangerous Drugs Act

IDENT identification (US Army)

IDES Brotherhood of the Divine Holy Ghost (Irmandade do Divino Espirito Santo—Portuguese)

IDEST Brotherhood of the Divine Holy Ghost and Trinity (Irmandade do Divino Espirito Santo e da Trinidade—Portuguese)

IDF intermediate distribution frame (telephone)

IDI Insurance Department and Inspectorate

IDIA Informativo de Investigaciones Agricolas (Argentina)

IDN In the Name of God (In Dei Nomine—Latin)

IDP International Driving Permit (automobile); license designating vehicle's country of origin

IDR Indian Defence Rules; Infantry Drill Regulations

IDRB Industrial Design Registration Bureau

i drug. and Company (i drugovi—Yugoslavian)

IDSM Indian Distinguished Service Medal

Id T Idaho Territory

ie that is (id est—Latin)

IE index error (navigation); Indian Empire; Indo-European; Initial Equipment (RAF); information and education (US Army)

I of E Institute of Export

IEA Insurance Executives Association; Italian East Africa

IEC Imperial Economic Committee; Industrial Emergency Board; Industrial and Engineering Chemistry (a publication); International Electro-Technical Commission International Emergency Committee

IEE Institution of Electrical Engineers

IEF Italian Expeditionary Force

IEFC International Emergency Food Committee

IEII Institution of Engineering Inspection Incorporated

I et L Indre-et-Loire (French Department)

IERX Inland Empire Refineries, Inc. (private car rr mark)

IES Illumination Engineering Society; Indian Educational Service; International Employment Service

IESA Insurance Economics Society of America

I et V Ille-et-Vilaine (French Department)

i f he did it himself (ipse fecit—Latin); intermediate frequency

if. according to (ifølge—Danish)

IF. International Fellowship

IFA Incorporated Faculty of Arts; International Fiscal Association

IFABSM Incorporated Association of Boot and Shoe Manufacturers

IFAC International Fellowship in Arts and Crafts

IFAHPF International Federation of

American Homing Pigeon Fanciers

IFALPA International Federation of Airline Pilots' Associations

IFAN Institut Français d'Afrique Noire

IFAP International Federation of Agricultural Producers

IFB Institute of Farm Brokers

IFBOA International Federation of Bank Officials' Associations

IFC International Food Conference; International Freighting Corporation

IFCA Independent Fundamental Churches of America

IFCC International Federation of Culture Collections of Micro-Organisms

IFCL International Fixed Calendar League

IFCTIO International Federation of Commercial Travelers Insurance Organizations

IFCTU International Federation of Christian Trade Unions

IF&DBD Inspector of Fortifications and Director of Bomb Disposal

IFDC Independent Food Distributors Council

IFE Institution of Fire Engineers

IFF identification of friend or foe (radar); International Film Foundation

IFFJ International Federation of Free Journalists

IFHA International Federation of Hand Arts

IFI Industrial Fasteners Institute

ifl according to (*ifølge*—Norwegian)

IFL International Fellowship League

IFLA International Federation of of Library Associations

IFLWU International Fur & Leather Workers Union

IFMA Industrial Furnace Manufacturers Association

IFMO Imperial and Foreign Money Orders

IFOG International Federation of Olive Growers

IFOR International Fellowship of Reconstruction

IFP Imperial and Foreign Post

IFPP Imperial and Foreign Parcel Post

IFR Indian Famine Relief; Instrument Flight Rules (ICAO); Iron Fireman Manufacturing Company (NYSE)

IFRB International Frequency Registration Board (of ITU)

IFRU French Institute of the United Kingdom (*Institut Français du Royaume Uni*—French)

IFS International Federation of Surveyors; Irish Free State

IFSMU Irish Free State Medical Union

IFSSO Irish Free State Stationery Office

IFT Institute of Food Technologists

IFTA International Federation of Teachers' Associations

IFTU International Federation of Trade Unions

IFUW International Federation of University Women

IFYHA International Federation of Youth Hostels Associations

IG Indo-Germanic; Inner Guard (freemasonry); Inspector-General (US Army); Intendant-General (military); Irish Guards; Iron Guard; trust, combine (*Interessengemeinschaft*—German)

IGA International Geneva Association

IGAA Independent Grocers Alliance of America

i gal. imperial gallon

IGAS International General Assembly of Spiritualists

IGB International Trades Union Office (*Internationales Gewerkschafts Büro*—German)

IGC Inspector General of Communications; International Grassland Congress

IGCR Intergovernmental Committee on Refugees

i/g/d illicit gold dealer

IGD Inspector General's Department (US Army)

IG'ds Irish Guards

IGF Inspector-General of Fortifications

IGFA International Game Fish Association

IGL Int'l Minerals & Chemicals (NYSE)

igla church (*iglesia*—Spanish)

ign ignition; unknown (*ignotus*—Latin)

Ign Ignacio; Ignatz

IGN International Great Northern Railroad Company (private car rr mark)

IGT Institute of Gas Technology

IGU International Geographical Union

IGWUA International Glove Workers Union of America

ih ice haulage; indirectly heated (valve); lies here (*iacet hic*—Latin); inside height (measurement)

IH Int'l Hydro-Electric System (NYSE)

IHB Indiana Harbor Belt Railroad Company; International Hydrographic Bureau

IHC International Hunting Council

IHCX International Harvester Company (private car rr mark)

IHFA Industrial Hygiene Foundation of America

IHLBNWU International Handbag, Luggage, Belt & Novelty Workers Union

IHM Jesus the Saviour of the World (*Iesus Mundi Salvator*—Latin)

IHN in His name

IHOU Institute of Home Office Underwriters

ihp indicated horsepower

ihp-hr indicated horsepower hour

IH Pr International Hydro-Elec. System (Pfd. $3.50 Ser.) (ASE)

IHS Jesus (Greek symbol)

IHSMA International Hotel Sales Management Association

IHV Irving Air Chute Company, Inc. (NYSE)

IHY MAT Isarco Hydro-Electric Company (ASE)

I/I indorsement irregular (banking); inventory and inspection report (US Army)

IIA Institute of Internal Auditors; Insurance Institute of America; International Information Administration

IICS International Solvay Institute of Chemistry

IICX Interlake Iron Corporation (private car rr mark)

IIE Institute of International Education; International Institute of Embryology

IIEIC International Institute Examinations Inquiry Committee

iIF Institute of International Finance

III International Isostatic Institute

IIL Institute of Industrial Launderers

IIMT International Institute of Milling Technology

IIRI International Industrial Relations Institute

IIST International Institute of Theoretical Sciences

iI of T Illinois Institute of Technology

i J in the year (*im Jahre*—German)

i J d W in the year of the world (*im Jahre der Welt*—German)

IJMA Infants and Juvenile Manufacturers Association

IJWU International Jewelry Workers' Union

i k inner keel

IK Interlake Iron Corporation (NYSE)

IKH His, Her or Your Royal Highness (*Ihre königliche*—German)

IKL Isänmaallinen Kansanluke

(National Patriotic Movement—
Finland)
IKN Interchemical Corporation
(NYSE)
i l inside length; interior length
IL Illinois Central Railroad Com-
pany (NYSE); Independence
League; interline; International
League (baseball); Investors'
League; Israel (IDP)
ILA International Law Association;
International Longshoremen's
Association
ILAAB International Law Associa-
tion, American Branch
ILC Instructor Lieutenant Com-
mander (naval); International
Labour Club; International Labour
Conference; International Law
Commission; Irrevocable letter
of credit
ILDX Incandescent Lamp Division
of General Electric Company
(private car rr mark)
ile illustrious (*ilustre*—Spanish)
ILGWU International Ladies' Garment Workers' Union
ILI Indiana Limestone Institute;
Institute of Life Insurance
ill. illumination; illustrated; illustration; most distinguished
(*illustrissimus*—Latin)
Ill Illinois
illinend to be smeared
(*illinendus*—Latin) (pharmacy)
illit illiterate
Ill. LRev Illinois Law Review
ill. mo most illustrious
(*illustrissimo*—Italian)
ILM Institute of Labour Management
ILMA Incandescent Lamp Manu-
facturers Association
ilmo most illustrious (*ilustríssimo*
—Portuguese); very illustrious
(*ilustrísimo*—Spanish)
i l o in lieu of
ILO International Labour Office;
International Labor Organiza-
tion
ILOUE in lieu thereof until ex-
hausted (US Army)
ILOWB International Labor Office,
Washington Branch
ILP Independent Labor Party
ILPBC International League of
Professional Baseball Clubs
ILR Industrial Rayon Corporation
(NYSE); International League of
Reform
ILS instrument landing (system);
Incorporated Law Society; Irish
Literary Society; International
Latitude Service; International
Salt Company (NYSE); Iota
Lambda Sigma (fraternity)

ILSA Improvement of Live Stock Act
ILSTM Incorporated Liverpool
School of Tropical Medicine
ILT Illinois Terminal Railroad Com-
pany (NYSE)
ilv supplement (*ilâve*—Turkish)
ILWU International Longshoremen's
and Warehousemen's Union
ILX Inland Molasses Company
(private car rr mark)
ILZ Illinois Zinc Company (ASE)
IM Idaho Maryland Mines Corpora-
tion (NYSE); imperial measure;
in memoriam; Isle of Man; Your
Majesty (*Ihre Majestät*—German)
I of M Instructor of Musketry; Isle of
Man
IMA Indian Military Academy; Irish
Medical Association
I Mar E Institution of Marine
Engineers (Canada)
IMB Institute of Micro-Biology
IMC International Missionary
Council; International Monetary
Conference; International Music
Council
IMCE Institution of Municipal and
County Engineers
IMCO Inter-Governmental Maritime
Consultative Organization
IMCS International Movement of
Catholic Students
IMD Indian Medical Department;
Industrial Machinery Division
IME Institute of Makers of Ex-
plosives; Institution of Mining
Engineers
IMEA Incorporated Municipal
Electrical Association; Independ-
ent Merchant Exporters Association
I Mech E Institution of Mechanical
Engineers
IMEI Institute of Marine Engineers
Incorporated
imep indicated mean effective
pressure
I Meth Independent Methodist
IMEX Indiana & Michigan Electric
Company (private car rr mark)
IMFWUNA International Molders and
Foundry Workers Union of North
America
IMG International Mining Corpora-
tion (NYSE)
IMIA International Metal Industries,
Ltd. (Com. Class "A") (ASE)
IMIB Inland Marine Insurance
Bureau
imit imitated; imitation; imitative
IMM International Mercantile Marine
Company
IMMAT immaterial (US Army)
immun immunology
immy immediately
IMNS Imperial Military Nursing

Service; Indian Military Nursing
Service
IMO Imperial Oil Ltd. (NYSE); in
memory of; International Meteorological Organization
Imp. Emperor (*Imperator*—Latin);
Empress (*Imperatrix*—Latin);
Imperial
imp. empire (*imperium*—Latin)
imperative; imperfect; imperial;
implement; import; imported; importer; impression; imprint; printer
(*imprimeur*—French); let it be
printed (*imprimatur*—Latin);
printing office (*impreuta*—Spanish)
IMP Imperial Chemical Indus., ADR
(NYSE); Imperial Chemical Industries, Ltd. (ASE); Institute of
Medical Psychology
imp. bu imperial bushel
impce importance (legal)
Imp'd ORM Improved Order of Red
Men
imper imperative
imperf imperfect; imperforate
impers impersonal
Imp. Inst Imperial Institute
impl implement
imposs impossible
IMPPA Independent Motion Picture
Producers Association
impr improved; improvement
impreg impregnated
improp improper
impt important
IMPT Inspector of Mines and
Petroleum Technologist
imptr importer
impv imperative
IMR Institute of Mortuary Research
IMRX Central States Oil Company
(private car rr mark)
IMS immersed midship section;
Independent Milk Supplies (Ltd);
Indian Medical Service; Industrial
Management Society; Institute of
Mathematical Statistics; Institute
of Mine Surveyors; Institute of Mine
Sweepers
IMSA International Municipal Signal
Association
IMSG Imperial Merchant Service
Guild
IMT Imperial Tobacco, Gt. Britain,
(NYSE); Institute of the Motor
Trade
IMTA Imported Meat Trade Associa-
tion; Institute of Municipal Treas-
urers and Accountants
IMTD Inspectors of the Military
Training Directorate
IMTP Industrial Mobilization Train-
ing Program (US Army)
IMU International Mailers Union
IMUA Inland Marine Underwriters'

Association

IMWA Independent Movers and Warehousemen's Association

IMWI Industrial Mineral Wool Institute

IMWU Interstate Metal Workers Union

in. inch

in.² square inch

in.³ cubic inch

IN. Illinois Northern Railway (rr mark); Indian Navy; Institute of Navigation

In Indonesia; indium

INA Indian National Airways; Institution of Naval Architects

INACT inactive(ate) (US Army)

inakt inactive (*inaktiv*—German)

in. aur to the ear (*in auri*—Latin) (pharmacy)

in, ball. in ballast (shipping)

inbd inboard

inc included; including; inclusive; incognito; income; incorporated; increase

Inc Incorporated

INC Indian National Congress; International Cigar Machinery Company (ASE); International Cigar Machinery Company (NYSE); International Nickel Company (Canada); in the Name of Christ (*in Nomine Christi*—Latin)

ince insurance

incept. inceptive

INCFO Institute of Newspaper Controllers and Finance Editors

incho inchoative

incid incidental

incl including; inclusive

INCL inclos(ure) (US Army)

incln inclusion

incog in secret (*incognito*—Latin)

incompat incompatibility

incor incorporated

incorr incorrect

Incpd Acctt Incorporated Accountant

incr increase; increasing

Incun Incunabula (earliest printed books)

ind independent; index; indication; indicative; indigo; industrial; industry

in. d daily (*in dies*—Latin) (pharmacy)

Ind Independent; India; Indian; Indiana; Indies; Indus (constellation)

IND in the name of God (*in Nomine Dei*—Latin); indorse(ment) (US Army)

ind du bois forestry (*industrie du bois*—French)

Ind E Industrial Engineer

indecl indeclinable (grammar)

indef indefinite

indemy indemnity

Ind Eur Indo-European

indic indicating; indicator

Ind Imp Emperor of India (*Indiae Imperator*)

indiv individual

Ind et L Indre-et-Loire (French Department)

indm indemnity

Ind Meth Independent Methodists

Indoch Indochina

INDOCT indoctrinate (US Army)

Indo-Eur Indo-European

Indo-Ger Indo-German

Indon Indonesia

indre indenture

ind reg induction regulator

Ind Rep Indiana Reports (legal)

indsl industrial

Ind Ter Indian Territory

induc induction

ined unpublished (*ineditus*—Latin)

in. ex at length (*in extenso*—Latin)

inf beneath, below (*infra*—Latin); infantry; infinitive; infirmary; information; lower (*inférieure*—French)

in. f in fine (finally)

inf l inflammable liquid

infl inflorescence (botany); influence; influx

info information

in. fol arg volvend to be silvered (*in folio argenti volvendae*—Latin) (pharmacy)

infra dig. beneath one's dignity (*infra dignitatem*—Latin)

infraptum written below (*infrascriptum*—Latin)

infric let it be rubbed in (*infricetur*—Latin) (pharmacy)

infricand to be rubbed in (*infricandus*—Latin) (pharmacy)

inf s inflammable solid

Ing engineer (*Ingenieur*—German)

INGAA Independent Natural Gas Association of America

Inh proprietor (*Inhaber*—German)

inhal inhalation (*inhalatio*—Latin) (pharmacy)

INI in the Name of Jesus (*In Nomine Iesu*—Latin)

in. init in the beginning (*in initio*—Latin)

inj injection (*injectio*—Latin) (pharmacy)

inject. injection

inj hyp hypodermic injection (*injectio hypodermica*—Latin) (pharmacy)

inkl inclusive (*inklusive*—German)

in-lb inch-pound

in lim at the outset (*in limine*—Latin)

in loc in its place (*in loco*—Latin)

in loc cit in the place cited (*in loco citato*—Latin)

in mem in memory of (*in memoriam*—Latin)

inns innings (cricket)

Innis Inniskilling

INOAVNOT if not available notify this office at once (US Army)

inorg inorganic

INP International News Photos

in. pr in the beginning (*in principio*—Latin)

INR International Silver Company (NYSE)

INRI Emperor Napoleon, King of Italy (*Imperator Napoleon Rex Italiae*—Latin); Jesus of Nazareth, King of the Jews (*Iesus Nazarenus Rex Juxaeorum*—Latin)

ins inches; inscribed; inspector; insulated; insulation; insurance

INS Immigration and Naturalization Service; International News Service

in. s in its original situation (*in situ*—Latin)

INSAIR Inspector of Naval Aircraft (US Navy)

insb especially (*insbesondere*—German)

insce insurance

inscr inscribed; inscription

insd val insured value

in/sec inches per second

INSENG Inspector of Naval Engineering Material (US Navy)

insep inseparable

Ins Gen Inspector General

ins int insurable interest

INSMACH Inspector of Naval Machinery (US Navy)

INSMAT Inspector of Naval Material (US Navy)

INSNAVMAT Inspector of Navigational Material (US Navy)

insol insoluble

insolv insolvent

INSORD Inspector of Ordnance (US Navy)

INSP inspect (US Army)

INSPETRES Inspector of Petroleum Reserves (US Navy)

inspir let it be inspired (*inspiretur*—Latin) (pharmacy)

INSRADMAT Inspector of Radio Material (US Navy)

inst installment; instant (the present month); instantaneous; institute; institution; instrument

INST in the Name of the Holy Trinity (*In Nomine Sanctae Trinitatis*—Latin)

Inst Act. Institute of Actuaries

Inst Bks Institute of Bankers

Inst CE Institution of Civil Engineers

Inst EE Institution of Electrical Engineers

instill. to be dropped in (*instillandus*—Latin) (pharmacy)

Inst ME. Institute of Marine Engineers

Inst Mech E Institution of Mechanical Engineers

Inst MM Institution of Mining and Metallurgy

Inst NA Institution of Naval Architects

instns instructions

INSTR instruct (US Army)

instr instructions; instructor; instrument; instrumental

Instr of M Instructor of Musketry

instrn instruction

instrns instructions

Inst RNVR Instructor of Royal Naval Volunteer Reserve

instrs instruments

instrum instrumentation

insuff an insufflation (*insufflatio*—Latin) (pharmacy)

INSURV Board of Inspection and Survey (US Navy)

int interchange; interest (*intérêt*—French); interim; interior; interjection; intermediate; internal; international; interpreter; interval; intransitive

INT Interstate Railroad (rr mark)

INTA International New Thought Alliance

int al amongst other things (*inter alia*—Latin)

intcl intercoastal

INTCP intercept (US Army)

intdd intended

Int Dept Department of the Interior

intens intensative; intensive

inter intermediate; interrogative

Intercom intercommunication

interj interjection

intern. internal

internat internotional

inter noct during the night (*inter noctem*—Latin) (pharmacy)

interp interpolation

Inter Sc Intermediate Science

Intl Bank International Bank for Reconstruction and Development

Intl Fund International Monetary Fund

INTMED intermediate (US Army)

intn intention

INTPR interpret (US Army)

INTR intransit (US Army)

intr intransitive; introduction

in trans in transit (*in transitu*—Latin)

Int Rev Internal Revenue

Intro introduced; introducing; introduction; introductory

intropta written within (*introscripta*—Latin)

inv he designed it (*invenit*—Latin); invective; invented; invention; inventor; inventory; inversion; investment; invoice

Inv Inverness

INVES investigate (US Army)

invest. investigations; investment

i o in order; inspecting order

Io ionium; Iowa

IO India Office; Inspecting Order; Intelligence Officer; Interpreter Officer (military)

IOA Institute of Actuaries; Institute of Arbitrators (Inc)

IOAE Institution of Automobile Engineers

IOB Institute of Bankers; Institute of Brewing; Institute of Builders

IOBA Independent Order B'rith Abraham

IOBB Independent Order of B'nai B'rith

IOBI Institute of Bankers in Ireland

IOBK Institute of Bookkeepers

IOBS Institute of Bankers in Scotland

IOC Imperial Opera Company; Institute of Chemistry; International Olympic Committee

IODE Imperial Order, Daughters of the Empire

IOE International Office of Epizootics; Inspectorate of Explosives; International Organization of Employers; Institution of Electronics

IOF Independent Order of Foresters; Institute of Fuel

IOFSI Independent Order of the Free Sons of Israel

IOGT Independent Order of Good Templars

IOH item(s) on hand (US Army)

I O J International Organization of Journalists; Institute of Journalists

IOM Indian Order of Merit; Institute of Metals

I of M Isle of Man

Ion Ionic

IOO Inspecting Ordnance Officer

IOOF Independent Order of Odd Fellows

IOP Institute of Painters in Oil Colours; Institute of Patentees (Inc); Institute of Petroleum; Institute of Physics; Iowa Power & Light (NYSE)

IOQ Institute of Quarrying

IOR Independent Order of Rechabites

I Organisation Organisation internationale des employeurs (OIE)

IORM Improved Order of Red Men

IOS Isle of Skye

IOSM Independent Order of the Sons of Malta

IOU I owe you (colloquial)

IOW Isle of Wight

I p afternoon (*iltapäivällä*—Finnish); identity preserved; improvement purchase; initial point; innings played (baseball); installment paid; intermediate pressure; iron pipe

IP imperial preference; inland post; input primary; International Paper (NYSE); Italian Patent (*Italienisches Patent*—German); Pasteur Institute (*Institut Pasteur*—French)

I&P Indexed and paged (of account books)

i p a including particular average (insurance)

IPA Imperial pale ale; Intermediate power amplifier; International Phonetic Association; International Powercycle Association; Institute of Public Administration

IPAA Independent Petroleum Association of America

IPC Illinois Power Company (NYSE); Institute of Paper Chemistry

IPCEA Insulated Power Cable Engineers Association

IPCX International Paper Company (private car rr mark)

IPD individual package delivery; in presence of the Lords (*in praesentia Dominorum*—Latin)

IPEA Independent Poster Exchanges of America

IPEAA Industrial Packaging Engineers Association of America

Ipecac Ipecacuanha (pharmacy and medicine)

IPEU International Photo-Engravers Union

IPFC Indo-Pacific Fisheries Council

ipi in the regions of the unbelievers (*in partibus infidelium*—Latin)

IPIMIGEO Pan American Institute of Mining Engineering and Geology

IPK International Packers (NYSE)

IPL Indianapolis Power & Light (NYSE)

IPL Pr Indianapolis Power & Light Co. (4% Pfd.) (ASE)

IPM Immediate Past Master (freemasonry)

IPR Institute of Pacific Relations

IPR CTFS Italian Power Realization Trust (ASE)

ips inches per second

i p s iron pipe size

IPS Incorporated Poetry Society; Indian Political (or Police) Service;

International Peace Society
IP size iron pipe size
IPT Independent Pneumatic Tool (NYSE); indexed, paged, and titled; Inspector of Physical Training; Institute of Petroleum Technologists
IPU International Paleontological Union; International Products Corporation (NYSE); Inter-Parliamentary Union
i p v instead of (in plaats van—Dutch)
IPW interrogation prisoner of war (US Army); Interstate Power Company (Del.) (NYSE)
IPWR Institute of Post War Reconstruction
i q the same as (idem quod—Latin)
I Q intelligence quotient
i q e d that which was to be proved (id quod erat demonstrandum—Latin)
IQS International Q Signal (see QS)
i r internal resistance
Ir Ireland; iridium; Irish
IR Immediate Reserve (RAF); India rubber; Ingersoll-Rand Company (NYSE); inland revenue; isoluble residue (chemical); interim report; Iran (Persia); Iranian Airways; Irish Rails; Irish Reports
I and R initiative and referendum
IRA Indian Rights Association; Industrial Recreation Association; Irish Republican Army
IRAA International Rodeo Association of America
Iran. Iranian; Iranic
Iraq. Iraqi
IRB Irish Republican Brotherhood
IRC Infantry Reserve Corps; irregular route carrier; International Red Cross; International Railways of Central America (NYSE); International Rice Commission
IRD Internal Revenue Department
Ire. Ireland
IRE Institute of Radio Engineers
Ired Iredell's Law Reports (legal)
IREM Institute of Real Estate Management
IRF International Road Federation
IRI Industrial Research Institute
ir Ko and company (ir Kompagniet—Lithuanian)
IRL Investors Royalty Company, Inc. (NYSE)
Ir LT Rep Irish Law Times Reports (legal)
IRM Improved Risk Mutuals
IRN Ironton Railroad Company (rr mark)
IRO Inland, or Internal, Revenue Office; International Refugee Organization

iron. ironic
IRQ Iraq (IDP)
Irr irredeemable; irregular
IRRC International Rescue and Relief Committee
irreg irregular
IRT Interborough Rapid Transit (NYC)
IRU Intercontinental Rubber (NYSE); International Relief Union; International Road Transport Union
IRY Intertype Corporation (NYSE)
i s internal shield; mean spherical candle power
is. interstate; island
Is. Isaiah (Biblical); Island[s]; Isle[s]; Isère (French Department)
IS. including sheeting (railway); India Society; input secondary (radio); International Society of Sculptors, Painters and Gravers; Inter-States; Irish Society
Isa Isaiah (Bible)
Isab Isabella
ISAB Institute for the Study of Animal Behavior
ISAL India Society of Art and Literature
ISALPA Incorporated Society of Auctioneers and Landed Property Agents
ISAP South American Petroleum Institute
ISAPC Incorporated Society of Authors, Playwrights and Composers
ISBA Incorporated Society of British Advertisers
isc interstate commerce
ISC Icelandic Steamship Company; Imperial Service College; Imperial Shipping Committee; Incorporated Society of Chiropodists; Indian Staff Corps; International Standards Conference; International Sericultural Commission; International Studies Conference; Iowa State College; Interlake Steamship Company (NYSE)
ISCA International Stewards and Caterers Association
ISCB International Society for Cell Biology
ISCC Inter-Society Color Council
ISCE International Society of Christian Endeavor
ISCM International Society for Contemporary Music
ISD Indian Store Department; Industrial Supplies Department; Interstate Department Stores (NYSE)
ISE Indian Service of Engineers; Institution of Sanitary Engineers; Institution of Structural Engineers

ISEA Industrial Safety Equipment Association
ISEC International Standard Electric Corporation
ISEOI Institute of Shortening and Edible Oils, Inc
ISEUNA International Stereotypers and Electrotypers Union of North America
ISF International Shipping Federation; International Socialist Forum
i s g imperial standard gallon
ISG Industrial Savings Groups; International Silk Guild
ISH Insuranshares Certificates (NYSE)
I S I International Statistical Institute; Iron and Steel Industry; Iron and Steel Institute
ising isinglass
ISIS Institute of Scrap Iron and Steel
ISIWM Incorporated Society of Inspectors of Weights and Measures
isl island; isle
ISM Imperial Service Medal; Incorporated Society of Musicians; Jesus, Savior of the World (Iesus Salvator Mundi—Latin)
ISO Imperial Service Order; International Standards Organisation
iso-Bu isobutyl (chemistry)
isoln isolation
isom isometric
Isostatic. Institut Isostatique International
isoth isothermal
ISP Iota Sigma Pi (society); Indiana Steel Products Company (NYSE)
Isr Israel
ISR Indian State Railways
iss issue
ISS International Shoe Company (NYSE); International Social Service; International Student Service
ISSAB International Social Service, American Branch
ISSB Inter-Service Security Board
ISSS International Society of Soil Science
IST Indiana State Teachers (college); Iowa State Teachers (college)
ISTA International Seed-Testing Association
ISTDA Institutional and Service Textile Distributors Association
i st f in place of (i stället för—Swedish)
isth isthmus
ISTX Interstate Tank Car Corporation (private car rr mark)
ISU International Seamen's Union; International Spinners Union; Iowa

Southern Utilities Company (rr mark); Iowa State University; Insurance Company of North America (NYSE); Southern Iowa Railway Company (rr mark)

ISWG Imperial standard wire gauge

it. item

i t in transit

It. Italian; Italy

IT. immediate transportation; income tax; Indian Territory; Inner Temple (legal); International Tel & Tel (NYSE); Iveagh Trust

ITA Institute of Transit Advertising; International Touring Alliance

ital italics; italicized

Ital Italian

ITC Illinois Terminal Railroad Company (rr mark); Imperial Tobacco Company of Canada (NYSE); Infantry Training Centre

ITCA International Typographic Composition Association

ITCP Institute of Trade and Commerce Professions

ITCPN International Technical Conference on Protection of Nature

ITCX Interstate Transport Company (private car rr mark)

i t d et cetera (*i tak dalej*—Polish)

ITE Institute of Traffic Engineers

ITF inland transit floater (insurance)

ITI International Theatre Institute

itin itinerary; itinerating

ITMA Institute for Training in Municipal Administration

ITO International Trade Organization

ITP The punctuation counts (QS)

ITS Iota Tau Sigma (fraternity)

ITT Institute of Textile Technology

ITU International Telecommunication Union; International Typographical Union

ITUA Industrial Trades Union of America

ITWF International Transport Workers' Federation

I U immunizing unit; international unit; Indiana University; Indian-

apolis Union Railway Company (private car rr mark); International Utilities (NYSE)

IUAI International Union of Aviation Insurers

IUB Interstate Underwriters Board

IUBS International Union of Biological Sciences

IUC International Union of Chemistry

IUCr International Union of Crystallography

IUCWL International Union of Catholic Women's Leagues

IUEC International Union of Elevator Constructors

IUGG International Union of Geodesy and Geophysics

IUHA Industrial Unit Heater Association

IUHS International Union of the History of Science

IUJHUSC International Union of Journeymen Horseshoers of the United States and Canada

IULIA International Union of Life Insurance Agents

IUMMSW International Union of Mine, Mill & Smelter Workers

IUMSWA Industrial Union of Marine and Shipbuilding Workers of America

IUOE International Union of Operating Engineers

IUOTO International Union of Official Travel Organizations

IUPAC International Union of Pure and Applied Chemistry

IUPAP International Union of Pure and Applied Physics

IUPN International Union for the Protection of Nature

IUS International Union of Students

IUSR International Union of Scientific Radio

IUSY International Union of Socialist Youth

IUTAM International Union of Theoretical and Applied Mechanics

IUUCLGW International Union, United Cement, Lime & Gypsum Workers

IUWWML International Union of Wood, Wire and Metal Lathers

IUX Industrias Unidas de Nuevo Laredo, South America (private car rr mark)

iv intravenous

i v increased value; invoice value; initial velocity; under the word (*in verbo*—Latin)

IVA Independent Voters' Association

i W inside diameter (*innere Weite*—German)

i w inside width (measurement)

IW Inspector of Works; Isle of Wight; isotopic weight (chemistry)

IWA Institute of World Affairs; International Woodworkers of America

IWC Inland Waterways Corporation (rr mark); International Whaling Commission

IWCANA International Wood Carvers Association of North America

IWCI Industrial Wire Cloth Institute

IWDGA Independent Wholesale Dry Goods Association

IWG Iowa-Illinois Gas & Electric; iron wire gauge

IWGC Imperial War Graves Commission

IWISTK issue while in stock (US Army)

IWLA Izaak Walton League of America

IWPCA Inland Water Petroleum Carriers Association

IWPR Institute of Women's Professional Relations

IWS International Wool Secretariat

IWSB Insect Wire Screening Bureau

IWT(D) Inland Water Transport (Department)

IWU Illinois Wesleyan University

IWW Industrial Workers of the World

IX Jesus Christ (*Iesus Christus*—Latin); (*Iesous Christos*—Greek)

Ixbre November (*Noviembre*—Spanish)

IY Imperial Yeomanry; International Petroleum, Ltd. (NYSE)

IYC International Youth Congress

izq left-handed (*izquierdo*—Spanish)

J

j newspaper (*journal*—French)

J Jack (cards); Jehovistic; Jew; Jewish; Joule (elec. unit); Judge (*Judex*—Latin); Julius; Jupiter; Justice; law (*jus*—Latin); year

(*Jahr*—German); Standard Oil Company (New Jersey) (NYSE)

Ja Jacob; Jacques; James; Japanese

JA Jewish Agency; joint account

Jac Jacobean; *Jacobus* (James)

JAC Joint Advisory Committee; Juvenile Advisory Council

Jacq J. F. Jacquin (botany)

JACS Journal of the American Chemical Society

J Adv   Judge Advocate
J Adv Gen   Judge Advocate General
JAE   Jaeger Machine Company (NYSE)
JAF   Judge Advocate of the Fleet
JAG   Judge Advocate General (US Army)
JAGC   Judge Advocate General's Corps (US Army)
JAGD   Judge Advocate General's Department
JAGN   Judge Advocate General of the Navy
Jahrb   yearbook (*Jahrbuch*—German)
Jahrg   year (*Jahrgang*—German)
JAJO   January, April, July, October (quarter months)
ja Ko   and company (*ja Komparriet*—Estonian)
Jal   Jalisco
JALX   Likely, Limited, Jos. A (private car rr mark)
Jam.   Jamaica; James (Biblical)
JAM   Journal of Applied Mechanics
Jan   January (*janeiro*—Portuguese); (*januar*—Norwegian); (*január*—Hungarian); (*januari*—Swedish); (*Januar*—Danish)
JANAP   Joint Army-Navy-Air Force Publication (US Army)
janv   January (*janvier*—French)
Jap   Japan; Japanese
JAP   Journal of Applied Physics
JARX   Roebling's Sons Company (private car rr mark)
Jas   James
Jasp   Jasper
JAT   Jugoslovenske Aerotransport (JAT)
jato   jet-assisted takeoff
Jav   Javanese
Jax   Jacksonville
Jb   year book (*Jahrbuch*—German)
JB   Bachelor of Law (*Jurum Baccalaureus*—Latin); Jim Brown Stores (NYSE); John Bull; joint bonds
JBT   Jewelers' Board of Trade
JC   Jesus Christ; Jesus College (Oxford and Cambridge); Jews' College; Jewish Congregations; Jockey Club; Johnson's Cases (legal); Julius Caesar; jurisconsult (*Jurisconsultus*—Latin); Justice Clerk; Juvenile Court
JCA   Jewelry Crafts Association; Jewish Colonization Association
JCB   Bachelor of Canon Law (*Juris Canonici Baccalaureus*—Latin); Bachelor of Civil Law (*Juris Civilis Baccalaureus*—Latin)
JC of C   Junior Chamber of Commerce
JCD   Doctor of Canon Law (*Juris Canonici Doctor*—Latin); Doctor of Civil Law (*Juris Civilis Doctor*—

Latin)
JCDHC   Judge of the Chancery Division of the High Court
J Ch   Johnson's Chancery Reports (legal)
JCL   Reader in Canon Law (*Juris Canonici Lector*—Latin); Licentiate in Canon Law (*Juris Canonici Licentiatus*—Latin)
JCOX   Jordan Company (private car rr mark)
JCP   Journal of Chemical Physics; Justice of the Common Pleas (legal); Penney (J. C.) Company (NYSE)
JCR   Junior Common Room
JCRNFE   Joint Committee on Reduction of Non-essential Federal Expenditures
JCRS   Jewish Consumptive Relief Society
JCS   Joint Chiefs of Staff (US Army); Journal of the Chemical Society
jct   junction
jct pt   junction point
JD   Doctor of Jurisprudence; Doctor of Law (*Juris Doctor*—Latin); Doctor of Laws (*Jurum Doctor*—Latin); Jenkins disc (plumbing); joined (US Army); Junior Dean; Justice Department
J & D   June and December
JDC   Joint Distribution Committee
J E   Joint Enterprise
J of E   Journal of Education
JEA   Jewish Education Association; Joint Export Agent
JEB   Joint Economy Board; Joint Emergency Board
Jed   Jedediah
JEE   Journal of Engineering Education
JEF   Jefferson Lake Sulphur Company (NYSE)
Jeff.   Jefferson's Reports (legal)
Jeho   Jehoshaphat
Jem   Jemima
JEM   Jerusalem and the East Mission
jentac   breakfast (*jentaculum*—Latin) (pharmacy)
Jer   Jeremiah; Jeremy; Jersey; Jerome; Jerusalem
Jes   Jesus
Jes Coll   Jesus College (Oxford and Cambridge)
jew.   jewelry
Jew.   Jewish
Jew. Chron   Jewish Chronicle
Jew. Hist Soc Eng   Jewish Historical Society of England
JF   Jordan Foundation
jfr   compare (*jämför*—Swedish)
jg   junior grade (US Navy)
Jg   Year (*Jahrgang*—German)

JGA   Jeannette Glass Company (NYSE); Jute Goods Association
JGTC   Junior Girls' Training Corps
JGW   Junior Grand Warden (freemasonry)
jh   young men (*jeunes hommes*—French)
Jhs   Jesus (*Jesús*—Spanish)
JHS   Journal of Hellenic Studies
JHU   Johns Hopkins University
JI   Case (J. I.) Company (NYSE)
JIC   Jewelry Industry Council; Joint Industrial Council
jj   judges; justices
J & J   January and July
JJN   Newberry (J. J.) Company (NYSE)
JKC   Julian & Kokenge Company (NYSE)
JKS   Kayser (Julius) & Company (NYSE)
jl   last (*jongstleden*—Dutch)
Jl   Joel
JL   Jones & Laughlin Steel (NYSE)
Jla   Julia
JLSX   Jones & Laughlin Steel Corporation (private car rr mark)
Jlt   Juliet
JLT   Junior Lord of the Treasury
JM   Johns-Manville Company (NYSE)
JMHX   Huber Corporation (private car rr mark)
JMJ   Jesus, Mary and Joseph
jms   never (*jamais*—French)
JMU   James Millikin University
jn   junction
Jn   John
jnd   just noticeable difference
jne   and so on (*ja niin edespäin*—Finnish)
JNF   Jewish National Fund
JNJ   Johnson & Johnson (NYSE)
jnlst   journalist
JNLX   Neils Lumber Company (private car rr mark)
Jno   John
jnr   junior
jnt   joint
jnt stk   joint stock
Jo   Joel; John
JO   Johore (IDP); St. Joseph Lead (NYSE)
Jo Bapt   John the Baptist
Jo'burg   Johannesburg
joc   jocose
JOC   joint operations center (US Army); Young Christian Workers (YCW)
Jo Div   John the Divine
Jo Evang   John the Evangelist
Joh   Johannes; St. John's College (Cambridge)
Johns Cas   Johnson's Cases (legal)
Johns Ch   Johnson's Chancery (legal)

join. joinery
JOJA July, October, January, April (quarter months)
JOM Jerry O'Mahony, Inc. (NYSE)
Jon Jonah (Bible)
Jona Jonathan
Jones & S Jones & Spencer (legal)
JORDAN Air Jordan
JORX Johnson Oil Refining Company (private car rr mark)
Jos Joseph; Joshua; Josiah
Josa Josepha
Jose Josephine
Josh. Joshua (Bible)
JOUAM Junior Order of the United American Mechanics
jour journal; journalist; journeyman
Jour Gen Microbiol Journal of General Microbiology
Jour Hort Sci Journal of Horticultural Science
JOY Joy Manufacturing (NYSE)
JP Justice of the Peace
j&p joists and planks (lumber)
JPB Joint Production Board
JPC Judge of the Prize Court
JPCAC Joint Production, Consulta-

tive and Advisory Committee
JPCX Powell Chemical Company, Inc. (private car rr mark)
j pp afternoon (jälkeen puolenpäivän —Finnish)
J Prob Judge of Probate
jr day (jour—French); journal; year (jòar—Dutch); junior; juror
JR Juvenile Rechabite; King James (Jacobus Rex—Latin); Johnson's Reports (legal)
j r joint resolution
JRF Julius Rosenwald Fund
JRLX Lawrence, J. R. (private car rr mark)
Jr OUAM Junior Order United American Mechanics
JS Japan Society; Johnson Society; Judaeo-Spanish
J & S Jones & Spencer's Reports (legal)
JSA Jewelers' Security Alliance
JSC Joint Standing Committee; Joint Stock Company
JSD Doctor of Science of Law; Doctor of Juristic Science
JSDM June, September, December,

March (quarter months)
JSLB Joint Stock Land Banks
JSMX Jewett & Sherman Company (private car rr mark)
JSS Johnson Stephens & Shinkle Shoe (NYSE)
JSSX Jacob Schlachter's Sons Company (private car rr mark)
JSX Stern & Sons, Inc., Jacob (private car rr mark)
JSYX Young Company, The J. S. (private car rr mark)
jt joint
JT Juvenile Templar (freemasonry)
JTA Jewish Telegraphic Agency
jt agt joint agent
JTB Jute Trade Board
JTC Junior Training Corps (in schools)
jtly jointly
jt r joint rate (shipping)
jt ten. wr of surv & not as ten. in com joint tenants with right of survivorship, and not as tenants in common
Judg Judges (Bible)
JW Jehovah's Witnesses

K

k Boltzmann constant; crown (korona —Hungarian); cumulus clouds (meteorology); karat; keg; kilo; knot; radius of gyration
K calyx; Calends (Kalendae—Latin); cathode (of a vacuum tube); company (Kaishia—Japanese); (Kompagnie —German); (Kompanict—Danish); Kelvin; King; Knight; Kiwanis Club; potassium; specific inductive capacity; visibility factor
Ko Company (Komppania—Finnish)
KA Kapok Association; King of Arms; Knight of St. Andrew (Russian)
kal calends (kalendae—Latin)
KAL Kalamazoo Stove & Furnace (NYSE)
KAN Kansas; Kansas Power & Light (NYSE); Knight of St. Alexander Nevskoi (Russian)
Kans Kansas
KA Kappa Alpha Order (fraternity)
Kap capital (Kapital—German); chapter (Kapitel—Danish)
kap chapter (kapitel—Swedish)
Kar Karafuto
KAR King's African Rifles
Kas Kansas
KAS Kappa Alpha Society (fraternity)

KAT Kappa Alpha Theta (sorority)
Kath Katharine
KAW Kawneer Company (NYSE)
KB King's Bench (legal); King's Bench Reports (legal); king's bishop (chess); kite baloon (RAF); Knight Bachelor; Knight of the Bath; limited partnership (Kommanditbolaget—Swedish)
k and b kitchen and bathroom
KBA Knight of St. Benedict of Avis (Portugal)
KBC King's Bench Court
KBD King's Bench Division
KBDC King's Bench Divisional Court
KBE Key Company (NYSE); Knight of the Black Eagle (Russian); Knight Commander of the Order of the British Empire
KBP Kappa Beta Pi (society)
KBS Knight of the Blessed Sacrament
kc kilocycles
KC Kansas City; Kennel Club; King's College (Cambridge and London); King's Counsel; Kiwanis Club; Knights of Columbus; Knight Commander; Knight of the Crescent (Turkey)

kcal kilocalorie(s)
KCB Knight Commander of the Order of the Bath
k c c kathodic closure contraction (electricity)
KCC King's College, Cambridge; Knight Commander of the Order of the Crown and the Congo Free State (Belgium)
KCCA Korean Chamber of Commerce in America
KCCH Knight Commander of the Court of Honor
KCCX Kimberly-Clark Corporation (private car rr mark)
KCDMA Kiln, Cooler, and Dryer Manufacturers Association
KCH Knight Commander of the Hanoverian Guelphic Order; King's College Hospital (London)
KCHS Knight Commander of the Holy Sepulchre
KCIE Knight Commander of the Order of the Indian Empire
KCL King's College, London; Kings County Lighting (NYSE)
KCL Pr Kings County Lighting Co. (4% Pfd.) (ASE)
KCLS Knight Commander of the Lion and the Sun

KCMG Knight Commander of the Order of St. Michael and St. George
KCNS King's College, Nova Scotia
KCP Knight Commander of the Order of Pius IX
KCPA Kaolin Clay Producers Association
kc/s kilocycles per second
KCS Kansas City Southern Railway Company; Knight of the Order of Charles III of Spain
KCSG Knight Commander of the Order of St. Gregory
KCSI Knight Commander of the Order of the Star of India
KCSS Knight Commander of the Order of St. Sylvester
KCT Kansas City Terminal Railway Company (rr mark)
k c te kathodic closure tetanus (electricity)
KCVO Knight Commander of the Royal Victorian Order
KCX Kingsford Chemical Company (private car rr mark)
KCY Kern County Land Company (NYSE)
kd killed
k d knocked down
KD kiln dried (timber); War Decoration (*Kriegs Dekoration*—German); Kappa Delta (sorority); Katz Drug Company (NYSE); Kentucky Derby
k d c l knocked down, in carloads
KDE Kappa Delta Epsilon (education society); Kidde (Walter) & Company, Inc. (NYSE)
k d f knocked down flat
KDF Strength through Joy (*Kraft durch Freude*—German)
KDG King's Dragoon Guards
k d l c l knocked down in less than carloads
KDR Kappa Delta Rho (fraternity)
KDY Kennedy's, Inc. (NYSE)
KE Kappa Epsilon (society); kinetic energy, (Denmark); Knight of the Elephant (Prussia); Knight of the Eagle
Keb Coll Keble College, Oxford
KECX Kuner-Empson Company (private car rr mark)
KEH King Edward's Horse (Regiment)
KEK Kappa Eta Kappa (fraternity)
Kel Ga Kelly's Reports, Georgia (legal)
Kem chemistry (*Kemi*—German)
Ken. Kentucky; Kenya
Ken. Dec Kentucky Decisions (legal)
KER Kerr-Addison Gold Mines (NYSE); Kerry (county in Ireland)
kern kernan (legal)

Kes cooperative society (*Keskusosuusliike*—Finnish)
KES Keystone Steel & Wire Company (NYSE)
KF Kaiser-Frazer Corporation (NYSE); Kellogg Foundation; Kent Foundation; Knight of Ferdinand (Spain); Kresge Foundation
KFC Kropp Forge Company (NYSE)
KFM Knight of St. Ferdinand and Merit (Naples)
KFSR Karakul Fur Sheep Registry
kg keg; kilogram; king
KG Knight of the Order of the Garter; Kresge (S. S.) Company (NYSE); limited (silent) partnership (*Kommanditgesellschaft*—German)
KGA Kitchen Guild of America
KGB Kewaunee, Green Bay & Western Railroad Company (rr mark)
KGC Knight of the Golden Circle; Knight Grand Commander; Knight of the Grand Cross
kg-cal kilogram-calorie
KGCB Knight of the Grand Cross of the Bath
KGE Knight of the Golden Eagle (German)
KGE Pr Kansas Gas & Elec. Co. (4½% Pfd.) (ASE)
Kgf Prisoner of War (*Kriegsgefangener*—German)
KGF Knight of the Golden Fleece
KGH Knight of the Guelphic Order of Hanover
KGK joint stock limited partnership (*Kabuskiki Goshi Kaisha*—Japanese)
kgl royal (*kongelig*—Danish); (*königlich*—German)
kgm kilogram-meter
kg/m³ kilograms per cubic meter
KGNX Kingan & Company (private car rr mark)
kg per cu m kilograms per cubic meter
kgps kilograms per second
kgs kegs
Kgs Kings (Biblical)
kg/s kilograms per second
KG ST J Knight of Grace of St. John of Jerusalem
KGV Knight of Gustavus Vasa (Sweden)
KH King's Hussars; Knight of Hanoverian Guelphic Order
KHC Honorary Chaplain to the King
KHM King's Harbour Master
KHP Honorary Physician to the King
KHS Honorary Surgeon to the King; Knight of the Holy Sepulchre
KI Kiwanis International
KIA killed in action (US Army)

KIC Kelley Island Lime & Transport (NYSE); Knight of the Iron Crown
KID Allied Kid Company (NYSE)
KiH Kaiser-i-Hind (Indian Medal)
kil kilderkin(s); kilogram; kilometer
kild kilderkin(s)
Kild Kildare (county in Ireland)
Kilk Kilkenny (county in Ireland)
kilo kilogramme
kilol kilolitre[s]
kilom kilometer (metric)
Kin Kinross (county in Scotland)
Kinc Kincardine
kingd kingdom
1 Kings, 2 Kings (Bible)
kir royal (*királyi*—Hungarian)
Kirk. Kirkcudbright (county in Scotland)
KJ Kimberley joint (plumbing); Knight of St. Joachim
K John King John
KJSt J Knight of Justice of St. John of Jerusalem
kk imperial-royal (*Kaiserlich-königlich*—German)
KK Joint stock company (*Kabushiki Kaisha*—Japanese)
K of K (Earl) Kitchener of Khartoum
k Kal small calorie (*kleine Kalorie*—German)
KKE Greek Communist Party
KKG Kappa Kappa Gamma (sorority)
KKK Ku Klux Klan
KKP Kappa Kappa Psi (society)
kl class (*klasse*—Danish); kiloliter; o'clock (*klockan*—Swedish); (*klokken*—Danish)
Kl class (*Klasse*—German)
KL[A] Knight of the Order of Leopold (Austria)
KLAX H. Earl Clock Company (private car rr mark)
KLB Knight of the Order of Leopold (Belgium)
KLH Knight of the Legion of Honor (French)
KLI King's Light Infantry; Klein (D. Emil) Company, Inc. (NYSE)
KLK Kirkland Lake Gold Mining (NYSE)
klm kilometer[s]
KLM Koninklijke Luchtvaart Maatschappij (Royal Dutch Airlines)
k-lo hour (*kello*—Finnish)
KLR Kleinert (I. B.) Rubber Company (NYSE)
KLT Kansas City Power & Light (NYSE)
KLU Kaiser Aluminum & Chemical (NYSE)
km kilometer; kingdom
km² square kilometer
km³ cubic kilometer
Km Kingdom

KM King's Messenger; Knight of Malta

KMC Knapp-Monarch Company (NYSE)

KME Kappa Mu Epsilon (society)

K Mess. King's Messenger

KMH Knight of Merit of Holstein

KMJ Knight of Maximilian Joseph (Bavaria)

km ph kilometers per hour

km/s kilometers per second

KMT Knight of Maria Theresa

kn knot (nautical)

KN Know-Nothing; Kappa Nu (fraternity); Kennecott Copper Corporation (NYSE)

Knick Knickerbocker

KNL Knight of the Netherland Lion

KNR King's National Roll

KNS Knight of the Order of the Royal Northern Star (Sweden)

Knt Knight

KNT Knott Hotels Corporation (NYSE)

Knt Bach Knight Bachelor

KNX Kinney (G. R.) Company, Inc. (NYSE)

k o keep off; keep out; knocked out; knockout

KO Coca-Cola Company (NYSE)

KOB Kobacker Stores, Inc. (NYSE)

k o c kathodic opening contraction (electricity)

KOC Coca-Cola International Corporation (NYSE); Knights of Columbus; Knight of the Order of the Oak Crown

Koeff coefficient (Koeffizient— German)

KO&G Kansas, Oklahoma & Gulf Railway Company

KOLI King's Own Light Infantry

Komp company (Kompagnie— German)

Konr Konrad

konz concentrated (konzentriert— German)

KOP Kappa Omicron Phi (society); Koppers Company, Inc. (NYSE)

KOPX Koppers Company, Inc. (private car rr mark)

Kor Korea

KORR King's Own Royal Regiment

KOSB King's Own Scottish Borderers

KOTX Kanotex Refining Company (private car rr mark)

KOYLI King's Own Yorkshire Light Infantry

K_p power factor

kp kingpost; kitchen police

Kp boiling point (Kochpunkt— German)

KP Kappa Pi (society); Kappa Psi (fraternity); Kellogg Pact; King's

Parade (Cambridge); king's pawn (chess); King's Proctor; Knight of the Order of St. Patrick; Knight of Pythias

KPA Kraft Paper Association

KPC Kirby Petroleum Company (NYSE)

KPC Pr Kirby Petroleum Co. (50¢ Pfd.) (ASE)

KPCX Koppers Company, Inc. (private car rr mark)

KPD Kommunistische Partei Deutschlands (German Communist Party)

KPK Kappa Phi Kappa (fraternity)

KPM King's Police Medal

KPP Keeper of the Privy Purse

KPT Kingston Products Corporation (NYSE)

Kpt captain (Kaptajn—Danish)

kr crown (krona—Swedish); (krone— Danish)

Kr district (Kreis—German); Krypton

KR King's Regiment; King's Regulations; Knight of the Order of the Redeemer (Greece); Kroger Company (NYSE)

KRC Knight of the Red Cross

KRCA King's Roll Clerks' Association

KRD King's Remembrancer's Department

KRE Knight of the Red Eagle (Prussia)

KRI King's Royal Irish Regiment

KRL Kroy Oils Ltd (NYSE)

k r p king's rook pawn (chess)

KRR King's Royal Rifles

KRRC King's Royal Rifle Corps

KRS Kinematograph Renters' Society

KRU Krueger (G.) Brewing Company (NYSE)

KRWX Kalamazoo Rendering Works (private car rr mark)

Ks Kansas

k S short sight (kurze Sicht—German)

ks compare (katso—Finnish)

KS Kappa Sigma (fraternity); keep standing (type); Kentucky State (college); King's Scholar; Knight of the Sword (Sweden); limited (silent) partnership (Kommanditselskabet—Danish)

KSA Knight of St. Anne (Russia)

KSC Kansas State College; King's School, Canterbury; Knight of St. Columba; Kress (S. H.) & Company (NYSE)

KSCX Kaiser Steel Corporation (private car rr mark)

KSE Knight of Saint-Esprit (France)

KSF Knight of San Fernando (Spain); Quaker State Oil Refining Company

(NYSE)

KSFM Knight of S. Ferdinand and Merit (Naples)

KSG Knight of St. George; Knight of St. Gregory

KSH Knight of St. Hubert (Bavaria)

KSI Knight of the Order of the Star of India

KSJ Knight of St. Januarius (Naples)

KSK ethyl iodoacetate (a lachrymatory gas); Kappa Sigma Kappa (fraternity)

ksl very soluble cold (kalt sehr löslich—German)

KSL Kinsel Drug Company (NYSE); Knight of the Sun and Lion (Persia)

KSLI King's Shropshire Light Infantry

KSM and SG Knight of St. Michael and St. George

KSMX Kosmos Portland Cement Company (private car rr mark)

K Soc Kamashastra Society

KSP Knight of St. Patrick; Knight of St. Stanislaus of Poland

KSS Knight of St. Sylvester; Knight of the Southern Star (Brazil); Knight of the Sword of Sweden

KST Kansas State Teachers College

K St J Knight [of Justice or of Grace] of the Order of St. John of Jerusalem

KSU Kansas City Southern Railway (NYSE); Kent State University

KSV Knight of St. Vladimir (Russia)

KSW Knight of Saint Wladimir

KSY King-Seeley Corporation (NYSE)

kt knight; knot

KT Kentucky & Tennessee Railway (rr mark); Kinsmen's Trust; Knight of the Order of the Thistle; Knight Templar; Missouri-Kansas-Texas (NYSE)

Kt Bach Knight Bachelor

Kt Ch Knight of Christ

KTEF Knights Templar Educational Foundation

ktl and so forth (kai ta loipa— Greek)

KTS Knight (of the Order) of the Tower and Sword

KTX Keith Railway Equipment Company (private car rr mark)

Kur Kuril Islands

Kuw Kuwait

kv kilovolt

k v kinematic viscosity

K of V Knights of Vartan

kva kilovolt-ampere

kvar kilovar

kvarh kilovar-hour

KVK Krieg Verdienst Kreuz

KVPX KVP Company, Limited, The (private car rr mark)

KVW Kansas City Kaw Valley Rail-

road, Inc. (rr mark)
kw kilowatt
KW Kelsey-Hayes Wheel, CI B (NYSE); Knight of William (Netherlands)
kw-an kilowatt-year (*kilowatt-an*—German)

Kwan Kwantung
KWE Knight of the White Eagle (Poland)
kwhr kilowatt-hour
Kwiec April (*Kwiecièn*—Polish)
k w l not very soluble cold (*kalt*

wenig löslich—German)
Kwst kilowatt hour (*Kilowattstunde*—German)
Ky Kentucky
Ky LR Kentucky Law Reporter (legal)

L

l elbow (plumbing); lady; ladyship; lake; latitude; law; leaf; league; left; lempira; length; leu; licentiate; lightning; liner; link; literate; little; low; lower; lumen; place (*locus*—Latin); pound (*livre*—French); read (*lies*—German)
L book (*liber*—Latin); elbow (plumbing); elevated railway, Labour; Latin; Liberal; Linnaeus (botany); London; Lord; Lordship; Lucius, Luke; Luxembourg
£ pound sterling
l a law agent; lead angle (gears); leasehold area; by the rules of the art (*lege artis*—Latin) (pharmacy); lightning arrester; local agent
la last (wool weight)
La lanthanum; Louisiana
LA American Locomotive Company (NYSE); law agent; Law Association; legal adviser; Legislative Assembly; Library Association; Lieutenant-at-Arms; light alloy; Literate in Arts; Liverpool Academy; Lloyd's Agent; local agent; Local Authority; loop aerial; Los Angeles; low altitude (US Army)
L/A landing account (shipping); Letter of Authority; lighter than air
l/a letter of advice (*lettre d'avis*—French)
£A pound Australian
L&A Louisiana & Arkansas Railway Company
LAA Lancashire Authors' Association; Licentiate of the Central Association of Accountants; Light anti-aircraft; Liverpool Academy of Arts; London Architectural Association of Certified Accountants
LAAOH Ladies' Auxiliary, Ancient Order of Hibernians
L A B low-altitude bombing
lab. labor; laborer; laboratory
Lab. Labour (English political party); Labrador; Labuan
LAB Labor Advisory Board; Legal Advisers' Branch; Lloyd Aereo Boliviano; Local Appeal Board; London Association for the Blind

Lab Stat Bull. Labor Statistics Bulletin
Lac Lacerta
LAC Lancashire Associated Collieries; Leading Aircraftman; Licentiate of the Apothecaries' Company; London Athletic Club; Liquidation Advisory Committee
LACSA Lineas Aereas Costarricenses
LACW Leading Aircraftwoman (WAAF)
LAD Light Aid Detachment; Lord Advocate's Department
LADE Lineas Aereas del Estado
ladp ladyship
L Adv Lord Advocate
laev laevus (left)
LAG L'Aiglon Apparel, Inc. (NYSE)
LAH Licentiate of Apothecaries' Hall
LAI Linee Aeree Italiane; Los Angeles Investment Company (NYSE)
lam laminated
LAM Lamarck (botany); Lamentations (Biblical); Lambert Company (NYSE); London Academy of Music; Master of the Liberal Arts (*Liberalium Artium Magister*—Latin)
LAMDA London Academy of Music and Dramatic Art
LAMSA Lineas Asociadas Mexicanas
L A N local apparent noon (navigation)
LAN Lanston Monotype Machinery Company (NYSE); Lineas Aerea Nacional
Lanc Lancaster
Lancs Lancashire
landw agricultural (*landwirt schaftlich*—German)
Lan Fus Lancashire Fusiliers
lang language
Lang Languedoc (France)
LANICA Lineas Aereas de Nicaragua
LANS Lansing (legal)
Lans Lansing's Supreme Court Reports (legal)
LANSA Lineas Aereas Nacionales

Lant Atlantic (US Navy)
LANY Linseed Association of New York
LAO Licensing Authorities' Office; Licentiate in Obstetrics
Lap. Lapland
LAP Loide Aereo Nacional
LAPX Linde Air Products Company, The (private car rr mark)
larg width (*largeur*—French); broadly (*largamente*) (music)
LARX Aetna Oil Company, Inc. (private car rr mark)
laryngol laryngological; laryngology
LAS Land Agents' Society; Licentiate of the Society of Apothecaries; Liverpool Architectural Society; London Apothecaries' Society; Lord Advocate of Scotland; Los Angeles Stock Exch.
LASX Lutz & Schramm, Inc. (private car rr mark)
lat wide (*latus*—Latin) (pharmacy); latitude
l a t local apparent time (navigation)
Lat Latin; Latvia
LAT Linseed Association Terms
latd latitude
lat def latent defect
lat dol to the painful side (*lateri dolenti*—Latin) (pharmacy)
lat ht latent heat
Lat pros Latin prosody
Latv Latvia
LAU Consolidated Laundries Corporation (NYSE)
LAUK Library Association of the United Kingdom
laun launched
Laur Laurence
LAV Linea Aeropostal Venezoliana
law. lawyer
LAW League of American Wheelmen; League of American Writers
Law Rep law reports
Lawr Lawrence
Laz Lazarus
lb lavatory basin; leg-bye (cricket); letter box; light bomber; pound (*libra*—Latin); local battery; local

board

LB Bachelor of Letters; (*Litterarum Baccalaureus*—Latin); to the kind reader (*lectori benevolo*—Latin); Ludwig Baumann & Company (NYSE)

lb ap pound, apothecaries'

lb av pound avoirdupois

LBC Land Bank Commission; London Bankruptcy Court

lb cal pound calorie

lb CHU pound centigrade heat unit

LBCM London Board of Congregational Ministers

LBD Legate of British Dramatists

L/Bdr Lance-Bombardier

lb ft pound foot

lb ft² pound per square foot

LBII Licensed Beverage Industries, Inc.

lb in. pound-inch

lb in² pound per square inch

LBMLA Little Business Men's League of America

LBP Length between perpendiculars (naval engineering)

LBPRC Laminated Bakery Package Research Council

lbr labor; lumber

LBR Labrador

LBRX Branchflower Co., Lyle (private car rr mark)

lbs to the benevolent reader greeting (*lectori benevolo salutem*—Latin); pounds

LBS London Botanical Society

LB & SCR London, Brighton & South Coast Railway

lb sq ft pound per square foot

lb t pound troy

l b w leg before wicket (cricket)

LBX Long-Bell Lumber Company, The (private car rr mark)

LBY Liberty Fabrics of New York (NYSE)

l c law courts; lead-covered (cables); leading cases; left center (stage); legal currency; legislative council; letter card; letter of credit; lead crossing; line of contract; loose coupler; lower case

LC deferred (telegram); label clause; Lance Corporal; Lancaster and Chester Railway Company (rr mark); landing craft; Lawrence College; League of Composers; Lee Conservancy; Liberation Committee; Library of Congress; Licencing Committee; Lieutenant Commander; Livestock Commissioner; London cheque; London clause (shipping); Lord Chamberlain; Lower California; Lower Canada

L/C letter of credit

l of c lines of communication

LCA Lake Carriers Association; Lake Central Airlines; Lambda Chi Alpha; Lords Commissioners of the Admiralty

LCATA Laundry and Cleaners Allied Trade Association

lcb longitudinal center of buoyancy

LCB Liquor Control Board; Lord Chief Baron

l c c landing craft control

LCC London Chamber of Commerce; London County Council

l c d lowest common denominator

LCD La Consolidada, Amer. 6% Pfd. (NYSE); London College of Divinity; Lord Chamberlain's Department; Lord Chancellor's Department; lower court decisions (legal)

lcdo licensed (*licenciado*—Spanish)

LCE Lone Star Cement Corporation (NYSE)

l c f least common factor; longitudinal center of flotation

LCFX Forman & Sons, Inc. L. C. (private car rr mark)

lcg longitudinal center of gravity

L Ch Licentiate in Surgery (*Licentiatus Chirurgiae*—Latin)

LCI Landing Craft Infantry

LCIX Liquid Carbonic Corporation (private car rr mark)

LCJ Lord Chief Justice

LCL less than carload (US Army); less than carload lot; local; Licentiate of Civil Law

l c m least common multiple (mathematics)

LCM Lagos Church Missions; Landing Craft Mechanized; London City Mission; London College of Music

LCMF Lancashire and Cheshire Manufacturers Federation

LCN Lehigh Coal & Navigation (NYSE)

l c n local civil noon (navigation)

L Corp lance corporal

LCP League of Coloured Peoples; Licentiate of the College of Preceptors

LCR Landing Craft Rubber

l/cr letter of credit (*lettre de crédit*—French)

l cr lieutenant commander

l c t local civil time (navigation)

LCT Landing Craft Tank

LCTA London Corn Trade Association

LCVP Landing Craft Vehicle Personnel

LCY Laclede-Christy Company (NYSE)

l d lady's day; lethal dose; light difference; line of departure; line of duty; low door; well said (*lepide dictum*—Latin)

ld land; lead; limited; load; lord

LD Doctor of Letters; Land Office Decisions; left door (theatre); Licentiate in Divinity; Light Dragoons; London Docks; Low Dutch; Praise be to God (*Laus Deo*—Latin)

l & d loss and damage; loans and discounts

L en D Licentiate of Law (*Licencié en Droit*—French)

lda limited (*limitada*—Portuguese)

LDBA Linens and Domestics Buyers of America

ldc lower dead center

LDCMMA Laundry and Dry Cleaners Machinery Manufacturers Association

LDD Local Defense Division

ldg landing; leading; loading; lodging

Ldg Acwm Leading Aircraftwoman (WAAF)

ldg & dely landing and delivery

ldgs lodgings

ld gt land grant

L d'H Legion of Honor (*Légion d'honneur*—French)

L Div Licentiate in Divinity

LDL Lambda Delta Lambda (society)

ld lmt load limit

LDM Licentiate of Dental Medicine

Ldn London

Ldp Laydship; Lordship

ldr laundry; leader; ledger

lds loads

LDS Latter-Day Saints; Licentiate in Dental Science; Licentiate in Dental Surgery; praise be to God (*Laus Deo*—Latin)

LDSR League of Distilled Spirits Rectifiers

l e left end; left eye

le lease

LE Labour Exchange; leading edge (RAF); low explosive (US Army)

£E Egyptian pound

lea league; leather; leave

LEA Local Education Authority

LEAA Lace and Embroidery Association of America

Leb Lebanon

LEC Electrolux Corporation (NYSE); Local Employment Committee

lect lecture

led. ledger

LED Lead Employers' Council; London Engine Drivers

L Ed United States Supreme Court Reports, Lawyer's Edition

LEDC League for Emotionally Disturbed Children

l e f liberty, equality, fraternity (*liberté, egalité, fraternité*—

French)

LEF Lake Erie, Franklin & Clarion Railroad Company (rr mark); Lefcourt Realty Corporation (NYSE)

Leg. alloy (*Legierung*—German)

leg. legal; legate; legato (music); legislation; legislative; legislature; he reads (*legit*—Latin); they read (*legunt*—Latin)

LEG. Legal [Department] (UN Secretariat)

leg.-b leg-bowled (cricket)

Leg. Canut Leges Canuti (Laws of King Canute)

Leg, Edm Leges Edmundi (Laws of King Edmund)

legg light and rapid (*leggiero*—music)

LEH Lehigh Valley Coal Corporation (NYSE)

leichtl easily soluble (*leichtlöslich*—German)

Leics Leicestershire

Leip Leipzig

Le Is. Leeward Islands

Leit Leitrim

LEL Laureate in English Literature

Lem Lemuel

LEM Lehman Corporation (NYSE)

Leon Leonard; Leonard's (Law Reports)

LER Lerner Stores Corporation (NYSE); London Electric Railway

LES Lees , James & Sons Company (NYSE); Leslie Salt Company (NYSE); Liverpool Engineering Society

L ès L Licentiate in Letters (*Licencié ès Lettres*—French)

L ès Sc Licencié ès Sciences

L et C Loir-et-Cher (French Department)

L et Ch Loir-et-Cher (French Department)

L et G *Lot-et-Garonne* (French department

let. letter; draft (*lettre*—French)

Lett Lettic; Lettish

lett hd letterhead

Lev Leviticus

lex lexicon

lexicog lexicographical; lexicographer; lexicography

Leyd Leyden

l f ledger folio; left field; light face (type); low frequency

lf leaf (botany)

LF Lancashire Fusiliers; Lakser Foundation

l f a local freight agent

LFB London Fire Brigade

l f c low-frequency current

LFC Lutheran Free Church

lfd current (*laufend*—German)

L F D least fatal dose (medicine)

LFE London Fur Exchange

lfg a portion (*lieferung*—German)

l f l late fee letter

LFM Lieutenant Field Marshal

LFPS Licentiate of the Faculty of Physicians and Surgeons

LFPSG Licentiate of the Faculty of Physicians and Surgeons, Glasgow

l Fr Law French

L F S late fee service

lft leaflet (botany)

l ft linear foot (lumber)

LFTB Louisville Freight Tariff Bureau

l g large grain; left guard (football); life guard

LG Laclede Gas Company (NYSE); landing ground (RAF); Leicester Galleries; Leper Guild (St. Francis'); Lewis gun; life guard; Lloyd George; London Gazette; Low German

LGAR Ladies of the Grand Army of the Republic

L G B local government board

LGCE Local Great Chamberlain of England

LGD Lambda Gamma Delta (society)

lge large

L Ger Low German

LGL Lynch Corporation (NYSE)

LGM Lloyd's Gold Medal

LGOC London General Omnibus Company

LGPA Luftgaupostamt (German)

L Gr late Greek; low Greek

LGSM Licentiate of Guildhall School of Music

lgth length

lg tn long ton

LGU Ladies' Golf Union

LGW Longines-Wittnauer Watch Company, (NYSE)

LGX Lehigh Gas (private car rr mark); Lehigh, Inc. (private car rr mark)

l h left hand; left handed; lever handle; luteinizing hormone (medicine)

LH Leath & Company (NYSE); Legion of Honor; licensing hours; light horse; lighthouse

LHA Lord High Admiral; local highway authority; local hour angle

LHAR London, Hull, Antwerp, or Rotterdam (shipping)

l h b left halfback (football)

LHC Lord High Chancellor

LHCCBCI London and Home Counties Conciliation Board of the Cinematograph Industry

LHCGACS Lord High Commissioner to the General Assembly of the Church of Scotland

LHCJEA London and Home Counties Joint Electricity Authority

LHD Doctor of Humanities (*Litterorum Humaniorum Doctor*—Latin)

l-hr lumen-hour

LHR Lehigh & Hudson River Railway Company, The (rr mark)

L&HR Lehigh and Hudson River Railway Company

LHT Lord High Treasurer

LHWCA Longshoremen's and Harbor Workers' Compensation Act

l i letter of introduction; longitudinal interval

li link; *lira* (Italian)

Li lithium

LI Leeward Islands; Licentiate of Instruction; Light Infantry; Lions international; Locomotive Institute; Long Island; Long Island Railroad Company

lia license (*licentia*—Latin)

LIA Lead Industries Association; Livestock Industry Act

LIAA Life Insurance Advertisers Association; Life Insurance Association of America

LIAMA Life Insurance Agency Management Association

lib book (*libro*—Spanish); liberal; librarian; library

Lib Liberia

lib cat. library catalogue

Lib Cong Library of Congress

Lib Nat Liberal National

libr librarian

Lic attorney (*Licenciado*—Spanish)

LIC Life Insurers Conference

Lic Med Licentiate in Medicine

LID League for Industrial Democracy

L&ID London and India Docks

Lieut Lieutenant

Lieut (jg) Lieutenant (junior-grade) (US Navy)

Lieut Col Lieutenant Colonel

Lieut Comdr Lieutenant Commander

Lieut Gen Lieutenant General

Lieut Gov Lieutenant Governor

Liech Liechtenstein

LIFPL Women's International League for Peace and Freedom (WILPF)

Lig Limoges (France)

LIG Lord Justice General

LIL Lily-Tulip Cup Corporation (NYSE)

Lim Limerick

LIMDAT limiting date (US Army)

lin boundary (*linea*—Spanish); lineal; linear; liniment

Linc Coll Lincoln College, Oxford
Lincs Lincolnshire
linct linctus (pharmacy)
Lindl Lindley (botany)
L Infre Loire-Inférieure (French Department)
lin ft linear foot
ling linguistics
Linn Linnaean; Linnaeus
lino linotype
LIO Lionel Corporation (NYSE)
lip. life insurance policy
Lip. July (*Lipiec*—Polish)
liq liquid; liquidation; liquor; solution (*liqueur*—French)
liq jud judicial liquidation (*liquidation judiciaire*—French)
liquon liquidation
LIRR Long Island Railroad Company
LIS Long Island Sound
Listop November (*Listopad*—Polish)
lit. liter; literal; literally; literary; literature
l lt Italian lires (*lire Italiane*—Italian)
Lit. Lawrence Institute of Technology
Lit D Doctor of Letters (*Litterarum Doctor*—Latin)
Lith Lithuania; Lithuanian
lithog lithography
lithol lithology
Lit Hum the Humanities (*Literæ Humaniores*—Latin)
litt littérateur; literary person
Litt B Bachelor of Letters (*Litterarum Baccalaureus*—Latin)
Litt D Doctor of Letters (*Litterarum Doctor*—Latin)
Litt L Licentiate in Letters (*Litterarum Licentiatus*—Latin)
Litt M Master of Letters
liturg liturgical; liturgics; liturgy
liv book; pound (*livre*—French); delivery (*livraison*—French)
Liv Jud Op Livingston's Judicial Opinions
liv st pound sterling (*livre sterling*—French)
l j current year (*laufen jahre*—German)
LJ Law Journal; Lord Justice; Libby, McNeill & Libby (NYSE); Library Journal
LJA Lord Justice of Appeal
LJJ Lords Justices
LJKB Law Journal, King's Bench (legal)
LJMX Laplace, L J & M (private car rr mark)
LJ Rep Law Journal Reports (legal)
Lk Luke (Biblical)
LK Lockheed Aircraft (NYSE)

LKB Link-Belt Company (NYSE)
lkg & bkg leakage and breakage (insurance)
LKHD Lockheed (aircraft)
LKK Lake Shore Mines, Ltd (NYSE)
LKQCPI Licentiate of the King and Queen's College of Physicians, Ireland
Lkr locker
LKS Lambda Kappa Sigma (society)
LKY Lakey Foundry Corporation (NYSE)
l l leased lines; lighterage limits; live load; loose leaf; do not end a line (typography); in the place quoted (*loco laudato*—Latin)
ll last, ultimate (*laatstleden*—Dutch)
Ll of laws (*Legum*—Latin); Lords
LL Late Latin; Law Latin; Lease-Lend; Lending Library; Limited Liability; London Lyceum; Lord Lieutenant; Lorillard, P., Company (NYSE); Low Latin
LLA Lady Literate in Arts (St. Andrews University)
LLAAII Their Imperial Highnesses (*Leurs Altesses Impériales*—French)
LLAARR Their Royal Highnesses (*Leurs Altesses Royales*—French)
L Lat Low Latin
LLB Bachelor of Laws (*Legum Baccalaureus*—Latin); Local Licensing Bench
Ll & Cos Lloyds' and Companies'
LL D Doctor of Laws (*Legum Doctor*—Latin)
LLD Legislative and Liaison Division (US Army)
LLEE Their Eminences (*Leurs Eminences*—French); Their Excellencies (*Leurs Excellences*—French)
LLGMA Luggage and Leather Goods Manufacturers of America
LLGSAA Luggage and Leather Goods Salesmen's Association of America
LLI Lord Lieutenant of Ireland
LLJJ Lords Justices
LL L Licentiate in Laws (*Legum Licentiatus*—Latin)
LLL Love's Labour's Lost; Liberal Liberty League; loose leaf ledger (paper)
LLM Master of Laws (*Legum Magister*—Latin)
LLMM Their Majesties (*Leurs Majestés*—French); Their Majesties (*Loro Maesta*—Italian)
LLN League for Less Noise
Lloyd's LR Lloyd's List Law Reports

Lloyd's Pr Cas Lloyd's Prize Case
LLPE Labor's League for Political Education
L & LS Londonderry and Lough Swilly (railway)
L l t London landed terms
LLT Long Island Lighting (NYSE)
LLX Louisiana Land & Exploration (NYSE)
l m long meter (music) [symbol for]; mechanical efficiency; place of the monument (*locus monumenti*—Latin)
l M of the current month (*laufenden Monats*—German)
LM Legion of Merit (US Army); Licentiate in Medicine; Licentiate in Midwifery; Liggett & Myers Tobacco (NYSE); London Museum; Lord Mayor
l & m labor and material bond (insurance)
LMA Last Manufacturers Association; Lingerie Manufacturers Association
LMAS London and Middlesex Archæological Society
l m c low middling clause (cotton trade)
LMC Labour Management Committee; Lamson Corporation of Delaware (NYSE); Lloyd's machinery certificate
LMCC Licentiate of Medical Council of Canada
l m d long meter double (music)
L Med Licentiate in Medicine
LMH Lady Margaret Hall (Oxford)
lm-hr lumen hour
L Mi Leo Minor (constellation)
LMLX Libby, McNeill & Libby (private car rr mark)
LMN lineman (US Army)
LMNA Label Manufacturers National Association
LMPB Labor-Management Public Board
LMRCP Licentiate in Midwifery of the Royal College of Physicians
LMRX Globe Oil & Refining Company (Illinois) (private car rr mark)
LMS Lamson & Sessions Company (NYSE); Licentiate in Medicine and Surgery; London Malacological Society; London Mathematical Society; London Medical Society; London Mendicity Society; London Microscopical Society; London, Midland and Scottish (Railway); London Missionary Society; London Municipal Society
l m s c let me see correspondence
LMSR London Midland and Scottish Railway
LM & SR London, Midland and Scottish Railway

LMSSA Licentiate in Medicine and Surgery of the Society of Apothecaries

l m t length, mass, time (physics); local mean time

lmtd limited

LMTX Libby, McNeill & Libby (private car rr mark)

LMVX Leas & McVitty, Inc. (private car rr mark)

l n north latitude (*latitude nord*—French)

lN liaison (US Army); lien; loan; logarithm natural

LN Air Liban; Louisville & Nashville Railroad (NYSE)

L&N Louisville & Nashville Railroad Company (rr mark)

L of N League of Nations

LNA Lithographers National Association

L Nat Liberal National

LNC League of Nations Covenant; Lincoln Printing Company (NYSE)

LND Lindsay Chemical Company (NYSE)

lndymn laundryman

LNE Lehigh and New England Railroad Company (rr mark)

LNER London and North-Eastern Railway

LNO Lion Oil Company (NYSE)

LNP Lehn & Fink Products Corporation (NYSE)

LNPX Lincoln Packing Company (private car rr mark)

Lnrk Lanark

L&N RR Louisville & Nashville Railroad

LNU League of Nations Union

LNWR London & North-Western Railway

LNY Lane Bryant, Incorporated (NYSE)

l o lubricating oil; their order (*leur ordre*—French)

lo local; lubricating; lubrication; in place (*loco*) (music)

LO Liaison Officer; lock out; London office; look out; lubrication order (US Army)

Lo Louth

LΩ legal ohm (electricity)

l o a length over all

LOAA Lace Operatives of America, Amalgamated

loadg & dischg loading and discharging

loadg pt loading port

l o b left on base (baseball)

LOB Loblaw Groceterias (NYSE)

LOB A Loblaw Groceterias A (NYSE)

LOB B Loblaw Groceterias B (NYSE)

l o c letter of credit

loc local; location

LOC location (US Army); Locke Steel Chain Company (NYSE)

loc cit at the place mentioned (*loco citato*—Latin)

loc cur. local currency

loc laud in the place cited (*loco laudato*—Latin)

locn location

loco locomotive

loc primo cit in the place first cited (*loco primo citato*—Latin)

LOCPUR local purchase order (US Army)

LOE League of the Empire; Loew's Boston Theatres Company (NYSE)

LOF Libbey-Owens-Ford Glass (NYSE)

LOFC line of communication (US Army)

LOFD line of departure (US Army)

LOFX Libbey-Owens-Ford Glass Company (private car rr mark)

log. logarithm (mathematics); logic; logistic

LOG Lambda Omicron Gamma (society)

LOL Louisiana P&L (NYSE)

LOM League of Mercy; Loyal Order of Moose

LOMA Life Office Management Association

LOMGEN Lombard General (Telegraphic Code)

LOMSHIP Lombard Shipping (Telegraphic Code)

LON Lonergan, Class B (NYSE)

Lond London; Londonderry

Lond R London Regiment

long. long (*longus*—Latin) (pharmacy); longitude; longitudinal

Long. Longford

longl longitudinal

LOOM Loyal Order of Moose

LOPM Liaison Office for Personnel Management

loq he (she) speaks (*loquitur*—Latin)

Lor Lorenzo

loran long-range [direction finding]

lösl soluble (*löslich*—German)

LOSX Los Angeles Soap Company (private car rr mark)

lot. lotion

LOT Polish State Airlines Lot

Lou Louisiana; Louth

LOU Louisville Gas & Elec. (Kentucky) (NYSE)

Louv Louvain

lox liquid oxygen

Loz Lozère (French department)

l p land plane; large paper; large post; long primer; low pressure

Lp Ladyship; Lordship

LP Labour Party; Last post; Lay preacher; Liberal Party; London Port; Lord Provost; Lord of the Privy Council

£P Palestine pound

LPC Lord President of the Council

LPCX Lehigh Portland Cement Company (private car rr mark)

LPGA Liquefied Petroleum Gas Association

LPI Louisiana Polytechnic Institute

LPM long particular meter (music); Lambda Phi Mu (society)

LPO Liberal Party Organization London Philharmonic Orchestra

Lpool Liverpool

LPPA Laminated Paperboard Package Association

LPS Le Play Society; London Parcels Section; London Philharmonic Society; Lord Privy Seal

LPT Lehigh Portland Cement Company (NYSE)

LPTB London Passenger Transport Board

LPVSA Limited Price Variety Stores Association

LPVX Louisville Provision Company (private car rr mark)

lpw lumens per watt

LQ Long-Bell Lumber Corporation (NYSE)

LQ Rev Law Quarterly Review

LQT Liquid Carbonic Corporation (NYSE); Liverpool Quay Terms

lR current account (*laufen Rechnung*—German)

l r log run (lumber)

Lr Laurence; Lawrence; Lira; Lorenzo

LR Land Registry; Law Reports; Lee Rubber & Tire Corporation (NYSE); Leicestershire Regiment; Lloyds' Register; long radius; Loyal Regiment

L & R lake and rail

LRA Lawyers' Reports, Annotated (legal)

LRAM Licentiate of the Royal Academy of Music

LRC Labour Representation Committee; Lincoln Relief Corps; London Rowing Club

LRCh App Law Reports, Chancery Appeal Cases

LRCM Licentiate of the Royal College of Music

LRCP Licentiate of the Royal College of Physicians

LRCPE Licentiate of the Royal College of Physicians of Edinburgh

LRCS Licentiate of the Royal

College of Surgeons

LRCSE Licentiate of the Royal College of Surgeons, Edinburgh

LRCSI Licentiate Royal College of Surgeons, Ireland

LRCVS Licentiate of the Royal College of Veterinary Surgeons

LRD London Recruiting Depot

lres letters (legal)

LRFPS Licentiate of the Royal Faculty of Physicians and Surgeons, Glasgow

LRFPSG Licentiate of the Royal Faculty of Physicians and Surgeons of Glasgow

LRHL Law Reports, House of Lords

LRIBA Licentiate of the Royal Institute of British Architects

LR KB Law Reports, King's Bench Division

LRMC Lloyd's refrigerating machinery certificate (shipping)

lr mco log run, mill culls out (lumber)

LRQB Law Reports, Queen's Bench

LRRO Land Revenue Record Office

Lrs Lancers

LRS Land Registry Stamp; Lloyd's Register of Shipping

LRSA Law Reports, South Australia (legal)

LRT last resort target (US Army)

l S long sight (lange Sicht—German)

ls land side; leading seamen; left side; letter service; letter signed; local sunset; lump sum; place of the seal (locus sigilli—Latin); south latitude (latitude sud—French)

LS Lamb Society; Law Society; Leading Seaman; Letter Service; Licentiate in Surgery; Light Sussex; Linnæan Society; Listed Securities; London Scottish; London Society; long shot; Lotta Suard (Finland's Women's Army)

l to s lighterage to shipside

l s a live stock agent

LSA Licentiate of the Society of Apothecaries; Linguistic Society of America

LSAA Linen Supply Association of America

LSAC London Sessions Appeal Committee; London Small Arms Company

l s b a leading sick-bay attendant

l s c in the place above cited (loco supra citato—Latin); lower school certificate

LSC London Salvage Corps; London Society of Compositors; London Survey Committee

LSCB Luscombe (aircraft)

lsd lightermen, stevedores and dockers; pounds, shillings, pence (librae, solidi, denarii—Latin)

lsd li leased line (railroad)

LSE left second entrance (theater); London School of Economics; London Stock Exchange

LSF Little Steel Formula; Local Security Force (Irish)

lsg solution (lösung—German)

LSG Lone Star Gas Company (NYSE)

LS (&) GCM Long Service and Good Conduct Medal (RAF)

L/Sgt Lance-Sergeant

LSHMH Lord Steward of His Majesty's Household

LSI Leaf Spring Institute

LS&I Lake Superior & Ishpeming Railroad Company

LSIA Lamp and Shade Institute of America

LSIOA Lake Superior Iron Ore Association

LSJM Praise be to Jesus and Mary (Laus sit Jesu et Maria—Latin)

LS & MS RY Lake Shore & Michigan Southern Railway

LSO Labour Supply Organization; Limitation of Supplies Order; London String Orchestra; London Symphony Orchestra; Louisiana Southern Railway Company (rr mark)

LSPX Lone Star Producing Company (private car rr mark)

LSS Life Saving Service; Life-Saving Station

LSSX Louis Stern Sons, Inc. (private car rr mark)

LST Landing-ship Tank; Lowenstein (M) & Sons (NYSE); local standard time

l stg pound sterling

LSU Louisiana State University

LSV Life Savers Corporation (NYSE)

LSWR London and South-Western Railway

LSX Lang & Son, Inc. C.C. (private car rr mark); La Salle Extension University (NYSE)

l t landed terms; lawn tennis; leading telegraphist; lieutenant; local time; long ton; low tension

lt In accordance with (laut—German); light

lT Turkish pound (lira Turca—Italian)

Lt Lieutenant

LT Lake Terminal Railroad Company; landing team or light (US Army); Law Times; Lawn Tennis; Leading Torpedoman; Legal Tender;

Liberty Ticket; Licentiate in Teaching; Licentiate in Theology; Low Tension; National Lead Company (NYSE); Turkish Pound

L/T Leading Telegraphist; Line Telegraphy

LTA Lawn Tennis Association; Linen Trade Association; London Teachers' Association

Lt Alt Alternating Marine Light

LTB London Transport Board; low-tension battery

LTCL Licentiate of Trinity College of Music, London

Lt Col Lieutenant Colonel

Lt Com Lieutenant Commander

ltd Limited

LTda limited (Limitada—Portuguese, Spanish)

LTEA Leaf Tobacco Exporters Association

LTF Lithographic Technical Foundation

Lt F Fl Fixed and Flashing Marine Light

Lt Fl Flashing Marine Light

ltge lighterage

Lt Gov lieutenant governor

lth lath (lumber)

lt h lighthouse

LTI Lowell Textile Institute

Lt Inf Light Infantry

LTL less than truckload

LTM Licentiate in Tropical Medicine

ltng arr lightning arrester

Lt Occ Occulting Marine Light

LTOS Law Times, Old Series (legal)

LTPCA Liquid Tight Paper Container Association

LTPX Lewis Tar Products Company (private car rr mark)

LTR letter; lighter (US Army)

LTRS Low Temperature Research Station

LT&SR London, Tilbury and Southend Railway

LTU LeTourneau (R.G.) Incorporated (NYSE)

lt-v light-vessel (shipping)

lt wt light weight

Lu lutecium

LU Langston University; Laval University; Lehigh University; Liberal Unionist; Loyola University

L & U loading and unloading (railway)

lub oil lubricating oil

lubric lubricate; lubricant; lubricator

LUC Lukens Steel Company (NYSE)

Lucr The Rape of Lucrece

l u e left upper entrance (theater)

lu h lumen hour (*lumen-heure*—French)
l u h f lowest useful high frequency
lum lumber
Lun Monday (*Lunes*—Spanish)
LUN League of United Nations
Lun Int Lunitidal Interval (navigation)
luo *luogo* (music)
Lup Lupus (constellation)
LUQ Laval University, Quebec
LUR London Underground Railways
Luth Lutheran
Lux Luxembourg
LUX Lion Oil Company (private car rr mark)
lv leave
l v legal volt (electricity); licensed victualler; low voltage
LV Lehigh Valley Railroad Company
LVI Praise to the Incarnate Word

(*Laus Verbo Incarnato*—Latin)
LVRR Lehigh Valley Railroad Company
lvs leaves (botany)
LVT landing vehicle, tracked
LVT(A) landing vehicle tracked (armored)
l w lap weed; long wave; low water; lumens per watt
l W internal diameter (*lichte Weite*—German)
LW Lake of the Woods Milling (NYSE); Lowe's Inc (NYSE); London waterguard; long wave (radio); low water
l w b long wheelbase
LWIU Laundry Workers International Union
l w l length on water line; load-water-line

LWL Lane-Wells Company (NYSE)
LWM Lloyd's War Medal; low water mark
l w o s t low water ordinary spring tides
l w p load water plane (shipping)
LWUI Longshoremen's and Warehousemen's Union International
LWV League of Women Voters
L&WV Lackawanna & Wyoming Valley Railroad Company (rr mark)
lx light (*lux*—Latin)
LX Uhited States Leather Company (NYSE)
LXX the Septuagint; Septuagint Version (of Bible)
Ly Lyon (France)
LY Lyons-Magnus (NYSE)
Lyn Lynx (constellation)
lyr lyric

M

m of death (*mortes*—Latin); hand (*main*—French); a handful (*manipulus*—Latin) (pharmacy); maiden (cricket); male; manual; mark; married; masculine; mass; measure; medicine; member; memorandum; meridian; meridional; meter; midday (*meridies*—Latin); mile; mill; minim; minor; minute; mist (meteorology); mixture (*mistura*—Latin) (pharmacy); molar (dentistry); in the morning (*mane*—Latin) (pharmacy); month; moon; morning; mountain; *musculus*
M atomic weight; bending moment; moment of flexion; intensity of magnetization; magnetic moment; Magistrate; Majesty; manual (music); Marcus; Mark (German coin); Marker beacon; mass; mate (naval); medical; of medicine (*medicinae*—Latin); member; Methodist; Metronome; Metropolitan; Middle (of languages); Militia; Minesweeper; Mix (*Misce*—Latin) (pharmacy); Moderate; Molar; Molecular weight; Moment of a force; Monday; Monsieur; Mother; Mountain; Mutual inductance (coefficient of); nautical mile; pole strength; Montgomery Ward & Company (NYSE); Montour Railroad Company (rr mark)
m/ month (*mois*—French)
m_{μ} minim (drop)
m^2 square meter
m^3 cubic meter
μa microampere

μ^3 cubic micron
μ^2 square micron
m a mill annealed
Ma masurium; Mary
mA milliangstrom
m/a my account
MA Magnesium Association; Mahogany Association; Maritime Administration; Master of Arts (*Magister Artium*—Latin); May Department Stores Company (NYSE); Metric Association; meter angle; Middle Ages; Military Academy; Military Assistant; Military Aviation; Mining Association; Ministry of Agriculture; Missionary, Apostolic (*Missionarius Apostolicus*—Latin); Missouri Appeals (legal); Montgomery Ward & Company, Inc. ("A" Stk.) (ASE); Mountain Artillery; for nonacceptance (*Mangels Annahme*—German); Postal (rr car)
M&A Missouri and Arkansas Railway Company; management and administration
MAA Manufacturers Aircraft Association; Master at Arms; Mathematical Association of America; Medical Abstainers' Association; Member of the Architectural Association; Motor Agents' Association
MAAF Mediterranean Allied Air Force
MAAGB Motor Agents' Association of Great Britain
MAAMC Motor Aircraft and Allied

Manufacturing Companies
MAB Magazine Advertisers Bureau; Magazine Advertising Bureau; Maracaibo Oil Exploration (NYSE); Medical Advisory Board; Metropolitan Asylums Board; Munitions Assignment Board
mac macadam; macerate; money of account
Mac Maccabees (Bible)
MAC McDonnell Aircraft Corporation (NYSE); mean aerodynamic chord; Metal Abrasive Council; Motor Ambulance Corps
MACA Mental After-Care Association
MACAF Mediterranean Allied Coastal Air Force
Macb Macbeth
Macc Maccabees (Bible)
M Acct Master of Accounts
Maced Macedonia
mach machine; machinery; machinist
MACH machine (US Army)
mach à vapeur steam machinery (*machines à vapeur*—French)
mach él electric machinery (*machines électriques*—French)
MA Christian Ed Master of Arts in Christian Education
Macl McLean's United States Circuit Court Reports (legal)
Mac NZ Macassey's New Zealand Reports (legal)
Mad. Madam
Madag Madagascar

MADCK Marine Aide-de-Camp to the King
Mad. H C Madras High Court Reports (legal)
Mad. Is. Madeira Islands
Madr Madras; Madrid
Mad. Univ Madison University; Madras University
Ma E Master in Engineering; Master of Aeronautical Engineering; Master of Art Education
MAE Master Electric Company (NYSE)
MA Ed Master of Arts in Education
MAEE Marine Aircraft Experimental Establishment
maest° majestically (*maestoso*—music)
MAF MacAndrews & Forbes Company (NYSE); Made in America Foundation
MA&F Minister of Agriculture and Fisheries
MAFL Manual of Air Force Law
mag magazine; magistrate; magnet; magnetic; magnetism; magneto; magnitude
Mag Magyar
MAG Magnavox Company (NYSE)
Mag Cas Magistrates' Cases (legal)
Mag Char Magna Carta
mag c i magnetic cast iron
mag c s magnetic cast steel
Magd Magdalen College (Oxford); Magdalene College (Cambridge)
magg maggiore (music); may (*maggio*—Italian)
M Agr Master of Agriculture
M Agr S Master of Agricultural Science
mah mahogany
MAH Mahoning Coal Railroad (NYSE)
MAHX Miller & Hart, Inc (private car rr mark)
Mai May (*Maius*—Latin)
MAI Master of Engineering (*Magister in Arte Ingeniaria*—Latin); Member of the Anthropological Institute; Midland Airways Limited
maint maintenance (legal)
MAINT maintenance (US Army)
máj May (*május*—Hungarian)
Maj Major
Maj Gen Major General
MAKSUTSUB make suitable substitutions (US Army)
Mal Malachi (Biblical); Malay; Malayan; Malta; Malaysian
MAL Malayan Airways Ltd.
malac malacology
MA LD Master of Arts in Law and Diplomacy
mal I malleable iron

mall. malleable
Mal St Malay States
m à m word for word (*mot à mot*—French)
Mam Mamercus
MAM medium automotive maintenance (US Army)
m & am compound myopic astigmatism (optics)
m amp milliampere
M Am Soc CE Member of the Amalgamated Society of Civil Engineers
man. gradually softer (*mancando*—Italian) (music); manual; manufactured
Man. Manchester; Manila; Manitoba
MANA Manufacturers Agents National Association
M Anaes Master of Anaesthesiology
manc gradually softer (*mancando*—Italian) (music)
Manch Manchester; Manchukuo; Manchuria
Manch R Manchester Regiment
Mand ap apostolic mandate (*mandatum apostolicum*—Latin)
man dir managing director
MANF May, August, November, February (quarter months)
manf manufacturer
Mang B Manganese bronze
Mang S Manganese steel
Manh Manhattan
Manit Manitoba
Manl Manuel
Man LR Manitoba Law Reports (legal)
man op manually operated
MANS Member of the Academy of Natural Sciences
manuf manufactory; manufacture
m a o in other words (*med andra ord*—Swedish); (*med andre ord*—Danish); (*med andre ord*—Norwegian)
MAO Master of Obstetric Art; Marshal of the Admiralty's Office
MAP Aeronautical Maps and Charts (ICAO); Maine Public Service (NYSE); Masco Screw Products Company (NYSE); maximum average price [regulation]; Ministry of Aircraft Production
MAPI Machinery and Allied Products Institute
MAPNY Maritime Association of the Port of New York
MA Public Adm Master of Arts in Public Administration
MAQ Madison Square Garden (NYSE); monetary allowance in lieu of quarters (US Army)
M Ar Master of Architecture
mar. marine; maritime; married
Mar. March; Margaret; Maria
MAR microanalytical reagent

(chemical); Maritime Central Airways
marc markedly (*marcato*)
màrc March (*màrcius*—Hungarian)
march. marchioness
M Arch Master of Architecture
M Arch CP Master of Architecture in City Planning
MARDET Marine Detachment (US Army)
Mar E Marine Engineer
marg margin; marginal
Margta Marguerite (*Margarita*—Spanish)
marg trans marginal translation
marit maritime
Mar. La Martin's Louisiana Reports (legal)
Mar. Mech E Marine Mechanical Engineers
Mar. NC Martin's North Carolina Reports (legal)
MAROC Air Maroc, S. A.
Marq Marquis
Marr Adm Marriott's Reports Admiralty (legal)
mars March (Swedish)
MARS Military Amateur Radio System (US Army)
Marshl Marischal
mart martyr; martyrology
Mart March (*Martius*—Latin); Martinique; Tuesday (*martes*—Spanish)
Mart (La) Martin's Louisiana Reports (legal)
Mart & Y (Tenn) Martin & Yerger's Tennessee Reports (legal)
Marv Marvel's Reports (legal)
MARVA Women's Naval Service (*Marine Vrouwen Afdeling*—Dutch)
MAS Manchester Astronomical Society; Master of Applied Science; Member of the Astronomical Society; Model Abattoir Society; Monetary Allowance in lieu of subsistence (US Army); Society of African Missions
masc masculine
masch machine (*maschine*—German)
MASME Member of the American Society of Mechanical Engineers
Masons Free and Accepted Masons or Prince Hall Masons
Mass. Massachusetts
Mass. LR Massachusetts Law Reporter, (legal)
mast. asph mastic asphalt
M Ast S Member of the Astronomical Society
masuko sons (Japanese)
mat. matinée; matins; maturity
MAT material, matériel (US Army); material (US Navy); Matson Navigation Company (NYSE); Multiple

Address Telegrams

Mat. Matthew

MATA Motorcycle and Allied

math mathematical; mathematics; mathematician

Math C Mathematics Corps

Math D Doctor of Mathematics

mat hdlg material handling

matr marriage (*matrimonium*— Latin)

Matric matriculated; matriculation

matrl material

MATS Military Air Transport Service (US Army)

Matt Matthew; Matthias

matut in the morning (*matutinus*— Latin) (pharmacy)

MAU Mount Allison University (Canada)

Maur Maurice; Mauritius [Island]

Maur Dec Mauritius Decisions (legal)

MAWX Mathieson Chemical Corporation (private car rr mark)

max. maxim; maximum

Max. Maximilian; Maxwell

max. cap maximum capacity

Max. Dig. Maxwell's Digest (legal)

MAY Mays (J.W.), Inc (NYSE)

mb millibar (meteorology)

MB Bachelor of Medicine (*Medicinae Baccalaureus*—Latin); Bachelor of Music (*Musicae Baccalaureus*— Latin); Medical Board; medium bomber; Metropolitan Borough; Ministry of Blockade; Mix-well (*Misce bene*—Latin); Mortar Board Society; motor boat ; Municipal borough; Baggage and Mail (rr car)

MBA Marine Biological Association; Master of Business Administration; Monument Builders of America; Metropolitan Boxing Alliance

MBAA Master Brewers Association of America; Mortgage Bankers Association of America

MBAD medical badge (US Army)

MBAN Member of the British Association of Neuropaths

MBAUS Mink Breeders Association of the United States

MBC Metropolitan Borough Council; Municipal Borough Council; Myers (F.E.) & Brothers Company (NYSE)

MBCM Bachelor of Medicine, Master of Surgery (*Baccalaureus Medicinae Chirurgiae Magister*—Latin)

MBCMC Milk Bottle Crate Manufacturers Council

MBCPE Member of British College of Physical Education

MBD Combination Mail, Baggage and Dormitory Car (rr car)

MBD IX Mtge. Bank of the Kingdom of Denmark (ASE)

MBE Member of the Order of the British Empire

MBE Combination Baggage, Mail and Express (rr car)

MBF et H Great Britain, France, and Ireland (*Magna Britannia, Francia, et Hibernia*—Latin)

MBH Michaels Brothers (NYSE)

MBI may be issued (US Army)

MBL mobile(ize) or (ization) (US Army)

MBM thousand board [foot] measure

MBMA Master Boiler Makers Association

MBP Michigan Bumper Corporation (NYSE)

MBR Mid-West Abrasive Company (NYSE)

MBRUU may be retained until unserviceable (US Army)

MBS Mandel Brothers, Inc (NYSE); Master of Business Science; Monumental Brass Society; Mutual Broadcasting System

MBST Member of the Boot and Shoe Industry

MBSX Suydam Division of Pittsburg Plate Glass Company (private car rr mark)

MBTA Metropolitan Board Teacher's Association

MBW Minneapolis Brewing Company (NYSE)

MBX Montrose Beef Company (private car rr mark)

mc megacycle (radio); millicurie(s); motorcycle

m c current money (*moneda corriente* —Spanish); current month (*mois courant*—French); magnetic course; marginal credit; marked capacity; metaling clause; meter candle; metric carat; moisture content; motor carrier

MC Machinery Certificate (shipping); Maintenance Command; Maine Central Railroad (NYSE); Manhattan College; Manufacturers' Conference; Maritime Commission; marriage certificate; Marshall College; Marymount College; Master of Ceremonies; Master Commandant; Master of Surgery (*Magister Chirurgiae*—Latin); Matrimonial Clauses (legal); Medical Corps; Medico-Chirurgical; Member of Congress; Member of Council; Mengel Company, The (NYSE); Mennonite Church; Mersey Conservancy; mess call; Mess Committee; Methodist chaplain; Methodist Church; Middlebury College; Military Col-

lege (Royal); military correspondent; Military Cross; Morse Code; Motor contact; Mount Carmel Fraternity; Movement control; Mundelein College

m/c my account (*mi cuenta*— Spanish)

MCA McCall Corporation (NYSE); Manufacturing Chemists Association; Master Clothworkers' Association; Matrimonial Causes Act; Mid-Continent Airlines; Motor Carrier Act; Music Corporation of America

MCAUS Manufacturing Chemists Association of the United States

MCAX Mather Stock Car Company (private car rr mark)

MCB Millwork Cost Bureau

MCC Marylebone Cricket Club; Member of the County Council; Mesta Machinery Company (NYSE); Middlesex County Council; Motor Carrier Case

McCah McCahon's Reports (legal)

McCr McCrary's United States Circuit Court Reports (legal)

MCCUS Mexican Chamber of Commerce of the United States

MCCX Mutual Chemical Company of America (private car rr mark)

MCD Doctor of Comparative Medicine; Member of the College of Dentists; Mining Corporation of Canada (NYSE); Minister for Coordination of Defence

MC Eng Master of Civil Engineering

MCEX Compania Mexicana de Comercio Exterior (private car rr mark)

MCF French Communist Movement (*Mouvement Communiste Français* —French)

Mcf One thousand cubic feet

MCG McGraw-Hill Publishing (NYSE); Millinery Creators Guild

M/C G Manchester Guardian

MCGFA Maraschino Cherry and Glacé Fruit Association

Mch March

M Ch Master of Surgery (*Magister Chirurgiae*—Latin)

M Ch D Master of Dental Surgery (*Magister Chirurgiae Dentalis*— Latin)

M Ch E Master of Chemical Engineering

M Ch Orth Master of Orthopædic Surgery (*Magister Chirurgiae Orthopædicæ*—Latin)

Mchr Manchester

M Chrom Master of Chromatics

mcht merchant

MCHX Montsanto Chemical Company, Merrimac Division (private car rr mark)

m c i malleable cast iron

MCK McKesson & Robbins, Inc (NYSE)

McL McLean's United States Circuit Court Reports (legal)

MCL Marine Corps League; Master of Civil Law; Moore-McCormack Lines (NYSE)

MCL Aux Marine Corps League Auxiliary

M Clin Psychol Master of Clinical Psychology

MCLX North Wester Refrigerator Line Company (private car rr mark)

MCM Manual for Courts Martial (US Army)

MCMES Member of the Civil and Mechanical Engineers' Society

MCMI Malleable Chain Manufacturers Institute

McMul Eq McMullan's Equity Reports (legal)

MCMT Michigan College of Mining and Technology

mço March (março—Portuguese)

MCO Main civilian occupation (US Army)

M Com Master of Commerce; Minister of Commerce (Ministère du Commerce—French)

MCP Master of City Planning; Member of the College of Preceptors; Member of Colonial Parliament

mcps megacycles per second

MCR McCord Corporation (NYSE)

MCRB Motor Carrier Rate Bureau

MC RR Michigan Central Railroad

MCRX McCook Rendering Company (private car rr mark)

Mcs Marcus

MCS Madras Civil Service; Malayan Civil Service; Master of Commercial Science; Merritt-Chapman & Scott (NYSE); Military College of Science

mcs megacycles per second

MCSB Milk Cap Statistical Bureau

MCT Michigan Steel Tube Products (NYSE)

m/cte my account (mon compte—French)

MCTI Metal Cutting Tool Institute

MCTS Moravian College and Theological Seminary

MCTX Michigan Chemical Corporation (private car rr mark)

MCU Motor Cycle Union

mcw modulated continuous waves

MCW McWilliams Dredging Company (NYSE)

MCX Mead Corporation (private car rr mark)

m d main deck; right hand (mano destro—Italian); (main droit—French) (music); as directed (more

dicto—Latin) (pharmacy); mentally deficient; middle door; months' date

md dealer (marchand—French)

Md Maryland

Mp molecular rotation

MD Doctor of Medicine (Medicinae Doctor—Latin); Managing Director; Market Day; Medical Department; Medicine and Duty; Mess Desk; Message dropping; Metropolitan District; Meteorology Department; Middle Dutch; military district; mine depot; Monroe Doctrine; Combination Mail and Dormitory Car (rr car)

M/d months after date

M/D Memorandum of deposit

m and d medicine and duty

MDA Magen David Adom (Jewish Red Cross); Marking Device Association

MDAAI Muscular Dystrophy Associations of America, Inc

MDAP mutual defense assistance program

mdat mandate, charge (mandat—French)

M-day Mobilization day

Md Ch Maryland Chancery Decisions (legal)

Mddx Middlesex

m de chap. conductor (maître de chapelle—French)

M Des Master of Design

MDG Medical Director General

Mdgr Madagascar

MDHB Mersey Docks and Harbour Board

M Di Master of Didactics

m di capp conductor (maestro di cappella—Italian)

M Dip. Master of Diplomacy

mdise merchandise

MDK Montana-Dakota Utilities (NYSE)

Mdlle Miss (Mademoiselle—French)

Mdm Madam

MDMA Metal Door Manufacturers Association

MDNA Machinery Dealers National Association

mdnt midnight

m d r minimum daily requirement

Mds ladies (Mesdames—French)

MDS Main Dressing Station; Master of Dental Surgery

MD&S Macon, Dublin & Savannah Railroad Company (rr mark)

MD Sc Master of Dental Science

mdse merchandise

MDSOR Monthly depot space and operating report (US Army)

M D S T mountain daylight saving time

MDT Merchants Despatch Transpor-

tation Corporation (private car rr mark)

M Du Middle Dutch

MDV Doctor of Veterinary Medicine; Metropolitan District Valuer; Mission Development Company (NYSE)

MDW Military Defence Works; Military District of Washington (US Army)

Mdx Middlesex (England)

MDY Midland Oil (NYSE)

Mg molecular weight (Molekulargewicht—German)

m e marbled edges

M° Master (maître—French)

m E in my opinion (meines Erachtens—German)

Me. Maine; Messerschmitt (German aircraft); methyl

ME marbled edges (bookbinding); Marine Engineer; Master of Elements; Master of Engineering; Mechanical Engineer; Methodist Episcopal; Middle East; Middle English; Military Engineer; Mining Engineer; Most Excellent

MEA Greek Home Guard; Mead Corporation (The) (NYSE); Meath (Ireland); Middle East Airlines

meas measure; measuring; measurable

Meas for M Measure for Measure

MeC Maine Central Railroad Company

MEC Maine Central Railroad Company (rr mark); Master of Engineering Chemistry; Member of the Executive Council; Middle East Command

mécan mechanic (mécanique—French)

MECH mechanic (US Army)

mech mechanic; mechanics

M E Ch Methodist Episcopal Church

Mech Can. Mechanician Candidate

Mech E Mechanical Engineer

mech eff mechanical efficiency

mech lub mechanical lubrication

MECL Mistress of English and Classical Literature

MECM Methodist Episcopal Church Mission

Me₂CO acetone

M Econ S Master of Economic Science

MECT Mellon Educational and Charitable Trust

MECZ mechanized (US Army)

med medalist; medical; medicine; medium; medieval; median

Med Mediterranean

MED Master of Education; Master of Elementary Didactics; medical (US Navy)

med jur medical jurisprudence

Med Lat Medieval Latin

Med L J Medico Legal Journal (legal)

Med ORC Medical Officers' Reserve Corps

Med RC Medical Reserve Corps

Med Sc D Doctor of Medical Science

Med Sch Medical School

med stl medium steel

MEE Master of Electrical Engineering; minimum essential equipment (US Army)

MEED Mechanical and Electrical Engineering Division

MEF Mediterranean Expeditionary Force

MEFO Company for Metallurgical Research (*Metalurgische Forschungsgesellschaft*—German)

meg megohm

MEGHP Most Excellent Grand High Priest

MEIC Member of Engineering Institute of Canada

Mej Miss (*Mejuffrouw*—Dutch)

MEL Master (or Mistress) of English Literature; Music Education League

Melan Melanesia; Melanie

M El Eng Master of Electrical Engineering

MELF Middle East Liberation Force

melodr melodrama

mem member; memento; memorandum; memoir; memorial

MEMA Motor and Equipment Manufacturers Association

meml memorial

Mem L J Memphis Law Journal (legal)

memo memorandum; memoranda

memo b/l memorandum bill of lading

MEMP Mechanical Engineering and Motive Power

men. less (*meno*—Italian) (music)

Men. Mensa (constellation)

MEN Menasco Manufacturing (NYSE)

MENC Music Educators National Conference

M Eng Master of Engineering; Mechanical, or Mining, Engineer

M Eng and PA Master in Engineering and Public Administration

mens by measure (*mensura*—Latin); month (*mensis*—Latin)

mensur mensuration

mentd mentioned (legal)

MEO Mining Engineering Officer

MeOH methyl alcohol, CH_3OH

mep mean effective pressure

m eq milliequivalent

Mer Mercury; Merivale (Law Reports)

mer mercantile; merchandise; mercury; meridian

merch merchantable

Merch V The Merchant of Venice

Meri Merionethshire (county of Wales)

mer rect mercury rectifier

Merry W Merry Wives of Windsor

MES Melville Shoe Corporation (NYSE); Methodist Episcopal Church South

M es A Master of Arts (*Maître ès Arts*—French)

MESA Mechanics Educational Society of America

MESC Middle East Supply Center

Mesd Ladies (*Mesdames*—French)

Messrs Gentlemen (*Messieurs*—French)

met. metaphor; metaphysics; metallurgical; meteorological; metronome; metropolitan

MET meteorology(ical) or (ist) (US Army)

métall metallurgy (*métallurgie*—French)

metath metathesis; metathetic

Met. E Metallurgical Engineer

Mete Ky Metcalfe's Kentucky Reports (legal)

météor. meteorology (*météorologie*—French)

meteor. meteorological; meteorology

meth methylated

Meth Methodist

M et L Maine-et-Loire (French department)

M et M Meurthe-et-Moselle (French department)

m et n morning and night (*mane et nocte*—Latin)

meton metonymy

Met. R Metropolitan Railway

metrol metrology

METX Modesto & Empire Traction Company (private car rr mark)

m e v million electron volts

Mev Mrs. (*Mevrouw*—Dutch)

MEW Ministry of Economic Warfare

MEWA Motor and Equipment Wholesalers Association

Mex Mexican; Mexico

MEZ Central European Time (*Mitteleuropäischezeit*—German)

mez half, medium (*mezzo*—Italian) (music)

mezzo mezzotint

mf moderately loud (*mezzo-forte*—music); millifarad

m f machine finish; medium frequency; mill finish; motor freight; intermediate frequency (*moyenne fréquence*—French)

mF micro-Farad

MF McColl-Frontenac Oil (NYSE); Malvern Festival; Marshall Field & Company (NYSE); Master of Forestry; Mineworkers' Federation

m/f my favor (*mi favor*—Spanish); months from date (*meses fecha*—Spanish)

m & f male and female

M of F Master of Foxhounds; Ministry of Food

μf microfarad (one-millionth of a farad)

MFA Master of Fine Arts; Mica Fabricators Association

MFA Arch. Master of Fine Arts in Architecture

MFA Art and Arch. Master of Fine Arts in Art and Archaeology

MFA Mus Master of Fine Arts in Music

MFB Metropolitan Fire Brigade; Millinery Fashion Bureau

MFCT major fraction thereof (US Army)

mfd manufactured

MFF MacFadden Foundation

mfg manufacturing

MFG McQuay-Norris Manufacturing (NYSE)

MFGA Master Furriers Guild of America

mfgr manufacturer

MFH Master of Fox hounds

mfr manufacturer

MIC Metalsmith First Class (US Navy)

m fl with others (*med flera*—Swedish); (*med flere*—Danish); (*med flere*—Norwegian)

m f l motor freight line

MFLX McColl-Frontenac Oil Company, Ltd. (private car rr mark)

MFMA Maple Flooring Manufacturers Association; Metal Finding Manufacturers Association

MFN most favored nation

MFP Mickelberry's Food Products (NYSE)

mfr manufacture; manufacturer

M Fr Middle French

mfrs manufacturers

MFS Malleable Founders Society; Mountain Fuel Supply Company (NYSE)

mfst manifest

m ft let a mixture be made (*mistura fiat*—Latin)

m f t motor freight tariff; motor freight terminal

m ft m mix to make a mixture (*misce fiat mistura*—Latin) (pharmacy)

MFV Motor Fleet Vessel

mfz mezzo forzando (music)

Mg magnesium; molecular weight (Ger.)

MG Graduate in Music; Major General; Master General; Medical Gymnast; Meso-Gothic; Minute Maid Corporation (NYSE); left hand

(*main gauche*—music); machine-
glazed; machine gun; mill-glazed

m g mixed grain (lumber); modified
guaranteed; motor generator

mg milligram; morning

m G Greenwich meridian (*méridien
de Greenwich*—French)

μg microgram

M&G Manning and Grainger (Law
Reports)

MGA Monongahela Connecting Railroad Company (rr mark); Music
Guild of America

MGB motor gunboat

MGC Machine-Gun Company; Machine Gun Corps

MGCA Mushroom Growers Cooperative Association

mgd million gallons per day

MGE Mangel Stores Corporation
(NYSE)

MGF Magic Chef, Inc (NYSE)

MGGS Major General , General Staff

M Gk Modern Greek

MGM Metro-Goldwyn-Mayer

M&GN Midland and Great Northern
Railway

MGO Master-General of Ordnance;
military government officer (US
Army)

MG PR Minnesota Pw. & Lt. Co.
(5% Pfd.) (ASE)

Mgr manager; Your Grace (*Monsei-
gneur*—French, *Monsignore*—
Italian)

M Gr Medieval Greek

MGR McGraw Electric Company
(NYSE)

MGRA Major General, Royal Artillery

MGRAT Major General of Royal
Artillery Training

MGT management (US Army)

MGU Michigan Sugar Company
(NYSE)

MGU Pr Michigan Sugar Company
(6% Pfd.) (ASE)

M & GWR Midland and Great Western
Railway

M Gyn and Obs Master of Gynecology
and Obstetrics

mh millihenry

MH Magdalen Hospital; main hatch;
Master of Horticulture; Master of
Hygiene; Medal of Honor; Medical
Household; Ministry of Health; Most
Honorable

MHA Member of the House of Assembly; Mental Hospitals Association; Ministry of Home Affairs

MHC Mount Holyoke College

mhcp mean horizontal candlepower

MHE materials handling equipment
(US Army)

MHG Middle High German

MHI Material Handling Institute;
Ministry of Health Inspectorate

MHK Member of the House of Keys

MHL Master of Hebrew Literature

MHLB Ministry of Health, Legal
Branch

mho [symbol for] unit of conductivity
(electricity)

MHR Member of the House of Representatives

MHS Massachusetts Historical Society; Member of the Historical
Society; Minister of Home Security

m h s c p mean hemispherical candle power

m h t as regards (*med hensyn til*—
Norwegian); (*med hensyn til*—
Danish)

MHTX Mangels, Herold Company,
Inc (private car rr mark)

m h w mean high water

MHW Minneapolis-Honeywell Regulator (NYSE)

M Hy Master of Hygiene

MHZX Matthiessen & Hegeler Zinc
Company (private car rr mark)

mi mile; mill; minute

Mi Mississippi

MI Medical Inspection; Miami Cop-
per Company (NYSE); Midwives'
Institute; Military Intelligence
(US Army); Minister of Information;
Mounted Infantry

M-I Missouri-Illinois Railroad Company

M of I Ministry of Information

m of i moment of inertia

MIA Marble Institute of America;
Master of International Affairs;
missing in action (US Army); Model
Industry Association

MIAE Member of the Institute of
Automobile Engineers

MIAe E Member of the Institution of
Aeronautical Engineers

MIAMA Member of the Incorporated
Advertising Managers' Association

Mic Micah; Micheas (Biblical)

MIC Marian Fathers

MICCI Milk and Ice Cream Can Institute

MICE Member of the Institute of
Civil Engineers

Mich Michael; Michaelmas; Michigan

Mich C C R Michigan Circuit Court
Reporter (legal)

MI Chem E Member of the Institution
of Chemical Engineers

Mich L Rev Michigan Law Review

Michoa Michoacán

Mich Pol Soc Michigan Political
Science Association (legal)

mic pan. crumb of bread (*mica panis*
—Latin) (pharmacy)

micro microphone

microcryst microcrystalline

micrometal micrometallurgy

micros microscopy

MICUM Interallied Commission for
the Control of Factories and Mines
(*Mission Interallié de Contrôle
d'Usines et Mines*—French)

MICX Mississippi Chemical Corporation (private car rr mark)

mid. middle; midshipman

Mid. Midlands

MID Mines Inspection Department

Middlx Middlesex (county of England)

Mid. Eng Middle English

Mid. L Midlothian (county of Scotland)

Mid. Lat Middle Latin

midn midshipman

Midr explanation (*Midrash*—Hebrew)

mid. sec midship section

Mids ND A Midsummer Night's Dream

MIEE Member of the Institution of
Electrical Engineers

Mierc Wednesday (*Miercoles*—
Spanish)

MIF Milk Industry Foundation

MI Fire E Member of the Institute of
Fire Engineers

Mig Michael (*Miguel*—Spanish)

MIG Mikoyan and Gurevich (U.S.S.R.
jet aircraft)

mih miles in the hour

MII military intelligence interpreter
(US Army)

MIIA Mine Inspectors Institute of
America

Mij joint-stock company (*Maat-
schapij*—Dutch)

MIK Micromatic Hone Corporation
(NYSE)

mil mileage; military; militia

Mil Miles' Reports (legal)

Mil Att Military Attaché

miles. thousandth (*milesima*—
Spanish)

mill. million

Mill. Const (S C) Mill's South
Carolina Constitutional Reports
(legal)

mil min military mining

MILoco E Member of the Institute of
Locomotive Engineers

Milt Milton

MILW Chicago, Milwaukee, St. Paul
& Pacific Railroad Company (rr
mark)

mim mimeograph

MIMA Magnesia Insulation Manufacturers Association

MI Mar. E Member of the Institute of
Marine Engineers

MIME Member of the Institute of
Mechanical Engineers; Member of
the Institute of Mining Engineers

MIMM Member Institution of Mining and Metallurgy
MIMT Member Institute of the Motor Trade
min mineral; mineralogy; minim; minimum; mining; ministerial; minor; minute
MIN mine; minecraft (US Navy)
MINA Member of the Institution of Naval Architects
min B/L minimum bill of lading
mineral. mineralogy
Minn Minnesota
mino minister (*ministro*—Spanish)
Min Plen Minister Plenipotentiary
min prem minimum premium (insurance)
Min Res Minister Resident
M Inst BE Member of the Institute of British Engineers
M Inst CE Member of the Institution of Civil Engineers
M Inst Gas E Member of the Institution of Gas Engineers
M Inst ME Member Institution of Mining Engineers
M Inst Met. Member of the Institute of Metals
M Inst MM Member of the Institution of Mining and Metallurgy
M Inst PT Member of the Institute of Petroleum Technologists
M Inst RA Member of the Institute of Registered Architects
M Inst T Member of the Institute of Transport
M Inst WE Member of the Institution of Water Engineers
M Int Med Master in Internal Medicine
min wt minimum weight
MINX Minnesota Mining and Manufacturing Company, Inc. (private car rr mark)
MIOB Member of the Institute of Builders
m i p marine insurance policy; mean indicated pressure
MIPE Member of the Institution of Production Engineers
mir mercifully (*misericorditer*—Latin)
M Ir Middle Irish
miraone pity (*miseratione*—Latin)
mis petty expenses (*menus frais*—French)
Mis Missouri
MIS Mission (US Navy)
misc miscellaneous; miscellany
Misc Miscellaneous Reports, New York
Misc Doc Miscellaneous Document
Miscel Miscellaneous Reports, New York (legal)
miscend to be mixed (*miscendus*—

Latin) (pharmacy)
mise merchandise (*marchandise*—French)
MISI Member of the Iron and Steel Institute
MISR major item status report (US Army)
miss. mission; missionary
Miss. Mississippi
Miss. C Mississippi Central Railroad Company
Miss. St Ca Mississippi State Cases (legal)
mist. mixture (*mistura*—Latin) (pharmacy)
mistrans mistranslation
MI Struct E Member Institution Structural Engineers
mit send (*mitte*—Latin) (pharmacy)
MIT Massachusetts Institute of Technology; military intelligence translator (US Army)
M It. Middle Italian
Mitt report (*Mitteilung*—German)
MIV Moody's Inv. Ser. (NYSE)
MIV P Pr Moody's Investors Service (Part. Pref.) (ASE)
MIWT Member of the Institute of Wireless Technology
mix. mixed; mixing
mixt mixture
MJ Manufacturers' Junction Railway Company (rr mark); Mead Johnson & Company (NYSE); Ministry of Justice; monkey jacket (colloquial)
MJI Member of the Institute of Journalists
MJS Member of the Japan Society
MJSD March, June, September, December (quarter months)
MJV Mojud Hosiery Company (NYSE)
mk mark (*markka*—Finnish)
MK Mittelland Kanal; Morrison-Knudsen Company (NYSE)
MKA Machine Knife Association
MKC McKeesport Connecting Railroad Company (rr mark)
mkd marked
mkd wt marked weight
m-kg meter-kilogram
MKH Mackintosh-Hemphill Company (NYSE)
MKM marksman (US Army)
MKO Muskogee Company (NYSE)
mkr microscopic (*mikroskopisch*—German)
MKS meter-kilogram-second
mkt market
MKT Missouri-Kansas-Texas Railroad Company
MKTT Missouri-Kansas-Texas Railroad Company of Texas (rr mark)
MKT of T Missouri-Kansas-Texas Railroad Company of Texas

MKW Military Knight of Windsor
MKY McKee (Arthur G.) & Company (NYSE)
m l mean level; muzzle-loading
ml mail; milliliter (cubic centimeter)
Ml Miss (*Matmazel*—Turkish)
M/L legal tender (*moneda legal*—Spanish)
ML Licentiate in Medicine (*Medicinae Licentiatus*—Latin); Licentiate in Midwifery; Martin (Glenn L.) Company (NYSE); Master of Laws (*Magister Legum*—Latin); Medieval Latin; Middle Latin; mine-layer; Ministry of Labour; Mission to Lepers; motor launch
μl microliter
MLA Master in Landscape Architecture; Master of Liberal Arts; Mechanical Lubricator Association; Medical Library Association; Member of Legislative Assembly; Modern Language Association
MLAA Modern Language Association of America
MLAN Miscellaneous List Advance Notice
ML Arch. Master of Landscape Architecture
MLAUS Maritime Law Association of the United States
MLC American Molasses Company (NYSE); major landing craft; Member of the Legislative Council; Modern Language Conference
m l d minimum lethal dose
mld molded
MLD Master of Landscape Design; Midland Railway Company of Manitoba (rr mark)
mldg molding (lumber)
mldr molder
mle pattern (*modèle*—French); maximum loss expectancy (insurance)
MLEA Metal Lath Export Association
ML 1C Molder First Class (US Navy)
MLG Middle Low German; Ministry of Labour Gazette: Most Loyal Gander (Order of the Blue Goose)
MLGA Merchants Ladies Garment Association
m l h c p mean lower hemispherical candle power
M Litt Master of Letters (*Magister Litterarum*—Latin)
MLL McLellan Stores Company (NYSE)
Mlle Miss (pl. Mlles) (*Mademoiselle*—French)
MLMA Metal Lath Manufacturers Association
MLN Monroe Loan Society (NYSE); Mouvement de la Libération Na-

tionale (French)

MLN A Monroe Loan Society ("A") (common stock, ASE)

mlnr milliner

MLNS Ministry of Labour and National Service

MLO Military Landing Officer; Military Liaison Officer

m l r muzzle loading rifle

MLR main line of resistance (US Army); Miller & Hart, Inc (NYSE)

MLS Manistique & Lake Superior Railroad (rr mark); Master of Library Science

MLSB Member London School Board

MLSC Member London Society of Compositors

ML2C Molder Second Class (US Navy)

MLT Mergenthaler Linotype (NYSE)

ML Trip. Modern Languages Tripos

m l w mean low water

MLW Miller-Wohl Company, Inc (NYSE)

MLW Pr Miller-Wohl Co., Inc. (The) (4½% Conv. Pfd.) (ASE)

m l w s mean low water springs (ocean tides)

MLX Master Lubricants Company (private car rr mark)

MLY Molybdenum Corporation of America (NYSE)

m m made merchantable; matrimony (*matrimonium*—Latin); and so forth (*med mera*—Swedish); motor mechanics; the necessary changes having been made (*mutatis mutandis*—Latin)

mm millimeter

Mm Mrs. (*Madam*—Turkish)

MM Maelzel's metronome; Master Mason (freemasonry); Marine Midland Corporation (NYSE); Master Mechanic; Medal of Merit (US Army); Medical Man; Mercantile Marine; Messageries Maritimes; Machinist's Mate; Military Medal; Military Motorization; Ministry of Mines; Ministry of Munitions; Missionary of Maryknoll; Money Market; Most deserving; Motor Mechanics; Music Master

mμ millimicron

μμ micromicron; pica (10⁻¹²)

mm² square millimetre

mm³ cubic millimetre

M/m made merchantable

m & m make and mend (naval)

M of M Ministry of Munitions

MMA MacRobertson-Miller Aviation Company Pty. Ltd.; Master Mechanics Association; Merchandise Marks Act; Metropolitan Museum of Art; Monorail Manufacturers Association; Museum of Modern Art

MMB Mixer Manufacturers Bureau

MMBA Mutation Mink Breeders Association

M Mde Merchant Marine (*Marine Marchande*—French)

Mme Mrs. (*Madame*—French)

MME Master of Mechanical Engineering; Master of Mining Engineering

MMEA Millinery Merchandising Executives Association

MMEC Machinery-Metals Export Club

M Mech Eng Master of Mechanical Engineering

Mmes Ladies (*Mesdames*—French)

M Met. E Master of Metallurgical Engineering

m m f magnetomagnetic force; magneto-motive force

μμF micro-micro-Farad (electricity)

MMF Milbank Memorial Fund

mmfd micromicrofarad

MM1C Machinist's Mate First Class (US Navy)

MMG Medium Machine Gun

MMIF Mutual Mortgage Insurance Fund

m mk material mark

MMLI Moore-McCormack Lines, Inc

mmm micromillimeter

MMMI Meat Machinery Manufacturers Institute

MMO Monarch Machine Tool Company (NYSE)

MMP Military Mounted Police

MMPANO Masters, Mates and Pilots of America, National Organization

MMPI Minnesota Multiphasic Personality Inventory

MMS Manchester Medical Society; Member of Council, Institution of Mining Engineers; Mercantile Marine Subsidy; Methodist Missionary Society; Moravian Missionary Society; Motor Mine Sweeper

MMSA Mining and Metallurgical Society of America

MM2C Machinist's Mate Second Class (US Navy)

m mu millimicron

M Mus Master of Music

M Mus Ed Master of Music Education

MMX Magma Copper Company (NYSE); Monarch Molasses Company (private car rr mark)

mn house (*maison*—French)

m n the name being changed (*mutato nomine*—Latin)

Mn Manganese

MN Master of Nursing; Merchant Navy

m/n national money (*moneda nacional*—Spanish)

M & N May and November

MNAS Member of the National Academy of Sciences

MNC Masonite Corporation (NYSE); Montreal Curb Market

MND Ministry of National Defence (Canada)

M&NE Manistee and Northeastern Railway Company (rr mark)

MNFF *Magyar Nemzeti Függetlensegi Front* (Hungarian National Independence Front)

mng managing

mngr manager; monsignor

MNI Madras Native Infantry

mnm minimum

MNM Muskegon Motor Spec. (NYSE)

Mnr mister (*Mijnheer*—Dutch)

MNS Minneapolis, Northfield and Southern Railway (rr mark); Member of the Numismatic Society; Mullins Manufacturing Corporation (NYSE)

mnt mononitrotoluene

MNU Manati Sugar Company (NYSE)

MNV Marion Power Shovel Company (NYSE)

MNX National Car Company (private car rr mark)

m o mail order; manually operated; mark off; money order; motor operated; municipal ownership

mo month; molded

Mo Missouri; molybdenum

MO Mailing Officer (WRNS); Marine Office(r); Mass observation; Master of Obstetrics; Master of Oratory; Medical Officer; Meteorological Office; method of operation (*modus operandi*—Latin); Philip Morris & Company Ltd (NYSE)

m/o my order (*mi orden*—Spanish, *mon ordre*—French)

M&O Mobile and Ohio Rail Road Company

MOA Metropolitan Oakland (California) Area

MOAA Mail Order Association of America

Mo App Rep. Missouri Appellate Reporter (legal)

mob. mobile; mobilization; mobilized

MOC Military Order of Cooties; Mozambique (IDP)

MOCX Missouri Portland Cement Company (private car rr mark)

mod moderate; moderato (music); modern; modified

MOD Mail Order Department; Modine Manufacturing Company (NYSE); Money Order Department

mod praescript in the manner directed (*modo praescripto*—Latin) (pharmacy)

Mods Moderations (Oxford)

MOGAS motor gasoline (US Army)
Mogl possible (*Möglich*—German)
Moh(am) Mohammedan(ism)
MOH Master of Otter Hounds; Medical Officer of Health; Metropolitan Opera House; Ministry of Health; Mohawk Airlines, Inc.
Moham Mohammedan
MOI Military Operations and Intelligence; Ministry of Information; Ministry of the Interior
m o i v mechanically operated inlet valve
MOK Mohawk Carpet Mills, Inc (NYSE)
mol molecule
MOL Ministry of Labour; Morrell (John) & Company (NYSE)
MOLL Military Order of the Loyal Legion
mol wt molecular weight
m o m middle of month
MOM Ministry of Munitions
MOM MAT Municipality of Medellin (ASE)
MoMM1C Motor Machinist's Mate First Class (US Navy)
MoMM2C Motor Machinist's Mate Second Class (US Navy)
mon house, firm (*maison*—French); monastery; monetary
Mon Monaco; Monday; Monitor; Monoghan (county of Ireland); Monmouthshire; Monoceros (constellation); Montana
MON Monogram Pictures Corporation (NYSE); Montreal Stock Exchange
Mon (B) Ben Monroe's Reports (legal)
Mong Mongolia
Mongh Monongahela Railway Company
monocl monoclinic
monog monograph
Mon R Monmouthshire Regiment
Mons Mister (*Monsieur*—French); monsignor (*monseñor*—Spanish)
Monsig my lord (*Monsignor*—Italian)
Mont Montgomeryshire (county of Wales); Montana
Mont LR Montreal Law Reports (legal)
Montour Montour Railroad Company
Montr Montreal
MONX Monsanto Chemical Company (private car rr mark)
Moo Francis Moore's Reports (legal)
Moo C P Moore's Common Pleas Reports (legal)
MOOIL motor oil (US Army)
Moore's Adj Moore's International Adjudications
Moore's Arb Moore's International Arbitrations
Moore's Dig. Moore's Digest of International Law
m o p mother of pearl
MOP Member of Parliament; Ministry of Pensions; Ministry of Production; mustering-out pay (US Army)
Mo P Missouri Pacific (rr)
Mo Pac Missouri Pacific Railroad Corporation
MOPH Military Order of the Purple Heart
MOPR manner of performance rating (US Army)
M Op S Member of the Optical Society
mor dying away (*morendo*—Italian) (music); morocco
Mor Moroccan; Morocco
MOR Ministry of Reconstruction
Morb Morbihan (French department)
M O R C Medical Officers' Reserve Corps
Morel Morelos
Mor Ia Morris' Iowa Reports (legal)
morn. morning
morph morphological; morphology
Morr Morris' Iowa Reports (legal)
mort mortuary
mortg mortgage
MORX Morrell & Company (private car rr mark)
Mos Moselle (French department); Mosely's English Chancery Reports (legal)
mos months
MOS Managers and Overlookers' Society; Member of the Ophthalmological Society; Military Occupational Specialty (US Army); Ministry of Supply
Most Rev Most Reverend
MOSX Martin Oil Service, Inc (private car rr mark)
mot motor
MOT Men of the Trees; Ministry of Transport; Motorola, Inc (NYSE)
mot & comb. int internal combustion motors (*moteurs à combustion interne*—French)
MOTARDIV Mobile Target Division (US Navy)
mot op motor operated
MOU Mountain States Tel & Tel (NYSE)
MOWB Ministry of Works and Buildings
MOWT Ministry of War Transport
MOWW Military Order of the World Wars
moy money
Moz Mozambique
MOZ MAT Mtge. Bank of Chile (ASE)
m p medium pattern; medium pressure; melting point; melting pot; mile post;

moderately soft (*mezzo piano*—Italian) (music); mooring pipe; mooring post; months after payment; motor passenger
MP Mandatory Power; Manifold Pressure; Marine Police; Master in Painting; McIntyre Porcupine Mines (NYSE); Meeting Point; Member of Parliament; Mercator's Projection; Methodist Protestant; Metropolitan Police; Military Police; *Millia Passuum* (Roman mile); Minister Plenipotentiary; Missouri Pacific Railroad Company (rr mark); Municipal Police; Postal (rr car)
M-P Postal Money Order (*Mandat-Poste*—French)
m/p memorandum of partnership
m & p material and process
MPA Master of Public Administration; Mechanical Packing Association
M&PA Maryland & Pennsylvania Railroad Company (rr mark)
MPAA Motion Picture Association of America
MPAUS Music Publishers Association of the United States
MPB Metropolitan Brick, Inc (NYSE)
MPBA Machine Printers Beneficial Association; Mechanical Press Builders Association
m p c mathematics, physics, chemistry
MPC Member of Parliament, Canada; Metropolitan Police College; Metropolitan Police Commissioner; Military Pioneer Corps; Missouri Portland Cement (NYSE); Morris Plan Corporation of America (NYSE)
MPCX Magnolia Petroleum Company (private car rr mark)
M Pd Master of Pedagogy
MPD Medusa Portland Cement (NYSE); Mines and Petroleum Department
MPDFA Master Photo Dealers and Finishers Association
M pdo last month (*meses pasado*—Spanish)
MPE Master of Physical Education; Middle States Petroleum (NYSE); Mu Phi Epsilon (music society)
MPEA Motion Picture Export Association
M Pen. Ministry of Pensions
m p f multi-purpose food
mpg miles per gallon
MPG Migne's *Patrologia Græca*; Museum of Practical Geology
MPGA Metropolitan Public Gardens Association; Ministry of Pensions General Administration
mph miles per hour
M Ph Master of Philosophy

MPH Master of Public Health; Murphy (G. C.) Company (NYSE)

mphps miles per hour per second

m p i mean point of impact

MPIC Motion Picture Industry Controllers

MPJ Member of the Profession of Journalism

MPKX Michigan Pickle Company (private car rr mark)

Mpl Montpellier (France)

MPL Master of Patent Law; Master of Polite Literature; Minnesota Power & Light (NYSE)

MPLX Mexican Petroleum Corporation (private car rr mark)

mpm meters per minute

m p m multi-purpose meal

MPMX Marathon Corporation (private car rr mark)

MPN Monongahela Power (NYSE)

MPN B Pr Monongahela Power Co. (4.80% Series "B" Pfd.) (ASE)

MPN C Pr Monongahela Power Co. (4.50% Series "C" Pfd.) (ASE)

MPN Pr Monongahela Power Co. (4.40% Pfd.) (ASE)

MPO Metropolitan Police Office; Midland Steel Products Company (NYSE); Military Post Office

MPO II Midland Steel Products Co. ($2 Non-Cum. Div. Shs.) (ASE)

MPP Member of Provincial Parliament

MPPA Music Publishers Protective Association

MPPDA Motion Picture Producers and Distributors of America

MPR Mapes Consolidated Manufacturing Company (NYSE)

MPRC Ministry of Production's Regionary Controller; Motion Picture Research Council

mp rdg map reading

M Prof Acc Master of Professional Accountancy

MP RR Missouri Pacific Railroad

MPRX Montana Power Company (private car rr mark)

mps meters per second

MPS marbled paper sides (bookbinding); Member of the Pharmaceutical Society [of Great Britain]; Member of the Philological Society; Member of the Physical Society; Ministry of Public Security; Motor Products Corporation (NYSE)

MPSC Military Provost Staff Corps

MPU Medical Practitioners' Union; message picking-up (RAF)

MPV Missouri Public Service (NYSE)

MPW Minneapolis-Moline Company (NYSE)

MPX Columbian Carbon Company,

Magnetic Pigment Division (private car rr mark)

Mpy company (*Maatschappij*—Dutch)

MPZ Mid-Continent Petroleum (NYSE)

MPZX Mineral Point Zinc Division of The New Jersey Zinc Company (private car rr mark)

MQ Mack Trucks, Inc (NYSE); metol-quinol (photography)

Mqe Martinique

m r mate's receipt; mill run; mine run; memorandum receipt; moment of resistance

Mr Master; Mister

MR machine records (US Army); McCloud River Railroad Company (rr mark); Map Reference; Maritime Regiment; Master of the Rolls; mate's receipt; Mersey Railway; Middlesex Regiment; Midland Railway; Ministry of Reconstruction; Minister Resident; Missionary Rector; Misrair (airline); moment of resistance; Municipal Reform; Postal Storage (rr car)

m/r my shipment (*mi remesa*—Spanish)

M/R memorandum receipt; morning report (US Army)

MRA Marathon Corporation (NYSE); Member of the Royal Agricultural College; Moral Re-Armament Association

MRAC Member of the Royal Agricultural College

MRAe S Member Royal Aeronautical Society

MRAF Marshal of the Royal Air Force

MRAS Member of the Royal Academy of Sciences; Member of the Royal Asiatic Society

MRC Marchant Calculators, Inc (NYSE); Medical Research Council; Medical Reserve Corps; Metals Reserve Company

MRCC Member of the Royal College of Chemistry

MRCO Member Royal College of Organists

MRCOG Member of Royal College of Obstetricians and Gynaecologists

MRCP Member of the Royal College of Physicians

MRCP E Member of Royal College of Physicians, Edinburgh

MRCPI Member Royal College of Physicians, Ireland

MRCS Member of the Royal College of Surgeons

MRCSE Member of Royal College of Surgeons, Edinburgh

MRCSI Member of the Royal College of Surgeons of Ireland

MRCVS Member of the Royal College of Veterinary Surgeons

MRE Master of Religious Education

MRF Meier & Frank Company, Inc (NYSE)

MRGS Member of the Royal Geographical Society

MRH Member of the Royal Household

MRI Malt Research Institute; Member of the Royal Institution

MRIA Member of the Royal Irish Academy

mrimonium matrimony (*matrimonium*—Latin)

MRIX Monarch Refineries, Inc (private car rr mark)

MRK Merck & Company (NYSE)

MRP Popular Republican Movement (*Mouvement Républicain Populaire*—French)

MRP Master in Regional Planning

MRR Market St. Railway (NYSE)

MRRX Mather Refrigerator Express (private car rr mark); Morrell & Company (private car rr mark)

Mrs. Mistress; gentlemen (*Messieurs*—French)

MRS Manufacturers Railway Company (private car rr mark); Medical Receiving Station; military railway service (US Army)

MR San I Member of Royal Sanitary Institute

MRSL Member of the Society of Literature

MRST Member of the Royal Society of Teachers

MRT Martin-Parry Corporation (NYSE)

MRTN Martin (aircraft)

MRU machine records unit (US Army)

MRUSI Member of Royal United Service Institute

MRW Motor Wheel Corporation (NYSE)

MRX Morrell Refrigerator Line (private car rr mark)

Mrz March (*Marzo*—Spanish)

m s machinery survey; mail steamer; margin of safety; maximum stress; medium steel; medium sweep; meters per second; mild steel; motor ship; multiple sclerosis

ms manuscript

MS McCrory Stores Corporation (NYSE); Massachusetts State (college); Master of Science; Master of Surgery; Medium shot (films); Memphis State (college); Mess Sergeant; Metric System; Military Secretary; Mine-Sweeper; Ministry of Supply; Missionary Fathers of La Salette; Missionary Society; Monitoring Service; Mail and Smoker (rr car)

m/s meters per second; months after sight

M & S March and September; Maule and Selwyn (Law Reports)

m s a mix skillfully (*misc secundum artem*—Latin) (pharmacy)

MSA Manufacturing Silversmiths Association; Master of Science and Arts; Master of Scientific Agriculture; Master Silversmiths' Association; Member of the Society of Apothecaries; Member of the Society of Architects; Member of the Society of Arts; Merchant Shipping Act; Military Service Acts; Mineralogical Society of America; Municipal School of Art

MSAE Member of the Society of Automotive Engineers

MS Agr Master of Scientific Agriculture

MS Agr Eng Master of Science in Agricultural Engineering

MS Agr Ex Master of Science in Agricultural Extension

MS Arch. Master of Science in Architecture

ms as. many years (*muchos años*—Spanish)

MSB Mesabi Iron Company (NYSE)

MS BA Master of Science in Business Administration

MSBL Member School Board, London

M S blk mild steel, black finish

M S brt mild steel, bright finish

MS Bus. Master of Science in Business

m s c authority without restriction (*mandatum sine clausula*—Latin); mile of standard cable; moved, seconded, and carried (parliamentary motion)

m sc machine screw

MSC Madras Staff Corps; Manchester Ship Canal; Medical Service Corps (US Army); Medical Staff Corps; Member of the Standing Committee; Metropolitan Special Constabulary; Michigan State College; Mile of Standard Cable; Millinery Stabilization Commission; Missionaries of the Sacred Heart (*Missionarii Sacratissima Cordis Jesu*—Latin); Mississippi State College; Montana State College; Morgan State College; [United Nations] Military Staff Committee

MSCC Missionary Society of the Canadian Church

MSCE Master of Science in Civil Engineering

MS ChE Master of Science in Chemical Engineering

MS Chem Master of Science in Chemistry

MS Com Master of Science in Commerce

mscp mean spherical candlepower

MSCW Mississippi State College for Women

M/s D Minesweeping Division (naval)

MSD Doctor of Medical Science; Master of Scientific Didactics; Master Surgeon Dentist

MS Dent. Master of Science in Dentistry

MSDMA Mayonnaise and Salad Dressing Manufacturers Association

MSE Massey-Harris Company Ltd (NYSE); Master of Science in Engineering; Midwest Stock Exchange; Mississippi Export Railroad Company (private car rr mark)

MSEB Marine Society for the Equipment of Boys

msec millisecond

M2C Metalsmith Second Class (US Navy)

MS Ed Master of Science in Education

MSEE Master of Science in Electrical Engineering

MSEM Master of Science in Engineering Mechanics

mses goods (*marchandises*—French)

MSF Congregation of the Missionaries of the Holy Family; Master of Science in Forestry; mobile striking force (US Army)

M S F Std master steam fitters' standard (plumbing)

MSFU Merchant Service Fighter Unit (RAF)

msg message

MSG Madison Square Garden; prefix indicating a message to or from the master of a ship concerning its operation or navigation (QS)

MS Gov't Management Master of Science in Government Management

MSGR messenger (US Army)

MS Group Work Ed Master of Science in Group Work Education

M Sgt Master Sergeant

MSH Manhattan Shirt Company (NYSE); Master of Staghounds

MSH Ec Master of Science in Home Economics

Mshl RAF Marshal of the Royal Air Force

MS Home Ec Master of Science in Home Economics

MS Hyg Master of Science in Hygiene

MS Hyg and Phys Educ Master of Science in Hygiene and Physical Education

MSI Member of the Chartered Surveyors' Institution; Milk Sugar Institute

MS Ind E Master of Science in Industrial Engineering

MSJ Master of Science in Journalism

MSK Muskegon Piston Ring (NYSE)

MSKX Milwaukee Solvay Coke Company (private car rr mark)

m s l mean sea level

MSL Minneapolis & St. Louis Railway (NYSE); missile (US Army)

MS & LR Manchester, Sheffield and Lincolnshire Railway

MSLS Master of Science in Library Science

MSM Madras and Southern Mahratta Railway; Master of Medical Science; Master of Sacred Music; Meritorious Service Medal; Minnesota, St. Paul & Sault Ste Marie Railroad (NYSE)

MSME Master of Science in Mechanical Engineering

MS Med Master of Medical Science

MS Mus Master of Science in Music

MSN Michigan State Normal (college)

MSNE Master of Science in Nursing Education

msngr messenger

MS Nurs Master of Science in Nursing

m-sopr mezzo-soprano

MSP Mutual Security Program

MSP E Master of Science in Physical Education

MSPEA Maine Sardine Packers Export Association

MSPH Master of Science in Public Health

MS Phar Master of Science in Pharmacy

MS PHE Master of Science in Public Health Engineering

MS Phy Ed Master of Science in Physical Education

MS PSM Master of Science in Public School Music

MS Public Adm Master of Science in Public Administration

MSR main supply road (US Army)

MSRD Merchant Ship Repairs Department

MS Ret Master of Science in Retailing

MSRI Metal Stamping Research Institute

MSRX Modern Sanitary Rendering Company (private car rr mark)

mss manuscripts

MSS Master of Social Service or Master of Social Science; Member of the Statistical Society; Mission Corporation (NYSE)

MS SE Master of Science in Sanitary Engineering

MS Social Adm Master of Science in

Social Administration

MS SS Master of Science in Social Service

M Soc Studies Master of Social Studies

MSST Missionary Servants of the Most Holy Trinity

MS SW Master of Science in Social Work

M Soc Wk Master of Social Work

MS Soc W Master of Science in Social Work

MST Mascot Oil Company (NYSE); Master of Sacred Theology; Mercantile Stores Company (NYSE) Inc; Mountain Standard Time

mst measurement

MSTA Manufacturers Surgical Trade Association

MS Tech Master of Technical Science (*Magister Scientiae Technicae* —Latin)

Msth mesothorium

M St J Ordinary Member of the Order of St John of Jerusalem

M&StL Minneapolis & St. Louis Railroad Company

MStP&SSM Minneapolis, St. Paul & Sault Ste. Marie Railway Company

mstr mech master mechanic

MS Trans Master of Science in Transportation

MS Trans E Master of Science in Transportation Engineering

MSTS military sea transportation service (US Army)

MSU Middle South Utilities (NYSE); Montana State University

M Sup p Ministry of Supply

M Surgery Master in Surgery

MSW Master of Social Work; Mountain States Power Company (NYSE)

MSX Morton Salt Company (private car rr mark); Seaboard Oil Company (Del.) (NYSE)

m t metric ton

mt empty; mountain

Mt Matthew; Mountain

MT empty [coach] (railway); Mandated Territory; Massoretic Text; mean time; Mechanical Transport; Meteorological Telegram; Middle Temple; Military Training; Motor Transport (US Army); Tangier (IDP)

M/T Mail transfer; measurement ton (US Army)

MTA Mine Tool Association; Music Teachers' Association

MTB Message to Base; Motor Transport Board; motor torpedo boat

MTC Marcus Tullius Cicero; Mechanical Transport Corps; Monsanto Chemical Company (NYSE); Mystic Terminal Company (private car rr mark)

MTCAUS Military Training Camps Association of the United States

mt ct cp mortgage certificate coupon

mtd mounted

MTD Manager Traffic Department; mean temperature difference

MT & E Morristown & Erie Railroad (rr mark)

Mter Manchester (England)

mtg meeting; mortgage; mounting

mtgd mortgaged

mtge mortgage

mtgee mortgagee

mtgor mortgagor

mth month

M Th Master of Theology

MTH Mathieson Chemical Corporation (NYSE)

MTI Metal Treating Institute

mties empties

mtl material

m t l mean tidal level

MTM Minnesota Mining & Manufacturing (NYSE)

MTNA Music Teachers National Association

MTO Mechanical Transport Officer

MTOUSA Mediterranean Theater of Operations, US Army

MTP mobilization training program (US Army); Montana Power Company (NYSE)

MTPI Member Town Planning Institute

MTR motor (US Army); Muter Company (NYSE)

MTRCL motorcycle (US Army)

Mt Rev Most Reverena

mtro master (*maestro*—Spanish)

mts mountains

MTS Manganese Track Society; Mechanical Transport Section; Merchant Taylors' School; Merchant Transport Service; Missions to Seamen

MT&S Mechanized Transport and Supply

MTV Motor Torpedo Vessel

MTX Metal Textile Corporation (NYSE); Morrell Tank Line (private car rr mark)

MTX P Pr Metal Textile Corp. (Part. Pref.) (ASE)

MTZ motorize (US Army)

mu micron; millimicron; murium

m u mache unit; mobile unit

MU McGill University; McMaster University; Marquette University; Mercer University; Miami University

mu a microampere

MUB Mueller Brass Company (NYSE)

Much Ado Much Ado About Nothing

m u f maximum usable frequency

mu f microfarad

muist note (*muistutus*—Finnish)

mult multiple

mu mu micromicron

mun municipal

MUN munitions (US Army); Munsingwear, Inc (NYSE)

munic municipal

MUNX Mather Refrigerator Express (private car rr mark)

MUO Municipal University of Omaha

Mur Murphey's Reports (legal)

MUR(F) United Renaissance Movement (*Mouvement Unifié de la Renaissance (Française)*—French)

mus museum; music; musician

Mus Musca (constellation)

m u s a multiple-unit steerable antenna

Mus B Bachelor of Music (*Musicae Baccalaureus*—Latin)

Mus D Doctor of Music (*Musicae Doctor*—Latin)

MUS1C Musician First Class (US Navy)

musicol musicology

Mus M Master of Music (*Musicae Magister*—Latin)

MUS2C Musician Second Class (US Navy)

mut mutilated; mutual

mu w microwatt

MUW Municipal University of Wichita

MUY Murray Corporation of America (NYSE)

mv market value; mean variation; medium voltage; with half voice (*mezza voce*—Latin); millivolt muzzle velocity

MV merchant vessel; Midland Valley Railroad Company; motor vessel; muzzle velocity; Veterinary Physician (*Medicus Veterinarius*—Latin)

μv microvolt

MVA Machinists' Vise Association; Medical Veterans Association; Missouri Valley Authority

MVC Midvale Company (NYSE)

MVM Mount Vernon-Woodberry Mills (NYSE)

MVMT movement (US Army)

MVO Member of the [Royal] Victorian Order

MV S Master of Veterinary Science

mvt movement

MVW Mount Vernon-Woodberry Mills, Inc (common stock, ASE)

MVX Milwaukee Vinegar Company (private car rr mark)

m w mixed widths (lumber); medium wave

mw megawatt; milliwatt

MW Middle Welsh; Most Worshipful; Most Worthy; to my knowledge

(Meines Wissens—German); Minnesota Western Railway Company (rr mark)

M & W Meason and Welsby (Law Reports)

MWA Modern Woodmen of America

MWAI Metal Wearing Apparel Institute

MWB Metropolitan Water Board; Ministry of Works and Buildings

MWD M & M Wood Working Company (NYSE)

MWEX Mars Incorporated (private car rr mark)

m w g music-wire gauge

MWG Section Gang or Track Inspection Car (rr cars)

MWGCP Most Worthy Grand Chief Patriarch

MWGM Most Worshipful Grand Master (freemasonry); Most Worthy Grand Master (freemasonry)

MWH Hand Car (rr cars)

MWI Metal Window Institute; Ministry of War Information

MWJ Ballast Unloader (rr cars)

MWK Snow-removing Car (rr cars)

MWKX Marden-Wild Corporation (private car rr mark)

MWL Hand Car (rr cars)

MWM Store-supply Car (rr cars)

MWO Midwest Oil Corporation (NYSE); modification work order (US Army)

MWP mechanical wood pulp (paper); Most Worthy Patriarch (freemasonry); Pile Driver (rr cars)

MWPA Married Women's Property Act

MWR Mid-West Refineries, Inc (NYSE); Muncie & Western Railroad Company (rr mark)

MWS Midwest Piping & Supply (NYSE); Montana, Wyoming & Southern Railroad Company (rr mark); Steam Shovel (rr cars)

MWT Ministry of War Transport; Mountain war time; Tool and Block Car (rr cars)

MWU Wrecking Derrick (rr cars)

MWV Masonic War Veterans; Mexican War Veteran; Wrecking Derrick (rr cars)

MWW Wrecking Derrick (rr cars)

MWX Boarding Outfit Car (rr cars)

MWZ Manischewitz (The B.) Company (common stock, ASE)

mxd mixed

Mx Maximilian; Middlesex (county of England)

mxm maximum

MXO Industria Electrica de Mex. (NYSE)

my. myopia (medicine); motor yacht

My. company *(Maatschappij*—Dutch)

M/Y marshalling yards (US Army)

MY motor yacht

mya myriare

mycol mycology

myg myriagram

MYG Maytag Company (NYSE)

My. and K Mylne and Keen (Law Reports)

myl myrialiter (metric)

MYLTR my letter (US Army)

mym myriameter

MYMSG my message (US Army)

MYO Murray Ohio Manufacturing (NYSE)

m y o b mind your own business (colloquial)

Myr Myrick's Probate Court Reports (legal)

MYSER my serial (US Army)

myst mysteries; mystery

myth. mythological; mythology

MZ Macy (R. H.) & Company (NYSE); for nonpayment *(Mangels Zahlung*—German)

mzo March *(marzo*—Spanish)

N

n born *(natus*—Latin); nails; name; nephew; net *(netto*—German); at night *(nocte*—Latin); nomen; nominative; noon; normal; note; number; our *(notre*—French); index of refraction; neuter; noun; born *(né, née*—French)

N index of refraction; International Nickel Company of Canada (NYSE); Nationalist; Naval Aircraft Factory; Navigator (naval); Name, *(nomen*—Latin); Negro (US Army); nitrogen; normal solution; north *(Nord*—French); North(ern) (US Army); Norse; Norway; number of turns of winding; Our *(Nostu*—Latin)

n a author's note *(nota del autor*—Spanish)

Na natrium (sodium)

n/a no account; non-acceptance

N/a no advice (banking)

NA National Academy; National Army; National Association: Nautical Almanac; Naval Accounts; Naval Architect; Naval Attaché; Naval Auxiliary; Naval Aviation; neutral axis (engineering); Neutrality Act; North America; North

American Company (NYSE); not above; not available (US Army); numerical aperture; Nursing Auxiliary

n a a not always afloat (shipping)

NAA National Aeronautic Association; National Arborist Association; National Artillery Association; National Automobile Association; Naval Aid Auxiliary; Naval Air Arm; Northern Architectural Association

NAABC National Association of American Business Clubs

NAABI National Association of Alcoholic Beverage Importers

NAACC National Association for American Composers and Conductors; National Association of Angling and Casting Clubs

NAACP National Association for the Advancement of Colored People

NAACS National Association of Accredited Commercial Schools

NAAFI Navy, Army and Air Force Institutes

NAAG National Association of Attorneys-General

NAAHU National Association of Ac-

cident and Health Underwriters

NAAI National Alliance of Art and Industry

NAAMIC National Association of Automotive Mutual Insurance Companies

NAAN National Advertising Agency Network

NAAO National Association of Amateur Oarsmen; National Association of Assessing Officers

NAAPPB National Association of Amusement Parks, Pools and Beaches

NAAUS National Archery Association of the United States

NAB National Association of Broadcasters; National Associated Businessmen

NABAC National Association of Bank Auditors and Comptrollers

NABCA National Alcoholic Beverage Control Association

NABET National Association of Broadcast Engineers and Technicians

NABIM National Association of Band Instrument Manufacturers

NABM National Association of Bedding Manufacturers; National Association of Blouse Manufacturers; National Association of Button Manufacturers

NABOM National Association of Building Owners and Managers

NABP National Association of Boards of Pharmacy

NABTE National Association of Building Trades Employers

NABTTI National Association of Business Teacher-Training Institutions

NAC National Air Council; National Archives Council; National Association of Chiropodists; National Association of Consumers; National Can Corporation (NYSE); Naval Aircraftman; North Atlantic Coast

NACA National Advisory Committee for Aeronautics; National Agricultural Chemicals Association; National Armored Car Association; National Association of Cost Accountants

NACAA National Association of County Agricultural Agents

NACC Norwegian-American Chamber of Commerce

NACDS National Association of Chain Drug Stores

NACE National Association of Corrosion Engineers

NACGM National Association of Chewing Gum Manufacturers

NACGN National Association of Colored Graduate Nurses

Nachf successor (*Nachfolger—* German)

nachm in the afternoon (*nachmittags* —German)

NACJ National Association of Credit Jewelers

NACLS National Association of Commission Lumber Salemen

NACM National Association of Cotton Manufacturers; National Association of Credit Men

NACO National Association of County Officials

NACPDCG National Association of Catholic Publishers and Dealers in Church Goods

NACS National Association of Civil Secretaries; National Association of College Stores

NACSDA National Association of Commissioners, Secretaries and Directors of Agriculture

NACW National Association of College Women; National Association of Colored Women

NACX Niagara Alkali Company (private car rr mark)

n a d no appreciable disease

NAD National Academy of Design; National Association of the Deaf; Naval Air Division; Naval Ammunition Depot (US Navy); Naval Armament Depot

NADA National Apple Dryers Association; National Automobile Dealers Association

NADAM National Association of Deans and Advisers of Men

NADEM National Association of Dairy Equipment Manufacturers

NADI National Association of Display Industries

NADSC National Association of Direct Selling Companies

NADW National Association of Deans of Women

NADX North American Car Corporation (private car rr mark)

NAEA Newspaper Advertising Executives Association

NAEB National Association of Educational Broadcasters

NAEBM National Association of Engine and Boat Manufacturers

NAEC National Association of Electric Companies

NAEGA North American Export Grain Association

NAEM National Association of Exhibit Managers

NAF National Association of Foremen; Naval Aircraft Factory (US Navy)

NAFC National Association of Food Chains

NAFD National Association of Flour Distributors

NAFFP National Association of Frozen Food Packers

NAFM National Association of Fan Manufacturers; National Association of Flag Manufacturers; National Association of Furniture Manufacturers

NAFTF National Association of Finishers of Textile Fabrics

NAG National Association of Gardeners

NAGCM National Association of Golf Club Manufacturers

NAGCP National Association of Greeting Card Publishers

NAGM National Association of Glue Manufacturers

Nah Nahum (Biblical)

NAHB National Association of Home Builders

NAHDM National Association of House Dress Manufacturers

NAHHVG National Association of Hot House Vegetable Growers

NAHM National Association of Hosiery Manufacturers

NAHO National Association of Housing Officials

NAHRMP National Association of Hotel and Restaurant Meat Purveyors

NAHS National Association of Horological Schools

NAHW National Association of Hardwood Wholesalers

NAHX North American Car Corporation (private car rr mark)

NAI National Airlines Incorporated; National Apple Institute

NAIA National Association of Insurance Agents

NAIB National Association of Insurance Brokers

NAIC National Association of Insurance Commissioners; National Association of Investment Companies

NAIDM National Association of Insecticide and Disinfectant Manufacturers

NAIHS National Association of Importers of Hides and Skins

NAII National Association of Ice Industries; National Association of Independent Insurers

NAIIA National Association of Independent Insurance Adjusters

NAIIU not authorized if issued under (US Army)

NAILM National Association of Institutional Laundry Managers

NAIRM National Association of Ice Refrigerator Manufacturers

NAITD National Association of Independent Tire Dealers

NAITT National Association of Industrial Teacher Trainers

NAIW National Association of Insurance Women

NAL National Air Lines

NALA National Agricultural Limestone Association

NALAO National Association of Legal Aid Organizations

NALC National Association of Letter Carriers

NALCM National Association of Lace Curtain Manufacturers

NALGM National Association of Leather Glove Manufacturers

NALGO National Association of Local Government Officers

NALH National Association of Ladies' Hatters

NALHI National Authority for the Ladies Handbag Industry

NALT National Association of the Legitimate Theater

NALU National Association of Life Underwriters

N Am. North America; North American

NAM Namm-Loeser's, Inc (common stock, ASE); National Association of Manufacturers

NAMA National Automatic Merchandising Association

NAMAC National Association of Men's Apparel Clubs

NAMB National Association of Merchandise Brokers

NAMBE National Association of Milk Bottle Exchanges

NAMBO National Association of Motor Bus Operators

NAMCC National Association of Motor Carriers Counsel; National Association of Mutual Casualty Companies

NAMD National Association of Marble Dealers

NAMDB National Association of Medical-Dental Bureaus

NAMF National Association of Metal Finishers

NAMI Newspaper Association Managers, Inc

NAMIA National Association of Mutual Insurance Agents

nǎml namely (*nǎmligen*—Swedish)

NAMM National Association of Margarine Manufacturers; National Association of Music Merchants

NAMMM National Association of Musical Merchandise Manufacturers

NAMMW National Association of Musical Merchandise Wholesalers

NAMO National Association of Marketing Officials

NAMOIM National Association of Miscellaneous and Ornamental Iron Manufacturers

NAMP National Association of Magazine Publishers; National Association of Master Plumbers

NAMPBG National Association of Manufacturers of Pressed and Blown Glassware

NAMPW National Association of Meat Processors and Wholesalers

NAMRA National Association of Marketing Research Agencies

NAMSC National Association of Mutual Savings Banks

NAMX Tank Car Corporation of America (private car rr mark)

NANA National Advertising Newspaper Association; North American Newspaper Alliance

NANAI National Association for Negroes in American Industry

NANE National Association for Nursery Education

NANX National Aniline Division of Allied Chemical & Dye Corporation (private car rr mark)

NAOA National Apartment Owners Association

NAOMM National Association of Ornamental Metal Manufacturers

Nap. Napoleon

NAP National Association of Postmasters; Non-Aggression Pact

NAPA National Association of Performing Artists; National Association of Purchasing Agents; National Automotive Parts Association

NAPBL National Association of Professional Baseball Leagues

NAPE National Alliance of Postal Employees; National Association of Power Engineers

NAPFM National Association of Packaged Fuel Manufacturers

NAPIM National Association of Printing Ink Makers

NAPL National Association of Photo-Lithographers

NAPM National Association of Photographic Manufacturers; National Association of Popcorn Manufacturers

NAPMM National Association of Produce Market Managers

NAPNE National Association for Practical Nurse Education

NAPNM National Association of Pipe Nipple Manufacturers

NAPOA National Association of Property Owners of America

NAPOMCE National Association of Post Office Mechanics and Custodial Employees

NAPP National Association of Play Publishers

NAPPO National Association of Plant Patent Owners

NAPRE National Association of Practical Refrigerating Engineers

NAPRM National Association of Printers Roller Manufacturers

NAPS. National Association of Postal Supervisors

NAPT National Association of Piano Tuners

NAR North American Rayon (NYSE); Northern Alberta Railways Company (rr mark)

NARB National Association of Referees in Bankruptcy

NARC National Association of Refrigeration Contractors; naval ordnance research calculator

NARCE National Association of Retired Civil Employees

NARCF National Association of Retail Clothiers and Furnishers

N Arch. Naval Architect

NARD National Association of Retail Druggists

NARDA National Appliance and Radio Dealers Association

NAREB National Association of Real Estate Boards

NARG National Association of Retail Grocers

NARHC National Association of River and Harbor Contractors

NARICM National Association of Retail Ice Cream Manufacturers

NARMD National Association of Retail Meat Dealers

NARND National Association of Radio News Directors

NARNH National Association of Registered Nursing Homes

NAR Pr North American Rayon Corporation ($3 Pfd.) (ASE)

narr complaint (*narratio*—Latin) (law)

NARSR National Association of Radio Station Representatives

NARTB National Association of Radio and Television Broadcasters

NARUC National Association of Railroad and Utilities Commissioners

NARW National Association of Refrigerated Warehouses

NAS Conde Nast Publications, Inc (NYSE); National Academy of Science; National Adoption Society; National Allotment Society; National Association of Sanitarians; National Association of Schoolmasters; National Association of Shopfitters; National Audubon Society; Naval Air Service; Naval Air Station; Nursing Auxiliary Service

NASA National Association of Securities Administrators; National Association of Subscription Agents

NASAB National Association of Shippers Advisory Boards

NASACT National Association of State Auditors, Comptrollers and Treasurers

NASAO National Association of State Aviation Officials

NASBO National Association of State Budget Officers

NASBP National Association of Surety Bond Producers

NASCS National Association of Shoe Chain Stores

NASD National Association of Securities Dealers

NASDM National Association of Special Delivery Messengers

NASE National Academy of Stationary Engineers; National Association of Steel Exporters

NASFCA National Automatic Sprinkler and Fire Control Association

NASL National Association of State Libraries

NASM National Association of Scale Manufacturers; National Association of Schools of Music; National Association of Silo Manufacturers; National Association of Slipper Manufacturers

NASMBCM National Association of Sanitary Milk Bottle Closure Manufacturers

NASMD National Association of Sheet Metal Distributors

NASPM National Association of Shirt and Pajama Manufacturers

NASPO National Association of State Purchasing Officials

NASRC National Association of State Racing Commissioners

NASS National Association of School Secretaries; National Association of Secretaries of State; National Association of Suggestion Systems

NASSA National Association of Schools of Social Administration

NASSB National Association of Supervisors of State Banks

NASSP National Association of Secondary School Principals

NASSW National Association of School Social Workers

NASU National Association of State Universities

NASW National Association of Science Workers; National Association of Shoe Wholesalers

NASWSO National Association of Soft Water Service Operators

nat national; native; natural; naturalized

Nat Natal; Nathan; Nathanael; Nathaniel

N At North Atlantic

NAT National Transit Company (NYSE); North Atlantic Treaty

NATA National Association of Tax Accountants; National Association of Tax Administrators; National Association of Teacher Agencies; National Association of Transportation Advertising; National Automobile Transporters Association; National Aviation Trades Association

NATB National Automobile Theft Bureau

NATD National Association of Tobacco Distributors

Nat Gal National Gallery

nat hist natural history

natl national

natl bk national bank

NATMA National Association of Teachers of Marketing and Advertising

NATMM National Association of Textile Machinery Manufacturers

NATO National Association of

Taxicab Owners; National Association of Travel Officials; North Atlantic Treaty Organization

nat ord natural order

NATOUSA Northern African Theater of Operations, U.S. Army

nat phil natural philosophy

NATS National Association of Training Schools; Navy Air Transport System

Nat Sc D Doctor of Natural Science

N Att Naval Attaché

NATTC Naval Air Technical Training Center (US Navy)

natur naturalist

NATX North American Car Corporation (private car rr mark)

NAUA National Automobile Underwriters Association

NAUM National Association of Uniform Manufacturers

naut nautical

naut mi nautical mile

nav naval; navigating; navigation

NAV National American Veterans

Nav Arch. Naval Architect

NAV Aux National American Veterans Auxiliary

Nav Const Naval Constructor

Nav E Naval Engineer

NAVED National Association of Visual Education Dealers

NAVGUN Naval Gun Factory (US Navy)

navig navigation; navigator

NAVOBSY Naval Observatory (US Navy)

NAVS National Association of Variety Stores

NAVTPM National Association of Vertical Turbine Pump Manufacturers

NAW National Association of Wholesalers

NAWA National Association of Women Artists; National Auto Wreckers Association

NAWB National Adequate Wiring Bureau

NAWCAS National Association of Women's and Children's Apparel Salesmen

NAWCEM National Association of Water Conditioning Equipment Manufacturers

NAWFM National Association of Wool Fibre Manufacturers

NAWGA National-American Wholesale Grocers Association

NAWHM National Association of Wood Heel Manufacturers

NAWL National Association of Women Lawyers

NAWLA National American Wholesale Lumber Association

NAWM National Association of Wool Manufacturers

NAWMD National Association of Waste Material Dealers

NAWWO National Association of Woolen and Worsted Overseers

Nay. Nayarit

NAYRU North American Yacht Racing Union

Nazi national socialist (*Nazionalsozialist*—German)

Nb nimbus (clouds); Niobium

n b mark well (*nota bene*—Latin); new boilers; new bonds; no ball (cricket); north bound

NB National Bellas Hess, Inc (NYSE); naval base; Netherland Brigade; New Brunswick; No bid; non-belligerent; North Borneo; North Butte Mining Company (NYSE); Northampton and Bath Railroad Company (rr mark); North Britain; North British

NBA National Bar Association; National Basketball Association; National Boxing Association; National Builders Association; National Button Association; North British Academy

NBAC National Book Awards Committee

NBAPC National Business Advisory and Planning Council

NBBB National Better Business Bureau

NBBDA National Burlap Bag Dealers Association

NBBMA National Beauty and Barber Manufacturers Association

NBBPVI National Board of Boiler and Pressure Vessel Inspectors

NBC National Baseball Congress; National Bowling Council; National Book Council; National Broadcasting Company; Naval Barracks, Chatham; Non-Combatant Corps; Northern Baptist Convention

NBCA National Baptist Convention of America

NBCL National Beauty Culturists League

NBCR National Bureau of Civic Research

NBCSDA National Broom Corn and Supply Dealers Association

NBCU National Bureau of Casualty Underwriters

NBD New British Dominion Oil (NYSE)

NBDA National Barrel and Drum Association

n b e north by east

NBEq Co New Brunswick Equity Cases (legal)

NBER National Bureau of Economic Research

NBFFO National Board of Fur Farm Organizations

NBFU National Board of Fire Underwriters

n b g no bloody good (colloquial)

NBGF National Beet Growers Federation

NBGQA National Building Granite Quarries Association

NBL National Basketball League; National Book League

NBMA National Broom Manufacturers Association

NBME National Board of Medical Examiners

NBOP National Brotherhood of Operative Potters

N Bor North Borneo

NBP National Business Publications

NBPA National Butane Propane Association

n br naval brass (colloquial)

N Br New Brunswick

n Br north latitude (*nördliche Breite* —German)

NBR North British Railway

NBRMP National Board of Review of Motion Pictures

NBS National Broadcasting Service (New Zealand); National Bureau of Standards; National Button Society; National Shares Corporation (NYSE)

NBSDI National Brands Soft Drink Institute

NBSHA National Bakers Supply House Association

nb st nimbo-stratus (clouds)

NBTA National Business Teachers Association; National Bus Traffic Association

n b w north by west

NBWA National Beer Wholesalers Association

NBYWCA National Board of the Young Women's Christian Association

n c new charter; new crop; nitrocellulose; non-callable; north country

n/c against us (*nuestro cargo*— Spanish); our account (*nuestra cuenta*—Spanish)

NC National Cash Register(NYSE); National Congress; National Council; Navy Cross; New Church; North Carolina; Northern Command; Nurse Corps; New Caledonia

N/C no change (US Army)

N&C Nashville, Chattanooga & St Louis Railway (rr mark)

NCA National Canners Association; National Cemetery Association; National Chiropractic Association;

National Costumers Association; National Cranberry Association; National Coal Association; National Coffee Association; National Confectioners Association; National Creameries Association; Northern Consolidated Airlines Inc

NCAA National Collegiate Athletic Association

NCAB New Council of American Business

NCAC National Concert and Artists Corporation

NCAI National Committee on Atomic Information; National Congress of American Indians

N Cal New Caledonia

NCAWE National Council of Administrative Women in Education

NCB National Coal Board; National Compliance Board; National Conservation Bureau

NCBA National Chinchilla Breeders of America

NCBBC National Council of Boards of Beauty Culture

NCBE National Conference of Bar Examiners

NCBM National Council on Business Mail

NCBPE National Conference of Business Paper Editors

NCBS National Council of Business Schools

NCBVA National Concrete Burial Vault Association

NCC Netherlands Chamber of Commerce

NCCA National Cotton Council of America

NCCC National Council of the Churches of Christ in the USA

NCCCWA National Cotton Compress and Cotton Warehouse Association

NCCD National Council for Community Development

NCCI National Council on Compensation Insurance

NCCJ National Conference of Christians and Jews

NCCM National Council of Catholic Men

NCCPA National Cinder Concrete Products Association

NCCPT National Congress of Colored Parents and Teachers

NCCRC National Conference of Commercial Receivable Companies

NCCUSL National Conference of Commissioners on Uniform State Laws

NCCVD National Council for Combating Venereal Disease

NCCW National Council of Catholic Women

NCD North Canadian Oils (NYSE)

NCE Newark College of Engineering

NCF National Cancer Foundation; National Civics Federation

NCFA National Consumer Finance Association

NCFC National Council of Farmer Cooperatives

NCFR National Council on Family Relations

NCGA National Cotton Ginners Association

NCGMA National Canvas Goods Manufacturers Association

NCGX Northern Refrigerator Line, Inc (private car rr mark)

NCH National Committee on Housing

NCHA National Contract Hardware Association; National Council of Housing Association

n Chr after Christ (*nach Christo*— German)

n c i no common interest

NCI National Cheese Institute; National Cooperatives, Inc; Natural Casing Institute

NCIPA National Council of Independent Petroleum Associations

NCJA National Conference of Juvenile Agencies

NCJCJ National Council of Juvenile Court Judges

NCJW National Council of Jewish Women

NCL National Church League; National Consumers League

NCLC National Child Labor Committee; National Council of Labor Colleges

NCLL National Conference on Labor Legislation

NCLX North American Cyanamid Limited (private car rr mark)

NCMA National Concrete Masonry Association; National Council of Millinery Associations

NCMH National Committee on Maternal Health; National Committee for Mental Hygiene

NCMLB National Council of Mailing List Brokers

NCMPF National Cooperative Milk Producers Federation

NCNW National Council of Negro Women

NCO non-commissioned officer; National Container Corporation (NYSE)

NCOX Newport Industries, Inc (private car rr mark)

n c p normal circular pitch (gears)

NCP National Collegiate Players

NCPE National Committee on Parent Education

NCPEI National Council of Parent Education, Inc

NCPIE National Council of Professional Industrial Engineers

NCPLA National Council of Patent Law Associations

NCPMI National Clay Pipe Manufacturers, Inc

NCPMTO National Council of Private Motor Truck Owners

NCPPL National Committee on Prisons and Prison Labor

NCPR National Congress of Petroleum Retailers

NCPW National Council for the Prevention of War

NCR North American Car Corporation (NYSE)

NCRC National Consumer-Retailer Council

NCRSA National Commercial Refrigerator Sales Association

NCSA National Civil Service Association; National Confectionery Salesmen's Association; National Crushed Stone Association; National Customs Service Association

NCSAB National Council of State Agencies for the Blind

NCSBEE National Council of State Boards of Engineering Examiners

NCSC National Council on Schoolhouse Construction

NCSGC National Council of State Garden Clubs

NCSI National Council for Stream Improvement

NCSIRB National Coat and Suit Industry Recovery Board

NCSL National Civil Service League

NCSLA National Conference of State Liquor Administrators

NCSO National Council of Salesmen's Organizations

NCSP National Conference on State Parks

NCSRA National Conference of State Retail Associations

NCSS National Conference on Social Security; National Council for the Social Studies

NCSSBA National Council of State School Board Associations

NCSSLS National Conference of State Small Loan Supervisors

NC&StL Nashville, Chattanooga & St. Louis Railway

NCSTSR National Conference of Superintendents of Training Schools and Reformatories

NCSW National Conference of Social Work

NCSX National Car Repair Shops, Inc (private car rr mark)

NCTC National Collection of Type Cultures

NCTF National Commercial Teachers Federation

NCTLE National Committee on Traffic Law Enforcement

NCTR National Council on Teacher Retirement

NCTS National Committee for Traffic Safety; National Council of Technical Schools

NCU National Cyclists' Union

NCUTAS National Conference on Uniform Traffic Accident Statistics

NCUTLO National Committee on Uniform Traffic Laws and Ordinances

n c v no commercial value

NCW National Council of Women

NCWA National Candy Wholesalers Association; National Cotton Waste Association

NCWC National Catholic Welfare Conference

NCWM National Conference on Weights and Measures

NCX Naugatuck Chemicals, Division of Dominion Rubber Company, Limited (private car rr mark); North Central Texas Oil Company (NYSE)

NCY National Cylinder Gas Company (NYSE)

nd low pressure (*niederdruck*—German)

n d no date; not dated

ND National Dairy Products (NYSE); national debt; natural draught; New Deal; North Dakota; Our Lady (*Notre Dame*—French)

Nd neodymium; Newfoundland Reports (legal)

n d a not dated [at] all

NDA National Dehydrators Association; National Dental Association; National Diploma in Agriculture; North Dakota Agricultural College

NDAC National Defense Advisory Commission

N Dak North Dakota

NDC National Dairy Council; National Defense Company; National Defense Corps; Notre Dame College

NDD National Diploma in Dairying

n de l'a author's note (*note de l'auteur*—French)

n de l'e editor's note (*note de l'éditeur*—French)

NDFA National Dietary Foods Association

NDGW Native Daughters of the Golden West

NDHA National District Heating Association

Ndl The Netherlands (*Nederland*—Dutch)

NDL North German-Lloyd (*Norddeutscher-Lloyd*—German)

NDMA National Door Manufacturers Association; National Dress Manufacturers Association

NDMB National Defense Mediation Board

n d p normal diametral pitch (gears)

NDPBC National Duck Pin Bowling Congress

ND spec Navy Department specifications

n d t translator's note (*note du traducteur*—French)

NDTC National Drug Trade Conference

NDU Notre Dame University

N/D/U none done up

NDX Nitrogen Division, Allied Chemical & Dye Corporation (private car rr mark)

n e new edition; no effects; nonessential; northeast; not exceeding

Ne neon

NE National Exchequer; National Executive; National Exhibition; Naval Engineer; New England; Northeastern; Northeastern Railway

NEA National Editorial Association; National Education Association; National Erectors Association; Newspaper Enterprise Association; Northeast Airlines Inc (NYSE)

neau new (*nouveau*—French)

NEAX Nealco-Monsanto Company (private car rr mark)

neb spray (*nebula*—Latin) (pharmacy)

Neb Nebraska

NEB National Employment Board; Neisner Brothers, Inc (NYSE)

nebe northeast by east

nebn northeast by north

n e c not elsewhere classified

NEC National Electrical Code; National Emergency Council; National Economic Council; National Exchange Club; New England Council; necessary (US Army)

NECA National Electrical Contractors Association

NEC Inst Northeast Coast Institution of Engineers and Shipbuilders

NE Code National Electrical Code

necy necessary; necessity

NED New English Dictionary

NEDA National Electronic Distributors Association

NED A New England Power Company (ASE)

NEF Near East Foundation

* NDLR = Note de la redaction

NEFA New England Freight Association

neg negation; negative

neg ins negotiable instrument

negt merchant (*négociant*—French)

Neh Nehemiah (Biblical)

n e i has not been found (*non est inventus*—Latin); not elsewhere indicated

NEI Netherlands East Indies

NEK Naval Equerry to the King

NEM Newmont Mining Corporation (NYSE)

NEMA National Electrical Manufacturers Association

nem con no one opposing; unanimously (*nemine contradicente*—Latin)

nem dis(s) nobody disagreeing (*nemine dissentiente*—Latin)

NEMI National Elevator Manufacturing Industry

NEMJSA New England Manufacturing Jewelers and Silversmiths Association

N Eng New England

NEO Northeast Oklahoma Railroad Company (rr mark)

n e p new edition pending; new economic policy

Nep Nepal; Neptune

NEPA National Egg Products Association

NER New England Reporter; North Eastern Railway; Northeastern Reporter (legal)

NERA National Emergency Relief Administration

n e s not elsewhere specified

NES New England Electric System (NYSE)

NESA National Electric Sign Association

N E (2d) Northeastern Reporter, Second Series

n e t not earlier than

Neth Netherlands

Neth Gu Netherlands Guiana

Neth Ind Netherlands Indies

Neth WI Netherland West Indies

n et m night and morning (*nocte et mane*—Latin) (pharmacy)

nett free from all deductions (*netto*—Italian)

n Eu northern Europe

NEUS northeastern United States

neut neuter; neutral

Nev Nevada

NEWA National Electrical Wholesalers Association

Newc L Newcastle-under-Lyme

Newf Newfoundland

NEWFO Newfoundland (US Navy)

new par new paragraph

New So W New South Wales

New Test. New Testament

n f noun feminine

nf nonfundable

n F new series (*neue Folge*—German)

N F National Formulary; New Forest; Newfoundland; New French; Norman-French; Normans Fund; Northumberland Fusiliers; Norwich Festival; Nutrition Foundation

N/F no funds (banking)

NFA National Alfalfa Dehydrating & Milling Company (Common Stock, ASE); National Fertilizer Association; National Founders Association; New Farmers of America

NFAS National Federation of American Shipping

NFBA National Federation of Beekeepers Associations; National Food Brokers Association

NFBPWC National Federation of Business and Professional Women's Clubs

NFCA National Fraternal Congress of America

NFCC National Farm Chemurgic Council; National Federation of Citizens Councils

NFCI National Film Carriers, Inc

NFCL National Federation for Constitutional Liberties

NFCTA National Fibre Can & Tube Association

NFDA National Food Distributors Association; National Funeral Directors Association

NFEAC National Foundation for Education in American Citizenship

NFF National Froebel Foundation

NFFA National Flying Farmers Association

NFFC National Film Finance Corporation

NFFE National Federation of Federal Employees

NFFLA National Frozen Food Locker Association

NFFS Non-Ferrous Founders Society

NFG National Fuel Gas Company (NYSE)

Nfg successor (*Nachfolger*—German)

NFGMIC National Federation of Grange Mutual Insurance Companies

NFI National Fisheries Institute

NFIP National Foundation for Infantile Paralysis

NFJMC National Federation of Jewish Men's Clubs

NFK Norfolk & Western Railway (NYSE)

NFL National Football League

Nfld Newfoundland

NFLU National Farm Labor Union

NFM Non-Ferrous Metal Products (NYSE)

NFMA November, February, May, August

NFMC National Federation of Music Clubs; National Film Music Council

NFOBA National Fats and Oils Brokers Association

NFP National Fireproofing Corporation (NYSE)

NFPA National Fire Protection Association

NFPOC National Federation of Post Office Clerks

NFPOMVE National Federation of Post Office Motor Vehicle Employees

NFPW National Federation of Press Women; National Federation of Professional Workers

NFPX National Fruit Product Company, Inc. (private car rr mark)

NFR no further requirement (US Army)

NFS National Federation of Settlements; National Fire Service

NFSE National Federation of Sales Executives

NFSI National Foundation for Science and Industry

NFSU National Federation of Salaried Unions

NFT National Federation of Textiles

NFTC National Foreign Trade Council

NFU National Farmers' Union

NFWA National Furniture Warehousemen's Association

NFWC National Fire Waste Council

NFWE National Federation of Women's Exchanges

NFWI National Federation of Women's Institutes

NFWRC National Federation of Women's Republican Clubs

NFX Naco Fertilizer Company (private car rr mark)

NFYF National Farm Youth Foundation

n g nitro-glycerine; new genus; not given (fire records)

NG National Gallery; National Government; National Guard; National Gypsum Company; New Granada; New Guinea; no good; Noble Grand; North German

NGA National Guard Association; Needlework Guild of America

NGAA National Gift and Art Association; Natural Gasoline Associa-

NEGRO New England Grass Roots Organization

tion of America
NGAC National Guard Air Corps
NGB National Guard Bureau
NGC New General Catalogue
NGCX Natural Gas Company (private car rr mark)
NGDA National Glass Distributors Association
NGE New York State Electric & Gas (NYSE)
NGHPD National Guild of Hy-Pure Druggists
NGI National Garden Institute
NGNY National Guard of New York
NGO Non-governmental Organizations
NGPT National Guild of Piano Teachers
N Gr New Greek
NGR National Guard Regulations
NGS National Geographic Society
NGSMA Natural Gasoline Supply Men's Association
ngt merchant (négociant—French)
NGTC National Grain Trade Council
N Gui Ter New Guinea Territory
NGUS National Guard of the United States
NH National Hospital; National Supply Company (NYSE); Naval Hospital; New Hampshire; New Haven (Connecticut); New York, New Haven & Hartford Railroad Company, The (rr mark)
NHA National Hay Association; National Health Association; National Hide Association; National Horse Association; National Housing Agency; New Homemakers of America
NHC National Health Council
NHCA National Hairdressers and Cosmetologists Association; National Horse Carriers Association
NHD Doctor of Natural History
NHDAA National Home Demonstration Agents Association
N Heb New Hebrew; New Hebrides
NHENMA National Hand Embroidery and Novelty Manufacturers Association
NHG New High German
NHHMA Northern Hemlock and Hardwood Manufacturers Association
NHHS New Hampshire Historical Society
NHI National Health Insurance; Nehi Corporation (NYSE)
NHIX Northern Refrigerator Line, Inc (private car rr mark)
NHLA National Hardwood Lumber Association
NHMA National Handle Manufacturers Association; National Housewares Manufacturers Association

NHOA National Heavy Outerwear Association
nhp nominal horsepower
NHPA National Horseshoe Pitchers Association
NHPOF National Home and Property Owners Foundation
NHRU National Home Reading Union
NHSA National Horse Show Association
NHSC National Home Study Council
NHUC National Highway Users Conference
NHV New Haven Clock & Watch (NYSE)
NHV Pr New Haven Clock & Watch Co. (4½% Conv. Pfd.) (ASE)
NHWA National Heating Wholesalers Association
NHWRA National Health and Welfare Retirement Association
Nⁱ numbers (Numeri—Italian)
Ni nickel
NI Native Infantry; Naval Instructor; Naval Intelligence; Netherlands Indies; New Ireland; non-intervention; Northern Ireland; North American Investment Corporation (NYSE); Northern Indiana Public Service (NYSE)
NIA National Indian Association; National Intelligence Authority; Navy Industrial Association
NIAA National Industrial Advertisers Association
NIAL National Institute of Arts and Letters
NIB National Industries for the Blind; National Information Bureau
Nic Nicaragua
NIC National Industrial Council; National Institute of Credit; National Interfraternity Conference; National Investors Council; Non-Intervention Committee
NICA National Industrial Conference Board
NICB National Industrial Conference Board
NICD National Institute of Cleaning and Dyeing
NICFC National Inter-Collegiate Flying Club
NICMA National Ice Cream Mix Association
ni crs nickel chromium steel
NICTOE National Institute for Commercial and Trade Organization Executives
NID Naval Intelligence Division
NIDS National Institute of Diaper Services
niedr low (neidrig—German)
NIF Northern Illinois Corporation (NYSE)
Nig Nigeria

NIGP National Institute of Governmental Purchasing
NIL I have nothing to send to you (QS); Niles-Bement-Pond Company (NYSE)
NILCA National Industrial Launderers and Cleaners Association
nim namely (nimittäin—Finnish)
NIM Niagara Share Corporation (NYSE)
NIMLO National Institute of Municipal Law Officers
n imp. new impression
NIMPA National Independent Meat Packers Association
9bre November (novembre—French)
ninupl ninuplicate
NIOSP National Institute of Oil Seed Products
NIP Nippon Electric Power Company Ltd. (ASE)
NIPA National Institute of Public Affairs
NI Pr Northern Indiana Public Service Company (4½% Pfd.) (ASE)
ni pri unless previously (nisi prius —Latin)
N(I)RA National (Industrial) Recovery Act
NIRB National Industrial Recovery Board
NIRC National Institute of Rug Cleaners
N Ire. Northern Ireland
NIREB National Institute of Real Estate Brokers
ni s nickel steel
NISA National Industrial Sand Association; National Industrial Service Association; National Industrial Stores Association
NISS National Institute of Social Sciences
NIST Northern Illinois State Teachers (college)
n i t none in town
NITL National Industrial Traffic League
NITPA National Institutional Teacher Placement Association
NITT National Institute for Traffic Training
N J New Jersey
NJA National Jail Association; National Jewelers' Association
NJC Central Railroad of N. J. (NYSE)
NJCW New Jersey College for Women
N J Eq New Jersey Equity Reports
NJLJ New Jersey Law Journal (legal)
NJP New Jersey Power & Light (NYSE)
NJWB National Jewish Welfare Board

NJZ New Jersey Zinc Company (NYSE)

NJZX New Jersey Zinc Company (of Pa.) (private car rr mark)

n/k not known

NKA National Kindergarten Association

NKM New Park Mining Company (NYSE)

NKOA National Knitted Outerwear Association

NKP New York, Chicago & St. Louis Railroad (NYSE)

NKPA National Kraut Packers Association

n/k/t none kept in town

n l it is not clear (*non liquet*—Latin) it is not permitted (*non licet*—Latin); new line; night letter; not far (*non longue*—Latin); not soluble (*nicht löslich*—German)

nl namely (*namelijk*—Dutch); (*nemlig*—Norwegian)

Nl National

NL Holland (IDP); National League; National Liberal; National Library; Navy League; Navy List; New Latin; North Latitude; North Library; Nuevo León

NLA National Lime Association; National Locksmiths Association

NLAPW National League of American Pen Women

N Lat North Latitude

NLB National Labor Board

NLC National League Club; National Liberal Club; New Orleans and Lower Coast Railroad Company (rr mark)

NLCA Norwegian Lutheran Church of America

NLCX Namarib Company (private car rr mark)

NLD National Legion of Decency; not in line of duty (US Army)

NLDA National Luggage Dealers Association

NLDPUS National League of District Postmasters of the United States

NLEA National Lumber Exporters Association

NLF National Labor Federation; National Liberal Federation

NLFC National Leather Fibre Conference

NLFG National Lighting Fixture Guild

NLG National Lawyers Guild

NLGI National Lubricating Grease Institute

NLI National Lifeboat Institution

NLMA Northeastern Lumber Manufacturers Association

NLMC National Labor-Management Council

NLNA National Landscape Nurserymen's Association

NLNE National League of Nursing Education

NLPBC National League of Professional Baseball Clubs

NLR North London Railway

NLRB National Labor Relations Board

NLS National Linen Service Corporation (NYSE)

NLSE National Live Stock Exchange

NLSFA National Leather and Shoe Finders Association

NLSMA National Lamp and Shade Manufacturers Association

NLSMB National Live Stock and Meat Board

NLSPA National Live Stock Producers Association

n l t not later than

NLTA National League of Teachers Associations

NLUS Navy League of the United States

NLV National Vulcanized Fibre (NYSE)

NLX Nichols Chemical Co., Ltd., The (private car rr mark)

n m nautical mile; night and morning (*nocte et mane*—Latin) (pharmacy); no marks; noun masculine

nm nutmeg

N/m no mark

NM Navy Minister; New Mexico; night message

N & M November and May

NMA National Medical Association; National Microfilm Association; Negligee Manufacturers Association

NMAA Navy Mutual Aid Association

N Mag Ca New Magistrates' Cases (legal)

NMAUS Newsprint Manufacturers Association of the United States

NMB National Maritime Board; National Mediation Board; Naval Meteorological Branch

NMBMA National Memorial Bronze Manufacturers Association

n m c no more credit

NMC National Mangement Council; National Manpower Council; National Metal Congress; National Music Council; New Mexico College

NMCA National Meat Canners Association; Navy Mothers Clubs of America

NME National Military Establishment (US Army)

NMEBA National Marine Engineers Beneficial Association

N Mex New Mexico

NMFA National Mineral Feeds Association

NMFC National Motor Freight Classification

NMHF National Mental Health Foundation

NMIC National Meat Industry Council

NMK Niagara Mohawk Power (NYSE)

NML National Mall, & Steel Cast (NYSE); National Municipal League

NMMA National Macaroni Manufacturers Association

NMONA National Mail Order Nurserymen's Association

NMPATA National Music Printers and Allied Trades Association

NMPC National Motion Picture Council

NMR Nestle-LeMur Company (NYSE)

NMS National Missionary Society

NMSA National Metal Spinners Association

NMSS National Multiple Sclerosis Society

NMST Northeast Missouri State Teachers (college)

NMSWF National Manufacturers of Soda Water Flavors

NMTA National Metal Trades Association

NMTBA National Machine Tool Builders Association

NMU National Manufacturer & Stores (NYSE); National Maritime Union

NMWA National Mineral Wool Association

n n neutralization number; no name

nn names (*nomina*—Latin); nouns

N/N not to be noted (bills of exchange)

NN Nevada Northern Railway Company (rr mark)

NNA National Notion Association

NNAC National Noise Abatement Council

n N Amer northern North America

NNB National Needlecraft Bureau

NNBA National Negro Bankers Association

NNBL National Negro Business League

NNCI National Nursing Council, Inc

NND Newport News Shipbuilding & Drydock (NYSE)

NNFDA National Negro Funeral Directors Association

NNG Northern Natural Gas Company (NYSE)

NNIA National Negro Insurance Association

NNNDA National Negro News Distributors Association

nno north-north-west (nord-nord-ouest—French)

NNPA National Newspaper Promotion Association

NNR New Nonofficial Remedies

n n w north-northwest

NNX Northern Central Railway (NYSE)

no. number

n o not out (cricket)

NO natural order (botany); naval officer; Navigation Officer; New Orleans; north-west (nordouest—French)

No. Net (Netto—German); Noah; norium; number (número—Turkish)

n/o our order (nuestra orden—Spanish); name of; no orders; not out

NOA Noma Electric Corporation (NYSE); not otherwise authorized (US Army)

NOAB National Outdoor Advertising Bureau, Inc

no acct no account

nob for our part (nobis—Latin)

NOB Northwest Bancorporation (NYSE)

n o c not otherwise classified

NOC Northrop Aircraft (NYSE)

NOD Naval Ordnance Department

n o e not otherwise enumerated

n1e nosed one edge (lumber)

NOFA National Office Furniture Association

NOFMA National Oak Flooring Manufacturers Association

NOG Novadel-Agene Corporation (NYSE)

n o h p not otherwise herein provided

n o i b n not otherwise indexed by name

NOIC Naval Officer-in-Charge

nol pros not wishing to prosecute (nolle prosequi—Latin)

nom nomenclature; nominal; nominative

NOM Natomas Company (NYSE)

NOMA National Office Management Association; National Oil Marketers Association

nom cap. nominal capital

NOMDA National Office Machine Dealers Association

nomin nominative

nomn nomination

nom nov new name (nomen novum—Latin)

nom nud naked name (nomen nudum—Latin)

nom std nominal standard

non cm non cumulative

non coll non collegiate

non com noncommissioned [officer]

noncon nonconformist

non-con non-content

non cul not guilty (non culpabilis-L)

n1e nosed one edge (lumber)

NO&NE New Orleans and Northeastern Railroad Company

non-mag c i non-magnetic cast iron

non obst notwithstanding (non obstante—Latin)

non pros does not prosecute (non prosequitur—Latin)

non-res non-resident

nonsect nonsectarian

non seq it does not follow (non sequitur—Latin)

non-vtg non-voting

n o p not otherwise provided

NOP Nopco Chemical Company (NYSE); North Pacific

no par no paragraph

NOPHN National Organization for Public Health Nursing

nor normal; north; northern

Nor Norma; Norman; Norway; Norwegian; Norwich

NOR Noranda Mines (NYSE); Norwich Pharmacal Company (NYSE)

NORC National Opinion Research Center

Norf Norfolk (county in England)

Nor Fr Norman French

norm. normalised

North & G North & Guthrie's Reports (legal)

Northants Northamptonshire (county in England)

Northumb Northumberland (county in England)

Northw Pr Northwest Provinces, India

Norvic of Norwich (Norvicensis—Latin)

n o s not otherwise specified

NOS New Orleans Stock Exchange

nostr our (noster—Latin)

n o t non-oiltight; not oil-tight

not. notice

NOTAM International Notices to Airmen

Not Dec Notes of Decisions (legal)

Not J Notaries Journal (legal)

NOT&M New Orleans, Texas & Mexico Railway Company

Nott&Hop. Nott & McCord's Reports (legal)

Nottm Nottingham

Nott & McC Nott & McCord's Reports (legal)

notwg notwithstanding

nov November (novembre—Italian); (novembre—French); (novembro—Portuguese)

nov novel; novelist

Nov Sc Nova Scotia

No West Rep Northwestern Reporter (legal)

NOX National Oil Company Inc (private car rr mark)

n o y not out yet

NOZ New Process Company (NYSE)

np neap tides; non participating (stocks)

n p for instance (na przyklad—Polish); net proceeds; new paragraph; nickel-plated; no paging; normal pitch

Np Neptunium

NP Naval Pensions; Neuropsychiatry (ic) or (ist) (US Army); New Providence; Nobel Prize; Norwegian patent; Northern Pacific Railway Company (NYSE); Northern Polytechnic; Notary Public

n p a normal pressure angle (gears)

NPA National Paperboard Association; National Parks Association; National Petroleum Association; National Pigeon Association; National Planning Association; National Preservers Association; National Production Authority; Newspaper Proprietors' Association

n p a o nickel plated all over (plumbing)

NPB National Planning Board

N & PB Norfolk & Portsmouth Belt Line Railroad Company (rr mark)

NPBEA National Poultry, Butter, and Egg Association

NPBI National Pretzel Bakers Institute

NPBMA National Paper Box Manufacturers Association

NPBSA National Paper Box Supplies Association

NPC National Panhellenic Conference; National Patent Council; National Peace Conference; National Peach Council; National Peanut Council; National Petroleum Council; National Potato Council; National Press Club; Naval Personnel Committee; Nisi Prius Case (legal)

NPCA National Pest Control Association

NPCHWS National Publicity Council for Health and Welfare Services

NPCI National Potato Chip Institute

n p d no payroll division; north polar distance

n p o r d no place or date

NPDA National Plywood Distributors Association

NPEA National Printing Equipment Association

n p f not provided for

NPFFG National Plant, Flower and Fruit Guild

NPGL National Popular Government League

NPHC National Public Housing Conference

N Ph D Doctor of Natural Philosophy

NPK National Pressure Cooker Company (NYSE)

NPKX Nuckolls Packing Company (private car rr mark)

n pl noun plural

NPL National Physical Laboratory

n p m national postal meter

NPM Neptune Meter Company of N.J. (NYSE)

NPMA National Piano Manufacturers Association; Northern Pine Manufacturers Association

NPMMA National Photographic Mount Manufacturers Association

n p n non-protein nitrogen

n p n a no protest for non-acceptance

NPOPR not paid on prior rolls (US Army)

n p p no passed proof

NPPA National Pickle Packers Association; National Press Photographers Association; National Probation and Parole Association

NPPC National Power Policy Committee

NPR North Pennsylvania Railroad Company (NYSE)

NP Ry Northern Pacific Railway

NPS National Park Service; Nipissing Mines Company, Ltd (NYSE)

NPSA National Paint Salesmen's Association

NPSB News Print Service Bureau

NPSPA National Pecan Shellers and Processors Association

n p t nickel plated trimmings (plumbing); normal pressure and temperature

NPT National Petroleum Corporation (NYSE); Nine-Power Treaty

NPTAUS National Paper Trade Association of the U.S.

n p v no par value

NPVLA National Paint, Varnish and Lacquer Association

NPX National Phoenix Industries, Inc. (common stock, ASE)

n & q notes and queries

n q a net quick assets

nr near

n r net register (shipping); no risk; not to be repeated (non repetatur —Latin)

Nr Number (Numer—Polish, Nummer

—German, Nummer—Danish)

NR National Redoubt; National Register; Naval Rating; Navy Regulations; North Riding; North River; Northern Rhodesia (Africa); number (US Army)

n/r our remittance (nuestra remesa— Spanish)

NRA National Radiator Company (NYSE); National Reclamation Association; National Recovery Administration; National Recreation Association; National Rehabilitation Association; National Renderers Association; National Restaurant Association; National Rifle Association

NRAA National Railway Appliances Association

NRAB National Railroad Adjustment Board

n r a d no risk after discharge

NRB National Resources Board; New York Air Brake Company (NYSE)

NRBX New River & Pocahontas Consolidated Coal Company (private car rr mark)

NRC National Research Corporation (NYSE); National Research Council; National Resources Committee; National Roadside Council; Northern Refrigerator Car Company (private car rr mark)

NRCA National Resources Council of America; National Retail Credit Association; National Roofing Contractors Association

NRCC National Republican Congressional Committee

NRCI National Red Cherry Institute

NRD National Recruiting Department

NRDGA National Retail Dry Goods Association

NRECA National Rural Electric Cooperative Association

NRF National Relief Fund

NRFA National Retail Florists Association; National Retail Furniture Association

NRFEA National Retail Farm Equipment Association

NRFI not ready for issue (US Army)

NRGSA National Retail Grocers Secretaries Association

N Rh Northern Rhodesia

NRHA National Retail Hardware Association

NRHC National Rivers and Harbors Congress

NRLCA National Rural Letter Carriers Association

NRLDA National Retail Lumber Dealers Association

NRLF National Religion and Labor

Foundation

NRLPSA National Retail Liquor Package Stores Association

NRMA National Rainwear Manufacturers Association

NRMCA National Ready Mixed Concrete Association

n r m e notched, returned, and mitred ends

NRMS Naval Reserve Midshipmen's School

Nro number (Numero—Italian); our (nuestro—Spanish)

NRPB National Resources Planning Board

NRRB National Recovery Review Board

n r s nonrising stem (plumbing)

NRS National Re-employment Service; Northern States Power (Minn.) (NYSE); National Rose Society

n r t net register tonnage

NRT National Reference Tribunal; Net Register tonnage (shipping)

NRTCMA National Retail Tea and Coffee Merchants Association

NRU National Rubber Machinery Company (NYSE)

N s near side; nickel steel; not specified; not sufficient (funds); so called (nün sauottu—Finnish)

Ns Nimbostratus (clouds)

NS National Socialism; National Society; National Steel Corporation (NYSE); Nevada Silver; New School; New Series; New Style Newspaper Society; nonstandard (US Army); Norfolk Southern Railroad Company; Northwestern State (college); Nova Scotia; Numismatic Society; Our Lord (Notre Seigneur —French)

n/s not sufficient (banking)

NSA National Service Acts; National Shellfisheries Association; National Sheriffs Association; National Showmen's Association; National Shuffleboard Association; National Skating Association; National Slag Association; National Slate Association; National Society of Auctioneers; National Stationers Association; National Student Association; Nursery School Association

NSAA National Ski Association of America; National Supply Association of America

NSAFA National Service Armed Forces Act

NS Amer northern South America

NSB National Service Board; National Society for the Blind; Participating Stock (NYSE)

NSBA National Sugar Brokers Association

NSBF New York Shipbuilding, Founders (NYSE)

NSBMA National Small Business Men's Association

NSC National Safety Council; National Savings Committee; National Security Council; Nesco Inc (NYSE)

NSCA National Shrimp Canners Association

NSCCA National Society for Crippled Children and Adults

NSCDA National Society of Colonial Dames of America

NSD Naval Supply Depot (US Navy)

NSDA National Sprayer and Duster Association; Naval Stores Dealers Association

NSDAR National Society of the Daughters of the American Revolution

NSEC National Service Entertainments Council

n s f not sufficient funds

NSF National Science Foundation; National Sharecroppers Fund

NSGA National Sand and Gravel Association; National Sporting Goods Association; National Swine Growers Association

NSGCI National Self Government Committee, Inc

NSGW Native Sons of the Golden West

NSHA National Steeplechase and Hunt Association; National Student Health Association

NSI National Society of Inventors; nonstandard item (US Army)

NSIC Our Saviour Jesus Christ (*Noster Salvator Iesus Christus* —Latin)

n sing. noun singular

NSJ Our Lord, Jesus Christ (*Nuestro Señor Jesucristo*— Spanish)

N-S J-C Our Saviour Jesus Christ (*Notre-Seigneur Jésus-Christ*— French)

NSKK Nazi German Automobile Corps (*Nazionalistische Sozialistische Kraftwagen Korps*—German)

NSL National Service League; National Steel Car Corporation (NYSE); National Story League; National Sunday League

NSLI National Service Life Insurance (US Army)

NSLL National Savings and Loan League

NSLRA National Society of Livestock Record Associations

NSLRB National Steel Labor Relations Board

NSLX National Silicates, Limited (private car rr mark)

NSMA National Scale Men's Association; National Shoe Manufacturers Association; National Soup Mix Association

NSMDA National Supply and Machinery Distributors Association

NSMI National Selected Morticians, Inc.

NSMPA National Screw Machine Products Association

NSN Nu Sigma Nu (fraternity)

NSO Naval Staff Officer

NSOPA National Society of Operative Printers and Assistants

NSOX North Star Oil Limited (private car rr mark)

n sp new species

NSP Nu Sigma Phi (society); National Starch Products (NYSE)

NSPA National Scholastic Press Association; National Society of Public Accountants; National Soybean Processors Association; National Split Pea Association; National Standard Parts Association

NSPB National Society for the Prevention of Blindness

NSPCA National Society for the Prevention of Cruelty to Animals

NSPCC National Society for the Prevention of Cruelty to Children

NSPE National Society of Professional Engineers

n s p f not specially provided for

NSPFA National Spray Painting and Finishing Association

n sr our mister (*notre sieur*— French)

NSRA National Shoe Retailers Association; National Shorthand Reporters Association

NSRB National Security Resources Board

NSRMCA National Star Route Mail Carriers Association

NSS National Sculpture Society; National Speleological Society; New Shakespeare Society; Newburgh & South Shore Railway Company, The (rr mark)

NSSA National Sanitary Supply Association; National Skeet Shooting Association; National Skirt and Sportswear Association

NSSC National Steam Specialty Club

NSSE National Society for the Study of Education

NSSI National School Service Institute

NSSR New School for Social Research

NSSTE National Society of Sales Training Executives

NST National-Standard Company (NYSE)

NSTA National Science Teachers Association; National Security Traders Association; National Shoe Travelers Association

NSTC National Shade Tree Conference

nstd nested (commerce)

NS Tripos, Natural Science Tripos

NSU National Sugar Refining Company (NYSE)

NSW New South Wales

NSWA National Social Welfare Assembly; National Stripper Well Association

NSWMA National Soft Wheat Millers Association

NSY New Scotland Yard

n t non-tight; net ton(shipping); non watertight; normal temperature

nt merchant (*négociant*—French)

N/t new terms; none in town

Nt nitron

NT National Trust; neap tide; New Testament; new translation; Newport Industries Inc (NYSE); night telegram; No Trumps; Northern Territory; not titled

NTA National Tavern Association; National Tax Association; National Technical Association; National Tuberculosis Association

NTAA National Travelers Aid Association

NTBMD National Truck Body Manufacturers Association

n t c negative temperature coefficient

NTC National Theatre Conference

NTCAVAL notice of availability (US Army)

n t d non-tight door

NTDMA National Tool and Die Manufacturers Association

NTEA National Tax Equality Association

NTF National Turkey Federation

ntfy notify

NT Gk New Testament Greek

n/30 net in 30 days (commercial)

nthn northern

NTL National City Lines, Inc. (NYSE)

NTLX Northern Tank Line Inc., The (private car rr mark)

ntm net ton mile

NTM National Tile & Manufacturing Company (NYSE)

NTMA National Terrazzo and Mosaic Association

n t o not taken out

NTO Naval Transport Officer

n t p normal temperature and

pressure; no title page

NTPG National Textile Processors Guild

NTR National Theatres, Inc (NYSE)

ntro our (*nuestro*—Spanish)

n t s not to scale

NTS Naval Transport Service

NT&SA National Trust & Savings Association

NTST North Texas State Teachers College

NTT New England Tel. & Tel. (NYSE)

NTTA National Tobacco Tax Association

NTTCI National Tank Truck Carriers, Inc.

Ntto net (*Netto*—German)

NTTTTI National Truck Tank and Trailer Tank Institute

NTWA National Toy Wholesalers Association

n2e nosed two edges (lumber)

nt wt net weight

NTY National Tea Company (NYSE)

n u name unknown

NU Northeastern University; Northwestern University; Norwich University; United Nations (*Nations Unies*—French)

NUCDA National Used Car Dealers Association

NUEA National University Extension Association

NUI National University of Ireland

NUJ National Union of Journalists

NUL National Urban League

num number; numeral

Num Numbers (Biblical)

NUM National Union of Manufacturers; National Union of Mineworkers; National Union Radio (NYSE)

NUMCS National Union of Marine Cooks and Stewards

numis numismatic; numismatology

númos numbers (*números*—Spanish)

NUN Nunn-Bush Shoe Company (NYSE)

nup nuptials (*nuptiae*—Latin)

NUP National Union of Protestants

NUR National Union of Railwaymen

NURA National Union of Ratepayer's Associations

nurs r nursery rhymes

NUS National Union of Students

NUSEC National Union of Societies for Equal Citizenship

NUT National Union of Teachers

N-u-T Newcastle-upon-Tyne

NUTN National Union of Trained Nurses

NUWSS National Union of Women's Suffrage Societies

NUWT National Union of Women Teachers

NUWW National Union of Women Workers

nux vom nux vomica (medical)

NUY North American Util. Secur. Corp. (common stock ASE)

n v naked vision

Nv nonvoting (stocks)

NV limited-liability company (*Naamloze Vennootschap*—Dutch); New Version (Bible); North American Aviation, Inc. (NYSE)

NVAI National Variety Artists, Inc.

NVB National Volunteer Brigade

NVF National Vitamin Foundation

NVGA National Vocational Guidance Association

NVGI National Voluntary Groups Institute

n v m non-volatile matter

NVM Nativity of the Virgin Mary

n w naked weight; narrow widths net weight

NW Now (QS); Chicago & North Western Railway (NYSE); Niagara Wire Weaving Company Ltd (NYSE) North Wales; northwest; Northwestern Reporter

N&W Norfolk and Western Railway Company

NWA National Wine Association; Northwest Airlines, Inc (NYSE)

NWAHACA National Warm Air Heating and Air Conditioning Association

NWARMI National Warm Air Register Manufacturers Institute

NWBA National Wooden Box Association

nwbn northwest by north

nwbw northwest by west

NWC National War College (US Army)

NWCA National Water Carriers Association

NWCMA National Work Clothing Manufacturers Association

NWCTU National Women's Christian Temperence Union

NWDA National Wholesale Druggists Association

NWF National Wildlife Federation

NWFA National Wholesale Furniture Association

NWFFDI National Wholesale Frozen Food Distributors, Inc

NWFGA Women's National Farm and Garden Association

NWFP North-West Frontier Province (India)

n w g national wire gauge

NWGA National Wholesale Garment Association; National Wool Growers Association

NWHA National Wholesale Hardware Association

NWI Netherlands West Indies

NWJA National Wholesale Jewelers Association

n w l natural wave-length

NWLB National War Labor Board

NWLDYA National Wholesale Lumber Distributing Yard Association

NWMA National Wool and Mohair Association

NWMC National Wool Marketing Corporation

NWMP North-West Mounted Police

NWNSA National Women's Neckwear and Scarf Association

NWP National Woman's Party; Northwestern Pacific Railroad Company (rr mark)

NWP North-West Provinces (India)

NWPMA National Wooden Pallet Manufacturers Association

NWPWA National Wall Paper Wholesalers Association

NWR Northwestern Reporter (legal)

NWRA National Wheel and Rim Association

N&W Ry Norfolk & Western Railway

n w s normal water surface

NWSA National Welding Supply Association; National Women's Suffrage Association

NWSB National Wage Stabilization Board

n w t non-watertight

n wt net weight

NWT Northwest Territory

NWTA National Wool Trade Association

n w t d non watertight door (shipbuilding)

NWTI National Wood Tank Institute

NWTUL National Women's Trade Union League

NWUMA National Women's Undergarment Manufacturers Association

NWX North Western Refrigerator Line Company (private car rr mark)

NX National Car Company (private car rr mark); National Department Stores (NYSE)

Ny Nancy (France)

NY New Year; New York

Nya Nyasaland

NYA National Youth Administration; New York Auction Company (NYSE)

NY Ann. Ca New York Annotated Cases (legal)

NYB New York City Omnibus Corporation (NYSE)

NYC New York Central Railroad Company; New York City; New York Curb Exchange

NYCAV Cavite Navy Yard (US Navy)

NYCE New York Cocoa Exchange; New York Commodity Exchange New York Cotton Exchange; New

York Curb Exchange
NYC & HR RR New York Central &
Hudson River Railroad
NY Cond Rep New York Condensed
Reports (legal)
NYCRR New York Central Railroad
NY Cr Rep New York Criminal Reports (legal)
NYCSE New York Coffee and Sugar
Exchange
NYC&StL New York, Chicago and
St. Louis Railroad Company
NYCT New York Community Trust
NYCt App New York Court of Appeals (legal)
n y d not yet diagnosed
NYD New York Dock Company
(NYSE)
NYDX Grand Trunk Western Railroad Company (rr mark); New York
Despatch Refrigerator Line (private
car rr mark)
NYF New York Foundation
NYH N. Y. & Honduras Rosario
Mining (NYSE)
NYHS New York Historical Society
nyk current (nykyinen—Finnish)
NYK Japan Mail Steamship Company
(Nippon Yusen Kaisha—Japanese)
NY Law Gaz New York Law Gazette
(legal)

NY Law Journ New York Law Journal (legal)
NYLC Anno New York Leading
Cases Annotated (legal)
NY Leg. News New York Legal
News
NY Leg. Reg New York Legal Register
NYLJ New York Law Journal
NYM New York Merchandise Company (NYSE)
NYME New York Mercantile Exchange
NYNG New York National Guard
NYNH&H New York, New Haven and
Hartford Railroad Company
NYNOR Norfolk Navy Yard
NYNYK New York Navy Yard
NYO&WRy New York, Ontario &
Western Railway
n y p not yet published
NYPE New York Produce Exchange
NYPEARL Pearl Harbor Navy Yard
NYPHIL Philadelphia Navy Yard
NYPL New York Public Library
NYPORT Portsmouth Navy Yard
NYPS Puget Sound Navy Yard
NYR not yet returned (US Army)
NYS New York State; New York
Stock Exchange; New York Supplement
NYSAC New York State Athletic
Commission

NYSCC New York State Crime Commission
NYSE New York Stock Exchange
NYSLRB Official reporter of New
York State Labor Relations Board
decisions
NYSPA New York State Power
Authority
NYS(2d) New York Supplement,
Second Series
NY St Rep New York State Reporter
(legal)
NY Supp New York Supplement (legal)
NYS&W New York, Susquehanna and
Western Railroad Company
NYT New York Times
NYU New York University
NYULQ Rev New York University
Law Quarterly Review
NYWASH Washington Navy Yard (US
Navy)
NZ New Mexico & Arizona Land
Company (ASE); Neutrality Zone;
New Zealand; New Zealand National Airways Corporation; Nova
Zembla (Russian)
NZAF New Zealand Air Force
NZD New Zealand Division
NZX National Zinc Company, Inc
(private car rr mark)

O

o the best (optimus—Latin); observe; occasional; ocean; octavo;
off; office; officer; ohm; old; only;
order; organ; ortho; over; overcast;
overseer; pint (octavus—Latin)
O East (Osten—German); Occupation [qualification]; October; office;
order, or ordinance (use in combination only) (US Army); Ohio; Ontario;
Operations; Orient (Freemasonry);
West (Ouest—French); owner; oxygen
(O) Observer Officer (RAF); Specialist in Ophthalmology (naval)
ǿ half farthing (ǿre—Norwegian)
o a among others (onder andere—
Dutch); and others (og annet—
Norwegian); over all (measurement)
o/A American gold (oro Americano
—Spanish)
OA Atlantic Ocean (Ocean Atlantique—French); Officers' Association; Official Assignee; Ordnance
Artificer; Osborne Association; Outdoor Associations
O & A October and April

OAA Food and Agriculture Organization (Organisation de l'Alimentation et de l'Agriculture—French)
OAAA Outdoor Advertising Association of America
OAC Overseas Automotive Club
OACI International Civil Aviation
Organization (ICAO)
OADR Office of Agricultural Defense Relations
OAF French Western Africa (Afrique
Occidentale Française—French)
OAK Oak Manufacturing Company
(NYSE)
OALMA Orthopedic Appliance and
Limb Manufacturers Association
OALX Oregon-American Lumber
Corporation (private car rr mark)
OA & M Oklahoma Agricultural and
Mechanical
OAMDG All to the greater Glory of
God (Omnia ad majorem Dei gloriam
—Latin)
OANDT organization and training
(US Army)
OAP Observation amphibian plane
(US Navy)

OAPC Office of Alien Property
Custodian
o appl open on application
OAS On Active Service; Open
Hearth Acid Steel; Organization of
American States
o a t one at a time
OAT Open-Air Theater; Overseas
Airways Transmission; Quaker
Oats Company
OAWR Office for Agricultural War
Relations
Oax Oaxaca
o b outside broadcast; single bearing;
one bearing; opening of banks; ordered back
ob he died (obiit—Latin); incidentally (obiter—Latin); oboe; obligation
Ob Obadiah (Bible)
OB oil bomb; oil immersed, airblast cooled; Old Bailey (legal);
order of battle (US Army); Order of
the Bath; Oscar Browning; Owens-
Illinois Glass Company (NYSE);
obstetrics
O/B opening of books (accounting)

OBB Old Battleship (US Navy)
obbl obbligato (music)
OBCA Outboard Boating Club of America
OBCCC Office of Bituminous Coal Consumers' Council
obdt obedient
OBE Officer of the Order of the British Empire; Order of the British Empire; Office of Business Economics
oberst oberstimme (music)
Ob in Xto died in Christ (*Obiit in Christo*—Latin)
obj object; objection
OBJ object (US Army)
obl oblong; obligation
OB/L order bill of lading
oblat cachet (*oblatum*—Latin) (pharmacy)
OBLI Oxford and Bucks Light Infantry
OBMA Outboard Boat Manufacturers Association
ob ph oblique photography (RAF)
obre October (*octubre*—Spanish)
obro October (*outubro*—Portuguese)
obs obscure; observation; observatory; obsolete; observe (*observera*—Swedish); obstetrician
OBS open hearth basic steel; Oxford Bibliographical Society
observng observation
OBSN observation (US Army)
obsol obsolescent
ob s p he died without issue (*obiit sine prole*—Latin)
obt obedient
obtd obtained
O Bulg Old Bulgarian
obv obverse
OBV Ocean Boarding Vessel
o c office copy; officer in charge; official classification; on center; only child; open charter; open scope; in the work cited (*opere citato*—Latin); order canceled; over the counter; of course
oc ocean; overcharge
o'c o'clock
o/c overcharge
OC Cistercian Order (*Ordo Cistercium*—Latin); Fathers of the Order of Charity (*Ordu Charitatis*); Oberlin College; Observer Corps; Occidental College; Ocean Club; occlusocervical (medical); Officer Candidate (US Army); Officer Commanding; Officers' Cook; Old Carthusian; Old Catholic; Old Cheltonian; Orderly Corporal; Order of the Coif (legal); Ordinance Corps; Orphans' Court; Oslo Convention; Ottawa Convention
OCA Officer of Controllers' Ac-

counts; Oxychloride Cement Association
OCAA Oklahoma City-Ada-Atoka Railway Company
O Camald Camaldolese Order
O Carm Order of Calced Carmelites, Carmelite Fathers
O Cart. Carthusian Order (*Ordo Cartusiensis*—Latin)
O Carth of the Carthusian Order (*Ordinis Carthusianorum*—Latin)
OCB Oil Control Board
Oc/B/L Ocean Bill of Lading
occ occasional; occurrence; western (*occidental*—French)
OCC Officer's Chief Cook (US Navy); Official Classification Committee; Ohio Circuit Court Reports (legal)
occas occasionally
occn occasion
occult occultism
occupon occupation (legal)
OCCWS Office of the Chief of Chemical Warfare Service
OCD the Barefoot Carmelites [Discalced Carmelites] (*Ordo Carmelitarum Discalceatorum*); Office of Civilian Defense (United States)
OCE Office of the Chief of Engineers
oceanog oceanographical; oceanography
OCEE European Economic Cooperation Organization (*Organisation de Cooperation Economique Européenne*—French)
OCF Owens-Corning Fiberglas (NYSE)
OC1C Officer's Cook First Class (US Navy)
OCIAA Office of Co-ordination of Inter-American Affairs
OCIC International Catholic Film Bureau (ICFB)
O Cist Cistercian Order
OCM Civil and Military Organization (*Organisation Civile et Militaire*—France)
OCO Office of the Chief of Ordnance
OCP Overland Common Points
OCR Office for Civilian Requirements; Order of the Crown of Rumania; Order of Reformed Cistercians (*Ordinis Cistercianorum Reformatorum*)
OCS Office of Civilian Supply; Office of Contract Settlement; officer candidate school (US Army)
OC2C Officer's Cook Second Class (US Navy)
OCSIGO Office of the Chief Signal Officer

OCSO Order of Cistercians of the Strict Observance, Trappists
oct octavo
Oct Octans (constellation); Octavius; Octavus; October
OCT Office of the Chief of Transportation; Office of Temporary Controls
OC3C Officer's Cook Third Class (US Navy)
OCTU Officer Cadet Training Unit
octupl octuplicate
OCU Oklahoma City University
ocul to the eyes (*oculis*—Latin) (pharmacy)
o d and the like (*och dylikt*—Swedish); every day (*omni die*—Latin); on demand; outside dimension; olive drab; on duty
od or (*oder*—German)
o/d overdraft (banking)
OD Doctor of Optometry; Ohio Decisions (legal); Office of Distribution; Officer of the day; Old Danish; Old Dutch; Omega Delta (fraternity); Operations Division (naval); Ordinary Seaman; ordnance datum; Ordnance Department; Ordnance Depot; outside diameter
ODB Office of Dependency Benefits
ODC Discalced Carmelite Fathers
o dgl or similarly (*oder dergleichen*—German)
Od HS Order of Hermann Sons (*Orden der Hermann-Söhne*—German)
ODHWS Office of Defense and Health Welfare Service
ODK Omicron Delta Kappa (fraternity)
ODM Office of Defense Mobilization; Order of Mercedarian Fathers
ODP Open Door Policy
ODT Office of Defense Transportation
OD&W Oneida & Western Railroad Company (rr mark)
o e omissions excepted
OE Officer of Education; Old English; Old Etonian; Oregon Electric Railway Company (rr mark)
OEA Organization of American States (OAS)
OEC Ohio Edison Company (NYSE)
OECE Organization for European Economic Co-operation (OEEC)
OECX Oldbury Electro-Chemical Company (private car rr mark)
OED Oxford English Dictionary
OEEC Organization for European Economic Co-operation
OEIU Office Employes International Union
OEL Organizational Equipment List (US Army)

OELX Linsin, Inc, O. E. (private car rr mark)

OEM Office for Emergency Management

OEMI Office Equipment Manufacturers Institute

OEP Omega Epsilon Phi (fraternity)

OER Officers' Emergency Reserve

OES Office of Economic Stabilization; Order of the Eastern Star

OESGGC Order of the Eastern Star, General Grand Chapter

OETA Occupied Enemy Territory Administration

OEW Office of Economic Warfare

o f oil filled (cable); oxidizing flame

OF Fatherland Front—Bulgaria (*Otechestven Front*); Odd Fellows; Officers' Federation; Old Face (type); Old French; Oliver Corporation (NYSE)

o f b oil-immersed forced-oil circulation with air-blast cooling

of c of course

OFC Office of Fishery Co-ordination; Overseas Food Corporation

ofcl official

OFd'I in A Order Sons of Italy in America

OFE French Publishing Office (*Office Français d'Édition*—French)

OFEA Office of Foreign Economic Administration

OFEC Office of Foreign Economic Co-ordination

off. offer; offered; office; officer; official; officinal

OFF Office of Facts and Figures; Officers' Families Fund

offg officiating

offic official

off. nom official nomenclature

offr officer

OFKX Koch Tank Line (private car rr mark)

o fl etc. (*og flere*—Norwegian)

OFL official (US Army)

OFM Order of Friars Minor (Franciscan); (*Ordinis Fratrum Minorum*)

OFMC Order of Friars Minor Conventual (*Ordinis Fratrum Minorum Conventualium*)

OFMCap Order of Friars Minor Capuchin

o f n oil-immersed forced-oil circulation with natural cooling

O Fr Old French

O Fris Old Frisian

OFRR Office of Foreign Relief and Rehabilitation

OFRRO Office of Foreign Relief and Rehabilitation Operations

OFS Orange Free State

OFTC Overland Freight Transfer Company

OG officer of the guard (US Army)

o g original gum (stamps)

OG Ogden Corporation (NYSE); Officer of the Guard; ogee (architecture); Olympic Games; Outside Guard; Outside Guardian

O Gael Old Gaelic

OGDANA Oyster Growers and Dealers Association of North America

OGE Oklahoma Gas & Electric (NYSE)

OGPU *Obyedinionnoye Gosudarstvennoye Politichiskoye Upravlenie* (Russian Political Police Department); Union State Political Administration (USSR)

OGR Office of Government Reports

o h hourly (*omni hora*—Latin) (pharmacy); open hearth [furnace]

O/H foreign trade company (*Overzuche Handelsmaatschappij*—Dutch)

o h a outside helix angle (gears)

OHBMS On His (or Her) Britannic Majesty's Service

OHCX Old Hickory Chemical Company (private car rr mark)

OHE Office of the Housing Expediter

OHG Old High German

OHIA Oil Heat Institute of America

ohm-cm ohm-centimeter

OHMS On His (or Her) Majesty's Service

OHO Ohio Oil Company (NYSE)

OHP Ohio Power (NYSE)

OHP Pr Ohio Power Co. (The) (4½% Pfd.)

o h s open-hearth steel

OHS Ohio Brass Company (corn exchange); Oxford Historical Society

OHS B Ohio Brass Co. ("B" Com.) (ASE)

o i oil-immersed

OI *Officier de l'Instruction publique* (French); Old Irish; Optimist International

OIA Oil Insurance Association

OIAA Office of Inter-American Affairs

OIC International Trade Organization (ITO); Office of International Information and Cultural Affairs; officer in charge (US Army)

OIE International Organization of Employers (IOE)

OIG Office of the Inspector General

OIJ International Organization of Journalists (IOJ)

OILX Oil Tank Line Company (private car rr mark)

OINA Oyster Institute of North

America

O Ir Old Irish

OIR Inter-American Radio Office; International Broadcasting Organization; International Refugee Organization (IRO)

o i s c oil-insulated self-cooled [transformer]

O It Old Italian

OIT International Labour Organisation (ILO)

OIV International Wine Office

o i w c oil-insulated water-cooled

OJA-G Office of the Judge-Advocate-General

OJAJ October, January, April, July (quarter months)

OJD Order of Job's Daughters

o k outer keel

OK all correct; without cost (*ohne Kosten*—German)

OKA Okalta Oils Ltd (NYSE)

OKG Oklahoma Natural Gas Company (NYSE)

Okla Oklahoma

Okl Cr Oklahoma Criminal Reports (legal)

OKO Okonite Company (NYSE)

OKU Omicron Kappa Upsilon (fraternity)

o l overhead line; overflow level; overload

Ol Oliver; Olympiad; Olympic

OL Officer of the Order of Leopold (Belgium); Old Latin; Ordnance Lieutenant; Overseas League

OLC Oak-Leaf Cluster (US Army)

OL Cr Ordnance Lieutenant-Commander

OLD Old Town Corporation (NYSE)

Old Test. Old Testament

oleo oleomargarine

OLG Old Low German

OLLA Office of Lend-Lease Administration

OLP Observation landplane (US Navy)

ol res oleoresin

OL & T owners, landlords, and tenants (insurance)

OLV Oliver United Filters (NYSE)

OLV B Oliver United Filters, Inc. ("B" Stk.) (ASE)

Olym Olympiad; Olympics

o m every morning (*omni mane*—Latin)

OM Greatest and Best (*Optimus Maximus*—Latin); Old Man (colloquial); Omnibus Corporation (NYSE); Order of Merit; Ordnance Map; organic matter; overturning moment

Om Oman

OMA Optical Manufacturers Association

OMC World-Wide Commerce Organi-

zation (*Organisation Mondiale du
Commerce*—French)
OM Cap. Order of Minor
Capuchins
OME Ordnance Mechanical Engi-
neer
OMEP World Organization for Early
Childhood Education
O Merced Order of our Lady of
Mercy
OMI Fathers of Mary Immaculate
(*Oblati Mariae Immaculatae*—
Latin); International Meteorological
Organization
OMIA Operating Maintenance Inter-
est and Adaptability
OMM Outboard, Marine & Manufac-
turing Company (NYSE)
OMMA Outboard Motor Manufacturers
Association
omn bih every two hours (*omni
bihora*—Latin) (pharmacy)
O(MN)F Officers' (Merchant Navy)
Federation
omn hor every hour (*omni hora*—
Latin) (pharmacy)
OMO ordinary money order
OMPS Overseas Motion Picture
Service
OMR Omar, Inc (NYSE)
OMS Organization for the
Maintenance of Supplies
OMV Master of Obstetrics
(Vienna)
OMX Oscar Mayer & Co., Davenport,
Ia. (private car rr mark)
o n every night (*omni nocte*—Latin)
(pharmacy); octane number; oil-
immersed natural cooling
On. Honorable (*Onorevole*—Ital-
ian)
ON Old Norse; Omicron Nu (soci-
ety)
O/N order-notify; own name
ONA Overseas News Association
on a/c on account
1 B one-base hit; first base (base-
ball)
1 Chron 1 Chronicles (Bible)
1 Cor 1 Corinthians (Bible)
1 Pet. 1 Peter (Bible)
1 Sam. 1 Samuel (Bible)
1 Thess 1 Thessalonians (Bible)
1 Tim. 1 Timothy (Bible)
ONF Old Norman French; Old North
French
ong about (*ongeveer*—Dutch)
ONG Non-Governmental Organizations (NGO)
ONO West North-West (*Ouest-nord-
ouest*—French)
onomat onomatopœia; onomatopœic
O North. Old Northumbrian
ONR Official Naval Reporter
Ont Ontario

ONT National Touring Office (*Of-
fice National du Tourisme*—
French); Ontario Northland Railway
(rr mark)
ONU Ohio Northern University;
United Nations Organization
(*Organisation des Nations-Unies*—
French)
ONUESC United Nations' Organiza-
tion for Education, Science and
Culture (*Organisation des Nations-
Unies Pour l'Education, la Science
et la Culture*—French)
onz ounce (*onza*—Spanish)
o o on order; or order
o/o order of
OO Observation Officer (RAF);
Oceanic Oil Company (NYSE); Op-
eration Order; Operations Officer;
Order of Owls; Orderly Officer;
Ordnance Officer
O/O on order
O & O Oriental and Occidental
(Steamship Company)
OOAA Olive Oil Association of
America
OOC Office of Censorship; Order of
the Child
OOG Officer of the Guard
OOQ Officer of the Quarters
OORX Chartrand's Traffic Service
(private car rr mark)
Ooty Ootacamund, Madras, India
(colloquial)
OOW Officer of the Watch (naval)
o p open pattern (plumbing); order
policy; original premium; out of
print
op excellent (*optimus*—Latin);
opera; operation; opus; overproof
Op Opera; Optime
OP Observation Post (US Army);
Occidental Petroleum Corporation
(NYSE); Old Persian; Old Play-
goers; old pieces; opaque; open
policy (insurance); Order of Precep-
tors; Order of Preachers (*Ordinis
Praedicatorum*); Orphans' Pensions;
Oslo Powers
OPA Office of Price Administration;
Overseas Parliamentary Association
OPACI Provisional International
Civil Aviation Organization
(PICAO)
OPACS Office of Price Administra-
tion and Civilian Supply
Op Att Gen Opinions of the Attorney
General
OPBMA Ocean Pearl Button Manu-
facturers Association
OPC Overseas Press Club
OPCA Overseas Press Club of
America
op cit in the work quoted (*opere
citato*—Latin)

OPCR One pass cold rolled [steel]
OPCW Office of Petroleum Coordi-
nator for War
Oph Ophiuchus (constellation)
ophthal ophthalmological; ophthal-
mology
OPI Office of Public Information
OPL outpost line (US Army)
OPLR outpost line of resistance
(US Army)
Opm remark (*Opmerking*—Dutch)
OPM Office of Production Manage-
ment
OPN operation (US Army)
opn operation; opinion; opposition
o p n pray for us (*ora pro nobis*—
Latin)
OPNAV Chief of Naval Operations
(US Navy)
o p p out of print at present
opp opposed; opposite; opposition
oppy opportunity
opr operator
O Prem Order of Premonstratensians
ops operations
OPS Operating Practices (ICAO);
Oppenheim, Collins & Company
(NYSE)
opt optative (grammar); optical
(*optique*—French); optics; optime;
optional; operation
Opt D Doctor of Optometry
optg operating
opt mineral. optical mineralogy
optns operations
OPX Ohio Power Company The
(private car rr mark)
OQMG Office of Quartermaster
General
o r official receiver; official
referee; organized reserve; owner's
risk
or. oratorio; other
o⁴ other
Or Orient; Oregon; Oriel [College]
(Oxford)
OR Orderly Room; Operating Room
o & r ocean and rail
ORA Official Records of the
Admiralty
orat orator; oration; oratorically
o r b omni-directional radio beacon;
owner's risk of breakage
o r c owner's risk of chafing
ORC Officers' Reserve Corps;
Orange River Colony; Order of the
Red Cross; Orderly Room Corporal;
Organized Reserve Corps (US Army)
ORCA Order of Railway Conductors
of America
orch orchestra; orchestration
orchl orchestral
ord ordained; order (*orden*—
Spanish); ordinal; ordinance; ordinary (*ordinaire*—French); ordnance

o r d owner's risk of damage; owner's risk of deterioration

ordentl ordinary (ordentlich—German)

Orderly Sgt orderly sergeant

Ord Sgt Ordnance Sergeant

Ore Oregon

Oreg Oregon

o r f owner's risk of fire

ORF Occupational Research Foundation

org organ; organist; organism; organization; organized

org chem organic chemistry

orgⁿ organization

Org Res Organized Reserves

ORHX Howard Tank Line (private car rr mark)

Orl Orion (constellation)

Orient. Oriental

orig origin; original; originated

orig bds original boards

Ork Orkney (county of Scotland)

Ork Is. Orkney Islands

o r l owner's risk of leakage

Orl Orlando; Orleans

ORMX Orme, D. L. (private car rr mark)

orn ornament; ornithological; ornithology

ornith ornithology

ORP Shall I decrease power? (QS)

orph orphan(age)

o r r owner's risk rates

ors others

o r s owner's risk of shifting

ORSA Order of Recollects of St. Augustine

orse otherwise (legal)

ORT Order of Railroad Telegraphers; Organization for Rehabilitation Through Training

orth orthography; orthopædic; orthopædy

ORTU Other Ranks Training Unit

ORT Union (Society for the Propagation of Agricultural and Manual Labour amongst the Jews of Russia)

o r w owner's risk of wetting

o s ocean station; on spot; only son; ordnance survey; other side; other sources

Os Osee (Bible); osmium (chemistry)

OS Observation Scout (US Navy); Old Saxon; Old School; Old Series; Old Side; Old Style; on sample; one side; Ophthalmological Society; Optical Society; Ordinary Seaman; Ordnance Survey; Oregon State (college); output secondary (radio); Outside Sentinel; outsides; outsize; overseas (US Army); Oxford Society

o/s gold currency (oro sellodo—Spanish); out of stock; outstanding

o s a an answer is requested (om svar anhalles—Swedish)

OSA Official Secrets Act; Office of Stabilization Administrator; Ontario Society of Artists; Operative Spinners' Association Optical Society of America; of the Order of St. Augustine (Ordinis Sancti Augustini)

OSA a reply is expected (Om Svar Anhålles—Swedish)

O Sax Old Saxon

OSB of the Order of St. Benedict (Ordinis Sancti Benedicti)

OSBM Order of St. Basil the Great

osc oscillating

Osc Oscar

O Sc Old Scandinavian

OSC Oblate of St. Charles; Ontario Services Club; Order of Scottish Clans; Overseas Settlement Committee

OS Cam Order of St. Camillus

O Scand Old Scandinavian

OSCC Official Spanish Chamber of Commerce

OSCR Canons Regular of the Holy Cross (Crosier Fathers)

OSCSA Ordnance Survey Civil Staff Association

OSD of the Order of St. Dominic (Ordinis Sancti Dominici—Latin); Ordnance Survey Department; Overseas Settlement Department

OS/D over, short, and damaged report (US Army)

o s & d over short and damage

OSE Union OSE Union

OSF Order of St. Francis

OSFC of the Order of St. Francis—Capuchins (Ordinis Sancti Francisci Capuccinorum—Latin)

OSFCW Office of Solid Fuels Coordinator for War

OSFI Open Steel Flooring Institute

OSFS Oblates of St. Francis de Sales

o/sg outstanding

OSG Office of the Secretary General

osh every hour (omni singula hora—Latin) (pharmacy)

OSH Order of St. Jerome (Hieronymites)

OSJ Oblates of St. Joseph

OSJD Order of St. John of God (Ordinis Sancti Joannis de Deo—Latin)

OSK Osaka Mercantile Steamship Company (Osaka Syosen Kaisha—Japanese

OSKX Mid-Continent Petroleum Corporation (private car rr mark); Oil States Tank Car Corporation (private car rr mark)

O Sl Old Slavonic

OSL RR Oregon Short Line Railroad

OSM Order of the Servants of Mary (Servites)

OSNC Orient Steam Navigation Company

OSO West South-West (Ouest-Sud-Ouest—French)

o s p died without issue (obiit sine prole—Latin)

O Sp Old Spanish

OSP Pan American Sanitary Organization (PASO)

OSRD Office of Scientific Research and Development

OSS Office of Strategic Services

O SS T Order of the Most Holy Trinity (Trinitarian)

o s t ordinary spring tides

osteo osteopath; osteopathy

OSU Ohio State University; Order of St. Ursula (Ursuline)

o s v and so forth (och sa vidare—Swedish, og så videre—Norwegian, og saa videre—Danish)

Osw Oswald

OSW Office of the Secretary of War

o s & w oak, sunk, and weathered (construction)

O Sw(ed) Old Swedish

o s &y outside screw and yoke (plumbing)

o t oil-tight; on track; on truck; oscillation transformer; overtime

Ot Otto's United States Supreme Court Reports (legal)

O/t old terms (grain trade)

OT Old Testament; Old Teutonic; Otis Elevator Company (NYSE); Overseas Trade

O & T Oyer and Terminer (legal)

OTA World Touring and Automobile Organization (WTAO)

OTANY Oil Trades Association of New York

OTB Office of Trade Boards; On the Bow (nautical)

otbd outboard

OTC Office of Temporary Controls; Officer in Tactical Command (US Navy); Officers' Training Camp

O Teut Old Teutonic

o t h oil-tight hatch

Oth Othello

OTM Old Turkey Mill (paper)

otol otological; otology

OTPX Otter Tail Power Company (private car rr mark)

OTQ on the quarter (nautical)

OTS Officers' Training School

ott octave (ottava—music)

Ott Ottawa

OTU Outlet Company (NYSE)

OTV Olympic Radio & Television (NYSE)

OU Oahu Sugar Company, Ltd

(NYSE); Oglethorpe University; Ohio University; Omega Upsilon (society); Oxford University

OUA Order of United Americans

OUAC Oxford University Athletic Club

OUAM Order of United American Mechanics

OUBC Oxford University Boat Club

OUCTA Order of United Commercial Travelers of America

OULC Oxford University Lacrosse Club

OULTC Oxford University Lawn Tennis Club

OUP Oxford University Press

OUSW Office of the Under Secretary of War

Out. Outerbridge's Reports (legal)

outs. outsider

ov egg (*ovis*—Latin); ovary; over-voltage; overture

OV Owners' Vans

ova octave (*ottava*—Italian) (music)

OVHL overhaul (US Army)

OVOX Grace & Company, W. R. (private car rr mark); Oriental Vegetable Oils Company (United States) (private car rr mark)

OVU Overseas Securities Company (NYSE)

o w one way

o W without value (*ohne Wert*—German)

OW New York, Ontario & Western Railway (rr mark); Office of Works; oil-immersed water-cooled

ö W Austrian currency (*österreichische Währung*—German)

OWI Office of War Information

OWIU Oil Workers International Union

OWM Office of War Mobilization

OWMR Office of War Mobilization and Reconversion

OWNA Osteopathic Women's National Association

OWRR&N Co Oregon-Washington

R.R. & Navigation Company

OWU Office of War Utilities; Ohio Wesleyan University

Ox Oxford

Oxf Oxfordshire (county in England)

Oxon, Oxonien of Oxford (*Oxoniensis*—Latin)

O/Y stock company (Osakeyhtio—Finnish)

oz ounce

OZA Ozark Air Lines, Inc

oz ap ounce, apothecaries'

oz av ounce avoirdupois

OZCX Ozark-Mahoning Company (private car rr mark)

oz-ft ounce-foot

oz-in ounce-inch

OZKX Ozark Tank Car Company (private car rr mark)

OZNA Section for the Defence of the People (*Odeljenje Zastite Naroda*—Yugoslav)

oz t ounce troy

OZX Ozone Company, Inc (private car rr mark)

P

p after (*post*—Latin); by (*per*—Latin); first (*primus*—Latin); for (*pour*—French); holy (*pius*—Latin); foot (*pied*—French); inch (*pouce*—French); little (*poco*) (music); page (*página*—Portuguese); park; part; participle; in port (*partim*—Latin); past (*passé*—French); passed; passing showers (meteorology); peak; pectoral (ichthyology); penny; pence; perch (area); perishable; peseta; peso; plaster; pint; pipe (measure); pole (measure); population; premolar; professional; protest (of bills) (*protêt*—French); soft (*piano*) (music); by weight (*poudere*—Latin)

P active power; anode (plate); brake; father (*Pére*—French); permeance; parson; pastor; Pawn (chess); performer; perianth; period (of time); person; personnel; Phillips Petroleum (NYSE); Philippine Scouts; phosphorus; people (*Populus*—Latin); Pope; port; Portugal; port side; post; Presbyterian; President; pressure; priest; Prince; probation; probate; Proconsul; Progressive; Protestant; protected; public; total load; vapor pressure

p a arithmetical progression (*progression arithmétique*—French);

atomic weight (*poids atomique*—French)

pa by authority (*par autorité*—French; *por autorización*—Spanish); care of (c/o) (*per adrés*—Dutch); participial adjective; particular average; patent applied; per annum; power amplifier; power of attorney; private account; printed sheet (*painoarkki*—Finnish); public address (system); for (*para*—Spanish); paper; participle; passive

p A care of (*per Adresse*—German)

Pa Pennsylvania; protoactinium

PA Pakistan Army; Parents' Association; Passenger Agent; Pedestrians' Association; Pennsylvania Railroad Company (NYSE); Personal Assistant; Phi Alpha (fraternity); Post Adjutant; power amplifier; Prefect Apostolic; Presbyterian Alliance; Press Agent; Press Association; Proprietary Association; Protestant Alliance; Prothonatary Apostolic; Provisional Alliance; Provisional Assembly; Public Address; Publishers' Association; Passenger (rr car)

p a a to be applied to the affected part (*parti affectœ applicandus*—Latin) (pharmacy)

PAA Pacific Alaska Airways; Pan American Airways; Peruvian American Association; Photographic Association of America; Potato Association of America

PAAA Premium Advertising Association of America

PAAC Pan American Association of Composers

PAADC Principal Air Aide-de-Camp

PAB Pabco Products Inc (NYSE); Panair do Brasil, South America; Petroleum Administrative Board; Price Adjustment Board

PABX private automatic branch exchange (telephone)

PAC Pacific Telephone & Telegraph (NYSE); Pan-American Coffee Bureau; Pan-American Congress; Political Action Committee; Public Assistance Committee; Passed Advanced Class; pursuant to authority contained in (US Army)

PACC Philippine-American Chamber of Commerce

PACI Public Affairs Committee, Inc

Pacif Pacific

Pac Oc Pacific Ocean

Pac R Pacific Reporter (legal)

Pac (2d) Pacific Reporter, Second Series

PAD. Phi Alpha Delta (fraternity)

PADA Past Arch Druidesses' Association

PADGT Past Assistant Deputy Grand Treasurer (freemasonry)

p adj participial adjective

pad. str paddle steamer

p æ equal parts (*partes æquales*—Latin) (pharmacy)

PAE Patino Mines & Enterprises (NYSE); port of aerial embarkation (US Army)

PAEA Pneumatic Automotive Equipment Association

p a f brake-horsepower (*puissance au frein*—French)

PAF Pan American Foundation

pág page (*página*—Spanish)

PAG Pacific Coast Aggregates (NYSE); Phi Alpha Gamma (fraternity)

PAGA Pan American-Grace Airways

PAHC Pan American Highway Confederation

Pai Paine's United States Circuit Court Reports (legal)

PAI Philippine Air Lines; Piedmont Aviation, Inc; Pioneer Air Lines, Inc; Public Affairs Institute; Pakistan International Airlines

pain. next (*prochain*—French)

paint. painting

PAIS Public Affairs Information Service

PAK Pakistan (IDP); Park Chemical Company (NYSE)

pal. paleontology

Pal. Palestine

PAL Pan American League; Police Athletic League

palæthnol paleethnology

paleobot paleobotany

palm. palmistry

pam. pamphlet; panoramic

PA & M Pittsburgh, Allegheny & McKees/Rocks Railroad Company (rr mark)

pamph pamphlet

pan. panchromatic; panoramic

Pan. Panama

PAN. Angola (IDP); Pantapec Oil (NYSE)

PANAGRA Pan American-Grace Airways, Inc.

Pan Am. Pan American; Pan-American World Airways

PANDA. personnel and administration (US Army)

pandi protection and indemnity (insurance)

PANDO plans and operations (US Army)

pant. pantomime

PANX Panoma Corporation (private car rr mark)

PAO Panhellenic Guerrilla Organization

pa p past participle

Pap. Papua

p app apparent power (*puissance apparente*—French)

Pap. Ter Papua Territory

par. paragraph; parallax; parallel; parallelogram; paraphrase; parish

Par. Paraguay; Paralipomenon (Bible)

parch. parchment

Par. Dec Parsons' Decisions (legal)

parens parentheses

parl parliament; parliamentary

Parl Agt Parliamentary Agent

parlars particulars

par. pas parallel passage

Pa RR Pennsylvania R.R.

part. participating; participial; participle; particular; partner; partnership

part. adj participial adjective

part. æq equal parts (*partes æquales*—Latin) (pharmacy)

PARX Producers & Refiners Corporation (private car rr mark)

Pas Easter Term (*Terminus Paschae*—Latin)

PAS passenger (US Army); Phi Alpha Sigma (fraternity); Public Administration Service; Combined Sleeping and Passenger (rr car)

PASA Pacific American Steamship Association

PASB Pan American Sanitary Bureau

PASI Professional Associate Chartered Surveyors' Institution

PASO Pan American Sanitary Organization

pass. everywhere (*passim*—Latin); passage; passenger; passive

Passed Asst Surg passed assistant surgeon

pass. tr passenger train

past. paste (pharmacy)

Pas T Paschal Term

pastill pastille (pharmacy)

PASUS Pan American Society of the United States

PASX Pan-Am Southern Corporation (private car rr mark)

pa t past tense

pat. patent; patented; pattern; patristus; patrol boat; atomic weight (*poids atomique*—French)

Pat Patrick

PAT. Patican Company, Ltd (NYSE); Phi Alpha Theta (fraternity); Pi Alpha Tau (sorority)

Pata Patagonia(n)

PATA Proprietary Articles Trade Association

patd patented

Pat. Dec Patent Decisions

path. pathology

patmkg patternmaking

Pat. Off. Patent Office

patt no. pattern number

PAU Pan American Union

paul a little (*paullum*—Latin) (pharmacy)

Paus Pausanias

PAUS Population Association of the United States

paux a little (*pauxillum*—Latin) (pharmacy)

Pav Pavo (constellation)

PAW Petroleum Administration for War United States

PAWA Pan American Women's Association; Pan American World Airways

PAX Private automatic exchange (telephone)

PAY Paymaster (US Navy)

p a y e pay as you earn; pay as you enter

Paym-Dir-Gen Paymaster Director-General

Paym-Gen Paymaster-General

Paymr Paymaster

Paymr-Capt Paymaster-Captain

Paym-Rear-Adml Paymaster-Rear-Admiral

payt payment

Październik October (*Październik*—Polish)

p b pocket book; privately bonded

Pb lead (plumbum)

PB Bachelor of Philosophy (*Philosophia Baccalaurus*); British Pharmacopoeia (*Pharmacopoeia Britannica*); Phi Beta (society); passenger (rr car); Patrol Bomber; pawnbroker; permanent bunkers; Picket Boat; Plymouth Brethren; Prayer Book; Primitive Baptist; Provisional Battalion; United Board & Carton Corporation (NYSE)

P-B Netherlands (*Pays-Bas*—French)

p b a permanent budget account

PBA Public Buildings Administration

PBB Private Boxes and Bags (GPO)

PBC Parlor Coach (rr car)

PBCP Political Bureau of the Communist Party

PBG Phi Beta Gamma (fraternity)

PBGX Protane Corporation (private car rr mark)

PBI Paper Bag Institute; Paving Brick Institute; Pitney-Bowes, Inc. (NYSE)

PBK Phi Beta Kappa (scholastic fraternity)

PBL preamble (QS)

pble possible (*posible*—Spanish)

PBM Pittsburgh Consolidation Coal (NYSE); Principal Beach Master (naval)

PBMA Peanut Butter Manufacturers Association

PBNE Philadelphia, Bethlehem and New England Railroad (rr mark)

PBO Parlor Coach Observation (rr car)

P Bor *Pharmacopoeia Borussica* (Prussian Pharmacopoeia)

PBP Phi Beta Phi (scholastic fraternity); Pi Beta Pi (fraternity); Pi Beta Pi (sorority)

PBR Patapsco & Back Rivers Railroad Company (private car rr mark)

PB Report Publication Board Report

PBREW Pittsburgh Brewing Company (NYSE)

PBT President of the Board of Trade

PBTB Paper Bag (or Box) Trade Board

PBX private branch (telephone) exchange

PBY Pep Boys-Manny, Moe & Jack (NYSE)

p c after meals (*post cibum*—Latin); avoirdupois (*pondus civile*—Latin); by the hundred (*per centum*—Latin); caused to be placed (*poni curairt*—Latin); freezing point (*point de congélation*—French); per cent (*por ciento*—Spanish); petty cash; pitch circle; post card; prime cost

pc piece

PC Communist Party (*Parti Communiste*—French); little calorie (*petite calorie*—French); first class (*première classe*—French); Pacific Coast Railroad Company (rr mark); Panama Canal; Parish Council(lor); Parliamentary Clerk; Paymaster-Cadet; Paymaster-Captain (naval); Paymaster-Commander (naval); Peace Commissioner; Penitentiary Commission; Perpetual Commissioner (legal); Perpetual Curate; Pharmacy Corps; Phi Chi (fraternity); Philippines Constabulary; Philharmonic Choir; Pioneer Club; Pioneer Corps; plate circuit (radio); Playwrights' Club; Police Constable; Portland Cement; Post Card; Post Commander; Prerogative Court of Canterbury; price current; prime cost; Prison Commission; Privy Council; Privy Councillor; Probation Committee; Psi Chi (society); Producers Council; Submarine Chasers; Steel-Hull (US Navy); Passenger, Parlor or Chair Car (rr mark)

P/C prices current

P & C put and call

p & c parge and core (building)

P-in-C Priest-in-Charge

PCA Paraffined Carton Association; Portland Cement Association; Production Code Administration; Progressive Citizens of America

PCB Pensions Commutation Board; Petty Cash Book

p c c true copy (*pour copie conforme*—French)

PCC Parks and Cemeteries Committee; Parochial Church Council; Portland Cement Concrete; Prerogative Court of Canterbury; Price Control Committee; Privy Council Cases; Production Credit Corporation; true copy (*pour copie conforme*—French)

PCCA Production Credit Corporations and Associations

PCCI Paper Cup and Container Institute

p c d pitch circle diameter

PCD Panama Canal Department; Petroleum Conservation Division

PCE Patrol Craft, Escort (US Navy)

PCE(R) Patrol Craft, Escort (Rescue) (US Navy)

PCES President's Committee on Economic Security

PCF Pacific American Fisheries (NYSE)

PCFA Pin, Clip and Fastener Association; Plastic Coatings and Film Association

PCFB Pacific Coast Freight Bureau

PCG Pacific Gas & Electric (NYSE)

PCG V A Rd Pr Pacific Gas & Electric Company (5% Red. 1st Pfd. "A") (ASE)

PCG V Rd Pr Pacific Gas & Electric Company (5% Red. 1st Pfd.) (ASE)

PCG V Pr Pacific Gas & Electric Company (5% 1st Pfd.) (Non-Redeemable) (ASE)

PCGN Permanent Committee on Geographical Names

PCG VI Pr Pacific Gas & Electric Company (6% 1st Pfd.) (Non-Redeemable) (ASE)

pchs purchase

pchsr purchaser

PCI Internationalist Communist Party (*Parti Communiste Internationaliste*—French); Pilot Club International

PCIMCO Preparatory Committee of the Inter-Governmental Maritime Consultative Organization

PCIRO Preparatory Commission for the International Refugee Organization

PCIX Pure Carbonic Company, A Division of Air Reduction Company, Incorporated; Shippers' Car Line Corp. (private car rr mark)

pck peck

PCK Pittsburgh Coke & Chemical Company (NYSE)

pcl(s) parcel(s)

PCL Pacific Coast League (baseball); Pancoastal Oil Corporation (NYSE)

p clk pay clerk

PCL V Pancoastal Oil Corp. C. A. (Registered Form) (Common Stock ASE)

PCLX Polymer Corporation Limited (private car rr mark)

p c m pulse code modulation; pulse count modulation

pc mk piece mark

PCMO Principal Colonial Medical Officer

PCN Pacific Can Company (NYSE)

PCO Pittston Company (NYSE)

PCP Past Chief Patriarch;

PCQI Pre-Conquest Quechua Indians (Peru)

PCRC Paraffined Carton Research Council

PCRCA pickled, cold rolled, and close annealed (steel sheets)

PCRS Poor Clergy Relief Society

pcs preconscious; pieces

PCS Patrol Craft, Sweeper (US Navy); permanent change of station (US Army); Principal Clerk of Session

PCSA Power Crane and Shovel Association

pct per cent; precinct

PCT Phi Chi Theta (society)

p/cta for account (*por cuenta*—Spanish)

PCUS Presbyterian Church in the United States; Propeller Club of the United States

PCUUS Portuguese Continental Union of the United States

PCUUSC Paving Cutters Union of the United States and Canada

PCX Pacific Coast Company (NYSE)

pd. paid; passed; foot (*pied*—French); postscript (*posdata*—Spanish)

p d by the day (*per diem*—Latin); daily paid; pitch diameter; pitch circle diameter; poop deck; post dues; position doubtful; potential difference; prism diopter; public document

Pd palladium; phenyl dichloride

PD Doctor of Philosophy (*Philosophiae Doctor*—Latin); Pack Drill; period (US Army); Personnel Department; Petroleum Department;

Physics Department; Plans Division; Police Department; Port Dues; Position Doubtful (naval); Postal District; Printer's Devil; Priorities Division; Probate Division; Tutor (*Privatdozent*—German); Tavern Car (rr car)

p&d pickup and delivery

pda to say good bye (*pour dire adieu*—French)

PDAD Probate, Divorce, and Admiralty Division

Pd B Bachelor of Pedagogy

PDC Parke, Davis & Company (NYSE); Phi Delta Chi (fraternity)

PDCA Painting and Decorating Contractors of America

Pd D Doctor of Pedagogy

PDD Phi Delta Delta (society)

PDE Phi Delta Epsilon (fraternity); Pi Delta Epsilon (society)

P de C *Pas-de-Calais*(French department)

P de D *Puy-de-Dôme* (French department)

PDF Panhandle Oil Corporation (NYSE)

PDG Paymaster Director-General; Peoples Drug Stores, Inc. (NYSE)

PDGX P.D. George Company, The (private car rr mark)

PDK Phi Delta Kappa (fraternity)

pdl poundal

pdm pulse duration modulation

Pd M Master of Pedagogy

PDMA Plumbing and Drainage Manufacturers Association

PDP Phi Delta Phi (fraternity); Phi Delta Pi (society); Pi Delta Phi (society)

p d q pretty damn quick

PDR Powdrell & Alexander, Inc. (NYSE)

PDS Combined Sleeping and Tavern (rr car)

PDSX Penn Dixie Cement Corporation (private car rr mark)

PDT Phi Delta Theta (fraternity)

PDY Peabody Coal Company (NYSE)

p e boiling point (*point d'ébullition* —French); equal parts (*parties égales*—French); for instance (*por ejemplo*—Spanish); pinion end; plain end; probable error; pulley end

PE Edinburgh Pharmacopoeia (*Pharmacopoeia Edinburgensis*); Pacific Electric Railway Company (rr mark); Petroleum Engineer; Peru (IDP); Philadelphia Electric Company (NYSE); Presiding Elder; Protestant Episcopal; Submarine Chaser (Eagle Boat Type (US Navy); Colonist or Emigrant (rr car)

PEA Phillips Exeter Academy; Portuguese East Africa; Potash Export Association

Pe B Bachelor of Pediatrics (*Pediatriae Baccalaureus*—Latin); Bachelor of Pedagogy

p e c photo-electric cell

PEC Protestant Episcopal Church

pect to the chest (*pectori*—Latin) (pharmacy)

PECX Pioneer Equipment Company (private car rr mark)

ped pedagogue; pedal; pedestal; pedestrian

Ped B Bachelor of Pedagogy (*Pedagogiae Baccalaureus*— Latin)

Ped D Doctor of Pedagogy (*Pedagogiae Doctor*—Latin)

pedet gradually (*pedetemptim*— Latin) (pharmacy)

PEEA Political Committee of National Liberation (*Politiki Epitropi Ethnikou Apeleftheroseos*—Greek)

Peeb Peebles

PEET Greek Committee of National Liberation

p ef personal effects floater

PEF Palestine Exploration Fund; Perfect Circle Company (NYSE)

Peg. Pegasus (constellation)

PEG Public Service Electric & Gas (NYSE)

PEI Porcelain Enamel Institute; Prince Edward Island (Canada)

p ej for instance (*por ejemplo*— Spanish)

Pek Pekingese

PEK Phi Epsilon Kappa (fraternity)

p e l proportional elastic limit

PEL Panhandle Eastern Pipe Line (NYSE); Personnel Licensing (ICAO)

Pemb Pembroke College (Cambridge); Pembrokeshire (county of Wales)

pen. brush (*penicillum*—Latin) (pharmacy); peninsula; penitentiary

PEN (International Association of) Poets, Playwrights, Editors, Essayists, and Novelists

PENB Poultry and Egg National Board

Pen. Code Penal Code

pend. weighing (*pendens*—Latin) (pharmacy)

Penn Pennsylvania

penol penological; penology

p e n r plain end not reamed (plumbing)

pent. pentagon; pentameter

Pent. Pentateuch; Pentecost

PENX Compania Minera de Penoles (private car rr mark)

peo people

PEO Petroleum Corporation of

America (NYSE)

Pe P Principal of Pedagogics

PEP Pepsi-Cola Company (NYSE); Persons by Express Post; Phi Epsilon Pi (fraternity); Political and Economic Planning; Portland Traction Company (rr mark)

PEPX Peppers Refining Company (private car rr mark)

p e r plain end reamed (plumbing)

per period; person

Per Pericles, Prince of Tyre; Perseus; Persia; Persian; Persic

PER Peoria & Eastern Railway Company (NYSE)

per an. by the year (*per annum*— Latin)

per cap. each (*per capita*—Latin)

% per cent; percentage

per cent by the hundred (*per centum* —Latin)

perd dying away (*perdendosi*) (music)

perf perfect; perforated (stamps); performance; performed

perh perhaps

Peri Perigee

perm permanent; permission

per M by the thousand

perp perpendicular; perpetual (bonds)

per pro by proxy (*per procurationem*—Latin) (legal)

pers person; personal

Pers Persia; Persian

PERS personnel (US Army)

persh perishable

persl personal (legal)

persp perspective

pert. pertaining

PERU Republic of Peru External Sinking Fund Dollar Bonds of 1947 (ASE)

Peruv Peruvian

pes peseta

PES Phi Eta Sigma (fraternity)

PESA Petroleum Equipment Suppliers Association

pess pessary (*pessus*—Latin) (pharmacy)

Pet. Peter (Biblical); Peterhouse College, Cambridge; petrol(eum); Peters' United States Supreme Court Reports (legal)

PET. Pet Milk Company (NYSE); Peterson's Telegraphic Code

I Pet. First Book of Peter (Bible)

II Pet. II Peter (Bible)

Pet. C C Peters' United States Circuit Court Reports (legal)

petn petition

petnr petitioner (legal)

petr petroleum

petr ether petroleum ether

Petriburg of Peterborough (*Petriburgensis*—Latin)

PETRL petroleum (US Army)

petrog petrography

PETX Petco Corporation, Great Lakes Refining Division (private car rr mark)

p ex for example (*par exemple*—French)

p f to congratulate (*pour féliciter*—French); dollars (*pesos fuertes*—Spanish); a little louder (*più or poco forte*) (music); melting point (*point de fusion*—French); plain face; power factor

pf perfect; preferred;

pF pico-farad (electrical engineering); water energy (p, logarithm; F, frequency)

Pf Pianoforte; *Pfennig*(German coin); *Pfund* (Pound—German); Preference (Stock Exchange)

PF frigates (US Navy); Penworkers' Federation; plain face (building); Procurator-Fiscal

p & f plumber and fitter

pf acc pianoforte accompaniment (music)

PFB Pfeiffer Brewing Company (NYSE); Provisional Frequency Board (of ITU)

Pfc private, first class

PFC Private Flying Corps

PFCI Protestant Film Commission, Inc.

pfd paraffined; preferred

Pfd pound (*Pfund*—German)

PFDA Pure Food and Drug Administration

pfd s preferred spelling

PFE Pacific Fruit Express Company (private car rr mark); Pfizer (Chas.) & Company, Inc. (NYSE)

PFER Pollak Foundation for Economic Research

PFFEA Pacific Fresh Fruit Export Association

PFG Pittsburgh Forgings Company (NYSE)

PFI Pacific Forest Industries; Photo Finishing Institute; Pipe Fabrication Institute

p f i & r part fill in and ram (building)

PFK Penick & Ford, Ltd., Inc. (NYSE)

PFMA Pipe Fittings Manufacturers Association; Progressive Fox Marketing Association; Propeller Fan Manufacturers Association

PFN Pacific Finance Corporation (NYSE)

P F P Postage Forward Parcels

PFS Pacific Mills (NYSE); Parliamentary and Financial Secretary

p f s a to say good-by (*pour faire ses adieux*—French)

PFSX Productos Forestales (private car rr mark)

PFT Pittsburgh, Ft. Wayne & Chicago Railway (NYSE)

p f v to make a call (*pour faire visite*—French)

pfx prefix

Pg Portugal; Portuguese

PG corvettes; gunboats (US Navy); German Pharmacopoeia (*Pharmacopoeia Germanica*); Pan Germanism; Past Grand (freemasonry); paste grain (bookbinding); paying guest; Philatelic Guild (United States); plate-glazed (paper); Princes' Galleries; Procter & Gamble Company (NYSE); Procurator-General; Provincial Government; pure gum (of envelopes)

PGA Professional Golfers Association

PGAA Professional Golfers Association of America

PGAD Past Grand Arch Druidess

PGAH Pineapple Growers Association of Hawaii

p g c d greatest common divisor (*plus grand commun diviseur*—French)

PGCOA Pennsylvania Grade Crude Oil Association

PGD Past Grand Deacon (freemasonry); Phi Gamma Delta (fraternity);

pgdo promissory note paid (*pagado*—Spanish)

pgdro payable (*pagadero*—Spanish)

PGE Pacific Great Eastern Railway Company (rr mark); Penn. Gas & Electric (NYSE)

PGE A Pennsylvania Gas & Electric Corp. ("A") (common stock, ASE)

PGJD Past Grand Junior Deacon (freemasonry)

PGL Peoples Gas Light & Coke (NYSE); Provincial Grand Lodge (freemasonry)

PGM Past Grand Master; Pi Gamma Mu (society); Provincial or Past Grand Master (freemasonry); Motor Gunboats (US Navy)

PGN pigeon (US Army); Phi Gamma Nu (society); Pig'n Whistle Corporation (NYSE)

PGR registered telegram (*pour garder recommandé*—French)

PGS Pennsylvania Glass Sand Corporation (NYSE)

PGSD Past Grand Senior Deacon (freemasonry)

PGSW Past Grand Senior Warden (freemasonry)

PGSX Propane Gas Service, Inc. (private car rr mark)

p g t per gross ton

PGT Passenger and Goods Transport; Past Grand Treasurer (freemasonry)

PGV Pierce Governor Company (NYSE)

ph phase; phone

pH acid-base scale; log of reciprocal of hydrogen ion concentration

Ph phenyl (chemistry); Philip

PH public health; Purple Heart

P of H Patrons of Husbandry

PHA Public Housing Administration

phar pharmaceutical; pharmacist; pharmacopoeia; pharmacy

Phar B Bachelor of Pharmacy (*Pharmaciae Baccalaureus*—Latin)

Phar D Doctor of Pharmacy

Phar M Master of Pharmacy (*Pharmaciae Magister*—Latin)

Ph B Bachelor of Philosophy (*Philosophiae Baccalaureus*—Latin); British Pharmacopoeia

PH B BA Bachelor of Philosophy in Business Administration

PH B Com Bachelor of Philosophy in Commerce

PH B J Bachelor of Philosophy in Journalism

PH B Sp Bachelor of Philosophy in Speech

ph bz phosphor bronze

Ph C Pharmaceutical Chemist; Philosopher of Chiropractic

PHC Philadelphia Company (Pitts.) (NYSE)

Ph D Doctor of Pharmacy (*Pharmaciae Doctor*—Latin); Doctor of Philosophy (*Philosophiae Doctor*—Latin)

PHD Doctor of Public Health

PH D Ed Doctor of Philosophy in Education

Phe Phoenix (constellation)

P H Eng Public Health Engineer

Ph G Graduate in Pharmacy

PHI Philippine Long Distance Telephone (NYSE)

PHIB amphibian; amphibious; Plumbing and Heating Industries Bureau

phil philharmonic; philological; philology; philosophical; philosophy

Phil Philadelphia; Philemon; Philip; Philippians; Philippine; Philippines

Phil Doc Doctor of Philosophy

Philem Philemon

Phil Eq Phillips' Equity Reports (legal)

Phil Is. Philippine Islands

Phil LD Doctor of Lithuanian Philology (*Philologiae Lituanicae Doctor*—Latin)

Phil Soc Philological, or Philosophical, Society

Phil Trans Philosophical Transactions; the Philosophical Transactions of the Royal Society of London

Ph L Licentiate of Pharmacy

PHL Philco Corporation (NYSE)

Ph M Master of Philosophy (*Philosophiae Magister*—Latin)

Ph & M Philip and Mary (*Philippus et Maria*—Latin)

PhM1c Pharmacist's Mate First Class (US Navy)

PHMI Prefabricated Home Manufacturers Institute

PhM2c Pharmacist's Mate Second Class (US Navy)

PhM3c Pharmacist's Mate Third Class (U S Navy)

Phoenix The Phoenix and the Turtle

PhoM1c Photographer's Mate First Class (US Navy)

PhoM2c Photographer's Mate Second Class (US Navy)

PhoM3c Photographer's Mate Third Class (US Navy)

phon phonetics

phonog phonography; phonographical

phonol phonology

Phos B phosphor bronze

phot photograph; photography

PHOTO photograph (er) (ic) (y) (US Army)

photom photometrical; photometry

Phot R Photographic Reconnaissance

p h p packing-house products

php pump horse power

PHP Phillips Packing Company (NYSE)

phr phrase; phraseology

Ph R Photographic Reconnaissance

phren phrenological; phrenology

PHS Pennsylvania Historical Society; Public Health Service

Ph Soc Philological Society

PHT Page-Hersey Tubes (NYSE)

phys physical (*physique*—French); physician; physics

phys chem physical chemistry

phys geog physical geography

physiog physiography

phys sci physical science

phys & surg physician and surgeon

phytogeog phytogeography

p i paper insulated; power input

pi piaster; pie (typography)

p&i protection and indemnity (insurance)

PI Packaging Institute; Philippine Islands; photo interpreter(ation) or program of instruction (US Army); polar inductor; Polytechnic Institute; Pyrene Manufacturing Company (NYSE)

PIA Penal Industries Association; Perfumery Importers Association; Phi Iota Alpha (fraternity); Postal Inspectors' Association; Printing Industry of America

Piang piangendo (music)

pianiss very softly (*pianissimo*) (music)

PIAT Infantry Anti-Tank Projector

PIB Polytechnic Institute of Brooklyn; Publishers Information Bureau, Inc.

PIBMM Permanent International Bureau of Motor Manufacturers

pic pictor

PIC Pacific Indemnity Company (NYSE); Preserve Industry Council

PICA Permanent International Commission of Agricultural Associations

PICAO Provisional International Civil Aviation Organization

PIC Gen C Permanent International Committee for Genetics Congresses

Pick. Pickering's Massachusetts Reports (legal)

PID Political Intelligence Department; Press Intelligence Department; Public Information Division (US Army)

PID A Piedmont Hydro-Electric Company (ASE)

PIEA Petroleum Industry Electrical Association

PIKPA Patriotic Foundation of Social Welfare and Relief (Greece)

pil pill (*pilula*—Latin)

Pin. Pinney's Reports (legal)

PIN. Public Service Company of Indiana (NYSE)

pinx he painted it (*pinxit*—Latin)

PIO Pioneer Gold Mines of B. C. (NYSE); public information officer (US Army)

PION pioneer (US Army)

PIP Piper Aircraft Corporation (NYSE)

PIT Pittsburgh Screw & Bolt (NYSE); Pittsburgh Stock Exchange

p i v positive infinity variable

PIWC Petroleum Industry War Council

pix pictures (slang)

PIX Publicker Industries, Inc. (private car rr mark)

pizz *pizzicato* (music)

PJ Justice of the Peace; Physical Jerks; Police Justice; Presiding Judge; Probate Judge

P of J Princes of Jerusalem

PJN Phillips-Jones Corporation (NYSE)

PJNWIU Playthings, Jewelry and Novelty Workers International Union

PJOX O'Donnell & Sons P.J. (private car rr mark)

pk pack (wool); park; peak; peck (measure)

pK $\log \dfrac{1}{K}$

PK Park Utah Consol. Mines (NYSE); Phi Kappa (fraternity)

PKA Pi Kappa Alpha (fraternity)

PKD Pi Kappa Delta (society)

PKDOM pack for domestic use (US Army)

pkg package; parking

PKL Pi Kappa Lambda (society)

PKMR packmaster (US Army)

PKO losing by a knockout (boxing) (*perdant par knockout*—French)

PKP Pi Kappa Phi (fraternity)

PKR packer (US Army); Parker Pen Company (NYSE)

PKR A Parker Pen Co. (The) ("A" Com) (ASE)

PKR B Parker Pen Co. (The) ("B" Com. (ASE)

PKS Phi Kappa Psi (fraternity); Phi Kappa Sigma (fraternity); Pi Kappa Sigma (sorority)

PKSEA pack for overseas (US Army)

pkt packet

PKT Park & Tilford Distillers (NYSE); Phi Kappa Tau (fraternity)

pkv peak kilovolts

pky pecky (lumber)

p l partial loss (insurance); perception of light; profit and loss; public laws; public liability

pl for instance (*például*—Hungarian); place; plain; plan; plate; platoon; plural

Pl Paul

PL Bureau of Personnel (UN Secretariat) Legal Procurator; London Pharmacopoeia (*Pharmacopoeia Londinensis*—Latin); Pamphlet Laws (Pa.); partial loss (insurance); Paymaster-Lieutenant; phase line (US Army); Plimsoll Line; Poet Laureate; Poland (IDP); position line; Primrose League; proportionality limit; Lounge (rr car)

p & l profit and loss account

PLA Port of London Authority

plat platform; platoon

Plat Platonic

Plaut Plautus

PLB Poor Law Board

plbg plumbing

plbr plumber

PLC Imperial Poet Laureate (*Poeta Laureatus Caesareus*); Paymaster Lieutenant-Commander; Poor Law Commission

PLCA Producers Livestock Commission Association

p l e primary loss expectancy

(insurance)

PLE Pittsburgh & Lake Erie Railroad (NYSE)

P&LE Pittsburgh and Lake Erie Railroad Company

plen plenipotentiary

plf plaintiff

PLG Poor Law Guardian

Plin Pliny (Latin)

PLK Phi Lambda Kappa (fraternity)

PLM Paris-Lyons-Mediterranean (Coast) Railway

pl n place-name

PLO Plough, Inc (NYSE)

PLP Pi Lambda Phi (fraternity)

PLPB Petroleum Labor Policy Board

p l & p d public liability and property damage (insurance)

p l r primary loss retention (insurance)

PL&R Postal Laws and Regulations

PLS Pi Lambda Sigma (sorority); Polaris Mining Company (NYSE)

Pl Sgt Platoon Sergeant

plstr plasterer

plt plate

PLT Pacific Lighting (NYSE); Pi Lambda Theta (society)

pltf plaintiff

pltg plating

Plt Off. Pilot Officer (RAF)

plu pluperfect; plural

PLU Phi Lambda Upsilon (society)

PLUNA Primeras Lineas Uruguayas de Navigacion Aerea

PLUTO pipe-line under the ocean

PLY U.S. Plywood Corporation (NYSE)

p m molecular weight (poids moléculaire—French); pari-mutuel; permanent magnet; phase modulation; pitch mark; purchase money; premium money

P/m. put of more (stock brokerage)

Pm promethium

PM Pacific Mail; parachute mine; Past Master (freemasonry); paymaster; peculiar meter (hymns); Peninsular Metal Products (NYSE); Pere Marquette (rr); Phi Mu (sorority); Pioneer Mills Company (NYSE); of pious memory (piae memoriae—Latin); Police Magistrate; Pope and Martyr; postmaster; Pratt & Lambert, Inc (NYSE) Prime Minister; prize money; Provost Marshal; purpose-made; in remembrance (pro memoria—Latin); afternoon (post meridiem—Latin)

PMA Pencil Makers Association; Phi Mu Alpha (fraternity); Production and Marketing Administration

PMAA Paper Makers Advertising Association

PMC Permanent Mandates Commission; plaster-molded cornice (building); president of the Mess Committee

PMCC Provisional Maritime Consultative Council

PMCX Peterson Manufacturing Company, Inc. (private car rr mark)

PMD Phi Mu Delta (fraternity)

PMDA Photographic Merchandising and Distributing Association

PME Pi Mu Epsilon (society)

PMEX Petroleos Mexicanos (private car rr mark)

PMF Pew Memorial Foundation

PMIC Patternmaker First Class (US Navy)

PMFPA Picture Moulding and Framed Products Association

PMG Pall Mall Gazette; Paymaster-General; Phi Mu Gamma (Fine Arts society); Postmaster-General; Provost Marshal General

p m i point of maximal impulse

PMI Pressed Metal Institute

p min feet per minute (pieds par minute—French)

pmk postmark

pmkd postmarked

PML Pomerania Elec. Company (ASE)

PMLA Publications of the Modern Language Association

PMLNA Pattern Makers League of North America

p m m purchase money mortgage

PMMA Plastic Materials Manufacturers Association

PMMI Packaging Machinery Manufacturers Institute

PMMIA Philippine Mahogany Manufacturers Import Association

pmo very soft (music) (pianissimo—Italian)

PMO Principal Medical Officer

PMOA Prospectors and Mine Owners Association

PM & OA Printers' Managers and Overseers Ass.

PMRR Pere Marquette Railroad Company

PMS Pickle Manufacturers Society; President Miniature Society

PM2C Patternmaker Second Class (US Navy)

PMST professor of military science and tactics (US Army)

PMT payment (US Army); Pittsburgh Metallurgical Company (NYSE)

PMWA Progressive Mine Workers of America

PMWCMA Paper Mill Wire Cloth Manufacturers Association

PMX private manual exchange

p n promissory note

pn partition; plane; pneumatic

PN Pan American World Airways (NYSE)

p/n please note

PNA Pacific Northern Airlines, Inc.; Paper Napkin Association; Printers National Association

PNAUS Polish National Alliance of the United States

PNCC Polish National Catholic Church

PND Pond Creek Pocahontas Company (NYSE)

pneu pneumatic

PNEU Parents' National Educational Union

PNF Penn Traffic Company (NYSE)

p n g unwelcome person (persona non grata—Latin)

PNLO Principal Naval Liaison Officer

PNO Pennroad Company (NYSE)

pnr pioneer

PNT decimal point (US Army)

pntd painted

pntr painter

PNU Pneumatic Scale Corporation Ltd. (NYSE)

P & NW Prescott & Northwestern Railroad Company (rr mark)

pnxt he painted it (pinxit—Latin)

PNYA Port of New York Authority

p o by order (per orden—Spanish); post office [box]; power output; prepaid order; public official; put out

po inch (pouce—French); peso; pole (measure)

Po Pedro; polonium

PO The Oratorians (Prêtres de l'Oratoire—French); Pacific Ocean; Paris-Orleans (railway); Parliamentary Offices; Patent Office; Personnel Officer; Petty Officer; Pilot Officer (RAF); post office; postal order; power-operated; Principal Officer; ordinary Professor (Professor Ordinarius); Province of Ontario; Psi Omega (fraternity); Publicity Officer; Pyrénées-Orientales (French department); Combined Observation and Parlor or Sleeping (rr car)

P & O Peninsular and Oriental (Steam Navigation Company); Peninsular and Occidental (Steamship Company); pickled and oiled (steel sheets)

POB Post Office Board; Post Office Box

poc cup (poculum—Latin) (pharmacy)

p o c port of call

POCA Processing Oils and Chem-

icals Association
pol political; politician; politics
Pol Poland; Polish
POL Patent Office Library; petroleum and its products (US Army)
POLA Public Ownership League of America
pol dist political district
pol econ political economy
poll. an inch (*pollex*—Latin) (pharmacy)
POLO. Post Office Liaison Officer
poly polytechnic
Polyb Polybius
Polyn Polynesia
pom pomological
POM Potomac Electric Power (NYSE); preparation for oversea movement (US Army)
POME Principal Ordnance Mechanical Engineer
pomerid in the afternoon (*post meridianus*—Latin) (pharmacy)
pomp. pompously (*pomposo*—Latin)
pon pontoon
p 100 per cent (*pour cent*—French)
pont bishop (*pontifex*)
Pont Max Supreme Pontiff (*Pontifex Maximus*—Latin)
po nto net weight (*peso neto*—Spanish)
pontus pontificate (*pontificatus*)
POO Post Office Order, Principal Ordnance Officer
p o p printing out paper
pop. popularly; population
POP Pi Omega Pi (society)
POPA Property Owners' Protection Association
p o r payable on receipt; pay on return (express)
por compare with (*porównaj*—Polish); portion; portrait
POR Personnel Occurrence Report (RAF); preparation for oversea movement of individual replacements (US Army); Poor & Company, C I B (NYSE)
porc porcelain
port. portfolio; portrait
Port. Portugal; Portuguese
Port. (Ala) Porter's Alabama Reports (legal)
Port. Gui Portuguese Guinea
Port. Timor Portuguese Timor
po sec inches per second (*pouces par seconde*—French)
pos positive; position; possession; possessive; possibility; possible
POS Prosperity Company Inc., Class B (NYSE)
POSB Post Office Savings Bank
POS B Prosperity Co. Inc. (The) (common stock, ASE)
posth posthumous

post. rcts postal receipts
pot. potential
potass potassium
P O Tel Petty Officer Telegraphist; Post Office Telephone
£ pound (see *under* L)
pouv cal calorific power (*pouvoir calorifique*—French)
P&OV Pittsburgh & Ohio Valley Railroad Company (rr mark)
pow powder; power
POW powder (US Navy); Post Office Worker; Power Coproration of Canada (NYSE); Prince of Wales; Prisoner of War
POW I Pr Power Corp. of Canada, Ltd. (6% 1st Pfd.) (ASE)
p p losing on points (*perdant aux points*—French); parcel post; parish priest; past participle; patent pending; pellagra preventive; picked ports (shipping); placed over; planned parenthood; postage paid (*post pagado*—Spanish); postpaid by power of attorney (*frangued pagado por poder*—Spanish)
pp pages; passport; between perpendiculars (shipbuilding); prepay; prepaid; very soft (*pianissimo*—Italian) (music)
p-p peak to peak
PP Chief Shepherd (*Pastor Primarius*); Father of His Country (*Pareus* or *Pater Patriae*); Fathers (*Patres*); Most Holy (*Pūssimus*); Papa (Greek priest); Parcel Post; parish priest; Past President; Pathfinder Pilot; Petrol Point; Phi Psi (fraternity); pilotless plane; Pluvius Policy (rain insurance); Pom-Pom (gun); power plant; Public Professor (*Professor Publicus*); Pusher Plane
ppa after shaking the bottle (*phiala prius agitata*—Latin) (pharmacy); per power of attorney
PPA Paper Pail Association; Paper Plate Association; Popcorn Processors Association; Poultry Publishers Association
PPAA Cardinals (*Patres Amplissimi*—Latin)
PPAI Point of Purchase Advertising Institute
Ppb bound in paper boards (*Pappband*—German)
PPB Private Posting Box
p p c picture post card
PPC Passport Control; People's Political Council; plain plaster cornice (building); Price Purchase Commission; Printers' Pension Corporation; Provincial Police College; to take leave (*pour prendre congé*—French)
p p c m least common multiple (*plus*

petit commun multiple—French)
PPCX Perfect Packed Products Company, Inc (private car rr mark)
ppd postpaid; precipitated; prepaid
PPD Public Prosecutions Department
PPDMG Popular Priced Dress Manufacturers Group
ppdo last month (*proximo pasado*—Spanish)
PPE Pacific Petroleums (NYSE); Philosophy, Politics, Economics (Oxford University)
PPFA Planned Parenthood Federation of America
PPG Pittsburgh Plate Glass Company (NYSE)
pph pamphlet
PPHX Pepper Packing Company (private car rr mark)
p p i parcel post insured; policy proof of interest
PPI Paisley Philosophical Institute; piston position indicator; plan position indicator
PPIX Pearl Packing Company (private car rr mark)
PPL Pr Pennsylvania Pw. & Lt. Co. (4½% Pfd.) (ASE)
ppm parts per million
PPM Patchogue-Plymouth Mills (NYSE); Postage Prepaid in Money
PPMA Plastic Products Manufacturers Association; Pulp and Paper Machinery Association
ppn precipitation
PPO Principal Priority Officer; Privy Purse Office
p p p built at his own expense (*propria pecunia posuit*—Latin)
PPPX Pepin Pickling Company (private car rr mark)
p pr present participle
PPR Pepperell Manufacturing Company (NYSE)
PPRB Press and Public Relations Branch
PPS Pan American Petroleum & Transportation (NYSE); Parliamentary Private Secretary; Political Private Secretary; a second postscript (*post-postscriptum*); Principal Private Secretary
ppse purpose
PPSG Piston and Pin Standardization Group
ppt precipitate; prompt loading
ppte precipitated (*précipité*—French)
pptg precipitating
PPTL Pulp and Paper Traffic League
PPU Pacific Public Service (NYSE); Peace Pledge Union
P&PU Peoria & Pekin Union Railway (rr mark)

PPU Pr Pacific Public Service Co. ($1.30 1st Pfd.) (ASE)

PPWA Ponderosa Pine Woodwork Association

PPW Pr Pacific Pw. & Lt. Co. (5% Pfd.) (ASE)

PPWX Pacific Wholesale Poultry Company (private car rr mark)

PPX Pioneer Products Company (private car rr mark)

p q previous question

P Q Province of Quebec

PQCX Philadelphia Quartz Company of California (private car rr mark)

p r in proportion (pro rata—Latin); pitch ratio (engineering); prize ring (boxing); proportional representation

pr for (pour—French); pair; powder (gun); preferred (stock); preposition· present; pressure; price (prix— French); priest; printer; prison; prove; proud; proven; pronoun; pronounced; proper

Pr praseodymium; propyl; Provençal; Provincial; Prussian (preussisch —German)

PR Parachute Regiment; Parliamentary Reports; parcel receipt; Pattern Rooms; Pershing Rifles; Pre-Raphaelite; Procurement Regulations (US Army); Proportional Representation; Public Relations; Puerto Rico; pure rubber river gunboats (US Navy)

P/R pay roll (US Army)

p & r plugged and reamed (plumbing)

P&R Philadelphia & Reading

Pr A Edition de luxe (Prachtausgabe —German)

PRA Paymaster-Rear-Admiral; President of the Royal Academy; President's Re-employment Agreement; Public Roads Administration

pract practitioner

pral principal (principal—Spanish)

prand dinner (prandium—Latin) (pharmacy)

PRATRA Philippines Relief and Trade Rehabilitation Administration

PRB Pre-Raphaelite Brotherhood

prb priest (presbyter)

Prc Proconsul

PRC after the founding of Rome (Post Roman conditam—Latin); Price Regulation Committee; Process Corporation (NYSE)

PRCA President of the Royal Cambrian Academy

PRCHST parachutist (US Army)

PRCHT parachute (US Army)

PRCP President of the Royal College of Physicians

PRCS President of the Royal College of Surgeons

p r d pro rata distribution (insurance)

PRD Public Relations Department

Pr Dec Printed Decisions (legal)

Pr Div Probate Division (legal)

pre prefix

PRE Petroleum Refining Engineer; Prussian Elec. Company (ASE)

preb prebend; prebendary

prec preceding; precentor; preceptor

Pre Cha Precedents in Chancery (law reports)

precip precipitate

pred predicate; predicatively

pref preface; preferably; preference; preferred; prefixed

Pref Preference; Preferred (Stock Exchange)

Pref Ap Prefect Apostolic

prehist prehistoric

prelim preliminary; preliminaries

prem premier; premium

premes premises

prep preparatory; preposition

PREP prepare (US Army)

prepd prepared

prepn preparation

pres preposition; presence; present; president; presidency; presumptive

Pres Presbyter; Presbyterian; Presidency; President

Presb Presbyterian

presdl presidential

presdᵗᵉ, president—presidente (Spanish)

press. pressure

pret preterit

pre-Teut pre-Teutonic

Preuss Prussian (Preussisch— German)

prev previous

PRF Plywood Research Foundation

PRIC Parachute Rigger First Class (US Navy)

PRFX Pringle & Company Inc (private car rr mark)

PRG Phila. & Reading Coal & Iron (NYSE)

PRGR proving ground (US Army)

PRH Petrol Railhead

PRHA President of the Royal Hibernian Academy

Pri Private (soldier); Prizeman

pri prison

PRI President Royal Institute of Painters in Water Colours

PRIBA President of the Royal Institute of British Architects

prid. the day before (pridie—Latin)

prim. primary; primate; primitive

prim. luc early in the morning (prima luce—Latin) (pharmacy)

prim. m early in the morning (primo mane—Latin) (pharmacy)

prin principal; principle

print. printing

PRIS prisoner (US Army)

pris coeff prismatic coefficient

priv privative (grammar); privilege (privilegio—Spanish)

private res private resolution

Priv Doz Privatdozent (German)

priv pr privately printed

PRK Parker Rust Proof Company (NYSE)

PRKX P. & P. Car Line, Inc., The (private car rr mark)

PRL Postal Reform League

PRLO Puerto Rican Labor Office

prm premium

PRMG Piston Ring Manufacturers Group

Pr Min Prime Minister

p r n as occasion demands (pro re nota—Latin) (pharmacy)

pro professional; progressive

Pro Provost

PRO Producers Corporation of Nevada (NYSE); Public Record Office; Public Relations Officer

prob probability; probable; probably; probate; problem

Prob Probate; Probationer

Prob Div Probate Division (legal)

Prob Div Mat Probate, Divorce and Matrimonial Cases (legal)

proc proceedings; process; proclamation; proctor; procurator

PROC procure (US Army)

Proc Am Soc Int Law. Proceedings of the American Society of International Law

pro capill for the hair (pro capillis— Latin) (pharmacy)

pro & con for and against (pro et contra—Latin)

Proc Prac Proctor's Practice (legal)

prod. produce; product

prodn production

prof professed; profession

Prof Professor

Prof Eng Professional Engineer

Pr of Manasses Prayer of Manasses

Prohib Prohibitionist

PROJ projectile (US Army)

prol prologue (prólogo—Spanish)

PROLT procurement lead time (US Army)

prom promenade; promontory; promoted

PROML promulgate (US Army)

pron pronominal; pronoun; pronounced; pronunciation

pron a pronominal adjective

pro no. progressive number

prop proper; property; proposition; proprietary; proprietor

PROP property (US Army)

propl proportional

propn proportion

props. properties (theater)

prop. shaft propeller shaft

pror attorney (*procurador*—Spanish)

pros prosecutor; prosodical; prosody

PROSIG procedure signal (US Army)

PROSINE procedure sign (US Army)

prot speedily (*protinus*—Latin) (pharmacy)

Prot protected (electricity); Protestant; prototype

protec protectorate

pro tem for the time being (*pro tempore*—Latin)

Prot Episc Protestant Episcopal

prov proverb; province; provincial; provisional; provost

Prov Provencal; Proverbs; Provost

PROV provide; provisional (US Army)

prove province (*provincia*—Spanish)

prov aws provided always

Prov GD of Cers Provincial Grand Director of Ceremonies (freemasonry)

Prov GM Provincial Grand Master (freemasonry)

provo proviso

provons provisions

prox of the next month (*proximo*—Latin)

prox acc he came next (*proxime accessit*—Latin)

Prox per cent (*Prozent*—German)

pr p present participle; prior preferred

PRP Petrol Refilling Point; Production Requirements Plan

pr pr about (*praeter propter*—Latin)

PRR Parkersburg Rig & Reel Company (NYSE); Pennsylvania Railroad (rr mark)

PRRA Puerto Rico Reconstruction Administration

PRRI Puerto Rico Rum Institute

prs pairs; printers

PRS Performing Right Society; Phi Rho Sigma (fraternity); President of the Royal Society; Preston East Dome Mines (NYSE); Proportional Representation Society; Protestant Reformation Society

PRSA President of the Royal Scottish Academy; Public Relations Society of America

PRSE President of the Royal Society of Edinburgh

PR2C Parachute Rigger Second Class (US Navy)

prsfdr pressfeeder

PRSL Pennsylvania-Reading Seashore Lines

prsmn pressman

pr spec process specification

pr st private statute

PR3C Parachute Rigger Third Class (US Navy)

PRTR1C Printer First Class (US Navy)

PRTR2C Printer Second Class (US Navy)

PRTR3C Printer Third Class (US Navy)

PRU Paramount Motors Corporation (NYSE); (RAF) Photographic Reconnaissance Units

Prus Prussia; Prussian

p r v to make a call (*pour rendre visite*—French)

PRX Palomar Oil and Refining Corporation (private car rr mark)

PRY Pittsburgh Railways Company (NYSE)

p s public sale; specific weight (*poids specifique*—French)

ps pesetas; pieces; postscript (*postskriptum*—Swedish); pseudonym

Ps Pasha (*Pasa*—Turkish); Psalm(s) (Biblical)

PS horsepower (*Pferdestärke*—German); paddle steamer; Palaeontological Society; Parliamentary Secretary; passenger steamer; Pastel Society; Pennsylvania State (college); Permanent Secretary; Phi Sigma (society); Philanthropical Society; Philippine Scouts (US Army); Philological Society; Philosophical Society; Physical Sciences; Physical Society; Pneumatic System; Poetry Society; Police Sergeant; postscript (*postscriptum*—Latin); Prehistoric Society; Pressed Steel Car Company (NYSE); Priority Service; Private Secretary; Privy Seal; prompt side (theater); proof stress; Provost-Sergeant; yield limit; yield point

P/S public sale

p & s planking and strutting; port and starboard

P&S Physicians and Surgeons; Pittsburgh & Shawmut Railroad Company

Psa Piscis Australis (constellation)

PSA Graduate of Royal Air Force Staff College; Graduate of Naval Staff College, Greenwich; Pacific Science Association; Passed School of Artillery; Photographic Society of America; Pi Sigma Alpha (society); Poetry Society of America; Poultry Science Association; Psi Sigma Alpha (fraternity); Dormitory Car (rr car)

PSAC Preferred Stock Advisory Committee

PSAL Public Schools Athletic League

PSANDT Pay, Subsistence, and Transportation (US Navy)

p s c per standard compass (navigation)

Psc Pisces (constellation)

PSC Pittsburgh Steel Company (NYSE); Public Service Commission

p s & c private siding and collected one end (railway)

PSCJ Society of Priests of the Sacred Heart of Jesus

PSD Pay Supply Depot; Personal Services Department; Phi Sigma Delta (fraternity); Postal Services Department

ps & d private siding and delivered one end (railway)

PSE Phi Sigma Epsilon (fraternity); Philadelphia Stock Exchange

PSEA Pacific Service Employees' Association; Pleaters, Stitchers, and Embroiderers Association

p sec feet per second (*pieds par seconde*—French)

pseud pseudonym; pseudonymous

psf pounds per square foot

P&SF Panhandle and Santa Fe Railway Company

ps fs dollars (*pesos fuertes*—Spanish)

PSG Phi Sigma Gamma (fraternity)

psi pounds per square inch (steel bars)

PSI Phi Sigma Iota (society); Public Seating Industry

p s i a pounds per square inch absolute

p s i g pounds per square inch gauge

PSIX Public Service Company of Northern Illinois (private car rr mark)

PSK Phi Sigma Kappa (fraternity)

PSL Paymaster Sub-Lieutenant

PSLX Portsmouth Division of Detroit Steel Corporation (private car rr mark)

PSM Pennsylvania Salt Manufacturing Company (NYSE); Pious Society of Missions (Piarist Fathers)

PSMX Pennsylvania Salt Manufacturing Company (private car rr mark)

PSN position (US Army); Patterson-Sargent Company (NYSE)

PS&N Pittsburgh, Shawmut Northern Railroad Company

PSNC Pacific Steam Navigation Company

PSP patrol seaplane (US Navy); phenol-sulphone-phthalein; Phi Sigma Pi (fraternity); Puget Sound Pulp and Timber (NYSE)

p spec specific weight (*poids specifique*—French)

ps and ps private siding and private siding (railway)

PSPX Phillips Petroleum Company (private car rr mark)

PSR Pennsylvania State Reports (legal); Public Service Company of Colorado (NYSE); Public Service Reserve

PSS Phi Sigma Sigma (sorority); Priests of Saint Sulpice; Psalms (Bible)

ps to s private siding to station (railway)

PSSC Pious Society of the Missionaries of Saint Charles

PSSMA Paper Shipping Sack Manufacturers Association

PSSS Private Secretary to the Secretary of State

p st pound sterling (*pond sterling* —Dutch)

PST Pacific Standard Time; Pacific Summer Time; Permanent Secretary to the Treasury; Phelps-Stokes Trustees

PSTA Public Service Transport Association

PSTMA Paper, Stationery, and Tablet Manufacturers Association

PSTO Principal Sea Transport Officer

PSTX Puget Sound Pulp & Timber Company (private car rr mark)

PSU South Porto Rico Sugar Company (NYSE)

p suiv following page (*page suivante*—French)

psv public service vehicle

PSW Phillips Screw Company (NYSE); Psychiatric Social Worker

PSX Pierce & Stevens, Inc. (private car rr mark)

PSY Pillsbury Mills, Inc. (NYSE)

psychiat psychiatrical; psychiatry

Psych & MLJ Psychological and Medico-Legal Journal

psychol psychological; psychology

psych res psychical research

PSYWAR psychological warfare (US Army)

p t parent teacher; past tense; per truck (railway); private terms; pupil teacher

pt continue (*perstetur*—Latin) (pharmacy); part; payment; pint; point; port; portable

Pt platinum

PT Pacific Standard Time; parcel ticket (railway); Patrol Torpedo-plane (US Navy Aircraft); physical training; Post Town; Postal Telegraph; Preferential Tariffs; Primary Target (US Army); Primary Trainer (US Army Aircraft); Priority Telegram; Prohibited Telegrams; Public

Trustee; pull-through; Purity Bakeries Corporation (NYSE); with full title (*pleno titulo*—Latin); for the time being (*pro tempore* —Latin); Tourist (rr mark)

PTA Parent Teachers' Association

pt aeq equal parts (*partes aequales* —Latin) (pharmacy)

ptbl portable

ptc participating

PTC Motor Submarine Chasers (US Navy); Pacific Tin Consolidated (NYSE); Physical Training Center; Postal and Telegraphic Censorship; Postal Telegraph Cable; Postal Telegraph Code; Power Transmission Council

PTD Passenger Transport Department

ptd a pointed arch (building)

pt/destin port of destination

pt/disch port of discharge

pte side (*parte*—Spanish); (military), private

PTE Parmelee Transportation Company (NYSE)

ptg printing

Ptg Portugal; Portuguese

Ptg Std Petrograd Standard (timber)

pt hd part heard (legal)

PTI Physical Training Instructor

p tjs for always (*pour toujours*— French)

PTL Peninsular Telephone Company (NYSE)

PTL Pr Peninsular Telephone Company (ASE)

PTLX Duredo Company (private car rr mark)

PTM passenger traffic manager; phase time modulation

PTN Prentice-Hall, Inc. (NYSE)

PTO please turn over; port transportation officer (US Army); Public Trustee Office

pt pf participating preferred

PTR Philadelphia Transportation (NYSE); Potter Company

PTR1C Painter First Class (US Navy)

ptrnmkr patternmaker

PTR2C Painter Second Class (US Navy)

PTR3C Painter Third Class (US Navy)

pts parts; pints; spring (*printemps*— French)

PTS Pi Tau Sigma (society); Pittsburgh Cincinnati, Chicago and St. Louis Railroad (NYSE)

pts et pts profit and loss (*profits et pertes*—French)

PTSX Keith Railway Equipment Company (private car rr mark)

PTT Cleveland & Pittsburgh (NYSE); Mail, Telegraphs and Telephones (*Postes, Télégraphes et Téléphones*—French)

PTTS Private Telegraph and Telephone Service

ptur is preferred (*praefertus*—Latin)

ptus aforesaid (*praefatus*—Latin)

PTX Pennsylvania-Conley Tank Line (private car rr mark)

pty party; proprietary

p u plant unit

pu pickup

Pu plutonium (chemistry)

PU pregnancy urine; Princeton University; Psi Upsilon (fraternity); Pullman, Inc (NYSE); Purdue University

PUAA Public Utilities Advertising Association

pub pubic; public; publican; public(ity) or publish (US Army); publicly; publication; published; publisher; publishing

pub doc public document

public. res public resolution

Pub No. Public Number (U.S. Congress)

púbo public (*público*—Spanish)

PUC after the building of the city (*post urbem conditam*—Latin); papers under consideration; pickup car; Public Utilities Commission

Pueb Puebla

pug. pugilist

PUL Publicker Industries, Inc (NYSE)

pulv powder (*pulvis*—Latin) (pharmacy)

pulv consper dusting powder (*pulvis conspersus*—Latin) (pharmacy)

PUM President of the United Mineworkers

PUMS Permanently Unfit for Military Service

pun. puncheon

punc punctuation

PUNS Permanently Unfit for Naval Service

PUO Phi Upsilon Omicron (society); pyrexia of unknown origin (trench fever)

Pup. Puppis (constellation)

pur purchase; purchaser; purchasing; pursuit

PURAVAL purchase availability (US Army)

PURCH purchase (US Army)

purch clk purchasing clerk

pur m purchase money

pur pr purchase price

purst pursuant

PUS Parliamentary Under-Secretary; Permanent Under-Secretary; Pharmacopoeia of the

United States (pharmacy); Pilgrims of the United States; President of the United States

PUW Puget Sound Power & Light (NYSE)

p v pipe ventilated

PV Freight train (*Petite Vitesse*— French); par value; Paravane; Patrol Vessel; post village; priest vicar

Pv B Bachelor of Pedagogy

p v c polyvinyl chloride compound

p vent. Pipe ventilated (electrical engineering)

p v f d pipe or duct ventilated forced draught

p v i d pipe or duct ventilated induced draught

p & vir pure and vulcanized rubber insulation

PVO Principal Veterinary Officer

PVOX Pacific Vegetable Oil Corporation (private car rr mark)

PV-P Past Vice-President

pvt private

p v t by telegraph (*par voie telegraphique*—French)

PVU Prairie View University

PVX Pennsylvania Coal & Coke Corporation (NYSE)

PVY Providence Gas Company (NYSE)

p w packed weight; water horsepower

PW Pittsburgh & West Virginia

Railway (NYSE); prisoner of war (US Army); Publishers' Weekly

P & W Penrose & Watts' Reports (legal)

PWA Portuguese West Africa; Public Works Administration

PWAP Public Works of Art Projects

PWC Pacific War Council; Prisoners of War Convention; Public Works Commissioner

PWD Public Works Department

PWEHC Public Works Emergency Housing Corporation

PWFA Papermakers Woven Felt Association

PWG "Promoted with Glory" (Salvation Army)

PWI Prince Edward Island

P Wms Peere Williams' (legal)

PWN Pleasant Valley Wine Company (NYSE)

PWO Pacific Western Oil (NYSE); Prince of Wales' Own (West Yorkshire Regiment)

PWP Past Worthy Patriarch; Past Worthy President; Pennsylvania Water & Power (NYSE)

PWPX Prentiss Wabers Products Company (private car rr mark)

pwr power

PWR Police War Reserve

PWRCB President's War Relief Control Board

pwt pennyweight

PWT Pacific War Time

PWTMI Plastic Wall Tile Manufacturers Institute

P & WV Pittsburgh and West Virginia Railway Company (rr mark)

PWWC Post War World Council

PX please exchange; post exchange; private exchange (telephone); Union Tank Car Co. (private car rr mark)

PXN Paramount Pictures Corporation (NYSE)

pxt painted it (*pinxit*—Latin)

PXY Phoenix Hosiery Company (NYSE)

Py pyridyl

PY converted yachts (US Navy); Pine Oil Company (NYSE)

PYA Pitts., Youngs. & Ash. Railway (NYSE)

Py B Bachelor of Pedagogy

PYC converted yachts, coastal (US Navy)

PYL Pyle-National Company (NYSE)

pymt payment

PYO Plymouth Oil Company (NYSE)

pyro pyrogallic acid; pyrotechnical; pyrotechnics

pyroelec pyroelectricity

Pyr Or. Pyrénées Orientales (French Department)

Pyx Pyxis (astronomy)

PZ may you live piously (*pie zeses*—Latin)

pza piece (*pieza*—Spanish)

Q

q almost (*quasi*—Latin); farthing (*quadraus*—Latin); look, inquire (*quaere*—Latin); quarto; quart; quarterly; quarter; queen; query; question; quintal; quire

Q dissipation constant of a coil; dissipation factor of a coil; dynamic pressure; quality factor; quality rating of a resonant circuit; quantity of heat; quantity of light; Quarter-Master's Department; Quebec; Queen; Queensland; question; quetzal; Quiller- Couch; Quintus (Latin name); squalls (meterology)

qa quiescent aerial

QA Quartermaster Association

QAB Queen Anne's Bounty

QAIMNS Queen Alexandra's Imperial Military Nursing Service

qal hundredweight (*quintal*—French)

QALAS Qualified Associate of the Land Agents' Society

QAMBA American Bantam Car Company (ASE)

QAP Quanah, Acme and Pacific Railway Company (rr mark)

QAPL Queensland Airlines Proprietary Ltd.

QARNNS Queen Alexandra's Royal Naval Nursing Service

q a s quick-acting scuttle

QB quarterback; Quarter Blue; Queen's Bays; Queen's Bench; Queen's Bishop (chess); quick break (colloquial); Quiet Birdman

QBACI Quality Bakers of America Cooperatives, Inc.

QBD Queen's Bench Division

QBOT Barcelona Trac. Light & Power Company Ltd. (ASE)

q b s m who kisses your hand (*que besa su mano*—Spanish)

q b s p kissing your feet (*que besa sus pies*—Spanish)

QC Quartermaster Corps; Quebec

Central Railway (rr mark); Queens' College; Queen's Counsel

QCA Queen Charlotte Airlines Ltd

QCI Quota Club International

QC Is. Queen Charlotte Islands

qcm square centimeter

q d as if one should say (*quasi dicat*—Latin); as if it were said (*quasi dictum*—Latin); four times a day (*quarter in die*—Latin) (pharmacy); which (*quodi*—Latin)

QD quarter deck

q d a quantity discount agreement

q d D g may he be in God's keeping (*que de Dios goce*—Spanish)

q e which is (*quod est*—Latin)

QEA Qantas Empire Airways

q e d which was to be proved (*quod erat demonstrandum*—Latin) (mathematics)

q e f which was to be done (*quod erat faciendum*—Latin) q e i   which was to be discovered (*quod erat inveniendum*—Latin) (mathematics)

q e p d   deceased (*que en paz descanse*—Spanish)

q f   quick-fire; quick-firing; quick freeze

QG   Headquarters (*Quartier-Général*—French)

q h   every hour (*quaque hora*—Latin) (prescription)

Q_H   (gross or higher) calorific value; (gross or higher) heating value

QH   Queen's Hall

QHC   Queen's Honorary Chaplain

QHP   Queen's Honorary Physician

QHS   Queen's Honorary Surgeon

q i d   four times a day (*quater in die*—Latin)

QIP   rest in peace (*Quiescat in Pace*—Latin)

QKt   Queen's Knight (chess)

QKtP   Queen's Knight's Pawn (chess)

ql   as much as you please (*quantus libet*—Latin) (pharmacy); hundredweight (*quintal*—Spanish)

Q_L   (lower or net) calorific value; (lower or net) heating value

Qld   Queensland

Q L R   Quebec Law Reports

qlty   quality

qm   in what manner (*quomodo*—Latin); square meter

QM   every morning (*quaque mane*—Latin); Quartermaster; Queen's Messenger

QMC   Quartermaster Corps

QM1C   Quartermaster First Class (US Navy)

QMG   Quartermaster-General

QMGB   Quartermaster General's Branch (military)

QM Gen   Quartermaster General

qmlbt   in any manner (*quomodo libet*—Latin)

QMOP   Missouri Pacific Railroad (NYSE)

QMORC   Quartermaster Officers' Reserve Corps

Qmr   Quartermaster

QMRC   Quartermaster Reserve Corps

QMS   Quartermaster Sergeant

QM2C   Quartermaster Second Class (US Navy)

QM3C   Quartermaster Third Class (US Navy)

q n   every night (*quaque nocte*—Latin) (prescription)

q^n   question; quotation

Q^n   Queen

Qns Coll   Queen's College (Oxford, Cambridge, Belfast)

qnty   quantity

qnty   quantity

q o   quick opening (plumbing)

QO   Qualified in Ordnance (naval); Quartermaster Operations

QOCH   Queen's Own Cameron Highlanders

q p   as much as seems good (*quantum placet*—Latin) (pharmacy); quartered partition (carpentry)

QP   Queen's Pawn (chess)

q pl   as much as seems good (*quantum placet*—Latin)

qq   in the capacity of (*qualitate qua*—Latin); quartos; questions; some (*quelque*—French)

QQ   Quartermaster (at Command Headquarters)

qq ch   something (*quelque chose*—French)

qqf   sometimes (*quelquefois*—French)

qq h   every hour (*quaque hora*—Latin) (pharmacy)

qq v   which see (*quae vide*—Latin)

q r   quarry reserve

qr   farthing (*quadrans*—Latin) quarter; quire

QR   Queen's Rook (chess)

QRA   What is the name of your station? (QS)

QRB   How far approximately are you from my station? (QS)

QRC   By what private enterprise (or State Administration) are the accounts for charges for your station settled? (QS)

QRD   Where are you bound and where are you from? (QS)

QRE   What is your estimated time of arrival at...(Place)? (QS)

QRF   Are you returning to...(Place)? (QS)

QRG   Will you tell me my exact frequency (or that of...)? (QS)

QRH   Does my frequency vary? (QS)

QRI   How is the tone of my transmission? (QS)

QRK   What is the readability of my signals (or those of...)? (QS)

QRL   Are you busy? (QS)

QRM   Are you being interfered with? (QS)

QRN   Are you being troubled by static? (QS)

QRO   Shall I increase power? (QS)

qrp   queen's rook's pawn (chess)

QRQ   Shall I send faster? (QS)

QRR   Are you ready for automatic operation? (QS)

qrs   quarters; quires

QRS   Shall I send more slowly? (QS)

QRT   Shall I stop sending? (QS)

QRU   Have you anything for me? (QS)

QRV   Are you ready? (QS)

QRW   Shall I inform...that you are calling him on...kc/s (or Mc/s)? (QS)

QRX   When will you call me again? (QS)

QRY   What is my turn? (QS)

QRZ   Who is calling me? (QS)

q s   as much as suffices (*quantum sufficit*—Latin); quarter section

QS   ''Q'' Signals (a series of abbreviated radio questions and answers; Quarter Sessions; quick sweep (construction)

QSA   What is the strength of my signals (or those of...)? (QS)

QSAC   Quarter Sessions Appeal Committee (legal)

QSAM   Samson United Corporation (NYSE)

QSB   Are my signals fading? (QS)

QSC   Are you a cargo vessel? (QS)

QSD   Is my keying defective? (QS)

QSG   Shall I send...telegrams at a time? (QS)

QSJ   What is the charge to be collected per word to...including your internal telegraph charge? (QS)

QSK   Can you hear me between your signals? (QS)

QSL   Can you acknowledge receipt? (QS)

QSM   Shall I repeat the last telegram which I sent you, or some previous telegram? (QS)

QSMX   Quaker State Oil Refining Corporation (private car rr mark)

QSN   Did you hear me? (QS)

QSO   Can you communicate with... direct or by relay? (QS)

QSP   Will you relay to...free of charge? (QS)

QSQ   Have you a doctor on board or is...(name of person) on board? (QS)

qss   quadruple screw-ship

QSTG   Sterling Engine Company (NYSE)

QSU   Shall I send or reply on this frequency or on...kc/s (or Mc/s) (with emissions of class...)? (QS)

QSV   Shall I send a series of V's on this frequency (or...kc/s (or Mc/s))? (QS)

QSW   Will you send on this frequency or on...kc/s (or Mc/s) (with emissions of class...)? (QS)

QSX   Will you listen to...(call sign(s) on...kc/s (or Mc/s)? (QS)

QSY   Shall I change to transmission on another frequency? (QS)

QSZ Shall I send each word or group more than once? (QS)

q t quantity; quart; quiet (colloquial)

QTA Shall I cancel telegram number ...as if it had not been sent? (QS)

QTB Do you agree with my counting of words? (QS)

QTC How many telegrams have you to send? (QS)

qtd quartered (lumber)

qt dx double quantity (*quantitas duplex*—Latin) (pharmacy)

QTE What is my TRUE bearing from you? (QS)

QTF Will you give me the position of my station according to the bearings taken by the direction finding stations which you control? (QS)

QTG Will you send two dashes of ten seconds each followed by your call sign (repeated...times) on... kc/s (or Mc/s)? (QS)

QTH What is your position in latitude and longitude (or according to any other indication)? (QS)

QTI What is your TRUE Track? (QS)

QTJ What is your speed? (QS)

QTK What is the speed of your aircraft in relation to the surface of the earth? (QS)

QTL What is your TRUE heading (TRUE course with no wind)? (QS)

QTN At what time did you depart from...(place)? (QS)

qtnus in so far as (*quatenus*—Latin)

qto quarto

QTO Have you left dock (or port)? (QS)

QTP Are you going to enter dock (or port)? (QS)

QTQ Can you communicate with my station by means of the International Code of Signals? (QS)

QTR What is the correct time? (QS)

qtr quarter; quarterly

qtrs quarters

qts quarts

QTS Will you send your call sign for...minute(s) now (or at... hours) on...kc/s (or Mc/s) so that your frequency may be measured? (QS)

QTU What are the hours during which your station is open? (QS)

QTV Shall I stand guard for you on the frequency of...kc/s (or Mc/s) (from...to...hours)? (QS)

QTX Will you keep your station open for futher communication with me until further notice (or until... hours)? (QS)

qty quantity

qu almost (*quasi*—Latin); quart; queen

QU Queen's University (Canada)

QUA Have you news of...(call sign)? (QS)

quad quadrangle; quadrant; quadrat; quadruple; qualified

QUAD quadruplicate (US Army)

quadr quadrupled

quadrupl quadruplicate

QUAL qualify; qualification (US Army)

quan quantity

quant quantitative

quant suff sufficient quantity (*quantum sufficit*—Latin) (pharmacy)

quar quarter; quarterly

quart. quarter; quarterly

QUART Quartermaster

4tette quartette (music)

quat four (*quattuor*—Latin)

QUB Can you give me, in the following order, information concerning: visibility, height of clouds, direction and velocity of ground wind at...(place of observation)? (QS); Queen's University, Belfast

QUC What is the number (or other indication) of the last message you received from me or from...(call sign)? (QS)

QUD Have you received the urgency signal sent by...(call sign of mobile station)? (QS)

Que Quebec

Queensl Queensland

Quer Querétaro

ques question

questn question

QUF Have you received the distress signal sent by...(call sign of mobile station)? (QS)

QUG Will you be forced to alight (or land)? (QS)

QUH Will you give me the present barometric pressure at sea level? (QS)

QUI Are your navigation lights working? (QS); Queen's University of Ireland

qui he rests (*quiescit*—Latin)

quin quintuple

Quinquag Quinquagesima Sunday

5tette quintette (music)

quintupl quintuplicate

QUJ Will you indicate the TRUE course for me to steer towards you (or...) with no wind? (QS)

QUK Can you tell me the condition of the sea observed at...(place or coordinates)? (QS)

QUL Can you tell me the swell observed at...(place or coordinates)? (QS)

QUM Is the distress traffic ended? (QS)

QUN Will vessels in my immediate vicinity (or in the vicinity of... latitude...longitude) (or of...) please indicate their position, TRUE course and speed? (QS)

QUO Shall I search for...(1. Aircraft; 2. Ship; 3. Survival craft) in the vicinity of...latitude... longitude (or according to any other indication)? (QS)

quor quorum

quot daily (*quotidie*—Latin) (pharmacy); quotation; quoted; quotient

quot os as often as needed (*quoties opus sit*—Latin) (pharmacy)

QUP Will you indicate your position by...(1. Searchlight; 2. Black smoke trail; 3. Pyrotechnic lights)? (QS)

QUQ Shall I train my searchlight nearly vertical on a cloud, occulting if possible and, if your aircraft is seen, deflect the beam up wind and on the water (or land) to facilitate your landing? (QS)

QUR Have survivors...(1. Received survival equipment; 2. Been picked up by rescue vessel; 3. Been reached by ground rescue party)? (QS)

QUS Have you sighted survivors or wreckage? If so, in what position? (QS)

QUSA Aerovias "Q," (airline)

QUT Is position of incident marked? (QS)

QUU Shall I home ship or aircraft to my position? (QS)

QUV What is my MAGNETIC bearing from you (or from...)? (QS)

QUX Will you indicate the MAGNETIC course for me to steer towards you (or...) with no wind? (QS)

q v as much as you like (*quantumvis volueris*—Latin) (pharmacy); which see (*quod vide*—Latin); who lived (*qui vixit*—Latin)

QVR Queen Victoria's Rifles

qx hundredweight (*quintaux*—French)

R

r rabbi; radical; radius; railroad; railway; rain; range; rank; rare; ratio; reaction; read; recipe; rector; redacto; registered; regular; residence; resides; resistance; response; retired; rifle; right; rises; river; road; rod; rogue; rood; rotor; run; royal; radium dosage

R bill or invoice (*Rechnung*— German); gas constant; King (*Rex*); Knight (*Ridder*—Danish); Queen (*Regina*); Rabbi; Radical; radiotelegram; Réaumur (thermometer); Recto; regulating or rifle (use in combination only) (US Army); Reynold's number; Reward; Robert; Roman; Rome; Rook (chess); Rotary wing Aircraft; Roumania (IDP); Rutland Railway Corporation (rr mark); street (*Rue*—French); US Rubber Company (NYSE)

ŕ remittance (*remesa*—Spanish)

ŗ recipe (pharmacy)

ŗ (magnet) reluctance

ṛ response

ŗ rupee

ŗa radio active; reduction of area; right ascension (navigation); rapid advance

Ra radium; Rachel

ŗA Argentine Republic (*Republica Argentina*—Spanish); Ratepayers' Association; Rear Admiral; Reduction of Area; Referees' Association; Regional Association; R-Insurance Agreement; Republic Aviation Corporation (NYSE); Resettlement Administration; Right Ascension (astronomy); Road Association; Royal Academician; Royal Academy; Royal Arcanum; Royal Arch (freemasonry); Royal Artillery; Brine-Tank Refrigerator (rr cars)

R/A refer to acceptor (banking); return to author (bookselling)

ŗA(A) Rear-Admiral of Aircraft Carriers

ŗAA Railway Assessment Authority; Royal Academy of Arts; Royal Artillery Association

ŗ ac radioactinium

ŗAAF Royal Australian Air Force

ŗab rabbi; rabbinical

ŗab discount (*Rabatt*—German)

ŗAC Royal Agricultural College; Royal Arch Chapter; Royal Armoured Corps; Royal Automobile Club; Rules of the Air and Air Traffic Control (ICAO)

ŗACC Regional Agricultural Credit Corporation

RA Ch D Royal Army Chaplains' Department

RACX Railway Accessories Company (private car rr mark)

rad radiant; radio; radius; root (*radix*—Latin)

Rad Radical; Radnorshire (Wales)

RA(D) Rear-Admiral (Destroyers)

RADA Royal Academy of Dramatic Art

radar radio detection and ranging

RADAR radio detector equipment (US Army)

RADDEF radiological defense (US Army)

raddol becoming gradually softer (*raddolcendo*—Italian) (music)

RADM Rear Admiral (US Navy)

radn radian

RADO Radiological Defense Officer (US Army)

Rad Sec radio section

RADWAR radiological warfare (US Army)

RAE Royal Aircraft Establishment

RAEC Royal Army Educational Corps

ra-em radium emanation

RAe S Royal Aeronautical Society

RAF Royal Aircraft Factory; Royal Air Force

RAFES Royal Air Force Educational Service

RAFFC Royal Air Force Ferry Command

RAFO Reserve of Air Force Officers

RAFR Royal Air Force Regiment

RAFVR Royal Air Force Volunteer Reserve

RAGC Royal and Ancient Golf Club (Saint Andrews)

RAGX North Western Refrigerator Line Company (private car rr mark)

RAH Royal Albert Hall

RAHX Rohm & Haas Company (private car rr mark)

RAI Resort Airlines, Inc.

ral gradually slower (*rallentando*— Italian) (music)

RAL Robinson Airlines

rallo gradually slower (*rallentando*— Italian)

RAM Brine Tank Refrigerator, similar to "RA" but equipped with beef rails (rr cars); Ronson Art Metal Works (NYSE); Royal Academy of Music; Royal Arch Masons

RAMC Royal Army Medical Corps

ramp. rampion

RAMS right ascension mean sun (navigation)

RAN Royal Australian Navy

Rand Randolph's Reports (legal)

RAOB Royal Antediluvian Order of Buffaloes

RAOC Royal Army Ordnance Corps

RAOX Roberts & Oake, Inc. (private car rr mark)

rap. rupees, annas, pies (Indian coinage)

RAPC Royal Army Pay Corps

Rap. NY Dig. Rapalje's New York Digest (legal)

rapp reporter (*rapporteur*—French)

RAR Royal Army Reserve

R Art. Royal Artillery

RAS Railway Air Services; Resettlement Advice Service; Royal Academy of Science; Royal Aeronautical Society; Royal African Society; Royal Agricultural Society; Royal Albert School; Royal Asiatic Society; Royal Astronomical Society

RASC Royal Army Service Corps

RASO Radiological Survey Officer (US Army)

RAT Rapeseed Association Terms (grain); rations (US Army)

Ra-Th radiothorium

RATO Rocket Assisted Take-Off

R Aux A F Royal Auxiliary Air Force

RAVC Royal Army Veterinary Corps

RAWX Riverside Acid & Inhibitor Company (private car rr mark)

RAY Raybestos-Manhattan, Inc (NYSE)

r b current year (*roku bieżącego*— Polish); rough body (plumbing)

Rb rubidium

RB Rifle Brigade; road bend (US Army); Beverage, Ice, Water of Vinegar Refrigerator (rr cars)

r&b ring and ball method

RBA Railway Business Association; Roadside Business Association; Royal Society of British Artists

RBC Richman Brothers Company (NYSE); Royal British Colonial Society of Artists

RBF Race Betterment Foundation; Rockefeller Brothers Fund

RBH regimental beachhead (US Army)

rbi receipt (*recibi*—Spanish)

r b i runs batted in

RBi Reed Roller Bit Company (NYSE)

RBM Robbins Mills, Inc (NYSE)

RBNX Fruit Growers Express Company (private car rr mark)

RBR Ruberoid Company (NYSE)

RBS Royal Society of British Sculptors

rbt repayment (*remboursement*—French)

r c compression ratio; reinforced concrete; release clause; resistance-capacitance; resistance-coupled; rest camp; rest cure; right center; roller chock; rough cutting (building); round corners (bookselling)

RC Radcliffe College; Radio Corporation of America; Rationing Committee; Reconstruction Committee; Recruiting Center; Red Cross; Reformed Church; Regional Commandant (RAF); Regional Commissioner; reinforced concrete; Rent Charge; Reply Coupon; Republican Convention; Research Committee; Rescue Committee; Reserve Corps; Rho Chi (society); Rider College; Roman Catholic

R/C reconsigned recovered

r&c rail and canal

RCA Radio Corporation of America; Radio Correspondents Association; Railway Clerks' Association; Reformed Church of America; Regional Communications Adviser; Rodeo Cowboys Association; Royal Cambrian Academy; Royal Canadian Academy; Royal College of Art

RCAA Railway Car Appliances Association

RCAF Red Cross Agricultural Fund; Royal Canadian Air Foce

RCC Railway and Canal Commissioners; Red Cross Commissioner; Representative Church Council (Scotland); Roman Catholic Chaplain; Roman Catholic Church; Rural Community Council

r&cc riots and civil commotions (insurance)

rcc & s riots, civil commotions, and strikes

rcd received

RCD Solid Carbon Dioxide Refrigerator (rr cars)

RCECA Railway Car Export Corporation of America

r c g reverberation-controlled gain (circuit)

RCH Chile (IDP)

RCIA Retail Clerks International Association; Retail Credit Institute of America

RCL Raymond Concrete Pile Company (NYSE); Ruling Case Law (legal)

rc&l rail, canal, and lake

RCLM reclaim, reclamation (US Army)

RCM Radar Counter Measures; Regimental Corporal-Major; Regimental Court-Martial; Roman

Catholic Managers; Royal College of Music

RCMP Royal Canadian Mounted Police

RCN Royal Canadian Navy

RCNC Royal Corps of Naval Constructors

RCNR Royal Canadian Naval Reserve

RCO Royal College of Organists

RCOC Royal Canadian Ordnance Corps

RCP Royal College of Physicians; Royal College of Preceptors

RCPA Research Council of Problems of Alcohol

rcpt receipt

RCR Receiver of Crown Rents (Scotland); Royal Canadian Rifles

RCS Revenue Cutter Service; Royal College of Surgeons; Royal College of Science; Royal Corps of Signals

RCSB Red Cedar Shingle Bureau

RCSE Royal College of Surgeons of Edinburgh

RCS (Eng) Royal College of Surgeons of England

RCSI Royal College of Surgeons in Ireland

RCSX Railway Tank Car Service, Inc (private car rr mark)

rct receipt

RCT recruit or regimental combat team (US Army)

RCVS Royal College of Veterinary Surgeons

RCWX Royster Chemical Works (private car rr mark)

r d right door (theater); right bank (*rive droite*—French); royal decree (*real decreto*—Spanish); running days

rd reduce; road; rood; round

RD Dominican Republic (*Republic Dominicana*—Spanish); Radio Department; reaction of degeneration (medical); Refer to Drawer; Research Department; research and development (US Army); Reserve Depot; Return to Drawer; rix dollars (coinage); Roads Department; Royal Dragoons; Royal Naval; Reserve Officers' Decoration; rural dean; Rural Delivery; rural district

r&d reamed and drifted (plumbing)

RDA Reda Pump Company (NYSE); Rolling Door Association

rd-ac radioactinium

RDB Research and Development Board (US Army)

r d c running-down clause (insurance)

RDC Royal Defence Corps; Rubber Development Corporation; Rural District Council

r d f radio direction finder; repeater distribution frame

RDF radio direction finder(ing) (US Army)

rdfn radiodiffusion

rdg reading; reducing

RDG Radio Directors Guild; Reading Company (rr mark); Rose de Guerre

rd hd round head

RDI Designer for Industry Royal Society of Arts

RDL Ritter Company, Inc (NYSE)

rdm random

Rdm1C Radarman First Class (US Navy)

Rdm2C Radarman Second Class (US Navy)

Rdm3C Radarman Third Class (US Navy)

rdo radio

RDP ration distributing point (US Army); Rouge Dragon Pursuivant (Heralds' College)

RDS Royal Drawing Society; Royal Dublin Society

RDT reserve duty training (US Army)

RDV rendezvous (US Army)

RDY Royal Dockyard

r e rate of exchange; real estate; red edges; right end (football); right eye

re prescription (*récipe*—Spanish); rupee

Re rhenium

RE Railway Eq & Realty Company, Ltd (NYSE); Reconnaissance Experimental; Reformed Episcopal; Right Excellent; Royal Engineers; Royal Exchange; Royal Society of Painter-Etchers and Engravers

r/e repayable to either (banking)

REA Rice Export Association; Rubber Export Association; Rural Electrification Administration

Read. Co Reading Company

re-af re-affirmed

REAL Real S/A-Transportes Aereos (airline)

Rear Adm Rear Admiral

REB Real Estate Board

rec receipt; received; receiver; reception; recipe; record; recorder; records; recovery; recreations

REC Railway Executive Committee; receive, receiving, receipt (US Army); recreation (US Army); Redwood Export Company

recap. recapitulation

recd received

recg reciting

recip reciprocal; reciprocity

recit recitative

RECM recommend (US Army)

RECNOFF record cannot be

located in this office (US Army)

RECOG recognize (US Army)

recogs recognizances

RECOGSIG recognition signal

RECON reconnaissance; reconnoiter (US Army)

recong reconsign

RECONST reconstruction (US Army)

recr receiver

recryst recrystallize

Rec Sec Recovery Section; Recording Secretary

rect rectified

Rect receipt; rectangle; rectified; rector; rectory

red. redeemed; reduced; reducer (photography); reduction

Red. editor (*Redaktór*—Danish)

RED Radio Equipment Department (naval); Red Bank Oil Company (NYSE); Research and Experimental Department

redemon redemption

Redf Sur Redfield's Surrogate (legal)

redisc rediscount

redupl reduplicated; reduplication; reduplicative

REE Reliance Elec. & Engineering (NYSE)

REEF Barrier Reef Airways Pty. Ltd

REENL re-enlist (US Army)

REEVE Reeve Aleutian Airways, Inc

re-ex re-examined

re-exp re-export

ref refer; referee; reference; referred; reform; reformed; reformer; refraction

Ref Reformation

REF reference (US Army)

refash refashioned

Ref Ch Reformed Church

Ref E Reformed Episcopal

refer. referendum

refg refrigerated; refrigeration

Refico Reconstruction Finance Corporation

refl reflection; reflective; reflectively; reflex; reflexively

Ref Lib Reference Library

ref mp referred mean pressure

REFORMA Aerovias Reforma (airlines)

Ref Pres Reformed Presbyterian

REFRG refrigerate (US Army)

refrig refrigerating; refrigeration

Ref Sp reformed spelling

reg regiment; region; register; registered; registrar; registry; regius; regular; regulation

Reg Regent; Reginald; Queen (*Regina*—Latin)

REG regulate (US Army)

Reg App Registration Appeals

Reg Bd Regional Board

Reg Brev Register of Writs

Reg Cas Registration Cases (legal)

regd registered

Reg-Gen Registrar-General

regl regimental

Reg Prof Regius Professor

Reg US Pat Off All Rts Res registered at U.S. Patent Office, all rights reserved

REHAB rehabilitation (US Army)

REIMB reimburse (US Army)

re-imp re-import

REINF reinforce (US Army)

REJD rejoined (US Army)

rel released; relating; relative; relatively; religion; religious; bound (of books) (*relié*); reluctance; remains (*reliquiae*)

REL relief, relieve (US Army)

rel pron relative pronoun

rem remainder; remark; remittance (*remise*—French)

Rem remittance (*Remesse*—German)

REMA Refrigeration Equipment Manufacturers Association

rembt reimbursement (*remboursement*—French)

REME Royal Electrical and Mechanical Engineers

remr remainder

remun remuneration

Ren Renaissance

Reneg Bd Renegotiation Board

Renf Renfrew (Scotland)

R Eng Royal Engineers

rep repeat; report; reporter; representative; republic; roentgen equivalent physical

Rep Republic; Republican

REP repair (US Army)

REPCAT report corrective action taken (US Army)

Rep Const Ct Reports of the Constitutional Court (legal)

repet let it be repeated (*repetatur*—Latin) (pharmacy)

REPHONE reference telephone conversation (US Army)

REPL replace (US Army)

repr represent; representative; represented; representing; reprinted

REPRO reproduction (US Army)

REPT report (US Army)

req request; require; requisition

requons requisitions (legal)

RER Railway Equipment Register

res resawed (lumber); research; reserve; residence; residue; resigned; resistance; resolution; resort

RES Reliable Stores Corporation (NYSE); reserve(ation) (US Army); reticulo-endothelial system (medicine); Royal Empire Society

RESC rescind, rescission (US Army)

rès des mat. material resistance (*résistance des (matériaux*—French)

resis resistance (naval engineering)

RESMA Railway Electric Supply Manufacturers Association

resp reply (*respuesta*—Spanish); respecting; respective (*respektio*—German); respiration; respirator; respond; respondent

Res Phys resident physician

resply respectively

respt respondent

rest. restored

restr restaurant

RESUP resupply (US Army)

resurr resurrection

Resz stock company (*Reszvenytarsasag*—Hungarian)

ret retain; retard; retired; return

Ret Reticulum (constellation)

RET retire (US Army)

retel referring to telegram

R et I King and Emperor (*Rex et Imperator*—Latin); Queen and Empress (*Regina et Imperatrix*)

retnr retainer

retrog retrogressive

rev revenue; reverse; review; revise; revision; revolving; revolution

Rev Revelation (Bible); Reverend

Rev A/c revenue account

revocon revocation

revon reversion

Revs plural of Rev

revs per min revolutions per minute

Rev St Revised Statutes

Rev Ver Revised version (Bible)

REWA Refrigeration Equipment Wholesalers Association

REX Railway Express Agency, Inc (private car rr mark); Rexall Drugs, Inc (NYSE)

r f radio frequency; range finder; rapid fire; rate free; refunding (stock exchange); rent free; right field (baseball); rough finish

RF French Republic (*République Française*); King of the Franks (*Rex Franconum*); Representative Fraction; Reserve Forces; Rockefeller Foundation

R F radiofrequency

RFA Radio Frequency Amplifier; Religious Films Association; Royal Field Artillery; Royal Fleet Auxiliary (naval)

RFC Radio Frequency Choke; Reconstruction Finance Corporation; Regional Fuel Controller; Royal Flying Corps (now RAF); Rugby Football Club

RFCMC Reconstruction Finance

Corporation Mortgage Company
RFD rural free delivery
rfg refunding; roofing
RFI ready for issue (US Army)
Rfn Rifleman
r f p retired on full pay
RFP Richmond, Fredericksburg & Potomac Railroad Company (rr mark)
RF&P Richmond, Fredericksburg and Potomac Railroad Company
RFPSG Royal Faculty of Physicians and Surgeons (Glasgow)
rfrs roofers
RFS Registrar of Friendly Societies; render, float, and set (building)
RFTEA Railway Fuel and Traveling Engineers Association
RFTY reformatory (US Army)
R Fus Royal Fusiliers
r f w reserve feed water
RFWASL Raw Fur and Wool Association of St. Louis
rfz with more emphasis (*rinforzando*—Italian) (music)
r g reduction gear; right guard
RGA Royal Garrison Artillery; Guernsey Artillery
RGB river gunboat
rg/e red under gold edges
RGG Royal Grenadier Guards
rglm regular (*regelmässig*—German)
RGS Rochester Gas & Electric (NYSE); Royal Geographical Society
RGS F Pr Rochester Gas & Elec. Corp. (4% "F" Pfd.) (ASE)
rgt regiment
RGV Rio Grande Valley Gas Company (NYSE)
r h relative humidity; right hand
Rh rhodium
RH Rhesus (blood factor); road haulage; Royal Highlanders; Royal Highness
RHA Royal Hibernian Academy; Royal Horse Artillery
rhap rhapsody
r h b right half back (football)
RHBX The R. H. Bogle Company (private car rr mark)
rhd railhead
RHE Rheem Manufacturing Company (NYSE)
rheo rheostat
rhet rhetoric; rhetorical
RHG Royal Horse Guards
rhinol rhinological
R Hist S Royal Historical Society
RHMS Royal Hibernian Military School
RHO Regional Hospital Officer
Rho Rhodesia
RHP Rath Packing Company (NYSE)
r h p c rapid hardening Portland cement

RHS Royal Historical Society; Royal Horticultural Society; Royal Humane Society
RHSMA Rubber Heel and Sole Manufacturers Association
r i repulsion - induction (motor)
RI Chicago, Rock Island & Pacific Railroad (NYSE); King Emperor (*Rex Imperator*—Latin); Queen Empress (*Regina Imperatrix*—Latin); Regimental Institute; Re-Insurance; repulsion induction (motor); Rhode Island; Rice Institute; Rotary International; Royal Institute of Painters in Water Colours; Royal Institution
RIA Railroad Insurance Association; Royal Irish Academy
RIAF Royal Iraqi Air Force
RIAM Royal Irish Academy of Music
RIASC Royal Indian Army Service Corps
RIB. Railway Information Bureau; Rural Industries Bureau
RIBA Royal Institute of British Architects
RIBS Royal Institute of British Sculptors
Ric Richard (*Ricardus*—Latin)
RIC Regolamento Internazionale Carozze (International Carriage and Van Union); Royal Irish Constabulary
Rich. Richard
Rich. Eq Richardson's South Carolina Equity Reports (legal)
Rich. II The Life and Death of King Richard II
Rich. III The Life and Death of King Richard III
RID Radio Intelligence Division
r i e retirement income endowment (insurance)
RIEC Royal Indian Engineering College
RIIA Royal Institute of International Affairs
RILEM International Conference of Research and Testing Laboratories for Materials and Structures
RIM. Royal Indian Marines
RIMS. Rockefeller Institute for Medical Research
RIN Royal Indian Navy
rinf gradually increasing the tone (*rinforzando*—Italian) (music)
rip. ripped (lumber); supplementary (*ripieno*—Italian)
RIP may he rest in peace (*requiescat in pace*—Latin)
RIR Rhode Island Red (poultry)
RIS Reis (Robert) & Company (NYSE); (Republik Indonesia Serikat) Republic of the United States of Indonesia; Rhode Island

State (college)
RISA Railway and Industrial Spring Association
rit gradually slower (*ritardando*—Italian) (music)
r i t refining in transit
RIT Rochester Institute Technology
riten slower (*ritenuto*—Italian) (music)
riv river; rivet
RIV Regolamento Internazionale Veicoli (International Wagon Union); Riverside Metal (NYSE)
RJ Reynolds (R. J.) Tobacco Company (NYSE); road junction (US Army)
RJA Royal Jersey Artillery
RJAX Allison Company, R. J., (private car rr mark)
RJLI Royal Jersey Light Infantry
RJM Royal Jersey Militia
RJRX Roesling and Company (private car rr mark)
r k rolling keel or fin
rk asph rock asphalt
RKG Rockingham Railroad Company (rr mark)
RKL Rickel (H. W.) & Company (NYSE)
RKO Radio-Keith-Orpheum
RKP RKO Pictures Corporation (NYSE)
RKT rocket (US Army)
RKTR rocketeer (US Army)
r k v a kilovar; reactive kilovolt-ampere
r l random lengths; restaurant license (liquor)
RL Lebanon (IDP); Reconstruction Loans; Reference Library; Richfield Oil Corporation (NYSE); Riding Lights; rocket launcher (US Army)
r & l rail and lake; right and left
r/l radiolocation (radar)
RLEA Railway Labor Executives Association
RLH rush like hell (colloquial)
RLM Reynolds Metals Company (NYSE)
RLO Railway Liaison Officer; Regional Liaison Officer; Returned Letter Office; Royalite Oil Company (NYSE)
rl & r rail, lake, and rail
RLS Reich Labour Service; Returned Letter Section; Robert Louis Stevenson
RLWA Rice Leaders of the World Association
rly railway
r m molecular refraction (*réfraction moléculaire*—French); ring micrometer
rm ream; room

RM German currency (*Reichsmarks—* German); Resident Magistrate; Royal Mail; Royal Marines

RMA Radio Manufacturers Association; Railway Mail Association; Rice Millers Association; Robert Morris Associates; Royal Marine Artillery; Royal Military Academy; Royal Military, or Marine, Asylum; Rubber Manufacturers Association

RMC regulated motor carriers; Reliance Manufacturing Company (NYSE); Royal Military College

RM Ch R. M. Charlton's Reports (legal)

R Met S Royal Meteorological Society

RMFA Retail Manufacturing Furriers of America

RM1C Radioman First Class (US Navy)

r m l rifled muzzle-loading

RMLI Royal Marine Light Infantry

RMM Religious Missionaries of Marianhill

RMMEA Rolling Mill Machinery and Equipment Association

RMNC Raw Materials National Council

RMO Radio Material Officer (US Navy); Royal Marine Office

RMP Royal Marine Police

RMR Royal Montreal Regiment

rms rooms

RMS Railway Mail Service; root mean square; Royal Mail Steamer; Royal Meteorological Society; Royal Microscopical Society; Royal Society of Miniature Painters

RM2C Radioman Second Class (US Navy)

RMSM Royal Military School of Music

RMSP Royal Mail Steam Packet

RM3C Radioman Third Class (US Navy)

RMWAA Roadmasters and Maintenance of Way Association of America

r n normal water surface (*retenue normale*—French)

Rn radon

RN Registered Nurse; Royal Navy; Ryan Aeronautical Company (NYSE)

RN of A Royal Neighbors of America

RNAAF Royal Norwegian Army and Air Force

RNAD Royal Navy Air Division

RNAF Royal Naval Air Force (now the Fleet Air Arm); Royal Norwegian Air Force

RNAS Royal Naval Air Service

RNAV Royal Naval Artillery Volunteers

RNB Royal Naval Barracks

RNC Republican National Committee; Royal Naval College

rnd round

RND Royal Naval Division

RNEIAF Royal Netherlands East Indies Air Force

RNEIN Royal Netherlands East Indies Navy

RNGW Rural Natural Gas Company (private car rr marks)

RNLI Royal National Lifeboat Institution

RNN Royal Norwegian Navy

RNNAS Royal Netherlands Naval Air Service

RNO Knight of the Order of the Pole Star (*Riddare of Nordstjerne Orden*—Swedish); Roan Antelope Copper Mines (NYSE)

RNP Rassemblement National Populaire (French)

RNPS Royal Naval Patrol Service

RNR Rayonier Incorporated (NYSE); Royal Naval Reserve

RNSC Royal Naval Staff College

RNS of M Royal Naval School of Mines

RNSR Royal Nova Scotia Regiment

RNSX Rausch Naval Stores, Company, Inc (private car rr mark)

RNVR Royal Naval Volunteer Reserve

RNVSR Royal Naval Volunteer Supplementary Reserve

RNWAR Royal Naval Wireless Auxiliary Reserve

RNWC Royal Naval War College

RNWMP Royal Northwest Mounted Police

RNWX Rainey Wood Coke Company (private car rr mark); Wood Steel Company, Alan (private car rr mark)

RNZAF Royal New Zealand Air Force

RNZN Royal New Zealand Navy

r o religious order; royal octavo

ro on the right-hand page (recto— Latin); road; rood; rough (building)

RO Receiving Office; Receiving Order; Record Office; Recruiting Officer; Reedham Orphanage; Regional Officer; Regulating Officer; Relieving Officer; Reserved Occupation; Returning Officer; Rodent Operative; Routine Order; Royal Observatory

r & o rail and ocean

R of O Reserve of Officers

ROA Railroad Owners Association

ROAUS Reserve Officers Association of the United States

r o b remain on board; ring oil bearing

Rob. Robert; Robinson's Reports (legal)

ROB Roos Brothers, Inc (NYSE)

Rob. La Robinson's Louisiana Reports (legal)

ROC Royal Observer Corps; Russian Orthodox Church

ROCA Rock and Ore Crusher Association

ROE Roeser & Pendleton, Inc (NYSE)

Roe Roven (France)

roentgenol roentgenology

ROF Robertshaw-Fulton Controls (NYSE); Royal Ordnance Factory

Roffen of Rochester

r o g receipt of goods

Rog Roger

ROG Royal Observatory, Greenwich

ROH Rohm & Haas Company (NYSE)

ROI Rosin Oil Institute; Royal Institute of Oil Painters

ROK Republic of Korea

Rol Roland

ROLFOR Patrol Force (US Navy)

r o m run of mine

rom change to roman letters (proofreading); romantic

Rom Roman; Romance; Romania; Romanian; Romans (Bible)

ROM Rome Cable Corporation (NYSE)

Roma Roman (*Romana*)

Romanes Romanesque

Rom Cath Roman Catholic

Rom & Jul Romeo and Juliet

RON Squadron (US Navy)

röntgenol röntgenological

ROO Railhead Ordnance Officer; Reserve of Officers

r o p run of paper (advertising)

ROP Russian Oil Products

r o r d return on receipt of documents

RORX Radio Oil Refineries, Ltd (private car rr mark)

Ros Roscommon

ROS Royal Order of Scotland

ROSC Reserve Officers' Sanitary Corps

Ross. Ross & Cromarty

rot. rotating; rotation

ROTC Reserve Officers Training Corps

rotn no. rotation number

Roum Roumania; Roumanian

r o w right of way

ROW Rowe Corporation (The) (NYSE)

ROW & PF Rake out, wedge, and point flashings (building)

ROX Richfield Oil Corporation (private car rr mark)

Rox Roxburgh

roy royal
ROY Rotary Electric Steel Company (NYSE)
r p rates of postage; regulating point; reply paid; reply prepaid; rescue party; reserve party; resident physicians; return premium (insurance); rider plate
rp reprint; republic (*republica*—Latin)
RP Radio Paris; Refilling Point; Reformed Presbyterian; Regimental Police; Regius Professor; regulating point (ground) (US Army); Reverend Father (*Révérend Père*—French) (*Reverendus Pater*—Latin); Robot Plane; Rotor Planes; Royal Society of Portrait Painters; Rules of Procedure (RAF); Mechanical Refrigerator (rr cars)
r-p reprinting
RPC Ralston Purina Company (NYSE); reply post card; Republican Party Conference
RPCX Robeson Process Company (private car rr mark)
RPD Recorded Programme Department (BBC); Regional Port Director; Regius Professor of Divinity; Doctor of political Science (*Rerum Politicarum Doctor*—Latin); Royal Parks Division
RPE Reformed Protestant Episcopal
rpf reichspfennig
RPF Rassemblement du Peuple Français (France)
rpgpm rounds per gun per minute
rp/h repairs, heavy
RPHX Roth Packing Company (private car rr mark)
RPI Rensselaer Polytechnic Institute
R of PICC Rules of Practise of Interstate Commerce Commission
rp/l repairs, light
rpm revolutions per minute
RPNC Republican Party National Convention
RPO railway post office
RPP reply paid postcard
RPRX Rath Packing Company (private car rr mark)
rps revolutions per second
RPS Royal Photographic Society
rpt report
RPT repeat (US Army); Republic Pictures Corporation (NYSE)
rptd repeated; reported; ruptured
RPTMC Rain Pipe and Trough Manufacturers Council
RPWAC Republican Post-War Advisory Council
RPWPA Republican Post-War Policy Association
RPWPDA Retail Paint and Wall

Paper Distributors of America
r q respiratory quotient
RQMS Regimental Quartermaster-Sergeant
RQMT requirement (US Army)
RQN requisition (US Army)
RQST request (US Army)
RQSTAD request advice to (US Army)
RQSTAUREQ request authority to requisition (US Army)
RQSTAUTH request authority (US Army)
RQSTCAN request cancellation (US Army)
RQSTFOLINFO request following information be forwarded this office (US Army)
RQSTSI request shipping instructions (US Army)
RQTRAC request tracer be initiated (US Army)
r r with all reserve (*reservatis reservandis*—Latin)
rr railroad; railway; rear; very rarely (*rarissime*—Latin)
RR Radio Research; Railroad; Raritan River; Rail Road Company (private car rr mark); Relative Rank; Remington Rand, Inc (NYSE); Right Reverend; Rights Reserved; Road Research; Rolls Royce; rural route
RRA Retraining and Re-employment Administration; Rubber Reclaimers Association
RRB Railroad Retirement Board
RRC regular route carrier; Royal Red Cross; Rubber Reserve Company
RRCC Reduced Rate Contribution Clause (insurance)
RRD Richmond Radiator Company (NYSE)
RRI Risk Research Institute
RRL regimental reserve line (US Army)
RRO Rolls-Royce, Ltd. (ASE)
RROTC Executive for Reserve and ROTC Affairs (US Army)
RRPM Representatives of Radio Parts Manufacturers
RRPP Reverend Fathers (*Révérends Pères*—French)
RRPWPA Regional Republican Post-War Policy Association
r s right side; specific resistance (*résistance spécifique*—French)
rs reis (former coinage of Brazil and Portugal); rupees
RS Radical Socialists (*Radicaux Socialistes*—French); Radiotelegram Service; Railex Service (GPO); Ray Society; reception station (US Army); Recording

Secretary; Recruiting Service; Republic Steel Corporation (NYSE); Revised Statutes (legal); road space (US Army); Roberval and Saguenay Railway Company (rr mark); Rolls Series; Rosicrucian Society; Royal Scorpion (sobriquet for Gibraltar-born); Royal Scots; Royal Society; Royal Standard; Rural Society; Russia Society; Bunker Refrigerator (rr car)
R/S report of survey (US Army)
RSA Redwood Shingle Association; Reynolds Spring Company (NYSE); Royal Scottish Academy or Academician; Royal Society of Antiquarians
RSAAF Royal South African Air Force
RSAF Royal Small Arms Factories
RSAI Royal Society of Antiquaries of Ireland
RS Arts Royal Society of Arts
RSBA Rail Steel Bar Association
RSC Railways Staff Conference; Raise the Standard Campaign; Road Safety Committee; Rules of the Supreme Court (legal)
RSCJ Religious of the Most Sacred Heart of Jesus (*Religiosa Sacratissimi Cordis Jesu*—Latin)
RSCX Republic Steel Corporation (private car rr mark)
RSD Royal Society of Dublin
r sdg rustic siding (lumber)
RSE Richmond Stock Exchange; Royal Society of Edinburgh
RSES Refrigeration Service Engineers Society
RSF Religious Society of Friends; Rough sunk face (building); Royal Scots Fusiliers; Russell Sage Foundation
RSFSR Russian Socialist Federated Soviet Republic
RSGD resigned (US Army)
RSGMR Registered Sporting Goods Manufacturers Representatives
RSH Regal Shoe Company (NYSE); Religious of the Sacred Heart
RSI Royal Sanitary Institute
R Sigs Royal Corps of Signals
r s j rolled steel joist (building)
RSK Russeks Fifth Avenue, Inc (NYSE)
RSL Royal Society of Literature; Royal Society of London
RSM Regimental Sergeant-Major; Royal School of Mines; Royal Scottish Museum; Royal Society of Medicine; San Marino (IDP); Bunker Refrigerator, similar to "RS" but equipped with beef rails (rr car)
R & SM Royal and Select Masters
RSMA Railway Supply Manufacturers Association

RSNA Royal Society of Northern Antiquaries

RSNT Railway Staff National Tribunal

RSO Railway sub-Office; Railway Sorting Office; Recruiting Staff Officer; Resident Surgical Officer

RSOA Railroad Security Owners Association

RSPCA Royal Society for the Prevention of Cruelty to Animals

RSQ rescue (US Army)

RSS Fellow of the Royal Society (*Regiae Societatis Sodalis—* Latin); Royal Statistical Society; Royal Stuart Society

Rss Russian (*Russe—*French)

R Suss R Royal Sussex Regiment

RSVP please reply (*Répondez s'il vous plaît—* French)

RSW Royal Scottish Watercolour Society

r s w c right side up with care

RSX Richter Sons Company (private car rr mark)

r t radio-telegraphy; radio-telephony; reading time; return ticket; right tackle (football); round trip

RT Received Text (Bible); reduction table(s) (US Army); Reuter's Trust; River Terminal Railway Company (rr mark); Rye Terms

r & t rail and truck

RTA Railway Tie Association; Reciprocal Trade Agreements; Regional Technical Adviser; Rescue Tug Auxiliary; Road Traffic Act

rt angle right angle

RTANY Rubber Trade Association of New York

RTC replacement training center (US Army); Reserve Training Corps; Royal Tank Corps

RTCX Republic Tank Car Company (private car rr mark)

RTDAI Retail Tobacco Dealers of America, Inc.

rte route

RT1C Radio Technician First Class (US Navy)

RTH RKO Theatres Corporation (NYSE)

Rt Hon Right Honorable

RTI Round Table International; Royal Typewriter Company, Inc. (NYSE)

rt m magnetic bearing (*relèvement magnétique—*French)

RTMA Radio-Television Manufacturers Association; Ring Traveler Manufacturers Association

RTN Raytheon Manufacturing Company (NYSE); return (US Army)

RTO Railway Transportation Office(r) (US Army)

RTR Royal Tank Regiment

Rt Rev Right Reverend

rts rights

RTS Religious Tract Society; Return to Sender; Royal Toxophilite Society

RT2C Radio Technician Second Class (US Navy)

RTTAA Railway Telegraph and Telephone Appliance Association

RT3C Radio Technician Third Class (US Navy)

rtty radio-teletype

RTU Reading Tube (common stock, NYSE)

RTUB Reading Tube Corp. (Class "B") (ASE)

Rt W Right Worshipful

RTYC Royal Thames Yacht Club

Ru Runic; ruthenium

RU Railway Underwriters (insurance); Rugby Union; Rutgers University

rub. red (*ruber—*Latin)

Rud Rudolph

r u e right upper entrance

RUI Royal University of Ireland

Rum. Rumania; Rumanian

Rup Rupert

RUP Ruppert (Jacob) (NYSE)

rur rural

RUR "Rossum's Universal Robots" (theatrical); Royal Ulster Rifles

RUSI Royal United Service Institution

RUSM Royal United Service Museum

RUSMAT Russian Govt. (Imperial) (ASE)

RUS Mus Royal United Service Museum

RUSNO Resident United States Naval Officer at—(US Navy)

russ russia (leather)

Russ Russia; Russian

RUSX Resinera Uruapan, South America (private car rr mark)

Rut. Rutland Railroad Company

Ruth Ruthenia

Rutl Rutlandshire (county of England)

RV Rahway Valley Railroad (rr mark); Rendezvous; Revised Version (Bible); Rifle Volunteers

r v a reactive volt ampere

Rva madam (*Rouva—*Finnish)

RVA Regular Veterans Association

RVB Revere Copper & Brass, Inc (NYSE)

RVC Rifle Volunteer Corps; Royal Victorian Chain

RVCI Royal Veterinary College of Ireland

RVF Roosevelt Field, Inc (NYSE)

RVO Royal Victorian Order

RVS Reeves Brothers, Inc (NYSE)

RVSVP please reply at once (*Répondez vite, s'il vous plaît—* French)

RVW River Raisin Paper Company (NYSE)

RVW Assn Regular Veterans Women's Association

r w random widths

rw railway

RW rail-water (US Army); Rice-Stix, Inc (NYSE); Right of Way; Right Worshipful; Right Worthy; Royal Warrant; Royal Warwickshire Regiment

r & w rail and water

RWA Member of Royal West of England Academy

R War R Royal Warwickshire Regiment

r w b rear wheel brakes

RWDGM Right Worshipful Deputy Grand Master (freemasonry)

RWDSU Retail, Wholesale, and Department Store Union

RWF(us) Royal Welch Fusiliers

RWGM Right Worshipful Grand Master (freemasonry)

RWGR Right Worthy Grand Representative (freemasonry)

RWGS Right Worthy Grand Secretary (freemasonry)

RWGT Right Worthy Grand Templar (freemasonry); Right Worthy Grand Treasurer (freemasonry)

RWGW Right Worthy Grand Warden (freemasonry)

RWJGW Right Worthy Junior Grand Warden (freemasonry)

RWK Royal West Kent (Regiment)

RWMA Resistance Welders Manufacturers Association

RWO Knight of the Order of the Order of Vasa (*Riddare af Wasa Order—*Swedish)

r w p rain water pipe

RWR rail-water-rail (US Army)

RWS Royal Society of Painters in Water Colours

RWSGW Right Worshipful Senior Grand Warden (freemasonry)

r w t h raised watertight hatch

r w t m h raised watertight manhole

rwy railway

Rx recipe; tens of rupees

rx rix-dollar

RY Reo Motors, Inc (NYSE); Rogue's Yarn (colored jute in ship's rope)

RYA Railroad Yardmasters of America

RYGD railway grand division (US Army)

RYH Ryerson & Haynes, Inc (NYSE)

RYN Ryan Consolidated Petroleum (NYSE)

RYNAI Railroad Yardmasters of North America, Inc
RYPG Rayon Yarn Producers Group

RYS Railway & Light Securities (NYSE); Royal Yacht Squadron
Ry Tel Railway Telegraph
RYU Railway & Util. Invest. Corp.

("A") (common stock, ASE)
R Z Régiment de Zouaves
RZSI Royal Zoological Society of Ireland

S

s buried (*sepulture*—Latin); century (*siècle*—French); half (*semi*—Latin); label (*signa*—Latin); left hand (*sinistra*) (music); page (*sahifa*—Turkish, *sida*—Swedish, *Seite*—German); sacral (anatomy); sacrum; school; scribe; second; section; see (of bishop); shilling (*solidus*—Latin); silver; sign; signed (*signé*—French); singular; snow; solo; son; soprano; southern; spherical; squadron; steamer; steel; stem; stocks; stratus cloud (meteorology); substantive; succeeded; suit; to be taken (*sumendus*—Latin) (pharmacy); super

S current density; page (*Seite*—German); Sabbath; Sailing Ship; Saint (*Sankt*—German); Saturday; Saxon; Scalar Scot; Scottish; Sears, Roebuck & Company (NYSE); Secretary; Senate (*Senatus*—Latin); Señor; sharpshooter or south(ern) (US Army); Signor; Socialist; Society; South (*Süd*—German); Southern; Spurius (Latin name); Statutes; Sun; Sunday; Sweden; sulphur

s/ over your or above your (*sobre su*—Spanish)

s a according to art (*secundum artem*—Latin); safe arrival; semi-annual; small arms; special agent; subject to approval; undated (*sine anno*—Latin); under the year (*sub anno*—Latin); see also (*siehe auch*—German)

Sa Sable (heraldry); Saturday; samarium

SA corporation (*Sociedad Anónima*—Spanish, *Sociedade Anonima*—Portuguese, *Società Anonima*—Italian, *Societate Anonima*—Rumanian, *Société Anonyme*—French); His or Her Highness (*Son Altesse*—French); Franciscans of the Atonement (*Societas Adunatonis*—Latin); Salvation Army; Savannah and Atlanta Railway Company (rr mark); Savings Association; Secretary of the Army (US Army); sex appeal (colloquial); Shops Act; Small Arms; Society of Antiquaries; Society of Apothecaries; South Africa; South African Airways;

South Australia; Southern Association (baseball); Storm Troop (*Sturm abteilung*—German); Supply Assistant; Third Order of St. Francis; Stock Car (rr car); South America

s/a subject to approval

s a a small arms ammunition

SAA Salvation Army Adjutant; Senior Assistant Architect; Shop Assistants Association; Small Arms Ammunition; Society for Applied Anthropology; South African Airways; Speech Association of America; Surety Association of America

SAAA Scottish Amateur Athletic Association; Southwestern Association of Advertising Agencies

SAAC Scientific Adviser to the Army Council

SAAD Small Arms Ammunition Depot

SAAF South African Air Force

SAAMI Sporting Arms and Ammunition Manufacturers Institute

Sab Saturday (*Sábado*—Spanish); Sabbath

SAB Science Advisory Board; Société Anonyme Belge d'Exploitation de la Navigation Aérienne; Society of American Bacteriologists

SABC South African Broadcasting Corporation

SABENA Société Anonyme Belge d'exploitation de la Navigation Aérienne

SAC School of Army Co-operation (RAF); Scientific Advisory Committee; Scottish Automobile Club; South Atlantic Coast; State Agricultural College; Strategic Air Command

S Acc limited partnership (*Società Accomandita*—Italian)

sacch sugar-coated (*saccharatae*—Latin) (pharmacy)

SACEUR Supreme Allied Commander Europe

SACX Columbia-Southern Chemical Corporation (private car rr mark); Southern Alkali (private car rr mark)

SADF South African Defence Forces

SADG Société des Architectes Diplômés par le Gouvernement

S Ad O Station Administrative Office (RAF)

SAE Sigma Alpha Epsilon (fratern-

ity); Society of American Etchers; Society of Automobile Engineers; Society of Automotive Engineers

saec century (*saeculum*—Latin)

SAF Sapphire Petroleums Limited (ASE); Society of American Foresters; Strategic Air Force

SAFE Braathens South-American & Far East Air-transport

SAFOH Society of American Florists and Ornamental Horticulturists

S Afr South Africa

S Afr D South African Dutch

SAG Screen Actors Guild; Stammerers Advisory Guild

SAH Supreme Allied Headquarters

SAHSA Servicio Aereo de Honduras, South America

SAI His Imperial Highness (*Son Altesse Impériale*—French); incorporated company (*Società Anonima Italiana*—Italian); senior army instructor (US Army); Sigma Alpha Iota (music society); Socialist Workers' Party (*Sozialistische Arbeiterpartei*—German); Southeast Asia Institute; Survey Associates, Inc

SAIE Services Aeriens Internationaux d'Egypte

SAIF South African Industrial Federation

SAJ St. Joseph Light & Power (NYSE)

Sal El Salvador

SAL Seaboard Air Line Railway Company; Sons of the American Legion

Salk Salkeld (Law Reports)

Salop Shropshire (county of England)

SALP South African Labor Party

SALR South Australian Law Reports (legal)

salri salutary (*salutari*—Latin)

SAL Ry Seaboard Air Line Railway

Salv Salvador

SALV salvage (US Army)

I Sam. I Samuel (Bible)

II Sam. II Samuel (Bible)

Sam. Samaria; Samaritan; Samoa, Samuel (Bible)

S Am. South America; South American

SAM Sigma Alpha Mu (fraternity); Society for the Advancement of Management; Society of American Magicians; surface to air missile (US Army)

SAMA Scientific Apparatus Makers of America

Samar Samaria; Samaritan

SAME. Society of American Military Engineers

SAMS South American Missionary Society

san sanatorium; sanitary

SAN School of Air Navigation

San C Sanitary Corps

Sand. Sandford's New York Reports (legal)

San D Doctor of Sanitation

Sandf Ch Sandford's Chancery (legal)

San E Sanitary Engineer

San Fran San Francisco

Sanh Sanhedrin

s a n r subject to approval no risk

Sans Sanskrit

SANS South African Naval Service

SAO Squadron Accountant Officer

SAOR Senior Assistant Official Receiver

sap. sapwood (lumber)

S Ap Scruple, Apothecaries

s a p semi-armor-piercing; soon as possible

SAP Scouting amphibian plane (US Navy); South African Party; South African Police

SAPC Shipowners Association of the Pacific Coast

SAPFT Special Adviser to the President on Foreign Trade

SAPI Salesmen's Association of the Paper Industry

sapon saponification

SAQC Sub-Area Quartering Commandant

Sar Sarawak; Sardinia

SAR His (Her) Royal Highness (*Son Altesse Royale*); search and rescue (ICAO); semiautomatic rifle (US Army); Society of Authors' Representatives; Solar Aircraft Company (NYSE); Sons of the American Revolution; South African Republic; Special Apparatus Rack

SAR & H South African Railways and Harbours

S A R L limited liability company (*Société à Responsabilité Limité*—French)

SARPS Standards and Recommended Practices (ICAO)

Sarum (Bishop of) Salisbury

SARX Salyer Refining Company, Inc (private car rr mark)

SAS His, Her Serene Highness (*Son

Altesse Sérénissime—French); Fellow of the Society of Antiquaries (*Societatis Antiquariorum Socius*—Latin); Scandinavian Airlines System; Ship Adoption Society; Special Air Service; Surgical Appliance Society

Sask Saskatchewan, Canada

SASO Senior Air Staff Officer

SASR Special Air Service Regiment

SASX Mathieson Chemical Corporation (private car rr mark); Southern Acid & Sulphur Company, Inc (private car rr mark)

Sat. Saturday; Saturn

sat. saturated

S At. South Atlantic

SAT. satisfactory (US Army); Scientific Adviser on Telecommunications

SATA Sociedade Açoriana de Transportes Aereas Ltda; South African Teachers' Association

S A T B soprano, alto, tenor, bass

SATC Students' Army Training Corps

satd saturated

satel satellite

Sat. Eve. Post Saturday Evening Post

satisfon satisfaction

sat. sol saturated solution

S Atto SS your obedient and faithful servant (*su atento y seguro servidor*—Spanish)

SAU South African Union

Sau Ar Saudi Arabia

sauf e ou o errors and omissions excepted (*sauf erreur ou omission*—French)

SAU&G San Antonio, Uvalde & Gulf Railroad Company

S Aus South Australia

Sav Savoie (French department)

S av scruple, avoirdupois

SAV stock at valuation

SAVS Scottish Anti-Vivisection Society

SAW. St. Lawrence Corporation Ltd (NYSE); S & W Fine Foods, Inc (NYSE)

SAWBET supply action will be taken (US Army)

SAWE Society of Aeronautical Weight Engineers

Sax Saxon; Saxony

SAX Simmons Oil & Refining Company (private car rr mark)

SAY Sayre & Fisher Brick Company (NYSE)

sb shipbuilding; southbound; substantive

s b separately billed; short bill; small bonds; standard bead

Sb antimony

SB Bachelor of Science (*Scientiae Baccalaureus*—Latin); Sam Browne (military); Savings Bank; School for the Blind; Scout Bomber (US Navy Aircraft); Serving Brother (freemasonry); Shipping Board; Sick Bay; Signal Boatswain; Simultaneous Broadcast; single breasted; Sound Beam (Morse); South Britain (England and Wales); Statistical Branch (military); Statute Book; steamboat; stretcher-bearer; Sunlight Bureau; supply bulletin (US Army); Sweet Briar (college)

s/b statement of billing

S&B sterilization and bath (US Army)

SBA Savings Bank Act; Scottish Bankers' Association; Seaboard & Western Airlines (NYSE); Silica Brickmakers' Association; Sick Bay Attendant (naval); Small Brewers Association; Sport Broadcasters Association; Solicitors' Benevolent Association; Small Business Administration

SBAC Society of British Aircraft Constructors

SBB Swiss Federal Railways (*Schweizer Bundesbahnen*—Ger)

SBC Ships Badges Committee; Signal Books Correct (naval); small bayonet; Southern Baptist Convention; Stokely-Van Camp, Inc. (NYSE)

SB Chem Bachelor of Science in Chemistry

SB Comm Bachelor of Science in Commerce

SBCPO Sick Bay Chief Petty Officer

SBD Savings Bank Department; Seaboard Air Line Railroad (NYSE)

s b e south by east

SB Ed. Bachelor of Science in Education

SB Engin Bachelor of Science in Engineering

SBF Stix, Baer & Fuller Company (NYSE)

SB Geol Bachelor of Science in Geology

SBH Scottish Board of Health

SBI Steel Boiler Institute; Sterchi Bros. Stores, Inc (NYSE)

SBIX Standard Brands Incorporated (private car rr mark)

SBK South Brooklyn Railway Company (rr mark)

SBL Blumenthal (Sidney) & Company (NYSE)

SB Med Bachelor of Science in Medicine

SBN South Bend Lathe Works (NYSE)

SBOAI Specialty Bakery Owners of America, Inc.

SBO Pr Simmons-Boardman Pub. Corp. ($3. Conv. Pref) (ASE)

SBOT Sacred Books of the Old Testament

SB Phar Bachelor of Science in Pharmacy

SBPW Special Board for Public Works

s Br south latitude (*südliche Breite* —German)

SBR Sterling Brewers, Inc. (NYSE)

SB&R San Benito & Rio Grande Valley Railway Company (rr mark)

Sbre September (*septiembre*—Spanish)

SBS Superintendent of Buildings and Supplies

SBT small boat (US Army)

s b w south by west

SBY Selby Shoe Company (NYSE)

s c salvage charges (insurance); same case; sharp cash; single column; single contact; shortened honors course; sole charge; steel cored; staff college (military)

sc he carved it (*sculpsit*—Latin); to know (*scitr*—Latin); namely (*scilicet*—Latin); scale; scene (*scène*—French); scarce; science; scientific; screw; scruple; supercharged; to wit (*scilicet*—Latin)

Sc Scandinavian; Scandium; Scotch; Scotland Scots; Scottish; Stratocumulus; scandium

SC decree of the Senate (*Senatus Consultum*—Latin); General Steel Cast (NYSE); Sacred Congregation (*Sacra Congregatio*—Latin); Salesion Congregation; Sanitary Corps; School Certificate; Senefelder Club; senior Controller; Service Certificate (naval); Services Committee; Short Course; Sion College; Sigma Chi (fraternity); Skidmore College; small capitals (type); Small Craft (naval); Smith College; Smithfield Club; Social Credit; South Carolina; Southern Command; Special Constable; Staff Captain (military); Staff College; Staff Corps; Statutory Committee; Studio Club; Submarine Chasers, wood-hulls (US Navy); supercalendered (paper); Superintending Cartographer (naval); Supervisory Commission; Supply Corps; Supreme Court (legal); Surgeon Captain; Surgeon-Commander (naval); Swimming Club

s/c his account (*son compte*—French); your account (*su cuenta*—Spanish); surcharge

S/C Set Course

s & c shipper and carrier; sized and calendered (paper)

SCA Department of Security Council Affairs (UN Secretariat); Science Clubs of America; Screen Composers Association; Shipbuilders Council of America; Stock Company Association

SCAEF Supreme Commander of Allied Expeditionary Force

SCAF Supreme Command of Allied Forces

SCAGF Supreme Commander, American Ground Force

sc ai steel-cored aluminum

Scand Scandinavia; Scandinavian

scan mag defamation of dignities (*scandalum magnatum*—Latin) (legal)

SCAP Supreme Commander for the Allied Powers (Japan)

SCAPA Society for Checking the Abuses of Public Advertising

s caps. small capitals (type)

SCARWAF special category Army personnel with Air Force (US Army)

SCAS Signal Corps Aviation School

SCAX Shell Oil Company of Canada, Limited (private car rr mark)

SCB Superintendent of the Chart Branch; Standing Council of the Baronetage

SCC Sea Cadet Corps; Siamese Cat Club; single cotton-covered (electric conductors); Society of Cosmetic Chemists; Special Criminal Court; Staff College, Camberley; State Corporation Commission; Sunday Chamber Concert

SCCC *Société de Commission et de Consignation Coloniale*

SCCUS Swedish Chamber of Commerce of the United States

SCCX Shell Oil Company, Inc. (private car rr mark)

scd screwed

SCD schedule (US Army); Doctor of Commercial Science

Sc D Doctor of Science (*Scientiae Doctor*—Latin)

Sc DHyg Doctor of Science in Hygiene

Sc DMed Doctor of Medical Science

sc dr screen door

s c e single cotton over enamel (insulation)

SCE Southern Cal. Edison Company (NYSE)

SCE A Southern California Edison Co. (ASE)

SCE B Southern California Edison Co. (ASE)

SCE C Southern California Edison Co. (ASE)

SCE D Southern California Edison Co. (ASE)

SC EE Sacred Congregation of Bishops and Regulars (*Sacra Congregatio Episcoporum et Regularium*—Latin)

SCE O Pr Southern California Edison Company (5% Part. Orig. Pfd.) (ASE)

scf standard cubic foot

SCF Save the Children Foundation; Shoe Corporation of America Cl A (NYSE)

SCF A Shoe Corporation of America (Class A Com.) (ASE)

SCG Screen Cartoonists' Guild; South Carolina Elec. & Gas (NYSE)

SCGB Ski Club of Great Britain

s c g s centimeter-gram-second system (physics) (*système cgs*—French)

sch note (*scholium*—Latin); scholar; scholarship; school; schooner

SCH Spencer Chemical Company (NYSE)

SCHC Select Committee of the House of Commons

sched schedule

scherz lively (*scherzando*—music)

schmp melting point (*Schmelzpunkt* —German)

Sch Mus B Bachelor of School Music

schol scholar; scholarly; scholarship; scholastic; scholiastic

schr schooner

Schupo police force or constable (*Schutzpolizei*—German)

SCHX Stauffer Chemical Company, Inc. (private car rr mark)

sci science; scientific

s c i soft cast iron

SCI Shipping Container Institute; Society of Chemical Industry

SCIC Ship's Cook First Class (US Navy)

sci fa let him know (*scire facias* —Latin) (legal)

Sci fa ad dis deb *Scire facias ad disprobandum debitum* (legal writ)

SCIT Special Commissioners of Income Tax

SCIX Samuel Cabot Inc. (private car rr mark)

SCJ Priests of the Sacred Heart (*Sacerdotum a Sacro Corde Jesu*); Supreme Court of Judicature

SCJX Spencer Chemical Company (private car rr mark)

scl. scale

SCL Society of Comparative Legislation; Student of Civil Law

s c m summary court-martial

Sc M Master of Science (*Scientiae Magister*—Latin)

sc m of holy memory (*sanctae memoriae*—Latin)

SCM Sacred Imperial Majesty (*Sacra Cæsarea Majestas*—Latin); Society of Coal Merchants; State Certified Midwife; Steward of Crown Manors; Student Christian Movement; Summary Court-Martial

s&cm surfaced one or two sides and center matched (lumber)

SCMA Silk Commission Manufacturers Association

Sc M Hyg Master of Science in Hygiene

SCMWA State, County and Municipal Workers of America

SCMX Shell Chemical Corporation (private car rr mark)

scn prot screen protected

SCNX Columbian Gasoline Corporation (private car rr mark)

Sco Scorpius

S/co against you (*su cargo*—Spanish)

SCO Scotten, Dillon Company (NYSE); Scovill Manufacturing Company (NYSE); Squadron Constructor Officer (naval)

s coln supply column

S Con Res (with number), Senate concurrent resolution

Scot. Scotch; Scottish; Scotland

scp script; spherical candlepower

SCP Social Credit Party; Standing Committee on Prices

SCPCU Society of Chartered Property and Casualty Underwriters

SCPI Structural Clay Products Institute

scr scratch; screwed; scrip; scruple

SCR Scurry Oils Ltd (NYSE); South Carolina Reports, (legal); Stone Container Corporation (NYSE)

SCRA Supreme Council of the Royal Arcanum

script. seventh; scripture

SCS Scottish Council of State; Society of Civil Servants; Soil Conservation Service; Superintendent Car Service

sc&s strapped, corded, and sealed

SCSA Soil Conservation Society of America

SC2C Ship's Cook Second Class (US Navy)

S Ct Supreme Court Reporter (legal)

SCT Smith (L.C.) & Corona Type (NYSE)

s/cta your account (*su cuenta*—Spanish)

SC3C Ship's Cook Third Class

SCTMI Sink and Counter Top Manufacturers Institute

SCTY security (US Army)

SCU Scottish Cycling Union;

Scullin Steel Company (NYSE)

sculp sculptor; sculptural; sculpture

sculps he engraved it (*sculpsit*—Latin)

SCV Sons of Confederate Veterans

SCW Society of Colonial Wars; Superintendent of Contract Work (naval)

SC of W State College of Washington

SCX Starrett (L.S.) Company (NYSE)

s d no date (*sans date*—French); safe deposit; the same day (*samma dag*—Swedish); same date (*samme dato*—Danish); see this (*siche dies*—German); semi-diameter; service dress; several dates; sight draft; single deck; soft drawn (wire); without day (*sine die*—Latin); solid drawn; special duty

sd he sat (*sedit*—Latin); said; sewed; signed; seasoned (lumber)

Sd boiling point (*Siedepunkt*—German)

SD by decree of the Senate (*Senatus decreto*—Latin); Doctor of Science (*Scientiae Doctor*—Latin); sends greetings (*salutum dicit*—Latin); Senior Deacon (freemasonry); servant of God (*servus Dei*—Latin); Service Dress; Security Service (*Sicherheitsdienst*—German); Signal Department; Solicitor's Department; solid drawn; South Dakota; Southern Department; Staff Duties; Standard Oil Company of California (NYSE); State Department; Stores Department; Stores Depot; Sub-marine Department; Supplies Division; Supply Depot; Surveyors' Department; Swaziland (IDP)

s/d sea damaged (grain trade)

s d a specific dynamic action

SDA Seventh Day Adventists; Soldiers' Dependants' Allowances

SDAA Servicemen's Dependants' Allowance Act; Skein Dyers Association of America

SDAE San Diego and Arizona Eastern Railway Company (rr mark)

S Dak South Dakota

SDAM Seventh Day Adventists' Mission

s d b l sight draft, bill of lading attached

SDC Sigma Delta Chi (fraternity); St. David's College; Society of the Divine Compassion

SDCID State Department's Current Information Division (United States)

S D Co Safe Deposit Company

SDCX Southern Dyestuff Corporation (private car rr mark)

s d d store door delivery

SDE Shattuck Denn Mining Corporation (NYSE); Sigma Delta Epsilon (society)

sdf except Sundays and holidays (*sauf dimanches et fêtes*—French)

SDF Social Democratic Federation; Southwark Diocesan Fund; Sudan Defence Force

sdg siding

SDG Glory to God alone (*Soli Deo Gloria*—Latin)

SDI Saudi Arabian Airlines

SDIX Smith-Douglass Company, Inc (private car rr mark)

SDJR Somerset and Dorset Joint Railway

sdk shelter deck

SDK Sigma Delta Kappa (fraternity)

SDM Sub-District Manager

SDMA Soap and Detergent Manufacturers Association

SDMJ September, December, March, June (quarter months)

SDN League of Nations (*Société des Nations*—French)

SDO Senior Dental Officer; Senior Duty Officer (RAF); Sharp & Dohme Inc (NYSE); Signal Distributing Officer; Squadron Dental Officer (naval)

S Doc Senate document

SDP Sigma Delta Pi (society); Sigma Delta Psi (society); Social Democratic Party

S Dpo Stores Depot (RAF)

SDR Standard Dredging Corporation (NYSE)

S & D(R) Somerset and Dorset (Railway)

SDR Pr Standard Dredging Corp. ($1.60 Pfd.) (ASE)

SDRX Sinclair Refining Company (private car rr mark)

SDS San Diego State (college); Simonds Saw & Steel Company (NYSE); Society of the Divine Saviour (Salvatorian Fathers)

SDT Sigma Delta Tau (sorority)

SDU Saint Dunstan's University (Canada)

SDUK Society for the Diffusion of Useful Knowlege

SDV Fathers of the Divine Word (RO) (*Societas Divini Verbi*—Latin)

SDX Squire Dingee Company (private car rr mark)

s e single entry (accounting); second entrance; semi-enclosed; screwed ends (plumbing); southeast (*sudeste*—Spanish)

Se selenium

SE His Excellency (*Su Excelencia*—Spanish); Saorstat Eirarm

(Irish Free State); Servel, Inc. (NYSE); Society of Engineers; Southeastern (postal district); Southeastern Reporter

S/E Stock Exchange

s & e surfaced one side and one edge (lumber)

sea. seaman

SEA. Service for Economic Action

SEAC South-East Asia Command

Sea. 1C Seaman, First Class

seapt seaport

SEATO Southeast Asia Treaty Organization

SEbE southeast by east

s e b s southeast by south

sec according to (*secundum*—Latin); secant (mathematics); second; secondary winding; secretary; section (*seccion*—Spanish)

SEC Secretary of the Education Committee; Securities Exchange Commission; South-Eastern Command; Sulphur Export Corporation; Supreme Economic Council

sec art according to the art (*secundum artem*—Latin) (pharmacy)

sec-ft second-foot

sech hyperbolic secant

sec leg. according to law (*secundum legem*—Latin)

Sec Leg. Secretary of Legation

sec nat according to nature (*secundum naturam*—Latin)

Sec Off. Section Officer

2d Dec Dig. Second Decennial Digest

secr secret; secretary

SECR South Eastern and Chatham Railway

sec reg according to rule (*secundum regulam*—Latin)

sect. chf chief of section

SED Scottish Education Department; German Social Unity Party (*Sozialistische Einheitspartei Deutschlands*—German)

SEE Seeman Brothers Inc. (common stock, ASE)

SE e O errors and omissions excepted (*salvis erroribus et omissis*—Latin)

SEF Southern Education Foundation

SEFA Southeastern Freight Association

seg follows (*segue*) (music); segment

SEG Segal Lock & Hardware Company (NYSE); Society of Economic Geologists

segms segments (botany)

seismol seismological; seismology

SEKF Sister Elizabeth Kenny Foundation

sel deceased (*selig*—German); selected; selection

SEL Seton Leather Company (common stock ASE)

Selk Selkirk (county of Scotland)

Sel Svc Selective Service

Selw Selwyn College, Cambridge

sem it seems (*semble*—French); semble; semicolon; seminar; seminary; week (*semaine*—French)

Sem Semitic

S Em His Eminence (*Son Eminence*—French)

SEMA Steam Engine Manufacturers Association

semp always the same style (*sempre*—Italian) (music)

sen senior; without (*senza*—Italian) (music)

Sen Senate; Senator

S en C limited partnership (*Sociedad en Comandita*—Spanish, *Sociedade en Commandita*—Portuguese, *Societé en Commandite*—French, *Societate en Commandita*—Rumanian)

sen clk senior clerk

SENL standard equipment nomenclature list (US Army)

S en NC joint stock company (*Société en Nom Colectif*—French); joint stock company (*Sociedad en Nombre Colectiva*—Spanish)

Sen Op Senior Optime

sent. sentence

SEO errors and omissions excepted (*sin errores y omisiones*—Spanish); Senior Engineer-Officer (naval)

SE&O errors and omissions excepted (*sauf erreur et omission*—French)

SEOC Serbian Eastern Orthodox Church

se ou o errors or omissions excepted (*sauf erreurs ou omissions*—French)

sep separate

SEP Saturday Evening Post (periodical); Sylvania Electric Prods (NYSE)

Sep September; Septuagint (Bible)

SEPEG International Study Weeks for Child War Victims

SEPM Society of Economic Paleontologists and Mineralogists

sept northern (*septentrional*—French)

Sept September (*septembre*—French)

Septuag (*Septuagesima*) 70th day before Easter

septupl septuplicate

seq and what follows (*sequenta*—Latin); it follows (*sequitur*—Latin); the following (*sequens*—Latin)

ser serial; series; sermon; serpens; service

Ser Servius

SER Sentry Safety Control Corporation (NYSE); serial service (telegrams); South Eastern Railway; Southeastern Reporter (legal)

Serb Serbia; Serbian

Sergt Sergeant

serv servant; service

Serv NC service not included (hotels) (*Service non compris*—French)

servor servant (*servidor*—Spanish)

SERX Service Tank Cars (private car rr mark); Shippers' Car Line Corporation (private car rr mark)

ses square edge siding (lumber)

SES Sigma Epsilon Sigma (society); Soil Erosion Service; Standards Engineers Society

SESAC Society of European Stage Authors and Composers

SESMMD Survey and Emigration Staff of the Mercantile Marine Department

SESO Senior Equipment Staff Officer (RAF)

sesquih an hour and a half (*sesquihora*—Latin)

sess session

sesunc an ounce and a half (*sesuncia*—Latin)

SESX Sessions Company Inc (private car rr mark)

Set September (*Setiembre*—Spanish)

SET Stetson (John B.) Company (NYSE)

SL Saône-et-Loire (French department)

S et M Seine-et-Marne (French department)

S et O Seine-et-Oise (French department)

sett September (*settembre*—Italian)

SEUA Southeastern Underwriters Association

s e u o error or omission excepted (*salvo error u omisión*—Spanish)

seur following (*seuraava*—Finnish)

SEUSS South-Eastern Union of Scientific Societies

sev several; severed

7bre September (*septembre*—French)

sex. section

Sex. Sextans (constellation); Sextus

Sexag (*Sexagesima*) 60th day before Easter

S Exc His Excellency (*Son Excellence*—French)

S Excia His Excellency (*Sua

Excellência—Portuguese)
sextupl sextuplicate
s f near the end (*sub finem*—
Latin); semi-finished; sunk face
(masonry); surface foot (lumber);
with sudden emphasis (*sforzando*,
sforzato—Italian) (music); without
charges (*sans frais*—French)
SF Atchison, Topeka & Santa Fe
(NYSE); Finland (IDP); San
Francisco; Scripps Foundation;
Senior Fellow; Sherwood Foresters;
Shipping Federation; Sinking Fund;
Sinn Fein; Sons of the Holy Family;
Strong Foundation
s/f your favor (*su favor*—Spanish)
S&F sound and flash (US Army)
s & f stock and fixtures (insurance)
SFA Scottish Football Association;
Solid Fuels Administration; Soy
Flour Association
S & FA Shipping and Forwarding
Agent
SFAW Solid Fuels Administrator
for War
SFBA Steamship Freight Brokers
Association
Sfc sergeant, first class
SFC Safety First Council; Sea-
Board Finance Company (NYSE)
sfce surface
sf ct safe conduct (*sauf-conduit*—
French)
SFDX Southern Fruit Distributors,
Inc (private car rr mark)
SF E OU O errors and omissions
excepted (*sauf erreurs ou omissions*
—French)
SFERT Laboratory of the European
Fundamental System of Reference
for Telephone Transmission
sff with sudden emphasis (*sforzando*
—Italian) (music)
SF1C Shipfitter First Class (US
Navy)
SFH Safe Harbor Water Power
Corporation (ASE)
SFIB Southern Freight Inspection
Bureau
S1C Seaman First Class (US Navy)
SFM San Francisco Mining Ex-
change
SFMA Soda Fountain Manufacturers
Association; Southern Furniture
Manufacturers Association
SFMAA Slide Fastener Manufac-
turers Association of America
SFMI Soft Fibre Manufacturers In-
stitute
SFO Standard Forgings Corporation
(NYSE)
S-4 supply officer (US Army)
S 4 S surfaced four sides (lumber)
SFS San Francisco State (college);
San Francisco Stock Exchange;

Society for Freedom in Science
SFSA Steel Founders Society of
America
SFSC Brothers of the Sacred Heart
SF2C Shipfitter Second Class (US
Navy)
SFSR Socialist Federation of So-
viet Republics
SF3C Shipfitter Third Class (US
Navy)
sftwd softwood (lumber)
SFX Saint Francis Xavier (college);
Stokely Foods, Inc. (private car
rr mark)
sfz with sudden emphasis (*sforzando*
—Italian) (music)
sg screen grid; singing; specific
gravity; surgeon
SG His, Her, Grace (*Sa Grâce*—
French); His Highness (*Sa Grandeur*
—French); for the sake of safety
(*salutis gratia*—Latin); Scots
Guards; screened grid (radio);
Seaman Gunner; Shipping Guild;
Society of Genealogists; Solicitor
General; Stage Guild; Standard
Gas & Electric (NYSE); State
Guard; Surgeon General (US Army)
s/g your draft (*su giro*—Spanish)
S/G Executive Office of the
Secretary General (UN Secretariat)
SGA Safety Glass Association;
Southern Natural Gas Company
(NYSE)
SGAA Stained Glass Association
of America
Sg C Surgeon-Captain
sgd signed
SGD Senior Grand Deacon (free-
masonry)
s g d g without Government guar-
antee [of patents] (*sans garantie
du gouvernement*—French)
Sge Sagittarius (constellation)
SGE Sigma Gamma Epsilon (society)
SGES Society of Grain Elevator
Superintendents
SGF Southern Counties Gas Com-
pany of California (ASE)
SGI Sun Glass Institute
sgl single
Sg L Cr Surgeon Lieutenant Com-
mander
SGM Sangamo Electric Company
(NYSE)
SGMA Southern Garment Manufac-
turers Association
SGO Squadron Gunnery Officer;
Surgeon-General's Office
SGP South American Gold &
Platinum (NYSE)
SGPS Secretary-General for Public
Security
SGPW Secretary-General for Prison-
ers of War

Sgr Sagittarius (constellation)
SGR School of General Reconnais-
sance (RAF)
Sg RA Surgeon-Rear-Admiral
SGS Secretary General Staff (US
Army); single green silk-covered;
Solicitor-General for Scotland
Sgt Sergeant
SGT A Southwestern Gas & Elec-
tric Company (ASE)
Sgt Maj Sergeant Major
SGW Salt-glazed ware; Senior
Grand Warden (freemasonry)
SGX Seeger Refrigerator Company
(NYSE)
s h schoolhouse; specified hours
sh shall; share; sheet; shilling
Sh Shipwright
SH His Highness (*Sa Hautesse*—
French); Sacred Heart Confraternity;
Sailors' Hostel; Schenley Indus-
tries, Inc (NYSE); Schleswig-
Holstein; Seton Hall (college);
Somerset Herald; Staghounds; Stop
Head (of account-book rulings);
Horse Car (rr car)
SHA Shawmut Association (NYSE);
Shellmar Products Corporation
(NYSE); Sidereal Hour Angle
(astronaval)
SHAEF Supreme Headquarters,
Allied Expeditionary Force
Shak Shakespeare
SHAPE Supreme Headquarters
Allied Powers (Europe)
sh d should
sh d shipping dry (lumber)
SHD Subsistence Homesteads Divi-
sion
sh dk shelter deck
SHE Sheaffer (W.A.) Pen Company
(NYSE)
Shef(f) Sheffield
SHEMA Steam Heating Equipment
Manufacturers Association
Sher F Sherwood Foresters
Shet Shetland (county of Scotland)
Shet Is. Shetland Islands
S & H exc Sundays and holidays
excepted
s h f superhigh-frequency
sh i sheet iron
ship. shipment or shipments
(lumber)
SHK Schick Incorporated (NYSE)
Sh L Shipwright Lieutenant
SHL Sheller Manufacturing Corpora-
tion (NYSE)
shlp shiplap (lumber)
SHM Shamrock Oil & Gas Corpora-
tion (NYSE); simple harmonic
motion
SHMI Saddlery Hardware Manufacturers Institute
shp shaft horsepower

SHP Smith (Howard) Paper Mills, Ltd. (common stock ASE)
SHPDTO ship on depot transfer order (number) (US Army)
SHPGO shipping order (US Army)
SHPI Southern Hardwood Producers, Inc
SHPIM ship immediately (US Army)
SHPMT shipment (US Army)
SHPREQ ship to apply on requisition (number) (US Army)
shpt shipment
SHPTARBY ship to arrive not later than (US Army)
SHPX First Corporation (private car rr mark); Shippers' Car Line Corporation (private car rr mark); Third Corporation (private car rr mark)
SHQ Supreme Headquarters
shr share; shares; sheets
sh s sheet steel
SHS Fellow of the Historical Society (*Societatis Historiae Socius*—Latin)
SHST Sam Houston State Teachers (college)
shtg shortage
sh tn short ton (2,000 pounds)
SHU Schulte (D.A.), Inc. (NYSE)
s h v under this word (*sub hoc voce,* or *sub hoc verbo*—Latin)
SHW Sherwin-Williams Company (The) (common stock ASE)
SHW Pr Sherwin-Williams Co. (The) (4% Pfd.) (ASE)
s i self induction; short interest (stocks)
Si silicon
SI Sandwich Islands; Secretary for India; *Seine-Inférieure* (French department); Shetland Isles; short interest (insurance); Society of Illustrators; Society of Jesus (Jesuits); Spokane International Railway Company; Sponge Institute; Staff Inspector; Star of India; Staten Island (New York); Surveyors' Institution; *Système International* (screw threads)
SIA Sanitary Institute of America; Self-Insurers Association
Sib Siberia; Siberian
SIB Statistics and Intelligence Branch
s i c specific inductive capacity (electricity)
Sic Sicilian; Sicily
SIC Sesame Imperial Club; Shriners Imperial Council; Specific Inductive Capacity
s i d once a day (*semel in die*—Latin) (prescription)
sid pages (*sidor*—Swedish)
SID his spirit is with God (*spiritus*

in Deo); Social Insurance Department; Society of Industrial Designers; Statistics and Intelligence Department
SIE Society of Industrial Engineers
Sier L Sierra Leone
Sierp August (*Sierpień*—Polish)
sig signal; signaller; signalman; signature; signifying
Sig Mr. (*Signor*—Italian); Mrs. (*Signora*—Italian)
SIG signal (US Navy); Southern Indiana Gas & Electric (NYSE)
SIGC Signal Corps (US Army)
sigill seal (*sigillum*—Latin)
Sig L Signal Lieutenant
sig mis signature missing
Sigmm Signalman
sign. signature
signe signature
Sig O Signal Officer
Sig-ri gentlemen (*Signori*—Italian)
sigte next (*siguiente*—Spanish)
sig unk signature unknown
SIHM International Society of the History of Medicine
SIK Sicks Breweries, Ltd. (common stock, ASE)
sil silver
Sil Silesia
SIL Singer Mfg. Company Ltd. (ASE)
Silv Cit Silvernail's Citations (legal)
SILX Jeffersonville Silgas, Inc (private car rr mark)
sim in like manner (*simile*) (music); similar; simile; similarly
Sim Simeon; Simon
SIM Sergeant-Instructor of Musketry; Simmons Company (NYSE); Sudan Interior Mission
SIMPP Society of Independent Motion Picture Producers
Sin. Sinaloa
sin. left hand (*sinistra*—Italian) (music); sine
sine com without commemoration (*sine commemoratione*—Latin)
sinf symphony (*sinfonia*) (music)
S-Infre *Seine-Inférieure* (French Department)
sing. of each (*singulorum*—Latin) (pharmacy); singular
Sing. Singapore
Singh Singhalese
singr singular
sinh hyperbolic sine
Sink. Sinkiang
s int senza interruzione (music)
SINU Southern Illinois Normal University
SIP Simplicity Pattern Company (NYSE); Society of the Institute

for Psychotherapy; standard inspection procedure (US Army)
SIPMHE Society of Industrial Packaging and Materials Handling Engineers
SIR Society of Industrial Realtors; Staten Island Rapid Transit Railway Company The (rr mark)
SIRB International Society of Radiobiology
SIRT Staten Island Rapid Transit Railway Company
sit. situate; situation; stopping in transit; storage in transit
SIT Stevens Institute of Technology
sit. rep situation report
SIUNA Seafarers International Union of North America
siv page, pages (*sivu, sivulla*—Finnish)
s i w self-inflicted wound
16 mo sextodecimo, sixteenmo (books)
64 mo sixty-fourmo (books)
sj under consideration (*sub judice*—Latin)
SJ Society of Jesus, Jesuit Fathers
SJAA St. John Ambulance Association
SJB St. Joseph Belt Railway Company (rr mark)
SJC Society of Jews and Christians; Standing Joint Committee; Supreme Judicial Court
SJD Doctor of Juridical Science (*Scientiae Juridicae Doctor*—Latin)
SJI Steel Joist Institute
SJ Res Senate joint resolution
SJS San Jose State (college)
Sjt Serjeant
SJU Saint John's University
s k so called (*sa kallad*—Swedish); safe keeping (commerce)
sk sack; sack (wool weight); street (*sokak*—Turkish)
SK Sigma Kappa (sorority)
s-ka company, association (*spolka*—Polish)
SKC Silver King Coalition Mines (NYSE)
SKCI Steel Kitchen Cabinet Institute
SK1C Storekeeper First Class (US Navy)
SKG Spencer Kellogg & Sons (NYSE)
SKKCA Supreme Knight of the Knights of Columbus of America
Skr Sanskrit
SKR South Korean Republic
Skrt Sanskrit
SK2C Storekeeper Second Class (US Navy)
SKSY Sikorsky (aircraft)

Skt Saint (*Sankt*—German)
SK3C Storekeeper Third Class (US Navy)
SKW Sparks-Withington Company (NYSE)
SKY Standard Oil Company (Kentucky) (NYSE)
s l without place (*sine loco*—Latin); salvage loss; seditious libel; separate lead (cables); sea level; sheer line; short lengths (building); single ledger; special lease; sprinkler leakage (insurance); without place (of printing) (*sine loco*—Latin)
sl slight (fire records); slow
SL Sarah Lawrence (college); Science Library; Second Lieutenant; Security List; Sierra Leone (Africa); Solicitor at Law; sound locator (US Army); South Latitude; Squadron Leader; Sub Lieutenant (naval); Sugar Land Railway Company (rr mark); Sunlight League; Saône-et-Loire (French department)
S/L on the Loire (river) (*Sur Loire*)
S & L Sudney & Louisburg Railway Company (rr mark)
SLA Showman's League of America; Slick Airways; Inc; Special Libraries Association; State Liquor Authority
sl & a without place and year (*sine loco et anno*—Latin)
S Lan R South Lancashire Regiment
s lat south latitude
Slav Slavic; Slavonian; Slavonic
SLAX St. Lawrence Starch Company Limited (private car rr mark)
SL B Simpsons, Ltd. ("B" Stk.) (ASE)
SLBA Sand-Lime Brick Association
SLC Statute Law Committee; Surgeon Lieutenant-Commander (naval)
sl & c shipper's load and count
S/LC Sue and Labour Clause
SLCI Supreme Legislative Council for India
sld sailed; sealed; sold
S Ldr Squadron Leader (RAF)
SLEA Southern Lumber Exporters Association; Steam Locomotive Export Association
slent becoming gradually slower (*slentando*—Italian) (music)
s l f straight-line frequency
SLF Service League Foundation
slg sailing
SLGA Stained and Leaded Glass Association
SLI Southwestern Louisiana Institute
SLIC Savings and Loan Insurance Corporation
SLK Real Silk Hosiery Mills, Inc (NYSE)

sll very readily soluble (*sehr leicht löslich*—German)
SLM Stahl-Meyer, Inc (NYSE)
s l n d without specifying place or date (*sine loco nec data*—Latin)
Slo Sligo (Ireland)
SLOF St. Louis and O'Fallon Railway Company, The (rr mark)
s l p without lawful issue (*sine legitima prole*—Latin)
SLP San Luis Potosi; scouting landplane (US Navy); Sea Level Pressure; Socialist Labour Party
s l r single lapping of pure rubber
SLRB Steel Labor Relations Board
SLRX St. Louis Refrigerator Car Company (private car rr mark)
SLS Salt Lake Stock Exchange
SLSF St. Louis-San Francisco Railway Company (rr mark)
slsmgr salesmanager
slsmn salesman
SLSX Swift Live Stock Express (private car rr mark)
SLT searchlight (US Army)
S Lt Sub-Lieutenant
sl & t shipper's load and tally
SLU Saint Lawrence University; Saint Louis University
s l w straight line wave-length
SLX Silex Company (NYSE)
sm centimetre (*santimetre*—Turkish); left hand (*sinistra mano*) (music); short meter; small
Sm samarium
s m sewing machine; short meter
SM His, Her, Majesty (*sa Majesté*—French); of holy memory (*sanctae memoriae*); Master of Science (*Scientiae Magister*); Sector Matron; Senior Magistrate; Sergeant Major; Silver Medallist; Simpson Multiplier (naval engineering); Society of Mary (*Societas Mariae*); Society of Miniaturists; Soldier's Medal (US Army); Sons of Malta; Spanish Morocco (Africa); Splinter Mats; Staff Major; State Militia; Sterling Market; Stipendiary Magistrate; Stock Market; Surgeon Major
s/M on the sea (*sur Mer*—French)
s&m surfaced and matched (lumber)
S&M September and March; Shropshire and Montgomery Railway; Stock and Machinery (insurance); Swansea and Mumbles Railway
S of M School of Musketry
SMA Safe Manufacturers' Association; Sales Managers' Association; Salt Manufacturers' Association; Saw Manufacturers' Association; Senior Military Attache (US Army); Sheffield Metallurgical Association; Shroud Manufacturers' Association; Shuttle Manufacturers' Association; Socialist Medical Association;

Society of African Missions (*Societas pro Missionibus ad Afros*—Latin); Society of Marine Artists; Spring Manufacturers Association; Stock Managers Association; Stoker Manufacturers Association; Surplus Marketing Administration
s/Ma on the Marne river (*sur Marne*—French)
S Mar. San Marino
SMAUS Saddlery Manufacturers Association of the United States
SMB His, Her, Britannic Majesty (*Sa Majesté Britannique*—French); Sulgrave Manor Board; Sunbeam Corporation (NYSE)
SMBL semimobile (US Army)
SMC His, Her, Catholic Majesty (of Spain) (*Sa Majesté Catholique*—French); Service Members' Committee; Smith (A.O.) Corporation (NYSE)
sm caps small capitals
SMCLN semicolon (US Army)
SMCNA Sheet Metal Contractors National Association
S/M CO Submarine Commanding Officer
Sm Cond Ala Smith's Condensed Alabama Reports (legal)
SMD short meter double; State Management Districts
SME Dutch Guiana (Surinam) (IDP); Holy Mother Church (*Sancta Mater Ecclesia*—Latin); School of Military Engineering
SM Engin Master of Science in Engineering
SMF Schurz Memorial Foundation; Singer Manufacturing Company (NYSE)
SM1C Signalman First Class (US Navy)
SMG submachine gun (US Army)
SMI His, Her, Imperial Majesty (*Sa Majesté Impériale*—French); Secondary Metal Institute; Super Market Institute
Smith. Inst Smithsonian Institution
SMIUNA Stove Mounters International Union of North America
sml compare (*sammenlign*—Danish)
SMLO Senior Military Liaison Officer (US Army)
SM Lond Soc Member of the London Medical Society (*Societatis Medicae Londiniensis Socius*—Latin)
SMM Holy Mother Mary (*Sancta Mater Maria*—Latin)
SMMMA Saw Mill Machinery Manufacturers Association
SMNA Safe Manufacturers National Association
SMO Senior Medical Officer; Squadron Medical Officer (RAF)

smorz dying away (*smorzando*) (music)

SMOX Standard Molasses Company (private car rr mark)

s m p without male issue (*sine mascula prole*—Latin)

SMPE Society of Motion Picture Engineers

SMR His, Her, Royal Majesty (*Sa Majesté Royale*—French)

SMRC Society of Minature Rifle Clubs; Special Military Revisory Court

SMRGC Sun Maid Raisin Growers of California

SMS His Swedish Majesty (*Sa Majesté Suédoise*—French); His Majesty's Ship (*Seiner Majestat Schiff*—German); State Medical Service

SM2C Signalman Second Class (US Navy)

SMS Fd'I Society for Mutual Help, Sons of Italy (*Societá Mutuo Soccorso Figli d'Italia*—Italian)

SMSSS Sheet Metal Screw Statistical Service

smstrs seamstress

SMSX Smith Company S, Morgan (private car rr mark)

SMTA Sewing Machine Trade Association

SMTC His Most Christian Majesty (*Sa Majesté très Chrétienne*—French)

SMTF His Most Faithful Majesty (*Sa Majesté très fidèle*—French)

SM3C Signalman Third Class (US Navy)

SMTO Senior Mechanical Transport Officer

SMU Southern Methodist University

SMWIA Sheet Metal Workers International Association

SMX Staley Milling Company (private car rr mark)

sn according to nature (*secundum naturam*—Latin); sanitation; without name (*sine nomine*—Latin); shipping note; sine of the amplitude (an elliptic function)

Sn tin (*stannum*—Latin)

SN Sergeant Navigator; Sigma Nu (fraternity); Standard Oil Company (Indiana) (NYSE); State Nurse

S/N (ratio) speech/noise (ratio); signal/noise (ratio)

SNA Soviet News Agency; Spanish News Agency

SNAME Society of Naval Architects and Marine Engineers

SNAX Sociedad Nacional de Productores de Alcohol (private car rr mark)

SNC Sanitary Corps; School of Naval Co-operation (RAF)

SNCF *Société Nationale des Chemins de Fer* (French)

Sn Col Sanitary Column

SND Superintendent of Net Defence

s n g without our guarantee (*sans notre garantie*—French)

SNG Securities Corporation General (NYSE)

SNIA salutary (*salutari*—Latin); opinion (*sententia*—Latin)

SNL standard nomenclature list (US Army); Sun Chemical Corporation (NYSE)

SNLR Services no longer required

SNO Senior Naval Officer; Senior Navigation Officer (RAF)

SNP Scottish Nationalist Party; Sigma Nu Phi (fraternity)

SNPA Southern Newspaper Publishers' Assn

SNPF en Angl National Society of French Professors in England (*Société Nationale des Professeurs de Français en Angleterre*—French)

snr senior

Sñr Mr. (*Señor*—Spanish)

SNR Society for Nautical Research

Snra Mrs. (*Senhora*—Portuguese)

Sñra Mrs. (*Señora*—Spanish)

Snrta Miss (*senhorita*—Portuguese)

SNS Sunstrand Machine Tool Company (NYSE)

s o ocean station (*station océanique*—French); seller's option; shipping order; ship's option; see above (*siehe oben*—German); side outlet (plumbing); single opening; (plumbing); special order; suboffice; that is (*se on*—Finnish)

so southeast (*sudoeste*—Spanish)

So South; Southern; Southern Reporter (legal)

SO Scottish Office; Scout Observation (US Navy Aircraft); Secretary's Office; Section Officer; Senior Officer; Ship's Option; sorting office; Southern Company (NYSE); Special Orders (US Army); Staff Officer; Standing Orders; Stationery Office; Statistical Office; Supply Officer; Symphony Orchestra

S-O South West (*Sud-Ouest*—French)

s/o your order (*su orden*—Spanish)

SOA Department of Social Affairs (UN Secretariat)

SOAD Staff Officer, Air Defence

soc society; sociology

Soc Socialist; Socialism; Socrates

SOC Shell Oil Company; Society of Organized Charity; Standard Oil Company; Superior Oil Company (Cal) (NYSE)

SO-in-C Signal Officer-in-Chief

Soc an⁰ limited company (*Société*

anonyme—French)

Soc Anon corporation (*Sociedad Anónima*—Spanish)

So. Car. South Carolina; South Carolina Reports (legal)

sociol sociology

Soc Is. Society Islands

SO Cist Cistercian Order of Common Observance

s o d seller's option to double

sod. sodium

SOD. seller's option to double; Shorter Oxford Dictionary

SOE Society of Engineers; Special Operations Executive

So East Rep Southeastern Reporter (legal)

SOED Shorter Oxford English Dictionary

SOF ST State of Maranhao (Brazil) (ASE)

sog so-called (*sogenannt*—German)

SOGX Shamrock Oil and Gas Corporation, The (private car rr mark)

SOH Standard Oil Company (Ohio) (NYSE)

SOI Signal operations instructions (US Army)

SOK Stroock (S.) & Company Inc (NYSE)

s o l shipowners' liability

sol solicitor; soluble; solution

Sol Solomon

SOL Ship Owner's Liability (marine insurance)

sol alcool alcoholic solution (*solution alcoolique*—French)

sol aq aqueous solution (*solution aqueuse*—French)

Sol Gen Solicitor General

solidif solidification

Sol Is. Solomon Islands

Sol J Solicitors' Journal

soln solution

solve. c cal dissolve by heating (*solve cum calore*—Latin) (pharmacy)

soly solubility

Som Somersetshire (England)

SOME. Senior Ordnance Mechanical Engineer

Somerset Somersetshire (England)

somet sometimes

SoM1C Soundman First Class (US Navy)

SoM2C Soundman Second Class (US Navy)

SoM3C Soundman Third Class (US Navy)

son. southern

Son. Sonora

SON Sonotone Corporation (NYSE)

SONAR submarine detection and ranging

S-1 Adjutant (US Army)

✱ SMSG - School Mathematics Study Group

s l e surfaced one edge (lumber)

s l s surfaced one side (lumber)

s l s l e surfaced one side and one edge (lumber)

s l s 2 e surfaced one side and two edges (lumber)

Song of Sol Song of Solomon

sonn sonnets

Sons of SAWV Sons of Spanish American War Veterans

SOO Minneapolis, St Paul & Sault Ste. Marie Railroad Company (rr mark)

sop soprano

SOP South Pacific; Staff Officer of Pensioners; standing operating procedure (US Army)

SOP (A) Senior Officer Present (Afloat) (US Navy)

SOPAT South China Patrol (US Navy)

Soph Sophomore; Sophonias (Biblical); Sophocles

SOP ST State of Parana (U. S. of Brazil) (ASE)

SOR Society for Occupational Research

SORC Signal Officers Reserve Corps

sord sordino (music)

So. Rep. Southern Reporter (legal)

s o s if necessary (si opus sit—Latin)

SOS distress signal; Soss Manufacturing Company (NYSE); Secretary of State; Senior Officers' School; Service of Supply (U.S.A.); Society of Schoolmasters

sos when needed (si opus sit) (pharmacy)

SOSB Order of St. Benedict; Sylvestrine Benedictines

sost sustained (sostenuto—Italian) (music)

SOTX Stoll Oil Refining Company, Inc (private car rr mark)

sou subscription (banking) (souscription—French)

Sou Southern Railway Company

SOU Southern Airways, Inc

sov sovereign

SOV Socony-Vacuum Oil Company, Inc (NYSE)

Sov Un Soviet Union

Sov Un Asia Soviet Union in Asia

So. West. Rep. Southwestern Reporter (legal)

SOY Savoy Oil Company (NYSE)

s p deceased (świętej pamięci— Polish); short page; single phase; single pole; so forth (sic porro— Latin); small pica; starting point; stirrup pump; stop payment; supra protest (banking); sustaining program; without issue (sine prole

—Latin); without pedal (senza pedale) (music)

sp seaport; species; specific; specimen; speed; spelling; spirit; velocity; spitze (music)

Sp Spain; Spaniard; Spanish

SP International Institute of Philology (Société Internationale de Philologie—French); Most Holy Father (Sanctissime Pater—Latin); sample post; School of Photography (RAF); self-propelled, special or supply point (US Army); Service Patrol (RAF); Shipping Port; Signal Publication; Sigma Phi (fraternity); Sigma Pi (fraternity); small paper (ordinary copies of books); South Penn Oil Company (NYSE); Southern Pacific (rr); Southern Pacific Lines West of Portland, Ogden, El Paso & Tucumcari (rr mark); St Peter (sanctus Petrus—Latin); Stretcher Party; Supreme Pontiff (summus Pontifex—Latin); Shore Patrol

s p a subject to particular average

spa. spacing; subpoena

S p A stock company (Società per Azioni—Italian)

SPA Salt Producers Association; Society of Philatelic Americans; Southern Pine Association; Surplus Property Administration

SPAA Systems and Procedures Association of America

SPAB Supply Priorities and Allocations Board

Span. Spanish

SPARS Women's Coast Guard Reserves

SPAS Member of the American Philosophical Society (Societatis Philosophicae Americanae Socius —Latin)

SPAUS Smoke Prevention Association of the United States

SPB Surplus Property Board

SPBA Specialty Paper and Board Affiliates

Spbre September (Septembre— French)

s p c single paper covered

SPC Society for the Prevention of Crime; South Pacific Commission; Soviet Purchasing Commission (United States); Steel Parts Corporation (NYSE)

s/p/c under protest to place to account (sotto protesto per mettere in conto—Italian)

SPCA Society for the Prevention of Cruelty to Animals

SPCBC Society and Pioneer Clinic for Birth Control

SPCC Society for Prevention of Cruelty to Children

SPCK Society for Promotion of Christian Knowledge

SPCM special court martial (US Army)

SP Co Southern Pacific Company

s p d he wishes much health (salutem plurimam dicit—Latin); steamer pays dues

SPD Seaplane Depot Ship; Sigma Phi Delta (fraternity); South Polar Distance; Standard Products Company (NYSE)

sp d t single-pole, double throw

SPE Sigma Phi Epsilon (fraternity); Society of Plastics Engineers; Society for Pure English

spec special; specially; specifically; specification; specimen; spectra; speculation; spectrum

SPEC specify; specification (US Army)

spec appt special appointment

spec emp specially employed

SPECL specialist, specialized (US Army)

SPEE Society for the Promotion of Engineering Education

Spens Spenser; Spenserian

SPERON Special Service Squadron

SPEX Southern Pine Extracts Company (private car rr mark)

spez specific (spezifisch—German)

spez Gew specific gravity (spezifisches Gewicht—German)

SPFA Steel Plate Fabricators Association

SPIC Specialist First Class (US Navy)

sp g specific gravity

spg spring

SPG Society for the Propagation of the Gospel

SPGA Southeastern Pecan Growers Association

SPGB Socialist Party of Great Britain

sp gr specific grant; specific gravity

Sp Gui Spanish Guinea

sph spherical

s ph single-phase

sp ht specific heat

SPHX Roth Packing Company (private car rr mark)

SPI Society of Photographic Illustrators; Society of the Plastic Industry

spirit. spiritualism; spiritualistic; with spirit (spiritoso) (music)

SPK Standard Packaging Corporation (NYSE)

SPK Pr Standard Packaging Corp (Conv. Pref.) (ASE)

spkr speaker; sprinkler

SPKX Shawinigan Products Corporation (private car rr mark)

spl special

s p l without legitimate issue (*sine prole legitima*—Latin)

SPL Southern Pipe Line Company (NYSE)

splty specialty

SPM Saint-Pierre et Miquelon (France); self-propelled mount (US Army); short particular meter (music); Society of the Fathers of Mercy

SPMA Soda Pulp Manufacturers Association; Sulphite Paper Manufacturers Association

Sp Mor Spanish Morocco

sp msgr special messenger

SPN Spencer Shoe Corporation (NYSE)

sp nov new species (*species nova*—Latin)

SPO sausages, potatoes and onions (colloqial); Stoker Petty Officer

sport. sporting; sportive

spp species (plural)

SPP Scott Paper Company (NYSE); Small Packets Post

SPPAI Screen Process Printing Association International

SPPI Saint Paul's Polytechnic Institute

s p q r small profits, quick returns

SPQR the Senate and People of Rome (*Senatus Populusque Romanus*—Latin)

s p r with request for return (*sub petito remissionis*—Latin)

spr sapper

SPR Society for Psychical Research; Superior Portland Cement (NYSE)

SPRA School Public Relations Association

SPRC Society for Prevention and Relief of Cancer

spre always (*siempre*—Spanish)

SPRL Society for the Promotion of Religion and Learning

SPRSI Portuguese Society of Queen Saint Isabel (*Sociedade Portuguesa Raînha Santa Isabel*—Portuguese)

s p s without surviving issue (*sine prole superstite*—Latin)

SPS St. Louis Public Service CI A (NYSE); Sigma Phi Sigma (fraternity); Sigma Pi Sigma (society); special services (US Army); Spokane, Portland & Seattle Railway Company (rr mark)

Sp Sah Spanish Sahara

SP2C Specialist Second Class (US Navy)

SPSO Senior Personnel Staff Officer (RAF)

SPSP St. Peter and St. Paul (The Papal Seal)

SPSSI Society for the Psychological Study of Social Issues

sp s t single-pole, single-throw

SPSX Stickney & Poor Spice Company (private car rr mark)

spt seaport

SPT School of Physical Training; support (US Army)

SP3C Specialist Third Class (US Navy)

SPUG Society for the Prevention of Useless Giving

SPVD Society for the Prevention of Venereal Disease

sp vol specific volume

SPWA Steel Products Warehouse Association

SPX Solvay Process Division, Allied Chemical & Dye Corporation (private car rr mark)

sq the following (*sequens*—Latin); squadron; square

SQ sick quarters; squadron (US Army)

sq ch square chain

sq cm square centimeter(s)

sq ft square foot (feet)

sq hd square head

sq in. square inch(es)

sq km square kilometer(s)

sq m square meter(s)

sq ml square mile(s)

sq mm square millimeter(s)

SQMS Staff Quartermaster-Sergeant

sq mu square micron(s)

Sqn Ldr Squadron Leader

Sqn QMS Squadron Quartermaster-Sergeant

Sqn SM Squadron Sergeant-Major

Sq O Squadron Officer (WAAF)

sqq the following (*sequentes*, *sequentia*—Latin)

sq rd square rod(s)

SQU Square D Company (NYSE)

sq yd square yard(s)

s r self-rectifying; shipping receipt; short rate (insurance); slip ring motor; slow running; specific resistance

sr stateroom

Sr Mr. (*Senhor*—Portuguese, *Señor*—Spanish, *Sieur*—French, *Signor*—Italian); strontium

SR Scottish Rifles; Senate Resolution; Sons of the Revolution; sound ranging (US Army); Southern Railway (NYSE); Southern Rhodesia (IDP); Special Regulations (US Army); Special Reserve; Supplementary Reserve; Swiss Air Transport Company, Ltd

s/r your remittance (*su remesa*—Spanish)

S/R service record (US Army); on the Rhône (river) (*Sur Rhône*—French)

SRA Society of Residential Appraisers; Special Refractories Association

SRC Sentinel Radio Corporation (NYSE); Signal Recruit Center; Signal Reserve Corps; Society of Retreat Conductors; Students' Representative Council; Surplus Relief Corporation

s r c c strikes, riots, and civil commotions (insurance)

SRCX Richardson Carbon Company (private car rr mark)

SRD "Service Rum Diluted"

SRE Holy Roman Church (*Sancta Romana Ecclesia*—Latin); Scientific Research and Experiments Department

S Rept Senate report

S Res Senate resolution

SRF Sugar Research Foundation

SRFI Self-Rising Flour Institute

s rg sound-ranging

SRGS Scottish Royal Geographical Society

S Rh Southern Rhodesia

SRH Supply Railhead

SRI Holy Roman Empire (*Sacrum Romanum Imperium*—Latin); Scrap Rubber Institute

srio secretary (*secretario*—Spanish)

srita young lady, Miss (*señorita*—Spanish)

SRJ ST State of Rio de Janeiro (Brazil) (ASE)

SRK Serrick Corporation, CI B (NYSE)

SRL Scranton Electric Company (NYSE)

SRLX Swift Refrigerator Line (private car rr mark)

SRM Mobile & Ohio (NYSE)

SRN State Registered Nurse

SRO Southland Royalty Company (NYSE); standing room only; Supplementary Reserve of Officers

SR & O Statutory Rules and Orders

SROX United States Atomic Energy Commission, Savannah River Operations Office (private car rr mark)

SRP Supply Refueling Point

SRPDAA Silk and Rayon Printers and Dyers Association of America

SRR Sun Ray Drug Company (NYSE)

SRS Fellow of the Royal Society (*Societatis Regiae Socius*—Latin); Scottish Record Society; Scottish Reform Society

SRSTA Society of Roller Skating Teachers in America

SRT St. Regis Paper Company (NYSE)

SRU Scottish Rugby Union; Seiberling Rubber Company (NYSE)

SRW Sherwin-Williams Co. of Can. Ltd. (The) (Ord.) (ASE)

SRX Sunland Refining Corporation (private car rr mark)

S Ry Southern Railway

SRY Standard Railway Equipment Manufacturing (NYSE)

s s screw steamer; simplified spelling; single screened; single sweep; south side; special subjects; superintendent of schools; sworn statement

ss namely (*scilicet*—Latin); sections; under (*sous*—French)

s S see page (*siehe Seite*—German)

SS Blessed Sacrament (*Saint-Sacrement*—Latin); His Holiness (*Sa Sainteté*—French); His Lordship (*Su Señoria*—Spanish); Holy Scripture (*Sacra Scriptura*—Latin); Most Holy (*Sanctiosimus*—Latin); pages (*Seiten*—German); Sabbath School; Scapa Society; *Schutzstaffel* (Nazi blackshirts); steamship; Second Secretary; Secondary School; Secretary for Scotland; Secretary of State; Secret Service; Selborne Society; Selden Society; Senior Sister (Princess Mary Nursing Service); Shell Shock; short sleeves; Signode Steel Strapping Company (NYSE); Silver Star (United States decoration); Smoke Screen; Society of Shuttlemakers; Society of Silurians; Song of Solomon (Bible); Staffordshire Society; Stair Society; Statistical Society; Steamship; Stewart Society; Straits Settlements; Sulpician Fathers; Sunday School; Supermarine Spitfire; submarines (US Navy); Surtees Society; Surveying Services (naval); *Su Servidor* (Spanish); Swedenborg Society; Synopsis Series of United States Treasury Decisions (legal); Saints

s & s screw and socket (plumbing); spigot and socket

S/S on the Seine (river) (*Sur Seine*—French)

s to s station to station

ssa subscribed (*subscripta*—Latin)

SSA Secretary of State for Air; Seismological Society of America; Selective Service Act; Senior Service Accountant (RAF); Soaring Society of America; Social Security Act; Society of Scottish Artists; Specialty Stores Association; Sunday School Association

s/Sa on the Saône (river) (*Sur Saône*—French)

SSAAII Their Imperial Highnesses (*Ses Altesses Imperiales*—French)

SSAARR Their Royal Highnesses (*Ses Altesses Royales*—French)

SSAFA Soldiers', Sailors', and Airmen's Families Association

SS Amer southern South America

SSB Bachelor of Sacred Scripture (*Sacrae Scripturae Baccalaureus*—Latin); Seafood Statistical Bureau; Secretary to Selective Board (military); Selective Service Board; Selective Service Bureau; Social Security Board; Social Service Board

SS Bde Special Service Brigade

SSC St. Columban's Foreign Missionary Society; Sculptors' Society of Canada; Secretary of State for the Colonies; single silk covered (electric conductors); Society of the Holy Cross (*Societas Sanctae Crucis*—Latin); Solicitor before the Supreme Court; Sunshine Mining Company (NYSE)

s & sc sized and supercalendered (paper)

s s and c same sea and country (shipping)

SS CC Fathers of the Sacred Hearts

SSc D Doctor of Social Science

SSCI Steel Shipping Container Institute

SSD Doctor of Sacred Scripture (*Sacrae Scripturae Doctor*—Latin); Most Holy Lord (the Pope) (*Sanctissimus Dominus*—Latin)

SSDA Secretary of State for Dominion Affairs

SSDB Superintendent of Sailing Directions Branch

SSE Scottish Society of Economists; single silk covering over enamel insulation; Society of St. Edmund; south-south-east

S2C Seaman Second Class (US Navy)

SSF Single-Seater Fighter (RAF); Special Service Force; standard Saybolt furol

SSGG the *Femgericht*: stick, stone, grass, groan (*Stock, Stein, Gras, Grein*—German)

S Sgt Staff Sergeant

SSH Sharon Steel Corporation (NYSE)

SSI standing signal instructions (US Army)

Ssi Company, Co. (*Sūrekasi*—Turkish)

SSIC Southern States Industrial Council

SSJ St. Joseph's Society of the Sacred Heart (Josephite Fathers)

SSJD Sisterhood of Saint John the Divine

SSJE Society of St. John the Evangelist

SSL Licentiate of Sacred Scripture (*Sacrae Scripturae Licentiatus*—Latin); Second Sea Lord (Admiralty); Social Security League

SSLOA Second Sea Lord's Office for Appointments

SSL X Semet-Solvay Division, Allied Chemical & Dye Corporation (private car rr mark)

SSM Society of the Sacred Mission; Squadron Sergeant-Major; Staff Squadron Major; Staff Sergeant-Major; surface to surface missile (US Army)

s & sm surfaced one or two sides and standard matched .(lumber)

SSMI Sodium Silicate Manufacturers Institute

SS MM Their, Your Majesties (*Sus Majestades*—Spanish)

SSMX Southwestern Sugar & Molasses Company (private car rr mark)

SSN specification serial number (US Army)

SSO Senior Staff Officer; Senior Supply Officer (military); south-south-west (*sud-sud ouest*—French); Special Service Officer (RAF); Squadron Signals Officer (naval)

S of Sol Song of Solomon (biblical)

s sord without mutes (*senza sordini*) (music)

SSP Pious Society of St. Paul; scouting seaplane (US Navy); Sigma Sigma Phi (fraternity)

SSP B Socket Screw Products Bureau

SSQ Station Sick Quarters

SSR Soviet Socialist Republic

SSRC Social Science Research Council

s s s single-screw ship; yours very truly (*su seguro servidor*—Spanish)

SSS Congregation of the Blessed Sacrament; Fathers of the Blessed Sacrament (Ro) (*Societas Sanctissimi Sacramenti*); School of Slavonic Studies; Secretary of State for Scotland; Selective Service System; Shore Signal Service; Sigma Sigma Sigma (sorority); Simplified Spelling Society; Single Screw Ship; single signal superheterodyne (radio); Small-Scale Savings; Social Service System; Stamp Savings Slips; your faithful servant (*Su Seguro Servidor*—Spanish); Standard Steel Spring Company (NYSE)

SSSA Soil Science Society of America

s s s c soft-sized super-calendered

s s t seamless steel tubing

SST Spear & Company (NYSE)

SSTI Seamless Steel Tube Institute

SSU Saybolt Universal seconds; Sunday School Union; Superior

Steel Corporation (NYSE)
SSVC Selective Service (US Army)
SSW Cotton Belt Route (rr mark);
St. Louis Southwestern Railway
Company (rr mark)
SSX South Coast Corporation
(NYSE)
s t short ton (2,000 lbs); single
throw (switch); sounding tube;
stopping in transit; storage in
transit
st let it stand (*stet*—Latin); shipping ticket; sounding tube; stanza;
state; stem (botany); stere; stone;
strait; street; strophe; studied;
stumped (cricket)
St individual piece (*Stück*—
German); Saint; Stary (old-Slavic
languages); Strait; Stratus clouds
(Beanfurt weather symbol)
ST Chicago, Milwaukee, St. Paul &
Pacific (NYSE); Seaman Torpedoman (naval); shipping ticket (US
Army); Shock Troops; Sigma Tau
(fraternity); Sons of Temperance;
Standard Time; State Teachers
(college); Superintendent of Trans-
portation; Summer Time
S/T short ton (US Army)
S & T Supply and Transport
S of T Sons of Temperance
sta stamen; station; stationary; sta-
tionery; stator
Sta female saint (*Santa*—Italian,
Spanish, Portuguese)
STA Scottish Temperance Alliance;
Scottish Travel Association; Scottish Typographical Association;
Standard Brewing Company of
Scranton (NYSE); Statistics
(JCAO); steel tape armored (ca-
bles); Summer Time Act
sta agt station agent
staatl State or Federal (*staatlich*—
German)
stacc distinct (*staccato*) (music)
sta com station complement
stae holy saints (*sanctae*)
sta eng stationary engineer
Staffs. Staffordshire (county of Eng-
land)
sta mi statute mile
stan stanchion
St Andr Saint Andrew's
STANHAF New Standard Halfword
(Telegraphic Code)
STANTER New Standard Three-letter
(Telegraphic Code)
STANY Security Traders Association of New York
STAT statistical (US Army)
Stat United States Statutes at Large
Stat Hall Stationers' Hall
statis statistical; statistics
STAX Stauffer Chemical Company
(private car rr mark)

stb et cetera (*és a többi*—
Hungarian)
st b steam boat
STB Bachelor of Sacred Theology
(*Sacrae Theologiae Baccalaureus*
—Latin); Bachelor of Theology
(*Scientiae Theologicae Baccallu-
reus*—Latin); Standard Tube Company Cl B (NYSE)
STB B Standard Tube Co. (The)
(Class "B" Com.) (ASE)
stbd starboard
s t c single trip container
STC Samuel Taylor Coleridge; Sea
Training Corps; Senior (Officers')
Training Corps; Senior Trade Com-
missioner; Small Traders' Commit-
tee; Standard Coil Products Com-
pany (NYSE); State Teachers Col-
lege
St Ch Cas Star Chamber Cases (le-
gal)
st-cu strato-cumulus (clouds)
std standard (timber trade)
Std hour (*Stunde*—German)
st d stopped diapasons
STD Doctor of Sacred Theology
(*Sacrae Theologiae Doctor*—Latin);
Doctor of Theology (*Scientiae
Theologicae Doctor*—Latin); Sea
Transport Department [Division];
Sigma Tau Delta (fraternity)
st diap Stopped diapason (music)
stds standards
Stdy Saturday
Ste Saint (feminine) (*Sainte*—French)
Sté Company (*Société*—French)
STE Society of Terminal Engineers;
special temporary enlistment; Steel
Company of Canada, Ord. (NYSE)
sten stencil; stenographer
s 10 d seller ten days to deliver
(NYSE)
STE NO stenographer (US Army)
stent stentando (music)
ster stereotype; sterling
STER sterilize (US Army)
stern. to the chest (*sterno*—Latin)
(pharmacy)
sternut snuff (*sternutamentum*—
Latin) (pharmacy)
STEV stevedore (US Army)
Stew. Stewart's Reports (legal)
STEW. Superintending Technical
Examiner of Works (military)
Stew. (NJ) Stewart's New Jersey
Equity Reports (legal)
St Ex Stock Exchange
stg sterling; storage; straight
STG Sigma Tau Gamma (fraternity);
Sterling Engine Company (common
stock, ASE)
STGAR staging area (US Army)
stge storage
stgs stringers

sth south
S Th Scholar in Theology
STH Standard Thomson Corporation
(NYSE)
sthn southern
S-3 operations and training officer
(US Army)
STHX Stauffer Chemical Company of
Nevada (private car rr mark)
STI Service Tools Institute; Steel
Tank Institute
stiff. stiffener
stip stipend; stipendiary; stipple;
stipulation
Stir. Stirling (county of England)
STIX Stauffer Chemical Company
(private car rr mark)
stk stock
STK Storkline Furniture Corporation
(NYSE)
stk mkt stock market
STL Lector of Sacred Theology
(*Sacrae Theologiae Lector*—
Latin); Licentiate of Sacred Theol-
ogy (*Sacrae Theologiae Licentiatus*
—Latin); Sterling, Inc (NYSE)
StL.B&M St. Louis, Brownsville and
Mexico Railway Company
STL.R semitrailer (US Army)
StL.-SF St. Louis-San Francisco
Railway Company
StL-SF&T St. Louis, San Francisco
and Texas Railway Company
StLSW St. Louis Southwestern Rail-
way Company
StL.SWofT St. Louis Southwestern
Railway Company of Texas
STL X Stauffer Chemical Company
(private car rr mark)
st m statute mile
STM Master of Sacred Theology
(*Sacrae Theologiae Magister*—
Latin); Master of Theology (*Sci-
entiae Theologicae Magister*—
Latin); Sterling Aluminum Products
(NYSE)
stmftr steamfitter
stn station
STN Stevens (J.P.) & Company, Inc
(NYSE)
STNA Scandinavian Telegraphic
News Agency
STNX Stauffer Chemical Company
(private car rr mark)
sto stoker
Sto Saint (*Santo*—Spanish)
STO Sea Transport Officer; Superior
Tool & Die Company (NYSE)
S'ton Southampton
stor storage
stp stamp
s t p standard temperature and pres-
sure
STP Professor of Sacred Theology
(*Sacrae Theologiae Professor*—
Latin); Sigma Tau Phi (fraternity);

Stop & Shop, Inc (NYSE)
str page (*stromia*—Polish); pressing (*stringendo*) (music); seater; steamer; strait; streak; strength; streptococcus (medicine); string; stringer; stroke
Str street (*Strasse*—German)
STR Scientific and Technological Research; Starrett Corporation (NYSE); strength (US Army)
STRAGL straggler line (US Army)
STRAT strategic (US Army)
Strat R Strategical Reconnaissance
St Rep. State Reporter; State Reports (legal)
string. stringendo (music)
str kpr storekeeper
Strob Strobhart's Law Reports (legal)
Str Sett Straits Settlements
s t s special treatment steel; station to station (railway)
sts stems (botany); stitches; streets
STS Scottish Text Society; Spokane Stock Exchange
STSLB Street and Traffic Safety Lighting Bureau
stsm statesman
STT School of Tank Technology; School of Technical Training (RAF); Stein (A) & Company (NYSE)
s t t l May the earth lie light on thee (*Sit tivi terra levis*—Latin)
St Tr State Trials
STU student (US Army)
s tube steel tube
stud. student
Stuka *Sturzkampf Flugzeug* (Dive Bomber—German)
St Vin Saint Vincent
stwd steward
S-2 intelligence officer (US Army)
s 2 e surfaced two edges (lumber)
s 2 s surfaced two sides (lumber)
s 2 s & cm surfaced two sides and center matched (lumber)
s 2 s & m surfaced two sides and center or standard matched (lumber)
s 2 s 1 e surfaced two sides and one edge (lumber)
s 2 s & s m surfaced two sides and standard matched (lumber)
STX Steffen & Company, Inc., M (private car rr mark); Stewart-Warner (NYSE)
sty story
STY Sterling Drug, Inc (NYSE)
Stycz January (*Styczeń*—Polish)
s u see below (*siehe unten*—German)
S u an answer is requested (*Svar udbedes*—Danish)
SU setup (freight); Siemens's mercury unit (electricity); Soviet Union; USSR (IDP); Shaw University;

Southeastern University; Stanford University; Studebaker Corporation (NYSE); Suffolk University; Susquehanna University; Syracuse University
Su Sunday; Susan
SUA Silver Users Association; State University Association
sub. subaltern; sub-editor; subject; subjunctive; submarine; subscription; substitute; suburb; suburban; subway; supply (*subandi*—Latin)
SUB submarine (US Army)
subch subchapter
subd subdivision
subj subject, subjunctive
subl sublimes
Sub-Lt Sub-Lieutenant
SUBOR subordinate (US Army)
subpar subparagraph
subrogn subrogation (insurance)
subs subscription; subsidiary; subsistence
subsec subsection
subseq subsequent
subseqtly subsequently
subst substantive
substtd substituted
subtrop subtropical (botany)
suc suction
succ success; successor; succeeded; succeeding
s u c l set up in carloads (transportation)
Sucs Successors (*Sucesores*—Spanish)
SUDAN Sudan Airways
sue & l sue and labor (insurance)
Suet. Suetonius, Roman historian
SUF sufficient (US Army)
suff sufficient; suffices (*sufficit*—Latin); suffix
Suff Suffolk; Suffragan
Suff B Suffragan Bishop
sufft sufficient
SUG Southern California Gas Company (ASE)
sugend to be sucked (*sugendus*—Latin) (pharmacy)
sug(g) suggested; suggestion
suiv following (*suivant*—French)
s u l c l set up in less than carloads (transportation)
Sult Sultan; Sultana
sum. let him take (*sumat*—Latin) (pharmacy)
Sum. Sumatra
SUM. Super Mold Corporation of California (NYSE)
SUMCM summary court martial (US Army)
Sumn Sumner's United States Circuit Court Reports (legal)
Sun. Sunday
SUN. Sun Oil Company (NYSE)
SUNA Switchmens Union of North

America
sund sundries
SUNX Sun Oil Company (private car rr mark)
sup. above (*supra*—Latin); petition (*súplica*—Spanish); super; superfine; superior; superlative; supplement; supplementary; supplies; supply
SUP supply (US Army); suppressor grid (vacuum tube); Sutherland Paper Company (NYSE)
SUPCON Superintending Constructor (US Navy)
Sup. Ct Superior Court; Supreme Court
Sup. Dpo Supply Depot
super. superficial; superfine; superior; superintendent; supernumerary
Super. Superior Court; Superior Court Reports (legal)
superl superlative
supers supersaturated
sup. gossyp on cotton wool (*super gossypium*—Latin) (pharmacy)
sup. lint. on lint (*super linteum*—Latin) (pharmacy)
Sup. O Supply Officer
SUPOHDU supply from stock on hand or due in (US Army)
supp supplement; supplementary
Supp New York Supplement Reports (legal)
Sup. P Supply Point
suppos suppository (pharmacy)
suppl supplement
Supp Rev Stat Supplement to the Revised Statutes
supr supreme
Sup. Sgt Supply Sergeant
SUPSHIP Supervisor of Shipbuilding (US Navy)
Supt Superintendent
SUPV supervise (US Army)
supvr supervisor
sur surface; surplus
Sur Surinam; Surrey (county of England)
surg surgeon; surgery; surgical
Surg-Comdr Surgeon-Commander
Surg Gen Surgeon General
Surg-Lt Comdr Surgeon-Lieutenant-Commander
Surg Maj Surgeon Major
Surg-Rear-Adml Surgeon-Rear-Admiral
SURR surrender (US Army)
Surr Surrogate
surv surveying; surveyor; surviving
SURV survey (US Army)
Surv Gen Surveyor General
survor survivor
Sus Susanna; Sussex (county of England)
SUS Saybolt Universal Seconds; Sun-

shine Biscuits, Inc (NYSE)

sus per coll hanging by the neck (*suspensio per collum*—Latin)

Suss Sussex

Suth Sutherland (county of Scotland)

SUV Saybolt universal viscosity

SUVCW Sons of Union Veterans of the Civil War

SUX Standard Ultramarine Company (private car rr mark)

SUY Sunray Oil Corporation (NYSE)

SUYX Sunray Oil Corporation (private car rr mark)

s v sailing vessel; same year (*samana vuonns*—Finnish); soft valve; under the word (*sub verbo*—Latin)

SV the holy Virgin (*Sancta Virgo*—Latin); sluice valve; stop valve; Sons of Veterans; swept volume (engines); Your Holiness (*Sanctitas Vestra*—Latin)

S & V sittings and vacations

svc service and wine included (hotels) (*service et vin compris*—French)

SVC service (US Army)

SVCX Schenectady Varnish Company, Inc (private car rr mark)

SVD Salvage Department; Society of the Divine Word (*Societas Verbi Divini*—Latin)

SVE Seagrave Corporation (NYSE)

SVM Savage Arms Corporation (NYSE)

SVMX Speas Company (private car rr mark)

s v p if you please (*s'il vous plaît*—French)

SVP Small Vessels Pool; Society of St. Vincent de Paul

s v r rectified spirit of wine (*spiritus vini rectificatus*—Latin)

s v t proof spirit of wine (*spiritus vini tenuior*—Latin)

s v v forgive the expression (*sit venia verbo*—Latin)

SVX Socony-Vacuum Oil Company, Inc., Central Region (private car rr mark)

s w sea water; sent wrong; shipper's weight; short wave; short-weight; specific weight; spot weld; stenciled weight; swell organ

sw swatch; switch

św saint (*świety*—Polish)

Sw Swabian; Sweden; Swedish; Swiss; Switzerland

SW Senior Warden (freemasonry);

Shelter Warden; South Wales; South-West; Southwestern; Southwestern Reporter (legal); Stone & Webster (NYSE)

SWAC Bureau of Standards' Western Automatic Computer

SWA single wire armored (cables); Society of Women Artists; Southwest Airways Company; South West Africa (IDP); Sweets Company of America (NYSE)

SW Afr Southwest Africa

s w a k sealed with a kiss

Swaz Swaziland

SWB short wheelbase (US Army)

swbd switchboard

s w b s southwest by south

s w b w southwest by west

SWC Supreme War Council

swchmn switchman

SWCX Sherwin-Williams Company of Canada, Limited, The (private car rr mark)

swd sewed

s w d sliding watertight door; stoneware drain

SWD Standard Power & Light (NYSE)

SWD B Standard Pw. & Lt. Corp. (Dela.) (Com. "B") (ASE)

SWD Pr Standard Pw. & Lt. Corp. (Dela.) ($7 Pfd.) (ASE)

Swed Sweden; Swedish

s w g standard wire gauge

SWG Screen Writers Guild; Society of Women Geographers

SWI Spring Washer Institute

Switz Switzerland

SWJX Supplee-Wills-Jones Milk Company (private car rr mark)

SWNCE the State War Navy Coordinating Committee

SWO Squadron Wireless Officer (naval); Squadron Wireless Operator; Station Warrant Officer (RAF); Swan-Finch Oil Corporation (NYSE)

SWP South West Penna. Pipe Lines (ASE)

SWPAC Sweet Wine Producers Association of California

SWPC Small War Plants Corporation; South-West Pacific Command

SWPX Shawinigan Chemicals Limited (private car rr mark)

s w r steel wire rope

SWR St. Louis Southwestern Railway (NYSE)

SWS Scranton-Spring Brook Water Service (NYSE); Shore Wireless

Service; single white silk covered; Static Water Supply

swtg switching

SWTX Swift Tank Line (private car rr mark)

s w u see below (*siehe weiter unten*—German)

SWUS southwestern United States

SWVB Social Work Vocational Bureau

SWW Shawinigan Water & Power (NYSE)

SWX Swift & Company (NYSE)

s x single cash ruled (stationery)

Sx Sussex

SX Southern Pacific Company (NYSE)

SXS Sigma Xi Society (society)

sy supply; survey

Sy Surrey

SY Seychelles (IDP); Sperry Corporation (NYSE); steam yacht

SYA Solvay America (NYSE)

SYB Society Brand Clothes (NYSE)

S Yd Scotland Yard

SYE Skelly Oil Company (NYSE)

syl syllable; syllabus

SYLX American Viscose Corporation, Sylvania Division (private car rr mark); Sylvania Industrial Corporation (private car rr mark)

sym symbol; symbolic; symmetrical; symmetry; symphony

symp orc symphony orchestra

syn synchronizing; synonym; synonymous

Syn Sons (*Synowie*—Polish)

synch synchronous motor or generator

synd syndicate

synop synopsis

Syn Ser Synopsis Series

Sy PO Supply Petty Officer (naval)

syr syrup (pharmacy)

Syr Syria; Syriac; Syrian

syst system

sz number (*szám*—Hungarian); honorable (*szanowny*—Polish)

sz(t) saint (*szent*—Hungarian)

SZ Symington-Gould Corporation (NYSE)

SZC Schwitzer-Cummins Company (NYSE)

szept September (*szeptember*—Hungarian)

SZPZ World Union of Poles Abroad

s zt then (*seiner zeit*—German)

T

t book (*tome*—French); in the time of (*tempore*—Latin); tare; target; tee; tempo; tenor; tense; t-bar; tension; terminal; territory; that; thunder (nautical); time; tome; ton; town; township; train; transit; transitive; triple bond; troy; *tutti* (music); volume (*tomus*—Latin)

T American Telephone & Telegraph (NYSE); Testament; Theodore; Theresa; Thomas; Tiler (freemasonry); *The Times*; Titus; Torpedoman (naval); transportation (use in combination only) (US Army); Treasury; Trinity (*Trinitas*—Latin); Tuesday; Turkish

t a additional taxes (*taxes additionelles*—French); tax agent; air transport (*transport aérien*—French); as the acts show (*testantibus actis*—Latin) (legal)

TA Tass Agency; Technical Adviser; Telegraphic Address; Territorial Army; Tissue Association; Tithe Annuity; Transamerica Corporation (NYSE); Treatment Allowance; Typographical Association

Ta tantalum

T/A table of allowances (US Army)

TAA Technical Assistance Administration; Territorial Army Association; Trans-Australia Airlines; Transportation Association of America

TAAN Transamerica Advertising Agency Network

tab. tablet (pharmacy); table; tableau

TAB Technical Assistance Board; Tobacco & Allied Stocks, Inc. (NYSE); Total Abstinence Brotherhood; Traffic Audit Bureau

TABSO Société Anonyme de Navigation Aerienne Civil Bulgar-Sovietique

Tac Tacitus, Roman historian

TAC tactic (US Army); Technical Assistance Committee

TACA TACA International Airlines (*Transportes Aeros Centro-Americanos*)

TACAO Townsville and Country Airways Pty. Ltd.

TACAV Linea Aerea TACA de Venezuela

TACIT Technical Advisory Committee on Inland Transport

Tac Sch Tactical School

T Adr telegraph address (*Telegraphische Adresse*—German)

TAE National Greek Airlines

TAF Tactical Air Force

TAFI Technical Association of the Fur Industry

TAG the Adjutant General (US Army); Telegraphist Air Gunner

TA&G Tennessee, Alabama and Georgia Railway Company (rr mark)

TAHQ theater army headquarters (US Army)

Tai Taiwan

TAI Compagnie de Transports Aeriens Intercontinentaux; Tobacco Associates, Inc

TAICE Transactions of the American Institute of Chemical Engineers

Tal Talmud; Talmudic

tal such (*talis*—Latin) (pharmacy)

TAL Trans-Atlantic League

TALOA Trans-Ocean Airlines

tal qual average quality (*talis qualis*—Latin)

tam land, air, sea (*terre, air, mer*—French)

Tam Tamaulipas; Tamil

tan. tangent (mathematics)

Tan. Taney's Circuit Court Reports (legal); Tanganyika

TAN. Transportes Aereos Nacionales

tan. bkt tangency bracket

tanh hyperbolic tangent

TANS Territorial Army Nursing Service

TAO Tau Alpha Omega (fraternity)

TAP Theta Alpha Phi (society); Transportes Aereos Portugueses

TAPPI Technical Association of the Pulp and Paper Industry

TAR. Société de Transports Aeriens en Extreme Orient

TARC theater army replacement command (US Army)

tars. ocul to the eyelids (*tarsis oculorum*—Latin) (pharmacy)

tart. tartar; tartaric (pharmacy)

Tas Tasmania; Tasmanian

TAS Travelers' Aid Society; true air speed

TASA the Assistant Secretary of the Army (US Army)

Tass Telegraph Agency of the USSR (*Telegrafnoe Agenstvo Soyusa Sovetskih Socialisticheskih Respublik*—Russian)

Tat. Tatar

TAT. to accompany troops (US Army)

Tau Taurus (constellation)

TAUS Tea Association of the United States; Tobacco Association of the United States

taut. tautological; tautology

TAY Third Avenue Transit Corporation (NYSE)

t a w twice a week (advertising)

TA&W Toledo, Angola & Western Railway Company (rr mark)

t b time base; times at bat (baseball); thorough bass (music)

Tb terbium; Tiberius

TB Tariff Bureau; Tea Bureau; techincal bulletin (US Army); Torpedo Boat (naval); Torpedo Bomber (US Navy aircraft); Tourist Bureau; tracer bullet; Training Battalion; Traffic Bureau; Trial Balance (accounting); tubercle bacilli; tuberculosis

t & b turned and bored (lumber)

t b a to be announced

TBA Television Broadcasters Association

TBAX Toronto Pipe Line Company (private car rr mark)

TBD torpedo-boat destroyer

TBGAA travel by Government automobile authorized (US Army)

TBL Through Bill of Lading

TBMAA travel by military aircraft authorized (US Army)

TBP Tau Beta Pi (fraternity)

tbsp tablespoon

TBTA Tennessee Burley Tobacco Association

t c take care; tariff circular; taxes included (*taxes comprises*—French); three strings [loud pedal] (*tre corde*) (music); till countermanded; time called; top center; towing chock

tc tierce

Tc technetium

TC the Republic of Turkey (*Türkiye Cümhuriyeti*—Turkish); Cameroun (IDP); Code Telegram; Tank Corps; Technical College; Technical Committee; telephone condenser; Temporary Constable; Tennessee Central Railway Company (rr mark); Tennis Club; Theta Chi (fraternity); Timber Corps; Touring Club; Town Clerk; Town Councillor; Traffic Commissioner; Training Center (US Army); Transport Command (RAF); Travellers Checks; Trinity College; Tuberculosis Committee; Tufts College

t & c threads and couplings (plumbing)

T & C Thompson & Cook's Supreme Court Reports (legal)

TCA Tanners Council of America; Trans-Canada Air Lines

TCAA Tile Contractors Association of America

TCC Tennessee Corporation (NYSE); triple cotton covered

TCD Theta Chi Delta (society); Trinity College, Dublin

TCF Touring Club de France; Twentieth Century Fund

TCFB Transcontinental Freight Bureau

TC1C Turret Captain First Class (US Navy)

TCG Tucson, Cornelia and Gila Bend Railroad Company (rr mark)

tchr teacher

TCIX Tennessee Coal, Iron & Railroad Company (private car rr mark)

TCL Trinity College London

TCLX Transit Company, Limited (private car rr mark)

TCMA Trailer Coach Manufacturers Association

T Corps Training Corps

TCOX Trinity Cotton Oil Division of Best Foods, Inc (private car rr mark)

TCP Traffic Control Post; Transport Command Pilots; Trichlorophenoxyacetic acid (insecticide); TriCresylPhosphate

TCPA Trans-Continental Passenger Association

TCPX Taylor-Colquitt Company (private car rr mark)

TCR Transportation Corps release (US Army)

TCS temporary change of station (US Army)

TCT Texas City Terminal Railway Company (rr mark)

TCTW Tin Can Tourists of the World

TCU Texas Christian University

TCW Tennessee College for Women

TCW & IB Transcontinental Weighing & Inspection Bureau

TCX The Texas Company (private car rr mark)

td tod (28 pounds—wool weight)

t d three times a day (ter in die) (pharmacy); time deposit

t-d tractor-drawn

TD Tactical Division (naval); Tank destroyer (US Army); Teachta Dala (Member of Parliament—Eire); Telecommunications Department (GPO); Telegraph Department; Telephone Department; Territorial Decoration; Tobacco Duty; Torpedo Depot (naval); Tractor-drawn (US Army); Trade Division (naval); Traffic Director; Treasury Department; Treasury Decisions; Trinidad and Tobago (IDP)

T/D table of distribution (US Army)

TDC Theta Delta Chi (fraternity)

td cu tinned copper

t d f trunk distribution frame

t d g twist drill gauge

TDI Textile Distributors Institute

TDN travel directed is necessary in the military service (US Army)

TDNA Trailercoach Dealers National Association

TDP Tau Delta Phi (fraternity)

TDPFO temporary duty pending further orders (US Army)

tdr all rights reserved (tous droits réservés—French)

TDWY treadway (US Army)

TDX Timken-Detroit Axle (NYSE)

TDY temporary duty (US Army)

t e totally enclosed; trailing edge

te telegram; telegraph; ton (toune —French)

Te Tellurium (chemistry)

TE Tampa Electric Company (NYSE); Theological Examination; Topographical Engineer; Trade Expenses; Triple Entente

T/E tables of equipment (US Army)

TEAL Tasman Empire Airways Limited

TEC the Executive Council (presidential)

T E C A totally enclosed, closed-air circuit (engineering)

tech technical; technics; technique; technology

Techn 3rd Gr Technician Third Grade

Tech Sgt Technical Sergeant

TED Toledo Edison Company (NYSE)

TEDPA Theater Equipment Dealers Protective Association

TED Pr Toledo Edison Co. (The) (4¼% Pfd.) (ASE)

t e f c totally enclosed, fan cooled

t e g top edge gilt

TEGMA Terminal Elevator Grain Merchants Association

TEI Tax Executives Institute

teilw partly (teilweise—German)

tel telegram; telegraph; telephone

TEL TelAutograph Corporation (NYSE)

Tel Bn Telegraph Battalion

TELECON telecommunication conference (US Army)

tel no. telephone number

Tel & Tel Telephone and Telegraph

TELX Pennsylvania Salt Manufacturing Company of Washington (private car rr mark)

TEM Ontario Northland Railway (rr mark); Temiskaming & Northern Ontario Railway (rr mark)

TEMA Tubular Exchanger Manufacturers Association

temp in the time of (tempora—Latin); temperance; temperature; template; tempo (music); temporal; temporary

Temp The Tempest (Shakespeare)

tempo 1 tempo primo (music)

ten. tenor (music); held; sustained

(tenuto) (music)

Tenn Tennessee; Tennyson

tens tensile

tens str tensile strength

TENX Tennessee Corporation (private car rr mark)

TEO Trans Empire Oils Ltd. (NYSE)

TEP Tau Epsilon Phi (fraternity)

ter rub (teratur) (pharmacy); terrace; territory

Ter Terence

TER Tau Epsilon Rho (fraternity)

terat teratological; teratology

term. terminal; termination; terminology; terminus

Ter Territory

tert tertiary; third (tertius—Latin)

te sep f totally enclosed, separately fan-cooled

TESMA Theater Equipment and Supply Manufacturers Association

test. testament; testator; testimonial

Test Testament

Test de Estate of (Testamentaria de—Spanish)

testmto will (testamento—Spanish)

testo witness (testigo—Spanish)

T et G Tarn-et-Garonne (French Department)

tetr tetragonal

Tetryl tetranitromethylaniline

Teut Teuton; Teutonic

t e w c totally enclosed, water cooled

t ex for instance (till exempel—Swedish)

Tex Texan; Texas

Tex App Texas Court of Appeals Reports (legal)

Tex Ct Rep Texas Court Reporter (legal)

Tex Mex Texas Mexican Railway Company

text. textile

text. rec received text (textus receptus—Latin)

t f till forbidden (advertising)

tf trifling (fire records)

TF penal servitude (travail forcé —French); task force or training film (US Army); Tax Foundation; Teagle Foundation; telegram for delivery by telephone; Territorial Forces; Textile Foundation; Tiffany Foundation; Torpedo Factory; Trainers' Federation; trench feet; trench fever; Trudeau Foundation; Twentieth Century-Fox Film (NYSE)

TFA Textile Fabrics Association; Tie Fabrics Association

TFC traffic (US Army)

TFI Textile Foundation Incorporated

T1C Telegrapher First Class (US Navy)

Tfl table (*Tafel*—German)
tfr transfer
TFR Fair (The) (NYSE)
TFS Transactions of the Faraday Society
. ʊ type genus
t & g tongued and grooved (lumber)
TG Texas Gulf Sulphur Company (NYSE)
T & G Tremont & Gulf Railway Company (rr mark)
TGA Toilet Goods Association
t g b tongued, grooved, and beaded (lumber)
TGCX Tank Gas Corporation (private car rr mark)
TGM Torpedo Gunner's Mate
TGT target (US Army)
TGWU Transport and General Workers' Union
th theater
t h tee handle (plumbing)
Th Thomas; Thursday; thorium
TH American Thread (NYSE); Territory of Hawaii; Toynbee Hall; Transport House; Trinity House
Th A Theological Associate
THA Taft-Hartley Act
Thad Thaddeus
Thai Thailand
Th B Bachelor of Theology
THB Toronto, Hamilton & Buffalo Railway Company (rr mark)
Thbd Theobald
thby thereby
Th & C Thompson & Cook's Supreme Court Reports (legal)
thd thread
Th D Doctor of Theology (*Theologiae Doctor*—Latin)
th em thorium emanation
Theo Theodore; Theodosia
Theoc Theocritus, Greek poet
theol theological; theologician; theology
Theoph Theophilus
theor theorem
theoret theoretic
theos theosophical; theosophy
therap therapeutic
thermochem thermochemistry
thermodyn thermodynamics (*thermodynamique*—French)
therm(om) thermometer; thermometric
Thesaur Amer Septent Sigil Seal of the Treasury of North America; Seal of the U.S. Treasury (*Thesaurus Americae Septentrionis Sigillum*—Latin)
Thess Thessalonians, Thessaly
I THESS First Thessalonians (Bible)
II THESS Second Thessalonians (Bible)
thfm therefrom

t h i time handed in
THI Thiokol Corporation (NYSE)
THIA theology (*theologia*—Latin)
3d Dec Dig. Third Decennial Digest
30 the end (newspapers)
32mo thirty-two mo, trigesimosecundo (books)
thk thick
THKX Thompson-Hayward Chemical Company (private car rr mark)
Thl part (*Theil*—German)
Th L Theological Licentiate
Th M Master of Theology (*Theologiae Magister*—Latin)
THM Thompson (John R.) Company (NYSE)
THMZ three hundred mile zone
tho though
THO Thompson Products (NYSE)
thof thereof
Thomp & C Thompson & Cook (legal)
thon thereon
thorac to the throat (*thoraci*—Latin) (pharmacy)
thoro thorough
Thos Thomas
thou thousand
thp thrust horsepower
TH Pr American Thread Co. (The) (5% Pfd.) (ASE)
THQ theater headquarters (US Army)
thr their; there
THR Thermoid Company (NYSE)
3B third base; three base hit (baseball)
3D three dimensions (motion pictures)
3-P three-pole (electricity)
throf thereof
THSA Traveling Hat Salesmen's Association
thto thereto
THU Teck-Hughes Gold Mines (NYSE)
Thurs Thursday
T H W M Trinity high-water mark
t i that is (*tudni illik*—Hungarian)
TI thallium; titanium; Tiberius (Latin); Tibet
TI Tax Institute; Thread Institute; Toastmasters International; Tuskegee Institute
TIA Tapioca Institute of America
TIC The Industrial Court
TICER Temporary International Council for Educational Reconstruction (of UNESCO)
tick tickler
t i d three times a day (*ter in die*—Latin) (prescription)
TIDX Tide Water Associated Oil Company (private car rr mark); Tide Water Oil Company (private car rr mark)
TI&ED Troop Information and Education Division

tier. tierce
Tiff Tiffany's Reports, (legal)
TIH Their Imperial Highnesses
t i m time is money
Tim Timothy (Bible)
1 Tim First Timothy (Bible)
11 Tim Second Timothy (Bible)
timb kettledrums (*timbales*—French) (music)
Timon Timon of Athens (Shakespeare)
timp drums (*timpani*) (music)
tinct tincture (pharmacy)
tip. printing office (*tipografia*—Spanish)
Tip. Tipperary (county of Ireland)
TIP troop information program (US Army)
tip bkt tipping bracket
TIS Tishman Realty & Construction (NYSE)
tit. name (*titulo*—Spanish); title (*titre*—French); titular
Tit. Titus (Biblical)
Tit. A Titus Andronicus (Shakespeare)
t j that is (*to jest*—Polish)
TJA trial judge advocate (US Army)
TJPOI Twisted Jute Packing and Oakum Institute
tjs always (*toujours*—French)
t k this month (*tämän kuun*—Finnish)
tk track; truck
TK tank (US Army); Technicolor, Inc (NYSE)
TKA Tau Kappa Alpha (fraternity)
TKE Tau Kappa Epsilon (fraternity)
t k o technical knockout
TKP Theta Kappa Phi (fraternity); Theta Kappa Psi (fraternity)
tkr tanker
TKR Timken Roller Bearing Company (NYSE)
tkt ticket
Tl part (*Teil*—German); thallium
t l time loan (banking); time loss; ton load; total loss (insurance); trade last (colloquial)
TL Telegraphist Lieutenant (naval); Texas League (baseball); time lengths or truckload (US Army); Torpedo Lieutenant (naval); Turkish pound (*Türk Lirasi*)
TLA Temperance League of America; Truck Line Association
Tlax Tlaxcala
TLC Talcott (James), Inc (NYSE)
TLCPA Truck Line-Central Passenger Association
TLCX Trinidad Leaseholds (Canada) Limited (private car rr mark)
t les j everyday (*tous les jours*—French)
t l o total loss only (insurance)
TLO Tilo Roofing Company Inc (NYSE)

t loc local tax (*taxe locale*—French)

TLP torpedo landplane

tlr teller (banking); tiler (free-masonry); trailer

TLR Times Law Reports; trailer (US Army)

TLRB Textile Labor Relations Board

tls taels

TLS Territorial Long Service; Times Literary Supplement

TLSX Tank Line Service Incorporated (private car rr mark)

TLX Trans-Lux Corporation (NYSE)

tm telegram with multiple addresses (*télégramme multiple*—French) turns per minute (*tours par minute* —French)

t m time modulation; trade-mark; trench mortar; true mean (value); twisting moment

Tm thulium

TM technical manual (US Army); Texas Mexican Railway Company; ton miles (railway); Traffic Manager; Trained Man (naval); Training Memorandum; Trainmaster

TMA Tile Manufacturers Association

TMAUS Tobacco Merchants Association of the United States

tmax maximum rate (*tarif maximum* —French)

TMC Thatcher Glass Manufacturing Company (NYSE)

TMEA Typewriter Manufacturers Export Association

TMFB Trans-Missouri Freight Bureau

TM1C Torpedoman's Mate First Class (US Navy)

TMG Track made good (navigation)

TMI Tag Manufacturers Institute; Thorofare Markets, Inc. (common stock, ASE)

tmkpr timekeeper

TML Three Mile Limit

TMO telegraph money order

TMOX Textiles Monterrey, (private car rr mark)

tmp temperature

t m s and so on (*tai muuta semmoista*—Finnish)

TM2C Torpedoman's Mate Second Class (US Navy)

TMSI Transportation Metal Sash Institute

TM3C Torpedoman's Mate Third Class (US Navy)

TMU Trench Mortar Unit

TMUSA Toy Manufacturers of the United States

TMX Mars Incorporated (private car rr mark)

t n tariff number; telephone number; true north

tn normal rate (*tarif normal*—French); ton; town

TN Texas & Northern Railway Company (rr mark); train (US Army)

Tna Tetranitroaniline

TNA The National Archives

tnd tinned

TNEC Temporary National Economic Committee

TNG training (US Army)

tnge tonnage

TNGX Texas Natural Gasoline Corporation (private car rr mark)

T & NO Texas and New Orleans Railroad Company (rr mark)

t no c threads no couplings (plumbing)

Tns Tunis (Africa)

TNT trinitrotoluene; trinitrotoluol

TNX trinitroxylene

TNZ Trunz, Inc. (ASE)

to volume (*tomo*—Spanish)

t o turn over; turnover

TO Technical Officer (military); Telegraph Office; Telephone Office; Torpedo Officer (naval); Torrington Company (NYSE); Trained Operator; Transport Officer (military)

T/o transfer order

T/O tables of organization (US Army)

t & o taken and offered

TOA Tall Oil Association; Theatre Owners of America; Trans Oceanic Airways Pty. Ltd.

t o b take off boost (engines)

Tob Tobiah; Tobias; Tobit

TOC theater of operations commander (US Army); Trooping of the Color

Toc H Talbot House

TOCX True's Oil Company (private car rr mark)

TOD Todd Shipyards Corporation (NYSE)

T/O & E tables of organization and equipment (US Army)

t o f to order from

togr together

TOK Toklan Royalty Corporation (NYSE)

Tol Toulouse (France)

TOL Tower of London

TOLX Petrolie Corporation, Limited (private car rr mark

t o m even (*till och med*—Swedish)

tom volume (*tomus*—Latin)

tonn tonnage

TONS Trans-Ocean News Service

t o o time of origin

t o p temporarily out of print

TOPNS theater of operations (US Army)

topog topographical; topography (*topographie*—French)

t o r time of reception

TOR Third Order Regular of St. Francis; Thor Corporation (NYSE); Toronto Stock Exchange

tor dep torpedo depot

torp torpedo

tot. total

TOT time on target (US Army)

tot enc totally enclosed

TOTFORF forfeiture of all pay and allowances due or to become due (US Army)

Towar association (*Towarzystwo*— Polish)

toxicol toxicology

t p postage stamp (*timbre poste*— French); title page; transit privileges

TP penal servitude for life (*travaux forcés à perpétuité*—French); Teaching Practice; Theta Psi (fraternity); Trade Post; Transvaal Province; Treaty Port

T & P Texas & Pacific Railway Company (rr mark)

TPA Theta Phi Alpha (sorority); Trans-Pacific Airlines, Ltd; travel by privately owned automobile is authorized (US Army); Travelers' Protective Association

TPB Township Planning Board

t p c triple paper covered

TPCX Colgate-Pamolive-Peet Company (private car rr mark)

TPDX Tennessee Products & Chemical Corporation (private car rr mark)

TPGI Tubular Plumbing Goods Institute

t p i teeth per inch (cog wheels); threads per inch (spur gears); tons per inch; turns per inch (screw system)

TPI Tennessee Polytechnic Institute

TPLX Pacific Lumber Company The (private car rr mark)

tpm revolutions per minute (*tours par minute*—French)

TPM Tonopah Mining Company of Nevada (NYSE)

tpo time (*tiempo*—Spanish)

t p r temperature, pulse, respiration (medical)

tpr trooper

TPRX Texas Power & Light Company (private car rr mark)

T & P Ry Texas & Pacific Railway Company

tps townships; troops

T P S earth telegraphy (*télégraphie par le sol*—French)

tpsf radio-telephony (*téléphonie sans fil*—French)

tpt transport; trumpet
TPTG turned plate turned grid (radio)
tptr trumpeter
t p w title page wanting
TP & W Toledo, Peoria & Western Railroad (rr mark)
TPX Texas & Pacific Railway Company (NYSE); Trojan Powder Company (private car rr mark)
t/q as is (*tale quale*) (grain trade)
t q d three or four times a day (*ter quaterve in die*—Latin) (pharmacy)
t r tariff rules; tons registered; transportation request; true radius; trust receipt
tr shake (*trillo*) (music); tare; terbium; trace; track (navigation); tragedy; train; transaction; transfer; transit (navigation); transitive; translated; translation; translator; transport; transpose; triangle; tribunal; troop; truck; trumpet (music); trustee
Tr draft (*Tratte*—German); tincture (pharmacy)
TR Tariff Reform; telegram to be called for at a telegraph office (*Télégraphe restant*—French); Term Reports (legal); Texas Gulf Producing Company (NYSE); Tirailleur Regiments; Tithe Redemption; transportation request (US Army); Trunk Road; Turkey (IDPI)
t/r trust receipt
t &r truck and rail
tra tincture (*tinctura*—Latin)
TRA Textile Refinishers Association; Tire and Rim Association; Trane Company (NYSE)
Tr A Triangulum Australe (constellation)
TRAC tractor (US Army)
TRACDR tractor-drawn (US Army)
trad tradition; traditional; traditionally
traf traffic
trag tragedian; tragedy; tragic
Tragk capacity (*Tragkraft*—German)
tram. tramways
tran transit
trans transaction; transferred; transformer; transitive; transitory; translated; translation; translator; transparent; transport(ation); transverse
Trans Transvaal
Transat Transatlantic
transcr transcribed
transfo transformer (*transformateur*—French)
Transj Trans-Jordan
translit transliterated; transliteration
Transpac Transpacific
Tr App Transcript Appeals (legal)

TRASTA Training station (US Navy)
tratt *trattenuto* (music)
TRAUS Thoroughbred Racing Associations of the United States
trav travel; traveler; works (*travaux*—French)
TRB troop basis (US Army)
TRC Thames Rowing Club; Tithes Rent Charge; Trona Railway Company (rr mark); Truax-Traer Coal Company (NYSE)
Tr Co Trust Company
tr coil tripping coil
Tr Coll Training College; Trinity College
Tr & Cr Troilus and Cressida (Shakespeare)
TREA Texas Rice Export Association
treas treasurer; treasury
tree trustee
t r f tuned radio frequency
trf tariff
TRF transfer (US Army)
TR F Ter Trieste Free Territory
TRFX Turpentine & Rosin Factors, Inc. (private car rr mark)
TRH Their Royal Highnesses
Tri doctor (*Tohtori*—Finnish); Triangulum (constellation)
TRI Department of Trusteeship and Information from Non-Self Governing Territories (UN Secretariat); Textile Research Institute
trib tribal; tribunal; tribune; tributary
TRICC Tariff Rules of the Interstate Commerce Commission
trig trigonometric; trigonometrical; trigonometry
trim quarter of a year (*trimestre*—French)
Trin Trinidad; Trinity
Trin Coll Trinity College
Trip Tripos
tripl triplicate; tripled
trit triturate
trk track; truck
TRKDR truck-drawn (US Army)
TRKHD truck head (US Army)
TRLP transport landplane (US Navy)
trm terminal
TRMT treatment (US Army)
trnfr transfer
troch lozenge (*trochiscus*—Latin) (pharmacy)
trom trombone (music)
tromp trumpet (*trompette*) (music)
trop tropic; tropical
TRP troop (US Army)
Tr Pl Tribune of the People (*Tribunus Plebis*—Latin)
Tr Pot by tribunician authority (*Tribunicia Potestate*—Latin)
TRRA Terminal Railroad Association of St. Louis (rr mark)

TRR of St L Terminal Railroad Association of St. Louis
trs transfer; transferred; transpose (type); trustees
TRS Technical Recruiting Staff; Torry Research Station; tough rubber sheathed (electric cables)
trsd transferred; transposed
TRSP transport seaplane (US Navy)
Tr S S triple screw ship
TRU True Temper Corporation (NYSE)
Tru Railw Rep Truman's Railway Reports (legal)
Truron of Truro (*Truronesis*—Latin)
trv traverse
tr&w truck rail and water
t s all by itself (*tutto solo*—Italian) (music); the key alone (*tasto solo*—Italian) (music); tensile strength; test solution; this side; tool steel; transport and supply; tub-sized (paper)
ts typescript
TS Tactical School (naval); Television Society; Texas Pacific Coal & Oil Company (NYSE); Theosophical Society; Training Ship; transit storage (US Army); Transport and Supply; Treasury Solicitor
t/s turns per second
T & S Trust and Savings
t s a total storage area
TSA Textile Salesmen's Association; Track Supply Association
TSAA Tobacco Salesmen's Association of America
tsc taxes and service included (*taxes et service compris*—French)
TSC Texas State College
TSCX Steel Company of Canada, Limited, The (private car rr mark)
TSD Tertiary of St. Dominic; theater shipping document (US Army)
TSDS Two-Speed Destroyer Sweeper
T2C Telegrapher Second Class (US Navy)
T2G Technician, Second Grade
TSF Two-Seater Fighter (RAF); wireless telegraphy (*télégraphie sans fil*—French)
TSFSR Transcaucasian Socialist Federal Soviet Republic
T Sgt Technical Sergeant
T/Sgt Top Sergeant
TSH Their Serene Highnesses
t s h thyroid stimulating hormone (medicine)
TSKREQ task force requisition (US Army)
TSL Thew Shovel Company (NYSE)
TSO Tidewater Southern Railway Company (rr mark); town suboffice
TSOA Tramp Ship Owners Association

tsp teaspoon
TSP Theta Sigma Phi (society); torpedo seaplane (US Navy)
t s r traveling stock reserve
TSRC Tubular and Split Rivet Council
TSS turbine steam ship; twin screw ship
TSSR Turkmenistan Socialist Soviet Republic
TST Thompson-Starrett Company (NYSE)
t s u this side up
TSU technical service unit (US Army); Theta Sigma Upsilon (sorority); Tobacco Securities Trust Co. Ltd. (ASE)
TSU D Tobacco Securities Trust Co. Ltd. (ASE)
TSW Transue & Williams Steel Forging (NYSE)
t t tank top
tt all (tout—French)
TT all yours (totus tuus—Latin); Tanganyika Territory; Tannu Tuva; Taylor Trust; Teetotaler; Theta Tau (fraternity); Telegraphic Transfer; Togoland (French) (IDP); Toledo Terminal Railroad Company (rr mark); torpedo tube (naval); Tourist Trophy; travel with troops (US Army); tuberculin tested
TTA Trans-Texas Airways
TTC Air Force, Technical Training Command
tte draft (traite—French) (commercial)
TTEX Tulsa Tank Line (private car rr mark)
TTG travel with troops going (US Army)
T3C Telegrapher Third Class (US Navy)
t t l to take leave
TTMA Truck Trailer Manufacturers Association; Tufted Textile Manufacturers Association
t t o this transaction only
TTR travel with troops returning (US Army)
t u thermal unit; toxic unit; traffic unit; transmission unit
Tu thulium; Tuesday
TU Taylor University; Temple University; Theta Upsilon (sorority); training unit (use in combination only) (US Army); Trengganu (IDP);

Trinity University; Tulane University
tub électron electronic tubes (tubes électroniques—French)
Tuc Tucana (constellation)
TUC Trades Union Congress; Trades Union Council
Tuck Surr Tucker's Surrogate Reports (legal)
Tues Tuesday
TUI Trade Union International
TUM Trades Union Movement
Tun Tunisia
tunic. let it be varnished (tunicetur) (pharmacy)
tunicat coated (tunicatœ) (pharmacy)
turbc turbulence
turbt turbulent
Turk. Turkey; Turkish
Turkn Turkistan
tus a cough (tussis—Latin)
tuss mol when the cough disturbs (tussi molesta) (pharmacy)
TUW Tung-Sol Electric, Inc (NYSE)
t v this year (tänä vuonna—Finnish)
T v successor (Tot vorsetting—Dutch)
tv transverse
TV television; terminal velocity; Tide Water Associated Oil (NYSE)
TVA Tennessee Valley Authority
TV & G Tavares & Gulf Railroad (rr mark)
TVL travel (US Army); Trav-ler Radio Corporation (NYSE)
TVOX Texas Vegetable Oil Company (private car rr mark)
TVR temperature variation of resistance (electricity)
t w tail water
TW Texas Wesleyan (college)
TWA Transcontinental & Western Air; Trans World Airlines, Inc. (NYSE)
TWAB Textile Work Assignment Boards
Twad Twaddell (hydrometer)
TWC Twin City Rapid Transit (NYSE)
TWE Textile Waste Exchange
Twel N Twelfth Night; or, What You Will (Shakespeare)
TWI Training Within Industry (Division of War Manpower Commission)
TWIMC to whom it may concern
TWIU Tobacco Workers Interna-

tional Union
twizn twilight zone
t w l top water-level
TWN Twin Coach Company (NYSE)
2B two-base hit; second base (baseball)
II Chron II Chronicles (Bible)
II Cor II Corinthians (Bible)
2,4 D insecticide
Two Gent Two Gentlemen of Verona (Shakespeare)
II Pet. II Peter (Bible)
2-p two-pole (electricity)
II Sam. II Samuel (Bible)
2/10,n-30 2 percent discount in 10 days, net in 30 days
II Thess II Thessalonians (Bible)
II Tim. II Timothy (Bible)
TWOX Tide Water Associated Oil Company (private car rr mark); Tide Water Oil Company (private car rr mark)
twp township
t w s timed wire service (telegraph)
tw-sc twin-screw
TWU Transport Workers Union
TWUA Transport Workers Union of America
TWX teletypewriter exchange message
tx barrels (tonneaux—French); tax or taxes
Tx radio transmitter
TX Theta Xi (fraternity)
TXCX Teas Extract Company (private car rr mark)
TXL Texas Pac. Land Tr. (NYSE)
txn taxation
TXP Texas Pr. & Lt., $4 Pfd (105) (NYSE)
TXT Textron Incorporated (NYSE)
TXU Texas Utilities Company (NYSE)
TXY Chicago Yellow Cab Company (NYSE)
ty territory; truly
TY Tri-Continental Corporation (NYSE)
TYC Thames Yacht Club; Two-Year-old Course
Tyl Tyler's Reports (legal)
typ typographer; typographical; typography
typw typewriter; typewritten
Tyr Tyrone (county of Ireland)
TZ I K Central Executive Committee (of the USSR) (Tzentralny Ispolnitelny Kommitet—Russian)

U

u   among (*unter*—German); and (*und*
—German); ugly threatening
weather (meteorology); uncle;
union; upper; velocity

U   clock, o'clock (*Uhr*—German);
Ulysses; Union; Unionist; unit
(use in combination only) (US
Army); United Corporation (NYSE);
University; uranium; Uriah; Utah

u a   among others; (*unter anderen*—
German); and others (*und andere*—
German)

UA   Ulster Association; Underwriting
Account; United Artists; Upsilon
Alpha (society)

U of A   University of Akron; Univer-
sity of Alabama; University of
Alaska; University of Alberta
(Canada); University of Arizona;
University of Arkansas

u a a O   and elsewhere (*und an
anderen Orten*—German)

UAB   Unemployment Assistance
Board

UABS   Union of American Biological
Societies

UAC   United Aircraft Corporation;
United States Air Conditioning
Corporation (NYSE)

UACX   Universal Atlas Cement
Company (private car rr mark)

UAFWBC   United American Free
Will Baptist Church

UAGBF   United Association of Great
Britain and France

UAL   United Air Lines, Inc.

u a m   and so forth (*und anderes
mehr*—German)

UAM   underwater to air missile
(US Army)

ua O   and elsewhere (*und andere
Orte*—German)

UAOD   United Ancient Order of
Druids

UAP   United Aircraft Products
(NYSE); United Australia Party;
utility amphibian plane (US Navy)

UAPRE   University Association for
Professional Radio Education

UAT   Union Aeromaritime de Transport

UAW   United Automobile Workers

u A w g   please reply (*um Antwort
wird gebeten*—German)

UAWU   United Automobile Workers

UAX   unit automatic exchange

ub   brought forward (*Übertrag*—
German)

üb   over (*über*—German)

UB   United Brethren in Christ;
Upper Bench (legal)

U of B   University of Buffalo

UBA   Union of Burma Airways

U of BC   University of Bishop's
College (Canada); University of
British Columbia (Canada)

UBCJA   United Brotherhood of Car-
penters and Joiners

UBCWA   United Brick and Clay
Workers of America

UBDMA   United Better Dress Manufacturers Association

UBEA   United Business Education
Association

übers   translated (*übersetzt*—German)

UBO   United States Tobacco Company (NYSE)

U-boat   German submarine (*Unter-
seeboot*—German)

UBS   Union des Banques Suisses;
United Biscuit of America (NYSE)

UBSOTA   United Beauty School
Owners and Teachers Association

uc   undercharge

u c   on, with, one string (*una corda*);
upper case (typography)

UC   the city being built (*urba
condita*—Latin); uncut edges
(bookbinding); Union College;
United Club; University College;
Upper Canada; Upper Chamber;
Upsala College; Ursinus College

U of C   University of California;
University of Chicago; University of Cincinnati; University of Colorado; University
of Connecticut

UCB   United Carbon Company
(NYSE)

UCBX   Union Carbon Company (private car rr mark)

UCC   United Electric Coal Companies (NYSE); Universal Correspondence College; Universities
China Committee; University
College, Cork

UCCD   United Christian Council
for Democracy

UCCW   United Council of Church
Women

UCD   University College, Dublin

UCEC   Union Central Executive
Committee

UCEI   Catholic Union of International Study

UCF   United-Carr Fastener Corporation (NYSE)

UCH   University College Hospital

UCI de SS   Catholic International
Union for Social Service (CIUSS)

UCL   Union Oil Dompany of California (NYSE); University College,
London

UCLA   University of California at

Los Angeles

UCL A Pr   Union Oil Co. of California ($3.75 "A" Pfd.) (ASE)

UCNW   University College of North
Wales

UCO   Universal Consolidated Oil
(NYSE)

UCOFS   University College of the
Orange Free State

UCP   United Country Party
(Australia)

UCR   United China Relief; Utah
Coal Route (rr mark)

UCS   Universal-Cyclops Steel
(NYSE); University Catholic So-
ciety; University College School;
University College of Swansea

UCT   United Commercial Travellers;
University of Capetown

UCT of A   United Commerical Travelers of America

UCTLV   United Committee for the
Taxation of Land Values

UCV   United Confederate Veterans

UCW   United Cigar-Whelan Stores
(NYSE)

u d   as directed (*ut dictum*—Latin)

ud   you (*usted*—Spanish)

UD   Undesirable Discharge (US
Army); United Dairies; Upper
Deck (naval); Urban District

U of D   University of Dayton; University of Denver; University of
Detroit

UDAX   North American Car Corporation (private car rr mark)

u d c   upper dead center

UDC   Union of Democratic Control;
United Daughters of the Confederacy; Urban District Council

u d f   and those following (*unde die
folgende*—German)

UDFI   Union Defence Force Institute

UDFMA   Upholstery and Drapery
Fabric Manufacturers Association

UDGA   United Date Growers Association

u dgl   and the like (*und dergleichen*
—German)

UDIX   Utilities Distributors, Inc.
(private car rr mark)

u dk   upper deck

UDM   United Merchants & Manufacturers (NYSE)

UDPC   United Dairy Products
Company

u drgl   and the like (*und dergleichen*
—German)

uds   you (*ustedes*—Spanish)

UDS   United Stores Corporation
(NYSE); Upsilon Delta Sigma
(fraternity)

UDSR *Union Démocratique et Socialiste de la Résistance* (French)
u d t underdeck tonnage
UDY United Dye & Chemical Corporation (NYSE)
u E our opinion (*unseres Erachtens* —German)
UE until exhausted (US Army); University Extension; upper entrance (theater)
ueb brought forward (*übertrag*—German)
UEBL Economic Union of Belgium and Luxembourg
UEC United Elastic Corporation (NYSE)
U Ed Your Honor (*Uwe Edelheid*—Dutch)
UEF United Engineering & Foundry (NYSE)
UEIC United East India Company
UEL United Empire Loyalist
u e m electromagnetic unit (*unité électromagnétique*—French)
UEO Unit Education Officer
UEP Union Electric of Missouri (NYSE)
UERMWA United Electrical, Radio and Machine Workers of America
UET Unit Equipment Table (RAF)
UETI United Engineering Trustees, Inc.
UEX Unexcelled Chemical Corporation (NYSE)
UF (International) United Free Church; United Fruit Company (NYSE); University Fellowship; urea-formaldehyde (plastics)
U of F University of Florida
UFA Universal Film Company (*Universal-Film-Aktiengesellschaft*—German)
UFC United Free Church (Scotland)
UFEMWA United Farm Equipment and Metal Workers of America
UFFVA United Fresh Fruit and Vegetable Association
UFG United States Freight Company (NYSE)
UFGX United Fuel Gas Company (private car rr mark)
UFMA United Fur Manufacturers Association
UFO United States & Foreign Securities (NYSE): unidentified flying object
Ug Uganda
UG United Gas Improvement (NYSE)
U of G University of Georgia
UGA Underwriters Grain Association
UGC United Gas Corporation (NYSE)
UGCCWA United Gas, Coke and Chemical Workers of America

UGI International Geographical Union (IGU)
UGLE United Grand Lodge of England (freemasonry)
UGSSS Union of Girls' Schools for Social Service
ugt urgent (telegrams)
UGWA United Garment Workers of America
U of H University of Hawaii; University of Houston
UHAA United Horological Association of America
UHCMWI United Hatters, Cap, and Millinery Workers International
UHCMWIU United Hatters, Cap, and Millinery Workers International Union
u h f ultra high frequency (waves)
UHRA United Hunts Racing Association
u i as below (*ut infra*—Latin)
UI Underwear Institute; Unemployment Insurance
U of I University of Idaho; University of Illinois
UIA International Union of Architects (*Union Internationale des Architectes*—French)
UIAA International Union of Aviation Insurers (IUAI)
UIBC International Union for the Issue of Combined Coupon Tickets
UIC International Union of Chemistry (IUC)
UICC International Union against Cancer
UICT International Union against Tuberculosis
UICWA United Infants and Children's Wear Association
UID Unemployment Insurance Department
UIHS International Union of the History of Science
UIJS International Union of Socialist Youth (IUSY)
UIN United States and International Securities (NYSE)
UINIPrWW U.S. & Intl. Secur. Corp. ($5 1st Pfd. with Wts.) (ASE)
UIOFEC International Union of Civil Register Officials
UIP Inter-Parliamentary Union (IPU)
UIPE International Union for Child Welfare
UIPN International Union for the Protection of Nature (IUPN)
UIR International Broadcasting Union
UIS International Relief Union; Utah-Idaho Sugar Company (NYSE)
UISA United Inventors and Scientists of America
UISC Unemployment Insurance

Statutory Committee
UIT International Telecommunications Union (ITU)
UIU Upper Iowa University
UIUNA Upholsterers International Union of North America
UIV Union Investment Company (NYSE)
UIWV United Indian War Veterans
UJ Union Jack
UJA United Jewish Appeal
UJC Union Jack Club
UJD Doctor of both Civil and Canon Law (*Utriusque Juris Doctor*—Latin)
UJECO United Jewish Educational and Cultural Organization
UK Union Carbide & Carbon (NYSE); United Kingdom
U of K University of Kansas; University of Kentucky
UKA Ulster King-of-Arms; United Kingdom Alliance
U of KC University of Kansas City; University of King's College (Canada)
UK/Cont United Kingdom or Continent (shipping)
UK/Cont (B-H) Bordeaux-Hamburg Range (shipping)
UK/Cont (H-H) Havre-Hamburg Range (shipping)
UKfo United Kingdom for orders (shipping)
UKHAD United Kingdom, Havre, Antwerp, or Dunkerque
UKML United Knitwear Manufacturers League
UKO United Milk Products Co (NYSE)
Ukr Ukraine; Ukrainian
Ukr SSR Ukrainian Soviet Socialist Republic
UL Underwriters Laboratories
U of L University of Louisville
ULA Universal American Corp. (NYSE)
U L A S T Latin American Union of Societies of Phtisiology
u & lc upper and lower case (typography)
ULCA United Lutheran Church in America
ULI Urban Land Institute
ULJD University of London Journalistic Diploma
ull ullage
ULP utility landplane (US Navy)
ult ultimate (*último*—Spanish); ultimately; in the preceding month (*ultimo*—Latin)
ultim ultimatum
ult praes prescribed last time (*ultimus praescriptus*—Latin)
ULWIU United Leather Workers International Union

u m under-mentioned
um unmarried
U of M University of Manitoba (Canada); University of Maine; University of Maryland; University of Miami; University of Michigan; University of Minnesota; University of Mississippi; University of Missouri; University of Montreal (Canada)
U Ma. Ursa Major (constellation)
UMA United Maritime Authority
UMC United Motor Courts
UMCA Universities Mission to Central Africa; Uraba, Medellin & Central Airways, Inc.
UMCC United Maritime Consultative Council
UME Uniform Manufacturers Exchange
UMFC United Methodist Free Churches
U MI Ursa Minor (constellation)
uml min revolutions per minute (umlaufungen pro minute—German)
UMO United Molasses Co. Ltd. (ASE)
ump umpire
UMPAC United Mink Producers Association, Cooperative
UMS Unfederated Malay States
UMTS Universal Military Training Service (System)
UMU United Mineworkers' Union
UMW United Mine Workers
UMWA United Mine Workers of America
un unified (bonds); union; united
UN Union Twist Drill Company (NYSE); United Nations
U of N University of Nebraska; University of Nevada
UNA United Nations Assembly; United Nations Association
unabr unabridged
UNAC United Nations Appeal for Children; United Nations Atomic Commission
UNAI Underwear-Negligee Associates, Inc.
unan unanimous
UNAPOC United National Association of Post Office Clerks
unatt unattached
UNAVA United Negro and Allied Veterans of America
U of NB University of New Brunswick (Canada)
unbd unbound (books)
unc uncertain
UNC United Nations Command; United Nations Commission; United Nations Conference
U of NC University of North Carolina
UNCCP United Nations Conciliation

Commission for Palestine
uncert uncertain
UNCE United Negro College Fund
UNCIO United Nations Conference on International Organization (San Francisco)
UNCIP United Nations Commission for India and Pakistan
UNCOK United Nations Commission on Korea
uncor uncorrected
UNCURK United Nations Commission for the Unification and Rehabilitation of Korea
und exception (undantag—Swedish)
U of ND University of North Dakota; University of Notre Dame
und dk under deck
UNDEB New Wales Union
undsgd undersigned
undtkr undertaker
UNEC United Nations Education Conference
UNEDA United Nations Economic Development Administration
UNESCO United Nations Educational, Scientific and Cultural Organization
unexpl unexplained; unexploded; unexplored
UNF United States Finishing Company (NYSE)
UNFAV unfavorable (US Army)
UNFB United Nations Film Board
UNFC United Nations Food Conference
ung about (ungefähr—German)
UNG Union Gas Company of Canada (NYSE)
UNGA United Nations General Assembly
U of NH University of New Hampshire
UNICEF United Nations International Children's Emergency Fund
UNIO United Nations Information Organization
UNIPED International Union of Producers and Distributors of Electric Power
unis unison; unisinö (music)
Unit. Unitarian; Unitarianism
univ universal; universally
Univ Universalist; University; University College (Oxford)
UNJSPB United Nations Joint Staff Pension Board
unk uncorrected (unkorrigiert—German)
unkn unknown
UNKRA United Nations Korean Reconstruction Agency
unl unlimited
unm unmarried
U of NM University of New Mexico
UNMC United Nations Mediterranean

Commission
UNO United Nations Organization
UNOECR United Nations Organization for Educational and Cultural Relations
unof unofficial
unop unopposed
unp unpaged
UNP Universal Products Company (NYSE)
UNPC United Nations Palestine Commission
UNPCC United Nations Conciliation Commission for Palestine
unpub unpublished
UNPX Union Petroleum Company (private car rr mark)
UNR Union Asbestos & Rubber (NYSE)
UNRPR United Nations Relief for Palestine Refugees
UNRPR Pool United Nations Relief for Palestine Refugees Pool
UNRRA United Nations Relief and Rehabilitation Administration
UNRR United Nations Relief and Rehabilitation Control
UNRWAPRNE United Nations Relief and Works Agency for Palestine Refugees in the Near East
uns unsymmetrical
UNS Union Sugar Company (NYSE); United Nations Society; United States Radiator Corporation (NYSE)
Un of S Afr Union of South Africa
UNSAT unsatisfactory (US Army)
UNSC United Nations Security Council; United Nations Social Commission
UNSCC United Nations Standards Co-ordinating Committee
UNSCCUR United Nations Scientific Conference on the Conservation and Utilization of Resources
UNSCOB United Nations Special Committee on the Balkans
UNSCOP United Nations Special Committee on Palestine
UNSG United Nations Secretary General
unsgd unsigned
UNSVC unserviceable (US Army)
unt below (unter—German)
UNTAA United Nations Technical Assistance Administration
UNTAB United Nations Technical Assistance Board
UNTC United Nations Trusteeship Council
UNTCOK United Nations Temporary Commission on Korea
UNTT United Nations Trust Territory
UNV Universal Insurance Company (ASE)
UNW United Wallpaper, Inc (NYSE)

UNWC United Nations War Crimes Commission

unwmkd unwatermarked

UNX Underwood Corporation (NYSE)

u ö and often (*und öfters*—German)

u & o use and occupancy (insurance)

U of O University of Oklahoma; University of Oregon; University of Ottawa (Canada)

UOCX Union Oil Co of California (private car rr mark)

UOPWA United Office and Professional Workers of America

UORM Independent Order of Red Men

UOS Union Stock Yards of Omaha (NYSE)

up. underproof; unpaged; upper

UP Postal Union (*Union Postale*— French); Ulster Parliament; Unemployable Pensions; Union Pacific Railroad (NYSE); United Parliament; United Party; United Presbyterian; United Press; United Provinces; University of Paris; University of Pennsylvania; University of Pittsburgh

UPA United Patternmakers' Association

UPAA United Press Association of America

U of Pa L Rev University of Pennsylvania Law Review

UPC United Presbyterian Church; United Protestant Council; United Specialties Company (NYSE)

UPCNA United Presbyterian Church of North America

UPDMA United Popular Dress Manufacturers Association

UP EC Portuguese Union of the State of California (*União Portuguesa do Estado da California*— Portuguese)

UPF United Profit-Sharing (NYSE)

UPF Pr United Profit Sharing Corp. (10% Pfd.) (ASE)

uphol upholsterer; upholstery

upm revolutions per minute (*umlaufungen pro minute*—German)

UPNAI United Practical Nurses Association, Inc

UPNCA United Pants and Novelties Contractors Association

u p o undistorted power output

UPP EC Portuguese Protective Union of the State of California (*União Portuguesa Protectora do Estado da California*—Portuguese)

UPR Union Pacific Railroad

U of PR University of Puerto Rico

UP RR Union Pacific Railroad

u p t urgent postal telegram

UPU Universal Postal Union (*Union Postale Universelle*—French)

UPX United Paramount Theatres (NYSE)

Ur Uruguay

UR Uniform Regulations; United Aircraft Corporation (NYSE); your (US Army)

U of R University of Redlands; University of Richmond; University of Rochester

Uran Uranus

urb urban

URCA United Roofing Contractors Association

URCLPWA United Rubber, Cork, Linoleum and Plastic Workers of America

URCX United Refining Company (private car rr mark)

URD Union Républicaine Démocratique (French)

urlet your letter

URL TR (reference) your letter (US Army)

URMSG (reference) your message (US Army)

URO United Rink Operators

urol urological; urology

URSER (reference) your serial (US Army)

URSI International Scientific Radio Union

URSS Union of Soviet Socialist Republics (*Union des Républiques Socialistes Soviétiques*—French equivalent of USSR)

urtel your telegram

URTX Union Refrigerator Transit Lines (private car rr mark)

URWA United Rubber Workers of America

URZ Ulen Realization Corporation (NYSE)

u s as above (*ut supra*—Latin); under seal (customs); uniform sales; where above mentioned (*ubi supra*—Latin)

US Under Secretary; Uncle Sam; uniform system (photography); United Service; United States; United States Reports; Universal Service (news); Unnamed Society

u/s unserviceable

U of S University of Saskatchewan (Canada); University of Scranton

USA Under-Secretary for Agriculture; Under-Secretary for Air; Unestablished Staff Association; Union of South Africa; United Society of Artists; United States of America; United States Army; United Steelworkers of America; University School of Agriculture; Urban Sanitary Authority; US Airlines, Inc

USAAC United States Army Air Corps

USAAF United States Army Air Forces

USABF United States Amateur Baseball Federation

USAC United States Air Corps; Utah State Agricultural College

USACSR United States Air Corps Specialist Reserve

USAEA United States Alkali Export Association

USAF United States Air Force

USAFBI United States Army Forces in the British Isles

USAFFE United States Armed Forces in the Far East

USAFI United States Armed Forces Institute (US Army)

USAFIK United States Army Forces in Korea

USAI South American Union of Engineers' Associations

USAIG United States Aircraft Insurance Group

USAMGIK United States Army Military Government in Korea

USAMP United States Army Mine Planter (US Army)

USANP United South African National Party

USAP B United States Aircraft Production Board

USAPWA United Stone and Allied Products Workers of America

USAR United States Army Reserve

USASI United States Air Staff Intelligence

USAT United States Army Transport

USATC United States Air Transport Command

USAVR United States Aviation Reports

USAX Department of the Army, Office of the Chief of Transportation (private car rr mark)

USBAE United States Board of Agricultural Economics

USBC United States Bureau of the Census

USC Ulster Savings Certificates; Under-Secretary for the Colonies; Unitarian Service Committee; United Services Corps; United States Club; United States Code (legal); United States Customs; United States of Colombia; upstage center; University of South Carolina; University of Southern California

USCA United States Code Annotated (legal); United States Copper Association

USCAA United States Coast Artillery Association

USCB United States Customs Bonded

USCC United States Chamber of Commerce; United States Circuit

Court; United States Court of
Claims (legal); United States Com-
mercial Company
USCCA United States Circuit Court
of Appeals
USCCPA United States Court of
Customs and Patent Appeals
USCG United States Coast Guard
USCGR United States Coast Guard
Reserve
USC&GS United States Coast and
Geodetic Survey
USCGSCF United States Coast
Guard Shore Communication Facil-
ities
U CM United States Conference of
ayors
SCNO United States Chief of
Naval Operations
Comp St United States Compiled
Statutes (legal)
US Comp St Supp United States
Compiled Statutes Supplement (le-
gal)
USCS United States Civil Service
Commission; United States Chief of
Staff; United States Conciliation
Service
USCSRA United States Cane Sugar
Refiners Association
USCSSB United States Cap Screw
Service Bureau
JSC Supp United States Code Sup-
plement (legal)
USCT United States Colored Troops
US Ct Cls United States Court of
Claims
USD United States Dispensatory
l of SD University of South Dakota
USDA United States Department of
Agriculture
USDAFDD United States Deputy Ad-
ministrator and Food Distribution
Director
JSDC United States District Court;
United States District of Columbia
USDFR United States Director of
Foreign Relief
US Dist Ct United States District
Court
USECC United States Employees'
Compensation Commission
USEF United States Expeditionary
Force
JSES United States Employment
Service
u s f and so forth (und so ferner—
German)
USF United Services Fund; United
States Foil Company, Inc., Cl B
(NYSE)
USFA Under-Secretary for Foreign
Affairs
USFAA United States Field Artil-
lery Association
USFARS United States Federation

of Amateur Roller Skaters
USF B United States Foil Company
(''B'') (common stock, ASE)
USFET United States Forces Euro-
pean Theater
USFHA United States Field Hockey
Association
USFSA United States Figure Skating
Association
U of SFX University of Saint
Francis Xavier (Canada)
USG United States Government;
United States Gypsum Company
(NYSE); United States standard
gauge
USGA United States Golf Associa-
tion
USGS United States Geodetic Sur-
vey; United States Geological Sur-
vey
USH United Shoe Machinery (NYSE)
USHA United States Housing Au-
thority
USHC United States High Commis-
sion; United States Housing Cor-
poration
USHG United States Home Guard
USHGA United States Hop Growers
Association
USHL United States Hockey League
USH Pr United Shoe Machinery Corp
(Pfd.) (ASE)
USI United Service Institution;
United States of Indonesia
USIA United States Infantry Associ-
ation
USIAC United States Inter-American
Council
USIBA United States International
Book Association (Inc.)
USIII United States Interim Inter-
national Information
USIRB United States Internal Reve-
nue Bonded
USIS United States Immigration Serv-
ice; United States Information Serv-
ice
USITA United States Independent
Telephone Association
USJCC United States Junior Cham-
ber of Commerce
USL United States Legation; United
States Lines Company (NYSE)
u s unemployed supernumerary list
(military)
USLSSA United States Live Stock
Sanitary Association
USLTA United States Lawn Tennis
Association
USM underwater to surface missile
(US Army); United States Mail;
United States Marines; United
States Mint
USMA United States Military Acad-
emy
USMC United States Marine Corps;

United States Maritime Commission
USMCA United States Marine Corps
Aviation
USMCR United States Marine Corps
Reserve
USMHS United States Marine Hos-
pital Service
US Mil Res United States military
reservation
USMMA United States Merchant
Marine Academy
USMP United States Military Police
USMS United States Maritime Serv-
ice
USMSSB United States Machine
Screw Service Bureau
USN Under-Secretary of the Navy;
United States Navy
USNA United Service for New Amer-
icans; United States National
Army; United States Naval Academy
USNAC United States Naval Air
Corps
USNAS United States Navy Depart-
ment
USND United States Navy Depart-
ment
USNFE United States Naval Forces
in Europe
USNG United States National Guard
USNH United States North of Cape
Hatteras (shipping)
USNR United States Naval Reserve
USNRF United States Naval Re-
serve Force
USNSCF United States Naval Shore
Communication Facilities
USNX Dept of the Navy (private car
rr mark)
USO United Service Organizations
USOA United States Olympic Asso-
ciation
USOFA Under Secretary of the Army
USP United States Patent; United
States Pharmacopoeia; United
States Playing Card Company
(NYSE)
USP A United States Polo Associa-
tion; United States Potters Associ-
ation
USP EC United States Paper Ex-
porters Council
USP F United States Pacific Fleet
US Pharm United States Pharma-
copoeia
USPHS United States Public Health
Service
USPM United States Provost Mar-
shal
USPO United States Post Office
USPPA United States Pulp Pro-
ducers Association
USPTA United States Paddle Ten-
nis Association
USQMC United States Quartermaster
Corps

USR United States Reserves; United States Supreme Court Reports (legal)

USRA United States Railroad Administration; United States Revolver Association

USRAD United States Fleet Shore Radio Station

USRCS United States Revenue Cutter Service

USRCSI United States Red Cedar Shingle Industry

USRS United States Reclamation Service; United States Revised Statutes

USRX United States Rubber Company (private car rr mark)

USS Under-Secretary of State; United States Scouts; United States Senate; United States Ship; United States standard (screws); United States Steamer

USSA United Saw Service Association; United States Salvage Association

USSAF United States Strategic Air Force

USSB United States Shipping Board

USSBEFC United States Shipping Board Emergency Fleet Corporation

USSC United States Steel Corporation; United States Supreme Court

USSEA United States Scientific Export Association

USSFA United States Soccer Football Association

USSIA United States Shellac Importers Association

USSLL United States Savings and Loan League

USSR Union of Soviet Socialist Republics

USSS United States Secretary of State; United States Steamship

USST United States Secretary of the Treasury

USSW United States Secretary for War

USSX United States Sugar Corporation (private car rr mark)

UST United Stockyards Corporation (NYSE)

USTA United States Trotting Association

USTB United States Tourist Bureau; United States Travel Bureau

USTC United States Tariff Commission

USTD United States Treasury Department

USTMA United States Trade Mark Association

US Treaty Ser United States Treaty Series

USTTA United States Table Tennis Association

USTX Union Starch and Refining Company (private car rr mark)

usu usual; usually

USU United States Rubber Reclaiming Company (NYSE)

usurp. to be used (*usurpandus*) (pharmacy)

USV United States Volunteers

u s w and so forth (*und so weiter*—German)

USW Under-Secretary for War; United Steel Workers

USWA United Shoeworkers of America

USWAB United States Warehouse Act Bonded

USWB United States Weather Bureau

USWD United States War Department

USWGA United States Wholesale Grocers Association

USWSA United States War Shipping Administration

USWSSB United States Wood Screw Service Bureau

USWV United Spanish War Veterans

USY A United Electric Service Company (ASE)

u t universal time

ut utility

Ut Utah

u/t untrained

UTA United Typothetae of America

UTC University Tutorial College

UTCX Union Tank Car Company (private car rr mark)

ut dict as directed (*ut dictum*—Latin)

utend to be used (*utendus*—Latin) (pharmacy)

UTIL utility (US Army)

ut inf as below (*ut infra*—Latin)

UTLX Union Tank Car Company (private car rr mark)

UTO United Telephone Organizations

UTP Utah Power & Light (NYSE)

UTS Union Theological Seminary

UTSEA United Transport Service Employees of America

ut sup. as above (*ut supra*—Latin)

UTWA United Textile Workers of America

UTX Union Tank Car Company (private car rr mark)

UU Union University

uu sometimes (*unter umständen*—German)

U of U University of Utah

u u r under usual reserves

UUTC Upjohn Unemployment Trustee Corporation

u u v errors and omissions excepted (*unter üblichen vorbehalt*—German)

u v ultraviolet

UV Unadilla Valley Railway (rr mark)

U of V University of Vermont; University of Virginia

UVCO United Veterans Council

UVL Universal Pictures Company (NYSE)

UVR United Veterans of the Republic

UVV Universal Leaf Tobacco (NYSE)

UVW United New Jersey Railroad & Canal (NYSE)

u/w underwriter

U of W University of Washington; University of Wisconsin; University of Wyoming

UWF United World Federalists

U of WO University of Western Ontario (Canada)

U WUA Utility Workers Union of America

ux wife (*uxor*—Latin)

UX uranium X

UXAA unexploded anti-aircraft

UXAPB unexploded anti-personnel bomb

UXB unexploded bomb

UXGB unexploded gas bomb

UXIB unexploded incendiary bomb

UXPM unexploded parachuted mine

UXTGM unexploded Type G mine

UY Uranium Y

UYT Udylite Corporation (NYSE)

u zw that is (*und zwar*—German)

V

v against (*versus*—Latin); city (*ville*—French); he, she lived (*vixit*—Latin); of, from (*von*—German); potential difference; see (*siehe*—German, *vide*—Latin, *véase*—Spanish); turn over (*voltare*—Italian) (music); vacuum tube; valve; vapor; velocity; ventral; verb; verse; version; very; vicar; vicarage; vicinal; voice (*voce*); year (*vuosi*—Finnish); volt

V N. Y., N. H. & Hartford Railroad

(NYSE); Friday (*Vendredi*—French); Vatican City (IDP); Venerable; Victor; Victoria; Viscount; Volunteers; you (*usted*—Spanish); vanadium; victory

v/ sight (*vista*—Spanish)

v a verb active; verbal adjective; volt-ampere

Va exchange equivalent (*Valuta*—German); viola (music); Virginia

VA Royal Order of Victoria and Albert; Vanadium Corp. of America (NYSE); Veneer Association; Veterans Administration; Vicar Apostolic; Vice Admiral; Victualling Allowance; Voice of America; Volunteer Artillery; Volunteers of America; Your Highness (*Vuestra Altezo*—Spanish); Fruit-Vegetable Ventilated Box (rr car)

V&A Victoria and Albert

vac vacant; vacation; vacuum

VAD Voluntary Aid Detachment

V Adm Vice-Admiral

VAE Your Electoral Highness (*Votre Altesse Électorale*—French)

val value; valued; valve; valvular

val exchange equivalent (*Valuta*—German); Valenciennes (lace); Valentine; Valencia (Spain)

VAL Valspar Corporation (NYSE)

val d at valued at (insurance)

valn valuation

VAL Pr Valspar Corp. (The) ($4 Conv. Pfd.) (ASE)

V Am. Vice Admiral

VAN Vanadium-Alloys Steel Company (NYSE); Vancouver Stock Exchange

vap vapor (*vapeur*—French)

var reactive volt-ampere; variant; variation; variegated; variety; various

VAR visual-aural range; your Royal Highness (*Votre Altesse Royale*—French)

Va R Virginia Reports (legal)

var cond variable condenser

VARIG Empresa de Viacao Aerea Rio Grandense (airline)

var lect varying reading (*varia lectio*—Latin)

VAS Vocational Advisory Service

Vat. Vatican

vaud vaudeville

v aux verb auxiliary

v b and others; et al (*ve baskalar*—Turkish)

verb Veterans Bureau; Volunteer Battalion

VBA Venetian Blind Association America

VBAUS Vanilla Bean Association of the United States

VBD Volta Bureau for the Deaf

vbl verbal

vb n verbal noun

VBR Virginia Blue Ridge Railway (rr mark)

v c color vision; valuation clause (insurance); visible capacity

vc for example (*verbi causa*—Latin); violoncello (music)

VC Before Christ (*Vor Christi*—German); Vassar College; Veterinary College; Veterinary Corps (US Army); Vice Chairman; Vice Chancellor; Vice Consul; Victoria Cross; Victory Corps; Villanova College; Virginia-Carolina Chemical (NYSE); Volunteer Corps; Volt-coulomb

v/c return mail (*vuelta de correo*—Spanish)

VCA Vitrified China Association

VCAS Vice-Chief of the Air Staff

VCC Vice-Chancellor's Court (legal)

VCCUS Venezuelan Chamber of Commerce of the United States

VCCX Virginia-Carolina Chemical Corporation (private car rr mark)

v cel celebrated man (*vir celeberrimus*—Latin)

v c g Vertical line through center of gravity

v Chr before Christ (*vor Christus*—German)

VCI Variety Clubs International

VCIGS Vice-Chief of the Imperial General Staff

v cl renowned man (*vir clarissimus*—Latin)

VCMA Vacuum Cleaner Manufacturers Association

VCOFSA Vice Chief of Staff, United States Army

VCPFA Vitreous China Plumbing Fixtures Association

VCR Long live Christ the King (*Viva Cristo Rey*—Spanish)

vcs voices

vct victor

VCW Victor Chemical Works (NYSE)

VCWX Victor Chemical Works (private car rr mark)

VCY Ventura County Railway Company (rr mark)

vd you (singular) (*usted*—Spanish)

vd vapor density; various dates

VD venereal disease; Viceroy-Designate; Victorian Decoration; Victualling Department (naval); Volunteer Officers' Decoration

Vda Widow (*Viuda*—Spanish)

VDA Verein für das Deutschtum im Auslande (Association for furthering Germanism abroad)

v def defective verb

v dep deponent verb (grammar)

VDG venereal disease, gonorrhea

VDH valvular disease of the heart

VDI Van Dorn Iron Works Company (NYSE)

VDL Van Diemen's Land

VDM Minister of the Word of God (*Verbi Dei Minister*—Latin)

VDMIE The word of the Lord endureth for ever (*Verbum Domini manet in eternum*—Latin)

vdrs vendors (legal)

VDS venereal disease, syphilis

VDT variable density wind tunnel; Vulcan Detinning Company (NYSE)

ve widow (*veuve*—French)

VE Victor Equipment Company (NYSE); Victory in Europe; Visalia Electric Railroad Company (rr mark); Your Eminence (*Votre Eminence*—French); Your Excellency (*Vossa Excel(l)ência*—Portuguese, Vuestra Excelencia—Spanish)

VEC Vertientes-Camaguey Sugar (NYSE); Viceroy's Executive Council

Ved Vedic

V-E Day Victory in Europe Day

vedr concerning (*vedrørende*—Danish)

veh vehicle

vel velocity; vellum

Vel Vela

VEL Virginia Electric & Power (NYSE)

VELX Cia Distribuidora de Gas; Vel-A-Gas (private car rr mark)

VEMC Visual Equipment Manufacturers Council

ven vene

Ven Venerable; Venetian; Venice; Venezuela; Venus

Ven & Ad Venus and Adonis (Shakespeare)

v en c value accounted for (*valor en cuenta*—Spanish)

vent. ventilation

Vent. Ventris's (Law Reports)

vent. pl ventilating plate

VENX Vendome Tank Car Company (private car rr mark)

ver verse; verses; version; vertex (navigation); united (*vereinigt*—German)

Ver society (*Verein*—German); Veracruz

verb. improved (*verbessert*—German); verbal

verb. sap. a word to the wise (*verbum sapienti*—Latin)

Verf author (*Verfasser*—German)

Vergl compare (*Vergleiche*—German)

Verh married (*Verheiratet*—German)

Verhandl proceedings (*Verhandlungen*—German)

verif verification (*verification*—French)

Verl publisher (*Verleger*—German)

Verm Vermont

Vern Vernon's (Law Reports)

vers versed sine (mathematics)

verson versine (mathematics)

Ver St United States (*Vereinigte Staaten*—German)

vert compare, cf (*vertaa*—Finnish); vertebrata; vertical

Very Rev Very Reverend

Verz catalogue (*Verzeichnis*—German)

ves vessel; vestry

Ves Vesey's (Law Reports)

VES Veterinary Evacuation Section

vesp in the evening (*vespere*—Latin) (pharmacy)

VET veteran; veterinarian; veterinary (US Army)

veter veterinary

Veterans Adm Veterans Administration

vet med veterinary medicine

Vet. Surg Veterinary Surgeon

V Exa Your Excellency (*Vossa Excell(l)ência*—Portuguese)

V Exc Your Excellency (*Votre Excellence*—French)

v f very fair; vision-frequency; video-frequency; voice-frequency; vulcanised fiber

Vf author (*Verfasser*—German)

V F Vicar Forane

v f o variable frequency oscillator

VFR visual flight rules

VFW Veterans of Foreign Wars of the United States

VFWUS Veterans of Foreign Wars of the United States

v g for example (*verbi gratia*—Latin); very good

V G Vicar-General; Vice-Grand; Your Grace (*Votre Grâce*—French)

VGAA Vegetable Growers Association of America

v g c viscosity gravity constant

vgl compare (*vergelijk*—Dutch; *vergleiche*—German)

vgl a see also (*vergleiche auch*—German)

VGN Virginian Railway Company, The (rr mark)

VGOX United Fuel Gas Company (private car rr mark); Virginian Gasoline & Oil Company (private car rr mark)

v gr for example (*verbigracia*—Spanish)

v H per cent (*vom Hundert*—German)

V/h formerly (*Vorheen*—Dutch)

v h c Very highly commended

v h f very-high frequency

v i see below (*vide infra*—Latin); verb intransitive; vertical interval;

viscosity index; volume indicator

Vi virginium

VI Vermiculite Institute; vertical interval; Victoria Institute; Virgin Islands

VIABRAS Viacao Aerea Brasil (airline)

vic times (*vices*—Latin) (pharmacy); vicar; vicarage;

Vic Vicente; Vicotria

VIC vicinity (US Army)

Vic Ap Vicar Apostolic

Vice Adm Vice Admiral

Vice-Chn Vice-Chairman; Vice-Chancellor

Vice Pres Vice President

Vice-Prin Vice-Principal

Vic Man. Victoria University of Manchester

Vict Victorian

VICX Van Iderstine Company, The (private car rr mark)

vid see (*vide*—Latin)

videl namely (*videlicet*—Latin)

Vier Friday (*Viernes*—Spanish)

VIK Vick Chemical Company (NYSE)

vil village

vila vilayet (Turkish province)

v imp. verb impersonal (grammar)

viol violet (*violaceus*—Latin); violin (*violino*—Italian) (music)

VIP very important person

v ir vulcanized indiarubber (cables)

Vir Virgo

virg virgin

virid green (*viridis*—Latin)

v irr verb irregular (grammar)

vis visibility (aviation); visiting

Vis Viscount or Viscountess

VIS American Viscose (NYSE); visual (US Army)

viv lively (*vivace*—Italian) (music)

vix he, she, lived (*vixit*—Latin)

viz namely (*videlicet*—Latin)

VJ victory over Japan

v J of the year (*vom jahre*—German)

V-J Day date of Japanese surrender in World War II

v k vertical keel (shipbuilding)

VKE Virginia Iron, Coal & Coke Company (NYSE)

VKG Visking Corp (NYSE)

VKS Vicksburg, Shreveport & Pacific Railway (NYSE)

v l see the place indicated (*vide locum*—Latin); terminal velocity (*vitesse limite*—French); variant reading (*varia lectio*—Latin); violin (*violino*—Italian)

VL Victoria League

V-L Vice-Lieutenant

vla viola

v l f very low frequency

v m ante meridian (*voormiddag*—Dutch)

vm great man (*vir magnificus*—Latin); voltmeter

Vm Your Worship (*Vuestra Merced*—Spanish)

v M ante meridian (vor *Mittag*—German); of the past month (*vorigen Monats*—German)

VM Virgin and Martyr; Your Grace (*Vossa Mercê*—Portuguese); Your Majesty (*Votre Majesté*—French); Fruit-Vegetable Ventilator (rr car)

VMA Valve Manufacturers Association

Vmcê Your Grace (*Vossa Mercê*—Portuguese)

VMD Doctor of Veterinary Medicine (*Veterinariae Medicinae Doctor*—Latin)

VMEV Association of Central European Railway Administrations (*Verein der Mitteleuropäischen Eisenbahnverwaltungen*—German)

VMH Victoria Medal of Honour (Royal Horticultural Society) for Horticulture

VMI Virginia Military Institute

v & mm vandalism and malicious mischief (insurance)

v n verb neuter; verbal noun (grammar)

VNA Visiting Nurse Association

vni *violini* (music)

vno *violino* (music)

VNT Van Norman Company (NYSE)

vo on the left-hand page (*verso*—Latin)

v o from the top (*von oben*—German)

VO Valuation Officer (Scotland); verbal orders (US Army); very old (liquor); Veterinary Officer; Victorian Order

VOA Vasa Order of America; Voice of America

voc vocative

vocab vocabulary

VOKS All-Union Society for Cultural Relations with Foreign Countries (*Vsesoyuznoe Obshchestvo Kulturnoy Svyazi s Zagranitsye*—Russian)

vol volcano; volume; voluntary; volunteer

Vol Volans (constellation)

VOL volunteer (US Army)

volc volcanic; volcano

vols volumes

volvend to be rolled (*volvendus*—Latin) (pharmacy)

VON Victorian Order of Nurses

V1 flying bomb, reprisal weapon (*Vergetungswaffe*—German)

v o p valued as in original policy

VOP very oldest procurable

VOPNAV Vice-Chief of Naval Operations (US Navy)

orm formerly (*Vormals*—German); in the morning (*vormittags*—German)

Vors chairman (*Vorsitzender*—German)

VOT Vogt Manufacturing Corporation (NYSE)

vou voucher

vox pop. voice of the people (*vox populi*—Latin)

voy see (*voyez*—French); voyage

v p vapor pressure; variable pressure; various places; various publishers; voting pool (stocks); vulnerable point

VP City of Paris (*ville de Paris*—French); Vice-President; Vice-Principal

VPA Village Produce Association

VPAC Vice-President of the Air Council

V Ph vertical photography

VPI Virginia Polytechnic Institute

V P K Vest Pocket Kodak

vpm volts per mil

VPMA Vegetable Parchment Manufacturers Association

⁹SB Veterans Placement Service Board

vr various

r verb reflexive; vocal resonance; voltage regulator tube; vulcanized rubber

R Queen Victoria (*Victoria Regnia*—Latin); Vermont Reports (legal); Vicar Rural; Volunteer Reserve; Vroom's Reports (legal)

rae your (*vestrae*—Latin)

vrbl variable

VRC Volunteer Rifle Corps

VRD Volunteer Reserve Decoration (England)

v refl verb reflexive

V Rev Very Reverend

vrg veering

VRI Victoria, Queen and Empress (*Victoria, Regina et Imperatrix*—Latin)

VRP Your Very Reverend Paternity

(*Vestra Reverendissima Paternitas*—Latin)

vrt compare, cf. (*vertaa*—Finnish)

VRT Van Raalte Company, Inc (NYSE)

VRY Virginian Railway Company (NYSE)

V S Vedanta Society; Venezuela Syndicate, Inc (NYSE); Veterinary Surgeon; Virginia State (college); Visual Signaling (RAF and Naval); Your Lordship (*Votre Seigneurie*—French)

vs against (*versus*—Latin); verse

v s and so forth (*ve saire*—Turkish); old style (*vieux style*—French); see above (*vide supra*—Latin); turn over quickly (*volti subito*—Italian) (music); vibration seconds; volumetric solution

VS Fruit-Vegetable Insulated Ventilator (rr car)

vsb visible

vsby visibility

VSC Volunteer Staff Corps

VSD vendor's shipping document (US Army)

vsn vision

VSO very superior old (liquor)

VSOP very superior old pale (liquor)

VSQ very special quality

VSR very special reserve

vss versions

V St United States (*Vereinigte Staaten*—German)

v s w very short waves; vitrified stoneware

VSX Virginia Smelting Company (private car rr mark)

v t per thousand (*von tausend*—German); vacuum tube (radio); verb transitive; voice tube

vt part by volume (*volumenteil*—French); voting

VT Old Testament (*Vetus Testamentum*—Latin); Victory Terminator (loans); Visual Telegraphy (military); Voting Trust

Vt Vermont

---

v/t your draft (*votre traite*—French)

VTA Varnished Tubing Association

v/ta sight (*vista*—Spanish)

VTC Volunteer Training Corps; voting trust certificate

vte sale (*vente*—French)

Vᵗᵉ Viscount (*Vicomte*—French)

Vᵗᵉˢˢᵉ Viscountess (*Vicomtesse*—French)

vtg voting

VTO vertical take-off

vt pl voting pool

v t vm vacuum tube voltmeter

V2 rocket bomb, reprisal weapon (*Vergetungswaffe*—German)

V TZ I K, VTZIK All-Russian Central Executive Committee (*Vserossiisky Tzentralny Ispolnitelny Kommitet*—Russian)

v u from the bottom (*von unten*—German); volume unit

VU Valparaiso University; Vanderbilt University

Vul Vulgate; Vulpecula (constellation)

vulg vulgar

VUU Virginia Union University

vv verbs; verses; first and second violins (music); volumes; your city (*votre ville*—French); you (plural) (*ustedes*—Spanish)

v v interchanged (*vice versa*—Latin); spoken aloud (*viva voce*—Latin)

v/v per cent volume in volume

vva widow (*viuva*—Portuguese)

Vve widow (*veuve*—French)

v/v/hr vibration velocity per hour

vv ll various readings (*variae lectiones*—Latin)

v v o very very old (liquor)

VW Very Worshipful

v w w velocity of wireless waves

v y various years

vy very

VY Victualling Yard

VZP Venezuelan Petroleum Company (NYSE)

W

w century (*wiek*—Polish); electrical energy; wanting; water; watt weather; week; weight; western; wet dew (nautical); wicket (cricket); wide; width; wife; with; word; work; work energy; wrong (proofreading)

W Wales; War Substantive Rank (RAF); Warden; Washington; Wednesday; Welsh; Wesleyan;

West; Western; with (US Army); William; wolfram (*tungsten*—German); Wednesday

w a will advise; wire armored; with average (insurance); work energy

Wa Walter; Watts' Reports

WA Wabash Railroad (NYSE); Webb Association; West Africa; Western Approaches; Western Australia; wire association; Woolknit Associ-

---

ates; Worcestershire Association

W & A Wight and Arnott (botany)

W long. western longitude

WofA Western Railway of Alabama

WAA War Assets Administration

WAAA Women's Amateur Athletic Association

WAAC West African Airways Corporation; Women's Army Auxiliary Corps

WAAE World Association for Adult Education
WAAF Women's Auxiliary Air Force
WAASC Women's Auxiliary Army Service Corps
Wab Wabash Railway Company
WAB Wagner Baking Corporation (NYSE); Work Allotment Board
WAB Pr Wagner Baking Corp. (7% Pfd.) (ASE)
WAC Gold Coast, Ashanti, Northern Territories, British Togoland (IDP); War Agricultural Committee; War Assets Corporation; Women's Army Corps; Women's Auxiliary Corps
WACA Women's Apparel Chains Association
WACLP Women's Action Committee for Lasting Peace
WAD. Work Allotment Division; World Association of Detectives
Wadh Wadham College, Oxford
w a e when actually employed
WAEC War Agricultural Executive Committee
w a f with all faults
WAF Women in the Air Force
WAFF West African Frontier Force
W Afr West Africa
W Afr R West African Regiment
WAFS Women's Auxiliary Ferrying Squadron
WAG Gambia (IDP); Walgreen Company
wal walnut
Wal Walachian; Walloon
WAL Sierra Leone (IDP); Waltham Watch Co (NYSE); Western Air Lines, Inc.
Wall. Wallace's U. S. Supreme Court Reports
WAN Nigeria and Cameroons (IDP)
WANS Women's Australian National Service
WAO Waco Aircraft Company (NYSE)
WAPOR World Association for Public Opinion Research
w a r with all risks (insurance)
war. warrant (securities)
War. Warwickshire (county of England)
WAR. West African Regiment
WARF Wisconsin Alumni Research Foundation
warrtd warranted
warrty warranty
Wash. Washington
Wash. Va Washington's Virginia Reports (legal)
WASP Women's Air Force Service Pilots
Wat Waterford (county of Ireland)
WAT Waitt & Bond, Inc. (NYSE)
WATC Women's Ambulance and Transport Corps

WAT Pr Waitt & Bond, Inc. ($2 Pfd.) (ASE)
watt-hr watt-hour
W Aus(t) Western Australia
WAVES Women Accepted for Voluntary Emergency Service
WAY World Assembly of Youth
wb weber
w b warehouse book; water ballast; (shipping); water board; waybill; west bound; word before
WB Warner Brothers Pictures, Inc (NYSE); Weather Bureau
WBA Woman's Benefit Association
WBEA Wine and Brandy Export Association
WB/EI West Britain/East Ireland
WBH Welsh Board of Health
WBI will be issued (US Army)
WBK Wisconsin Bankshares Corporation (NYSE)
WBM Women's Board of Missions
WBMA Wirebound Box Manufacturers Association
w b n west by north
WBRX Riley Company, Inc. (private car rr mark)
w b s west by south; without benefit of salvage (insurance)
w c water closet; without charge
WC War Cabinet; War Communications; War Council; War Credits; Watch Committee; Wellesley College; Wesleyan Chapel; West Central; Western Command; Wheat Commission; Wheaton College; Whitley Council; Whitman College; Whittier College; Williams College; Wing Commander; Wittenberg College; working capital; Workmen's Circle
w/c watts per candle
WCA War Charities Act; Water Companies' Association; West Coast Airlines, Inc.; Women Citizens' Association; Women's Christian Association; Workmen's Compensation Act; World Calendar Association
WCACTC West Coast Air Corps Training Center
WCC War Crimes Commission; Washington's Circuit Court Reports; Welsh Church Commission; Workmen's Compensation Cases (legal); World Council of Churches
WCDFMA Water Cooler and Drinking Fountain Manufacturers Association
WCEU World Christian Endeavour Union
WCF Watson characterization factor; Wool Carbonizers' Federation; World Congress of Faiths
WCFA Wholesale Commission Florists of America

WCHX Walter Haffner Company (private car rr mark)
WCK West Virginia Coal & Coke Corporation (NYSE)
WCLA West Coast Lumbermen's Association
WCLX Wilson Car Lines (private car rr mark)
WCOF Women's Catholic Order of Foresters
WC & PR Weston, Cleveland and Portishead Railway
WCSA West Coast of South America (shipping)
WCSAC War Cabinet Scientific Advisory Committee
WCTU Woman's Christian Temperance Union
WCTX Roesling and Company (private car rr mark)
wd ward; warranted; wood; word; would; wound
w d whole depth (gears); without date
WD War Department; War Division in Department of Justice; Ward Baking Company (NYSE); warp dresser; Whisky Duty; Wife's Divorce [suit] (legal); withdrawn (US Army); Works Department
W/D Wind Direction (navigation)
WDC War Damage Commission (or Contribution); War Damage Corporation; War Department Citation; War Department Constabulary; Workers' Defense Committee
wdf waterfront dock facilities
WDFOA War Department Fleet Officers' Association
wdg winding; wording
WDGI Wholesale Dry Goods Institute
WDL Woodall Industries, Inc (NYSE); Workers Defense League
WDLX Waddell Coal Mining Company, Inc (private car rr mark)
WDM White (S.S.) Dental Manufacturing Company (NYSE)
Wdr L Wardmaster Lieutenant
wd sc wood screw
wdt width
WDV War Department Vehicle
WD WS Ward Baking Company (warrants) (ASE)
w e watch error (navigation); week end
WE War Establishment; Warrant Engineer (naval)
WEA weather (US Army); Workers' Educational Association
WEAEA Washington Evaporated Apple Export Association
WEBA Workers Education Bureau of America
Webst Dict Webster's Dictionary
WEC Wartime Emergency Commit-

tee; Winnipeg Electric Company (NYSE); Women's Emergency Corps; Women's Engineering Committee; World Engineering Conference

WECX Westinghouse Electric Corporation (private car rr mark)

Wed. Wednesday

wef with effect from

Wel Welsh

w e n waive exchange if necessary

WEN Wentworth Manufacturing (NYSE)

Wend. Wendell's Reports (legal)

WEP West Penn Electric Company (NYSE)

WEPI War Emergency Pipelines, Inc

Wes Wesleyan

WES Women's Engineering Society; World Economic Survey

WESC Walnut Export Sales Company

Westm Westmeath (county of Ireland);Westminster; Westmorland (county of England)

West Res Coll Western Reserve College

Wes Univ Wesleyan University

Wex Wexford (county of Ireland)

WEY Weyenberg Shoe Manufacturing (NYSE)

wf won on foul; wrong font

WF Wake Forest (college); Watumull Foundation; Wells Fargo Bank & Union Trust (NYSE); White Fathers, Missionaries of Africa; Whitney Foundation; Wieboldt Foundation; Wilson Foundation; Woman's Foundation

w & f water and feed (transportation)

WFA War Food Administration; Women Flyers of America

WFBI Wood Fibre Blanket Institute

WFD War Finance Division (Treasury)

WFDY World Federation of Democratic Youth

w f e with food element

WFEA World Federation of Education Associations

WFEX Western Fruit Express Company (private car rr mark)

WFI Wheat Flour Institute

WFL Women's Freedom League

WFLX St. Regis Paper Company, West Fork Logging Division (private car rr mark); West Fork Logging Company (private car rr mark)

WFMH World Federation for Mental Health

WFP Warren Foundry & Pipe Corporation (NYSE)

WFPX Western Food Products Company (private car rr mark)

WFSW World Federation of Scientific Workers

WFTU World Federation of Trade Unions

WFUNA World Federation of United Nations Associations

wg weight guaranteed; wire gauge

WG W. G. Grace (famous cricketer); Grenada (IDP); Welsh Guards; Westminister Gazette; West Germanic; Wing (US Army)

WGC Worthy Grand Chaplain (freemasonry); Worthy Grand Conductor (freemasonry)

WGCLA Window Glass Cutters League of America

WGDA Watermelon Growers and Distributors Association

W Gds Welsh Guards

W Ger West Germanic

WGG Worthy Grand Guardian (freemasonry); Worthy Grand Guide (freemasonry)

wght weight

WGI Work Glove Institute

WGL Washington Gas Light Company (NYSE)

WGM Worthy Grand Master (freemasonry)

WGMA Wet Ground Mica Association

Wg Off. Wing Officer (WAAF)

WGS Worthy Grand Sentinel

WGSX Warden, Leonard (private car rr mark)

wgt weight

WGWTU Waterproof Garment

wh watt-hours; which

Wh Wheaton's United States Supreme Court Reports (legal)

WH White Motor Company (NYSE)

WHA World Health Assembly

whas whereas

whatsr whatsoever

whby whereby

W & HC Welfare and Health Council

WHCA White House Correspondents Association

WHD Western Homestead Oils (NYSE)

WHE Wheeling Stock Exchange

Wheat. Wheaton's U.S. Supreme Court Reports

whf wharf

whfg wharfage

WHI Whitman (William) Company Inc (Ohio) (common stock ASE)

WHIA Woolen Hosiery Institute of America

WHIX Western Fruit Express Company (private car rr mark)

whm weighmaster

WHMA Women's Home Missionary Association; Wood Heel Manufacturers Association

WHMAA Wool Hat Manufacturers

Association of America

WHO World Health Organization

whp water horse power

whr watt-hour; whether

WHR Whirlpool Corporation (NYSE)

whrin wherein

whr m watt-hour meter

whs warehouse

whsle wholesale

whsmn warehouseman

whsng warehousing

whs rec warehouse receipt

whs stk warehouse stock

WHU Warner-Hudnut, Inc (NYSE)

whvs wharves

WHX Wheeling Steel Corporation (NYSE)

w i wrought iron

WI War Information; West Indian; West Indies; Windward Islands; Wine Institute; Women Inspectors; Women's Institute

w & i weighing and inspection

WIA wounded in action (US Army)

WIBC Women's International Bowling Congress

Wick. Wicklow (county of Ireland)

WID West India Dock; West Indies Sugar (NYSE)

WIDF Women's International Democratic Federation

WIE Wieboldt Stores, Inc (NYSE)

WIEN Wien Alaska Airlines

WIF West India Fruit & Steamship Company, Inc (rr mark)

Wig. Wigtown (county of Scotland)

Wigorn signature Bishop of Worcester

WIIU Workers' International Industrial Union

WIL Wilson & Company (NYSE)

Will. William (*Willelmus*—Latin)

WILPF Women's International League for Peace and Freedom

Wilts Wiltshire (county of England)

w i m c whom it may concern

WIN Winn & Lovett Grocery (NYSE)

W Ind West Indian; West Indies

Wind I Windward Islands

Win Eq Winston's Equity Reports (legal)

Wing-Cdr Wing-Commander (RAF)

Winton of Winchester (*Wintoniensis* —Latin)

Wint T The Winter's Tale (Shakespeare)

WIR West India Regiment

WIRES Women in Radio and Electrical Service

Wis Wisconsin

WIS Wisconsin Central Airlines, Inc; Wisconsin Power & Light (NYSE)

Wisd of Sol Wisdom of Solomon

WIS Pr Wisconsin Pw. & Lt. Co. (4½% Pfd.) (ASE)

WIST Western Illinois State Teachers (college)
witht without
witned witnessed
witneth witnesseth
WITX Witco Chemical Company (private car rr mark)
WIX Wickes Corporation (The) (NYSE)
WIZO Women's International Zionist Organization
W & J Washington and Jefferson (college)
WJC World Jewish Congress
WJCC Women's Joint Congressional Committee
wk week; work
w k well-known
WK Westinghouse Air Brake (NYSE)
WKB Walker & Company (NYSE)
wkds weekdays
WKR wrecker (US Army)
WKST Western Kentucky State Teachers (college)
wkt wicket
WKT Wayne Knitting Mills (NYSE)
WKU Waukesha Motor Company (NYSE)
WKWX Warren Foundation, The William K. (private car rr mark)
WKY West Kentucky Coal (NYSE)
w l wagons-lit (France); water line; water-line coefficient; water-plane coefficient; wave length
WL St. Lucia (IDP); War Loan; Wardmaster-Lieutenant (naval); West Lothian (county of Scotland); Western Lines; White Leghorn (poultry); Women's Legion
W & L Washington and Lee (University)
WLA Wescosa Lumber Association; Women's Land Army
WLB Wilson Brothers (NYSE)
WLBD War Labor Board Directives
WLB Pr Wilson Brothers (5% Pfd.) (ASE)
wl coeff water-line coefficient
WLE Wheeling & Lake Erie Railway Company (NYSE)
WLF Women's Liberal Federation
WLHA Wagner Labor Relations Act (United States)
WLJ Wilson Jones Company (NYSE)
WLM Williams (R.C.) & Company, Inc (NYSE)
w long. west longitude
WLS Western Leaseholds, Ltd (NYSE)
wm wattmeter
w m wavemeter; white metal; anti-friction metal; wire mesh
Wm William
WM Western Maryland Railway Company (NYSE); Western Michigan

(college); Worshipful Master (free-masonry)
w/m weight or measurement
W & M Washburn and Moen (gauge); William and Mary
WMA Warrant Master-at-Arms; Workers' Musical Association
WMB War Mobilization Board
WMBA Wire Machinery Builders Association
WMC War Manpower Commission; Ways and Means Committee
WMD War Mobilization Director
WMF Wire Mattress Federation
WM 1 Pr Western Maryland Rwy. Co. (7% 1st Pfd.) (ASE)
WMI War Materials Incorporated; Webbing Manufacturers Institute; Westmoreland, Inc (NYSE); Wild-life Management Institute
wmk watermark
wmkd watermarked
WMKX Whiting Milk Company (private car rr mark)
WMO World Meteorological Organization
WMPC War Man Power Commission
WMR Westmoreland Coal Company (NYSE)
WMS Wesleyan Missionary Society
WMSC Women's Medical Specialist Corps (US Army)
Wms Saund Williams' Edition of Saunders' (Law Reports)
WMTC Women's Mechanized Transport Corps
WMU Washburn Municipal University
WMV War Munition Volunteers
WN Webb & Knapp, Inc (NYSE)
WNA Winter North Atlantic (shipping)
WNAA Womens National Aeronautical Association
WNB Weekly Newspaper Bureau
WNDC Women's National Democratic Club
WNE Weston Electrical Instrument (NYSE)
WNF Winfield Railroad Company, The (rr mark)
WNG warning (US Army)
WNI Women's National Institute
WNLF Women's National Liberal Federation
WNO Wesson Oil & Snowdrift Company (NYSE)
W&NO Wharton and Northern Railroad Company (rr mark)
WNP Wayne Pump Company (NYSE); Welsh Nationalist Party; wire nonpayment
WNPC Women's National Press Club
WN Pr Webb & Knapp, Inc. (Pref. of $6 Series) (ASE)
WNRC Women's National Republican

Club
WNSEA Wood Naval Stores Export Association
WNU Western Newspaper Union (ASE)
w n w west-northwest
WNW Wood Newspaper Machinery (NYSE)
w o above (weiter oben—German); as above (wie oben—German); wait order; walk over
WO War Office; Warrant Officer; Wireless Operator; Willys-Overland Motors, Inc (NYSE)
W/O without (US Army)
WOA Wharf Owners' Association
WO/AG Wireless Operator/Air Gunner
w o b washed overboard (shipping)
WOBX Western Fruit Express Company (private car rr mark)
wo c without compensation
WOCB War Office Casualty Branch
WOCCI War Office Central Card Index
Woch weekly (Wochenschrift—German)
WOCL War Office Casualty List
WOD Woodward Iron Company (NYSE)
WOFI Wood Office Furniture Institute
w o g with other goods
WOJG Warrant Officer (junior grade)
w o l wharfowners' liability
WOLX Westland Oil Company (private car rr mark)
WOM War Mobilization Office; Wireless Operator Mechanic
WOO Warrant Ordnance Officer (naval)
Wood Tech Wood Technologist
Wool. Woolworth's United States Circuit Court Reports (legal)
W Op AG Wireless Operator Air Gunner
Wor Worshipful
Worcs Worcestershire (county of England)
work. comp workmen's compensation (insurance)
workho workhouse
World WCTU World's Woman's Christian Temperance Union
WOSL Women's Overseas Service League
WOTP World Organization of the Teaching Profession
W&OV Warren & Ouachita Valley Railway (rr mark)
WOW Woodmen of the World
W/O WN without winch (US Army)
WOX Wasatch Oil Company, Idaho Division (private car rr mark)
WOY Woodley Petroleum Company (NYSE)

Wp Worshipful

w p waste paper; weather permitting; white paper; wire payment; without prejudice

WP Ware Police; War Policy; Warrant Photographer (naval); West Point; Western Pacific Railway Company; will proceed to (US Army); Worthy Patriarch (freemasonry); Worthington Corporation (NYSE)

w p a with particular average (insurance)

WPA Western Pine Association; Works Progress Administration

w p b waste-paper basket

WPB War Production Board

wpc watts per candle

WPC War Pensions Committee; War Problems Committee; Wisconsin Electric Power (NYSE); Woman Power Committee; Women Peers Committee; World Power Conference

WPD Works Progress Division

WPF War Production Fund; War Purposes Fund; World Peace Foundation; World Prohibition Federation

WPG West Point Graduate

WPI Wall Paper Institute; Waste Paper Institute; Waxed Paper Institute; Worcester Polytechnic Institute; World Peaceways, Inc

wpm words per minute

WPMA Writing Paper Manufacturers Association

WPN weapon (US Army); West Penn Traction Company (ASE)

w p p waterproof paper packing (shipping)

WPP Women Police Patrol

WPR Willson Products, Inc (NYSE)

WPRR Co Western Pacific Railroad Company

WPT Westates Petroleum Company (NYSE)

WPTA Wooden Pail and Tub Association

w r war risk (insurance); warehouse receipt; wash room; with rights (securities) writing paper

WR King William (*Willelmus Rex*—Latin); War Reserve (police); Ward Room (naval); Wassermann Reaction; water-rail (US Army); West Riding (of Yorkshire); Wirral Railway

w & r water and rail

w/r was received (shipping)

WRA War Relocation Authority Wireless Retailers' Association; Working Rules Agreement

WRAC Women's Royal Army Corps

WRAF Women's Royal Air Force

wrang wrangler

WRB War Refugee Board

WRC War Resources Council; Women's Relief Corps

WRCX Wisconsin Rendering Company (private car rr mark)

Wrens Women's Royal Naval Service (England)

WRETA Wire Rope Export Trade Association

wrfg wharfage

WRI War Resisters International; War Risks Insurance; Wellcome Research Institution; Wire Reinforcement Institute; Wire Rope Institute; Women's Rural Institute

WRIA War Risks Insurance Act

WRL War Resisters League

WRLX Winona Refrigerator Car Corporation (private car rr mark)

WRN Warren Petroleum Corporation (NYSE)

WRNS Women's Royal Naval Service ("Wrens")

wrnt warrant

WRNWCA Western Red and Northern White Cedar Association

WRNX Warren Petroleum Corporation (private car rr mark)

w r o war risk only (insurance)

WRO Wichita River Oil Corporation (NYSE)

WRS Western Pacific Railroad Company (NYSE)

WRSSR White Russian Socialist Soviet Republic

WRSX Wheeler, Reynolds & Stauffer (private car rr mark)

WRT Warrior River Terminal Company (rr mark); Wright-Hargreaves Mines, Ltd (NYSE)

WRU Welsh Rugby Union; Wesleyan Reform Union; Western Reserve University

WRX Western Refrigerator Line Company (private car rr mark)

Wrzes September (*Wrzesień*—Polish)

Ws water (*Wasser*—German)

w s water surface; weather station

WS War scale; War-Substantive; Wayne Screw Products Company (NYSE); West Saxon; Western Department Stores (NYSE); Women's Size (clothing); Women's Suffrage; Writer to the Signet (Scotland); Wilderness Society; Wildlife Society

w & s whisky and soda

w and s wait and see

WSA War Shipping Act; War shipping Administration

WSAP Women's South African Party

WSAUS Wholesale Stationers Association of the United States

WSB Webster Tobacco Company (NYSE)

WSE Washington Stock Exchange

WSFI Water Softener and Filter Institute

WS gu please turn over (*Wenden Sie gefälligt um*—German)

WSI Window Shade Institute; Wool Stock Institute

WS of J White Shrine of Jerusalem

WSLX Wheeling Steel Corporation (private car rr mark)

WSNSCA Washable Suits, Novelties, and Sportswear Contractors Association

WSP water supply point (US Army); West Penn Power Company (NYSE)

WSPU Women's Social and Political Union

WSR World Student Relief

WSS War Savings Stamp; Winston-Salem Southbound Railway Company (rr mark)

WSSF World Student Service Fund

WST Western Auto Supply Company (NYSE)

WSTIB Woolen and Silk Textiles Industries Board

W SUP water supply (US Army)

w s w west-southwest

WSW White Sewing Machine Corporation (NYSE)

WSWA Wine and Spirits Wholesalers of America

WSX Weirton Steel Company (private car rr mark); Western Air Lines Inc (NYSE)

w t war tax; watch time (navigation); watertight; wireless telegraphy; withholding tax

wt warrant; weight; without

WT War Transport; Warrant Telegraphist (naval); Wireless Technology; Wireless Telegraphy; Wireless Telephony; Woolworth (F.W.) Ltd, (NYSE)

WTAO World Touring and Automobile Organization

WTB Western Tablet & Stationery (NYSE)

WT Bn Wireless Beacon

w t d watertight door (shipbuilding)

W/TDF Wireless Direction Finding Station

w t f b watertight flush bolted (hatch)

WT1C Water Tender First Class (US Navy)

wth width

WTLA Western Trunk Line Association

w t m h watertight manhole

Wt/Off Warrant Officer

wt prej without prejudice

w t q a d watertight quick-acting door

wtr waiter; winter; writer

WTR Wrightsville and Tennille Railraod Company (rr mark)

wts   weights
WTS   War Training Service
WTSB   Wood Turners Service Bureau
WT2C   Water Tender Second Class (US Navy)
WTST   West Texas State Teachers (college)
WTUC   World Trade Union Conference
WTUF   World Trade Union Federation
WTWA   World Trade Writers Association
WTX Pr   West Texas Util. Co. ($6 Pfd.) (ASE)
WU   Washington University; Wayne University; Wesleyan University; Western Union Telegraph (NYSE); Wilberforce University; Williamette University
WUA   Western Underwriters Association
WUSL   Women's United Service League
WV   St. Vincent (IDP)
w/v   per cent of weight in volume; wind velocity

W Va   West Virginia
WVCX   Westvaco Chemical Division, Food Machinery and Chemical Corporation (private car rr mark)
WVP   West Virginia Pulp & Paper Company (NYSE)
WVS   West Virginia State (college); Women's Voluntary Service
WVU   West Virginia University
w w   warehouse warrants; with warrants; wood wheel
ww   waterworks
WW   Walworth Company (NYSE) Warrant Writer (naval); White Wyandotte (poultry); Woodmen of the World
w/w   per cent of weight in weight
w w a   with will annexed
WWB   Writers War Board
w w d   weather working-days
Wwe   widow (*Witwe*—German)
WWF   Woodrow Wilson Foundation
WW & IB   Western Weighing & Inspection Bureau
W/WN   with winch (US Army)
WWNA   Woolen Wholesalers National Association

WWO   Wing Warrant Officer (RAF)
WW I   World War I
WWP   Washington Water Power (NYSE)
WWPA   Woven Wire Products Association
WWPX   W. & W. Pickle & Canning Company (private car rr mark)
WWII   World War II (US Army)
WWV   Walla Walla Valley Railway Company (rr mark)
WWWVI   Women World War Veterans, Inc
WWY   Wrigley (Wm.) Jr., Company (NYSE)
WX   Westinghouse Electric Corporation (NYSE)
WXC   Wilcox Oil Company (NYSE)
WXY   Waldorf System, Inc (NYSE)
wy   wey (wool weight, 14 pounds)
WY   American Woolen Company (NYSE)
Wyo   Wyoming
WYO   Wyandotte Worsted Company (NYSE)
Wyo T   Wyoming Territory
WYR   West Yorkshire Regiment
WZO   World Zionist Organization

X

X   extra; Specialist in Radiology (naval); Christ; Christian; Cross; reactance; reconditioned; an unknown quantity; United States Steel Corporation (NYSE); Xavier; Xerxes; Xenon (chemistry); xenophone; explosive
XA   Crucible Steel Company of America (NYSE)
Xbre   December (*décembre*—French), (*diciembre*—Spanish)
Xc   Christ (*Christus*—Latin)
x car   from car (shipping)
x c l   excess current liabilities (insurance)
xcp   without coupon (NYSE)
x c & u c   exclusive of covering and uncovering (railway)
Xcut   crosscut
xd   without dividend (NYSE)
xdIv   without dividend (NYSE)
Xdr   Crusader
Xe   xenon (chemistry)
xg   crossing
X heavy   extra heavy
'   ex interest, without next interest

(NYSE)
x in.   without interest (bonds)
Xing   (road) crossing; (railroad) crossing
XL   Ex-Cell-O Corporation (NYSE)
xlnt   excellent
xl & ul   exclusive of loading and unloading (railway)
Xmas   Christmas
Xmo   tithe (*diezmo*—Spanish)
xmtr   transmitter
x n   ex new (NYSE)
Xn   Christian
Xnty   Christianity
Xo   cross-out
Xos   extra outsize (clothing)
X out   cross out
Xp   fire resistive protected (insurance)
x p   express paid
x per   without privileges
Xper   Christopher
x p p   express paid letter (*exprès payé lettre*—French)
XPP   Xi Psi Phi (fraternity)
x pr   without privileges (securities)

x p t   express paid telegraph (*exprès payé télégraphe*—French)
x q   cross-question
Xr   Christopher; cruiser (*Kreuzer*—German); without rights (NYSE)
Xref   cross-reference
x rts   without rights (NYSE)
Xs   atmospherics
XSP   Xi Sigma Pi (fraternity)
X strong   extra strong
Xt   Christ
Xtian   Christian
Xtiany   Christianity
xtry   extraordinary
Xts   Christ's College, Cambridge
Xu   fire resistive unprotected (insurance)
XU   Xavier University
x w   without warrants (securities)
XX   double strength ale; double strength paper
XX heavy   double extra heavy
XX strong   double extra strong
XXX   triple strength [ale or paper]; urgency signal (QS)

Y

y   an unknown quantity; yard; year; yen; you; youngest

Y   Allegheny Corporation (NYSE); Serving with Yeomanry; Young Men's (Women's) Christian Association; yttrium

Y/A   York-Antwerp (Rules) (marine insurance)

YABA   Yacht Architects and Brokers Association

Yale L J   Yale Law Journal

YAM   Yates-American Machine Company (NYSE)

YAR   York-Antwerp Rules (marine insurance)

YAT   Yale & Towne Manufacturing Company (NYSE)

Yb   ytterbium

y b   year-book

YB   Youngstown Sheet & Tube (NYSE)

YC   Yale College; Yeshiva College; Youngstown College

YCL   Youth Communist League

YCW   Young Christian Workers

yd   yard

ydg   yarding

yds   yards

Yem   Yemen

yeo   yeomanry

yesty   yesterday

Y1C   Yeoman First Class (US Navy)

YG   Young (L.A.) Spring & Wire (NYSE)

YHA   Youth Hostels Association

YHWH   Jehovah (God)

yieldg   yielding

Yks   Yorkshire

Y & L   York and Lancaster

YLI   Yorkshire Light-Infantry; Young Ladies' Institute

Y and LR   York and Lancaster Regiment

y m   etc (yannä muuta—Finnish)

YMA   Yarn Merchants Association

YMBT   Young Men's Board of Trade

YMCA   Young Men's Christian Association

YM Cath A   Young Men's Catholic Association

YMCU   Young Men's Christian Union

YMFS   Young Men's Friendly Society

YMHA   Young Men's Hebrew Association

YMI   Young Men's Institute

YMS   Motor Minesweepers (US Navy)

Y & MV RR   Yazoo & Mississippi Valley Railroad

y o   year old

YOK   York Corporation (NYSE)

Yorks   Yorkshire (county in England)

y p   yield point; yield limit

YP   Yellow Peril; Young People

YPSCE   Young People's Society of Christian Endeavor

yr   junior (den yugre—Norwegian); year; your; younger

YRA   Yacht Racing Association

yrs   years; yours

YRS   Yugoslav Relief Society

y s   yard super; yield strength

YS   Youngstown & Southern Railway Company (rr mark)

YSD   Youngstown Steel Door Company (NYSE)

Y2C   Yeoman Second Class (US Navy)

yst   youngst

YSTX   Youngstown Sheet & Tube Company, The (private car rr mark)

y t   yoke top (plumbing)

YT   Yukon Territory

Y3C   Yeoman Third Class (US Navy)

YU   Yale University; Yugoslavia (IDP)

Yuc   Yucatán

Yugo   Yugoslavia

Yuk   Yukon

YWCA   Young Women's Christian Association

YWCA (World's)   World's Young Women's Christian Association

YWCTU   Young Woman's Christian Temperance Union

YWHA   Young Women's Hebrew Association

YWS   Young Wales Society

Z

z   atomic number; an unknown quantity; zee bar; zero; zone; zenith distance

Z   customs duty (Zoll—German) inch (zoll—German); line (zeile—German); Woolworth (F.W.) Company (NYSE); Zachary; Zebadiah; zone (use in combination only) (US Army); zinc

za   approximately (zirka—German)

ZA   American Zinc, Lead & Smelt (NYSE); South Africa (IDP)

Zab   Zabriskie's Reports (legal)

Zac   Zacatecas

Zach   Zacharias (Biblical); Zachary

Zan   Zanzibar

z B   for example (zum Beispiel—German)

ZB   Crown Zellerbach Corporation (NYSE)

ZBT   Zeta Beta Tau (fraternity)

ZC   Zionist Congress

z d   zenith distance; zone descrip-

tion (navigation)

ze   for example (zum exempel—German)

ZE   Zenith Radio Corporation (NYSE)

Zeb   Zebadiah; Zebedee

Zech   Zechariah (Bible)

Zeitschr   journal (Zeitschrift—German)

Zeph   Zephaniah (Bible)

z f   zero frequency

ZF   zone of fire (US Army)

Z F O   French Zone of Occupation; (zone Française D'Occupation—French)

ZG   Zoological Gardens

z H   attention of (zu Händen—German)

z hr   zero hour

ZI   zone of interior (US Army); Zonta International

ZIP   Talon, Inc., class A (common stock, NYSE)

ZM   Callahan Zinc-Lead Company (NYSE)

ZMRI   Z-Metals Research Institute

Zn   son (Zoon—Dutch); zinc

Znen   Sons (Zoonen—Dutch)

ZNP   Polish National Union of America

ZO   Occupied Zone (Zone Occupée—French)

ZOA   Zionist Organization of America

zoochem   zoochemical; zoochemistry

zoogeog   zoogeographical; zoogeography

zool   zoological; zoology

zooph   zoophytology

ZP   Zeta Psi (fraternity); Zonite Products Corporation (NYSE)

ZPE   Zeta Phi Eta (society)

Zr   zirconium

Zs   periodical (Zeitschrift—German)

ZS   Zoological Society

ZSN   Zoological Station of Naples

ZSSR Polish equivalent of USSR
ZST Zone Standard Time

z T in part (*zum Teil*—German)
ZT Torrid Zone (Zone *Torride*—French)

ZTA Zeta Tau Alpha (sorority)

Ztg newspaper (*Zeitung*—German)
Ztr hundred-weight (*Zentner*—German)

Ztschr periodical (*Zeitschrift*—German)

zus together, total (*zusammen*—German)

z V at disposal (*ze Verfügung*—German)
zw between (*zwischen*—German)
z Z at the time, acting (*zur Zeit*—German)
z Zt at this time (*zu Zeit*—German)

APPENDIX

Signs and Symbols

+ plus
− minus
± plus or minus
∓ minus or plus
× multiplied by
÷ divided by
= equal to
≠ or ≠ not equal to
≈ or ≈ nearly equal to
≡ identical with
≢ not identical with
⇔ equivalent
≎ difference between
∼ or ∸ difference
≅ congruent to
⊏ or > greater than
≯ or ≧ not greater than
⊐ or < less than
≮ or ≦ not less than
: is to; ratio
:: as; proportion
∷ geometric proportion
≐ approaches
→ approaches limit of
∝ varies as
⊣ is part of
∥ parallel
⊥ perpendicular
∠ angle
∟ right angle
△ triangle
□ square
▭ rectangle
▱ parallelogram
○ circle
⌒ arc of circle
⟂ equilateral
≜ equiangular
√ radical; root; square root
∛ cube root
∜ fourth root
Σ sum
! or ⌊ factorial product
∞ infinity
∫ integral
ʃ function
∂ or δ differential; variation
π pi
∴ therefore
∵ because
‾ vinculum (above letter)
( ) parentheses
[ ] brackets
{ } braces

° degree
′ minute
″ second
HP horsepower
Δ increment
ω ohm
Ω microhm
MΩ megohm
Φ magnetic flux; farad
Ψ dielectric flux; electrostatic flux
ρ resistivity
γ conductivity
Λ equivalent conductivity
ℛ reluctance
→ direction of flow
⇄ electrical current
⬡ benzene ring
→ yields
⇌ reversible reaction
↓ precipitate
↑ gas
‰ salinity
☉ or ⊙ Sun
● or ● New Moon
☽ First Quarter
☽ or ⊕ Full Moon
☾ Last Quarter
☿ Mercury
♀ Venus
⊖ or ⊕ Earth
♂ Mars
♃ Jupiter
♄ Saturn
♅ Uranus
♆ or L Neptune
♇ Pluto
♈ Aries
♉ Taurus
♊ Gemini
♋ Cancer
♌ Leo
♍ Virgo
♎ Libra
♏ Scorpio
♐ Sagittarius
♑ Capricornus
♒ Aquarius
♓ Pisces
☌ conjunction
☍ opposition
△ trine
□ quadrature
✳ sextile
☊ dragon's head, ascending node
☋ dragon's tail, descending node

♄ Ceres
⚴ Pallas
⚵ Juno
⚶ Vesta
⚶ rain
✳ snow
⊠ snow on ground
← floating ice crystals
▲ hail
△ sleet
∨ frostwork
⊔ hoarfrost
≡ fog
∞ haze; dust haze
⊤ thunder
⚡ sheet lightning
⊕ solar corona
⊕ solar halo
⚡ thunderstorm
↖ direction
○ or ⊙ or ① annual
⊙⊙ or ② biennial
♃ perennial
♂ or ♂ male
♀ female
□ male, in charts
○ female, in charts
℞ take (from Latin *Recipe*)
ÂÂ or Ā or āā of each (in doctor's prescription)
℔ pound
℥ ounce
ℨ dram
Ə scruple
O pint
f℥ fluid ounce
fʒ fluid dram
℩ minim
& or & and; ampersand
℀ per
number
/ virgule; solidus; separatrix; shilling
´ acute
` grave
~ tilde
ˆ circumflex
‾ macron
˘ breve
¨ dieresis
¸ cedilla
∧ caret

From Government Printing Office Style Manual.

Braille Alphabet and Numerals

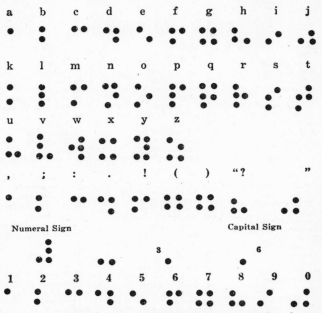

The six dots of the Braille cell are arranged and
numbered thus:

$$\begin{array}{ccc} 1 & \bullet & 4 \\ 2 & \bullet & 5 \\ 3 & \bullet & 6 \end{array}$$

The capital sign, dot 6,
placed before a letter, makes it a capital. The
numeral sign, dots 3, 4, 5, 6, placed before a
character, makes it a figure and not a letter. The
apostrophe, dot 3, like the other punctuation
marks, is formed in the lower part of the cell.

Roman Numerals

A repeated letter repeats its value; a letter placed after one of greater value adds to it; a letter placed before one of greater value subtracts from it; a dashline over a letter denotes multiplied by 1,000.

I	1	XXIX	29
II	2	XXX	30
III	3	XXXV	35
IV	4	XXXIX	39
V	5	XL	40
VI	6	XLV	45
VII	7	XLIX	49
VIII	8	L	50
IX	9	LV	55
X	10	LIX	59
XV	15	LX	60
XIX	19	LXV	65
XX	20	LXIX	69
XXV	25	LXX	70

LXXV	75	DC	600
LXXIX	79	DCC	700
LXXX	80	DCCC	800
LXXXV	85	CM	900
LXXXIX	89	M	1,000
XC	90	MD	1,500
XCV	95	MM	2,000
XCIX	99	MMM	3,000
C	100	MMMM or MV̄	4,000
CL	150	V̄	5,000
CC	200	M̄	1,000,000
CCC	300		
CD	400		
D	500		

GENERAL

Term	Symbol	Units
Accleration	a	(ft./sec.)/sec., (ft./hr.)/hr.
Acceleration of gravity	g	(ft./sec.)/sec., (ft./hr.)/hr.
do., standard value	g_0	(ft./sec.)/sec., (ft./hr.)/hr.
Activity	a	
Activity coefficient, molal basis	γ (gamma)	(f also is used)
Angle	α (alpha)	degrees, radians. (θ and ϕ also are used)
Area	A, S	sq.ft.
Base of natural logarithms	e	
Breadth, width	b	ft.
Coefficient of expansion, linear	α (alpha)	(ft./ft.)/°F., (ft./ft.)/°C.
Coefficient of expansion, volumetric	β (beta)	(cu.ft./cu.ft.)/°F., (cu.ft./cu.ft.)/°C.
Compressibility factor	z	pV/RT
Concentration, volumetric	c	lb./cu.ft., lb. moles/cu.ft.
Cross section	S, A	sq.ft.
Density	ρ (rho)	lb./cu.ft.
Diameter	D	ft.
Difference, finite; often that causing flow	Δ (capital delta)	
Differential operator	d	
Diffusivity, thermal	α (alpha)	sq.ft./hr.
Diffusivity of vapor	D_v	sq.ft./hr.
Efficiency	η (eta)	
Energy, in general	E	B.t.u., B.t.u./lb. mole, P.c.u., P.c.u./lb. mole
Enthalpy	H	B.t.u., B.t.u./lb. mole, P.c.u., P.c.u./lb. mole
Enthalpy, per unit weight	h	B.t.u./lb., P.c.u./lb. (i is used when necessary to distinguish)
Entropy	S	B.t.u./(°R.) or B.t.u./(lb. mole) (°R.), P.c.u./(°K.) or P.c.u./(lb. mole) (°K.)
Entropy, per unit weight	s	B.t.u./(lb.) (°R.), P.c.u./(lb.) (°K.)
Fluidity	$1/\mu$	(sec.) (ft.)/lb.
Force, total load	F	lb. force
Free energy, Gibbs	G	($H - TS$) (F also has been used)
Free energy, Helmholtz	A	($U - TS$), B.t.u., B.t.u./lb. mole, P.c.u., P.c.u./lb. mole
Fugacity	f	lb. force/sq.ft., atm.
Function	ϕ, ψ, χ (phi, psi, chi)	
Gas constant, universal	R	Where necessary to distinguish, use R_0
Internal energy	U	B.t.u., B.t.u./lb. mole, P.c.u., P.c.u./lb. mole
Internal energy per unit weight	u	B.t.u./lb., P.c.u./lb.
Latent heat of evaporation	λ (lambda) h_{fg}	B.t.u./lb., P.c.u./lb.
Length	L	ft.
Mass	m	lb.
Mechanical equivalent of heat	J	(ft.) (lb. force)/B.t.u., (ft.) (lb. force)/P.c.u.
Molecular weight	M	
Moment of inertia	I	(ft.)⁴
Newton law of motion, conversion factor in	g_c	(lb.) (ft.)/(sec.)²(lb. force)
Number in general	N	
Power	P	(ft.) (lb. force)/sec.
Pressure	p	lb. force/sq.ft., atm.
Quantity of matter, weight	W	lb.
Radius	r	ft.
Rate of rotation	n	rev./min.
Solid angle	ω (omega)	
Specific heat	c	B.t.u./(lb.) (°F.), P.c.u./(lb.) (°C.)
Specific heat, at constant pressure	c_p	B.t.u./(lb.) (°F.), P.c.u./(lb.) (°C.)
Specific heat, at constant volume	c_v	B.t.u./(lb.) (°F.), P.c.u./(lb.) (°C.)
Specific heats, ratio of	k, κ (kappa)	c_p/c_v [γ (gamma) also is used]
Specific volume	v	cu.ft./lb.
Surface per unit volume	a	sq.ft./cu.ft.
Surface tension	σ (sigma)	lb. force/ft., dynes/cm.
Temperature	t	°F. or °C. (θ is used in some lists)
Temperature, absolute	T	°K. or °R. (Rankine)
Thermal conductivity	k	B.t.u./(hr.) (sq.ft.) (°F./ft.), P.c.u./(hr.) (sq.ft.) (°C./ft.)
Time	t, r (tau)	sec., hr. (θ also has been used)
Velocity, angular	ω (omega)	
Viscosity, absolute	μ (mu)	lb./(sec.) (ft.), lb./(hr.) (ft.) η (eta) also is used
Viscosity, kinematic	ν (nu)	sq.ft./sec., sq.ft./hr.
Viscosity, relative to water	μ/μ_w	
Volume, total or per mole	V	cu.ft., cu.ft./lb. mole

Weignt, quantity of matter	W	lb.
Width, breadth	b	ft.
Work	W	B.t.u., P.c.u. (Where necessary to distinguish, use W_k)
Work, external	W_e	B.t.u., P.c.u.

FLOW OF FLUIDS

Coefficient, of discharge, etc.	C	
Depth	y	ft.
Distance in direction of flow	x	ft.
Distance above datum plane	Z	ft.
Friction, in energy balance	F	(ft.) (lb. force)/lb.
Friction factor, Fanning	f	($F = 2fLV^2/g_cD$)
Hydraulic radius	R_H	ft., sq.ft./ft.
Mass flow rate	w	lb./sec., lb./hr.
Mass velocity	G	lb./(hr.) (sq.ft.), lb./(sec.) (sq.ft.)
Rate of flow, volumetric	q	cu.ft./sec., cu.ft./hr.
Tractive force per unit area	r (tau)	lb. force/sq.ft.
Velocity, acoustic	V_a	ft./sec. (c also is used)
Velocity, average	V	ft./sec., ft./hr.
Velocity, local	v	ft./sec., ft./hr.
Weight rate of flow per unit of breadth	Γ (capital gamma)	lb./(hr.) (ft.), lb./(sec.) (ft.)

HEAT TRANSMISSION

Absorptivity (for radiation)	α (alpha)	
Coefficient of heat transfer, individual	h	B.t.u./(hr.) (sq.ft.) (°F.), P.c.u./(hr.) (sq.ft.) (°C.)
Conductance	$1/R$, C	B.t.u./(hr.) (°F.), P.c.u./(hr.) (°C.)
Emissivity (for radiation)	ϵ (epsilon)	
Film thickness, effective	B	ft.
Fraction by volume	x_v	
Fraction by weight	x_w	
Heat transfer coefficient, over-all	U	B.t.u./(hr.) (sq.ft.) (°F.), P.c.u./(hr.) (sq.ft.) (°C.)
Heat transfer factor	j	$(h/cG)\phi(c\mu/k)$
Quantity of heat transferred	Q	B.t.u., P.c.u.
Radiation, intensity of	N	B.t.u./(hr.) (sq.ft.), P.c.u./(hr.) (sq.ft.)
Rate of heat transfer	q	B.t.u./hr., P.c.u./hr.
Resistance, thermal	R	°F./(B.t.u./hr.), °C./(P.c.u./hr.)
Stefan-Boltzmann constant	σ (sigma)	
Unit conductance	$1/RA$	B.t.u./(hr.) (sq.ft.) (°F.), P.c.u./(hr.) (sq.ft.) (°C.)

EVAPORATION
HUMIDIFICATION, DEHUMIDIFICATION

Humidity	H	lb./lb. dry air
Humid heat	c_s	B.t.u./(lb. dry air) (°F.), P.c.u./(lb. dry air) (°C.)
Humid volume	v_H	cu.ft./lb. dry air
Relative humidity	H_R	

GAS ABSORPTION AND EXTRACTION

Height of transfer unit "H.T.U."	H_t	ft. (Z_t also is used)
Henry's law constant, c/p	H	(lb. moles/cu.ft.)/atm.
Mass transfer coefficient, individual	k	lb. moles/(hr.) (sq.ft.) (atm.)
gas film	k_G	lb. moles/(hr.) (sq.ft.) (atm.)
liquid film	k_L	lb. moles/(hr.) (sq.ft.) (lb. mole/cu.ft.)
Mass transfer coefficient, overall	K	lb. moles/(hr.) (sq.ft.) (atm.)
on gas film basis	K_G	
on liquid film basis	K_L	
Mass velocity of liquid	L	lb./(hr.) (sq.ft.)
Mole fraction, in liquid	x	
Mole fraction, in vapor,	y	
do., equilibrium value	y^*	
Mole ratio, in liquid	X	
Mole ratio, in vapor	Y	
Rate of transfer	N	lb. moles/hr.
Slope of equilibrium curve	m	dy^*/dx
"Transfer units," number of	N_t	

DISTILLATION

Distillate rate	D	lb. moles/hr.
Entrainment ratio	E	lb./lb., lb. moles/lb. mole
Equilibrium constant, $y = K_x$	K	(K^* also is used)
Feed rate	F	lb. moles/hr.
Height equivalent to a theoretical plate, "H.E.T.P."	H_p	ft.
Liquid rate,	L	lb. moles/hr.
above feed	L_n	lb. moles/hr.
below feed	L_m	lb. moles/hr.
Plates, number of	N_p	
Reflux ratio	R	Use R_D for L/D, and R_v for L/V
Relative volatility	α (alpha)	$\alpha_{AB} = (y^*_A/x_A)/(y^*_B/x_B)$
Residue, waste, bottoms	W, B	lb. moles/hr.
Thermal condition of feed $(L_m - L_n)/F$	q	
Vapor rate	V	lb. moles/hr.

DRYING

Free moisture content	W	lb./lb.
Production rate	R	lb./hr.

CLASSIFICATION, SEDIMENTATION, SETTLING, ETC.

Coefficient of resistance	C	

FILTRATION

Equivalent resistance of cloth	r	
Exponent of compressbility of cake	s	
Specific cake resistance	α (alpha)	

SCREENING AND SAMPLING

Aperture	A, a	in.
Mesh	M, m	1/in.

CRYSTALLIZATION

Evaporation	E	lb.
Solubility	S	lb./100 lb. solvent
Solvent present	H_o	lb.

CENTRIFUGATION

CRUSHING AND GRINDING

Coefficient of friction	f	
Reduction ratio	R_R	
Specific surface	s	sq.ft./lb., sq.cm./g.

DIMENSIONLESS NUMBERS USED IN CHEMICAL ENGINEERING

Reynolds number	N_{Re}, R	$\dfrac{DV\rho}{\mu}$
Froude number	N_{Fr}, F	V^2/gD
Mach number	N_{Ma}	V/V_a
Nusselt number	N_{Nu}	$\dfrac{hD}{k}$
Prandtl number	N_{Pr}	$\dfrac{c\mu}{k}$
Peclet number	N_{Pe}	$\dfrac{DV\rho c}{k}$
Graetz number	N_{Gz}	$\dfrac{wc}{kL}$
Grashof number	N_{Gr}	$\dfrac{L^3\rho^2\beta g\Delta t}{\mu^2}$
Stanton number	N_{St}	$\dfrac{h}{cV\rho}$
Condensation number	N_{Co}	$\dfrac{h}{k}\left(\dfrac{\mu^2}{\rho^2 g}\right)^{1/3}$
Biot number	N_{Bi}	$\dfrac{hL}{k}$
Fourier number	N_{Fo}	$\dfrac{kr}{\rho c L^2}$
Schmidt number	N_{Sc}	$\dfrac{\mu}{\rho D_v}$
Number used in condensation of vapors	N_{Cv}	$\dfrac{L^3\rho^2 g\lambda}{k\mu\Delta t}$

ARRANGED ALPHABETICALLY BY SYMBOLS

a	Acceleration	(ft./sec.)/sec., (ft./hr.)/hr.
	Activity	
	Aperture (see A)	in.
	Surface per unit volume	sq.ft./cu.ft.
A	Aperture (see a)	in.
	Area	sq.ft.
	Cross section	sq.ft.
	Free energy, Helmholtz, $(U - TS)$	B.t.u., B.t.u./lb. mole, P.c.u., P.c.u./lb. mole
b	Breadth, width	ft.
B	Film thickness, effective	ft.
	Residue, waste, bottoms	lb. moles/hr.
	Concentration, volumetric	lb./cu.ft., lb. moles/cu.ft.
	Specific heat	B.t.u./(lb.) (°F.), P.c.u./(lb.) (°C.)
	See V_a (Velocity, acoustic)	
c_p	Specific heat, at constant pressure	B.t.u./(lb.) (°F.), P.c.u./(lb.) (°C.)
c_s	Humid heat	B.t.u./(lb. dry air) (°F.), P.c.u./(lb. dry air) (°C.)
c_v	Specific heat, at constant volume	B.t.u./(lb.) (°F.), P.c.u./(lb.) (°C.)
C	Coefficient, of discharge, etc.	
	Coefficient of resistance	
	Conductance (see 1/R)	B.t.u./(hr.) (°F.), P.c.u./(hr.) (°C.)
d	Differential operator	
D	Diameter	ft.
	Distillate rate	lb. moles/hr.
D_v	Diffusivity of vapor	sq.ft./hr.
e	Base of natural logarithms	
E	Energy, in general	B.t.u., B.t.u./lb. mole, P.c.u./lb. mole
	Entrainment ratio	lb./lb., lb. moles/lb. mole
	Evaporation	lb.
f	Coefficient of friction	
	Friction factor, Fanning	$(F = 2fLV^2/g_cD)$
	Fugacity	lb. force/sq.ft., atm.
	Activity coefficient, molal basis	
	See γ (Activity coefficient)	
F	Feed rate	lb. moles/hr.
	Force, total load	lb. force
	Friction in energy balance	(ft.) (lb. force)/lb.
	See G (Free energy, Gibbs)	
g	Acceleration of gravity	(ft./sec.)/sec., (ft./hr.)/hr.
g_c	Newton law of motion, conversion factor in	(lb.) (ft.)/(sec.)²(lb. force)

Symbol	Quantity	Units
g_0	Acceleration of gravity, standard value	(ft./sec.)/sec., (ft./hr.)/hr.
G	Free energy, Gibbs $(H - TS)$	(F also has been used)
	Mass velocity	lb./(hr.) (sq.ft.), lb./(sec.) (sq.ft.)
h	Coefficient of heat transfer, individual	B.t.u./(hr.) (sq.ft.) (°F.), P.c.u./(hr.) (sq.ft.) (°C.)
	Enthalpy, per unit weight	B.t.u./lb., P.c.u./lb. (i is used when necessary to distinguish)
h_{fg}	Latent heat (see λ)	B.t.u./lb., P.c.u./lb.
H	Enthalpy	B.t.u., B.t.u./lb. mole P.c.u., P.c.u./lb. mole
	Henry's law constant c/p	(lb. moles/cu.ft.)/atm.
	Humidity	lb./lb. dry air
H_o	Solvent present	lb.
H_p	Height equivalent to a theoretical plate, "H.E.T.P."	ft.
H_R	Humidity, relative	
H_t	Height of transfer unit, "H.T.U."	ft.
i	See under Enthalpy, per unit weight	
I	Moment of inertia	(ft.)⁴
j	Heat transfer factor	$(h/cG)\phi(c\mu/k)$
J	Mechanical equivalent of heat	(ft.) (lb. force)/B.t.u., (ft.) (lb. force)/P.c.u.
k	Mass transfer coefficient, individual	lb. moles/(hr.) (sq.ft.) (atm.)
	Specific heats, ratio of κ (kappa) and γ (gamma) also are used c_p/c_v	
	Thermal conductivity	B.t.u./(hr.) (sq.ft.) (°F./ft.), P.c.u./(hr.) (sq.ft.) (°C./ft.)
k_G	Mass transfer coefficient, gas film	lb. moles/(hr.) (sq.ft.) (atm.)
k_L	Mass transfer coefficient, liquid film	lb. moles/(hr.) (sq.ft.) (lb. mole/cu.ft.)
K	Equilibrium constant, $y = Kx$	
	Mass transfer coefficient, overall	lb. moles/(hr.) (sq.ft.) (atm.)
K_G	Mass transfer coefficient, on gas film basis	
K_L	Mass transfer coefficient, on liquid film basis	
L	Length	ft.
	Liquid rate	lb. moles/hr.
	Mass velocity of liquid	lb./(hr.) (sq.ft.)
L_m	Liquid rate, below feed	lb. moles/hr.
L_n	Liquid rate, above feed	lb. moles/hr.
m	Mass	lb.
	Mesh (see M)	1/in.
	Slope of equilibrium curve	$dy*/dx$
M	Mesh (see m)	1/in.
	Molecular weight	
n	Rate of rotation	rev./min.
N	Number in general	
	Rate of transfer	lb. moles/hr.
	Radiation, intensity of	B.t.u./(hr.) (sq.ft.), P.c.u./(hr.) (sq.ft.)
N_p	Plates, number of	
N_t	"Transfer units," number of	
p	Pressure	lb. force/sq.ft., atm.
P	Power	(ft.) (lb. force)/sec.
q	Rate of flow, volumetric	cu.ft./sec., cu.ft./hr.
	Rate of heat transfer	B.t.u./hr., P.c.u./hr.
	Thermal condition of feed, $(L_m - L_n)/F$	
Q	Quantity of heat transferred	B.t.u., P.c.u.
r	Equivalent resistance of cloth	
	Radius	ft.
R	Gas constant, universal	Where necessary to distinguish, use R_o
	Production rate	lb./hr.
	Reflux ratio	Use R_D for L/D, and R_V for L/V
	Resistance, thermal	°F./(B.t.u./hr.), °C./(P.c.u./hr.)
R_H	Hydraulic radius	ft., sq.ft./ft.
R_R	Reduction ratio	
s	Entropy, per unit weight	B.t.u./(lb.) (°R.), P.c.u./(lb.) (°K.)
	Exponent of compressibility of cake	
	Specific surface	sq.ft./lb., sq.cm./g.
S	Area	sq.ft.
	Cross section	sq.ft.
	Entropy	B.t.u./(°R.) or B.t.u./(lb. mole) (°R.), P.c.u./(°K.) or P.c.u./(lb. mole) (°K.)
	Solubility	lb./100 lb. solvent
t	Temperature	°F. or °C. (θ is used in some lists)
	Time [see r (tau)]	sec., hr. (θ also has been used)
T	Temperature, absolute	°K. or °R. (Rankine)
u	Velocity, local	ft./sec., ft./hr.
	Internal energy per unit weight	B.t.u./lb., P.c.u./lb.
U	Heat transfer coefficient, overall	B.t.u./(hr.) (sq.ft.) (°F.), P.c.u./(hr.) (sq.ft.) (°C.)
	Internal energy	B.t.u., B.t.u./lb. mole P.c.u., P.c.u./lb. mole
v	Specific volume	cu.ft./lb.
v_H	Humid volume	cu.ft./lb. dry air
V	Vapor rate	lb. moles/hr.
	Velocity, average	ft./sec., ft./hr.
	Volume, total or per mole	cu.ft., cu.ft./lb. mole
V_a	Velocity, acoustic	ft./sec. (c also is used)
w	Mass flow rate	lb./sec., lb./hr.
W	Free moisture content	lb./lb.
	Residue, waste, bottoms	lb. moles/hr.
	Work	B.t.u., P.c.u. Where necessary to distinguish use W_k
	Weight, quantity of matter	lb.
W_a	Work, external	B.t.u., P.c.u.

W_k	See W	
x	Distance in direction of flow	ft.
	Mole fraction, in liquid	
x_v	Fraction by volume	
x_w	Fraction by weight	
X	Mole ratio, in liquid	
y	Depth	ft.
	Mole fraction, in vapor	
y^*	Mole fraction, in vapor, equilibrium value	
Y	Mole ratio, in vapor	
z	Compressibility factor	pV/RT
Z	Distance above datum plane	ft.
α (alpha)	Angle	degrees, radians (θ and ϕ also are used)
	Coefficient of expansion, linear	(ft./ft.)/°F., (ft./ft.)/°C.
	Diffusivity, thermal	sq.ft./hr.
	Absorptivity (for radiation)	
	Relative volatility	
	Specific cake resistance	
β (beta)	Coefficient of expansion, volumetric	(cu.ft./cu.ft.)/°F., (cu.ft./cu.ft.)/°C.
γ (gamma)	Activity coefficient, molal basis	f also is used
	See κ (kappa) and γ (gamma)	

Γ (capital gamma)	Weight rate of flow per unit of breadth	lb./(sec.) (ft.), (lb./(hr.) (ft.)
Δ (capital delta)	Difference, finite; often that causing flow	
ϵ (epsilon)	Emissivity (for radiation)	
η (eta)	Efficiency	
	See μ (viscosity, absolute)	
θ (theta)	See τ (tau), α (alpha)	
κ (kappa)	Specific heats, ratio of: c_p/c_v	k and γ (gamma) also are used
λ (lambda)	Latent heat of evaporation. See h_{fg}	B.t.u./lb., P.c.u./lb.
μ (mu)	Viscosity, absolute	lb./(sec.) (ft.), η (eta) also is used lb./(hr.) (ft.)
ν (nu)	Viscosity, kinematic	sq.ft./sec., sq.ft./hr.
ρ (rho)	Density	lb./cu.ft.
σ (sigma)	Surface tension	lb. force/ft., dynes/cm.
	Stefan-Boltzmann constant	
τ (tau)	See t (Time)	sec., hr. (θ also has been used)
	Tractive force per unit area	lb. force/sq.ft.
ϕ (phi)	Function	
	See α (alpha)	
ψ (psi)	Function	
χ (chi)	Function	
ω (omega)	Solid angle	
	Velocity, angular	

absolute .... abs
acre .... spell out
acre-foot................... acre-ft
air horsepower .... air hp
alternating-current (as adjective)..a-c
ampere .... amp
ampere-hour ....amp-hr
amplitude, an elliptic function... am.
Angstrom unit .... A
antilogarithm .... antilog
atmosphere .... atm
atomic weight .... at. wt
average .... avg
avoirdupois .... avdp
azimuth .... az or α

barometer .... bar.
barrel .... bbl
Baumé .... Bé
board feet (feet board measure) .. fbm
boiler pressure .... spell out
boiling point .... bp
brake horsepower .... bhp
brake horsepower-hour .... bhp-hr
Brinell hardness number .... Bhn
British thermal unit[1] ....Btu or B
bushel .... bu

calorie .... cal
candle c
candle-hour .... c-hr
candlepower .... cp
cent .... c or ¢
center to center .... c to c
centigram .... cg
centiliter cl
centimeter .... cm
centimeter-gram-second (system)..cgs
chemical .... chem
chemically pure .... cp
circular .... cir
circular mils .... cir mils
coefficient .... coef
cologarithm .... colog
concentrate .... conc
conductivity .... cond
constant .... const
continental horsepower ..... cont hp
cord .... cd
cosecant .... csc
cosine .... cos
cosine of the amplitude,
  an elliptic function .... cn
cost, insurance, and freight ...... cif
cotangent .... cot
coulomb .... spell out
counter electromotive force ..... cemf
cubic .... cu
cubic centimeter .. cu cm, cm³ (liquid,
  meaning milliliter, ml)
cubic foot .... cu ft

cubic feet per minute ....ctm
cubic feet per second .... cfs
cubic inch .... cu in.
cubic meter .... cu m or m³
cubic micron ..... cu μ or cu mu or μ³
cubic millimeter ...... cu mm or mm³
cubic yard .... cu yd
current density .... spell out
cycles per second .... spell out or c
cylinder .... cyl

day .... spell out
decibel .... db
degree[2] .... deg or °
degree centigrade C
degree Fahrenheit .... F
degree Kelvin .... K
degree Réaumur .... R
delta amplitude,
  an elliptic function .... dn
diameter .... diam
direct-current (as adjective) .....d-c
dollar .... $
dozen .... doz
dram .... dr

efficiency........................eff
electric...................... elec
electromotive force............ emf
elevation .... el
equation .... eq
external .... ext

farad ....spell out or f
feet board measure (board feet) .. fbm
feet per minute .... fpm
feet per second .... fps
fluid ....fl
foot ....ft
foot-candle .... f-c
foot-Lambert .... ft-L
foot-pound .... ft-lb
foot-pound-second (system) ....fps
foot-second (see cubic feet
  per second)
franc ....fr
free aboard ship.......... spell out
free alongside ship .... spell out
free on board .... fob
freezing point .... fp
frequency .... spell out
fusion point .... fnp

gallon .... gal
gallons per minute .... gpm
gallons per second .... gps
grain .... spell out
gram .... gm
gram-calorie .... g-cal
greatest common divisor .... gcd

haversine .... hav
hectare .... ha
henry ....h
high-pressure (adjective) .... h-p
hogshead .... hhd
horsepower .... hp
horsepower-hour.............. hp-hr
hour .... hr
hour (in astronomical tables).......h
hundred C
hundredweight (112 lb) .... cwt
hyperbolic cosine .... cosh
hyperbolic sine .... sinh
hyperbolic tangent............. tanh

inch .... in.
inch-pound .... in-lb
inches per second.............. ips
indicated horsepower .... ihp
indicated horsepower-hour..... ihp-hr
inside diameter .... ID
intermediate-pressure (adjective).. i-p
internal .... int

joule........................... j

kilocalorie .... kcal
kilocycles per second............kc
kilogram .... kg
kilogram-calorie............ kg-cal
kilogram-meter .... kg-m
kilograms per cubic meter
  .... kg per cu m or kg/m³
kilograms per second ....kgps
kiloliter....................... kl
kilometer .... km
kilometers per second .... kmps
kilovolt .... kv
kilovolt-ampere .... kva
kilowatt .... kw
kilowatthour .... kwhr

lambert L
latitude .... lat or φ
least common multiple .... lcm
linear foot................... lin ft
liquid......................... liq
lira .... spell out
liter l
logarithm (common) .... log
logarithm (natural)........ log. or ln
longitude .... long. or λ
low-pressure (as adjective)....... l-p
lumen .... l*
lumen-hour .... l-hr*
lumens per watt .... lpw

*The International Commission on Illu-
mination has changed the symbol for lumen to lm, and the symbol for lumen-hour
to lm-hr. This nomenclature is used in
American Standard for Illuminating Engineering Nomenclature and Photometric
Standards (ASA Z7.1-1942).

Note: These forms are recommended for readers whose familiarity with the terms used makes possible a maximum of abbreviations.
For other classes of readers editors may wish to use less contracted combinations made up from this list. For example, the list
gives the abbreviation of the term "feet per second" as "fps." To some readers ft per sec will be more easily understood.
[1] Abbreviation recommended by the A.S.M.E. Power Test Codes Committee. B = 1 Btu, kB = 1000 Btu, mB = 1,000,000 Btu. The
A.S.H.&V.E. recommends the use of Mb = 1000 Btu and Mbh = 1000 Btu per hr.
[2] There are circumstances under which one or the other of these forms is preferred. In general the sign ° is used where space
conditions make it necessary, as in tabular matter, and when abbreviations are cumbersome, as in some angular measurements,
i.e., 59° 23′ 42″. In the interest of simplicity and clarity the Committee has recommended that the abbreviation for the temperature
scale, F, C, K, etc., always be included in expressions for numerical temperatures, but, wherever feasible, the abbreviation for
"degree" be omitted; as 69 F.

*Extracted from "American Standard Abbreviations for Scientific and Engineering Terms," ASA Z10.1—1941, with the permission of
the publisher, The American Society of Mechanical Engineers, 29 West 39 Street, New York 18, N. Y.*

mass .... spell out
mathematics (ical) .... math
maximum .... max
mean effective pressure .... mep
mean horizontal candlepower ... mhcp
megacycle .... spell out
megohm .... spell out
melting point .... mp
meter .... m
meter-kilogram .... m-kg
mho ....spell out
microampere .... μa or mu a
microfarad .... μf
microinch .... μin.
micromicrofarad .... μμf
micromicron .... μμ or mu mu
micron .... μ or mu
microvolt .... μv
microwatt .... μw or mu w
mile......................spell out
miles per hour .... mph
miles per hour per second .... mphps
milliampere .... ma
milligram .... mg
millihenry .... mh
millilambert .... mL
milliliter .... ml
millimeter .... mm
millimicron .... mμ or m mu
million .... spell out
million gallons per day .... mgd
millivolt .... mv
minimum .... min
minute .... min
minute (angular measure).........
minute (time)
  (in astronomical tables)......... m
mole .... spell out
molecular weight .... mol. wt
month .... spell out

National Electrical Code .... NEC

ohm .... spell out or Ω
ohm-centimeter .... ohm-cm

ounce .... oz
ounce-foot .... oz-ft
ounce-inch .... oz-in.
outside diameter .... OD

parts per million .... ppm
peck............................pk
penny (pence)...................d
pennyweight .... dwt
per .... (See Fundamental Rules)
peso .... spell out
pint .... pt
potential .... spell out
potential difference........ spell out
pound........................... lb
pound-foot.................... lb-ft
pound-inch .... lb-in.
pound sterling .... £
pounds per brake horsepower-
  hour .... lb per bhp-hr
pounds per cubic foot.... lb per cu ft
pounds per square foot .... psf
pounds per square inch .... psi
pounds per square inch absolute
  .... psia
power factor......... spell out or pf

quart..........................qt

radian .... spell out
reactive kilovolt-ampere........ kvar
reactive volt-ampere .... var
revolutions per minute .... rpm
revolutions per second .... rps
rod.................... spell out
root mean square.............. rms

secant .... sec
second .... sec
second (angular measure) .... ''
second-foot (see cubic feet per
  second)

second (time)
  (in astronomical tables) .... s
shaft horsepower .... shp
shilling....................... s
sine .... sin
sine of the amplitude,
  an elliptic function............ sn
specific gravity .... sp gr
specific heat................. sp ht
spherical candle power .... scp
square......................... sq
square centimeter ...... sq cm or cm²
square foot.................... sq ft
square inch .... sq in.
square kilometer .... sq km or km²
square meter .... sq m or m²
square micron ... sq μ or sq mu or μ²
square millimeter ..... sq mm or mm²
square root of mean square...... rms
standard .... std
stere .... s

tangent .... tan
temperature................... temp
tensile strength .... ts
thousand .... M
thousand foot-pounds........ kip-ft
thousand pound................ kip
ton..................... spell out
ton-mile.................. spell out

versed sine................... vers
volt v
volt-ampere .... va
volt-coulomb .... spell out

watt........................... w
watthour .... whr
watts per candle............... wpc
week.................... spell out
weight........................ wt

yard.......................... yd
year.......................... yr

Proofreaders' Marks

∧	Make correction indicated in margin.
Stet	Retain crossed-out word or letter; let it stand.
. . . . Stet	Retain words under which dots appear; write "Stet" in margin.
×	Appears battered; examine.
≡	Straighten lines.
√√	Unevenly spaced; correct spacing.
‖	Line up; i.e., make lines even with other matter.
run in	Make no break in the reading; no ¶
no ¶	No paragraph; sometimes written "run in."
out see copy	Here is an omission; see copy.
¶	Make a paragraph here.
tr	Transpose words or letters as indicated.
₰	Take out matter indicated; dele.
₰̂	Take out character indicated and close up.
¢	Line drawn through a cap means lower case.
⊚	Upside down; reverse.
⁐	Close up; no space.
#	Insert a space here.
⊥	Push down this space.
□	Indent line one em.
[	Move this to the left.
]	Move this to the right.
⌐¬	Raise to proper position.
└┘	Lower to proper position.
////	Hair space letters.
w.f.	Wrong font; change to proper font.
Qu?	Is this right?
l.c.	Put in lower case (small letters).
s.c.	Put in small capitals.
Caps	Put in capitals.
C&s.c.	Put in caps and small caps.
rom.	Change to Roman.
ital.	Change to Italic.
≡	Under letter or word means caps.
=	Under letter or word, small caps.
—	Under letter or word means Italic.
~~	Under letter or word, bold face.
,/	Insert comma.
;/	Insert semicolon.
:/	Insert colon.
⊙	Insert period.
/?/	Insert interrogation mark.
(!)	Insert exclamation mark.
/-/	Insert hyphen.
’	Insert apostrophe.
“ ”	Insert quotation marks.
∨	Insert superior letter or figure.
∧	Insert inferior letter or figure.
[/]	Insert brackets.
(/)	Insert parenthesis.
1/m	One-em dash.
2/m	Two-em parallel dash.

Greek Alphabet

Alpha	A	a α*
Beta	B	β
Gamma	Γ	γ
Delta	Δ	δ ∂*
Epsilon	E	ϵ
Zeta	Z	ζ
Eta	H	η
Theta	Θ	θ ϑ*
Iota	I	ι
Kappa	K	κ
Lambda	Λ	λ
Mu	M	μ
Nu	N	ν
Xi	Ξ	ξ
Omicron	O	o
Pi	Π	π
Rho	P	ρ
Sigma	Σ	σ s†
Tau	T	τ
Upsilon	Υ	υ
Phi	Φ	ϕ φ*
Chi	X	χ
Psi	Ψ	ψ
Omega	Ω	ω

* *Old-style characters*   † *Final letters*

Abbreviations in Greek

A. E.	Αὐτοῦ 'Εξοχότης, His Excellency
A. M.	Αὐτοῦ Μεγαλειότης, His Majesty
B. Δ.	Βασιλικὸν Διάταγμα, Royal Decree
βλ.	βλέπε, see
δηλ.	δηλαδή, that is, namely, to wit
δρ.	δραχμή, drachma
δράμ.	δράμιον, dram
Δ. Φ.	Διδάκτωρ Φιλοσοφίας, Ph. D.
Δ. N.	Διδάκτωρ Νομικῆς, LL. D.
ἔ. ἀ.	ἔνθα ἀνωτέρω, loc. cit.
ἰδ.	ἰδέ, see
I. X.	'Ιησοῦς Χριστός, Jesus Christ
Καθ.	Καθηγητής, Prof.
Κος	Κύριος, Mr.
Κα	Κυρία, Mrs.
κτλ.	καὶ τὰ λοιπά, etc.
κ. τ. δ.	καὶ τά ὅμοια, and the like
κφλ.	κεφάλαιον, chapter
λπτ.	λεπτά, lepta
μέρ.	μέρος, part
μ. μ.	μετὰ μεσημβρίαν, p. m.
μ. X.	μετὰ Χριστόν, A. D.

N. Δ.	Νέα Διαθήκη, New Testament; Νομοθετικὸν Διάταγμα, Legislative Ordinance
ν. ἡμ.	νέον ἡμερολόγιον, New Style
O'	'Εβδομήκοντα, Septuagint
Π. Δ.	παλαιὰ Διαθήκη, Old Testament; Προεδρικὸν Διάταγμα, Presidential Order
πλ.	πληθυντικός, plural
π. μ.	πρὸ μεσημβρίας, a. m.
πρβλ.	παραβάλε, compare, cf.
π. X.	πρὸ Χριστοῦ, B. C.
π. χ.	παραδείγματος χάριν, for example, e. g.
σεβ.	σεβαστός, Hon.
σελ.	σελίς, page
στήλ.	στήλη, column
σύγκρ.	σύγκρινε, compare, cf.
τ. ἔ.	τοῦτ' ἔστιν, that is, i. e.
τόμ.	τόμος, volume
T. Σ.	τόπος σφραγίδος, L. S., loco sigilli
τρ. ἔτ.	τρέχοντος ἔτους, current year
φ.	φύλλον, folio
χιλ.	χιλιόμετρον, kilometer

German Alphabet

𝔄 𝔅 ℭ 𝔇 𝔈 𝔉 𝔊 ℌ 𝔍 𝔎 𝔏 𝔐 𝔑 𝔒 𝔓 𝔔 ℜ 𝔖 𝔗 𝔘 𝔙 𝔚 𝔛 𝔜 𝔷 &

a b c d e f g h i j k l m n o p q r s t u v w x y z
fl fi ff ſſ ſi ſt ll ß tz ck ch &c.

Russian Alphabet

А	а	a
Б	б	b
В	в	v
Г	г	g
Д	д	d
Е	е	e, ye
Ё	ё	ë, yë
Ж	ж	zh
З	з	z
И	и	i
Й	й	y
К	к	k
Л	л	l
М	м	m
Н	н	n
О	о	o
П	п	p
Р	р	r
С	с	s
Т	т	t
У	у	u
Ф	ф	f
Х	х	kh
Ц	ц	ts
Ч	ч	ch
Ш	ш	sh
Щ	щ	shch
Ъ	ъ	”
Ы	ы	y;
Ь	ь	’
Э	э	e
Ю	ю	yu
Я	я	ya

Амер.	Американский,	American
АХР	Ассоциация Художников Революции,	Association of Artists of the Revolution
ВКП(Б)	Всесоюзная Коммунистическая Партия (Большевиков),	Communist (Bolshevik) Party of the Soviet Union
вм.	вместо,	instead of
ВОКС	Всесоюзное Общество Культурной Связи с Заграницей,	All-Union Society for Foreign Cultural Relations
ВЦИК	Всероссийский Центральный Исполнительный Комитет,	All-Russian Central Executive Committee
г.	город,	city; год, year
Г.	Господин,	Mr.
Гжа	Госпожа,	Mrs. Miss
гл.	глава,	chapter
ж. д.	железная дорога,	railroad
и мн. др.	и многие другие,	and many others
и пр.	и прочее,	etc.
и т. д.	и так далее,	etc.
и т. п.	и тому подобное,	and such like
км.	километр,	kilometer
КП	Коммунистическая Партия,	Communist Party
м.	метр,	meter
мм.	миллиметр,	millimeter
м. п.	место печати,	place of seal, L. S.
на пр.	на пример,	for example
н. ст.	новый стиль,	new style
по Р. Х.	по рождестве Христове,	anno Domini
см.	сантиметр,	centimeter; смотри, see, cf.
СССР	Союз Советских Социалистических Республик,	Union of Soviet Socialist Republics
с. ст.	старый стиль,	old style
США	Соединенные Штаты Америки,	United States of America
ст.	статья,	article
стр.	страница,	page
т. е.	то есть,	that is
ЦИК	Центральный Исполнительный Комитет,	Central Executive Committee
ч.	часть,	part

Hebrew Alphabet

אבגדהוזחטיכלמנסעפצקרשת

The names of the letters and their transliterations (reading
from right to left in the alphabet) are:

Name	Transliteration	Name	Transliteration
'Alef	' or omit	Zayin	z
Bēth	b, v	Ḥēth	ḥ
Gīmel	g	Ṭēth	ṭ
Daleth	d	Yōd	y
Hē	h	Kaf	k, kh
Wāw	w	Lamed	l

Name	Transliteration	Name	Transliteration
Mēm	m	Ṣadē	ṣ
Nūn	n	Qōf	q
Samekh	s	Rēsh	r
'Ayin	'	Śin, Shīn	ś, sh
Pē	p, f	Tāw	t

Sir, Master, Mr.; thousand	א', אדון אלף
Aleph Beth (the alphabet)	א"ב, אלף בית
Said our learned ones of blessed memory	אחז"ל, אמרו חכמינו זכרונם לברכה
The Land of Israel (Palestine)	א"י, ארץ ישראל
God willing	איה, אם ירצה השם
Synagogue	בהכנ"ז, בית הכנסת
Sons of Israel, the Jews	ב"י, בני ישראל
In these words, viz	בזה"ל, בזה הלשן
The author	בע"מ, בעל מחבר
Gaon (title of Jewish princes in the Babylonian exile), His Highness, His Majesty.	ג', גאון
The laws of Israel	ד"י, דיני ישראל
The Holy One, Blessed be He (the Lord)	הקב"ה, הקדוש ברוך הוא
Destruction of the First Temple	חב"ר, חרבן בית ראשן
Destruction of the Second Temple	חב"ש, חרבן בית שני
Exodus from Egypt	יצ"מ, יציאת מצרים
As it was said; as it was written	כמ"ש, כמו שאמר; כמו שכתב
A. M. (anno mundi)	לב"ע, לבריאת עולם
The Holy Language (Hebrew)	להק, לשן הקדש
Good luck; I congratulate you	מז"ט, מזל טוב
The Sacred Books	סה"ק, ספרים הקדושים
The Holy Scroll	ס"ת, ספר תורה
May he rest in peace	ע"ה, עליו השלום
In the Hereafter	עוה"ב, עולם הבא
New Year's Eve	ער"ה, ערב ראש השנה
Sabbath Eve	ע"ש, ערב שבת
Verse; chapter	פ', פסוק; פרק
The judgment of the court	פב"ד, פסק בית דין
Saint (St.); Zion	צ', צדיק; ציון
Recognition of God's justice	צה"ד, צדוק הדין
The reading of the Holy Scroll	קה"ת, קראית התורה
First of all	קק"ך, קדם כל דבר
Our Rabbis of Blessed Memory	רו"ל, רבותינו זכרונם לברכה
Rabbi Moses, son of Maimon (Maimonides)	רמב"ם, ר' משה בן מימון
Catalog	רש"ס, רשימת ספרים
Year; line; hour	ש , שנה; שורה; שעה
Sabbath days and holidays	שרי"ט, שבתות וימים טובים
As stated	שנ', שנאמר
Babylonian Talmud	ת"ב, תלמוד בבלי
The Books of the Law, the Prophets, and Hagiographa (Old Testament).	תנ"ך, תורה, נביאים, כתובים